ADDISON-WESLEY MATHEMATICS 12

NATIONAL EDITION

Brendan Kelly
Professor of Mathematics
Faculty of Education
University of Toronto
Ontario

Bob Alexander
Assistant Co-ordinator
of Mathematics
Toronto Board of Education
Toronto, Ontario

Paul Atkinson
Principal
Cameron Heights
Collegiate Institute
Kitchener, Ontario

Contributing Author
A. George Ditto
Assistant Principal
Bowness Senior High School
Calgary, Alberta

Addison-Wesley Publishers Limited

Don Mills, Ontario
Reading, Massachusetts
Menlo Park, California
Wokingham, England
Amsterdam • Bonn
Sydney • Singapore
Tokyo • Madrid
San Juan

Design
John Zehethofer
Assembly and Technical Art
Frank Zsigo
Editorial
Lesley Haynes
Typesetting
Q Composition
Printer
The Bryant Press

Photographic Credits

The publisher wishes to thank the following sources for photographs and other illustrative
materials used in this book. We will gladly receive information enabling us to rectify any errors
or references in credits.
Cover, Richard Simpson; 1, Ministry of Fisheries and Oceans; 2, Allsport/Masterfile; N. Serba/
Miller Comstock Inc.; Bob Alexander; 13, Lesley Haynes; 14, Bob Alexander; 32, NASA; Carl
Zeiss Canada Ltd.; 41, Province of British Columbia; 47, Schnepel Photography; 85, Paul
Atkinson; 90, © R. Kinne/Science Source/Masterfile; 92, Addison-Wesley photo library; 95,
J.A. Kraulis/Masterfile; 101, Global Television Network; 113, Allsport/Masterfile; 120, Allsport/
Masterfile; 131, Bob Alexander; 151, Roberts/Miller Comstock Inc.; 193, Nova Scotia Power
Corporation; 196, Roberts/Miller Comstock Inc.; 225, Addison-Wesley photo library; 232,
Lambert/Miller Comstock Inc.; 237, Palomar Observatory Photograph; 267, Nova Scotia
Communications and Information Centre; 299, Vincent van Gogh Foundation/National Museum,
Vincent van Gogh, Amsterdam; 345, Addison-Wesley photo library; 357, Roberts/Miller
Comstock Inc.; 369, Mastefile; 370, Addison-Wesley photo library; 374, Addison-Wesley photo
library; 381, Ministry of Agriculture and Food; 393, T. Rosenthal; 393, Government of Quebec,
Tourist Branch; 407, © M.C. Escher c/o Cordon Art-Baarn Holland; 416, Yale University/
M. Marsland/1989; 417, Chris D'Arcy; 429, John de Visser/Masterfile; 483, Ontario Lottery
Corporation; 484, Miller Comstock Inc.; 497, Douglas Mawson; 514, Stanford News Service

Written, printed, and bound in Canada

ISBN   0-201-19276-4

A B C D E F – BP – 96 95 94 93 92 91

Features of Mathematics 12

CONCEPT DEVELOPMENT

Mathematics 12 is carefully sequenced to develop concepts in mathematics. Concepts are explained with several examples, each of which has a detailed solution.

10-6 APPLICATIONS OF COMBINATORICS TO PROBABILITY

The counting techniques involving permutations and combinations are part of a branch of mathematics called *combinatorics*. These techniques are important in helping us enumerate favorable and possible outcomes in probability experiments and thereby calculate theoretical probabilities. Sometimes we can calculate probabilities using either permutations or combinations. Both methods are equivalent, as shown in the following example.

Example 1. Two cards are picked at random from a deck of 52 regular playing cards. What is the probability that they are both aces?

Solution. *Using combinations*
The number of ways of choosing two aces from the four aces is $_4C_2$.
The number of ways of choosing two cards from 52 cards is $_{52}C_2$.
The probability of choosing 2 aces in a selection of 2 cards from 52 is

$$P(2 \text{ aces}) = \frac{_4C_2}{_{52}C_2}$$
$$= \frac{\frac{4!}{2!2!}}{\frac{52!}{50!2!}}$$
$$= \frac{4!50!}{2!52!}$$
$$= \frac{1}{221}$$

REINFORCEMENT

An abundance of exercises is provided to reinforce skills and concepts. These exercises are graded by difficulty with an appropriate balance of A, B, and C exercises. The A exercises may sometimes be completed mentally and the answers given orally or the questions may be discussed with the students. The B exercises are intended for the students to consolidate their learning of the concepts that were taught. The C exercises present a challenge and usually involve extensions of the concepts taught in that section.

Review Exercises and *Cumulative Reviews* provide additional practice. Answers to all questions are included in the text.

TECHNOLOGY

A contemporary mathematics program must reflect the impact of calculators and computers on society.

Mathematics 12 assumes that students will use scientific calculators where appropriate. It is up to the students to familiarize themselves with their calculators.

 COMPUTER POWER

Graphing Functions

A computer is ideally suited for graphing functions, since it can rapidly calculate the values of a function for many values of x. The graph can be displayed on the computer screen or printed on paper. The most primitive programs plot symbols on the screen, which normally consists of about 20 rows of 40 characters each. The program below is of this type, and can be used on almost any computer. For more accurate graphs, other programs must be used, but the commands are specific to particular computers.

This program can be used to obtain an approximation to the graph of any function that can be defined by an equation. When the program is run, the computer asks for the first and last values of x to be used in the

```
READ(Y1,Y2); WRITELN;
WRITELN('WHAT PLOTTING
SYMBOL DO YOU WANT?');
S := READKEY; WRITELN;
XAXIS := TRUNC(22-(Y1*22
/ (Y2-Y1)));
YAXIS := TRUNC((-X1*40 /
(X2-X1)));
FOR X := 1 TO 40 DO BEGIN
  FOR Y := 1 TO 22 DO BEGIN
    P[X,Y] := CHR(32);
  END;
END;
FOR X := 1 TO 40 DO
P[X,XAXIS] := CHR(46);
FOR Y := 1 TO 22 DO
P[YAXIS,Y] := CHR(46);
XT := X1;
I := 0;
REPEAT
  I := SUCC(I);
  { UNCOMMENT ONE OF THESE
```

COMPUTER POWER features provide opportunities for students to explore mathematical problems using a computer. It is assumed that students know how to enter a program in PASCAL, but is not necessary for them to understand the program.

APPLICATIONS OF MATHEMATICS

Students can better understand mathematical principles when they are related to their applications. For this reason, applications are integrated throughout *Mathematics 12*.

Every chapter begins with an applied problem that is solved as an example in the chapter.

5 Trigonometric Functions

The tides in the Bay of Fundy are among the highest in the world. Suppose you know how high the water is at high tide, and the time of day this occurs, and also how high it is at low tide, and the time it occurs. How can you determine the height of the water at any other time of the day? (See Section 5-13 *Example 1*.)

Many sections begin with an application which illustrates the necessity for the mathematics that follows.

1-3 COMPOSITION OF FUNCTIONS

Consider the problem of expressing the cost of fuel, when taking a trip by car, as a function of the distance driven.

The cost of fuel, C cents, is a function of the amount of fuel consumed. If fuel costs 50 ¢/L, the cost for x litres of fuel is given by this equation.

$$C = 50x \ldots \text{①}$$

The amount of fuel consumed is a function of the distance driven. If the car consumes fuel at the rate of 8.0 L/100 km, then in travelling d kilometres the amount of fuel consumed is given by this equation.

$$x = 0.080d \ldots \text{②}$$

We can express the cost of fuel as a function of the distance driven

Applications are also included throughout the exercises.

8. The performance of a bicycle can be greatly improved by streamlining, which reduces the effective frontal area of vehicle and rider.
   a) Assuming that the riders can sustain the speeds indicated in the graph, determine the distance travelled in each position illustrated, during 8 h of cycling.
   b) State the domain and the range of the function shown in the graph.
   c) Describe what changes there would be in the graph if it were drawn to represent the speeds sustained for a much shorter period, such as one minute. What change, if any, would there be in the domain? in the range?

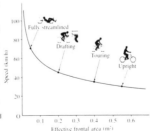

Speed sustained for 8 h by a good athlete

PROBLEM SOLVING

Problem solving is integrated throughout the program, with many of the exercises providing challenging problems for the students to solve. In addition, special features are included which promote the development of problem-solving skills.

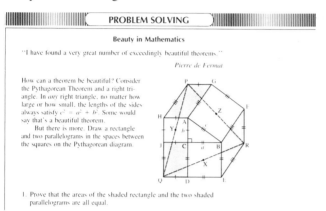

PROBLEM SOLVING

Beauty in Mathematics

"I have found a very great number of exceedingly beautiful theorems."

Pierre de Fermat

How can a theorem be beautiful? Consider the Pythagorean Theorem and a right triangle. In *any* right triangle, no matter how large or how small, the lengths of the sides always satisfy $c^2 = a^2 + b^2$. Some would say that's a beautiful theorem.

But there is more. Draw a rectangle and two parallelograms in the spaces between the squares on the Pythagorean diagram.

1. Prove that the areas of the shaded rectangle and the two shaded parallelograms are all equal.

The *PROBLEM SOLVING* feature is a two-page spread in every chapter which extends the strategies that were developed in earlier grades. The problems are graded by difficulty into B, C, and D problems. The B problems may require some ingenuity to solve. The C problems are challenging, and are similar to the problems that are found in mathematics contests. Some of the D problems are extremely difficult, and may approach the level of difficulty of the problems that occur in olympiad competitions. It is not expected that many students will solve the D problems.

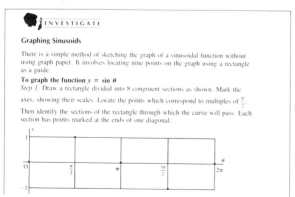

INVESTIGATE

Graphing Sinusoids

There is a simple method of sketching the graph of a sinusoidal function without using graph paper. It involves locating nine points on the graph using a rectangle as a guide.

To graph the function $y = \sin \theta$

Step 1. Draw a rectangle divided into 8 congruent sections as shown. Mark the axes, showing their scales. Locate the points which correspond to multiples of $\frac{\pi}{2}$.

Then identify the sections of the rectangle through which the curve will pass. Each section has points marked at the ends of one diagonal.

Frequent *INVESTIGATE* features are starting points for mathematical investigations to help the student develop analytic skills. These features always relate to the concepts that are developed in the sections in which they occur.

The *MATHEMATICS AROUND US* features outline applications of mathematics in the sciences, the arts, business, and industry.

MATHEMATICS AROUND US

The Waggle Dance of Honeybees

In 1973, Karl von Frisch received a Nobel Prize for his research in animal behaviour. One of his discoveries concerns a method used by honeybees to communicate the location of a food source to other bees inside a hive. Von Frisch observed bees returning to the hive when they had discovered a food source. Shortly after a bee returned, hundreds of bees left the hive, and went directly to the food source, although the bee which had found the food remained inside the hive. Somehow, the bee had informed the others where the food was located.

By marking the bees with paint, and using glass-walled hives, von Frisch learned how they do this. The bee which found the food performs a dance on the honeycomb inside the hive. It follows a figure-8 pattern and wags its body in the central part. Von Frisch observed that:
- the orientation of the central portion indicates the direction of the food source.
- the speed of the dance indicates the distance to the food.

Von Frisch made thousands of observations, comparing the speeds of the bees' dances with the distances to the food, and summarized his results on a graph like the one shown.

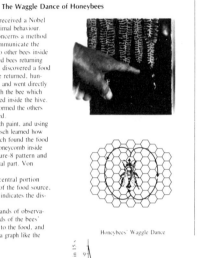

Honeybees' Waggle Dance

QUESTIONS

1. If the food is 1 km away, how many complete cycles does the bee make in

THE MATHEMATICAL MIND features offer insights into the work of mathematicians and the historical development of mathematics. Anecdotes of human interest that are part of history are included. In this feature, problems related to the topic are presented for the student to solve.

THE MATHEMATICAL MIND

The Cubic Equation Controversy

One of the most important mathematical achievements of the sixteenth century was the discovery by Italian mathematicians of formulas for the solution of cubic and quartic equations. This accomplishment occurred at a time when discoveries were often kept secret, and rivals were challenged to solve the same problem.

About 1510, a professor at the University of Bologna revealed to a student a method he had found of solving cubic equations without a quadratic term, such as $x^3 + 5x = 8$.

Nicolo Tartaglia
1499-1557

In 1535, when Nicolo Tartaglia claimed to have found a method of solving cubic equations without a linear term, such as $x^3 + 2x^2 = 6$, the former student challenged him to a public equation-solving contest. But before the contest, Tartaglia learned how to solve an equation of the first type as well, and he won the contest triumphantly.

Girolamo Cardano
1501-1576

Later, Girolamo Cardano urged Tartaglia to show him his method. When Cardano promised to keep it secret, Tartaglia gave it to him. But in 1545 Cardano published his *Ars Magna*, a Latin text on algebra, and included Tartaglia's solution of cubic equations. When Tartaglia protested the breach of his promise, Cardano claimed to have received his information from another party, and accused Tartaglia of plagiarism from the same source. There followed a bitter dispute between the two men over the question of who was the first to discover the formula for solving cubic equations.

Tartaglia's solution gave only one root, and later mathematicians found improved solutions. They also discovered formulas for quartic equations. Much work was done attempting to find a formula for quintic equations, but without success. This was

Contents

1 Functions

From studies of waves, oceanographers have learned that certain properties of waves are related. If you know its wavelength (distance between crests), how can you determine the velocity of a wave? (See Section 1–5 *Example 1.*)

1-1 FUNCTIONS

In everyday language, we use the word "function" to express the idea that one thing depends on another.

The time to complete the course is a function of the skipper's skill.

The time of free fall is a function of the plane's altitude.

The number appearing on the tape counter of a videocassette recorder is a function of the time of playing. The operator's manual for one machine contains the following table. Both the table and the graph show how the counter number is related to the playing time.

Graph of counter number against playing time

Time (h)	Counter Number
0	0
1	2250
2	3182
3	3897
4	4500
5	5031
6	5511

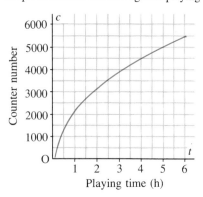

The relation between the counter number and the playing time in hours can be expressed as a set of ordered pairs.

{(0,0), (1,2250), (2,3182), (3,3897), (4,4500), (5,5031), (6,5511)}

This relation can also be expressed with an equation. The equation relating the counter number c with the playing time t hours, is $c = 2250\sqrt{t}$. You can verify that this equation is correct by substituting values for t from the table and using a calculator to calculate the values for c.

On the graph, a smooth curve was drawn through the plotted points. This curve represents the times and the corresponding counter numbers between those given. It is impossible to include all the points in the table of values or the set of ordered pairs because there are infinitely many of them. We can represent these points in a set, using a notation called *set-builder notation*, as follows.

$$\{(x,y) \mid y = 2250\sqrt{x},\ 0 \leq x \leq 6,\ x \in R\}$$

The set . . .   . . . all ordered   . . . such $y = 2250\sqrt{x}$ . . . and *x* is a

of . . .   pairs (*x*,*y*) . . .   that . . .   real number.

     where *x* is between 0 and 6 . . .

Since there cannot be two different counter numbers for the same playing time, this set of ordered pairs has a special property. No two ordered pairs have the same first coordinate. A set of ordered pairs with this property is called a function.

> A *function* is a set of ordered pairs in which no two ordered pairs have the same first coordinate.

A function can be represented in different ways. The requirement that the ordered pairs must have different first coordinates can be seen in each.

- A table of values

x	*y*
0	0
1	2250
2	3182
3	3897
4	4500
5	5031
6	5511

All the entries in the first column are different.

- A graph

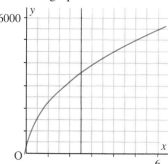

No two points can be joined by a vertical line.

- An equation

$$y = 2250\sqrt{x}$$

For any value of *x*, there is only one value of *y*.

> **Tests for a Function**   (Either of these tests is sufficient.)
>
> *Vertical-Line Test.* If no two points on a graph can be joined by a vertical line, then the graph represents a function.
>
> *Equation Test.* If a value of *x* can be found which produces more than one value of *y* when substituted in an equation, then the equation *does not* represent a function. If there is no such value of *x*, then the equation *does* represent a function.

Example 1.   Given the equations $y = (x - 2)^2$ and $y^2 = x$
  a) Graph the equations and use the graphs to determine which represents a function.
  b) Use the equations to determine which represents a function.

Solution.   a) $y = (x - 2)^2$

x	y
-1	9
0	4
1	1
2	0
3	1
4	4
5	9

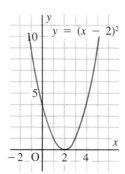

$y^2 = x$

x	y
0	0
1	± 1
4	± 2
9	± 3

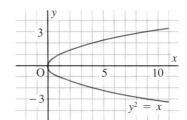

The vertical-line test shows that $y = (x - 2)^2$ is a function, and that $y^2 = x$ is not a function.
  b) For the equation $y = (x - 2)^2$, only one value of y can be calculated for any value of x. Therefore, $y = (x - 2)^2$ is a function.
  For the equation $y^2 = x$, there are values of x for which more than one value of y can be calculated; for example, when $x = 4$, $y = 2$ or $y = -2$. Since there is more than one value of y when $x = 4$, $y^2 = x$ is not a function.

Example 2.   Determine which equations define functions.

  a) $x^2 + y^2 = 10$ b) $y = 2^x$ c) $y = \dfrac{x}{x^2 - 1}$

Solution.   a) $x^2 + y^2 = 10$
  When $x = 0$, $y^2 = 10$
  $$y = \pm\sqrt{10}$$

  Since there are two values of y when $x = 0$, $x^2 + y^2 = 10$ is not a function.
  b) For the equation $y = 2^x$, only one value of y can be calculated for any value of x. Therefore, $y = 2^x$ is a function.

c) The expression $\dfrac{x}{x^2 - 1}$ is not defined when $x = 1$ or when $x = -1$.

For any other value of x, there is only one value of y. Therefore, there is no value of x which produces more than one value of y when substituted in the equation. Therefore, $y = \dfrac{x}{x^2 - 1}$ defines a function if $x \neq 1$ or $x \neq -1$.

Consider again the example of the tape counter on a videocassette recorder, discussed earlier.

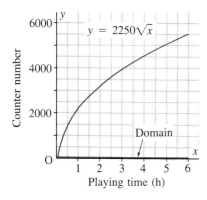

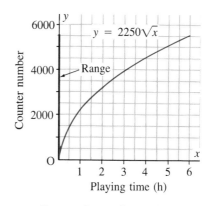

The set of first coordinates is $\{x \mid 0 \leqslant x \leqslant 6, x \in R\}$.
This is the set of possible playing times in hours, and is called the domain of the function.

The set of second coordinates is $\{y \mid 0 \leqslant y \leqslant 5511, y \in R\}$.
This is the set of counter numbers (for playing times up to 6 h), and is called the range of the function.

Given the *graph* of a function

The *domain* is the set of x-values represented by the graph.

The *range* is the set of y-values represented by the graph.

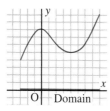

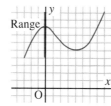

Given the *equation* of a function

The *domain* is the set of all values of x for which the equation is defined.

The *range* is the set of all values of y which are defined for values of x in the domain.

Example 3. Find the domain and the range of the function $y = \sqrt{x^2 - 1}$.

Solution. Since square roots of negative numbers are not real numbers,
$$x^2 - 1 \geq 0$$
$$x^2 \geq 1$$
$$x \geq 1 \text{ or } x \leq -1$$
The domain is the set of all real numbers greater than or equal to 1, or less than or equal to -1. In set-builder notation, the domain is $\{x \mid x \geq 1 \text{ or } x \leq -1, x \in R\}$.
Since the radical sign indicates a positive square root, the expression $\sqrt{x^2 - 1}$ is never negative. That is, $y \geq 0$. Therefore, the range is the set of all non-negative real numbers. In set-builder notation, the range is $\{y \mid y \geq 0, y \in R\}$.

EXERCISES 1-1

Ⓐ

1. Which graphs represent functions?

   a)

   Temperature of melting ice

   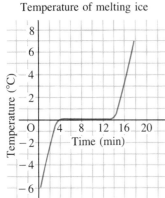

   b)

   World records for the marathon run

   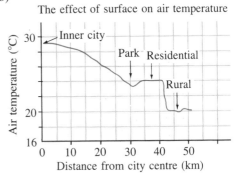

2. State the domain and the range for each function.

   a)

   Value of
   Canadian dollar in U.S. cents

   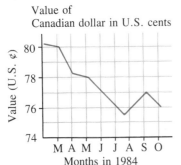

   b)

   The effect of surface on air temperature

3. Determine if each graph represents a function.

a)

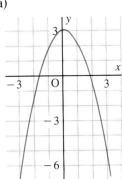

b)

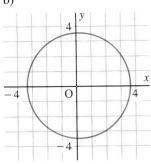

c)

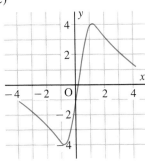

Ⓑ

4. Determine if each equation represents a function. If it does, state the domain and the range.

a) $y = 2x - 4$
b) $y = x^2$
c) $y = \sqrt{x + 1}$
d) $y^2 = x$
e) $y = 10^x$
f) $x^2 - y^2 = 4$

5. State the domain and the range for each function.

a) $y = 2 - 3x$
b) $y = x^3$
c) $y = \sqrt{1 - x}$
d) $y = \dfrac{1}{x}$
e) $y = \dfrac{1}{x^2 - 1}$
f) $y = \dfrac{x^2}{x^2 - 4}$

6. Graph each function.

a) $y = 2x + 3$
b) $y = 5 - 2x$
c) $y = x^2$
d) $y = (x + 2)^2$
e) $y = \sqrt{x}$
f) $y = \sqrt{x + 3}$

7. Air pressure is a function of altitude.
   a) Use the graph to find the air pressure at each location.

Location	Altitude (m)
i) Sea level	0
ii) Banff, Alberta	1 383
iii) Mexico City	2 240
iv) Peak of Mount Everest	8 848
v) Jet liner	12 000

b) At what altitude is the air pressure 50% of the pressure at sea level?
c) State the domain and the range of the function, as graphed.

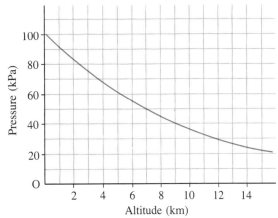

Pressure variations with altitude

8. The performance of a bicycle can be greatly improved by streamlining, which reduces the effective frontal area of vehicle and rider.
   a) Assuming that the riders can sustain the speeds indicated in the graph, determine the distance travelled in each position illustrated, during 8 h of cycling.
   b) State the domain and the range of the function shown in the graph.
   c) Describe what changes there would be in the graph if it were drawn to represent the speeds sustained for a much shorter period, such as one minute. What change, if any, would there be in the domain? in the range?

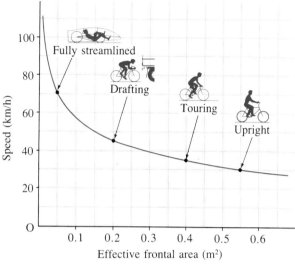

Speed sustained for 8 h by a good athlete

9. Graph each function.
   a) $y = 3x - 5$
   b) $y = (x + 3)^2$
   c) $y = \sqrt{2x - 4}$
   d) $y = \dfrac{1}{x}$
   e) $y = \dfrac{5}{x^2 + 1}$
   f) $y = \dfrac{5x}{x^2 + 1}$

Ⓒ

10. High-speed photographs have shown that the hand of a karate expert can reach speeds of 12 m/s or greater during certain karate manoeuvres.
    a) For each graph shown
       i) Find the speed of the hand after 0.05 s; after 0.10 s.
       ii) Find the hand's greatest speed.
    b) What happens to the speed of the hand during the forward karate punch between 0.12 s and 0.14 s? Why does this not happen during the hammer-fist strike?

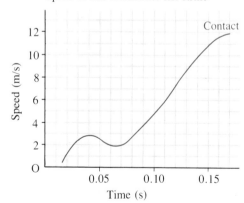

Speed of fist in hammer-fist strike

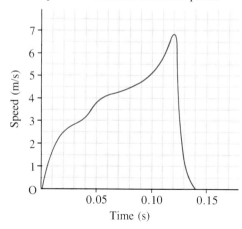

Speed of fist in forward karate punch

1-2 FUNCTION NOTATION

In the preceding section we saw that a function can be represented by a set of ordered pairs, a table of values, a graph, and an equation. A function can also be represented using a special notation, called *function notation*. For example, we may write:

$f(x) = 5x^2 - 6x + 1$. We say, "f of x equals $5x^2 - 6x + 1$." This notation simplifies recording the values of the function for several values of x. For example, $f(-3)$ is the value of $f(x)$ when we substitute -3 for x everywhere x occurs in the expression.

$$f(x) = 5x^2 - 6x + 1$$

$$f(-3) = 5(-3)^2 - 6(-3) + 1$$
$$= 45 + 18 + 1$$
$$= 64$$

Example 1. If $f(x) = 3x + \dfrac{1}{x}$, find:

a) $f(2)$

b) $f\left(-\dfrac{1}{2}\right)$

Solution. a) Substitute 2 for x.

$$f(x) = 3x + \frac{1}{x}$$

$$f(2) = 3(2) + \frac{1}{2}$$

$$= 6.5$$

b) Substitute $-\dfrac{1}{2}$ for x.

$$f(x) = 3x + \frac{1}{x}$$

$$f\left(-\frac{1}{2}\right) = 3\left(-\frac{1}{2}\right) + \frac{1}{-\frac{1}{2}}$$

$$= -1.5 - 2$$
$$= -3.5$$

Algebraic expressions may be substituted for variables in the equation of a function.

Example 2. If $g(x) = \dfrac{x - 3}{x}$, $x \neq 0$, find:

a) $g(1 - 2x)$

b) $g\left(\dfrac{5}{y}\right)$

Solution. a) $g(x) = \dfrac{x - 3}{x}$

Substitute $1 - 2x$ for x.

$$g(1 - 2x) = \frac{(1 - 2x) - 3}{1 - 2x}$$

$$= \frac{-2 - 2x}{1 - 2x}$$

$$= \frac{2x + 2}{2x - 1}, x \neq \frac{1}{2}$$

b) $g(x) = \dfrac{x - 3}{x}$

Substitute $\dfrac{5}{y}$ for x.

$$g\left(\frac{5}{y}\right) = \frac{\frac{5}{y} - 3}{\frac{5}{y}} \times \frac{y}{y}$$

$$= \frac{5 - 3y}{5}, y \neq 0$$

Function notation can be used even when an equation relating the variables is not given.

Example 3. From the graph of $y = f(x)$, find:

a) $f(1)$ b) $f(-2)$ c) $f(5)$ d) $f(0)$.

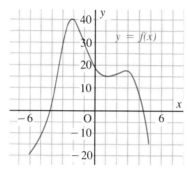

Solution.

a) $f(1)$ is the value of y when $x = 1$. To find this value, draw a vertical line, $x = 1$, to intersect the graph. Then, draw a horizontal line to intersect the y-axis.

$f(1)$ appears to be 15.

b) $f(-2)$ appears to be 40.

c) $f(5)$ appears to be -15.

d) $f(0)$ appears to be 20.

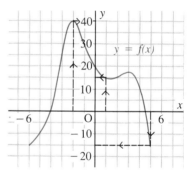

Example 4. Let n be a natural number, and let $f(n)$ represent the number of factors of n.

a) Find $f(5)$, $f(6)$, and $f(9)$.

b) Draw the graph of $y = f(n)$ for values of n from 1 to 12.

Solution.

a) The factors of 5 are 1 and 5. Since there are two factors, $f(5) = 2$.
The factors of 6 are 1, 2, 3, and 6. Since there are four factors, $f(6) = 4$.
The factors of 9 are 1, 3, and 9. Since there are three factors, $f(9) = 3$.

b) Make a table of values and draw the graph.

n	1	2	3	4	5	6	7	8	9	10	11	12
$f(n)$	1	2	2	3	2	4	2	4	3	4	2	6

Factors of natural numbers

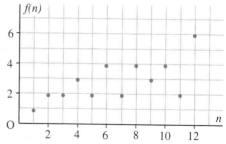

EXERCISES 1-2

1. If $f(x) = x^2 + 3$, find:
   a) $f(1)$ b) $f(2)$ c) $f(0)$ d) $f(-1)$ e) $f(-2)$ f) $f(-3)$.

2. If $g(x) = 1 - 2x$, find:
   a) $g(1)$ b) $g(-2)$ c) $g(-5)$ d) $g(0)$ e) $g(6)$ f) $g\left(-\dfrac{1}{2}\right)$.

3. Find $f(-3)$, $f(4)$, and $f(-0.5)$ for each function.
   a) $f(x) = 5x - 2$ b) $f(x) = x^2 - 5$ c) $f(x) = x^2 + x$

4. For each graph of $y = f(x)$, find $f(-4)$, $f(0)$, and $f(6)$.
   a)   b)

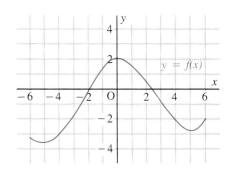   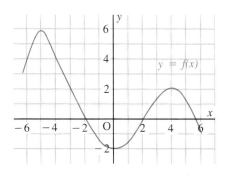

5. If $f(x) = 3x^2 - 5x + 2$, find:
   a) $f(4)$ b) $f(-2)$ c) $f(1)$ d) $f(-1)$ e) $f(0)$ f) $f(1.5)$.

6. If $g(x) = -2x^2 + 3x - 6$, find:
   a) $g(1)$ b) $g(2)$ c) $g(-2)$ d) $g(0)$ e) $g(-4)$ f) $g(-0.5)$.

7. Let n be a positive integer, and let $d(n)$ represent the number of digits of n. For example, $d(15) = 2$, since 15 has 2 digits.
   a) Find. i) $d(6)$ ii) $d(47)$ iii) $d(803)$
   b) How many positive integers n are there such that:
      i) $d(n) = 1$ ii) $d(n) = 2$ iii) $d(n) = 3$?

8. If $f(x) = 2x + 1$, and $g(x) = 3 - x$, find:
   a) $f(a)$ b) $f(3a)$ c) $f(1 + y)$ d) $f(x + 1)$
   e) $g(y)$ f) $g(2 - y)$ g) $g(z - 1)$ h) $g(2x - 3)$
   i) $2f(x)$ j) $5g(n)$ k) $-3f(x)$ l) $-2g(a)$.

9. Graph each function and state its domain and range.
   a) $f(x) = 2x + 1$ b) $f(x) = x^2$ c) $f(x) = \sqrt{x}$

10. If $f(x) = 2 - 5x$, and $g(x) = x^2 - x - 1$, evaluate each expression.
    a) $f(1) + g(1)$ b) $f(2) + g(2)$ c) $f(-1) + g(-1)$
    d) $f(-1) - g(-1)$ e) $f(-3) - g(-3)$ f) $f(0) - g(0)$

11. If $g(x) = \dfrac{x+1}{x-1}$, $x \neq 1$, find:

   a) $g(2x)$ b) $g(-x)$ c) $-g(x)$ d) $g\left(\dfrac{1}{x}\right)$

   e) $g(x+1)$ f) $-g(x-1)$ g) $g(2x+1)$ h) $g(1-2x)$.

12. If $f(x) = 2x - 3$, and $g(x) = 1 - 4x$, find a value of x that satisfies each equation.
   a) $f(x) = g(x)$ b) $f(x) = g(-x)$ c) $f(-x) = g(x)$
   d) $f(x+1) = g(x-1)$ e) $f(2x-1) = g(x+1)$

13. If $f(x) = 3x - 5$, solve each equation.
   a) $f(x) = 0$ b) $f(x) = 1$ c) $f(x) = -4$
   d) $f(x) = f(-x)$ e) $f(x+1) = f(x-1)$

14. Let n be a positive integer, and let $s(n)$ represent the sum of the digits of n.
   a) Find.   i) $s(15)$ ii) $s(68)$ iii) $s(509)$
   b) Give examples of positive integers n such that: i) $s(n) = 1$ ii) $s(n) = 2$.
   c) How many solutions do these equations have?
     i) $s(n) = 1$ ii) $s(n) = 2$

Ⓒ

15. If $f(x) = 1 + \dfrac{1}{x}$, prove that $f(x) + f\left(\dfrac{1}{x}\right) = f(x)f\left(\dfrac{1}{x}\right)$.

16. Let n be a positive integer, and let $f(n)$ represent the number of different prime factors of n.
   a) Find.   i) $f(1)$ ii) $f(6)$ iii) $f(9)$ iv) $f(20)$
   b) What is the least number n such that: i) $f(n) = 3$ ii) $f(n) = 4$?

17. Let n be a natural number, and let $g(n)$ be the largest factor of n, other than n.
   a) Explain why $g(n) \leqslant \dfrac{1}{2}n$ for all values of n.
   b) Give an example of a natural number n such that:
     i) $g(n) = \dfrac{1}{2}n$ ii) $g(n) < \dfrac{1}{2}n$.

18. $f(x)$ is a function with the following properties.
   ● The domain of $f(x)$ is the set of real numbers.
   ● $f(0) = 0$
   ● $f(x+1) = f(x) + 2x + 1$ for all real values of x
   a) Find.   i) $f(1), f(2), f(3), f(4)$
           ii) $f(-1), f(-2), f(-3), f(-4)$
   b) Describe the function $f(x)$.

19. Given $f(x) = 2^x$, show that:
   a) $f(x)f(y) = f(x+y)$ b) $f(nx) = [f(x)]^n$, where $n \in N$.

20. In *Exercise 19*, find another example of a function $f(x)$ such that
   $f(x)f(y) = f(x+y)$ and $f(nx) = [f(x)]^n$, $n \in N$.

MATHEMATICS AROUND US

The Waggle Dance of Honeybees

In 1973, Karl von Frisch received a Nobel Prize for his research in animal behaviour. One of his discoveries concerns a method used by honeybees to communicate the location of a food source to other bees inside a hive. Von Frisch observed bees returning to the hive when they had discovered a food source. Shortly after a bee returned, hundreds of bees left the hive, and went directly to the food source, although the bee which had found the food remained inside the hive. Somehow, the bee had informed the others where the food was located.

By marking the bees with paint, and using glass-walled hives, von Frisch learned how they do this. The bee which found the food performs a dance on the honeycomb inside the hive. It follows a figure-8 pattern and wags its body in the central part. Von Frisch observed that:

- the orientation of the central portion indicates the direction of the food source,
- the speed of the dance indicates the distance to the food.

Von Frisch made thousands of observations, comparing the speeds of the bees' dances with the distances to the food, and summarized his results on a graph like the one shown.

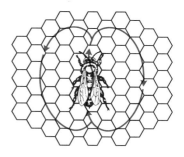

QUESTIONS

1. If the food is 1 km away, how many complete cycles does the bee make in 15 s? in 1 min?

2. If the bee makes 10 complete cycles in one minute, how far away is the food?

3. How would the graph differ if it were drawn to show the number of complete cycles in one minute instead of 15 s?

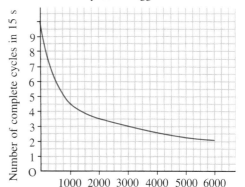

Honeybees' Waggle Dance

1-3 COMPOSITION OF FUNCTIONS

Consider the problem of expressing the cost of fuel, when taking a trip by car, as a function of the distance driven.

The cost of fuel, C cents, is a function of the amount of fuel consumed. If fuel costs 50 ¢/L, the cost for x litres of fuel is given by this equation.

$$C = 50x \ldots ①$$

The amount of fuel consumed is a function of the distance driven. If the car consumes fuel at the rate of 8.0 L/100 km, then in travelling d kilometres the amount of fuel consumed is given by this equation.

$$x = 0.080d \ldots ②$$

We can express the cost of fuel as a function of the distance driven by substituting $0.080d$ for x in ①.

$$C = 50x$$
$$= 50(0.080d)$$
$$C = 4.0d \ldots ③$$

The cost of fuel to drive a distance of d kilometres is $C = 4.0d$, or 4 cents per kilometre.

When two functions are applied in succession, the resulting function is called the *composite* of the two given functions. The function described by equation ③ is the composite of the functions described by equations ① and ②.

Function composition can be illustrated with mapping diagrams.

Distance	Litres	Cost
100	8.0	400
200	16.0	800
300	24.0	1200
400	32.0	1600

Consider the functions $f(x) = 2x + 3$ and $g(x) = x^2 - 1$. There are two different ways to form the composite of these functions.

Apply f first and g second	**Apply g first and f second**
Double and add 3, then . . . square and subtract 1.	Square and subtract 1, then . . . double and add 3.

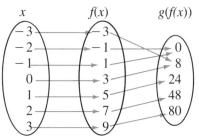

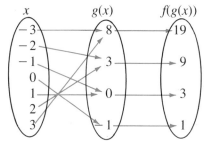

The composite function relates the numbers in the first set to those in the third, and is written as $g(f(x))$, or $g \circ f(x)$. We say, "g of f of x".

In this case, the composite function is written as $f(g(x))$, or $f \circ g(x)$.

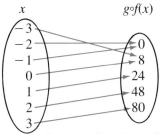

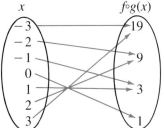

To express $g \circ f(x)$ as a function of x, substitute $f(x)$ for x in $g(x)$.

$$g(x) = x^2 - 1$$

$$g(f(x)) = (f(x))^2 - 1$$
$$= (2x + 3)^2 - 1$$
$$= 4x^2 + 12x + 9 - 1$$
$$= 4x^2 + 12x + 8$$

To express $f \circ g(x)$ as a function of x, substitute $g(x)$ for x in $f(x)$.

$$f(x) = 2x + 3$$

$$f(g(x)) = 2g(x) + 3$$
$$= 2(x^2 - 1) + 3$$
$$= 2x^2 - 2 + 3$$
$$= 2x^2 + 1$$

Example 1. Given $f(x) = 3x - 5$ and $g(x) = x^2 - x$
   a) Find $f \circ g(3)$ and $g \circ f(3)$.
   b) Express $f \circ g(x)$ and $g \circ f(x)$ as functions of x.

Solution.   a)

$$g(x) = x^2 - x$$
$$g(3) = 3^2 - 3$$
$$= 6$$
$$f \circ g(3) = f(g(3))$$
$$= f(6)$$
$$= 3(6) - 5$$
$$= 18 - 5$$
$$= 13$$

$$f(x) = 3x - 5$$
$$f(3) = 3(3) - 5$$
$$= 4$$
$$g \circ f(3) = g(f(3))$$
$$= g(4)$$
$$= 4^2 - 4$$
$$= 16 - 4$$
$$= 12$$

b)
$$f \circ g(x) = f(g(x))$$
$$= 3(g(x)) - 5$$
$$= 3(x^2 - x) - 5$$
$$= 3x^2 - 3x - 5$$

$$g \circ f(x) = g(f(x))$$
$$= (f(x))^2 - f(x)$$
$$= (3x - 5)^2 - (3x - 5)$$
$$= 9x^2 - 30x + 25 - 3x + 5$$
$$= 9x^2 - 33x + 30$$

   When finding the composite of two functions, it is not necessary for the functions to be different. In other words, we can find the composite of a function with itself.

Example 2. Given $f(x) = 3x - 1$, find $f \circ f(x)$.

Solution.
$$f \circ f(x) = f(f(x))$$
$$= 3(f(x)) - 1$$
$$= 3(3x - 1) - 1$$
$$= 9x - 4$$

EXERCISES 1-3

(A)

1. Given $f(x) = 2x + 1$ and $g(x) = 3x + 1$, find:
   a) $f(3)$ b) $g(f(3))$ c) $g(3)$ d) $f(g(3))$.

2. For the functions in *Exercise 1*, find $g(f(x))$ and $f(g(x))$.

3. Given $f(x) = x^2 + 1$ and $g(x) = 2x$, find:
   a) $f(2)$ b) $g \circ f(2)$ c) $g(2)$ d) $f \circ g(2)$.

4. For the functions in *Exercise 3*, find $g \circ f(x)$ and $f \circ g(x)$.

5. Find $f(g(x))$ and $g(f(x))$ for each pair of functions.
   a) $f(x) = 3x + 4$; $g(x) = -2x + 5$
   b) $f(x) = x^2 + 5x$; $g(x) = 2x + 1$
   c) $f(x) = 2x^2 - 3x + 1$; $g(x) = 7 - 4x$

6. Given $f(x) = 3x^2 - 1$, find $f(g(x))$ and $g(f(x))$ for each function $g(x)$.
   a) $g(x) = x + 2$ b) $g(x) = 1 - 2x$ c) $g(x) = x^2$

   d) $g(x) = x^2 + x$ e) $g(x) = 2x^2 - 3x$ f) $g(x) = \dfrac{1}{x}, x \neq 0$

7. The area A of a circle is a function of its radius r, where $A = \pi r^2$. Express the area as a function of the diameter d.

8. The volume V of a sphere is a function of its radius r, where $V = \dfrac{4}{3}\pi r^3$. Express the volume as a function of the diameter d.

(B)

9. Given $f(x) = 2x - 1$ and $g(x) = 1 - 3x$, find:
   a) $f(g(2))$ b) $g(f(2))$ c) $f(f(2))$ d) $g(g(2))$.

10. For the functions in *Exercise 9*, find:
    a) $f(g(x))$ b) $g(f(x))$ c) $f(f(x))$ d) $g(g(x))$.

11. Given $f(x) = 4 - x$ and $g(x) = x^2 + x$, find:
    a) $f \circ g(-1)$ b) $g \circ f(-1)$ c) $f \circ f(-1)$ d) $g \circ g(-1)$.

12. For the functions in *Exercise 11*, find:
    a) $f \circ g(x)$ b) $g \circ f(x)$ c) $f \circ f(x)$ d) $g \circ g(x)$.

13. For each pair of functions, find $f \circ g(x)$, $g \circ f(x)$, $f \circ f(x)$, and $g \circ g(x)$.
    a) $f(x) = \sqrt{x}$; $g(x) = 4 - 2x$ b) $f(x) = \sqrt{2x}$; $g(x) = 1 + 3x$

    c) $f(x) = \dfrac{x}{x + 1}$; $g(x) = x^2 - 1$ d) $f(x) = 2^x$; $g(x) = 3x - 4$

14. The area A and perimeter P of a square are functions of its side length S. Express the area as a function of the perimeter.

15. Express the area of a square as a function of the length of its diagonal.

16. Given $f(x) = \dfrac{1}{x}$ and $g(x) = x^2$, show that $f(g(x)) = g(f(x))$.

17. Given $f(x) = 1 - x$ and $g(x) = \dfrac{x}{1 - x}$, $x \neq 1$

   a) Show that $g(f(x)) = \dfrac{1}{g(x)}$.   b) Does $f(g(x)) = \dfrac{1}{f(x)}$?

18. The temperature of the Earth's crust is a linear function of the depth below the surface. An equation expressing the relationship is $T = 0.01d + 20$. T is the temperature in degrees Celsius, and d is the depth in metres. If you go down the shaft in an elevator at the rate of 5 m/s, express the temperature as a function of the time of travel t seconds.

19. For each pair of functions, determine values of x such that $f(g(x)) = g(f(x))$.

   a) $f(x) = 2x + 3$; $g(x) = x^2 - x + 3$ b) $f(x) = \dfrac{1}{x}$; $g(x) = 2x + 1$

20. From the functions listed in the box, find two whose composite function is $h(x)$.

   a) $h(x) = (x + 1)^2$
   b) $h(x) = \sqrt{x - 3}$
   c) $h(x) = x^2 - 6x + 9$
   d) $h(x) = x - 2$

$e(x) = x - 3$	$f(x) = x^2$
$g(x) = \sqrt{x}$	$k(x) = x + 1$

21. Find two functions whose composite function is $k(x)$.

   a) $k(x) = x^6 + 2x^3 + 1$ b) $k(x) = (x - 4)^2 + 3(x - 4) + 4$

   c) $k(x) = \sqrt{3x - 2}$ d) $k(x) = \dfrac{1}{x + 3}$

22. Given $f(x) = x - 3$ and $g(x) = \sqrt{x}$, find:
   a) $f{\circ}g(x)$ b) the domain of $f{\circ}g(x)$ c) the range of $f{\circ}g(x)$
   d) $g{\circ}f(x)$ e) the domain of $g{\circ}f(x)$ f) the range of $g{\circ}f(x)$.

23. Given $f(x) = x^2 + 1$ and $g(x) = \sqrt{x - 1}$, find:
   a) $f{\circ}g(x)$ b) the domain of $f{\circ}g(x)$ c) the range of $f{\circ}g(x)$
   d) $g{\circ}f(x)$ e) the domain of $g{\circ}f(x)$ f) the range of $g{\circ}f(x)$.

24. Find $f(f(x))$ for each function.

   a) $f(x) = \dfrac{1}{1 - x}$, $x \neq 1$ b) $f(x) = \dfrac{x - 1}{x + 1}$, $x \neq -1$

Ⓒ

25. Given $f(x) = 2x + 1$
   a) Find. i) $f{\circ}f(x)$ ii) $f{\circ}f{\circ}f(x)$ iii) $f{\circ}f{\circ}f{\circ}f(x)$
   b) On the basis of the results in part a), predict what these functions would be.
      i) $f{\circ}f{\circ}f{\circ}f{\circ}f(x)$ ii) $f{\circ}f{\circ}f \ldots {\circ}f(x)$ (n functions)

26. Repeat *Exercise 25* using $f(x) = \dfrac{x}{x + 1}$, $x \neq -1$.

27. Given $f(x) = ax + b$, $g(x) = cx + d$, and $f(g(x)) = g(f(x))$, how are a, b, c, and d related?

COMPUTER POWER

Graphing Functions

A computer is ideally suited for graphing functions, since it can rapidly calculate the values of a function for many values of *x*. The graph can be displayed on the computer screen or printed on paper. The most primitive programs plot symbols on the screen, which normally consists of about 20 rows of 40 characters each. The program below is of this type, and can be used on almost any computer. For more accurate graphs, other programs must be used, but the commands are specific to particular computers.

This program can be used to obtain an approximation to the graph of any function that can be defined by an equation. When the program is run, the computer asks for the first and last values of *x* to be used in the table of values. To reduce the length of the program, it is necessary that the first value be negative, and the second value positive. Also, the least and greatest *y*-values desired must be entered. Once again, the first must be negative, and the second positive.

To get the graph of $y = x^3 - 12x + 8$, delete the brace brackets which precede and follow the equation in the line that follows {UNCOMMENT ONE OF THESE LINES}.

```
LABEL 250;
VAR
  P : ARRAY [1..40,1..22] OF CHAR;
  S,CH : CHAR;
  X1,X2,Y1,Y2,XT : REAL;
  XAXIS,YAXIS,X,Y,I,XI :
  INTEGER;
BEGIN  { FUNCTION GRAPHS }
       WRITELN('FIRST AND LAST
       X-VALUES? ');
       READ(X1,X2); WRITELN;
       WRITELN('LEAST AND
       GREATEST Y-VALUES? ');
```

```
       READ(Y1,Y2); WRITELN;
       WRITELN('WHAT PLOTTING
SYMBOL DO YOU WANT? ');
S := READKEY; WRITELN;
XAXIS := TRUNC(22-(Y1*22
/ (Y2-Y1)));
YAXIS := TRUNC((-X1*40 /
(X2-X1)));
FOR X := 1 TO 40 DO BEGIN
  FOR Y := 1 TO 22 DO BEGIN
    P[X,Y] := CHR(32);
  END;
END;
FOR X := 1 TO 40 DO
P[X,XAXIS] := CHR(46);
FOR Y := 1 TO 22 DO
P[YAXIS,Y] := CHR(46);
XT := X1;
I := 0;
REPEAT
  I := SUCC(I);
  { UNCOMMENT ONE OF THESE
LINES }
  { Y := TRUNC((XT*XT*XT) -
12 * XT + 8); }
  { Y := TRUNC(XT * XT - 4 *
XT); }
  { Y := 1 SHL TRUNC(XT); }
  { Y := TRUNC(ABS(2 * XT
+ 1)); }
  { IF (XT + 3 < 0) THEN GOTO
250; Y := TRUNC(SQRT(XT +
3)); }
  IF (Y >= Y1) AND (Y<=Y2)
THEN
    P[I,TRUNC(22-((Y-Y1)
    * 22 / (Y2-Y1)))] := S;
250:  XT := XT + ((X2 - X1) /
39);
UNTIL XT >= X2;
FOR Y := 1 TO 22 DO BEGIN
  FOR X := 1 TO 40 DO BEGIN
    CH := P [X,Y];
    WRITE(CH);
  END;
  WRITELN;
END;
CH := READKEY;
END.
```

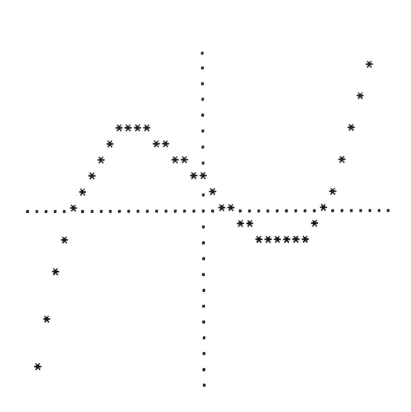

The sample output shows this function graphed for values of *x* between −5 and 5, with values of *y* between −50 and 50.

```
FIRST AND LAST X-VALUES? -5,5
LEAST AND GREATEST Y-VALUES? -50,50
WHAT PLOTTING SYMBOL DO YOU WANT? *
```

The program allows you to graph 4 other functions: $y = x^2 - 4x$; $y = 2^x$; $y = |2x + 1|$; $y = \sqrt{x + 3}$. Replace the brace brackets around the line representing $y = x^3 - 12x + 8$ and delete the brackets around the function selected. To graph any other function, insert its equation in the program without the brace brackets.

Error messages will result if values of *x* for which the function is not defined are used. For example, with reciprocal functions, a denominator of 0 must be avoided. Similarly, with square root functions, square roots of negative numbers must be avoided.

1-4 THE INVERSE OF A FUNCTION

Consider the functions $y = f(x)$ and $y = g(x)$ represented by the following mapping diagrams.

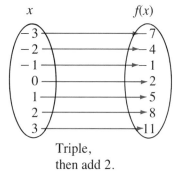

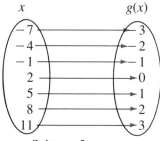

Triple,
then add 2.

Subtract 2,
then divide by 3.

The diagram on the right reverses the mapping of the diagram on the left, and vice versa. The ordered pairs of the function $y = g(x)$ are obtained by interchanging the members of the ordered pairs of $y = f(x)$. We say that the functions $y = f(x)$ and $y = g(x)$ are inverses of each other.

The *inverse* of a function is the set of ordered pairs obtained by interchanging the members of each ordered pair of the function.

We can compare the graphs of the functions $y = f(x)$ and $y = g(x)$ by drawing them on the same grid.

    The graphs appear to be reflections of each other in the line $y = x$. This is what we should expect since the members of the ordered pairs of one function are interchanged to obtain the ordered pairs of the other function.

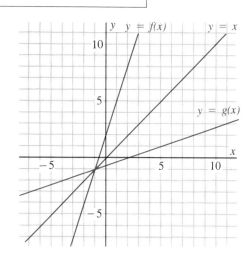

Reflection Property
When the members of each ordered pair of a function are interchanged, the graph of the function is reflected in the line $y = x$.

We can prove this reflection property as follows.

Given:
The graphs of $y = f(x)$ and its inverse $y = g(x)$

Required to Prove:
$y = g(x)$ is the reflection of $y = f(x)$ in the line $y = x$.

Analysis:
If we can prove that the line $y = x$ is the perpendicular bisector of
the line segment joining two corresponding points on the graphs of
$y = f(x)$ and $y = g(x)$, then $y = x$ must be the line of reflection
for those graphs.

Proof:
Let P(a,b) be a point on the graph of $y = f(x)$.
Since $y = g(x)$ is the inverse of $y = f(x)$, Q(b,a) is the
corresponding point on the graph of $y = g(x)$.
Since each coordinate of the midpoint of a line segment
is the mean of the corresponding coordinates of the
endpoints,

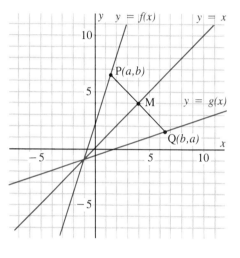

$$M\left(\frac{a + b}{2}, \frac{b + a}{2}\right) \text{ is the midpoint of PQ.}$$

Since the coordinates of M are equal, M lies on the
line $y = x$.
Hence, $y = x$ bisects PQ.

Assuming $a \neq b$, the slope of PQ is $\dfrac{a - b}{b - a} = \dfrac{a - b}{-(a - b)}$
$$= -1$$

The slope of the line $y = x$ is 1.

Since their slopes are negative reciprocals, PQ is perpendicular to the
line $y = x$.
We have proved that the line $y = x$ bisects PQ, and is perpendicular
to PQ.
Therefore, the line $y = x$ is the perpendicular bisector of PQ.

This proves that $y = g(x)$ is the reflection of $y = f(x)$ in the line $y = x$.

When a function is defined by an equation, we can obtain its inverse by interchanging x and y in the equation rather than in the ordered
pairs. In the above example, the equation of the function $y = f(x)$ is
$y = 3x + 2$. We can find the equation of the inverse by interchanging
x and y.
$$x = 3y + 2$$
It is customary to solve this equation for y.
$$3y = x - 2$$
$$y = \frac{x - 2}{3}$$
Therefore, the equation of the inverse function is $y = \dfrac{x - 2}{3}$.

The inverse function of a given function $y = f(x)$ is written with a special notation, $y = f^{-1}(x)$. We say, "y equals the inverse function of x." For the function $f(x) = 3x + 2$, we write $f^{-1}(x) = \dfrac{x - 2}{3}$.

Example 1. a) Find the inverse of the function $f(x) = \dfrac{1}{x + 2}$.

b) Show that the inverse is a function and write it using function notation.

c) Determine the domain and the range of the inverse.

Solution. a) Write the equation of the function.

$$y = \frac{1}{x + 2}$$

Interchange x and y.

$$x = \frac{1}{y + 2}$$

Solve for y.

$$xy + 2x = 1$$
$$xy = 1 - 2x$$
$$y = \frac{1 - 2x}{x}$$

b) For each value of x, only one value of y can be calculated. Therefore, the inverse is a function.

In function notation, the inverse function is $f^{-1}(x) = \dfrac{1 - 2x}{x}$.

c) The inverse function is defined for all values of x except $x = 0$.
Therefore, the domain of the inverse function is $\{x \mid x \neq 0, x \in R\}$.
The domain of the given function is all values of x except $x = -2$.
Since the ordered pairs are interchanged when finding the inverse, this corresponds to the range of the inverse.
Therefore, the range of the inverse function is $\{y \mid y \neq -2, y \in R\}$.

Example 2. a) Find the inverse of the function $f(x) = (x - 3)^2$.

b) Graph the function $y = f(x)$ and its inverse on the same grid.

c) Is the inverse a function?

Solution. a) Write the equation of the function.
$$y = (x - 3)^2$$
Interchange x and y, and then solve for y.
$$x = (y - 3)^2$$
Take the square root of both sides, assuming $x \geq 0$.
$$\pm\sqrt{x} = y - 3$$
$$y = \pm\sqrt{x} + 3$$

b) We graph $f(x) = (x - 3)^2$ by making a table of values. Then we can graph the inverse by reflecting the graph of $y = f(x)$ in the line $y = x$.

$f(x) = (x - 3)^2$

x	y
0	9
1	4
2	1
3	0
4	1
5	4
6	9

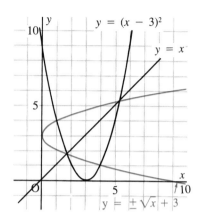

c) The inverse is not a function, since there are two values of y corresponding to a value of x. This is indicated by the term $\pm\sqrt{x}$ in the equation, and by the fact that the graph of the inverse does not pass the vertical-line test.

When the inverse of a function is not a function, we can usually restrict the domain of the given function so that its inverse is a function. Two ways of doing this for the function in *Example 2* are shown below. In principle, there are infinitely many ways of doing this.

Restrict the domain of $y = (x - 3)^2$ to values of $x \geqslant 3$.
Then, the inverse is $y = \sqrt{x} + 3$.

or

Restrict the domain of $y = (x - 3)^2$ to values of $x \leqslant 3$.
Then, the inverse is $y = -\sqrt{x} + 3$.

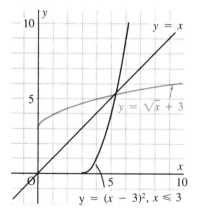

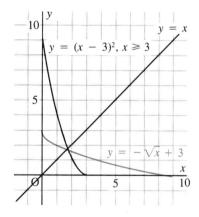

In both cases, the inverse is a function because its graph passes the vertical-line test.

Properties of the Inverse of a Function
- The inverse of a function is obtained by:
  - — reversing the mapping diagram
  - — interchanging the ordered pairs of the function
  - — interchanging x and y in the equation, and solving for y
  - — reflecting the graph of the function in the line $y = x$.
- The domain of the inverse is the range of the original function.
- The range of the inverse is the domain of the original function.
- The inverse of a function is not necessarily a function.

EXERCISES 1-4

(A)

1. On each grid, is $y = g(x)$ the inverse of $y = f(x)$?

 a)

 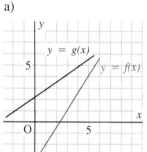

 b)

 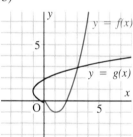

 c)

 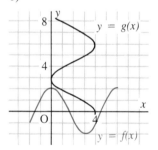

2. Find the equation for the inverse of each function. Is the inverse a function?

 a) $y = 2x + 5$

 b) $3x^2 - y = 4$

 c) $5x + 2y = 10$

 d) $f(x) = 4x^2 - 1$

 e) $f(x) = \dfrac{x - 3}{x}$

 f) $f(x) = \dfrac{2x + 3}{4}$

(B)

3. Graph each function, its inverse, and the line $y = x$ on the same grid.

 a) $f(x) = 5 - 2x$

 b) $f(x) = \dfrac{1}{2}x^2 - 2, \; x \geq 0$

 c) $f(x) = \dfrac{2x - 1}{x}, \; x > 0$

 d) $f(x) = (x - 1)^2 + 2, \; x \geq 1$

4. Find the inverse of each function, and state whether the inverse is also a function. If the inverse is a function, state its domain and range.

 a) $f(x) = 2x + 3$

 b) $g(x) = 2x^2 - 3$

 c) $h(x) = \dfrac{1}{x + 1}$

 d) $f(x) = (x + 1)^2$

 e) $g(x) = \dfrac{x + 1}{x}$

 f) $\{(x,y) \mid y = \sqrt{x - 2}\}$

5. Restrict the domain of each function so that its inverse is a function. Illustrate the function and its inverse on a grid.
   a) $y = x^2 - 2$
   b) $y = 2(x + 1)^2 - 3$
   c) $y + x^2 = 5$
   d) $f(x) = 4 - x^2$
   e) $f(x) = (x - 1)^2 - 1$
   f) $f(x) = 4 - (x - 3)^2$

6. Find the inverse of each function.
   a) $f(x) = \dfrac{1}{1 - x}, x \neq 1$
   b) $f(x) = \dfrac{x - 2}{x + 2}, x \neq -2$
   c) $f(x) = \dfrac{2x^2}{x^2 - 4}, x \neq 2, -2$
   d) $f(x) = \dfrac{1}{3x^2 + 4}$

7. Two functions are described in words. Is each function the inverse of the other?
   a) i) The value of x is increased by 3.
      ii) The value of x is decreased by 3.
   b) i) Twice the value of x is decreased by 1.
      ii) Half the value of x is increased by 1.
   c) i) Twice the value of x is subtracted from 5.
      ii) The value of x is subtracted from 5, then divided by 2.
   d) i) x is reduced by 1, then squared and increased by 3.
      ii) x is reduced by 3, then the square root is found, which is then increased by 1.

8. Given $f(x) = 2x + 5$, find an expression for each function.
   a) $f^{-1}(x)$
   b) $f \circ f^{-1}(x)$
   c) $f^{-1} \circ f(x)$

9. Given $f(x) = \dfrac{x - 1}{x + 1}$, find an expression for each function.
   a) $f^{-1}(x)$
   b) $f \circ f^{-1}(x)$
   c) $f^{-1} \circ f(x)$

10. If $f(x)$ is any function which has an inverse, what do $f \circ f^{-1}(x)$ and $f^{-1} \circ f(x)$ represent?

Ⓒ

11. Show that $f(f^{-1}(x)) = x$ and $f^{-1}(f(x)) = x$, where $f^{-1}(x)$ is the inverse of $f(x)$.

12. Is the inverse of every linear function also a function? If you think it is, explain why. If you think it is not, give a counterexample.

13. Find the inverse of the inverse of each function. Is the inverse of the inverse of a given function always a function?
    a) $f(x) = \dfrac{3x - 5}{2}$
    b) $g(x) = 2(x - 1)^2 + 3$
    c) $h(x) = \dfrac{2x - 3}{x}$

14. Find two ways to restrict the domain of each function so that its inverse is a function.
    a) $g(x) = 2(x + 1)^2 - 5$
    b) $y = \dfrac{4 - x^2}{3}$
    c) $f(x) = |2x + 3| - 5$

 INVESTIGATE

Find examples of functions that are equal to their own inverse functions. What property do these functions have in common?

1-5 QUADRATIC FUNCTIONS

Suppose we drop a stone from a bridge 60 m above a river. The height of the stone above the water is expressed as a function of the elapsed time t seconds by the equation $f(t) = 60 - 4.9t^2$. This is an example of a *quadratic function*. Its graph has horizontal intercepts of approximately 3.5 and -3.5. We say that the *zeros* of the function are approximately 3.5 and -3.5. The positive zero represents the time for the stone to hit the water.

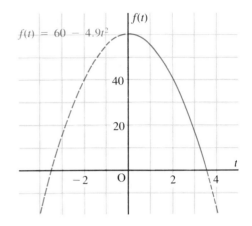

We can calculate the zeros of the function algebraically as follows. Let $f(t) = 0$ and solve for t.

$$60 - 4.9t^2 = 0$$
$$4.9t^2 = 60$$
$$t = \pm \sqrt{\frac{60}{4.9}}$$
$$\doteq \pm 3.5$$

Since the function represents the height of the stone only for the values of t between 0 and approximately 3.5, its domain is restricted to this interval. We indicate this on the graph by using a solid curve for these values of t.

Example 1. In the open sea, the length of a wave is a function of its velocity. The equation $L = 0.64v^2$ expresses the wavelength L metres as a quadratic function of the velocity v metres per second.
a) If the wavelength is 15 m, what is the velocity?
b) What increase in wavelength is needed to double the velocity?

Solution. a) Substitute 15 for L in $L = 0.64v^2$.
$$15 = 0.64v^2$$
$$v = \sqrt{\frac{15}{0.64}}$$
$$\doteq 4.8$$
If the wavelength is 15 m, the velocity is approximately 4.8 m/s.
b) Substitute $2v$ for v in $L = 0.64v^2$.
$$L = 0.64(2v)^2$$
$$= 4(0.64v^2)$$
If the velocity is doubled, the wavelength increases 4-fold.

The general quadratic function is $y = ax^2 + bx + c$, where $a \neq 0$. Its zeros can be calculated by solving the corresponding quadratic equation $ax^2 + bx + c = 0$. Many quadratic equations can be solved by factoring.

Example 2. Find the zeros of each function.

a) $f(x) = x^2 - x - 12$ b) $g(t) = 4t^2 - 20t + 25$

Solution.   a) Let $x^2 - x - 12 = 0$

$(x - 4)(x + 3) = 0$

Either $x - 4 = 0$ or $x + 3 = 0$

$x = 4$ $x = -3$

The zeros of f are 4 and -3.

b) Let $4t^2 - 20t + 25 = 0$

$(2t - 5)(2t - 5) = 0$

$2t - 5 = 0$

$t = 2.5$

The function g has only one zero, 2.5.

In *Example 2a*, the quadratic equation has two different roots. In *Example 2b*, we say that the equation has two equal roots.

Since the graph of every quadratic function is a parabola, we can use its zeros, if they exist, as an aid to sketch its graph.

Example 3. Sketch the graph of the quadratic function $f(x) = 2x^2 + 5x - 12$.

Solution.   Let $2x^2 + 5x - 12 = 0$

$(2x - 3)(x + 4) = 0$

Either $2x - 3 = 0$ or $x + 4 = 0$

$x = 1.5$ $x = -4$

The graph is a parabola with x-intercepts -4 and 1.5.

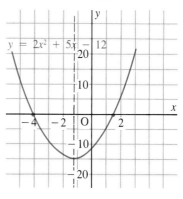

The y-intercept is $f(0) = -12$.

We locate the points $(-4, 0)$ and $(1.5, 0)$ on the x-axis, and the point $(0, -12)$ on the y-axis. The graph is a parabola passing through these points, and with axis of symmetry midway between the two x-intercepts.

Example 4. a) Write two different quadratic functions with zeros 1 and 4.

b) Graph the functions in part a).

Solution.   a) The function $y = (x - 1)(x - 4)$

or $y = x^2 - 5x + 4$

has zeros 1 and 4. Any multiple of this function also has zeros 1 and 4. For example, the function

$y = 2(x - 1)(x - 4)$

or $y = 2x^2 - 10x + 8$

also has zeros 1 and 4.

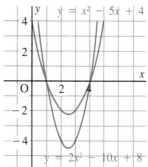

Example 4 shows that a function is not uniquely defined by its zeros. To determine the function uniquely, some additional information would be needed.

Many quadratic equations cannot be solved by factoring. But all quadratic equations can be solved using the method of *completing the square*.

Example 5. Solve $x^2 + 8x + 2 = 0$

Solution. $x^2 + 8x + 2 = 0$

Isolate the constant term.

$$x^2 + 8x = -2$$

Add the square of one-half the coefficient of x to both sides.

$$x^2 + 8x + 16 = -2 + 16$$
$$(x + 4)^2 = 14$$

Take the square root of both sides.

$$x + 4 = \pm\sqrt{14}$$
$$x = -4 \pm \sqrt{14}$$

The method of completing the square can be used to prove the formula for solving any quadratic equation.

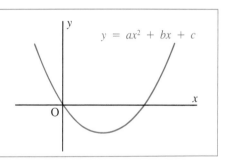

Quadratic Formula

The roots of the quadratic equation

$$ax^2 + bx + c = 0 \qquad (a \neq 0)$$

are $x = \dfrac{-b \pm \sqrt{b^2 - 4ac}}{2a}.$

These are the zeros of the corresponding quadratic function

$$f(x) = ax^2 + bx + c \qquad (a \neq 0)$$

$y = ax^2 + bx + c$

Example 6. Solve. $9x^2 - 12x + 2 = 0$

Solution.

$$x = \frac{-b \pm \sqrt{b^2 - 4ac}}{2a}$$

$$= \frac{-(-12) \pm \sqrt{(-12)^2 - 4(9)(2)}}{2(9)} \qquad \begin{aligned} a &= 9 \\ b &= -12 \\ c &= 2 \end{aligned}$$

$$= \frac{12 \pm \sqrt{72}}{18}$$

$$= \frac{12 \pm 6\sqrt{2}}{18}$$

$$= \frac{2 \pm \sqrt{2}}{3}$$

The roots of the equation are $\dfrac{2 + \sqrt{2}}{3}$ and $\dfrac{2 - \sqrt{2}}{3}$.

The equation in *Example 6* has two different real roots. If the equation had been $9x^2 - 12x + 4 = 0$, the solution would differ only in the number under the radical sign, $b^2 - 4ac = (-12)^2 - 4(9)(4)$, or 0. Hence the equation $9x^2 - 12x + 4 = 0$ has two equal roots, $\frac{2}{3}$.

And, if the equation had been $9x^2 - 12x + 5 = 0$, the number under the radical sign would be $b^2 - 4ac = (-12)^2 - 4(9)(5)$, or -36. Since the square root of a negative number is not a real number, the equation $9x^2 - 12x + 5 = 0$ has no real roots.

Hence, the number under the radical sign indicates the types of roots the equation has. This number is called the *discriminant* of the equation.

Properties of Quadratic Equations
- The roots of the equation $ax^2 + bx + c = 0$, $a \neq 0$, are:
$$\frac{-b + \sqrt{b^2 - 4ac}}{2a} \text{ and } \frac{-b - \sqrt{b^2 - 4ac}}{2a}.$$
- The nature of the roots is indicated by the discriminant.
  If $b^2 - 4ac > 0$, there are two different real roots.
  If $b^2 - 4ac = 0$, there are two equal real roots.
  If $b^2 - 4ac < 0$, there are no real roots.

EXERCISES 1-5

Ⓐ

1. Solve, expressing the roots to two decimal places.
   a) $6x^2 = 45$
   b) $19m^2 = 608$
   c) $5.8c^2 - 29 = 0$
   d) $37a^2 = 1776$
   e) $2.7t^2 - 13.77 = 0$
   f) $0.38x^2 - 5.85 = 0$

2. Solve and check.
   a) $x^2 - 9x + 14 = 0$
   b) $m^2 - 2m - 15 = 0$
   c) $x^2 - 14x + 33 = 0$
   d) $t^2 + 12t + 32 = 0$
   e) $y^2 + 7y - 18 = 0$
   f) $x^2 + 15x + 54 = 0$

Ⓑ

3. Find the zeros of each function.
   a) $f(x) = x^2 + 5x + 6$
   b) $y = x^2 - 4x$
   c) $y = 2x^2 + 5x - 3$
   d) $g(x) = 2 + x - 3x^2$
   e) $h(x) = 6x^2 - 7x - 3$
   f) $y = 4 - 4x + x^2$

4. Sketch the graph of each quadratic function.
   a) $y = x^2 - 6x + 5$
   b) $f(x) = x^2 + 3x - 4$
   c) $g(x) = 3x - x^2$
   d) $y = x^2 - 4x + 4$
   e) $y = \frac{1}{2}x^2$
   f) $p(x) = 0.2x^2$

5. Solve and check.
   a) $3x^2 - 5x + 2 = 0$ b) $5x^2 + 6x + 1 = 0$ c) $2x^2 - 6x - 1 = 0$
   d) $4x^2 - 24x + 36 = 0$ e) $2x^2 - 13x + 10 = 0$ f) $4x^2 - 4x - 3 = 0$

6. Solve.
   a) $x^2 + 7x - 12 = 0$ b) $x^2 - 8x + 14 = 0$ c) $3x^2 + 5x + 1 = 0$
   d) $4x^2 - 9x + 5 = 0$ e) $2x^2 + 5x + 6 = 0$ f) $5x^2 + 4x + 2 = 0$

7. Find the zeros of each function.
   a) $f(x) = 4x^2 + 20x + 10$ b) $g(x) = 4x^2 + 20x + 21$
   c) $h(x) = 4x^2 + 20x + 25$

8. Write a quadratic equation with the given roots.

   a) 3, 7   b) -4, 9   c) $\frac{2}{3}$, -5

9. Write two different quadratic functions with the given zeros.

   a) 4, -1 b) -3, 2   c) $\frac{3}{5}$, $-\frac{4}{3}$

10. A quadratic function has zeros 1 and 3. Find the equation of the function if its
    graph has a y-intercept of: a) 8   b) 4.

11. A quadratic function $y = f(x)$ has zeros -1 and 1. Find the equation of the function
    if: a) $f(0) = -2$ b) $f(0) = 1$ c) $f(2) = 12$.

12. The speed with which water flows out
    of a hole at the bottom of a reservoir
    is related to the depth of the water.
    According to Torricelli's theorem,
    $d \doteq 0.05s^2$, where d is the depth of
    the water in metres and s is the speed
    in metres per second.
    a) Solve the formula for s.
    b) What is the speed to 1 decimal place
       of the water if the depth is:
       i) 1 m   ii) 2 m   iii) 5 m?
    c) What happens to the speed if the
       depth is: i) doubled   ii) tripled?

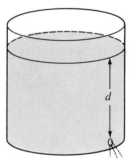

13. In a certain programming language, the instruction CALL -856 executes a delay
    loop of length t microseconds, where $t = 2.5x^2 + 13.5x + 13$, and x is a number
    stored in memory. What number x should be stored to have a delay loop of length:
    a) 1 s   b) 30 s?

14. Find the discriminant of each equation.
    a) $3x^2 + 7x + 4 = 0$ b) $2x^2 + 3x - 8 = 0$ c) $5x^2 - x + 2 = 0$
    d) $4x^2 + 12x + 9 = 0$ e) $2x^2 - 9x - 5 = 0$ f) $3x^2 + 4x + 7 = 0$

15. Which equations in *Exercise 14* have:
    a) 2 different real roots   b) 2 equal real roots   c) no real roots?

16. A square with sides of length 6 cm is divided into 3 right triangles and a larger isosceles triangle. The three right triangles have equal areas.
    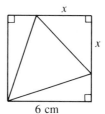
    6 cm
    a) Find the value of x.
    b) Find the area of the larger isosceles triangle.

17. Determine the nature of the roots of each equation.
    a) $4x^2 + 7x - 2 = 0$ b) $2x^2 - 7x - 15 = 0$ c) $3x^2 - 8x + 7 = 0$
    d) $7x^2 + 10x - 3 = 0$ e) $16x^2 + 8x + 1 = 0$ f) $12x^2 - 9x + 5 = 0$

18. Solve.
    a) $5x^2 + 4x - 1 = 0$ b) $2x^2 - 8x + 5 = 0$ c) $3x^2 + 5x + 1 = 0$
    d) $4x^2 + 7x + 5 = 0$ e) $3x^2 - 8x + 4 = 0$ f) $2x^2 - 4x + 5 = 0$

19. Solve.
    a) $5x(x + 3) = (3x + 2)(x - 1)$
    b) $(2x + 5)(x - 3) = (4x + 7)(3x - 1)$
    c) $(x + 2)(5x + 1) = 5x - (2x + 1)(2x + 2)$
    d) $(2x + 7)(x + 4) = (3x + 5)(x - 2)$

20. Solve.
    a) $\dfrac{x^2 + 5}{3} - \dfrac{7}{2} = \dfrac{x + 8}{2}$
    b) $\dfrac{4}{x + 1} - \dfrac{1}{x + 3} = \dfrac{2}{3}$
    c) $\dfrac{8}{x} + \dfrac{5}{x + 2} = 1$
    d) $\dfrac{3}{2x + 1} - \dfrac{x + 2}{3x - 1} = \dfrac{x - 3}{2x + 1}$

Ⓒ

21. In $\triangle PQR$, $QR = 10\sqrt{2}$, $\angle P = 90°$, and D is a point on QR such that PD is perpendicular to QR. If $QD = 4\sqrt{2}$, find the length of PD.

22. In $\triangle ABC$, $\angle C = 60°$; the lengths of the three sides in such a triangle are related by the formula
    $c^2 = a^2 + b^2 - ab$.
    If $AC = 8$ cm and $AB = 7$ cm, find the length of BC. Explain why there are two answers.
    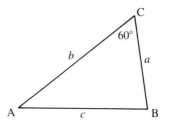

23. In *Exercise 22*, if $\angle C = 60°$ and $AC = 8$ cm, how long would side AB have to be such that there is only one value for the length of BC?

24. Determine whether or not there are any real numbers x and y with the property that the reciprocal of their sum is equal to the sum of their reciprocals.

25. a) Show that the product of two consecutive natural numbers can never be a perfect square.
    b) If n is a natural number, determine the least value of x such that $n + x$ is a rational number and $n(n + x)$ is a perfect square.

PROBLEM SOLVING

A Short History of Problem Solving

Mathematics, a product of the human mind, has been used to solve significant problems of the past and present.

What is the shape of the universe?
For centuries people believed that the world was flat. Eventually it was discovered that the Earth was round and that anyone travelling far enough in any direction would, in time, return to the starting point. In 1917, Albert Einstein made known his General Theory of Relativity which suggests that, like the Earth, the universe is finite. A space traveller covering a distance of 10^{11} light years in any given direction would eventually return to her or his original position.

What is the chance of inheriting a hereditary disease?
Genetics is the study of inherited characteristics. This important field of science relies heavily on a branch of mathematics called probability theory. Using probability, geneticists can predict the likelihood that a particular person will inherit a hereditary disease. They can also predict the likelihood that a contagious disease contracted by a given number of people will generate an epidemic.

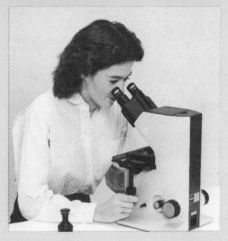

Most significant mathematical problems that have been studied in the past have turned out to have important applications. Here is an example.

What curves result when a plane intersects a cone?

About 200 B.C. the Greek geometer Apollonius of Perga wrote a book which described the curves that result when a plane intersects a cone, and their properties. The curves were studied for their own sake, and without concern for any applications they might have.

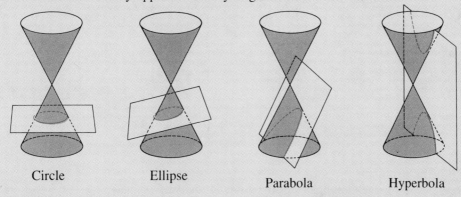

Circle   Ellipse   Parabola   Hyperbola

Who would have thought that 1800 years later the German physicist Johannes Kepler would use Apollonius' work to describe the orbits of the planets?

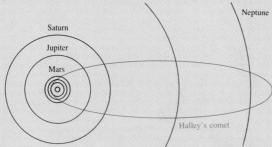

Saturn

Jupiter

Mars

Neptune

Halley's comet

To solve the problems in the *PROBLEM SOLVING* pages of this book, you may need to use mathematical concepts from the entire curriculum. Strategies you have learned in the past may be helpful. You may have your own strategies for solving certain problems. Several problems can be solved in more than one way, using different strategies. Be persistent — try a problem, set it aside, try it again later, or try another strategy. Do not be surprised if it takes several days (or even longer) to solve a problem. Considerable ingenuity may be needed to solve some of them. Some problems are extremely difficult. Do not be disappointed if you never solve them.

PROBLEM SOLVING

Don't Make the Problem Harder

"... mathematics is more than arithmetic and ... the problem-solving process is more than a single right answer."

Jean Kerr Stenmark

Find the equation of the line which passes through the point of intersection of the lines
L_1: $5x - 3y - 6 = 0$
L_2: $3x + 4y - 12 = 0$

and which also has slope $\frac{1}{2}$.

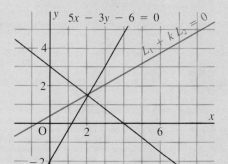

Understand the problem
- We could solve for the coordinates of the point of intersection, and then find the equation of the required line, but the solution will be encumbered with fractions with denominator 29.
- Do we have to know the point of intersection?

Think of a strategy
- According to a property of linear systems studied in earlier grades, when two lines intersect, we can add multiples of their equations together without changing the solution.
- Hence, for any value of k, the equation $L_1 + kL_2 = 0$ represents a line passing through the point of intersection of L_1 and L_2.

Carry out the strategy
- Let $5x - 3y - 6 + k(3x + 4y - 12) = 0$ represent the required line, where k is a constant to be determined.
- Write the equation in the form $Ax + By + C = 0$, and then write an expression for the slope of the line as a function of k.
- Since the slope is $\frac{1}{2}$, you should be able to determine k.
- Substitute back to find the equation of the required line.

Look back
- Check that this method is easier than solving for the point of intersection.
- Does $L_1 + kL_2 = 0$ represent every line through the point of intersection?

PROBLEMS

Ⓑ

1. a) Find a positive number that becomes its own reciprocal by subtracting 1.
   b) Show that the number in part a) also becomes its own square by adding 1.

2. Give some examples of natural numbers which can be expressed as the difference of two perfect squares. Can you find a way of telling whether or not a given natural number can be expressed as the difference of two squares?

3. What fraction of the triangular region is shaded?

4. Here is an arrangement of the natural numbers from 1 to 5:   2 4 5 3 1. Notice that the sum of any two adjacent numbers is composite.
   a) If $n < 5$, prove that it is impossible to arrange the natural numbers from 1 to n such that the sum of any two adjacent numbers is composite.
   b) If $n \geqslant 5$, prove that it is always possible to arrange the natural numbers from 1 to n such that the sum of any two adjacent numbers is composite.

5. Find the equation of the line which passes through the point of intersection of the lines $7x - 2y + 9 = 0$ and $6x + 5y - 2 = 0$, and which also passes through the point $(5, -1)$.

Ⓒ

6. The product of the first n natural numbers is $1 \times 2 \times 3 \times 4 \ldots \times n$. This product is called *factorial n* and is written $n!$ Find the largest power of 2 which divides 100!

7. How many natural numbers less than 1000 are divisible by 2, 3, or 5?

8. Find the equation of the line which passes through the points of intersection of the circles defined by $(x - 2)^2 + y^2 = 16$ and $x^2 + (y - 3)^2 = 16$.

Ⓓ

9. A line $y = mx + b$ and a point $A(x_1, y_1)$ are given. Determine the coordinates of the point B such that the given line is the perpendicular bisector of AB.

1-6 COMPLEX NUMBERS

Prior to the middle of the seventeenth century, when mathematicians encountered quadratic equations with negative discriminants they dismissed them as impossible or absurd. They considered that the equations had no roots because no meaning was given to square roots of negative numbers. They did not realize that meaning could be given to these quantities by extending the number system.

The idea of extending a number system to include all formally derived roots of equations was one of the important advances in mathematical thinking. Consider these examples.

- The equation $x + 3 = 0$ has no solution in the set of natural numbers. But it does have a solution, -3, in the set of integers.
- The equation $2x + 1 = 0$ has no solution in the set of integers. But it does have a solution, $-\frac{1}{2}$, in the set of rational numbers.
- The equation $x^2 - 2 = 0$ has no solution in the set of rational numbers. But it does have two solutions, $\pm\sqrt{2}$, in the set of real numbers.

Similarly, an equation such as $x^2 + 1 = 0$ has no solution in the set of real numbers. But by extending the number system, we can give meaning to the solution of this equation. We do this by defining the number i with the property that:

$$i^2 = -1, \text{ or } i = \sqrt{-1}$$

With this definition of i, $x^2 + 1 = 0$ has two roots, i and $-i$.

When $x = i$,
L.S. $= i^2 + 1$ R.S. $= 0$
     $= -1 + 1, \text{ or } 0$
When $x = -i$,
L.S. $= (-i)^2 + 1$ R.S. $= 0$
     $= i^2 + 1$
     $= -1 + 1, \text{ or } 0$

Since there is no real number with the property that its square is negative, the number i is not a real number. It cannot be expressed as a decimal, and it cannot be represented by a point on the number line. For these reasons, the square roots of negative numbers were called *imaginary* numbers. This is an unfortunate name because it suggests that these numbers are somehow less valid than the real or decimal numbers to which we have become accustomed. All numbers are imaginary in the sense that they are abstractions.

Once mathematicians had learned to understand and work with this new kind of number, they found that the numbers had many applications in science, engineering, and electronics.

The number i can be used to define the square root of any negative number.

Since $\sqrt{-16} = \sqrt{16 \times (-1)}$
we can define $\sqrt{-16} = \sqrt{16} \times \sqrt{-1}$
$$= 4 \times i$$
$$= 4i$$

If $k > 0$, we define: $\sqrt{-k} = \sqrt{k} \times \sqrt{-1}$
$$= \sqrt{k}\,i$$

This definition permits us to solve quadratic equations with a negative discriminant.

Example 1. Solve. $x^2 - 6x + 13 = 0$

Solution. Use $x = \dfrac{-b \pm \sqrt{b^2 - 4ac}}{2a}$

$a = 1$
$b = -6$
$c = 13$

$$x = \frac{-(-6) \pm \sqrt{(-6)^2 - 4(1)(13)}}{2(1)}$$

$$= \frac{6 \pm \sqrt{-16}}{2}$$

$$= \frac{6 \pm 4i}{2}$$

$$= 3 \pm 2i$$

The roots of the equation are $3 + 2i$ and $3 - 2i$.

In *Example 1*, the roots of the equation are examples of complex numbers. We can check that they satisfy the equation, by using $i^2 = -1$.
Check the root $x = 3 + 2i$.

L.S. $= x^2 - 6x + 13$ R.S. $= 0$
$= (3 + 2i)^2 - 6(3 + 2i) + 13$
$= 9 + 12i + 4i^2 - 18 - 12i + 13$
$= 9 - 4 - 18 + 13$
$= 0$

Hence, $3 + 2i$ is a root of the equation $x^2 - 6x + 13 = 0$. We can also check the root $3 - 2i$. These two roots are called conjugates, since they differ only in the sign of the term containing i.

- An expression of the form $a + bi$, where a and b are real numbers, and $i^2 = -1$, is called a *complex number*.
- The complex numbers $a + bi$ and $a - bi$ are called *conjugates*.
- The set of complex numbers includes real numbers since any real number x can be written in the form $x + 0i$.

Example 2. Write as a complex number.

a) $\sqrt{-9}$ b) $\sqrt{-32}$ c) $(2 + i) + (5 - 3i)$

d) $i(4 - 5i)$ e) i^6 f) $(1 + 2i)(1 - 2i)$

Solution.

a) $\sqrt{-9} = \sqrt{9 \times (-1)}$
$= 3 \times \sqrt{-1}$
$= 3i$

b) $\sqrt{-32} = \sqrt{32 \times (-1)}$
$= 4\sqrt{2} \times \sqrt{-1}$
$= 4\sqrt{2}i$

c) $(2 + i) + (5 - 3i)$
$= 2 + i + 5 - 3i$
$= 7 - 2i$

d) $i(4 - 5i) = 4i - 5i^2$
$= 4i - 5(-1)$
$= 4i + 5$
$= 5 + 4i$

e) $i^6 = (i^2)^3$
$= (-1)^3$
$= -1$

f) $(1 + 2i)(1 - 2i)$
$= 1 - 2i + 2i - 4i^2$
$= 1 - 4i^2$
$= 1 - 4(-1)$
$= 5$

Examples 2e and *2f* show that operations with complex numbers sometimes result in real numbers.

Example 3. Find two numbers with a sum of 10 and a product of 40. Check the result.

Solution. Let the numbers be represented by x and $10 - x$.

Since their product is 40,

$x(10 - x) = 40$
$10x - x^2 = 40$
$x^2 - 10x + 40 = 0$

$x = \dfrac{-b \pm \sqrt{b^2 - 4ac}}{2a}$ $a = 1$
$b = -10$
$c = 40$

$x = \dfrac{10 \pm \sqrt{(-10)^2 - 4(40)}}{2}$

$= \dfrac{10 \pm \sqrt{-60}}{2}$

$= 5 \pm \sqrt{-15}$

$= 5 \pm \sqrt{15}i$

The numbers are $5 + \sqrt{15}i$ and $5 - \sqrt{15}i$

Check. Sum: $5 + \sqrt{15}i + 5 - \sqrt{15}i = 10$

Product: $(5 + \sqrt{15}i)(5 - \sqrt{15}i) = 25 - 15i^2$
$= 25 + 15$
$= 40$

The solution is correct.

EXERCISES 1-6

(A)

1. Write as a complex number.
   a) $\sqrt{-5}$
   b) $\sqrt{-49}$
   c) $(3 + 2i) - (1 + 5i)$
   d) $i(8 + 3i)$
   e) $(2 + i)(5 - 3i)$
   f) $(7 - 4i)^2$

2. Show that both i and $-i$ are roots of the equation $x^2 + 1 = 0$.

3. Show that $2 + \sqrt{2}i$ and $2 - \sqrt{2}i$ satisfy the equation $x^2 - 4x + 6 = 0$.

4. Show that $\dfrac{-3 + i}{2}$ and $\dfrac{-3 - i}{2}$ are the roots of the equation $2x^2 + 6x + 5 = 0$.

5. Solve and check.
   a) $x^2 + 4 = 0$
   b) $x^2 + 9 = 0$
   c) $x^2 + 25 = 0$
   d) $x^2 + 12 = 0$
   e) $x^2 + 18 = 0$
   f) $x^2 - 2x + 2 = 0$

(B)

6. Write as a complex number.
   a) $2i(3 - 5i)$
   b) $(5 - 3i)(5 + 3i)$
   c) $(2 - 7i) + (5 + 3i)$
   d) $(7 + 2i)(5 - 4i)$
   e) $2i(3i^2 - 4i - 5)$
   f) $3i(2 + 5i)^2$

7. Solve and check.
   a) $x^2 + 3x + 5 = 0$
   b) $x^2 - 4x + 5 = 0$
   c) $x^2 + x + 2 = 0$
   d) $x^2 - 2x + 3 = 0$
   e) $x^2 - 5x + 7 = 0$
   f) $2x^2 + 3x + 2 = 0$

8. Solve.
   a) $3x^2 - 4x + 2 = 0$
   b) $3x^2 - 2x + 2 = 0$
   c) $x^2 + \sqrt{2}x + \dfrac{1}{2} = 0$
   d) $x^2 - 2x + 5 = 0$
   e) $7x^2 - 4x + 2 = 0$
   f) $-7 + 4x + x^2 = 0$

9. Find two numbers which have a sum of 2 and a product of 2.

 **INVESTIGATE**

Dividing Complex Numbers

To divide $3 + 2i$ by $1 - 2i$ we can use either of these methods.

Using conjugates

Write $\dfrac{3 + 2i}{1 - 2i} = \dfrac{3 + 2i}{1 - 2i} \times \dfrac{1 + 2i}{1 + 2i}$

Simplify the product on the right side and write the result in the form $a + bi$.

Equating real and imaginary parts

Let $\dfrac{3 + 2i}{1 - 2i} = a + bi$

Hence, $3 + 2i = (1 - 2i)(a + bi)$ Simplify the expression on the right side and compare with the number on the left side. For what values of a and b are they equal?

Try other examples. Can these methods be used to divide any two complex numbers?

Review Exercises

1. Graph each function. State the domain and the range.
   a) $y = \dfrac{2x + 1}{3}$
   b) $y = (x - 2)^2 - 3$
   c) $y = \dfrac{x + 3}{x}$

2. If $f(x) = 5x - 2$, find:
   a) $f(-3)$
   b) $f(2a)$
   c) $f(x + 1)$
   d) $f(3n - 2)$.

3. If $f(x) = 4 - 3x$ and $g(x) = x^2 + 2x - 5$, find:
   a) $f(2)$
   b) $g(-3)$
   c) $f(2x^2 + 1)$
   d) $g(x - 1)$
   e) $f(g(x))$
   f) $g(f(x))$
   g) $2f(x) + g(x)$
   h) $g(x) - f(x)$.

4. If $f(x) = 2x^2 - 5x + 1$, solve each equation.
   a) $f(x) = -1$
   b) $f(x) = 13$
   c) $f(2a) = 13$

5. If $g(x) = \dfrac{x + 1}{x - 1}$, $x \neq 1$, find:

   a) $g(3)$
   b) $g\left(\dfrac{1}{2}a\right)$
   c) $g\left(\dfrac{2x - 1}{x}\right)$
   d) $g^{-1}(x)$.

6. Given $f(x) = 3x + 2$ and $g(x) = 2x - 1$, find:
   a) $f(g(2))$
   b) $g(f(-2))$
   c) $f(f(3))$
   d) $g(g(-1))$
   e) $f \circ g(x)$
   f) $f^{-1} \circ g(x)$
   g) $g \circ f^{-1}(x)$
   h) $g^{-1}(f(x))$.

7. If $f(x) = 2x + 5$ and $g(x) = x^2 - 3x + 2$, find:
   a) $f \circ g(x)$
   b) $g \circ f(x)$
   c) $f \circ f(x)$
   d) $g \circ g(x)$
   e) $f^{-1} \circ g(x)$
   f) $g \circ f^{-1}(x)$
   g) $f^{-1} \circ f(x)$
   h) $f^{-1} \circ f^{-1}(x)$.

8. Find the inverse of each function. Is the inverse a function?
   a) $y = \dfrac{7 - x}{3}$
   b) $y = \dfrac{2x^2 - 1}{5}$
   c) $y = \dfrac{3x + 1}{x - 2}$

9. Graph each function and its inverse on the same axes. State the domain and the range of the inverse. Is the inverse a function?
   a) $f(x) = 4 - 2x$
   b) $y = (x - 2)^2 + 3$
   c) $y = 2\sqrt{x + 1} - 2$

10. Find the zeros of each function.
    a) $f(x) = 2x^2 - 5x - 12$ b) $g(x) = 4x^2 + 8x - 5$ c) $h(x) = 3x^2 + 14x + 8$

11. Determine the nature of the roots of each equation.
    a) $4x^2 + 5x + 6 = 0$ b) $5x^2 + 6x - 7 = 0$ c) $9x^2 + 6x + 1 = 0$

12. Solve.
    a) $6x^2 - 12x + 5 = 0$ b) $7x^2 + 3x - 6 = 0$

13. Write as a complex number.
    a) $3i(2 + 3i)$ b) $(3 + 2i)(3 - 2i)$ c) $7i(1 - 2i)^2$

14. Solve.
    a) $x^2 - x + 3 = 0$ b) $3x^2 - 7x + 7 = 0$ c) $2x^2 + 3x + 4 = 0$

2 Polynomial Functions

The Bloedel Conservatory in Vancouver, British Columbia, is an example of a geodesic dome in the shape of a spherical segment. If you know the base radius and the volume of space it encloses, how can you determine its height? (See COMPUTER POWER, page 70, *Question 4.*)

2-1 POLYNOMIAL FUNCTIONS

When we drop a stone into a well, we cannot see it hit the water, but we can hear the splash. The time interval t seconds for a well 100 m deep can be calculated from this equation.

$0.015t^3 - 4.9t^2 + 100 = 0$

This is an example of a cubic equation. The corresponding *cubic function* is $y = 0.015x^3 - 4.9x^2 + 100$. Quadratic and cubic functions are special cases of a more general type of function called a *polynomial function*. Here are some other examples of polynomial functions.

Quartic function (fourth degree): $f(x) = x^4 + 2x^3 - 6x^2 + 3x + 1$

Quintic function (fifth degree): $g(x) = 3x^5 + 2x^4 - 5x^2 - 3$

Polynomial equations with a cubic term, such as $x^3 - 12x + 8 = 0$, first appeared in Babylonian tablets dated about 2000 B.C. Although the Babylonians lacked a general technique for solving such equations, they developed numerical methods for solving certain types of cubic equations. During the last four thousand years, a number of different methods have been developed to solve such equations. The most useful method is one that has been employed only recently — in most practical applications, computers are now used to solve polynomial equations.

One method of solving a polynomial equation is to graph the corresponding polynomial function. The zeros of the function are the roots of the equation.

Example 1. Solve by graphing. $\quad x^3 - 12x + 8 = 0$

Solution. Let $y = x^3 - 12x + 8$. Make a table of values for various values of x, plot the ordered pairs (x, y) on a grid, and draw a smooth curve through them.

x	y
-5	-57
-4	-8
-3	17
-2	24
-1	19
0	8
1	-3
2	-8
3	-1
4	24
5	73

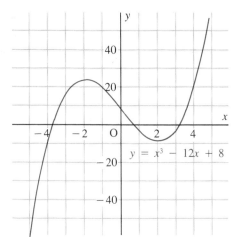

The zeros of the function $y = x^3 - 12x + 8$ are approximately -3.8, 0.7, and 3.1. These are the roots of the equation $x^3 - 12x + 8 = 0$.

Example 2. Solve graphically. a) $x^3 - 12x - 16 = 0$ b) $x^3 - 12x + 32 = 0$

Solution. Compare the given equation with the equation in *Example 1*.

a) Since the constant term in $y = x^3 - 12x - 16$ is 24 less than the constant term in $y = x^3 - 12x + 8$, the table of values can be written directly. Each y-value for $y = x^3 - 12x - 16$ is 24 less than the corresponding y-value for $y = x^3 - 12x + 8$.

b) Similarly, each y-value for $y = x^3 - 12x + 32$ is 24 greater than the corresponding y-value for $y = x^3 - 12x + 8$.

Plot the ordered pairs and draw the graphs.

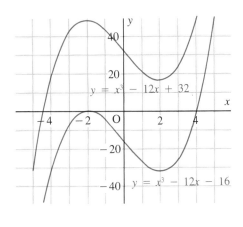

	a)	b)
x	y	y
-5	-81	-33
-4	-32	16
-3	-7	41
-2	0	48
-1	-5	43
0	-16	32
1	-27	21
2	-32	16
3	-25	23
4	0	48
5	49	97

a) The graph of $y = x^3 - 12x - 16$ appears to cross the x-axis at one point and touch it at another. The equation $x^3 - 12x - 16 = 0$ has three real roots, two of which are equal: -2, -2, and 4.

b) The graph of $y = x^3 - 12x + 32$ intersects the x-axis at only one point. The equation $x^3 - 12x + 32 = 0$ has one real root, which is approximately -4.4.

Example 3. Approximate the real zeros of $f(x) = x^4 - 20x^2 + 10x + 30$.

Solution. Make a table of values for the equation $y = x^4 - 20x^2 + 10x + 30$ and graph the ordered pairs.

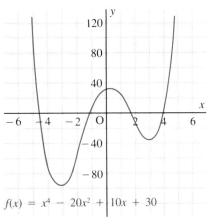

x	y
-5	105
-4	-74
-3	-99
-2	-54
-1	1
0	30
1	21
2	-14
3	-39
4	6

The zeros of the function $f(x) = x^4 - 20x^2 + 10x + 30$ are approximately -4.6, -1.0, 1.6, and 3.9. There are four real zeros.

EXERCISES 2-1

Ⓐ

1. Use the graph to estimate the zero(s) of each function.
   a) $f(x) = x^3 + 2x^2 - 10$ b) $g(x) = -x^3 - 3x^2 + 5x + 16$

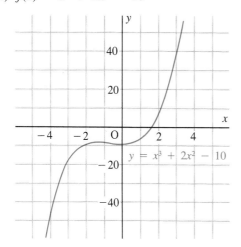
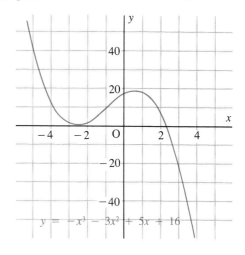

   c) $h(x) = x^4 - 10x^2 - 5x + 5$ d) $p(x) = x^5 - 10x^3 + 15x$

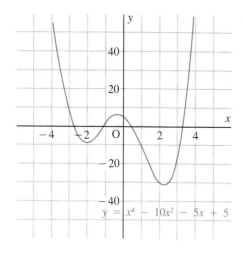
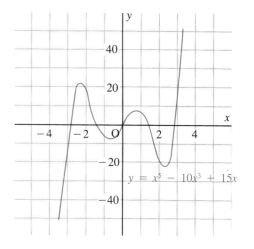

Ⓑ

2. Solve graphically.
   a) $x^3 - 10x = 0$ b) $x^3 - 10x + 12 = 0$
   c) $x^3 - 10x - 12 = 0$ d) $x^3 - 10x - 24 = 0$

3. Use a graph to approximate the real zeros of each function.
   a) $p(x) = x^3 - 15x - 10$
   b) $q(x) = x^3 + x - 15$
   c) $f(x) = x^4 - 15x^2 + 20$
   d) $g(x) = x^4 - 5x^2 - 10x - 25$

4. Approximate the real zeros of each function.
   a) $f(x) = x^3 + 10x - 20$
   b) $f(x) = x^3 - 3x^2 + x - 10$
   c) $f(x) = x^4 - 10x^2 + 5x + 7$
   d) $f(x) = x^4 - 4x^3 + 16x - 25$

5. In *Exercise 1 b)*, is it possible to tell for certain if there are two equal negative zeros? If there are not two equal negative zeros, then what other possibilities are there for this function?

6. Explain why every cubic function has at least one real zero.

7. Sketch an example of a cubic function which has:
   a) three equal zeros
   b) two equal zeros and a third zero which is less than they are
   c) two equal zeros and a third zero which is greater than they are
   d) only one real zero.

8. Sketch an example of a quartic function which has:
   a) four equal zeros
   b) two pairs of two equal zeros
   c) one pair of equal zeros and two other real zeros
   d) only one pair of equal zeros.

9. Solve the equation given on page 42 to determine how long it is between dropping a stone into a well 100 m deep and hearing the stone hit the water.

10. It is given that the equations $x^3 - 12x + 16 = 0$ and $x^3 - 12x - 16 = 0$ both have two different real roots.
    a) Which of the equations below have:
       i) three different real roots   ii) only one real root?
       $$x^3 - 12x + 20 = 0 \qquad x^3 - 12x + 10 = 0 \qquad x^3 - 12x - 20 = 0$$
    b) For what values of k does the equation $x^3 - 12x + k = 0$ have:
       i) 3 different real roots   ii) 2 different real roots   iii) only 1 real root?

---

11. A Babylonian tablet gives the values of $n^3 + n^2$ for integral values of n from 1 to 30.
    a) Make a table of values for $n = 1$ to 10.
    b) Use your table to find a root of the equation $x^3 + 2x^2 = 441$.
    c) Determine whether or not the equation $x^3 + 2x^2 = 441$ has any other real roots.

12. Individual packets of juice measure 6.4 cm by 3.8 cm by 10.3 cm. The packets contain 250 mL of juice. The manufacturer plans to introduce a new line of juice in packets containing twice as much juice. If each dimension of the original packets is increased by the same amount, find the dimensions of the new packets.

COMPUTER POWER

Using Factoring to Evaluate Polynomials

When we make a table of values for a given polynomial, we need to evaluate the polynomial for several values of the variable. We can often simplify the calculation by factoring the polynomial before substituting. For example, suppose we evaluate $x^2 + 12x + 27$ for $x = 8$. The calculation could proceed in either of two ways.

Without factoring

$$x^2 + 12x + 27 = 8^2 + 12(8) + 27$$
$$= 64 + 96 + 27$$
$$= 187$$

This solution requires two multiplications and two additions.

With factoring

$$x^2 + 12x + 27 = (x + 9)(x + 3)$$
$$= (8 + 9)(8 + 3)$$
$$= (17)(11)$$
$$= 187$$

This solution requires two additions and only one multiplication.

Since the solution using the factored form involves one less multiplication, it is the more efficient procedure. If a polynomial is to be evaluated for many values of x, it is worth factoring the polynomial before substituting.

Not all polynomials can be factored. However, any polynomial in one variable can be expressed in a *nested form* by successive grouping and factoring. For example, the polynomial $3x^4 - 5x^3 + 7x^2 - 4x + 2$ can be expressed as follows.

$$3x^4 - 5x^3 + 7x^2 - 4x + 2 = (3x^3 - 5x^2 + 7x - 4)x + 2$$
$$= ((3x^2 - 5x + 7)x - 4)x + 2$$
$$= (((3x - 5)x + 7)x - 4)x + 2$$

When $x = 3$, the value of the polynomial can be found as follows.

Using the original form

$$3x^4 - 5x^3 + 7x^2 - 4x + 2$$
$$= 3(81) - 5(27) + 7(9) - 4(3) + 2$$
$$= 243 - 135 + 63 - 12 + 2$$
$$= 161$$

This solution requires calculating the powers, four multiplications, and four additions.

Using the nested form

$$(((3x - 5)x + 7)x - 4)x + 2$$
$$= (((9 - 5)3 + 7)3 - 4)3 + 2$$
$$= ((19)3 - 4)3 + 2$$
$$= (53)3 + 2$$
$$= 161$$

This solution requires four multiplications and four additions.

It is easier to evaluate the polynomial using the nested form than it is using the original form.

1. Write each polynomial in nested form, and then evaluate it for $x = 1, 2, 3,$ 4, and 5.
   a) $5x^3 + 2x^2 - 7x + 8$
   b) $2x^3 - 5x^2 + 3x - 9$
   c) $6x^3 + x^2 - 4x + 12$
   d) $2x^4 + 3x^3 - 5x^2 + 6x - 11$

2. a) Evaluate $f(x) = x^2 + 12x + 11$ for $x = 1, 2, 3, \ldots, 10$
   b) For what value(s) of x is $f(x)$ a perfect square?
   c) For what value(s) of x is each polynomial a perfect square?
      i) $x^2 + 7x + 6$ ii) $x^2 + 8x - 9$ iii) $x^2 - 11x + 24$

3. The program on the next page can be used to compare the time a computer takes to evaluate a polynomial, for a large number of values of x, when it is written in its usual form, with the time it takes to evaluate the polynomial, for the same values of x, when it is written in nested form. For convenience, it is assumed that the coefficient of every term is 3, and that the values of x start at 0 and increase by 0.01. The program can be used for polynomials up to the tenth degree.
   a) When the program is run, the computer prints out the times when the program starts and stops. Run the program and determine how long the computer takes to evaluate a cubic polynomial 250 times using both methods.
   b) Copy and complete the table.

Degree of polynomial	1	2	3	...	10
Time to evaluate 250 terms in original form					
Time to evaluate 250 terms in nested form					

   c) Draw a graph of the results in part b).
   d) The time required to evaluate the polynomial 250 times is a function of its degree. What kind of function does it appear to be?

```
VAR
  CH : CHAR;
  X,Y,XP : REAL;
  C,H,I,K,N : INTEGER;
  STH,STM,STS,STD : WORD;
  ETH,ETM,ETS,ETD : WORD;
BEGIN      { CALCULATING TEST }
    REPEAT
          WRITELN('WHAT IS THE DEGREE? ');
          READ(N); WRITELN;
          WRITELN('HOW MANY VALUES ARE DESIRED? ');
          READ(H); WRITELN;
          WRITELN('ENTER 1 - POLYNOMIAL, 2 - NESTED ');
          READ(C); WRITELN;

          GETTIME(STH,STM,STS,STD);
          IF C = 1 THEN BEGIN
            WRITELN('CALCULATING USING POLYNOMIAL FORM');
            X := 0;
            FOR K := 1 TO H DO BEGIN
                Y := 3;
                XP := X;
                FOR I := 1 TO N DO BEGIN
                    Y := Y + 3 * XP;
                    XP := XP * X;
                END;
                X := X + 0.01;
            END;
          END;
          IF C = 2 THEN BEGIN
            WRITELN('CALCULATING USING NESTED FORM');
            X := 0;
            FOR K := 1 TO H DO BEGIN
                Y := 3;
                FOR I := 1 TO N DO BEGIN
                    Y := Y * X + 3;
                END;
                X := X + 0.01;
            END;
          END;
          GETTIME(ETH,ETM,ETS,ETD);

          WRITELN('STARTED AT',STH,':',STM,':',STS,':',STD);
          WRITELN('   ENDED AT',ETH,':',ETM,':',ETS,':',ETD);
          WRITELN('PRESS S TO STOP, R TO REPEAT');
          CH := READKEY;
          WRITELN;
    UNTIL CH = CHR(83);
END.
```

2-2 DIVIDING A POLYNOMIAL BY A POLYNOMIAL

Dividing a polynomial by a polynomial is similar to long division in arithmetic. Compare the steps in these two examples.

$$
\begin{array}{r}
32 \\
21\overline{)679} \\
63 \\
\hline
49 \\
42 \\
\hline
7
\end{array}
\qquad
\begin{array}{r}
3x + 2 \\
2x + 1\overline{)6x^2 + 7x + 9} \\
6x^2 + 3x \\
\hline
4x + 9 \\
4x + 2 \\
\hline
7
\end{array}
$$

— Divisor
— Quotient
— Dividend
— Remainder

To check, multiply the divisor by the quotient and add the remainder.
The result should be the dividend.

$21 \times 32 + 7 = 679 \qquad (2x + 1)(3x + 2) + 7 = 6x^2 + 7x + 9$

Example 1. Divide $2x^2 + 5x - 2$ by $x + 3$ and check. Assume that $x \neq -3$.

Solution.

$$
\begin{array}{r}
2x \\
x + 3\overline{)2x^2 + 5x - 2}
\end{array}
$$
Divide $2x^2$ by x to get $2x$.

$$
\begin{array}{r}
2x \\
x + 3\overline{)2x^2 + 5x - 2} \\
2x^2 + 6x \\
\hline
-x
\end{array}
$$
Multiply $2x$ by $x + 3$ to get $2x^2 + 6x$.
Subtract $2x^2 + 6x$ from $2x^2 + 5x$ to get $-x$.

$$
\begin{array}{r}
2x - 1 \\
x + 3\overline{)2x^2 + 5x - 2} \\
2x^2 + 6x \\
\hline
-x - 2
\end{array}
$$
Bring down the -2.
Divide $-x$ by x to get -1.

$$
\begin{array}{r}
2x - 1 \\
x + 3\overline{)2x^2 + 5x - 2} \\
2x^2 + 6x \\
\hline
-x - 2 \\
-x - 3 \\
\hline
1
\end{array}
$$
Multiply -1 by $x + 3$ to get $-x - 3$.
Subtract $-x - 3$ from $-x - 2$ to get 1.

Since the remainder has a lower degree than the divisor, the division is now complete.

Check. $(x + 3)(2x - 1) + 1 = 2x^2 + 5x - 3 + 1$
$$= 2x^2 + 5x - 2$$

Example 2. Divide $-4x^3 + 6x^2 + 4x - 7$ by $2x - 3$.

Solution.

$$
\begin{array}{r}
-2x^2 \qquad + 2 \\
2x - 3\overline{)-4x^3 + 6x^2 + 4x - 7} \\
-4x^3 + 6x^2 \\
\hline
0 + 4x - 7 \\
+ 4x - 6 \\
\hline
-1
\end{array}
$$
Since the remainder is zero, bring down the next *two* terms.

The quotient is $-2x^2 + 2$ with a remainder of -1.

If a power is missing in the dividend, it must be included using zero as the coefficient.

Example 3.   Divide $t^4 - 25t^2 + 62t - 36$ by $t^2 + 3t - 18$.

Solution.

$$
\begin{array}{r}
t^2 - 3t + 2 \\
t^2 + 3t - 18{\overline{\smash{\big)}\,t^4 + 0t^3 - 25t^2 + 62t - 36}} \\
\underline{t^4 + 3t^3 - 18t^2} \\
-3t^3 - 7t^2 + 62t \\
\underline{-3t^3 - 9t^2 + 54t} \\
2t^2 + 8t - 36 \\
\underline{2t^2 + 6t - 36} \\
2t
\end{array}
$$

The quotient is $t^2 - 3t + 2$, with a remainder of $2t$.

When dividing polynomials, we must write both expressions in descending (or ascending) powers of the variable.

Example 4.   Divide $-7x - 6 + x^3$ by $x + 1$ and check.

Solution.   Write $-7x - 6 + x^3$ as $x^3 + 0x^2 - 7x - 6$.

$$
\begin{array}{r}
x^2 - x - 6 \\
x + 1{\overline{\smash{\big)}\,x^3 + 0x^2 - 7x - 6}} \\
\underline{x^3 + x^2} \\
-x^2 - 7x \\
\underline{-x^2 - x} \\
-6x - 6 \\
\underline{-6x - 6} \\
0
\end{array}
$$

Check. $(x^2 - x - 6)(x + 1) = x^3 - 7x - 6$

In *Example 4*, the quotient can be factored.
We can write $x^3 - 7x - 6 = (x^2 - x - 6)(x + 1)$
$$= (x - 3)(x + 2)(x + 1)$$
This example illustrates that if one factor of a polynomial is known, other factors can be found by dividing, and then factoring the quotient.

Example 5.   Show that $x - 5$ is a factor of $x^3 - 2x^2 - 33x + 90$ and use the result to factor the polynomial.

Solution.

$$
\begin{array}{r}
x^2 + 3x - 18 \\
x - 5{\overline{\smash{\big)}\,x^3 - 2x^2 - 33x + 90}} \\
\underline{x^3 - 5x^2} \\
3x^2 - 33x \\
\underline{3x^2 - 15x} \\
-18x + 90 \\
\underline{-18x + 90} \\
0
\end{array}
$$

Since the remainder is 0, $x - 5$ is a factor of the given polynomial.
Since the quotient can be factored, we can factor the polynomial.
$$x^3 - 2x^2 - 33x + 90 = (x - 5)(x^2 + 3x - 18)$$
$$= (x - 5)(x + 6)(x - 3)$$

It is possible to reduce the amount of writing required when we divide polynomials. For example, we can delete the variables and record only the coefficients. This is called the method of *detached coefficients*.

Example 6. Divide $x^3 - 2x^2 - 33x + 90$ by $x - 5$ using detached coefficients.

Solution.

$$
\begin{array}{r}
1 + 3 - 18 \\
1 - 5)\overline{1 - 2 - 33 + 90} \\
\underline{1 - 5} \\
3 - 33 \\
\underline{3 - 15} \\
-18 + 90 \\
\underline{-18 + 90} \\
0
\end{array}
$$

The quotient is $x^2 + 3x - 18$, and there is no remainder.

Compare the above solution with that of *Example 5*; the only difference is that the variables have been omitted. The solution of *Example 6* can be compacted even further, by using a procedure called *synthetic division*.

Example 7. Divide $x^3 - 2x^2 - 33x + 90$ by $x - 5$ using synthetic division.

Solution.

$$
\begin{array}{r|rrrr}
-5 & 1 & -2 & -33 & 90 \\
& & & & \\ \hline
& 1 & & &
\end{array}
$$
Write only the constant term of the divisor, and the coefficients of the dividend. Write the first coefficient under the line.

$$
\begin{array}{r|rrrr}
-5 & 1 & -2 & -33 & 90 \\
& & -5 & & \\ \hline
& 1 & 3 & &
\end{array}
$$
Multiply 1 by -5, record the product above the line, and subtract.

$$
\begin{array}{r|rrrr}
-5 & 1 & -2 & -33 & 90 \\
& & -5 & -15 & \\ \hline
& 1 & 3 & -18 &
\end{array}
$$
Multiply 3 by -5, record the product above the line, and subtract.

$$
\begin{array}{r|rrrr}
-5 & 1 & -2 & -33 & 90 \\
& & -5 & -15 & 90 \\ \hline
& 1 & 3 & -18 & 0
\end{array}
$$
Multiply -18 by -5, record the product above the line, and subtract.

$$\underbrace{1 \quad 3 \quad -18}_{\text{quotient}} \quad \underset{\text{remainder}}{0}$$

The quotient is $x^2 + 3x - 18$, and there is no remainder.

The method illustrated above can be used when the divisor is a binomial with a leading coefficient of 1. Synthetic division can be extended to cases where the divisor is any polynomial.

EXERCISES 2-2

Ⓐ

1. Find each quotient and remainder. Assume that the divisor is not equal to zero.
   a) $(x^2 + 7x + 14) \div (x + 3)$ b) $(x^2 - 3x + 5) \div (x - 2)$
   c) $(c^2 + c - 2) \div (c + 3)$ d) $(n^2 - 11n + 6) \div (n + 5)$

2. Divide.
   a) $x^3 - 5x^2 + 10x - 15$ by $x - 3$ b) $m^3 - 5m^2 - m - 10$ by $m - 2$
   c) $3s^3 + 11s^2 - 6s - 10$ by $s + 4$ d) $2x^3 + x^2 - 27x - 36$ by $x + 3$

3. When a certain polynomial is divided by $x + 2$, the quotient is $x^2 - 4x + 1$ and the remainder is 8. What is the polynomial?

4. When a certain polynomial is divided by $x - 3$, the quotient is $x^2 + 2x - 5$ and the remainder is -3. What is the polynomial?

Ⓑ

5. Divide.
   a) $2x^2 - 1 + 5x$ by $x + 1$ b) $3x^2 - 5 + 2x$ by $x - 2$
   c) $25u^2 + 1$ by $5u + 3$ d) $6x^2 - 3$ by $2x + 4$
   e) $8x^2 + 11 - 6x$ by $2x - 3$ f) $9m^2 - 5$ by $3m + 2$

6. Divide.
   a) $c^3 + 13c^2 + 39c + 20$ by $c + 9$ b) $x^3 + x - 8x^2 + 37$ by $x - 2$
   c) $6 + 7n - 11n^2 - 2n^3$ by $6 + n$ d) $x^3 - 12x - 20$ by $2 + x$
   e) $5a^3 - 5a + 3a^2 + 3$ by $a - 1$ f) $m^3 - 19m - 24$ by $m - 3$

7. Divide.
   a) $x^3 - 10x - 15 + 7x^2$ by $x + 8$
   b) $-2a^2 + 29a - a^3 - 40$ by $-3 + a$
   c) $-6m^3 + 7m + 29m^2 - 13$ by $2m - 1$
   d) $4s^3 - 13s - 6$ by $2s + 1$

8. Divide each polynomial by $x - 2$ and factor the quotient.
   a) $x^3 - 9x^2 + 26x - 24$ b) $3x^3 - 8x^2 + 3x + 2$
   c) $-x^3 + 3x + 2$ d) $5x^3 - 56x + 13x^2 + 20$
   e) $16x^3 - 2x^2 - 51x - 18$ f) $-10x^3 + x - 6 + 21x^2$

9. Divide.
   a) $x^3 + 5x^2 - 2x - 24$ by $x^2 + 7x + 12$
   b) $y^3 - y^2 + 4y + 15$ by $y^2 + 2y - 3$
   c) $10a^4 - a^3 + 11a^2 + 7a + 5$ by $5a^2 + 2a - 1$
   d) $6t^4 + 4t^3 - 13t^2 - 10t - 5$ by $2t^2 - 5$

10. Find each quotient.
   a) $\dfrac{x^3 + 3x^2 - 4x - 12}{x - 2}$ b) $\dfrac{2m^3 - 3m^2 - 8m - 3}{2m + 1}$
   c) $\dfrac{3x^3 + 2x^2 - 11x - 12}{x + 1}$ d) $\dfrac{a^3 - 28a - 41}{a + 4}$

11. Find each quotient then factor it.
    a) $(x^3 + x^2y - 9xy^2 - 9y^3) \div (x + y)$
    b) $(-x^3 - 5x^2y - 2xy^2 + 8y^3) \div (x - y)$
    c) $(-8a^3 + 37a^2b - 33ab^2 - 18b^3) \div (a - 2b)$
    d) $(-15m^3 + 47mn^2 + 28m^2n + 12n^3) \div (5m + 4n)$

12. Find the quotient.
    a) $(x^3 + 4x^2 - 3x - 12) \div (x + 4)$
    b) $(6a^3 + 4a^2 + 9a + 6) \div (3a + 2)$
    c) $(9m^3 + 6m - 15m^2 - 10) \div (3m - 5)$
    d) $(4x^3 - 10x^2 + 6x - 15) \div (2x - 5)$

13. One factor of $4x^3 + 15x^2 - 31x - 30$ is $x - 2$. Find the other factors.

14. Two factors of $12a^4 - 39a^2 + 8a - 8a^3 + 12$ are $a - 2$ and $2a + 1$. Find the other factors.

15. Find the quotient.
    a) $(x^4 + x^3 + 7x^2 - 6x + 8) \div (x^2 + 2x + 8)$
    b) $(-2a^3 - 10 + 16a + 39a^2 - 15a^4) \div (2 - 4a - 5a^2)$
    c) $(s^5 - 4s^3 + 19s^2 - 2s^4 + 15 - 31s) \div (s^3 - 7s + 5)$

Ⓒ

16. Find the quotient.
    a) $(x^3 + 1) \div (x + 1)$ b) $(a^5 - 1) \div (a - 1)$
    c) $(s^4 + s^2t^2 + t^4) \div (s^2 + st + t^2)$ d) $(m^4 + 4n^4) \div (m^2 + 2mn + 2n^2)$

17. When $10x^3 + mx^2 - x + 10$ is divided by $5x - 3$, the quotient is $2x^2 + nx - 2$ and the remainder is 4. Find the values of m and n.

18. Find the value of k such that when $2x^3 + 9x^2 + kx - 15$ is divided by $x + 5$, the remainder is 0.

19. Divide $x^3 + (a + b)x^2 + (ab + c)x + ac$ by $x + a$.

20. a) Divide $x^3 + (a + b + c)x^2 + (ab + bc + ac)x + abc$ by $x + a$.
    b) Using the result of part a), predict the quotient when
       $x^3 + (a + b + c)x^2 + (ab + bc + ac)x + abc$ is divided by:
       i) $x + b$ ii) $x + c$.

INVESTIGATE

1. Let $f(x) = x^3 - 2x^2 + 7x - 4$.
   a) Divide $f(x)$ by $x - 1$, and note the remainder.
   b) Evaluate $f(1)$ and compare with the result of part a).
   c) Find the remainders when $f(x)$ is divided by $x - 2$ and by $x + 3$, and compare the results with $f(2)$ and $f(-3)$.
   d) Based on your results in parts b) and c), state a probable conclusion.

2. Investigate whether similar relations hold for other polynomials.

2-3 THE REMAINDER THEOREM

In some problems involving division, only the remainder is needed. For example, to find the day of the week 60 days from now, it is necessary to divide 60 by 7.

$$
\begin{array}{r}
8 \longleftarrow \text{Quotient} \\
\text{Divisor} \quad 7\overline{)60} \longleftarrow \text{Dividend} \\
\underline{56} \\
4 \longleftarrow \text{Remainder}
\end{array}
$$

Since the remainder is 4, in 60 days the day of the week will be four days after today.

In algebra, we can find remainders without actually dividing. To understand the method, it is necessary to recognize the relations among the dividend, divisor, quotient, and remainder in a division problem. For the division illustrated above, we can write:

$$
\begin{array}{ccccc}
60 & = & (7)\,(8) & + & 4 \\
\downarrow & & \downarrow \;\; \downarrow & & \downarrow
\end{array}
$$

dividend = (divisor) (quotient) + remainder

> **Division Statement**
> In any division problem,
> dividend = (divisor)(quotient) + remainder

Example 1. Given $f(x) = x^3 + 4x^2 + x - 2$, find the remainder when $f(x)$ is divided by $x - 1$. Write the corresponding division statement.

Solution.

$$
\require{enclose}
\begin{array}{r}
x^2 + 5x + 6 \\
x - 1 \overline{)x^3 + 4x^2 + \;\;\; x - 2} \\
\underline{x^3 - \;\; x^2} \\
5x^2 + \;\; x \\
\underline{5x^2 - 5x} \\
6x - 2 \\
\underline{6x - 6} \\
4
\end{array}
$$

The corresponding division statement is
$$x^3 + 4x^2 + x - 2 = (x - 1)(x^2 + 5x + 6) + 4$$

In *Example 1*, notice that the remainder is a constant, otherwise we could have continued the division. Notice also what happens if we substitute 1 for x in both sides of the division statement.

In the left side, the result is $\qquad$ In the right side, the result is
$$1^3 + 4(1)^2 + 1 - 2 = 4 \qquad \begin{aligned}(1 - 1)(1^2 + 5(1) + 6) + 4 &= 0(12) + 4 \\ &= 4\end{aligned}$$

Hence, $f(1) = 4$

Therefore, $f(1)$ is equal to the remainder. In other words, when the polynomial $x^3 + 4x^2 + x - 2$ is divided by $x - 1$, the remainder is $f(1)$.

This is an example of a general result which is true for any polynomial, and is called the remainder theorem.

> **Remainder Theorem**
> When a polynomial $f(x)$ is divided by $x - a$, the remainder is $f(a)$.

This theorem is proved below.

Given:
A polynomial $f(x)$ is divided by $x - a$.

Required to Prove:
The remainder is $f(a)$.

Analysis:
If we can write the division statement, then we can use the same reasoning that we used above. We should substitute a for x in the division statement.

Proof:
When $f(x)$ is divided by $x - a$, the division can be continued until the remainder is a constant, r.
If $q(x)$ represents the quotient, then the division statement is
$f(x) = (x - a)q(x) + r$.
Substitute a for x in both sides of the division statement.
In the left side, the result is $f(a)$.
In the right side, the result is $(a - a)q(a) + r$, or r.
Since these two results must be equal, $f(a) = r$
Therefore, the remainder is $f(a)$.

We can use the remainder theorem to find the remainder without actually dividing.

Example 2. Find the remainder when $x^3 - 4x^2 + 5x - 1$ is divided by:
a) $x - 2$ b) $x + 1$.

Solution.
a) Let $f(x) = x^3 - 4x^2 + 5x - 1$.
The remainder when $f(x)$ is divided by $x - 2$ is $f(2)$.
$$f(2) = 2^3 - 4(2)^2 + 5(2) - 1$$
$$= 8 - 16 + 10 - 1$$
$$= 1$$
The remainder is 1.

b) Since $x + 1 = x - (-1)$, the remainder when $f(x)$ is divided by $x + 1$ is $f(-1)$.
$$f(-1) = (-1)^3 - 4(-1)^2 + 5(-1) - 1$$
$$= -1 - 4 - 5 - 1$$
$$= -11$$
The remainder is -11.

Example 3. When $x^3 + 3x^2 - kx + 10$ is divided by $x - 5$, the remainder is 15. Find the value of k.

Solution. Let $f(x) = x^3 + 3x^2 - kx + 10$.
The remainder when $f(x)$ is divided by $x - 5$ is $f(5)$.
$$f(5) = 5^3 + 3(5)^2 - 5k + 10$$
$$= 125 + 75 - 5k + 10$$
$$= 210 - 5k$$
Since the remainder is 15,
$$210 - 5k = 15$$
$$-5k = -195$$
$$k = 39$$

EXERCISES 2-3

Ⓐ

1. Divide, and write the corresponding division statement.
   a) $a^2 - 2a - 13$ by $a + 3$ b) $x^3 + x^2 + x + 11$ by $x + 2$
   c) $2p^3 + 5p^2 - 2p - 3$ by $p + 1$ d) $2s^3 - 7s^2 + 16s - 22$ by $2s - 3$

2. Find the remainder when $x^3 + 3x^2 - 5x + 4$ is divided by each binomial.
   a) $x - 1$ b) $x - 2$ c) $x - 3$
   d) $x + 1$ e) $x + 2$ f) $x + 3$

3. Find the remainder when each polynomial is divided by $x - 2$.
   a) $x^2 - 5x + 2$ b) $x^3 + x^2 - 2x + 3$
   c) $-x^3 - x^2 + 10x - 8$ d) $3x^3 - 5x^2 + 2x + 8$
   e) $2x^3 + x^2 + 4x - 7$ f) $-x^4 - 3x^3 + 2x^2 - 5x - 1$

4. Without using long division, find each remainder.
   a) $(2a^2 + 6a + 8) \div (a + 1)$
   b) $(n^2 + 4n + 12) \div (n - 4)$
   c) $(y^3 + 6y^2 - 4y + 3) \div (y + 2)$
   d) $(-p^3 + 2p^2 + 5p + 9) \div (p + 1)$
   e) $(3m^3 + 7m^2 - 2m - 11) \div (m - 2)$
   f) $(-c^4 + 3c^2 - c + 1) \div (c + 2)$

5. What is the remainder when each polynomial is divided by x?
   a) $x^2 + 3x$ b) $x^3 - 2x + 8$ c) $-x^3 - 7x^2 + 4x - 6$
   d) $-x^4 + 2x^2 + 1$ e) $x^3 - x^2 + 5x$ f) $-x^4 - 3x^3 + 2$

Ⓑ

6. Find each remainder.
   a) $(2m^2 + m - 6) \div (m + 3)$
   b) $(-a^3 + 2a^2 - 5a + 1) \div (a - 2)$
   c) $(2x^3 + 7x^2 - 3x + 10) \div (1 + x)$
   d) $(n^3 - n^2 + 7n + 4) \div (n - 3)$
   e) $(-3y^3 - 9y^2 + 12) \div (2 + y)$
   f) $(-2x^4 + 3x^2 - 5x + 14) \div (-2 + x)$

7. Find k.
   a) When $x^3 + kx^2 + 2x - 3$ is divided by $x + 2$, the remainder is 1.
   b) When $x^4 - kx^3 - 2x^2 + x + 4$ is divided by $x - 3$, the remainder is 16.
   c) When $2x^3 - 3x^2 + kx - 1$ is divided by $x - 1$, the remainder is 1.

8. When $kx^3 + px^2 - x + 3$ is divided by $x - 1$, the remainder is 4. When this polynomial is divided by $x - 2$, the remainder is 21. Find the values of k and p.

9. When $x^3 + kx^2 + 2x + 9$ is divided by $x - 1$, the remainder is 7. What is the remainder when $x^3 + kx^2 + 2x + 9$ is divided by $x + 1$?

$\copyright$ ───────────────────────────────────────

10. $f(x)$ is a polynomial which leaves a remainder of 3 when it is divided by $x + 2$. Find the remainder when each polynomial is divided by $x + 2$.
    a) $f(x) + 1$ b) $f(x) + x + 2$ c) $2f(x)$

11. When the polynomial $f(x)$ is divided by $x - a$, the quotient is $q(x)$ and the remainder is r. Show that the remainder is equal to each of these expressions.
    a) $f(0) + aq(0)$ b) $f(a + 1) - q(a + 1)$ c) $f(a - 1) + q(a - 1)$
    Illustrate your answers with an example in which $f(x)$ is a cubic polynomial and $q(x)$ is a quadratic polynomial.

12. Without using long division, find the remainder.
    a) $(6x^2 - 10x + 7) \div (3x + 1)$ b) $(-8a^2 - 2a - 3) \div (4a - 1)$
    c) $(-4x^3 - 9x + 10) \div (1 - 2x)$ d) $(6m^3 - 15m^2 + 3) \div (2m + 1)$

13. a) If a fourth-degree polynomial is divided by a quadratic polynomial, would it be possible for the remainder to be: i) a cubic polynomial
    ii)   a quadratic polynomial   iii)   a linear polynomial?
    b) Use the result of part a) to find the remainder when $x^4 + 2x^3 - 5x^2 + x + 3$ is divided by $x^2 + x - 2$.

14. Without using long division, find the remainder.
    a) $(x^3 + 3x^2 - x - 2) \div (x + 3)(x + 1)$
    b) $(2x^3 + x^2 - 4x + 12) \div (x^2 + x - 2)$
    c) $(x^4 - 4x^2 + 2) \div (x - 1)(x + 1)(x - 2)$

15. Find the remainder if the polynomial $f(x)$ is divided by each expression.
    a) $ax + b$ b) $(x - a)(x - b)$

16. If $f(x) = (x - a)q(x) + r$, where r is a constant, what multiples of $x - a$ are closest to $f(x)$? Illustrate your answer with an example in which $f(x)$ is a cubic polynomial and $q(x)$ is a quadratic polynomial.

 INVESTIGATE

The remainder theorem was proved by substituting a for x in the division statement $f(x) = (x - a)q(x) + r$. Investigate what happens if values of x other than a are substituted in this statement. Illustrate your results with specific examples.

2-4 THE FACTOR THEOREM

According to the remainder theorem, if a number a is substituted for x in a polynomial, the value obtained is the remainder when the polynomial is divided by $x - a$. If this remainder is 0, then $x - a$ is a factor of the polynomial. This special case of the remainder theorem is called the factor theorem.

> **Factor Theorem**
> If $x = a$ is substituted into a polynomial in x, and the resulting value is 0, then $x - a$ is a factor of the polynomial.

Example 1.   a) Find the remainder when $x^3 - 4x^2 + x + 6$ is divided by $x - 3$.
   b) State a factor of $x^3 - 4x^2 + x + 6$.

Solution.   a) Let $f(x) = x^3 - 4x^2 + x + 6$.
   The remainder when $f(x)$ is divided by $x - 3$ is $f(3)$.
   $f(3) = 3^3 - 4(3)^2 + 3 + 6$
   $= 27 - 36 + 3 + 6$
   $= 0$
   b) By the factor theorem, $x - 3$ is a factor of $x^3 - 4x^2 + x + 6$.

The factor theorem provides a simple method for determining whether a binomial of the form $x - a$ is a factor of a given polynomial.

Example 2.   Determine which binomials are factors of $x^3 - 6x^2 + 3x + 10$.
   a) $x - 2$ b) $x - 3$ c) $x + 1$ d) $x - 5$

Solution.   Let $f(x) = x^3 - 6x^2 + 3x + 10$.
   a) $f(2) = 2^3 - 6(2)^2 + 3(2) + 10$
   $= 8 - 24 + 6 + 10$
   $= 0$
   Since $f(2) = 0$, $x - 2$ is a factor of $x^3 - 6x^2 + 3x + 10$.
   b) $f(3) = 3^3 - 6(3)^2 + 3(3) + 10$
   $= 27 - 54 + 9 + 10$
   $= -8$
   Since $f(3) \neq 0$, $x - 3$ is not a factor of $x^3 - 6x^2 + 3x + 10$.
   c) $f(-1) = (-1)^3 - 6(-1)^2 + 3(-1) + 10$
   $= -1 - 6 - 3 + 10$
   $= 0$
   Since $f(-1) = 0$, $x + 1$ is a factor of $x^3 - 6x^2 + 3x + 10$.
   d) $f(5) = 5^3 - 6(5)^2 + 3(5) + 10$
   $= 125 - 150 + 15 + 10$
   $= 0$
   Since $f(5) = 0$, $x - 5$ is a factor of $x^3 - 6x^2 + 3x + 10$.

In *Example 2*, we found three factors of $x^3 - 6x^2 + 3x + 10$. The product of these three factors must be $x^3 - 6x^2 + 3x + 10$. This can be checked by multiplication.

$(x - 5)(x + 1)(x - 2) = x^3 - 6x^2 + 3x + 10$

Notice that the product of the constant terms in the factors is $(-5)(+1)(-2)$, or 10. This is also the constant term in the polynomial. This suggests the following property of the factors of a polynomial.

Factor Property
If a polynomial has any factor of the form $x - a$, then the number a is a factor of the constant term of the polynomial.

The factor property indicates which factors to test when attempting to factor a polynomial.

Example 3. Find one factor of the polynomial $x^3 + 2x^2 - 5x - 6$.

Solution. Let $f(x) = x^3 + 2x^2 - 5x - 6$.
We must find a value of x such that $f(x)$ has a value of 0.
According to the factor property, the numbers to test are the factors of -6: that is, 1, 2, 3, 6, -1, -2, -3, and -6.
Try $x = 1$. $\quad f(1) = 1^3 + 2(1)^2 - 5(1) - 6$
$\qquad\qquad\qquad = 1 + 2 - 5 - 6$
$\qquad\qquad\qquad \neq 0$
$x - 1$ is not a factor of $x^3 + 2x^2 - 5x - 6$.
Try $x = -1$. $\quad f(-1) = (-1)^3 + 2(-1)^2 - 5(-1) - 6$
$\qquad\qquad\qquad\quad = -1 + 2 + 5 - 6$
$\qquad\qquad\qquad\quad = 0$
$x + 1$ is a factor of $x^3 + 2x^2 - 5x - 6$.
Therefore, one factor of $x^3 + 2x^2 - 5x - 6$ is $x + 1$.

From *Example 3*, we know that $x + 1$ is one factor of $x^3 + 2x^2 - 5x - 6$. The other factors can be found using either of the following strategies.

Using long division

$$
\begin{array}{r}
x^2 + x - 6 \\
x + 1 \overline{)x^3 + 2x^2 - 5x - 6} \\
\underline{x^3 + x^2} \\
x^2 - 5x \\
\underline{x^2 + x} \\
- 6x - 6 \\
\underline{- 6x - 6} \\
0
\end{array}
$$

The other factor is $x^2 + x - 6$. Therefore,
$$x^3 + 2x^2 - 5x - 6 = (x + 1)(x^2 + x - 6)$$
$$\qquad\qquad\qquad\qquad = (x + 1)(x + 3)(x - 2)$$

By equating coefficients

One factor of $x^3 + 2x^2 - 5x - 6$ is $x + 1$. Let the other factor be $x^2 + bx + c$. Then,

$(x + 1)(x^2 + bx + c) = x^3 + 2x^2 - 5x - 6$

When the product on the left side is expanded, the constant term must equal the constant term on the right side. Also, the term containing x must equal the term containing x on the right side. These terms are found as follows.

The constant term: $(x + 1)(x^2 + bx + c) = x^3 + 2x^2 - 5x - 6$
$$+ 1c$$
$$c = -6$$

The x term: $(x + 1)(x^2 + bx + c) = x^3 + 2x^2 - 5x - 6$
$$cx$$
$$+ 1bx$$
$$cx + bx = -5x$$
$$(c + b)x = -5x$$

Since this equation is true for all values of x, the coefficients are equal.
$$c + b = -5$$
$$-6 + b = -5$$
$$b = 1$$

The other factor of $x^3 + 2x^2 - 5x - 6$ is $x^2 + x - 6$. Therefore,
$$x^3 + 2x^2 - 5x - 6 = (x + 1)(x^2 + x - 6)$$
$$= (x + 1)(x + 3)(x - 2)$$

Example 4.   Factor fully. $x^3 - 6x^2 - x + 30$

Solution.   Let $f(x) = x^3 - 6x^2 - x + 30$.

Since the constant term 30 is much larger than the coefficients of the other terms, we can see that substituting $x = 1$ or $x = -1$ would not give zero.

Try $x = 2$. $f(2) = 2^3 - 6(2)^2 - 2 + 30$
$$= 8 - 24 - 2 + 30$$
$$\neq 0$$

Try $x = -2$. $f(-2) = (-2)^3 - 6(-2)^2 - (-2) + 30$
$$= -8 - 24 + 2 + 30$$
$$= 0$$

Therefore, $x + 2$ is one factor of $x^3 - 6x^2 - x + 30$.

The other factor can be found using long division or by equating coefficients. We use the method of equating coefficients.

Let the other factor be $x^2 + bx + c$. Then,
$$(x + 2)(x^2 + bx + c) = x^3 - 6x^2 - x + 30$$

Equate coefficients.

Since the constant term is 30, $2c = 30$
$$c = 15$$

Since the term containing x is $-x$, $2b + c = -1$
$$2b + 15 = -1$$
$$b = -8$$

Therefore, the other factor of $x^3 - 6x^2 - x + 30$ is $x^2 - 8x + 15$.
$$x^3 - 6x^2 - x + 30 = (x + 2)(x^2 - 8x + 15)$$
$$= (x + 2)(x - 3)(x - 5)$$

Example 5. Factor fully. $2x^3 + 7x^2 + 2x - 3$

Solution. Let $f(x) = 2x^3 + 7x^2 + 2x - 3$.
Try $x = -1$. $f(-1) = 2(-1)^3 + 7(-1)^2 + 2(-1) - 3$
$$= -2 + 7 - 2 - 3$$
$$= 0$$

Therefore, $x + 1$ is one factor of $2x^3 + 7x^2 + 2x - 3$.

We use the method of equating coefficients to find the other factor.

Let the other factor be $ax^2 + bx + c$. Then,
$$(x + 1)(ax^2 + bx + c) = 2x^3 + 7x^2 + 2x - 3$$
Equate coefficients.
Since the term containing x^3 is 2, $a = 2$
Since the term containing x^2 is 7, $a + b = 7$
$$2 + b = 7$$
$$b = 5$$
Since the constant term is -3, $c = -3$
Therefore, the other factor of $2x^3 + 7x^2 + 2x - 3$ is $2x^2 + 5x - 3$.
$$2x^3 + 7x^2 + 2x - 3 = (x + 1)(2x^2 + 5x - 3)$$
$$= (x + 1)(2x - 1)(x + 3)$$

In *Example 5*, since $2x - 1$ is a factor of $2x^3 + 7x^2 + 2x - 3$,

substituting $x = \frac{1}{2}$ into the polynomial should give a value of zero.

That is, $f(x) = 2x^3 + 7x^2 + 2x - 3$

$$f\left(\frac{1}{2}\right) = 2\left(\frac{1}{2}\right)^3 + 7\left(\frac{1}{2}\right)^2 + 2\left(\frac{1}{2}\right) - 3$$

$$= \frac{1}{4} + \frac{7}{4} + 1 - 3$$
$$= 0$$

EXERCISES 2-4

1. Given $f(x) = x^3 + x^2 - 9x - 9$
   a) Show that $f(3) = 0$.
   b) Use long division to show that $x - 3$ is a factor of $f(x)$.

2. Given $g(x) = x^3 + 4x^2 + 5x + 2$
   a) Show that $g(-2) = 0$.
   b) Use long division to show that $x + 2$ is a factor of $g(x)$.

3. Given $p(x) = 2x^3 + x^2 - 27x - 36$
   a) Show that $p(-3) = 0$.
   b) Use long division to show that $p(x)$ is divisible by $x + 3$.

4. If $x + 7$ is a factor of $f(x)$, then what is the value of $f(-7)$?

5. If $f(5) = 0$, then what must be a factor of $f(x)$?

6. Which polynomials have $x - 2$ as a factor?
   a) $x^3 - 3x^2 - 4x + 12$
   b) $x^3 + x^2 - 16x + 20$
   c) $-x^3 + 3x - 2$
   d) $x^4 - 8x^3 + 24x^2 - 32x + 16$

7. Which polynomials have $x + 3$ as a factor?
   a) $x^3 + 2x^2 - 9x - 18$
   b) $-x^3 - 2x^2 + 21x - 18$
   c) $x^3 + 6x^2 + 9x$
   d) $-x^4 - 8x^3 - 14x^2 + 8x + 15$

8. Which of the following polynomials has $x - 2$ as a factor?
   a) $x^3 - 5x^2 - 17x + 21$
   b) $-x^3 - 5x^2 + 2x + 24$
   c) $x^3 - x^2 - 17x - 15$
   d) $x^3 + 7x^2 + 7x - 15$

9. a) Which polynomial in *Exercise 8* has $x + 5$ as a factor?
   b) Which polynomial in *Exercise 8* has $x - 7$ as a factor?

10. If $y^3 + 2y^2 - 5y - 6$ has a value of 0 when -1, 2, and -3 are substituted for y, then what are the factors of $y^3 + 2y^2 - 5y - 6$?

11. Determine which binomials are factors of $x^3 - 4x^2 + x + 6$ without dividing.
   a) $x - 2$
   b) $x + 2$
   c) $x - 3$

12. Given $f(x) = x^3 - 3x^2 - 6x + 8$, determine which binomials are factors of $f(x)$.
   a) $x + 1$
   b) $x - 2$
   c) $x - 4$
   d) $x - 1$

13. Given $p(x) = 2x^3 + 11x^2 - 7x - 6$, determine if $p(x)$ is divisible by each binomial.
   a) $x - 1$
   b) $x + 6$
   c) $x + 2$

Ⓑ

14. Show that the first two binomials are factors of the cubic polynomial, and use the results to factor the polynomial.
   a) $a - 2$, $a - 1$; $a^3 - 6a^2 + 11a - 6$
   b) $a + 2$, $a - 2$; $a^3 + 3a^2 - 4a - 12$
   c) $x + 3$, $x + 2$; $x^3 + 4x^2 + x - 6$

15. Determine whether each binomial is a factor of the higher-degree polynomial, without dividing.
   a) $x - 1$; $x^2 - 7x + 6$
   b) $x + 2$; $x^2 + 8x + 6$
   c) $x - 2$; $x^3 - 3x^2 - 4x + 12$
   d) $x - 3$; $x^3 + 6x^2 - 2x + 3$
   e) $x + 1$; $x^7 - 5x^4 - 4x + 2$
   f) $2x - 1$; $4x^3 - 6x^2 + 8x - 3$

16. Find a linear factor of each polynomial.
   a) $x^3 - 4x + 3$
   b) $x^3 + x^2 + x + 1$
   c) $-y^3 - 19y^2 - 19y - 1$
   d) $x^3 - 27$
   e) $-y^3 + y^2 + y + 2$
   f) $x^3 + 2x^2 + 5x + 4$

17. a) Show that both $x - 1$ and $x + 2$ are factors of $x^3 - 3x^2 - 6x + 8$.
    b) Find another factor of $x^3 - 3x^2 - 6x + 8$.

18. a) Show that both $x - 2$ and $x - 3$ are factors of $2x^3 - 11x^2 + 17x - 6$.
    b) Find another factor of $2x^3 - 11x^2 + 17x - 6$.

19. Three students were discussing their methods of factoring cubic polynomials.

Scott, "After finding one factor by the factor theorem, I always use long division to get another factor."

Megan, "I don't like using long division, so I always use the method of equating coefficients."

Ivan, "I have found a faster method. I try to use the factor theorem three times. If I can get three values of x which make the expression equal 0, then I know what the three factors are."

Megan, "But that method won't work for all cubic polynomials."

a) Factor $x^3 - 8x^2 + 19x - 12$ using Ivan's method.

b) Give two examples which show that Megan is correct.

20. Factor completely.

a) $x^3 + 5x^2 + 2x - 8$ b) $x^3 + 9x^2 + 23x + 15$
c) $x^3 + 2x^2 - 19x - 20$ d) $x^3 - 7x - 6$
e) $5x^3 - 7x^2 - x + 3$ f) $x^3 - 9x^2 + 17x - 6$
g) $x^3 + 8x^2 + 17x + 10$ h) $2x^3 - x^2 - 13x - 6$

21. Factor completely.

a) $x^3 - 8x^2 + 17x - 6$ b) $x^3 - 3x^2 - 24x - 28$
c) $x^3 + 6x^2 - 31x - 36$ d) $x^3 - 28x - 48$
e) $3x^3 + 2x^2 - 11x - 10$ f) $10x^3 - 21x^2 - x + 6$
g) $x^3 - 39x - 70$ h) $3x^3 + 4x^2 - 35x - 12$

22. Find k.

a) $x - 2$ is a factor of $x^3 - 6x^2 + kx - 6$.
b) $x + 4$ is a factor of $3x^3 + 11x^2 - 6x + k$.
c) $x - 3$ is a factor of $x^3 + kx^2 + kx + 21$.

Ⓒ

23. Is $2x + 1$ a factor of $2x^3 - x^2 - 13x - 6$?

24. Is $x^2 - 1$ a factor of $2x^4 - 3x^3 + 3x^2 + 3x - 5$?

25. Is $x^3 - 6x^2 + 3x + 10$ divisible by $x^2 - x - 2$?

26. Solve by factoring.

a) $x^3 - 2x^2 - 19x + 20 = 0$ b) $x^3 - 8x^2 + x + 42 = 0$
c) $6x^3 + 13x^2 - 16x - 3 = 0$ d) $5x^3 - 13x^2 - 56x - 20 = 0$

27. Prove that $x - y$ is a factor of $x^n - y^n$ for all values of $n \in N$.

28. Prove that $x + a$ is a factor of $(x + a)^5 + (x + c)^5 + (a - c)^5$.

29. Show that for any polynomial $f(x)$ there exists a polynomial $g(x)$ such that $f(x) = xg(x) + c$, where c is a constant.

 INVESTIGATE

Investigate whether or not $x + y$ is a factor of $x^n + y^n$ for all values of $n \in N$. If it is not, then for what values of n is $x + y$ a factor of $x^n + y^n$?

2-5 SOLVING POLYNOMIAL EQUATIONS BY FACTORING

Although there are formulas for solving cubic and quartic equations, they involve cube and fourth roots, and are too complicated to be of practical significance. There are no formulas for solving polynomial equations of degree higher than the fourth.

Some polynomial equations can be solved by factoring.

Example 1. Solve for x. $x^3 - x = 0$

Solution. The left side of the equation has a common factor.
$$x^3 - x = 0$$
$$x(x^2 - 1) = 0$$
$$x(x - 1)(x + 1) = 0$$
Either $x = 0$ or $x - 1 = 0$ or $x + 1 = 0$
$$x = 1 \qquad\qquad x = -1$$

Example 2. Solve for x. $x^3 - 3x^2 - 4x + 12 = 0$

Solution. We recognize that the left side can be factored by grouping because a factor of $x - 3$ remains when common factors are removed from the first two terms and from the last two terms.
$$x^3 - 3x^2 - 4x + 12 = 0$$
$$x^2(x - 3) - 4(x - 3) = 0$$
$$(x - 3)(x^2 - 4) = 0$$
$$(x - 3)(x + 2)(x - 2) = 0$$
Either $x - 3 = 0$ or $x + 2 = 0$ or $x - 2 = 0$
$$x = 3 \qquad\qquad x = -2 \qquad\qquad x = 2$$

Example 3. Solve for x. $x^3 + 9x^2 + 13x + 5 = 0$

Solution. Since grouping does not produce a common factor, we try the factor theorem.
Let $f(x) = x^3 + 9x^2 + 13x + 5$.
The factors of 5 are ± 1 and ± 5.
By inspection, we see that $f(1) \neq 0$. All the terms are positive and hence cannot have a sum of zero.
$$f(-1) = (-1)^3 + 9(-1)^2 + 13(-1) + 5$$
$$= -1 + 9 - 13 + 5$$
$$= 0$$
Since $f(-1) = 0$, $x + 1$ is a factor of the left side of the given equation. Also, 5 is the last term in the quadratic factor. The quadratic factor can be found by long division, or by equating coefficients.

$$\text{Let } (x + 1)(x^2 + bx + 5) = x^3 + 9x^2 + 13x + 5.$$

The term containing x is $5x + bx$ on the left side, and $13x$ on the right side. Since the coefficients are equal,

$$5 + b = 13$$
$$b = 8$$

Therefore, the given equation can be written in the form

$$(x + 1)(x^2 + 8x + 5) = 0$$

Either $x + 1 = 0$ or $x^2 + 8x + 5 = 0$

$$x = -1$$

$$x = \frac{-8 \pm \sqrt{8^2 - 4(1)(5)}}{2}$$

$$= \frac{-8 \pm \sqrt{64 - 20}}{2}$$

$$= \frac{-8 \pm \sqrt{44}}{2}$$

$$= -4 \pm \sqrt{11}$$

Example 4.   Solve for x. $x^3 + 1 = 0$

Solution.   The left side of the equation is a sum of cubes.

$$x^3 + 1 = 0$$
$$(x + 1)(x^2 - x + 1) = 0$$

Either $x + 1 = 0$ or $x^2 - x + 1 = 0$

$$x = -1$$

$$x = \frac{1 \pm \sqrt{(-1)^2 - 4(1)(1)}}{2}$$

$$= \frac{1 \pm \sqrt{-3}}{2}$$

There is only one root, $x = -1$, in the set of real numbers.

Example 5.   A rectangular piece of cardboard measuring 10 cm by 8 cm is made into an open box by cutting squares from the corners and turning up the sides. If the box is to hold a volume of 48 cm³, what size of square must be removed?

Solution.   Draw a diagram.
Let the side of the square to be removed be represented by x centimetres. Then the volume of the box is given by this expression.

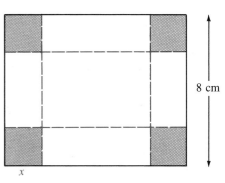

$$V = x(10 - 2x)(8 - 2x)$$

Since the volume is 48 cm³,

$$x(10 - 2x)(8 - 2x) = 48$$
$$4x(5 - x)(4 - x) = 48$$
$$x(20 - 9x + x^2) = 12$$
$$x^3 - 9x^2 + 20x = 12$$
$$x^3 - 9x^2 + 20x - 12 = 0 \qquad \dots \text{①}$$

Solve using the factor theorem.
Let $f(x) = x^3 - 9x^2 + 20x - 12$.

$$f(1) = 1^3 - 9(1)^2 + 20(1) - 12$$
$$= 1 - 9 + 20 - 12$$
$$= 0$$

Since $f(1) = 0$, $x - 1$ is a factor of the left side of equation ①. The other factors can be found by division, by inspection, or by using the factor theorem again.

$$f(2) = 2^3 - 9(2)^2 + 20(2) - 12$$
$$= 8 - 36 + 40 - 12$$
$$= 0$$

Since $f(2) = 0$, $x - 2$ is a factor of the left side of equation ①.
Since $x - 1$ and $x - 2$ are factors, using the factor property the third factor has the form $x - a$, where

$$(-1)(-2)(-a) = -12$$
$$a = 6$$

Therefore, the third factor is $x - 6$.
That is, the equation may be written $(x - 1)(x - 2)(x - 6) = 0$.
Either $x = 1$, $x = 2$, or $x = 6$

When $x = 1$, the dimensions of the box are 8 cm by 6 cm by 1 cm, and it has a volume of 48 cm³.

When $x = 2$, the dimensions are 6 cm by 4 cm by 2 cm, and the volume is also 48 cm³.

It is impossible for x to be 6 since four squares with sides of this length cannot be cut from the cardboard.

Therefore, four squares with 1 cm sides, or four squares with 2 cm sides can be removed to form a box with a volume of 48 cm³.

As the above examples suggest, only certain polynomial equations can be solved by factoring. More general methods are needed to solve other polynomial equations.

EXERCISES 2-5

1. Solve for x.
   a) $x(x - 2)(x + 5) = 0$
   b) $x(2x + 3)(x - 4) = 0$
   c) $x(x^2 + 10x + 21) = 0$
   d) $x(6x^2 + 5x - 21) = 0$
   e) $x^3 - 4x = 0$
   f) $2x^3 + 10x^2 + 12x = 0$

2. a) One root of each equation below is the same for every equation. What is this root?
   i) $10x^3 - 25x^2 - 15x = 0$
   ii) $12x^3 = 27x$
   iii) $6x^3 + 45x = 33x^2$
   iv) $3x^4 + 14x^3 + 8x^2 = 0$
   v) $18x^4 - 50x^2 = 0$
   vi) $35x^2 - 5x^3 = 60x$
   b) Find the other roots of each equation in part a).

Ⓑ

3. Solve.
   a) $x^3 - 2x^2 + 3x - 6 = 0$ b) $x^3 + 5x^2 - 9x - 45 = 0$
   c) $2x^3 - 3x^2 - 11x + 6 = 0$ d) $3x^3 - 2x^2 - 12x + 8 = 0$

4. Solve.
   a) $x^3 + 3x^2 - 10x - 24 = 0$ b) $x^3 - x^2 + 9x - 9 = 0$
   c) $2x^3 - 3x^2 - 5x + 6 = 0$ d) $8x^3 + 4x^2 - 18x - 9 = 0$

5. Solve.
   a) $x^3 + x - 10 = 0$ b) $2x^3 - 4x^2 - 18x + 36 = 0$
   c) $2x^3 + 10x^2 + 13x + 5 = 0$ d) $3x^3 - 2x^2 + 75x - 50 = 0$

6. Find three consecutive integers with a product of: a) -24 b) -120.

7. What number and its cube differ by: a) 24   b) -120?

8. A rectangular piece of cardboard measuring 12 cm by 8 cm is made into an open box by cutting squares from the corners and turning up the sides. If the volume of the box is 60 cm³, what are its dimensions?

Ⓒ

9. The product of the squares of two consecutive integers is 256 036. Find the integers.

10. Write a polynomial equation with these roots.
    a) 2, 5, 1   b) $-1, 2 + \sqrt{3}, 2 - \sqrt{3}$
    c) $-\dfrac{1}{2}, 3, -3, 1$ d) $-1, \dfrac{3 + 2\sqrt{5}}{2}, \dfrac{3 - 2\sqrt{5}}{2}$

11. If one root is 2, find each value of k, and the other roots.
    a) $2x^3 - 13x^2 + kx + 10 = 0$ b) $25x^4 + kx^2 + 16 = 0$
    c) $3x^3 - 15x^2 + kx - 4 = 0$ d) $3x^4 - kx^3 + 49x^2 - 23x - 14 = 0$

12. Solve.
    a) $3x^4 - 15x^2 + 12 = 0$ b) $\dfrac{3}{x^2} + \dfrac{2x}{x + 2} = \dfrac{3x}{x + 2} + \dfrac{1}{x^2}$

13. The diagrams show the first four pyramidal numbers. The number of balls in each layer of the pyramids is a perfect square. An expression for the nth pyramidal number is $\dfrac{n(n + 1)(2n + 1)}{6}$.

    a) Verify that the expression is correct by using it to find the number of balls in the pyramids shown in the diagrams.
    b) The only pyramidal number (other than 1) which is a perfect square is 4900. How many layers are in the pyramid for this number?

COMPUTER POWER

Solving Polynomial Equations

The computer is an ideal tool for solving polynomial equations such as $x^3 - 12x + 8 = 0$ (see *Example 1* in Section 2-1). The program below can be used to find decimal approximations to the roots of polynomial equations up to the tenth degree.

```
VAR
  CH : CHAR;
  I,N,K,Q : INTEGER;
  D,DT,T,X,XT,Y,Y1,Y2 : REAL;
  A : ARRAY [0..255] OF REAL;

BEGIN    { POLYNOMIAL EQUATIONS }
        WRITELN('WHAT IS THE DEGREE? ');
        READ(N); WRITELN;
        WRITELN('ENTER ',N+1,' COEFFICIENTS');
        FOR I := 0 TO N DO READ(A[I]);
        WRITELN('WHAT IS THE FIRST VALUE OF X? ');
        READ(X); WRITELN;
        T := 0;
        WRITELN('WHAT IS THE INCREMENT? ');
        READ(D);
        Y1 := 0; Y2 := 0;
        CH := CHR(1);
        REPEAT
          FOR K := 1 TO 11 DO BEGIN
            Y := A[0];
            FOR I := 1 TO N DO Y := Y * X + A[I];
            Y2 := Y1; Y1 := Y;
            WRITELN(X:5:8,' ',Y:5:8);
            IF Y = 0 THEN BEGIN
              WRITELN; WRITELN(X:5:8,'IS A ROOT');
            END;
            IF (Y1 * Y2) < 0 THEN BEGIN
              WRITELN;
              WRITELN('THERE IS A ROOT BETWEEN ',X-D:5:8,'
              AND ',X:5:8);
              WRITELN('ENTER 1 - FOR A MORE ACCURATE
              APPROXIMATION');
              WRITELN('      2 - TO CONTINUE');
              WRITELN('      3 - TO REPEAT');
              WRITELN('      4 - TO STOP');
              READ (Q);

              IF T = 0 THEN BEGIN
                XT := X;
                DT := D;
              END;
```

```
              CASE Q OF
                   1:
                     BEGIN
                     T := T + 1; Y1 := 0; Y2 := 0;
                     X := X - D; D := D / 10;
                     END;
                   2:
                     BEGIN
                     T := 0; X := XT; D := DT;
                     END;
                   3:
                     T := 0;
                   4:
                     CH := CHR(0);
                END;
           END;
                X := X + D;
           END;
      UNTIL CH = CHR(0);
 END.
```

When the program is run, the computer first asks for the degree of the polynomial, and then for the coefficients. These must be entered in descending order, including zero coefficients for missing terms. For example, to solve the equation $x^3 - 12x + 8 = 0$, the degree is 3 and the coefficients are 1, 0, -12, and 8.

The program instructs the computer to evaluate the polynomial for eleven successive values of x. You must enter the first value of x desired, and the increment. For example, if you enter -5 for the first value of x, and 1 for the increment, the computer will evaluate the polynomial for these values of x: $-5, -4, -3, \ldots,$ 5. For the polynomial $x^3 - 12x + 8 = 0$, the computer is calculating the table of values shown on page 42. In this table, notice that some of the y-values are negative, while others are positive. Also, a root of the equation occurs between the values of x for which the corresponding values of y change sign. The program uses this fact to calculate the root of the equation.

When the computer encounters two consecutive values of y with opposite signs, it indicates that a root exists between the two corresponding values of x. At this point, four options are given. Simply follow the instructions on the screen. For example, if you indicate that a more accurate approximation is desired, the computer will calculate values of x between those found, using a smaller increment. If this option is chosen several times in succession, the root can be found very accurately.

The following result was obtained for the root of the equation
$x^3 - 12x + 8 = 0$ which lies between -4 and -3.

```
THERE IS A ROOT BETWEEN -3.8 AND -3.7
THERE IS A ROOT BETWEEN -3.76 AND -3.75
THERE IS A ROOT BETWEEN -3.759 AND -3.758
THERE IS A ROOT BETWEEN -3.7588 AND -3.7587
THERE IS A ROOT BETWEEN -3.75878 AND -3.75877
THERE IS A ROOT BETWEEN -3.758771 AND -3.75877
THERE IS A ROOT BETWEEN -3.7587705 AND -3.7587704
```

This shows that one root of the equation is $-3.758\ 770$, to six decimal places.

Use the program to answer these questions.

1. Find the other roots of the equation $x^3 - 12x + 8 = 0$, to six decimal places.

2. Each equation has a root between -3 and $+3$. Find this root to four decimal places.
   a) $x^3 + 6x^2 + 5x - 15 = 0$
   b) $x^5 + 5x^4 + 5x^3 - 5x^2 - 6x - 40 = 0$
   c) $x^3 - 3x - 5 = 0$

3. Find all the real roots of each equation, to four decimal places.
   a) $x^3 + 2x^2 - 11x - 5 = 0$
   b) $x^4 - 4x^3 - 4x^2 + 16x - 1 = 0$
   c) $x^5 - 2x^3 + x^2 - 10x + 25 = 0$

4. The volume V of a spherical segment
   with base radius a and height h is
   given by this formula.

   $$V = \frac{1}{6}\pi h(3a^2 + h^2)$$

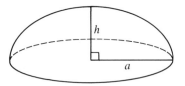

   A domed stadium is designed to be in the shape of a spherical segment with a base radius of 150 m. If the dome is to contain a volume of 3 500 000 m³, find the height of the dome at its centre, to the nearest tenth of a metre.

5. Give an example of a polynomial equation which has a real root that would not likely be found by the program. Use the program to illustrate that it cannot be found this way.

THE MATHEMATICAL MIND

The Cubic Equation Controversy

One of the most important mathematical achievements of the sixteenth century was the discovery by Italian mathematicians of formulas for the solution of cubic and quartic equations. This accomplishment occurred at a time when discoveries were often kept secret, and rivals were challenged to solve the same problem.

About 1510, a professor at the University of Bologna revealed to a student a method he had found of solving cubic equations without a quadratic term, such as $x^3 + 5x = 8$.

Nicolo Tartaglia
1499-1557

In 1535, when Nicolo Tartaglia claimed to have found a method of solving cubic equations without a linear term, such as $x^3 + 2x^2 = 6$, the former student challenged him to a public equation-solving contest. But before the contest, Tartaglia learned how to solve an equation of the first type as well, and he won the contest triumphantly.

Tartaglia knew that, by substituting $y - \dfrac{b}{3a}$ for x, any cubic equation $ax^3 + bx^2 + cx + d = 0$ could be reduced to the form $y^3 + my = n$.
He proved that a root of this equation is

$$y = \sqrt[3]{\sqrt{\left(\frac{m}{3}\right)^3 + \left(\frac{n}{2}\right)^2} + \frac{n}{2}}$$
$$- \sqrt[3]{\sqrt{\left(\frac{m}{3}\right)^3 + \left(\frac{n}{2}\right)^2} - \frac{n}{2}}.$$

Girolamo Cardano
1501-1576

Later, Girolamo Cardano urged Tartaglia to show him his method. When Cardano promised to keep it secret, Tartaglia gave it to him. But in 1545 Cardano published his *Ars Magna*, a Latin text on algebra, and included Tartaglia's solution of cubic equations. When Tartaglia protested the breach of his promise, Cardano claimed to have received his information from another party, and accused Tartaglia of plagiarism from the same source. There followed a bitter dispute between the two men over the question of who was the first to discover the formula for solving cubic equations.

Tartaglia's solution gave only one root, and later mathematicians found improved solutions. They also discovered formulas for quartic equations. Much work was done attempting to find a formula for quintic equations, but without success. This was proved to be impossible in 1824 by the Norwegian mathematician, Niels Henrik Abel.

QUESTIONS

1. Use a calculator and the formula given above to solve these cubic equations. Verify each solution.
    a) $y^3 + 6y = 2$
    b) $y^3 + 4y + 3 = 0$
    c) $x^3 - 3x^2 + 5x + 4 = 0$

2-6 THE ROOTS OF POLYNOMIAL EQUATIONS

During the last two centuries, mathematicians have devoted much time and effort to the problem of solving polynomial equations. In this work it is often possible to prove something about the roots of an equation without knowing what they are. For example, if we calculate the value of the discriminant $b^2 - 4ac$, we can determine the nature of the roots of a quadratic equation $ax^2 + bx + c = 0$ without solving the equation.

The graphs of some cubic functions are shown below.

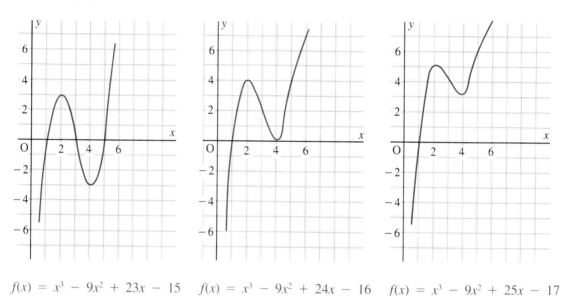

$$f(x) = x^3 - 9x^2 + 23x - 15 \qquad f(x) = x^3 - 9x^2 + 24x - 16 \qquad f(x) = x^3 - 9x^2 + 25x - 17$$

In each case, the graph intersects the x-axis at least once. These examples suggest that the graph of every cubic function intersects the x-axis at least once. There is a simple reason for this.

If x is a negative number with a large absolute value, such as -100 or -1000, the value of the cubic term will be a very large negative number. This dominates the other terms, leaving a negative number for the value of the polynomial. Conversely, if x is a very large positive number, the value of the cubic term will be a very large positive number. This dominates the other terms, leaving a positive number for the value of the polynomial. Therefore, the graph of a cubic function proceeds from the lower left to the upper right, and must cross the x-axis.

This reasoning applies to all cubic functions whose coefficient of x^3 is positive. If the coefficient is negative, the analysis is similar, but the graph proceeds from the upper left to the lower right.

Since the graph of every cubic function intersects the x-axis at least once, we conclude that every cubic equation has at least one real root. Then, what are the possibilities for the other roots?

Consider the equations below. These correspond to the three graphs on the opposite page. Each equation has $x = 1$ as a root. The other roots are found by dividing each polynomial by $x - 1$.

Equation 1. $x^3 - 9x^2 + 23x - 15 = 0$

$(x - 1)(x^2 - 8x + 15) = 0$

In addition to $x = 1$, there are two other roots, which are the roots of this quadratic equation.

$x^2 - 8x + 15 = 0$

$(x - 3)(x - 5) = 0$

$x = 3$ or $x = 5$

This equation has three different real roots. These occur at the points where the graph of the corresponding function intersects the x-axis.

Equation 2. $x^3 - 9x^2 + 24x - 16 = 0$

$(x - 1)(x^2 - 8x + 16) = 0$

In addition to $x = 1$, there are two other roots, which are the roots of this quadratic equation.

$x^2 - 8x + 16 = 0$

$(x - 4)^2 = 0$

$x = 4$

The cubic equation has three real roots, two of which are equal. These equal roots occur at the point where the graph of the corresponding function touches the x-axis.

Equation 3. $x^3 - 9x^2 + 25x - 17 = 0$

$(x - 1)(x^2 - 8x + 17) = 0$

In addition to $x = 1$, there may be two other real roots, which are the roots of this quadratic equation.

$x^2 - 8x + 17 = 0$

Use the quadratic formula.

$$x = \frac{-b \pm \sqrt{b^2 - 4ac}}{2a}$$

$$= \frac{8 \pm \sqrt{64 - 4(17)}}{2}$$

$$= \frac{8 \pm \sqrt{-4}}{2}$$

There are no other real roots. The one real root occurs at the point where the graph of the corresponding function crosses the x-axis.

These examples suggest the following properties of cubic equations.

> **Property of Cubic Equations**
> • Every cubic equation has one, two, or three roots.

We can analyze higher-order polynomial equations in a similar manner. The graph of a 4th degree polynomial may intersect the x-axis up to four times. Hence, a 4th degree polynomial equation has at most four real roots. If the graph intersects the x-axis less than four times, then two or more of the roots are real and equal. Similar results occur for polynomial equations of the 5th degree and higher degrees.

> **Property of Polynomial Equations**
> • Every polynomial equation of degree n has at most n real roots.

Example 1. Write a polynomial equation with these four roots: -3, 4, and a double root of $-\frac{1}{2}$.

Solution. By the factor theorem, the factors of the polynomial are $(x + 3)$, $(x - 4)$, $\left(x + \frac{1}{2}\right)$, and $\left(x + \frac{1}{2}\right)$. Hence, the equation is:

$$(x + 3)(x - 4)\left(x + \frac{1}{2}\right)^2 = 0$$

or $(x + 3)(x - 4)(2x + 1)^2 = 0$

The equation in *Example 1* is a 4th degree equation. Although it is not necessary to do so, the factors may be multiplied and the equation written as

$4x^4 - 51x^2 - 49x - 12 = 0 \ldots \textcircled{1}$

If we had left the equation as $(x + 3)(x - 4)\left(x + \frac{1}{2}\right)^2$ and multiplied the factors, the result would have been

$x^4 - \frac{51}{4}x^2 - \frac{49}{4}x - 3 = 0 \ldots \textcircled{2}$

Equations $\textcircled{1}$ and $\textcircled{2}$ are equivalent because $\textcircled{1}$ can be obtained from $\textcircled{2}$ by multiplying by 4. These equations have the same roots. That is, multiplying both sides of an equation by a constant does not change the roots of the equation.

Similarly, multiplying a function by a constant does not change its zeros, but it does yield a different function. For example, the polynomial functions corresponding to ① and ② are

$$p(x) = 4x^4 - 51x^2 - 49x - 12$$

$$q(x) = x^4 - \frac{51}{4}x^2 - \frac{49}{4}x - 3$$

Both $p(x)$ and $q(x)$ have the same zeros; that is, -3, 4, and a double zero of $-\frac{1}{2}$.

But $p(x)$ and $q(x)$ are different functions. The graph of $p(x)$ is expanded vertically by a factor of 4 relative to the graph of $q(x)$. Since the coefficients of $p(x)$ are integers, $p(x)$ is an example of an *integral polynomial function*.

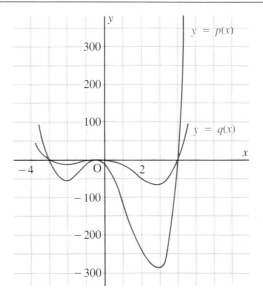

Hence, we can see that a polynomial function is not uniquely defined by its zeros. That is, the zeros alone are not sufficient to determine a polynomial function. Some additional information must be given, such as another point on its graph.

Example 2. A cubic function has zeros -3, -1, and 2. The y-intercept of its graph is 12.

a) Sketch the graph of the function.
b) Determine the function.

Solution. a) The x-intercepts of the graph are -3, -1, and 2. Infinitely many cubic curves can be drawn through these points, but only one of them has a y-intercept of 12.

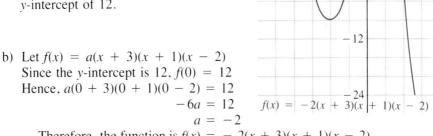

b) Let $f(x) = a(x + 3)(x + 1)(x - 2)$
Since the y-intercept is 12, $f(0) = 12$
Hence, $a(0 + 3)(0 + 1)(0 - 2) = 12$
$$-6a = 12$$
$$a = -2$$
Therefore, the function is $f(x) = -2(x + 3)(x + 1)(x - 2)$
or $f(x) = -2x^3 - 4x^2 + 10x + 12$

In *Example 2* the zeros of the polynomial $f(x)$ are -3, -1, and $+2$. These zeros are factors of the constant term of the polynomial, 12. This is a direct consequence of the factor theorem, and is known as the Integral Zero Theorem.

Integral Zero Theorem

Let $p(x)$ be an integral polynomial function which has an integral zero $x = a$. Then, a is a factor of the constant term of the polynomial.

Proof: Since $x = a$ is a zero of the polynomial, $p(a) = 0$. Hence, by the factor theorem, $p(x) = (x - a)q(x)$, where $q(x)$ is an integral polynomial. Therefore, the constant term of $p(x)$ is $-a$ times the constant term of $q(x)$. That is, a is a factor of the constant term of $p(x)$.

Corollary   Rational Zero Theorem

Let $p(x)$ be an integral polynomial function which has a rational zero $x = \frac{a}{b}$, $a \in I$, $b \in I$, $b \neq 0$. Then, a is a factor of the constant term of the polynomial, and b is a factor of the coefficient of the highest-degree term.

Example 3.   List the possible rational roots of the equation
$2x^3 + 11x^2 + 17x + 5 = 0$.

Solution.   If the equation has a rational root $\frac{a}{b}$, then by the rational zero theorem, a is a factor of the constant term 5, and b is a factor of the coefficient of x^3, 2. The only possibilities for a and b are $a = \pm 1, \pm 5$, and $b = \pm 1, \pm 2$. Hence, the only possible rational roots are $1, -1, 5, -5, \frac{1}{2}, -\frac{1}{2}, \frac{5}{2}$, and $-\frac{5}{2}$.

In *Example 3*, to determine which if any of the possible rational roots are, in fact, roots of the equation, we would have to substitute each one in turn into the left side and see if the expression simplifies to 0. For this particular equation, the work is simplified considerably if we observe that it is impossible for the equation to have a positive root, since the left side of the equation is positive if $x > 0$. Hence, we would only need to check the possible negative roots. If we did this, we would find that $x = -\frac{5}{2}$ is the only rational root of the equation.

EXERCISES 2-6

1. What is the greatest number of real roots each equation could have?
   a) $x^3 + 5x^2 - 6x - 3 = 0$
   b) $7x^2 - 12x + 4 = 0$
   c) $2x^3 - x^2 + 8x - 9 = 0$
   d) $5x^4 + 3x^2 - x - 12 = 0$
   e) $3x^3 + 17x + 15 = 0$
   f) $x^3 + 10x = 3x^5 - 8x^2 + 4$

2. Write a cubic equation with the given roots.
   a) 1, 2, 3   b) 2, 2, 5   c) $-4, 1, 0$ d) 2, 2, 2

3. Write a polynomial equation with the given roots.
   a) 1, 2, 3, 4   b) 5, -2, 1, 2   c) 1, 1, 2, 2, 3, 3

4. Polynomial functions of degree 2, 3, 4, 5, 6, and 7 are graphed below. What is the degree of the function in each graph?

a)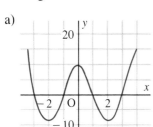

b)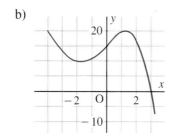

c)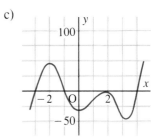

d)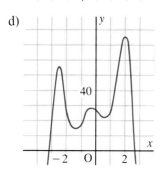

e)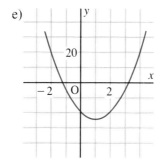

f)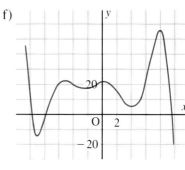

(B)

5. A cubic function has zeros -2, 1, and 4. The y-intercept of its graph is 24.
   a) Sketch the graph of the function.
   b) Determine the function.

6. Sketch the graph of each polynomial function and determine the function.
   a) zeros -2, 2, 2; graph has y-intercept -16.
   b) zeros -3, 2, 5; graph has y-intercept 45.
   c) zeros -2, -1, 1, 2; graph has y-intercept 20.
   d) zeros 0, 2, 4; graph passes through $(3, 9)$.

7. a) Find an integral root of the cubic equation $x^3 - 10x + 9 = 0$.
   b) Show that the equation in part a) has only one integral root.

8. List the possible integral roots of each equation.
   a) $x^3 - 2x^2 + 6x - 5 = 0$ b) $x^3 - x^2 - 4x + 4 = 0$
   c) $x^3 - x^2 - 3x - 9 = 0$ d) $2x^3 - 7x - 6 = 0$

9. List the possible integral zeros of each polynomial.
   a) $x^3 - 3x^2 - x + 3$ b) $2x^3 + x^2 - 13x + 6$
   c) $3x^3 - 20x^2 + 23x + 10$ d) $4x^4 + 3x^2 - 1$

10. Prove that the equation $x^5 + 9x^3 + 7x^2 + x + 1 = 0$ has no positive roots.

11. Prove that the equation $x^4 - 4x^3 + 5x^2 - 3x + 6 = 0$ has no negative roots.

12. List the possible rational roots of each equation.
    a) $5x^3 + 13x^2 + 9x + 1 = 0$
    b) $2x^5 - x^4 - 2x + 1 = 0$
    c) $2x^3 - 3x^2 - x - 2 = 0$
    d) $4x^3 + 2x^2 + 2x + 1 = 0$
    e) $5x^3 + 17x^2 - 17x + 3 = 0$
    f) $6x^4 - 4x^3 + 3x^2 - 8x + 4 = 0$

13. State which of the five equations listed has:
    a) a root of 2   i) $3x^3 - 4x^2 + x = 0$
    b) a root of -5 ii) $3x^3 - 5x^2 - 4x + 4 = 0$
    c) a root of $\frac{2}{3}$ iii) $x^3 + 8x^2 + 16x + 5 = 0$
                                       iv) $x^3 + 8x^2 + 17x + 10 = 0$
    d) at least one real root   v) $x^4 + 3x^3 - 11x^2 - 3x + 10 = 0$
    e) no positive root.

14. Find all three roots of each cubic equation.
    a) $2x^3 + x^2 - 13x + 6 = 0$
    b) $x^3 - 1 = 0$
    c) $2x^3 + 11x^2 + 17x + 5 = 0$
    d) $6x^3 + 7x^2 - 7x - 6 = 0$

Ⓒ

15. Explain why a polynomial equation of degree n has at least one real root if n is odd.

16. Consider the three cubic functions graphed on page 72.
    $y = x^3 - 9x^2 + 23x - 15$
    $y = x^3 - 9x^2 + 24x - 16$
    $y = x^3 - 9x^2 + 25x - 17$
    a) Note the pattern in the coefficients. Assuming that this pattern is continued, write the next three functions in the list.
    b) Describe what happens to the shape of the graph of the function $f(x) = x^3 - 9x^2 + (24 + k)x - (16 + k)$ as k increases through positive values.
    c) If the pattern is continued in the opposite direction, write the preceding three functions in the list.
    d) Describe what happens to the shape of the graph of the function $f(x) = x^3 - 9x^2 + (24 + k)x - (16 + k)$ as k decreases through negative values.

2-7 SOLVING POLYNOMIAL INEQUALITIES

The graph below shows the polynomial function $y = x^3 - 2x^2 - 5x + 6$.
The graph divides the x-axis into three different sets of values of x.

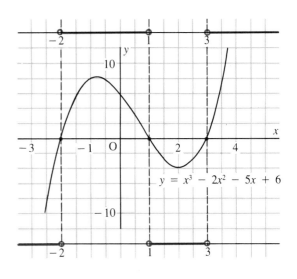

$y = x^3 - 2x^2 - 5x + 6$

- The values of x which satisfy the inequality $x^3 - 2x^2 - 5x + 6 > 0$; these are the values of x where the graph is above the x-axis. We say that the solution set of the inequality is $\{x \mid -2 < x < 1 \text{ or } x > 3\}$.

- The values of x which satisfy the equation $x^3 - 2x^2 - 5x + 6 = 0$; these are the values of x where the graph intersects the x-axis. The roots of the equation are -2, 1, and 3.

- The values of x which satisfy the inequality $x^3 - 2x^2 - 5x + 6 < 0$; these are the values of x where the graph is below the x-axis. The solution set of the inequality is $\{x \mid x < -2 \text{ or } 1 < x < 3\}$.

Any polynomial inequality can be solved by graphing. But notice in the above example that the roots of the corresponding equation determine the endpoints of the intervals in the solutions of the inequalities. Hence, a more efficient method of solving a polynomial inequality is to solve the corresponding equation and test values of x in the intervals defined by the roots of the equation.

Example 1. Solve the inequality $6 - 5x^2 < 13x$.

Solution. *Step 1.* Solve the equation $6 - 5x^2 = 13x$.

By factoring, or using the quadratic formula, we find that the roots are -3 and $\frac{2}{5}$. These divide the x-axis into three intervals: A, B, and C.

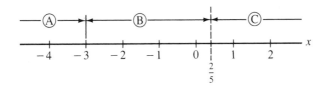

Step 2. Select a value of x in each interval, and substitute it in both sides of the given inequality. If the inequality is satisfied, all values of x in the interval are solutions of the inequality.

A value of x in interval A is -10. Substitute -10 for x.

Left side $= -494$ Right side $= -130$

This value of x satisfies the inequality.

A value of x in interval B is 0. Substitute 0 for x.
Left side = 6   Right side = 0
This value of x does not satisfy the inequality.

A value of x in interval C is 1. Substitute 1 for x.
Left side = 1   Right side = 13
This value of x satisfies the inequality.

Step 3. Write the solution set of the inequality, or illustrate the solution set on a number line.

The solution set is $\left\{ x \mid x < -3 \text{ or } x > \frac{2}{5} \right\}$.

In *Example 1*, the numbers -3 and $\frac{2}{5}$ are not part of the solution set. If the inequality had been $6 - 5x^2 \leqslant 13x$, these numbers would satisfy the inequality, and the solution set would be written as
$\left\{ x \mid x \leqslant -3 \text{ or } x \geqslant \frac{2}{5} \right\}$.

Polynomial inequalities of higher degree can be solved in the same way. The initial step of solving the corresponding equation can be carried out by factoring or by using a computer.

EXERCISES 2-7

1. Use each graph to write the solution set of the inequalities given below it.

   a)

   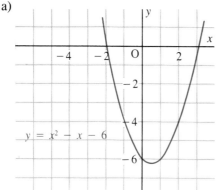

   $y = x^2 - x - 6$

   i) $x^2 - x - 6 < 0$
   ii) $x^2 - x - 6 > 0$

   b)

   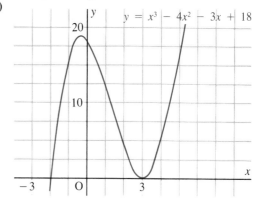

   $y = x^3 - 4x^2 - 3x + 18$

   i) $x^3 - 4x^2 - 3x + 18 < 0$
   ii) $x^3 - 4x^2 - 3x + 18 > 0$

2. Solve each inequality.
   a) $(x - 2)(x + 2) > 0$ b) $(x + 1)(x + 2) \leqslant 0$
   c) $x(x - 5) > 0$ d) $x(x - 2)(x - 4) \leqslant 0$
   e) $(a - 1)(a - 2)(a - 3) < 0$ f) $(n + 1)(n - 3)(n + 5) \geqslant 0$

(B)

3. Solve each inequality.
   a) $(x - 2)(x + 2)(x - 6) > 0$
   b) $(c + 4)(c - 3)^2 < 0$
   c) $s(s + 3)(s + 5) \geqslant 0$
   d) $x(x - 2)(x^2 - 16) \leqslant 0$
   e) $(x + 2)^2 (x - 5)^2 > 0$
   f) $(u - 1)(u - 2)(u - 3) < (u - 1)(u - 3)$

4. Solve each inequality.
   a) $x^2 - 5x < 0$
   c) $18 - 3y - y^2 \geqslant 0$
   e) $x^3 - 4x^2 > 0$
   b) $m^2 - 2m \geqslant 8$
   d) $x^2 + 4 > 4x$
   f) $a^2 + 15 \leqslant 17a - a^3$

5. Solve each inequality.
   a) $2z^3 - z^2 - 8z + 4 > 0$
   c) $2x^3 + x^2 + 2x < 0$
   e) $x^4 - 10x^2 + 9 \geqslant 0$
   b) $x^3 + 3x^2 - 9x - 27 < 0$
   d) $n^2 - 6n + 11 > 0$
   f) $r^4 - r \leqslant 3r^3 - 3$

6. For what values of x does the parabola $y = x^2 - 4x$ lie above the line $y = 2x - 5$?

7. For what values of x does the graph of the cubic function $y = x^3 + 2x^2 + 3x + 4$ lie above the parabola $y = x^2 + 2x + 3$?

8. Which real numbers are less than their square roots?

(C)

9. Prove that every cubic inequality has infinitely many real solutions.

10. Give an example of a polynomial inequality that has no real solution.

11. Give an example of a polynomial inequality whose solution set is the set of all real numbers except:
    a) 3
    b) 3 and -3.

12. Write a polynomial inequality whose solution set is each given graph.

    a)
    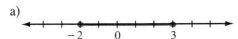

    b)
    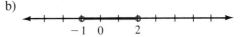

    c)

    d)

    e)

    f)
    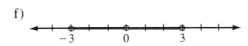

PROBLEM SOLVING

The Crossed Ladders Problem

"Not all problems can be solved within the confines of one mathematics lesson; some need to be "mulled over" for longer periods of time."

Marilyn N. Suydam

In an alley, two ladders, 6 m and 9 m long, lean against opposite walls, and cross at a point 3 m above the ground. Determine the distance between the walls.

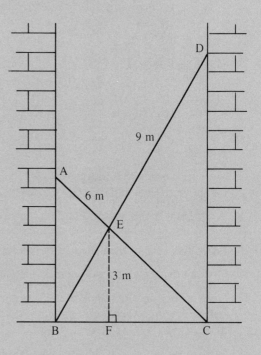

Think of a strategy
- Try using similar triangles.

Carry out the strategy
- If x represents the length of BC, can you use similar triangles to find an equation in x? If not, try letting x represent the length of BE.
- Since some of the triangles are right triangles, the Pythagorean Theorem may be useful.
- Can you use similar triangles and the Pythagorean Theorem to obtain an equation in x? Do not be surprised if it is a polynomial equation of the fourth degree.

Look back
- If you can obtain a polynomial equation in x, the problem about the ladders is essentially solved. You can use systematic trial or the computer program on page 68 to solve the equation.
- In the past, this problem was popular because it leads to a fourth degree equation. Since there were no computers, the challenge of solving the problem was replaced with the challenge of solving the equation!
- Does the equation have any negative roots? Only a positive root can be a solution of the crossed ladders problem.
- Is there any way to check the answer?

PROBLEMS

1. Two cardboard strips with small holes in each end are linked with a paper fastener at P. Point A is held fixed and a pencil is placed at point B.
   a) If AP $= x$ cm and PB $= y$ cm, describe the region in which B is free to move.
   b) Describe the region if point B is held fixed and the pencil is placed at point A.

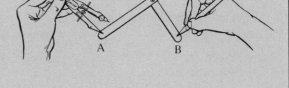

2. Given $ab = cd$ and $bc = ad$
   a) Prove that either $a^2 = c^2$ or $b^2 = d^2$ or both.
   b) Give a numerical example in which $a^2 = c^2$ and $b^2 = d^2$, and another numerical example in which $a^2 = c^2$ and $b^2 \neq d^2$.

3. Two consecutive odd numbers that are powers of positive integers are $25 = 5^2$ and $27 = 3^3$. Determine whether or not it is possible for two consecutive even numbers to be powers of positive integers. If it is possible, give a numerical example. Otherwise, prove that it is impossible.

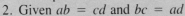

4. A semicircular piece of paper has a radius of 6 cm. Edges OA and OB are joined to form a cone. Find the height of the cone.

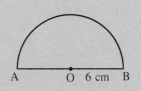

5. There is only one two-digit number that becomes a perfect square when it is doubled, and a perfect cube when it is tripled. What is this number?

6. Prove that the area A of any $\triangle ABC$ is given by the formula $A = rs$, where r is the radius of the inscribed circle, and s is the *semi-perimeter*,
$$s = \frac{1}{2}(a + b + c).$$

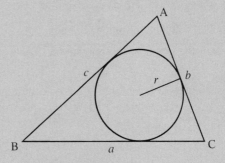

7. Prove that the graph of every cubic function has *point symmetry*. That is, a point F can be found such that for every other point P on the graph, there is a point Q on the graph such that F is the midpoint of PQ.

Review Exercises

1. Solve graphically.

   a) $x^3 - 5x + 9 = 0$

   b) $\dfrac{x^3}{3} - 3x = 0$

2. Divide, then factor the quotient if possible.
   a) $2a^3 - 5a^2 - 9a + 18$ by $a + 2$
   b) $2x^3 - 13x + 5x^2 - 30$ by $x + 3$
   c) $6x^3 + 17x^2y - 26xy^2 + 8y^3$ by $x + 4y$
   d) $32x^3 - 18x - 16x^2 + 9$ by $2x + 1$

3. Find the remainder when $x^3 + 2x^2 - x + 3$ is divided by each binomial.
   a) $x - 1$ b) $x + 3$ c) $x + 2$

4. When $x^4 - 3x^3 - kx^2 + 5x - 2$ is divided by $x - 3$, the remainder is -5. Find the value of k.

5. Which polynomials have $x - 3$ as a factor?
   a) $x^3 - 29x + 2x^2 + 40$
   b) $x^3 - 9x^2 + 26x - 24$
   c) $5x^3 - 18x^2 - 5x + 42$
   d) $8x^3 + 33x - 37x^2 + 18$

6. Factor completely.
   a) $x^3 + 3x^2 - 4x - 12$
   b) $x^3 - 3x - 2$
   c) $x^3 + 5x^2 + 2x - 8$
   d) $x^3 + x^2 - 9x - 9$

7. Find k if $x + 2$ is a factor of $x^3 - 5x^2 + kx - 4$.

8. Solve.
   a) $(x^2 + 4x)^2 - 9(x^2 + 4x) - 36 = 0$
   b) $x^3 - 4x^2 + x + 6 = 0$
   c) $x^3 - x^2 - 4x + 4 = 0$
   d) $x^4 - 3x^3 - 2x^2 + 12x - 8 = 0$

9. Write a cubic equation with roots -4, 2, and 5.

10. Sketch the graph of the polynomial function with zeros -2, 1, and 4, and y-intercept 16.

11. List the possible rational roots of each equation.
    a) $3x^3 - 4x^2 + 6x - 10 = 0$ b) $4x^4 + 7x^3 - 6x + 3 = 0$

12. Solve each inequality.
    a) $(x + 3)(x - 4)(x + 6) > 0$ b) $(a - 1)(a + 2)(a - 5) \leq 0$

3 Quadratic Relations

Some bridges have curved arches like this one. If the type of arch is known, and if the height and the width at its base are known, how can the height be determined at any other point under the arch? (See Section 3-10, *Example 1.*)

3-1 LOCUS

To make this photograph, a point source of light was mounted on a wheel. A camera recorded the light at split-second intervals as the wheel rolled along a flat surface. The path traced out by the light is an example of a locus. Another example of a locus is the path traced out by a pencil point when compasses are used to construct a circle.

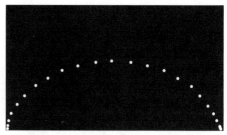

A *locus* is the path traced out by a point which moves according to a given condition. If the given condition is simple enough, we can find an equation which represents the path.

Example 1.   A point moves such that it is always 3 units from the point A(2, 0).
   a) Identify the locus.
   b) Find the equation of the locus.

Solution.   a) The locus is a circle with centre (2, 0) and radius 3.
   b) Let P(x, y) be any point on the locus. Then,

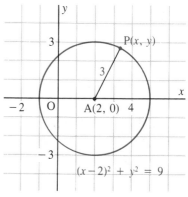

$$AP = 3$$
$$\sqrt{(x - 2)^2 + (y - 0)^2} = 3$$

Square both sides.

$$(x - 2)^2 + y^2 = 9$$

The equation of the locus is
$$(x - 2)^2 + y^2 = 9,$$
or $x^2 + y^2 - 4x - 5 = 0$

Example 2.   Let N be the point (1, −2). A point P moves such that the slope of the segment NP is always $\frac{3}{4}$.

   a) Identify the locus.
   b) Find the equation of the locus.

Solution.   a) The locus is a straight line with slope $\frac{3}{4}$, passing through N(1, −2).

   b) Let P(x, y) be any point on the locus.

Then, since the slope of NP is $\frac{3}{4}$,

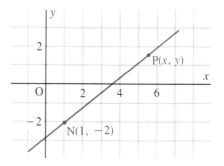

$$\frac{y + 2}{x - 1} = \frac{3}{4}$$
$$3x - 3 = 4y + 8$$
$$3x - 4y - 11 = 0$$

The equation of the locus is
$$3x - 4y - 11 = 0$$

In *Examples 1* and *2* we could identify the locus before we found its equation. If the given condition is more complicated, it may not be possible to do this.

Example 3. A point P moves such that it is always the same distance from the point F(5, 1) as it is from the line defined by $y = -1$.
a) Find the equation of the locus.
b) Identify the locus and sketch its graph.
c) Find the value of y_1 if T(11, y_1) is on the graph.

Solution. a) Let P(x, y) be any point on the locus.
Then according to the given condition,
$$PF = PN$$
$$\sqrt{(x - 5)^2 + (y - 1)^2} = y + 1$$
Square both sides.
$$(x - 5)^2 + (y - 1)^2 = (y + 1)^2$$
$$x^2 - 10x + 25 + y^2 - 2y + 1 = y^2 + 2y + 1$$
$$4y = x^2 - 10x + 25$$
$$y = \tfrac{1}{4}(x - 5)^2$$

b) The locus is a parabola with vertex (5, 0), and axis of symmetry $x = 5$. The parabola opens up, and is congruent to the parabola defined by $y = \tfrac{1}{4}x^2$.

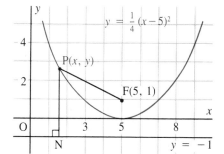

c) Substitute 11 for x and y_1 for y in the equation.
$$y = \tfrac{1}{4}(x - 5)^2$$
$$y_1 = \tfrac{1}{4}(11 - 5)^2$$
$$= 9$$
Hence, if T(11, y_1) is on the graph, $y_1 = 9$.

In the above examples we used the following fundamental properties of a locus.

Properties of a Locus
- The coordinates of every point on a locus satisfy the equation of the locus.
- Every point whose coordinates satisfy the equation of a locus is on the locus.

EXERCISES 3-1

Ⓐ

1. Describe each graph as a locus.

a)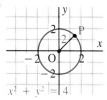
$x^2 + y^2 = 4$

b)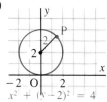
$x^2 + (y - 2)^2 = 4$

c)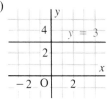
$y = 3$

d)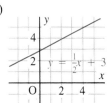
$y = \frac{1}{2}x + 3$

e)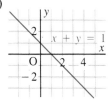
$x + y = 1$

f)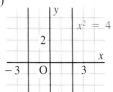
$x^2 = 4$

2. Describe the graph of each equation as a locus.
   a) $y = -5$ b) $x = -2$ c) $x^2 + y^2 = 49$
   d) $y = x + 2$ e) $(x - 1)^2 + (y + 4)^2 = 16$ f) $(x - 1)^2 + y^2 = 1$

Ⓑ

3. A point P moves such that it is always 6 units from the point B(0,3).
   a) Identify the locus.
   b) Find the equation of the locus.

4. A point P moves such that it is always 5 units from the point C($-1,2$).
   a) Find the equation of the locus.
   b) Identify the locus and sketch its graph.
   c) Find the value of y_1 if A(3,y_1) is on the graph.

5. Find the equation of the locus of P. Identify the locus and sketch its graph.

   a) The slope of the line through P and M(3, -1) is $\frac{2}{3}$.

   b) P is equidistant from the point F(0,1) and the line defined by $y = -1$.
   c) P is equidistant from the point F(3, -1) and the line defined by $y = 1$.

6. A point P moves such that it is always equidistant from the point G(2,5) and the line defined by $y = 3$.
   a) Find the equation of the locus.
   b) Identify the locus and sketch its graph.
   c) Find the value of y_1 if B($-4,y_1$) is on the graph.

7. Find the equation of the locus of P. Identify the locus and sketch its graph.
   a) P is always the same distance from A($-2,3$) as it is from B(8, -1).
   b) P is always twice as far from A(8,0) as it is from B(2,0).
   c) The slope of the line through P and A(2,1) is equal to the slope of the line through P and B($-1,4$).

8. A point P moves such that the slope of the line through P and S(2,0) is always 2 greater than the slope of the line through P and T(-2,0).
   a) Find the equation of the locus.
   b) Identify the locus and sketch its graph.
   c) Find the value of x_1 if M(x_1,16) is on the graph.

9. A point P moves such that the product of the slopes of the line segments joining P to Q(-5,0) and to R(5,0) is -1.
   a) Find the equation of the locus.
   b) Identify the locus and sketch its graph.
   c) Find the value of y_1 if the point D(2,y_1) lies on the graph.

10. Perpendicular lines are drawn through A(4,0) and B(-4,0).
   a) Find the equation of the locus of the point of intersection of these lines.
   b) Identify the locus and draw its graph.

Ⓒ

11. A line segment 10 units long has its endpoints on the x- and y-axes. Find the equation of the locus of its midpoint, and sketch its graph.

12. Find the equation of the locus of P. Sketch the graph of the locus.
   a) P is 3 units from the x-axis.
   b) The product of the distances from P to the x- and y-axes is 6.
   c) The sum of the distances from P to the x- and y-axes is 5.
   d) The difference of the distances from P to the x- and y-axes is 3.
   e) P is equidistant from the x- and y-axes.
   f) P is always twice as far from the x-axis as it is from the point V(0,3).

13. Find the equation of the locus of a point P which moves such that the slope of the line segment joining P to A(-3,0) is half the slope of the line segment joining P to B(3,0). Identify the locus and sketch its graph.

14. Find the equation of the locus of P.
   a) The sum of the distances from P to A(2,0) and B(-2,0) is 8.
   b) The difference of the distances from P to C(4,0) and D(-4,0) is 2.

15. In △ABC, ∠C = 90° and C is the point (5,3). If A is on the x-axis and B is on the y-axis, find the equation of the locus of the midpoint of AB.

 INVESTIGATE

A circle can be defined as the locus of a point which moves such that its distance to a given point is constant. By examining the examples and exercises of this section:
a) list some other possible definitions of a circle
b) list some possible definitions of: a straight line; a parabola.

3-2 INTRODUCTION TO QUADRATIC RELATIONS

The ancient Greeks defined a cone as the surface generated when a line is rotated about a fixed point P on the line. Notice that the cone has two symmetric parts on either side of P.

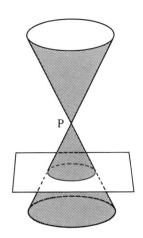

The curves that result when a plane intersects a cone are called *conic sections*, or *conics*. The Greeks discovered many properties of conics, but they were not interested in practical applications. In the seventeenth century, Isaac Newton proved that the orbit of a body revolving around another in accordance with the law of gravitation is a conic.

When a plane intersects a cone, the angle of inclination of the plane with respect to the cone determines the shape of the curve that results.

The Circle

In the drawing above, the plane is parallel to the base of the cone. In this case the curve of intersection is a *circle*. Hence, a circle is a conic.

The orbits of satellites and planets are nearly circular. The spectacular photographs we see of a total solar eclipse are caused by the fact that both the sun and the moon appear to us as circular discs of about the same size.

Although the conics are defined as sections of a cone, they also occur as the graphs of certain equations in x and y.

Example 1. Graph the relation $x^2 + y^2 = 16$.

Solution. We could use a table of values to draw the graph. A more efficient method is to observe that the equation expresses the condition that the distance from a point $P(x,y)$ to $O(0,0)$ be 4 units. Hence, the graph is a circle, with centre $(0,0)$ and radius 4.

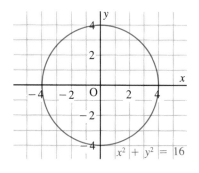

The Ellipse

If the intersecting plane is inclined to the base of the cone as shown, an *ellipse* results. As the angle of the intersecting plane increases, the shape of the ellipse changes from circular to long and elongated.

Satellites, planets, and some comets travel in elliptical orbits. Halley's comet, which returns to the sun approximately every 76 years, has a very long elliptical orbit.

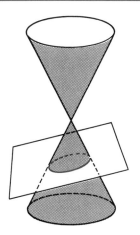

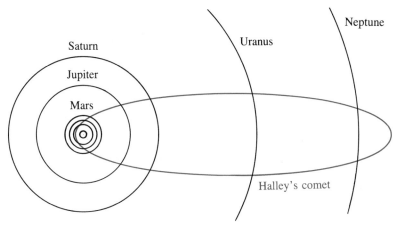

Example 2. Graph the relation $4x^2 + 9y^2 = 36$ using a table of values.

Solution. To prepare a table of values, we first solve the equation for y.

$$4x^2 + 9y^2 = 36$$
$$9y^2 = 36 - 4x^2$$
$$y = \frac{\pm\sqrt{36 - 4x^2}}{3}$$

x	y	x	y
0	± 2.00	0	± 2.00
0.5	± 1.97	-0.5	± 1.97
1.0	± 1.89	-1.0	± 1.89
1.5	± 1.73	-1.5	± 1.73
2.0	± 1.49	-2.0	± 1.49
2.5	± 1.11	-2.5	± 1.11
3.0	0	-3.0	0

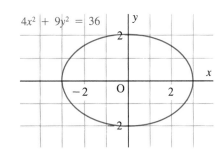

The Parabola

In this diagram, the intersecting plane is
parallel to the line AB on the cone. The
resulting curve is a *parabola*. Hence, a
parabola is a conic.

Parabolas have many applications in
astronomy. The mirrors in some telescopes
have surfaces whose cross sections are
parabolas. Many comets have orbits which
extend far beyond the outermost planets.
In the vicinity of the sun, these orbits are
nearly parabolic. Also, as the photograph
below suggests, a parabolic shape is sometimes formed by the coma and dust tail of
a comet.

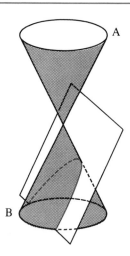

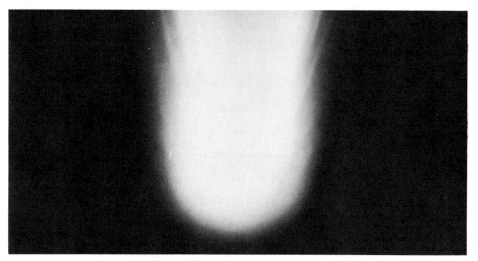

Example 3. Graph the relation $x^2 - 4y = 0$.

Solution. We could use a table of values to
draw the graph. A more efficient
method is to solve the equation
for y and use our knowledge of
the transformations of functions.
$$x^2 - 4y = 0$$
$$y = \frac{1}{4}x^2$$

The graph is a parabola with vertex
(0,0), axis of symmetry the y-axis,
and opens up. It is a vertical
compression of the parabola
$y = x^2$.

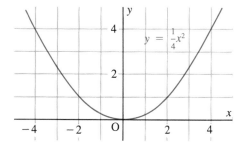

The Hyperbola

If the plane intersects the cone as shown, the resulting curve is called a *hyperbola*. Note that a hyperbola intersects both parts of the cone. Hence, a hyperbola has two distinct parts, or branches.

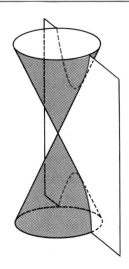

   Some comets travel along paths which are slightly hyperbolic. As a result, they only appear once near the sun, and do not return. If a star passes another star, each is deflected along a hyperbolic path by the other. Another example of a hyperbolic path is provided by the Voyager 2 space probe which was launched to the outer planets in August, 1977. The diagram shows Voyager's path as it passed by Uranus in January, 1986.

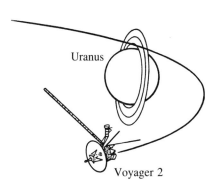

Uranus

Voyager 2

Example 4. Graph the relation $x^2 - y^2 = 4$ using a table of values.

Solution. To prepare a table of values, we first solve the equation for y.

$$x^2 - y^2 = 4$$
$$y^2 = x^2 - 4$$
$$y = \pm\sqrt{x^2 - 4}$$

x	y
2	0
3	± 2.24
4	± 3.46
5	± 4.58
6	± 5.66

x	y
-2	0
-3	± 2.24
-4	± 3.46
-5	± 4.58
-6	± 5.66

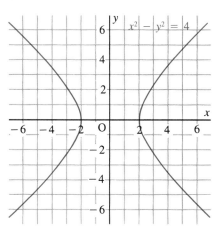

Each equation in the above examples has terms of the second degree in x or y. Any relation whose defining equation contains terms of the second degree, but no terms of higher degree, is called a *quadratic relation*.

These are quadratic relations.

$x^2 + 9y^2 = 18$
$2x^2 + xy - 2x = 14$

These are not quadratic relations.

$y = x^3$
$x^2 + 2xy^2 + 3y = 6$

In this chapter we will develop techniques for graphing certain quadratic relations without making tables of values.

EXERCISES 3-2

1. Which of these are quadratic relations?
   a) $x^2 - y^2 = 9$
   b) $2x^3 + y^3 = 24$
   c) $3x^2 + 2y^2 = 12$
   d) $x^2 + 3x^2y = 6$
   e) $x^2 - 2y^2 + x - y = 7$
   f) $xy = 12$

2. Graph each relation and identify the curve.
   a) $x^2 + y^2 = 9$
   b) $4x^2 + y^2 = 16$
   c) $4x^2 - y^2 = 16$
   d) $y = \dfrac{x^2}{8}$
   e) $4x^2 + 25y^2 = 100$
   f) $4x^2 - 25y^2 = 100$

3. a) Graph each relation.
   i) $x^2 + y^2 = 0$
   ii) $x^2 - y^2 = 0$
   iii) $(x - y)^2 = 0$
   b) Explain how the graphs of the relations in part a) could result when a plane intersects a cone.

4. A jet breaking the sound barrier creates a shock wave which has the shape of a cone. Describe the shape of the shock wave on the ground if the jet is:
   a) flying parallel to the ground
   b) gaining altitude
   c) losing altitude.

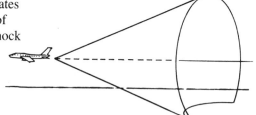

INVESTIGATE

Models of the Conics
You can make models of the conics using styrofoam cones, which can be obtained from a craft store. Cut some styrofoam cones with a fine-toothed saw to create a circle, an ellipse, a parabola, and a hyperbola. Paint the surfaces.

Can you make four cuts in one cone to show a circle, an ellipse, a parabola, and a hyperbola?

3-3 THE CIRCLE

Many farms in western North America use an automated centre-pivot irrigation system. A long pipe sprays water as it rotates about the centre. Distinctive circular traces are left by the wheels, and, since the end of the pipe is always the same distance from the centre, the area watered forms a circle.

A circle is the locus of a point which moves such that it is always the same distance from a fixed point called the *centre*. This distance is called the *radius*. We can find the equation of any circle with centre $C(h, k)$ and radius r. Let $P(x, y)$ be any point on the circle. Then

$$CP = r$$
$$\sqrt{(x - h)^2 + (y - k)^2} = r$$

Square both sides.

$$(x - h)^2 + (y - k)^2 = r^2$$

This is the *standard equation* of a circle with centre (h, k) and radius r.

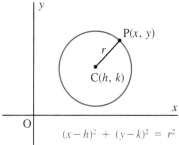

$$(x - h)^2 + (y - k)^2 = r^2$$

Standard Equation of a Circle
The equation of a circle with centre (h, k) and radius r is
$$(x - h)^2 + (y - k)^2 = r^2.$$
If the centre is $(0, 0)$, the equation is
$$x^2 + y^2 = r^2.$$

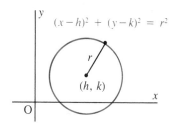

$$(x - h)^2 + (y - k)^2 = r^2$$

Example 1. A circle has centre $(2, -1)$ and radius 5 units.

a) Write the equation of the circle.

b) If $(4, y_1)$ is on the circle, find the value of y_1 to two decimal places.

Solution. a) The equation of the circle is
$$(x - 2)^2 + (y + 1)^2 = 25$$

b) Substitute 4 for x and y_1 for y.
$$(4 - 2)^2 + (y_1 + 1)^2 = 25$$
$$4 + y_1^2 + 2y_1 + 1 = 25$$
$$y_1^2 + 2y_1 - 20 = 0$$
$$y_1 = \frac{-2 \pm \sqrt{84}}{2}$$
$$= -1 \pm \sqrt{21}$$
$$\doteq 3.58 \text{ or } -5.58$$

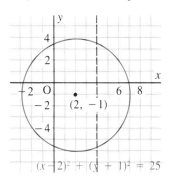

$$(x - 2)^2 + (y + 1)^2 = 25$$

In *Example 1* we can expand the left side of the equation of the circle.

$$(x - 2)^2 + (y + 1)^2 = 25$$
$$x^2 - 4x + 4 + y^2 + 2y + 1 = 25$$
$$x^2 + y^2 - 4x + 2y - 20 = 0$$

The form in which this equation is written is called the *general form* of the equation. When the equation of a circle is written in general form, the radius and the coordinates of the centre cannot be seen in the equation. But we can determine the radius and the coordinates of the centre using the method of *completing the square*.

Example 2. A circle has the equation $x^2 + y^2 - 6x + 14y + 10 = 0$. Determine the radius and the coordinates of the centre.

Solution. We collect the terms containing x, and the terms containing y and then use the method of completing the square.

$$x^2 + y^2 - 6x + 14y + 10 = 0$$
$$x^2 - 6x + y^2 + 14y + 10 = 0$$

Add the squares of $\frac{1}{2}(-6)$ and $\frac{1}{2}(14)$ to both sides.

$$(x^2 - 6x + 9) + (y^2 + 14y + 49) + 10 = 9 + 49$$
$$(x - 3)^2 + (y + 7)^2 = 48$$

The radius is $\sqrt{48}$, or $4\sqrt{3}$, and the centre is $(3, -7)$.

The general equation of a circle is usually written as $x^2 + y^2 + 2Gx + 2Fy + C = 0$. We can use the method of *Example 2* to find expressions for its centre and radius.

$$x^2 + y^2 + 2Gx + 2Fy + C = 0$$
$$x^2 + 2Gx + y^2 + 2Fy + C = 0$$

Complete each square.

$$x^2 + 2Gx + G^2 + y^2 + 2Fy + F^2 + C = G^2 + F^2$$
$$(x + G)^2 + (y + F)^2 = G^2 + F^2 - C$$

This equation represents a circle with centre $(-G, -F)$ and radius $\sqrt{G^2 + F^2 - C}$, provided that $G^2 + F^2 - C \geqslant 0$.

General Equation of a Circle
- The equation $x^2 + y^2 + 2Gx + 2Fy + C = 0$ represents a circle, provided that $G^2 + F^2 - C \geqslant 0$.
- The coordinates of the centre are $(-G, -F)$.
- The radius is $\sqrt{G^2 + F^2 - C}$.

Observe that in the general equation of a circle the quadratic terms are $x^2 + y^2$.

Example 3. Which equations represent circles? Find the coordinates of the centre, and the radius, of each circle.
a) $x^2 + y^2 + 8x - 12y + 42 = 0$
b) $2x^2 + 2y^2 - 12x + 9y + 27 = 0$
c) $x^2 + 2y^2 + 6x - 10y - 3 = 0$
d) $x^2 - y^2 - 4x + 7y = 0$
e) $x^2 + y^2 - 2x + 3y + 4 = 0$

Solution. The equations in parts c) and d) do not represent circles because they cannot be written in a form in which the quadratic terms are $x^2 + y^2$.

a) $x^2 + y^2 + 8x - 12y + 42 = 0$

For this equation, $G = \frac{1}{2}(8)$ $F = \frac{1}{2}(-12)$ $C = 42$

$\qquad\qquad\qquad = 4 \qquad\qquad = -6$

$G^2 + F^2 - C = 4^2 + (-6)^2 - 42$

$\qquad\qquad\quad = 10$

The equation represents a circle with radius $\sqrt{10}$ and centre $(-4, 6)$.

b) $2x^2 + 2y^2 - 12x + 9y + 27 = 0$

Divide both sides by 2 to write the equation in general form.

$x^2 + y^2 - 6x + \frac{9}{2}y + \frac{27}{2} = 0$

For this equation, $G = \frac{1}{2}(-6)$ $F = \frac{1}{2}\left(\frac{9}{2}\right)$ $C = \frac{27}{2}$

$\qquad\qquad\qquad = -3 \qquad\qquad = \frac{9}{4}$

$G^2 + F^2 - C = (-3)^2 + \left(\frac{9}{4}\right)^2 - \frac{27}{2}$

$\qquad\qquad\quad = 9 + \frac{81}{16} - \frac{27}{2}$

$\qquad\qquad\quad = \frac{9}{16}$

The equation represents a circle with radius $\sqrt{\frac{9}{16}}$, or $\frac{3}{4}$, and centre

$\left(3, -\frac{9}{4}\right)$.

e) $x^2 + y^2 - 2x + 3y + 4 = 0$

For this equation, $G = \frac{1}{2}(-2)$ $F = \frac{1}{2}(3)$ $C = 4$

$\qquad\qquad\qquad = -1 \qquad\qquad = \frac{3}{2}$

$G^2 + F^2 - C = (-1)^2 + \left(\frac{3}{2}\right)^2 - 4$

$\qquad\qquad\quad = -0.75$

Since this expression is negative, the given equation does not represent a circle.

EXERCISES 3-3

(A)

1. Determine if each point is on the circle defined by $x^2 + y^2 = 85$.
   a) $(9, -2)$ b) $(-5, 8)$ c) $(-7, -6)$ d) $(4, 8)$

2. State the radius and the coordinates of the centre of the circle defined by each equation.
   a) $x^2 + y^2 = 64$ b) $x^2 + y^2 = 12$
   c) $(x - 3)^2 + (y + 4)^2 = 81$ d) $(x + 2)^2 + (y - 1)^2 = 5$
   e) $(x + 4)^2 + y^2 = 15$ f) $x^2 + (y - 6)^2 = 48$

3. Write the equation of the circle with each given centre and radius.
   a) $(0, 0)$, 3   b) $(0, 0)$, 7   c) $(5, 3)$, 4   d) $(-2, 6)$, 5

   e) $(4, 0)$, 6   f) $(0, -3)$, 9   g) $(0, 0)$, $\sqrt{5}$ h) $(3, -5)$, $\sqrt{10}$

4. Convert each equation to general form.
   a) $(x - 3)^2 + (y + 2)^2 = 25$ b) $(x - 1)^2 + (y - 6)^2 = 30$
   c) $(x + 4)^2 + (y - 2)^2 = 11$ d) $(x + 5)^2 + y^2 = 25$

5. Convert each equation to standard form.
   a) $x^2 + y^2 - 4x + 10y + 13 = 0$ b) $x^2 + y^2 + 8x - 6y - 25 = 0$

(B)

6. Sketch the circles defined by these equations on the same grid.
   a) $x^2 + y^2 = 9$ b) $(x - 4)^2 + y^2 = 9$
   c) $x^2 + (y - 5)^2 = 9$ d) $(x - 4)^2 + (y - 5)^2 = 9$

7. A circle has centre $(0, 0)$ and radius 6 units.
   a) Find the equation of the circle.
   b) Find the value of y_1 if $(4, y_1)$ is on the circle.

8. A circle has centre $(3, 2)$ and radius 5 units.
   a) Find the value of x_1 if $(x_1, 3)$ is on the circle.
   b) Find the value of y_1 if $(2, y_1)$ is on the circle.

9. Which equations represent circles? Find the radius, and the coordinates of the centre of each circle.
   a) $x^2 + y^2 - 10x + 4y + 20 = 0$ b) $x^2 + y^2 - 6x - 2y - 15 = 0$
   c) $x^2 + y^2 + 6x - 2y + 12 = 0$ d) $x^2 + y^2 + x + y - 4 = 0$
   e) $2x^2 + 2y^2 - 4x + 3y - 5 = 0$ f) $3x^2 + 3y^2 + 5x - 9y + 40 = 0$

10. Sketch the circle represented by each equation.
    a) $x^2 + y^2 - 6x + 5 = 0$ b) $x^2 + y^2 + 2y - 8 = 0$
    c) $x^2 + y^2 - 2x - 6y = 0$ d) $x^2 + y^2 + 6x - 4y + 9 = 0$
    e) $x^2 + y^2 - 6x + 10y + 25 = 0$ f) $x^2 + y^2 + 8x + 8y + 16 = 0$

11. Under what condition(s) does the equation $x^2 + y^2 + 2Gx + 2Fy + C = 0$ represent a circle:
    a) with centre on: i) the x-axis   ii) the y-axis   iii) both axes
    b) which passes through the origin
    c) which is tangent to: i) the x-axis   ii) the y-axis   iii) both axes.

12. Suggest why the coefficients of x and y in the general equation of a circle contain the factor 2.

13. A point P moves such that it is always twice as far from A(6, 0) as it is from the origin.
    a) Find the equation of the locus.
    b) Identify the locus and sketch its graph.
    c) Verify from the graph that points on the graph are twice as far from A as they are from the origin.

14. Determine the equation of the circle defined by the given conditions.
    a) The centre is C(3, −2), and R(−1, 1) is a point on the circle.
    b) The endpoints of a diameter are M(5, 1) and N(−3, 3).
    c) The circle passes through A(2, 2) and B(5, 3), and the centre is on the line defined by $y = x + 1$.

15. The three circles shown have the same centre, and the middle circle has a radius of 1. If the colored region has the same area as the shaded region, what is the relation between x and y?

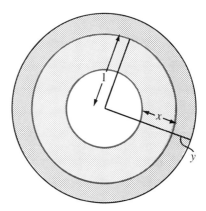

16. Determine if the circles defined by each pair of equations intersect.
    a) $x^2 + y^2 - 8x - 4y + 12 = 0$; $x^2 + y^2 + 4x - 12y + 22 = 0$
    b) $x^2 + y^2 - 6x + 2y + 5 = 0$; $x^2 + y^2 - 2x + 4y - 27 = 0$
    c) $x^2 + y^2 - 10x + 2y + 17 = 0$; $x^2 + y^2 + 6x + 14y + 9 = 0$
    d) $x^2 + y^2 - 4x - 6y + 9 = 0$; $x^2 + y^2 - 2x - 4y - 8 = 0$

ⓒ

17. Given the circles defined by $x^2 + y^2 + 2G_1x + 2F_1y + C_1 = 0$ and $x^2 + y^2 + 2G_2x + 2F_2y + C_2 = 0$, what conditions must be satisfied by G_1, F_1, C_1, G_2, F_2, and C_2 if the circles intersect?

18. Determine the equation of the circle which passes through the points J(−3, 2), K(4, 1), and L(6, 5).

19. A circle has x-intercepts 0 and a, and y-intercepts 0 and b. Determine the equation of the circle.

20. Two points $A_1(a_1, 0)$ and $A_2(a_2, 0)$ are given on the x-axis, and two points $B_1(0, b_1)$ and $B_2(0, b_2)$ are given on the y-axis. What condition(s) must be satisfied by a_1, a_2, b_1, and b_2 if a circle passes through all four points?

Constructing a Parabola

To construct a parabola, follow these steps. You will need compasses and a sheet of ordinary lined paper. For a unit of measure, let the distance between two adjacent lines on the paper be one unit.

Step 1. Draw a line *d* on any of the lines of the paper. Label the lines above *d* according to their distances from *d* as line 1, line 2, line 3, ... Mark any point F on line 2.

Step 2. Mark point V on line 1, 1 unit from F and 1 unit from *d*. Then, with compasses point on F, mark two points on each of line 2, line 3, line 4, . . . whose distances from *d* are as follows.
- On line 2, 2 units from *d*
- On line 3, 3 units from *d*
- On line 4, 4 units from *d*, and so on

Step 3. Draw a smooth curve through the marked points.

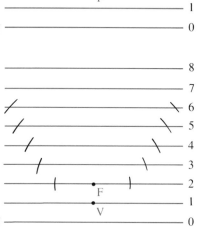

1. Construct a parabola by following the above steps.

2. For any point on the parabola, how does its distance from F compare with its distance from the line *d*?

3. Write a definition of a parabola based on this construction. F is called the *focus*, and *d* is called the *directrix* of the parabola.

4. Investigate the effect on the appearance of the parabola of changing the position of F relative to *d*.

3-4 THE PARABOLA: VERTEX (0, 0)

When major league baseball games are televised, a parabolic reflector microphone is often used to pick up the voices of the players and umpires. A cross section of the microphone has the shape of a parabola. Another example from baseball is the parabolic path of the ball when it is hit or thrown.

A parabola is defined as follows.

A *parabola* is the locus of a point P which moves such that it is always the same distance from a fixed point F and a fixed line *d*.
The point F is called the *focus* of the parabola.
The line *d* is called the *directrix*. The point V, halfway between F and *d* is the *vertex*. The line through F perpendicular to the directrix is the *axis*.

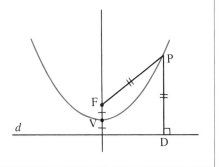

We can use the defining property to develop the equation of a parabola. The equation depends on the positions of the focus and the directrix.

For example, suppose the vertex is the origin and the focus in on the *x*-axis. Then the focus is F(p, 0) and the directrix is the line $x = -p$. Let P(x, y) be any point on the parabola. Then, if D is the point $(-p, y)$,

$$PF = PD$$
$$\sqrt{(x - p)^2 + y^2} = \sqrt{(x + p)^2}$$

Square both sides.

$$(x - p)^2 + y^2 = (x + p)^2$$
$$x^2 - 2px + p^2 + y^2 = x^2 + 2px + p^2$$
$$y^2 = 4px$$

This is the *standard equation* of a parabola with vertex (0, 0) and focus F(p, 0) on the *x*-axis. Similarly, the standard equation of a parabola with vertex (0, 0) and focus F(0, p) on the *y*-axis is $x^2 = 4py$. In these equations, p may be positive or negative.

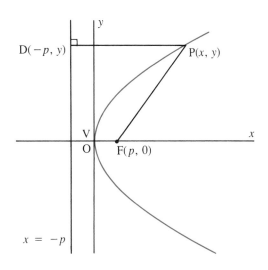

Standard Equations of a Parabola with Vertex (0, 0)

The equation of a parabola with vertex (0, 0) and focus on the *x*-axis is $y^2 = 4px$.

The equation of a parabola with vertex (0, 0) and focus on the *y*-axis is $x^2 = 4py$.

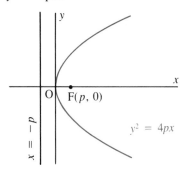

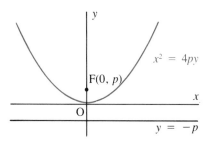

Coordinates of focus: $(p, 0)$
Equation of directrix: $x = -p$
If $p > 0$, the parabola opens right.
If $p < 0$, the parabola opens left.

Coordinates of focus: $(0, p)$
Equation of directrix: $y = -p$
If $p > 0$, the parabola opens up.
If $p < 0$, the parabola opens down.

Example 1. A parabola has the equation $y^2 = -6x$. Sketch the parabola, showing the coordinates of the focus and the equation of the directrix.

Solution. Compare the given equation $y^2 = -6x$ with the standard equation $y^2 = 4px$.

Hence $4p = -6$

$$p = -\frac{3}{2}, \text{ or } -1.5$$

The coordinates of the focus are $(-1.5, 0)$, and the equation of the directrix is $x = 1.5$.

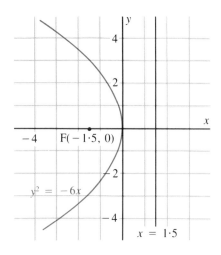

Example 2. A parabola has vertex (0, 0) and focus on the *y*-axis.
   a) Find the equation of the parabola if it passes through the point A(4, 12).
   b) Find the value of y_1 if B(3, y_1) is on the parabola.

Solution.　a) Let the equation of the parabola be $x^2 = 4py$. Since A(4, 12) is a point on the parabola, its coordinates satisfy the equation. Substitute 4 for x and 12 for y in $x^2 = 4py$.

$$x^2 = 4py$$
$$4^2 = 4p(12)$$
$$p = \frac{1}{3}$$

The equation of the parabola is

$$x^2 = \frac{4}{3}y$$

or $y = \frac{3}{4}x^2$

b) Substitute 3 for x and y_1 for y in $y = \frac{3}{4}x^2$.

$$y_1 = \frac{3}{4}(3)^2$$
$$= \frac{27}{4}$$

Hence, if B(3, y_1) is on the parabola, $y_1 = \frac{27}{4}$.

EXERCISES 3-4

(A)

1. Determine if each point is on the parabola defined by $y = 3x^2$.
   a) $(-1, 3)$　　　　b) $(3, 9)$　　　　c) $(-2, -12)$　　d) $(-2, 12)$.

2. State the coordinates of the focus and the equation of the directrix of the parabola defined by each equation.
   a) $y^2 = 4x$　　　　b) $y^2 = 12x$　　　c) $y^2 = -6x$　　　d) $x^2 = 8y$
   e) $x^2 = -2y$　　　f) $x^2 = 3y$　　　g) $y^2 = -9x$　　　h) $x^2 = -5y$

(B)

3. Sketch the parabola defined by each equation, showing the coordinates of the focus and the equation of the directrix.
   a) $y^2 = 8x$　　　b) $y^2 = -3x$　　　c) $x^2 = 4y$　　　d) $x^2 = -10y$

4. A parabola has vertex $(0, 0)$ and focus on a coordinate axis. Write the equation of the parabola if:
   a) the focus is:　i) $(4, 0)$　　ii) $(-6, 0)$　　iii) $(0, 3)$
   b) the directrix is the line defined by $y = 8$.

5. A parabola has vertex $(0, 0)$ and focus on the y-axis. Find the equation of the parabola if it passes through each point.
   a) $(2, 8)$　　　　b) $(4, 6)$　　　　c) $(-4, 10)$　　　d) $(4, -2)$

6. A parabola has vertex (0, 0) and focus on the x-axis. Find the equation of the parabola if it passes through each point.
   a) (20, 8)   b) (12, 10)   c) (5, −6)   d) (3, 7)

7. A parabola has vertex (0, 0) and focus on the y-axis.
   a) Find the equation of the parabola if it passes through each point.
      i) (8, 8)   ii) (5, 5)   iii) (−3, −3)   iv) (−7, −7)
   b) What conclusion can you make about the equation of a parabola if it passes through a point whose x- and y-coordinates are equal?

8. The focus of a parabola is F(5, 0) and the directrix is the line $x = -5$. Use the definition of a parabola to derive the equation of this parabola.

9. Use the definition to derive the equation of a parabola with focus F(0, p) on the y-axis and directrix the line $y = -p$.

10. A rectangle has a perimeter of 50 cm, and a length of x centimetres.
    a) Write the area A square centimetres as a function of the length.
    b) Draw a graph of the function in part a).

11. Use the definition of a parabola to prove that a parabola is symmetric about its axis. That is, if P_1 is any point on a parabola, and if the axis is the perpendicular bisector of P_1P_2, then P_2 is also on the parabola.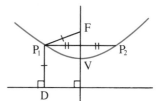

12. A line passing through the focus of a parabola, and perpendicular to the axis intersects the parabola at L and R. Prove that the length of LR is four times the distance between the focus and the vertex.

©────────────────────────────────

13. In the second diagram on page 101, find the coordinates of P if △PFD is:
    a) an equilateral triangle   b) a right triangle.

 INVESTIGATE

Parabolas and Pythagorean triples
Three natural numbers, such as 5, 12, and 13, which satisfy the equation $a^2 + b^2 = c^2$ are called *Pythagorean Triples*.

1. a) Sketch the graph of the parabola defined by $y^2 = 4px$. Locate points on the parabola whose x-coordinates are p, $4p$, $9p$, $16p$, . . .
   b) Let P be any of the points in part a). Let N be the point on the x-axis with the same x-coordinate as P. Prove that the lengths of the sides of △PNF are Pythagorean triples. (Assume p is a natural number.)

2. Use the result of *Question 1* to find formulas for some Pythagorean triples.

3-5 THE PARABOLA: VERTEX (h, k)

We can use the definition of a parabola to find the equation of a parabola with any vertex $V(h, k)$. We let p represent the distance from the vertex to the focus and to the directrix.

If the axis of symmetry is horizontal, the coordinates of the focus are $F(h + p, k)$ and the equation of the directrix is $x = h - p$.

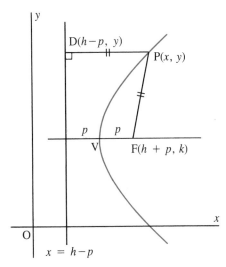

Let $P(x, y)$ be any point on the parabola. Then, if D is the point $(h - p, y)$,

$$PF = PD$$
$$\sqrt{(x - h - p)^2 + (y - k)^2} = \sqrt{(x - h + p)^2}$$

Square both sides.

$$(x - h - p)^2 + (y - k)^2 = (x - h + p)^2$$
$$x^2 + h^2 + p^2 - 2hx - 2px + 2hp + (y - k)^2 = x^2 + h^2 + p^2 - 2hx + 2px - 2hp$$
$$(y - k)^2 = 4p(x - h)$$

This is the standard equation of a parabola with vertex (h, k) and a horizontal axis of symmetry. Similarly, the standard equation of a parabola with vertex (h, k) and a vertical axis of symmetry is $(x - h)^2 = 4p(y - k)$.

Standard Equations of a Parabola with Vertex (h, k)

Horizontal axis of symmetry:

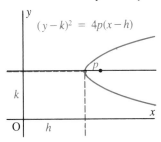

$(y - k)^2 = 4p(x - h)$

Vertical axis of symmetry:

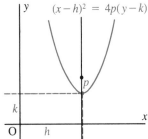

$(x - h)^2 = 4p(y - k)$

Coordinates of focus: $(h + p, k)$
Equation of directrix: $x = h - p$
Equation of axis: $y - k = 0$
Opening: right if $p > 0$, left if $p < 0$

Coordinates of focus: $(h, k + p)$
Equation of directrix: $y = k - p$
Equation of axis: $x - h = 0$
Opening: up if $p > 0$, down if $p < 0$

Example.   Sketch the parabola defined by each equation. Show the vertex and the focus, and the equations of the directrix and the axis.

a) $(y + 3)^2 = -8(x - 4)$ b) $(x + 1)^2 = 6(y - 2)$

Solution.   a) Compare $(y + 3)^2 = -8(x - 4)$
with the standard equation
$(y - k)^2 = 4p(x - h)$.
Hence, $4p = -8$ $h = 4$
      $p = -2$ $k = -3$
Vertex: $V(4, -3)$
Axis: $y = -3$
Since the parabola opens to the left,
the coordinates of the focus are
$F(4 - 2, -3)$ or $F(2, -3)$, and the
equation of the directrix is
$x = 4 - (-2)$, or $x = 6$.

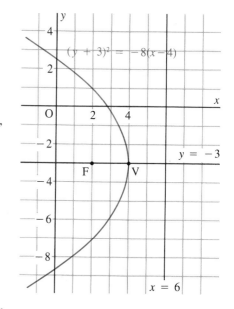

b) Compare $(x + 1)^2 = 6(y - 2)$ with
the standard equation
$(x - h)^2 = 4p(y - k)$.
Hence, $4p = 6$ $h = -1$
      $p = 1.5$ $k = 2$
Vertex: $V(-1, 2)$
Axis: $x = -1$
Since the parabola opens up,
the coordinates of the focus are
$F(-1, 2 + 1.5)$, or $F(-1, 3.5)$,
and the equation of the directrix is
$y = 2 - 1.5$, or $y = 0.5$.

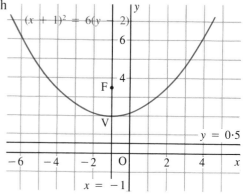

In the equations of the *Example*, the binomial squares may be expanded, and the equations written in *general form*. For example, in general form the equation $(y + 3)^2 = -8(x - 4)$ becomes
$$y^2 + 6y + 9 = -8x + 32$$
$$y^2 + 8x + 6y - 23 = 0$$
In general form the coordinates of the vertex cannot be seen in the equation.

EXERCISES 3-5

1. State the coordinates of the vertex, the equation of the axis, and the direction of opening of the parabola defined by each equation.
   a) $(y - 2)^2 = 4(x - 3)$
   b) $(y + 1)^2 = -8(x - 2)$
   c) $(x + 1)^2 = 4(y + 5)$
   d) $(x - 4)^2 = -12(y - 1)$
   e) $(y - 3)^2 = 8x$
   f) $x^2 = 16(y - 2)$

2. Convert each equation to general form.
   a) $(y + 3)^2 = 2(x - 1)$
   b) $(y - 1)^2 = -(x + 3)$
   c) $(x + 5)^2 = -4(y - 2)$
   d) $(x - 2)^2 = 3y$

3. Convert each equation to standard form.
   a) $x^2 - 2x - 3y - 8 = 0$
   b) $x^2 + 6x + 5y - 1 = 0$
   c) $y^2 - 4x + 4y + 24 = 0$
   d) $y^2 + 3x - 2y + 7 = 0$

Ⓑ

4. Sketch the parabola defined by each equation. Show the coordinates of the vertex and the focus, and the equations of the axis and the directrix on your sketch.
   a) $(y + 2)^2 = 4(x - 1)$
   b) $(y - 3)^2 = -2(x + 4)$
   c) $(x - 3)^2 = 2(y + 2)$
   d) $x^2 = -3(y - 1)$
   e) $y^2 = -8(x - 2)$
   f) $x^2 = 4(y + 1)$

5. Determine the equation of the parabola defined by the given conditions.
   a) The vertex is V(1, 2) and the focus is F(3, 2).
   b) The vertex is V(-1, 3) and the equation of the directrix is $x - 2 = 0$.
   c) The focus is F(2, 0) and the equation of the directrix is $y + 6 = 0$.

6. A point P moves such that it is always the same distance from the point F(3, 0) as it is from the line defined by $x - 1 = 0$.
   a) Find the equation of the locus.
   b) Identify the locus and sketch its graph.
   c) Verify from the graph that points on the graph are equidistant from F(3, 0) and the line defined by $x - 1 = 0$.

7. A point P moves such that it is always equidistant from the point F(-1, 2) and the line defined by $y - 6 = 0$. Find the equation of the locus.

Ⓒ

8. A point P moves such that it is always 2 units farther from the line defined by $x + 4 = 0$ than it is from the point F(4, 0). Find the equation of the locus of P.

9. Investigate whether the locus of a point, which moves such that the difference of its distances from a fixed point and a fixed line is constant, is a parabola.

10. What condition(s) must be satisfied by p, h, and k, if each equation represents a parabola whose focus is the origin?
    a) $(y - k)^2 = 4p(x - h)$
    b) $(x - h)^2 = 4p(y - k)$

3-6 SOLVING RADICAL EQUATIONS

In coordinate geometry the expression for the distance between two points contains a radical. When this expression occurs in an equation, as it did in earlier sections of this chapter, we eliminate the radical by squaring both sides of the equation. Some locus problems involve the sum or the difference of two distances. Hence the corresponding equations will contain two radicals. To eliminate two radicals from such equations we isolate one of the radicals and square both sides. Usually, one radical will remain after squaring. Hence, we isolate that radical and square again.

Example 1.   Solve. $\sqrt{2x + 5} - \sqrt{x - 2} = 3$

Solution.   Isolate one of the radicals.
$$\sqrt{2x + 5} = 3 + \sqrt{x - 2}$$
Square both sides.
$$(\sqrt{2x + 5})^2 = (3 + \sqrt{x - 2})^2$$
$$2x + 5 = 9 + 6\sqrt{x - 2} + (\sqrt{x - 2})^2$$
$$2x + 5 = 9 + 6\sqrt{x - 2} + x - 2$$
Isolate the remaining radical.
$$x - 2 = 6\sqrt{x - 2}$$
Square both sides again.
$$(x - 2)^2 = (6\sqrt{x - 2})^2$$
$$x^2 - 4x + 4 = 36(x - 2)$$
$$x^2 - 40x + 76 = 0$$
$$(x - 38)(x - 2) = 0$$
Either $x = 38$ or $x = 2$

Check.

When $x = 38$,
L.S. $= \sqrt{2(38) + 5} - \sqrt{38 - 2}$
$= \sqrt{81} - \sqrt{36}$
$= 9 - 6$
$= 3$
R.S. $= 3$

When $x = 2$,
L.S. $= \sqrt{2(2) + 5} - \sqrt{2 - 2}$
$= \sqrt{9} - \sqrt{0}$
$= 3 - 0$
$= 3$
R.S. $= 3$

Both 38 and 2 are roots of the equation.

In *Example 1*, there are no extraneous roots. But other equations containing two radicals may contain one or more extraneous roots.

Radical equations containing two radicals arise in the problem of calculating the altitude of a triangle when the lengths of its three sides are given.

Example 2.   From town A, a highway runs 7.0 km due east to town B. A third town C is 4.0 km from A and 6.0 km from B. A north-south highway is being planned from C to meet the road AB at N. How long is the section of highway CN?

Solution. Let x represent the distance, in kilometres, from C to N. By the Pythagorean Theorem,

In $\triangle CAN$, $\quad AN = \sqrt{4^2 - x^2}$
$$= \sqrt{16 - x^2}$$

In $\triangle CBN$, $\quad NB = \sqrt{6^2 - x^2}$
$$= \sqrt{36 - x^2}$$

Since $AN + NB = 7$,
$$\sqrt{16 - x^2} + \sqrt{36 - x^2} = 7$$

Isolate one of the radicals.
$$\sqrt{16 - x^2} = 7 - \sqrt{36 - x^2}$$

Square both sides.
$$(\sqrt{16 - x^2})^2 = (7 - \sqrt{36 - x^2})^2$$
$$16 - x^2 = 49 - 14\sqrt{36 - x^2} + (\sqrt{36 - x^2})^2$$
$$16 - x^2 = 49 - 14\sqrt{36 - x^2} + 36 - x^2$$

Isolate the radical.
$$14\sqrt{36 - x^2} = 69$$
$$\sqrt{36 - x^2} = \frac{69}{14}$$

Square both sides.
$$(\sqrt{36 - x^2})^2 = \left(\frac{69}{14}\right)^2$$
$$36 - x^2 = \left(\frac{69}{14}\right)^2$$
$$x^2 = 36 - \left(\frac{69}{14}\right)^2$$
$$\doteq 11.71$$
$$x \doteq \sqrt{11.71}$$
$$\doteq 3.42$$

The section of highway is about 3.4 km long.

[Diagram: right triangle with apex C at top, base from A to B. N is the foot of the perpendicular from C to AB (right angle at N). Side CA = 4 km, side CB = 6 km, and AB = 7 km.]

EXERCISES 3-6

1. Solve.
   a) $2\sqrt{x - 4} = \sqrt{3x - 5}$
   b) $\sqrt{x} - \sqrt{x - 5} = 5$
   c) $\sqrt{x + 5} + 5 = \sqrt{x}$
   d) $x - 2\sqrt{x} = 3\sqrt{x} - 6$
   e) $\sqrt{x + 7} - \sqrt{x + 2} = 1$
   f) $\sqrt{x + 6} + \sqrt{x + 1} = 5$

2. Solve.
   a) $\sqrt{3x + 1} - \sqrt{x - 1} = 2$
   b) $x + \sqrt{x^2 + 9} = 9$
   c) $\sqrt{2x - 3} = 1 + \sqrt{x + 2}$
   d) $\sqrt{x + 9} - \sqrt{x - 1} = 2$
   e) $\sqrt{x - 2} + 3 = \sqrt{3x - 5}$
   f) $\sqrt{3x - 2} = \sqrt{2x - 2} + 1$

3. Solve.
   a) $\sqrt{x} + \sqrt{1 - x} = 1$
   b) $\sqrt{6x + 1} - \sqrt{3x + 4} = 1$
   c) $10 - \sqrt{25 + 9x} = 3\sqrt{x}$
   d) $\sqrt{x + 11} + \sqrt{x - 1} = 6$
   e) $\sqrt{3x + 1} + \sqrt{x - 1} = 6$
   f) $\sqrt{4x + 1} - 1 = \sqrt{3x - 2}$

4. From town A, a highway runs 5.0 km due east to town B. A third town C is 4.0 km from A and 3.0 km from B. A north-south highway runs through C meeting the road AB at N. How long is the section of highway CN?

5. A roof truss has the measurements shown in the diagram (below left). What is the height of the peak X above the rafter YZ?

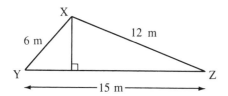
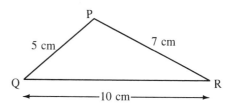

6. In △PQR (above right) find the length of the altitude from P to QR.

7. Solve.
   a) $\sqrt{1 + \sqrt{x}} = 2$
   b) $\sqrt{7 - \sqrt{x - 1}} = 3$
   c) $\sqrt{1 - \sqrt{x + 3}} = 1$
   d) $\sqrt{x + \sqrt{x - 2}} = 2$

Ⓒ

8. Solve.
   a) $\sqrt{2x - 1} - \sqrt{x - 1} = x$
   b) $\sqrt{8x + 1} - \sqrt{x + 1} = \sqrt{3x}$
   c) $2\sqrt[3]{5x - 1} - 3 = 5$
   d) $\sqrt[3]{x + 2} = \sqrt{x - 2}$

9. Solve.
   a) $\sqrt{x} + \sqrt{2x} = 5$
   b) $3 - \sqrt{2x + 1} = \sqrt{x}$
   c) $\sqrt{2x - 1} + \sqrt{x + 1} = 2$
   d) $\sqrt{3x - 2} - \sqrt{x - 1} = 3$

10. Triangle ABC has sides of length a, b, and c.
    a) Find an expression for the length of the altitude from A to BC in terms of a, b, and c.
    b) Show that the area of △ABC is given by this formula (known as Heron's formula).
       $A = \sqrt{s(s - a)(s - b)(s - c)}$, where s is the semi-perimeter and
       $s = \frac{1}{2}(a + b + c)$

11. Use the formula in *Exercise 10b)* to find the area of each triangle with the given sides, to 1 decimal place.
    a) 5 cm, 8 cm, 9 cm
    b) 3 cm, 4 cm, 5 cm
    c) 6 m, 7 m, 10 m
    d) 5 m, 5 m, 5 m

12. A regular polygon with sides of length x is inscribed in a circle with radius R. The diagram shows that a regular polygon with twice as many sides can be constructed using the perpendicular bisector of each side. The length of the sides of the larger polygon is given by this formula.

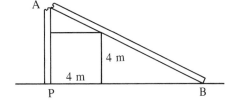

$$s = \sqrt{2R^2 - R\sqrt{4R^2 - x^2}}$$

Solve this formula for x.

13. A square is inscribed in a circle with radius 10 cm.
    a) Find the length of each side of the square.
    b) If a regular octagon is inscribed in the same circle, use the result of *Exercise 12* to find the length of each side of the octagon.

14. An equilateral triangle is inscribed in a circle with radius 10 cm.
    a) Find the length of each side of the triangle.
    b) If a regular hexagon is inscribed in the same circle, use the result of *Exercise 12* to find the length of each side of the hexagon.

15. A 20 m pole, which is standing vertically at P, breaks at A and just clears the 4 m by 4 m obstruction shown, in such a way that the top of the pole just touches the ground at B. Find the height, to the nearest centimetre, of the point where the pole broke.

16. a) Solve.
    i) $\sqrt{x + \sqrt{x + 1}} = 2$ ii) $\sqrt{x + \sqrt{x + 2}} = 2$
    iii) $\sqrt{x + \sqrt{x + 3}} = 2$ iv) $\sqrt{x + \sqrt{x + 4}} = 2$
    b) For what natural number values of n does $\sqrt{x + \sqrt{x + n}} = 2$ have an integral root?

17. Solve  $\sqrt{x + \sqrt{x + \sqrt{x + \ldots}}} = 2$, where . . . indicates that the pattern continues indefinitely.

![INVESTIGATE icon] **INVESTIGATE**

In the solution of the radical equation in *Example 1*, a quadratic equation resulted. The radical equation had no extraneous roots. Find, if possible, an example of a radical equation which has:
a) one extraneous root   b) two extraneous roots.

INVESTIGATE

Constructing an Ellipse

To construct an ellipse, follow these steps. You will need a piece of corrugated cardboard, some string, some tape, and two paper fasteners.

Step 1

Tape a piece of paper to the cardboard, and push the paper fasteners through it, about 6 cm apart. Tie the string into a loop about 16 cm long.

Step 2.

Place the loop around the paper fasteners.

Use a pencil to keep the string taut.

Step 3.

Keeping the string taut, move the pencil to trace out an ellipse.

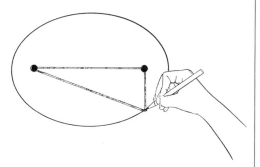

1. Construct an ellipse by following the above steps.

2. Write a definition of an ellipse based on this construction.

3. For the ellipse you constructed, mark the points F_1 and F_2 where the paper fasteners were located.
    a) Mark any point P on the ellipse. Measure PF_1 and PF_2, and calculate the sum $PF_1 + PF_2$. Repeat for other points P on the ellipse.
    b) Locate the points A_1 and A_2 where the line F_1F_2 intersects the ellipse. How does the length of A_1A_2 compare with the sum $PF_1 + PF_2$ for any point of the ellipse?

4. Use your definition to show that, for any point P on an ellipse, the sum $PF_1 + PF_2$ is always equal to the length of A_1A_2.

5. Investigate the effect on the shape of the ellipse of changing the length of the loop of string, or changing the distance between the paper fasteners.

3-7 THE ELLIPSE

A spotlight is often used in skating shows. The light rays form a cone of light which illuminates an elliptical region on the ice.

An ellipse also results when a cylindrical tube is cut at an angle. In machinery, elliptical gears are sometimes used to provide a powerful stroke followed by a quick return.

An ellipse may be defined as follows.

An *ellipse* is the locus of a point P which moves such that the sum of its distances from two fixed points F_1 and F_2 is constant.

F_1 and F_2 are called the *foci* of the ellipse. PF_1 and PF_2 are called *focal radii*.

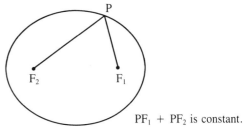

$PF_1 + PF_2$ is constant.

Let the line F_1F_2 intersect the ellipse at A_1 and A_2. Let the perpendicular bisector of F_1F_2 intersect the ellipse at B_1 and B_2.

- A_1 and A_2 are called the *vertices*.
- Line segment A_1A_2 is called the *major axis*; its length is represented by $2a$.
- Line segment B_1B_2 is called the *minor axis*; its length is represented by $2b$.
- Since A_1A_2 is longer than B_1B_2, $a > b > 0$.
- A_1A_2 and B_1B_2 intersect at the *centre*, O.
- OA_1 is called the *semi-major axis*, and has length a.
- OB_1 is called the *semi-minor axis*, and has length b.
- The distance from the centre to either focus is represented by c.
- Both the major axis and the minor axis are lines of symmetry of the ellipse.

Properties of the Ellipse

According to the definition, $PF_1 + PF_2$ is constant for all positions of P on the ellipse. In particular, P could be at A_1 or at B_1.

Suppose P is at A_1. $PF_1 + PF_2 = A_1F_1 + A_1F_2$
$$= A_2F_2 + A_1F_2 \quad \text{(by symmetry)}$$
$$= A_1A_2, \text{ or } 2a.$$

Hence, for all positions of P on the ellipse, $PF_1 + PF_2$ is equal to the length of the major axis.

Suppose P is at B₁. $PF_1 + PF_2 = B_1F_1 + B_1F_2$
$$= 2B_1F_1 \quad \text{(by symmetry)}$$
$$= 2a$$

Hence, $B_1F_1 = a$. That is, the distance from the endpoints of the minor axis to either focus is equal to the length of the semi-major axis.
Since $\triangle OB_1F_1$ is a right triangle,
$$B_1F_1^2 = OB_1^2 + OF_1^2$$
$$a^2 = b^2 + c^2$$

Focal Radii Property	**Pythagorean Property**
	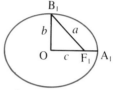
$PF_1 + PF_2 = 2a$	$a^2 = b^2 + c^2$

The Equation of an Ellipse
We can use the defining property to find the equation of any ellipse.

Example 1. The foci of an ellipse are $F_1(3, 0)$ and $F_2(-3, 0)$, and the sum of the focal radii is 10 units. Find the equation of the ellipse.

Solution. Let $P(x, y)$ be any point on the ellipse. Since the sum of the focal radii is 10 units,
$$PF_1 + PF_2 = 10$$
$$\sqrt{(x-3)^2 + y^2} + \sqrt{(x+3)^2 + y^2} = 10$$
Isolate one of the radicals and square both sides.
$$\sqrt{(x-3)^2 + y^2} = 10 - \sqrt{(x+3)^2 + y^2}$$
$$(\sqrt{(x-3)^2 + y^2})^2 = (10 - \sqrt{(x+3)^2 + y^2})^2$$
$$(x-3)^2 + y^2 = 100 - 20\sqrt{(x+3)^2 + y^2} + (x+3)^2 + y^2$$
$$x^2 - 6x + 9 + y^2 = 100 - 20\sqrt{(x+3)^2 + y^2} + x^2 + 6x + 9 +$$
Isolate the radical and square both sides again.
$$20\sqrt{(x+3)^2 + y^2} = 100 + 12x$$
$$5\sqrt{(x+3)^2 + y^2} = 25 + 3x$$
$$25(x^2 + 6x + 9 + y^2) = 625 + 150x + 9x^2$$
This equation simplifies to
$$16x^2 + 25y^2 = 400$$
or
$$\frac{x^2}{25} + \frac{y^2}{16} = 1$$

Hence, the equation of the ellipse is $\dfrac{x^2}{25} + \dfrac{y^2}{16} = 1$.

We can use the method of *Example 1* to derive the standard equation
of an ellipse with centre (0, 0) and foci on the *x*-axis.
Let the coordinates of the foci be $F_1(c, 0)$ and $F_2(-c, 0)$.
Let $P(x, y)$ be any point on the ellipse.
Then, by the focal radii property, the sum of the focal radii is $2a$.

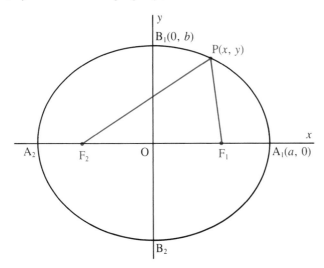

$$PF_1 + PF_2 = 2a$$
$$\sqrt{(x - c)^2 + y^2} + \sqrt{(x + c)^2 + y^2} = 2a$$

Isolate one of the radicals and square both sides.

$$\sqrt{(x - c)^2 + y^2} = 2a - \sqrt{(x + c)^2 + y^2}$$
$$(\sqrt{(x - c)^2 + y^2})^2 = (2a - \sqrt{(x + c)^2 + y^2})^2$$
$$(x - c)^2 + y^2 = 4a^2 - 4a\sqrt{(x + c)^2 + y^2} + (x + c)^2 + y^2$$
$$x^2 - 2cx + c^2 + y^2 = 4a^2 - 4a\sqrt{(x + c)^2 + y^2} + x^2 + 2cx + c^2 + y^2$$

Isolate the radical and square both sides again.

$$4a\sqrt{(x + c)^2 + y^2} = 4a^2 + 4cx$$
$$a\sqrt{(x + c)^2 + y^2} = a^2 + cx$$
$$a^2(x^2 + 2cx + c^2 + y^2) = a^4 + 2a^2cx + c^2x^2$$

This equation may be written as

$$(a^2 - c^2)x^2 + a^2y^2 = a^2(a^2 - c^2)$$

By the Pythagorean property, $a^2 - c^2 = b^2$. Hence, the equation becomes

$$b^2x^2 + a^2y^2 = a^2b^2$$

or

$$\frac{x^2}{a^2} + \frac{y^2}{b^2} = 1$$

This is the *standard equation* of an ellipse with centre (0, 0) and
foci on the *x*-axis. Similarly, the standard equation of an ellipse with
centre (0, 0) and foci on the *y*-axis is $\dfrac{x^2}{b^2} + \dfrac{y^2}{a^2} = 1$.

Standard Equations of an Ellipse with Centre (0, 0)

The equation of an ellipse with centre (0, 0) and major axis on the x-axis is $\frac{x^2}{a^2} + \frac{y^2}{b^2} = 1$, where $a > b$.

The equation of an ellipse with centre (0, 0) and major axis on the y-axis is $\frac{x^2}{b^2} + \frac{y^2}{a^2} = 1$, where $a > b$.

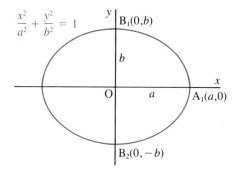

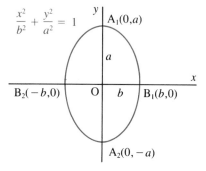

Length of major axis: $2a$
Length of minor axis: $2b$
Vertices: $(a, 0)$ and $(-a, 0)$
Foci: $(c, 0)$ and $(-c, 0)$
   where $c^2 = a^2 - b^2$

Length of major axis: $2a$
Length of minor axis: $2b$
Vertices: $(0, a)$ and $(0, -a)$
Foci: $(0, c)$ and $(0, -c)$
   where $c^2 = a^2 - b^2$

We can always tell whether the major axis is on the x-axis or the y-axis from the standard equation. If the larger denominator occurs in the term containing x, the major axis is on the x-axis; if it occurs in the term containing y, the major axis is on the y-axis.

Example 2.   Given the equation $4x^2 + 25y^2 = 100$

a) Show that this equation represents an ellipse. Determine the lengths of the major and minor axes, the coordinates of the vertices, and the coordinates of the foci.

b) Graph the ellipse.

Solution.   a) Since the standard equation has 1 on the right side, we divide both sides of the equation by 100.

$$\frac{4x^2}{100} + \frac{25y^2}{100} = 1$$

$$\frac{x^2}{25} + \frac{y^2}{4} = 1$$

b)

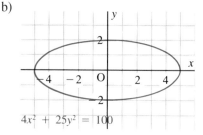

Hence, the equation represents an ellipse.

For this equation, $a = 5$ and $b = 2$
The major axis has length $2a$, or 10.
The minor axis has length $2b$, or 4.

Since the larger denominator occurs under x^2, the major axis lies on the x-axis. The coordinates of the vertices are $(5, 0)$ and $(-5, 0)$.

$$c^2 = a^2 - b^2$$
$$= 25 - 4$$
$$= 21$$
$$c = \sqrt{21}$$

The coordinates of the foci are $(\sqrt{21}, 0)$ and $(-\sqrt{21}, 0)$.

EXERCISES 3-7

1. Determine if each point is on the ellipse defined by $x^2 + 4y^2 = 20$.
   a) $(4, 1)$ b) $(-2, 2)$ c) $(0, -5)$ d) $(0, \sqrt{5})$

2. State the coordinates of the vertices, the coordinates of the foci, and the lengths of the major and minor axes of the ellipse defined by each equation.
   a) $\dfrac{x^2}{16} + \dfrac{y^2}{9} = 1$
   b) $\dfrac{x^2}{36} + \dfrac{y^2}{25} = 1$
   c) $\dfrac{x^2}{4} + \dfrac{y^2}{9} = 1$
   d) $\dfrac{x^2}{16} + \dfrac{y^2}{49} = 1$
   e) $\dfrac{x^2}{64} + \dfrac{y^2}{16} = 1$
   f) $\dfrac{x^2}{9} + \dfrac{y^2}{25} = 1$

3. An ellipse has centre $(0, 0)$ and major axis on the x-axis. Write the equation of the ellipse if:
   a) $a = 5$ and $b = 3$
   b) $a = 8$ and $b = 6$
   c) $b = 4$ and $c = 2$
   d) the x-intercepts are ± 7 and the y-intercepts are ± 3
   e) the minor axis has length 6, and the sum of the focal radii is 10
   f) one vertex is $A_1(6, 0)$ and one focus is $F_1(4, 0)$.

4. For each ellipse whose equation is given below
   i) Write the standard equation.
   ii) Determine the lengths of the major and minor axes, the coordinates of the vertices, and the coordinates of the foci.
   iii) Graph the ellipse.
      a) $4x^2 + 9y^2 = 36$ b) $x^2 + 4y^2 = 16$ c) $16x^2 + 9y^2 = 144$
      d) $25x^2 + 16y^2 = 400$ e) $9x^2 + y^2 = 9$ f) $2x^2 + 3y^2 = 6$

5. The foci of an ellipse are $F_1(2, 0)$ and $F_2(-2, 0)$, and the sum of the focal radii is 6 units. Use the definition of an ellipse to derive the equation of this ellipse.

6. Use the definition to derive the equation of an ellipse with sum of focal radii $2a$ and foci $F_1(0, c)$ and $F_2(0, -c)$ on the y-axis.

7. An ellipse has centre $(0, 0)$ and one vertex $A(10, 0)$.
   a) Find the equation of the ellipse if it passes through $R(6, 4)$.
   b) Find the value of x_1 if $S(x_1, 3)$ is on the ellipse.
   c) Find the value of y_1 if $T(5, y_1)$ is on the ellipse.

8. Is a circle an ellipse? Justify your answer.

9. A point P moves such that it is always twice as far from the line $x = 8$ as it is from the point $(2, 0)$.
   a) Find the equation of the locus.
   b) Identify the locus and sketch its graph.
   c) Verify from the graph that points on the graph are twice as far from the line $x = 8$ as they are from the point $(2, 0)$.

10. On page 113, O was defined to be the midpoint of F_1F_2. Use the definition of an ellipse to prove that O is also the midpoint of A_1A_2.

11. Use the definition of an ellipse to prove that an ellipse is symmetric about the minor axis. That is, if P_1 is any point on the ellipse, and if B_1B_2 is the perpendicular bisector of P_1P_2, then P_2 is also on the ellipse.

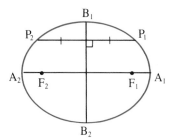

12. Use the definition of an ellipse to prove that an ellipse is symmetric about its major axis.

Ⓒ

13. Describe how the graph of the ellipse $\dfrac{x^2}{a^2} + \dfrac{y^2}{b^2} = 1$ changes if:
   a) b is kept constant and a varies
   b) a is kept constant and b varies.

14. Given the equation $Ax^2 + By^2 + C = 0$, what conditions must be satisfied by A, B, and C if this equation represents an ellipse with foci on:
   a) the x-axis
   b) the y-axis?

15. Draw a diagram to represent the ellipse defined by $\dfrac{x^2}{a^2} + \dfrac{y^2}{b^2} = 1$. Let P be any point on this ellipse.
   a) On the same diagram, draw the circle defined by $x^2 + y^2 = a^2$. Draw a vertical line through P to intersect this circle at Q and the x-axis at R. Prove that $\dfrac{PR}{QR} = \dfrac{b}{a}$.
   b) On the same diagram, draw the circle defined by $x^2 + y^2 = b^2$. Draw a horizontal line through P to intersect this circle at S and the y-axis at T. Prove that $\dfrac{PT}{ST} = \dfrac{a}{b}$.

Constructing a Hyperbola

To construct a hyperbola, follow these steps. You will need a piece of corrugated cardboard, some string, some tape and two paper fasteners.

Step 1.
Tape a piece of paper to the cardboard, and push the paper fasteners through it, about 10 cm apart. Make a knotted loop in the string to hold a pencil.

Step 2.
Pass the string around the paper fasteners as shown. Hold the ends of the string together, and keep the string taut with the pencil.

Step 3.
Keeping the string taut, move the pencil to trace out a hyperbola; repeat by reversing the position of the string to form the other branch of the hyperbola.

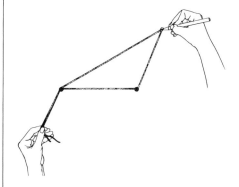

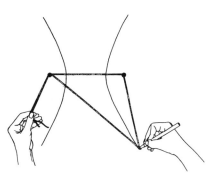

1. Construct a hyperbola by following the above steps.

2. Write a definition of a hyperbola based on this construction.

3. For the hyperbola you constructed, mark the points F_1 and F_2 where the paper fasteners were located.
   a) Mark any point P on the hyperbola. Measure PF_1 and PF_2, and calculate the difference $|PF_1 - PF_2|$. Repeat for other points P on the hyperbola.
   b) Locate the points A_1 and A_2 where the line F_1F_2 intersects the hyperbola. How does the length of A_1A_2 compare with the difference $|PF_1 - PF_2|$ for any point P on the hyperbola?

4. Use the above definition to show that, for any point P on a hyperbola, the difference $|PF_1 - PF_2|$ is always equal to the length of A_1A_2.

5. Investigate the effect on the shape of the hyperbola of changing the distance between the paper fasteners.

3-8 THE HYPERBOLA: FOCI ON *x*-AXIS

The *Saddledome* was built for the figure skating and hockey events of the 1988 Olympic Winter Games in Calgary, and it is used by the Calgary Flames hockey team. Horizontal cross-sections of its saddle-shaped roof are hyperbolas; when viewed from the side the roof outlines a parabola. The roof is an example of a geometrical surface called a hyperbolic paraboloid.

A hyperbola may be defined as follows.

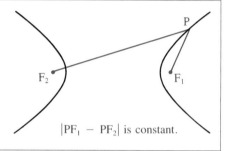

A *hyperbola* is the locus of a point P which moves such that the difference of its distances from two fixed points F_1 and F_2 is constant. F_1 and F_2 are called the *foci* of the hyperbola. PF_1 and PF_2 are called the *focal radii*.

$|PF_1 - PF_2|$ is constant.

Let the line F_1F_2 intersect the hyperbola at A_1 and A_2, and construct the perpendicular bisector of F_1F_2.
● A_1 and A_2 are called the *vertices*.
● Line segment A_1A_2 is called the *transverse axis*; its length is represented by $2a$.
● The midpoint of F_1F_2 is the *centre* O.
● OA_1 is called the *semi-transverse axis*, and has length a.
● The distance from the centre to either focus is represented by c, where $c > a > 0$.
● Both the transverse axis and its perpendicular bisector are lines of symmetry of the hyperbola.

Focal Radii Property

According to the definition, $|PF_1 - PF_2|$ is constant for all positions of P on the hyperbola. In particular, P could be at A_1.
Suppose P is at A_1.
$$\begin{aligned}|PF_1 - PF_2| &= |A_1F_1 - A_1F_2|\\ &= |A_2F_2 - A_1F_2| \quad \text{(by symmetry)}\\ &= A_1A_2\\ &= 2a\end{aligned}$$

Hence, for all positions of P on the hyperbola, $|PF_1 - PF_2|$ is equal to the length of the transverse axis.

The Equation of a Hyperbola

We can use the defining property to find the equation of any hyperbola.

Example 1. The foci of a hyperbola are $F_1(5, 0)$ and $F_2(-5, 0)$, and the difference of the focal radii is 8 units. Find the equation of the hyperbola.

Solution.

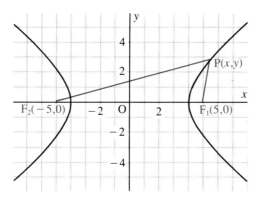

Let $P(x, y)$ be any point on the hyperbola. Since the difference of the focal radii is 8 units,

$$PF_1 - PF_2 = \pm 8$$
$$\sqrt{(x - 5)^2 + y^2} - \sqrt{(x + 5)^2 + y^2} = \pm 8$$

Isolate one of the radicals and square both sides.

$$\sqrt{(x - 5)^2 + y^2} = \pm 8 + \sqrt{(x + 5)^2 + y^2}$$
$$(\sqrt{(x - 5)^2 + y^2})^2 = (\pm 8 + \sqrt{(x + 5)^2 + y^2})^2$$
$$(x - 5)^2 + y^2 = 64 \pm 16\sqrt{(x + 5)^2 + y^2} + (x + 5)^2 + y^2$$
$$x^2 - 10x + 25 + y^2 = 64 \pm 16\sqrt{(x + 5)^2 + y^2} + x^2 + 10x + 25 + y^2$$

Isolate the radical and square both sides again.

$$-20x - 64 = \pm 16\sqrt{(x + 5)^2 + y^2}$$
$$-5x - 16 = \pm 4\sqrt{(x + 5)^2 + y^2}$$
$$25x^2 + 160x + 256 = 16(x^2 + 10x + 25 + y^2)$$

This equation simplifies to

$$9x^2 - 16y^2 = 144$$

or

$$\frac{x^2}{16} - \frac{y^2}{9} = 1$$

Hence, the equation of the hyperbola is $\dfrac{x^2}{16} - \dfrac{y^2}{9} = 1$.

In *Example 1* we can find the x-intercepts of the hyperbola by substituting 0 for y to obtain $\dfrac{x^2}{16} = 1$, or $x = \pm 4$. These x-intercepts correspond to the vertices $A_1(4, 0)$ and $A_2(-4, 0)$. The graph shows that there are no y-intercepts. This is also shown by the equation; if we substitute 0 for x, we obtain $-\dfrac{y^2}{9} = 1$, or $y^2 = -9$, which has no real solution.

Nevertheless, it is useful to consider the term $\dfrac{y^2}{9}$ without the negative sign, and to identify two points $B_1(0, 3)$ and $B_2(0, -3)$ on the y-axis. These points are not on the hyperbola, but they are related to it, as explained below.

The diagram shows the graph of *Example 1* with a rectangle centred at the origin. The points A_1, A_2, B_1, and B_2 are the midpoints of the sides of this rectangle. We see that the hyperbola lies between the lines containing its diagonals. As $|x|$ increases, the hyperbola comes closer to these lines. We can see why by solving the equation of the hyperbola for y.

$$\frac{x^2}{16} - \frac{y^2}{9} = 1$$

$$\frac{y^2}{9} = \frac{x^2}{16} - 1$$

$$\frac{y^2}{9} = \frac{x^2 - 16}{16}$$

$$y = \pm\frac{3}{4}\sqrt{x^2 - 16}$$

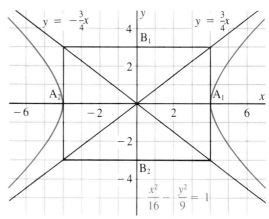

If $|x|$ is large, then x^2 is very large compared with 16. Hence,

$$y \doteq \pm\frac{3}{4}\sqrt{x^2}$$

$$\doteq \pm\frac{3}{4}x$$

The lines defined by $y = \dfrac{3}{4}x$ and $y = -\dfrac{3}{4}x$ are called the *asymptotes* of the hyperbola. The line segment B_1B_2 is called the *conjugate axis*.

We can use the method of *Example 1* to derive the standard equation of a hyperbola with centre $(0, 0)$ and foci on the x-axis.
Let the coordinates of the foci be $F_1(c, 0)$ and $F_2(-c, 0)$.
Let $P(x, y)$ be any point on the hyperbola.
Then, by the focal radii property, the difference of the focal radii is $2a$.

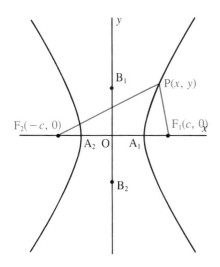

$$PF_1 - PF_2 = \pm 2a$$

$$\sqrt{(x-c)^2 + y^2} - \sqrt{(x+c)^2 + y^2} = \pm 2a$$

Isolate one of the radicals and square both sides.

$$\sqrt{(x-c)^2 + y^2} = \pm 2a + \sqrt{(x+c)^2 + y^2}$$

$$(\sqrt{(x-c)^2 + y^2})^2 = (\pm 2a + \sqrt{(x+c)^2 + y^2})^2$$

$$(x-c)^2 + y^2 = 4a^2 \pm 4a\sqrt{(x+c)^2 + y^2} + (x+c)^2 + y^2$$

$$x^2 - 2cx + c^2 + y^2 = 4a^2 \pm 4a\sqrt{(x+c)^2 + y^2} + x^2 + 2cx + c^2 + y^2$$

Isolate the radical and square both sides again.

$$-4a^2 - 4cx = \pm 4a\sqrt{(x+c)^2 + y^2}$$

$$-a^2 - cx = \pm a\sqrt{(x+c)^2 + y^2}$$

$$a^4 + 2a^2cx + c^2x^2 = a^2(x^2 + 2cx + c^2 + y^2)$$

This equation may be written as

$$(c^2 - a^2)x^2 - a^2y^2 = a^2(c^2 - a^2)$$

To simplify this equation, we *define* $b^2 = c^2 - a^2$.

Hence, the equation becomes

$$b^2x^2 - a^2y^2 = a^2b^2$$

or

$$\frac{x^2}{a^2} - \frac{y^2}{b^2} = 1$$

This is the standard equation of a hyperbola with centre $(0, 0)$ and foci on the *x*-axis.

Since we defined $b^2 = c^2 - a^2$, we can identify points $B_1(0, b)$ and $B_2(0, -b)$ on the *y*-axis, which are the endpoints of the conjugate axis. And, as we saw in the above example, we can use the points A_1, A_2, B_1, and B_2 to draw a rectangle centred at $(0, 0)$ whose diagonals are the asymptotes of the hyperbola. Observe that for the hyperbola there is no restriction that a be greater than b as there was for the ellipse.

Hence, every equation of the form $\dfrac{x^2}{a^2} - \dfrac{y^2}{b^2} = 1$ represents a hyperbola

with foci on the x-axis for all positive values of a and b.

Standard Equation of a Hyperbola with Centre (0, 0) and Foci on the x-axis

The equation of a hyperbola with centre (0, 0) and foci on the x-axis

is $\dfrac{x^2}{a^2} - \dfrac{y^2}{b^2} = 1$.

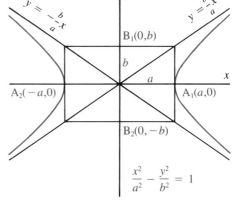

Length of transverse axis: $2a$
Length of conjugate axis: $2b$
Vertices: $(a, 0)$ and $(-a, 0)$
Foci: $(c, 0)$ and $(-c, 0)$
      where $c^2 = a^2 + b^2$
Asymptotes: $y = \dfrac{b}{a}x$ and $y = -\dfrac{b}{a}x$

Example 2.   Given the equation $9x^2 - 16y^2 = 144$
   a) Show that this equation represents a hyperbola. Determine the lengths of the transverse and conjugate axes, the coordinates of the vertices, and the coordinates of the foci.
   b) Write the equations of the asymptotes.
   c) Graph the hyperbola.

Solution.   a) The standard equation has 1 on the right side. Hence, we divide both sides of the equation by 144.

$$\frac{9x^2}{144} - \frac{16y^2}{144} = 1$$

$$\frac{x^2}{16} - \frac{y^2}{9} = 1$$

Hence, the equation represents a hyperbola.

For this equation, $a = 4$ and $b = 3$
Length of transverse axis: $2a = 8$
Length of conjugate axis: $2b = 6$
Vertices: $(4, 0)$ and $(-4, 0)$

$$c^2 = a^2 + b^2$$
$$= 16 + 9$$
$$= 25$$
$$c = 5$$

Foci: $(5, 0)$ and $(-5, 0)$

b) The equations of the asymptotes are $y = \frac{3}{4}x$ and $y = -\frac{3}{4}x$.

c) To graph the hyperbola, locate the vertices and draw a rectangle centred at the origin, with length 8 units and width 6 units. Next, draw the asymptotes, which are the diagonals of this rectangle. Then sketch the hyperbola.

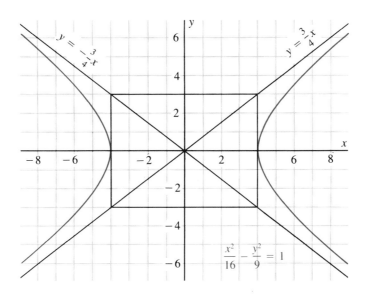

Example 3. The LORAN (LOng RAnge Navigation) system of navigation is based on the definition of a hyperbola. Equipment on a ship determines the difference of the distances to two transmitters on shore by measuring the time difference for simultaneous signals to reach the ship from the transmitters. If the transmitters are 300 km apart and the ship is 200 km farther from one transmitter than the other, determine an equation of the hyperbola on which the ship is located.

Solution.   Use a system of coordinates in which the transmitters have coordinates $F_1(150, 0)$ and $F_2(-150, 0)$. Let $S(x, y)$ represent the position of the ship. Then S is on a hyperbola with foci F_1 and F_2. For this hyperbola,

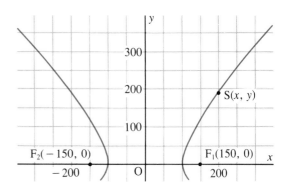

$c = 150$ and $2a = 200$

$\qquad a = 100$

$b^2 = c^2 - a^2$

$\quad = 22\ 500 - 10\ 000$

$\quad = 12\ 500$

The equation of the hyperbola is $\dfrac{x^2}{a^2} - \dfrac{y^2}{b^2} = 1$

$$\frac{x^2}{10\ 000} - \frac{y^2}{12\ 500} = 1$$

or $\qquad 5x^2 - 4y^2 = 50\ 000$

In *Example 3*, if a second pair of transmitters is used, a second hyperbola on which the ship is located can be determined. Then the position of the ship can be found since it is on both hyperbolas.

EXERCISES 3-8

1. Determine if each point is on the hyperbola defined by $3x^2 - 2y^2 = 10$.
   a) $(-2, 1)$ b) $(5, 6)$ c) $(6, -7)$ d) $(0, \sqrt{5})$

2. State the coordinates of the vertices, the coordinates of the foci, and the lengths of the transverse and conjugate axes of the hyperbola defined by each equation.
   a) $\dfrac{x^2}{4} - \dfrac{y^2}{16} = 1$ b) $\dfrac{x^2}{25} - \dfrac{y^2}{9} = 1$ c) $\dfrac{x^2}{81} - \dfrac{y^2}{49} = 1$

(B)

3. A hyperbola has centre $(0, 0)$ and transverse axis on the *x*-axis. Write the equation of the hyperbola if:
   a) $a = 6$ and $b = 3$
   b) $a = 3$ and $b = 2$
   c) $b = 4$ and $c = 6$
   d) the conjugate axis has length 14, and the difference of the focal radii is 10
   e) one vertex is $A_1(2, 0)$ and one focus is $F_1(3, 0)$
   f) one *x*-intercept is 7 and one asymptote is defined by $y = -x$.

4. For each hyperbola whose equation is given below
   i) Write the standard equation.
   ii) Find the lengths of the transverse and conjugate axes, the coordinates of the vertices and foci, and the equations of the asymptotes.
   iii) Graph the hyperbola.
   a) $9x^2 - 4y^2 = 36$ b) $x^2 - 9y^2 = 36$ c) $25x^2 - 9y^2 = 225$
   d) $4x^2 - y^2 = 16$ e) $x^2 - 3y^2 = 12$ f) $4x^2 - 5y^2 = 20$

5. The foci of a hyperbola are $F_1(6, 0)$ and $F_2(-6, 0)$, and the difference of the focal radii is 4 units. Use the definition of a hyperbola to derive the equation of this hyperbola.

6. A hyperbola has centre $(0, 0)$ and one vertex $A(\sqrt{6}, 0)$.
   a) Find the equation of the hyperbola if it passes through $J(9, 5)$.
   b) Find the value of x_1 if $K(x_1, 2)$ is on the hyperbola.
   c) Find the value of y_1 if $L(3, y_1)$ is on the hyperbola.

7. A *rectangular hyperbola* is one whose transverse axis and conjugate axis have the same length.
   a) Write the equation of a rectangular hyperbola with vertices $A_1(3, 0)$ and $A_2(-3, 0)$.
   b) For the hyperbola in part a), determine the coordinates of the foci and the equations of the asymptotes.

8. A point P moves such that it is always twice as far from the point $(4, 0)$ as it is from the line $x = 1$.
   a) Find the equation of the locus.
   b) Identify the locus and sketch its graph.
   c) Verify from the graph that points on the graph are twice as far from the point $(4, 0)$ as they are from the line $x = 1$.

9. On page 120, O was defined to be the midpoint of F_1F_2. Use the definition of a hyperbola to prove that O is also the midpoint of A_1A_2.

10. Use the definition of a hyperbola to prove that a hyperbola is symmetric about:
    a) the conjugate axis   b) the transverse axis.

11. Prove that the length of the perpendicular from a focus of a hyperbola to an asymptote is equal to the length of the semi-conjugate axis.

Ⓒ

12. Describe how the graph of the hyperbola defined by $\dfrac{x^2}{a^2} - \dfrac{y^2}{b^2} = 1$ changes if:

    a) b is kept constant and a varies   b) a is kept constant and b varies.

13. Since the ellipse defined by $\dfrac{x^2}{b^2} + \dfrac{y^2}{a^2} = 1$ has its foci on the y-axis, one might think that the hyperbola defined by $\dfrac{x^2}{b^2} - \dfrac{y^2}{a^2} = 1$ has its foci on the y-axis. Investigate whether this is true.

3-9 THE HYPERBOLA: FOCI ON y-AXIS

In the preceding section we found that the equation $\dfrac{x^2}{a^2} - \dfrac{y^2}{b^2} = 1$
represents a hyperbola with centre $(0, 0)$ and foci $(\pm c, 0)$ on the
x-axis, where $c^2 = a^2 + b^2$. To obtain the equation of a hyperbola
with foci on the y-axis, we interchange x and y in the equation above.
This has the effect of reversing the coordinates of the points which satisfy the equation. Hence, the graph of the hyperbola is reflected in the
line defined by $y = x$.

If we interchange x and y in the equation above, we obtain

$$\frac{y^2}{a^2} - \frac{x^2}{b^2} = 1$$

or $\quad \dfrac{x^2}{b^2} - \dfrac{y^2}{a^2} = -1$

Hence, this equation represents a hyperbola with centre $(0, 0)$ and foci
$(0, \pm c)$ on the y-axis, where $c^2 = a^2 + b^2$. This equation can also
be obtained using the locus definition of a hyperbola; the derivation is
left to the exercises.

**Standard Equation of a Hyperbola with Centre (0, 0) and Foci
on the y-axis**

The equation of a hyperbola
with centre $(0, 0)$ and
foci on the y-axis is
$$\frac{x^2}{b^2} - \frac{y^2}{a^2} = -1.$$

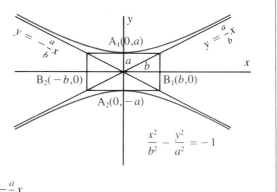

Length of transverse axis: $\quad 2a$
Length of conjugate axis: $\quad 2b$
Vertices: $\quad (0, a)$ and $(0, -a)$
Foci: $\quad (0, c)$ and $(0, -c)$
$\qquad$ where $c^2 = a^2 + b^2$

Asymptotes: $\quad y = \dfrac{a}{b}x$ and $y = -\dfrac{a}{b}x$

We can always tell whether the transverse axis of the hyperbola is
on the x-axis or the y-axis from the standard equation. If there is a 1
on the right side, the transverse axis is on the x-axis; if there is a -1
on the right side, the transverse axis is on the y-axis. In either case, the
value of a occurs in the term on the left side that has the same sign
as the term on the right side.

Example. Given the hyperbola defined by $x^2 - 2y^2 = -8$
a) Determine the lengths of the transverse and conjugate axes, the coordinates of the vertices and the coordinates of the foci.
b) Graph the hyperbola.

Solution. a) Divide both sides of the equation by 8.
$$\frac{x^2}{8} - \frac{y^2}{4} = -1$$
For this equation, $a^2 = 4$ and $b^2 = 8$
$$a = 2 \qquad b = 2\sqrt{2}$$
Length of transverse axis: $2a = 4$
Length of conjugate axis: $2b = 4\sqrt{2}$
Vertices: $(0, 2)$ and $(0, -2)$
$$c^2 = a^2 + b^2$$
$$= 4 + 8$$
$$= 12$$
$$c = \sqrt{12}, \text{ or } 2\sqrt{3}$$
Foci: $(0, 2\sqrt{3})$ and $(0, -2\sqrt{3})$

b) To graph the hyperbola, locate the vertices and draw a rectangle, centred at the origin, with length $4\sqrt{2}$ units and width 4 units. Draw the diagonals, and extend them to form the asymptotes. Then sketch the hyperbola.

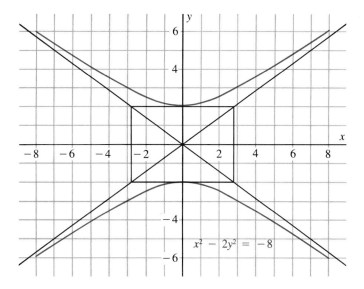

EXERCISES 3-9

1. Determine if each point is on the hyperbola defined by $7x^2 - 3y^2 = -20$.
   a) $(-1, 3)$ b) $(2, -4)$ c) $(5, 8)$ d) $(-7, -11)$

2. State the coordinates of the vertices, the coordinates of the foci, and the lengths of the transverse and conjugate axes of the hyperbola defined by each equation.
   a) $\dfrac{x^2}{16} - \dfrac{y^2}{9} = -1$ b) $\dfrac{x^2}{4} - \dfrac{y^2}{25} = -1$ c) $\dfrac{x^2}{64} - \dfrac{y^2}{36} = -1$

(B)

3. A hyperbola has centre $(0, 0)$ and transverse axis on the y-axis. Write the equation of the hyperbola if:
   a) $a = 3$ and $b = 4$
   b) $a = 7$ and $c = 8$
   c) $b = 3$ and $c = 6$
   d) the transverse axis has length 10 and one focus is $F_1(0, 4\sqrt{2})$
   e) one focus is $(0, 2\sqrt{5})$ and one asymptote is defined by $y = 2x$.

4. For each hyperbola whose equation is given below
   i) Write the standard equation.
   ii) Find the lengths of the transverse and conjugate axes, the coordinates of the vertices and foci, and the equations of the asymptotes.
   iii) Graph the hyperbola.
        a) $4x^2 - 9y^2 = -36$ b) $x^2 - 4y^2 = -16$ c) $16x^2 - 25y^2 = -400$
        d) $4x^2 - y^2 = -100$ e) $x^2 - 2y^2 = -50$ f) $3x^2 - 4y^2 = -24$

5. The foci of a hyperbola are $F_1(0, 3)$ and $F_2(0, -3)$, and the difference of the focal radii is 2 units. Use the definition of a hyperbola to derive the equation of this hyperbola.

6. Use the definition to derive the equation of a hyperbola with difference of focal radii $2a$ and foci $F_1(0, c)$ and $F_2(0, -c)$ on the y-axis.

(C)

7. Describe how the graph of the hyperbola defined by $\dfrac{x^2}{b^2} - \dfrac{y^2}{a^2} = -1$ changes if:

   a) b is kept constant and a varies   b) a is kept constant and b varies.

8. Given the equation $Ax^2 + By^2 + C = 0$, what conditions must be satisfied by A, B, and C if this equation represents a hyperbola with transverse axis on the y-axis?

9. Two hyperbolas are called *conjugate hyperbolas* if the transverse axis of one is the conjugate axis of the other.
   a) Give an example of the equations of two conjugate hyperbolas.
   b) If the equation of a hyperbola is given in standard form, how can you find the equation of the conjugate hyperbola?

MATHEMATICS AROUND US

The Shadow of a Sphere

This photograph suggests that the shadow of a sphere is an ellipse. Since the sun is so far away that we can assume its rays are parallel, the rays of light intercepted by the sphere form a cylinder. Hence, we can prove that the shadow of a sphere in sunlight is an ellipse if we can prove that the curve formed when a plane intersects a cylinder is an ellipse.

QUESTIONS

1. A plane intersects a cylinder, forming a closed curve. Two spheres, each of which is tangent to the plane, are inscribed in the cylinder. Let F_1 and F_2 be the points of contact of the spheres and the plane. Let Q_1 and Q_2 be points of contact of the spheres and the cylinder. Let P be any point on the curve. Prove that the curve is an ellipse by showing that $PF_1 + PF_2$ is constant.

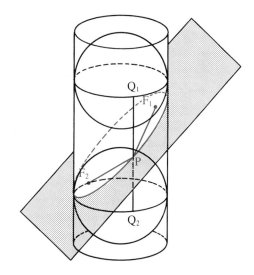

2. Obtain a large ball, such as a basketball, and set it on a level surface in direct sunlight, preferably in the late afternoon when it will cast a long shadow.
   a) Measure the lengths of the major and minor axes of the elliptical shadow as accurately as you can.
   b) Determine the positions of the foci of the ellipse.
   c) Use the result of part a) to determine the angle of elevation of the sun at the time the measurements were taken.

Planes and Cones

"Beautiful and fascinating in their many aspects, [conic sections] offer a rare opportunity to blend analytic and solid geometry, locus, similar triangles, circles and spheres, and so on, into a potpourri of unusual and unexpected results."

Roselyn Teukolsky

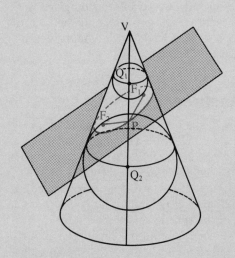

A plane intersects a cone, forming a closed curve. Two spheres, each of which is tangent to the plane, are inscribed in the cone. Let F_1 and F_2 be the points of contact of the spheres and the plane. Then, if P is any point on the curve, prove that $PF_1 + PF_2$ is a constant.

Understand the problem
- What curves are formed by the points of contact of the spheres and the cone?

Think of a strategy and carry it out
- Draw a line on the surface of the cone through P and the vertex V. Let Q_1 and Q_2 be the points on the spheres which lie on this line.
- Compare the lengths of PF_1 and PQ_1. Why are they equal?
- Similarly, why are the lengths of PF_2 and PQ_2 equal?
- Hence, what does $PF_1 + PF_2$ equal?

Look back
- Lines on the cone passing through the vertex are called *generators* of the cone. Why is this name appropriate?
- Use this diagram to prove a similar property for the hyperbola.

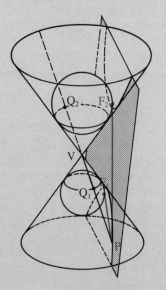

PROBLEMS

Ⓑ

1. a) Find two powers that differ by 11.
   b) Given any odd number, explain how to find two powers that differ by that number.

2. Solve the equation $\dfrac{x+1}{x^2} + \dfrac{x^2}{x+1} = \dfrac{5}{2}$.

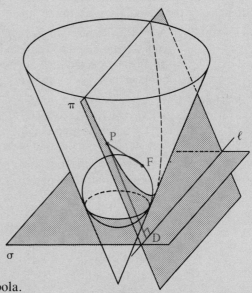

3. A plane π, parallel to a generator of a cone, intersects the cone to form a curve as shown. A sphere, which is tangent to the plane, is inscribed in the cone touching the cone on a circle. This circle lies in a *plane of contact*, σ. The planes π and σ intersect in a line l. Prove that if P is any point on the cone, then PF = PD, where D is the foot of the perpendicular from P to l. Hence, the curve of intersection is a parabola.

Ⓒ

4. Give an example of two triangles, $\triangle$ABC and $\triangle$PQR, in which the three angles of $\triangle$ABC are equal to the three angles of $\triangle$PQR, and two sides of $\triangle$ABC are equal to two sides of $\triangle$PQR, but $\triangle$ABC and $\triangle$PQR are *not* congruent.

5. Prove that the sum of any positive number and its reciprocal is greater than or equal to 2.

6. Sketch the graph of each function.
   a) $y = |x^2 - 6x + 5|$ b) $y = x^2 - |6x| + 5$ c) $y = x^2 - |6x + 5|$

7. An ellipse has centre O(0,0) and one focus F(2,0). If the ellipse also passes through the point S(2,1), determine its equation.

8. An ellipse with centre O(0,0) and foci on the *x*-axis passes through the point P(6,2). If the distance from P to the closest focus is $2\sqrt{2}$, find the equation of the ellipse.

Ⓓ

9. Determine the equation of an ellipse and a hyperbola, with axes parallel to the coordinate axes, which pass through A(3, 1), B(2, 7), and C(-1, 3).

3-10 APPLICATIONS OF QUADRATIC RELATIONS

Quadratic relations have many applications in astronomy, and in construction and design. The problems are usually solved by using the given data to determine an equation of a conic in standard form, and then using the equation to determine some unknown quantity.

Example 1.   A bridge over a river is supported by a parabolic arch which is 40 m wide at water level. The maximum height of the arch is 16 m.
a) Write an equation to represent the arch.
b) How high is the arch at a point 10 m from the centre?

Solution.   a) Use a coordinate system as shown.
Let the equation of the arch be $y = ax^2$. From the given information, and the diagram, the point $M(20, -16)$ is on the parabola. Hence, these coordinates satisfy the equation. Substitute 20 for x and -16 for y in $y = ax^2$.

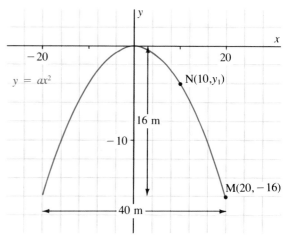

$$-16 = a(20)^2$$
$$-16 = 400a$$
$$a = -\frac{16}{400}$$
$$= -0.04$$

The equation of the parabola is $y = -0.04x^2$.

b) Let $N(10, y_1)$ represent a point on the arch which is 10 m from the centre. Then these coordinates satisfy the equation. Substitute 10 for x and y_1 for y in $y = -0.04x^2$.
$$y_1 = -0.04(10)^2$$
$$= -4$$

A point 10 m from the centre is 4 m below the highest point, and therefore 12 m above the water level. Hence, the arch is 12 m high at a point 10 m from the centre.

In *Example 1* we used the standard form of the equation of a parabola given in the previous section, $y = ax^2$. We could also have used the standard form, $x^2 = 4py$. Both forms are equivalent, because they are derived from the equation $y = x^2$ by multiplying one side of the equation by a constant.

Example 1 was solved using the fundamental property of a locus. That is, the coordinates of every point on the graph of a relation satisfy its equation; and, every point whose coordinates satisfy the equation of a relation is on its graph.

Example 2. The arch of a bridge has the shape of a rectangular hyperbola. The base is 120 m wide, and the vertex is 30 m above the base.
a) Find an equation of the hyperbola.
b) Find the height of the arch at a point 25 m from the centre.

Solution.   a) Let the equation of the hyperbola be
$x^2 - y^2 = -a^2$. The co-ordinates of vertex A_2 are $(0, -a)$. Let P be a point 60 m to the right of A_2 and 30 m below A_2. Hence, the coordinates of P are $(60, -a - 30)$. Since P is on the hyperbola, its coordinates satisfy the equation. Substitute 60 for x and $-a - 30$ for y in $x^2 - y^2 = -a^2$.

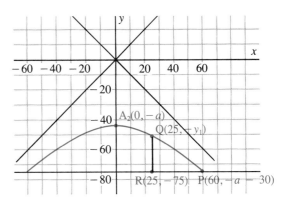

$$3600 - (-a - 30)^2 = -a^2$$
$$3600 - (a^2 + 60a + 900) = -a^2$$
$$a = \frac{2700}{60}$$
$$= 45$$

Hence, the equation of the hyperbola is $x^2 - y^2 = -45^2$, or $x^2 - y^2 = -2025$.

b) Let $Q(25, -y_1)$ represent a point on the arch 25 m from the centre. Then these coordinates satisfy the equation. Substitute 25 for x and $-y_1$ for y.

$$x^2 - y^2 = -2025$$
$$625 - y_1^2 = -2025$$
$$y_1^2 = 2650$$
$$y_1 = \sqrt{2650}$$
$$\doteq 51.5$$

The coordinates of Q are $(25, -51.5)$. From part a), the coordinates of P are $(60, -75)$. Hence, the coordinates of R are $(25, -75)$, and the length of segment QR is $75 - 51.5$, or 23.5. Hence, the arch is 23.5 m high at a point which is 25 m from the centre.

EXERCISES 3-10

Ⓑ

1. The cables of a suspension bridge hang in a curve which approximates a parabola. The road bed passes through the vertex. If the supporting towers are 720 m apart and 60 m high, find:
   a) an equation of the parabola
   b) the height of the cables at a point 30 m from the vertex.

2. A stone thrown horizontally from a bridge 25 m above a river splashes in the water 40 m from the base of the bridge. If the stone falls in a parabolic path, find its equation relative to the position from which it was thrown.

3. The supporting structure for the roof of a curling rink has parabolic arches anchored at ground level. If the arches are 15.3 m high, and span 70 m, find:
   a) an equation of the parabola
   b) the height of the arches at a point 10 m from the centre.

4. A pool has the shape of an ellipse. The major axis has length 10 m and the minor axis has length 6 m.
   a) Write an equation of the ellipse.
   b) Find the width of the pool at a point on the major axis which is 2 m from the centre.

5. A retractable dome on a sports stadium has the shape of an ellipse. Its height is 125 m and it spans 300 m.
   a) Write an equation of the ellipse.
   b) Calculate the height of the dome at a point on the major axis which is 20 m from the centre.

6. A tunnel is built under a river for a road 12 m wide with a 2 m sidewalk on either side. The top of the tunnel is semi-elliptical. A local bylaw stipulates that there must be a clearance of at least 3.6 m at all points on the road. If the smallest possible ellipse is used, find the clearance at the centre of the road.

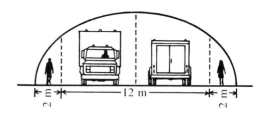

7. A bridge over a river is supported by a hyperbolic arch which is 200 m wide at the base. The maximum height of the arch is 50 m. How high is the arch at a point 30 m from the centre?

Ⓒ

8. The orbit of a satellite is an ellipse with the centre of the Earth on its major axis. One satellite has an orbit with major axis 15 540 km and minor axis 15 490 km. The centre of the orbit is 600 km from the centre of the Earth. The radius of the Earth is 6370 km. Calculate the height of the satellite at:
   a) its lowest point (the *perigee*)   b) its highest point (the *apogee*).

3-11 THE ELLIPSE AND THE HYPERBOLA: CENTRE (h, k)

In the preceding sections the ellipses and the hyperbolas had centres
(0,0). We could use the definitions of these conics to find their equations when their centres are not (0,0), but it is simpler to consider the
effect of adding or subtracting a constant to the variables in the equations.

Compare these two equations.

$$\frac{x^2}{9} + \frac{y^2}{4} = 1 \dots ①$$

$$\frac{(x-5)^2}{9} + \frac{(y+1)^2}{4} = 1 \dots ②$$

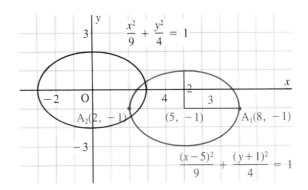

Equation ① represents an ellipse
with centre $(0, 0)$.
For this ellipse, $a = 3$ and $b = 2$
The major axis has length $2a$, or 6.
The minor axis has length $2b$, or 4.
The coordinates of the vertices are $(3, 0)$
and $(-3, 0)$
We can use this information to sketch the
graph of equation ②. Both equation ①
and equation ② state that the sum of two
numbers is 1.
In equation ②, to give the same numbers adding to 1 as in equation
①, the values of x must be 5 *greater* than those in equation ①. Similarly, the values of y must be 1 *less* than those in equation ①. Every
point whose coordinates satisfy equation ② must be 5 units to the *right*
of, and 1 unit *below* the corresponding point whose coordinates satisfy
equation ①. Hence, equation ② represents an ellipse that has been
translated 5 units to the right and 1 unit down relative to the first ellipse.
Therefore, its centre is $(5, -1)$. Since the major axis has length 6,
the coordinates of the vertices are $(5 \pm 3, -1)$; that is, $(8, -1)$ and
$(2, -1)$. The minor axis has length 4, and the coordinates of its endpoints
are $(5, -1 \pm 2)$; that is, $(5, 1)$ and $(5, -3)$.
  Equations ① and ② may be written as follows.
$$4x^2 + 9y^2 = 36 \dots ③$$
and $\qquad 4(x - 5)^2 + 9(y + 1)^2 = 36$
$$4x^2 + 9y^2 - 40x + 18y - 73 = 0 \dots ④$$
Observe that equations ③ and ④ contain the same quadratic terms.
That is, the quadratic terms were not affected by the translation.

  The above analysis can be applied to the equation of any quadratic
relation and its graph.

Translation Property of a Relation

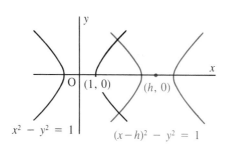

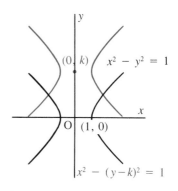

- If x is replaced with $x - h$ in the equation of a relation, the graph is translated h units horizontally.
- If y is replaced with $y - k$ in the equation of a relation, the graph is translated k units vertically.
- These replacements do not change the quadratic terms in the equation.

Example. Given the equation $\dfrac{(x - 3)^2}{25} + \dfrac{(y + 4)^2}{4} = 1$

    a) Identify the conic represented by the equation.

    b) Graph the conic, showing the coordinates of the centre and the coordinates of the vertices.

    c) Determine the coordinates of the foci.

Solution.   a) Since the squared terms are separated by a $+$ sign, the equation represents an ellipse.

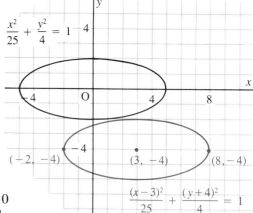

    b) The graph is translated 3 units to the right and 4 units down relative to the graph of the ellipse defined by $\dfrac{x^2}{25} + \dfrac{y^2}{4} = 1$.

    For this ellipse,

$$a^2 = 25, \text{ so } a = 5$$

and $b^2 = 4$, so $b = 2$

Length of major axis: $2a$, or 10

Length of minor axis: $2b$, or 4

Centre: $(3, -4)$

Vertices: $(3 + 5, -4)$ or $(8, -4)$ and $(3 - 5, -4)$ or $(-2, -4)$

    c) For an ellipse,

$$c^2 = a^2 - b^2$$
$$= 25 - 4, \text{ or } 21$$
$$c = \sqrt{21}$$

Foci: $(3 + \sqrt{21}, -4)$ and $(3 - \sqrt{21}, -4)$

In the *Example*, observe how the graph helps us determine the coordinates of the vertices and foci. First, note that the major axis is horizontal. This means that the vertices and foci are on the same horizontal line as the centre. Hence, to find the vertices we add and subtract a to the x-coordinate of the centre. To find the foci, add and subtract c to the x-coordinate of the centre.

Similar methods apply for ellipses with foci on the y-axis, and for hyperbolas.

The equation in the above example was written in standard form.

Equations of Ellipses and Hyperbolas in Standard Form, Centre (h, k)

Ellipse with centre (h,k)

Major axis horizontal

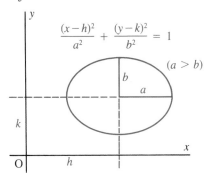

$$\frac{(x-h)^2}{a^2} + \frac{(y-k)^2}{b^2} = 1$$

$$(a > b)$$

Major axis vertical

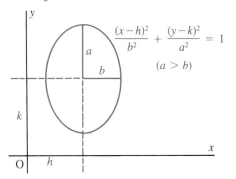

$$\frac{(x-h)^2}{b^2} + \frac{(y-k)^2}{a^2} = 1$$

$$(a > b)$$

Hyperbola with centre (h,k)

Transverse axis horizontal

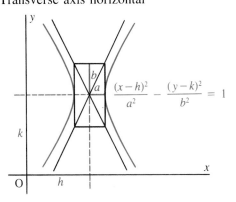

$$\frac{(x-h)^2}{a^2} - \frac{(y-k)^2}{b^2} = 1$$

Transverse axis vertical

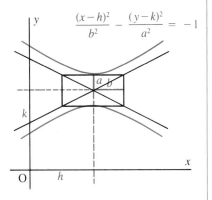

$$\frac{(x-h)^2}{b^2} - \frac{(y-k)^2}{a^2} = -1$$

EXERCISES 3-11

Ⓐ

1. Write an equation to represent each conic.

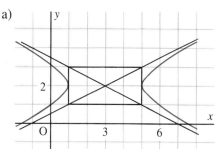

a)

b)

Ⓑ

2. Identify the conic represented by each equation. Graph the conic, showing the coordinates of the centre and the coordinates of the vertices. Determine the coordinates of the foci.

a) $\dfrac{(x-2)^2}{16} + \dfrac{(y+3)^2}{49} = 1$

b) $\dfrac{(x+5)^2}{16} + \dfrac{(y-3)^2}{4} = 1$

c) $\dfrac{(x-4)^2}{9} - \dfrac{(y+6)^2}{4} = 1$

d) $\dfrac{(x-2)^2}{9} - \dfrac{y^2}{25} = 1$

e) $\dfrac{(x+3)^2}{18} + \dfrac{(y+3)^2}{9} = 1$

f) $\dfrac{(x-5)^2}{36} - \dfrac{(y-1)^2}{9} = -1$

3. Identify the conic represented by each equation. Graph the conic, showing the coordinates of the centre and the coordinates of the vertices. Determine the coordinates of the foci.

a) $4(x-3)^2 + 9(y-2)^2 = 36$

b) $4(x+1)^2 - (y-3)^2 = 16$

c) $(x+5)^2 - 4(y+4)^2 = -36$

d) $3(x-2)^2 + 4(y+2)^2 = 24$

e) $3x^2 - (y-2)^2 = 27$

f) $(x+5)^2 + 6y^2 = 36$

 INVESTIGATE

Degenerate Conics

1. In Section 3-2, diagrams were shown illustrating four ways in which a plane can intersect a cone. In what other ways can a plane intersect a cone?

2. *Question 1* suggests that a second-degree equation in *x* and *y* may have a graph which is not a circle, ellipse, parabola, or hyperbola. What other possible graphs are there? Write an example of an equation to represent each possibility.

3-12 WRITING EQUATIONS IN STANDARD FORM

When the equation of a quadratic relation is written in standard form, the numbers in the equation indicate certain properties of its graph. For example, we can tell that the equation

$$\frac{(x-2)^2}{9} + \frac{(y-1)^2}{16} = 1$$

represents an ellipse with these properties.

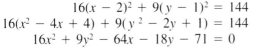

Centre: $(2, 1)$
Length of major axis: $2a$, or 8
Length of minor axis: $2b$, or 6
The major axis is vertical.
Vertices: $(2, 1 + 4)$, or $(2, 5)$
    and $(2, 1 - 4)$, or $(2, -3)$
For an ellipse, $c^2 = a^2 - b^2$
        $= 16 - 9$, or 7
        $c = \sqrt{7}$
Foci: $(2, 1 + \sqrt{7})$ and $(2, 1 - \sqrt{7})$

The above equation can also be written as follows.
$$16(x - 2)^2 + 9(y - 1)^2 = 144$$
$$16(x^2 - 4x + 4) + 9(y^2 - 2y + 1) = 144$$
$$16x^2 + 9y^2 - 64x - 18y - 71 = 0$$

This form of writing the equation is called the *general form*. When an equation is written in general form we cannot read the properties of the graph from the equation. To determine the properties we must first write the equation in standard form.

Example 1. Given the conic defined by $4x^2 - 9y^2 + 32x + 18y + 91 = 0$
    a) Write the equation in standard form.
    b) Describe and sketch the graph of the conic.

Solution. a) We collect the terms containing x, and the terms containing y.
$$4x^2 - 9y^2 + 32x + 18y + 91 = 0$$
$$4x^2 + 32x - 9y^2 + 18y + 91 = 0$$
$$4(x^2 + 8x) - 9(y^2 - 2y) + 91 = 0$$
Complete each square.
$$4(x^2 + 8x + 16 - 16) - 9(y^2 - 2y + 1 - 1) + 91 = 0$$
$$4(x + 4)^2 - 64 - 9(y - 1)^2 + 9 + 91 = 0$$
$$4(x + 4)^2 - 9(y - 1)^2 = -36$$
$$\frac{(x + 4)^2}{9} - \frac{(y - 1)^2}{4} = -1$$

b) The equation represents a
hyperbola.
Centre: $(-4, 1)$
Length of transverse axis:
$2a$, or 4
Length of conjugate axis:
$2b$, or 6
The transverse axis is
vertical.
Vertices:
$(-4, 1 + 2)$, or $(-4, 3)$;
$(-4, 1 - 2)$, or $(-4, -1)$

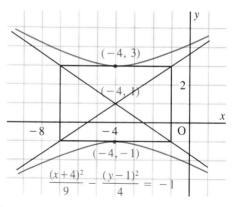

For a hyperbola, $c^2 = a^2 + b^2$
$$= 4 + 9, \text{ or } 13$$
$$c = \sqrt{13}$$
Foci: $(-4, 1 + \sqrt{13})$ and $(-4, 1 - \sqrt{13})$

In *Example 1* we could have predicted that the given equation
represents a hyperbola since the quadratic terms are separated by a −
sign.
Equations that represent a parabola contain only one squared term;
hence, only one square can be completed.

Example 2.   Given the conic defined by $x^2 + 10x + 4y + 13 = 0$
a) Write the equation in standard form.
b) Describe and sketch the graph of the conic.

Solution.   a) $x^2 + 10x + 4y + 13 = 0$
$$x^2 + 10x + 25 - 25 + 4y + 13 = 0$$
$$(x + 5)^2 + 4y - 12 = 0$$
$$4(y - 3) = -(x + 5)^2$$
$$y - 3 = -\left(\frac{x + 5}{2}\right)^2$$

b) The equation represents a parabola.
Vertex: $(-5, 3)$
Direction of opening: down
Axis: $x = -5$

Congruent to $y = \frac{1}{4}x^2$

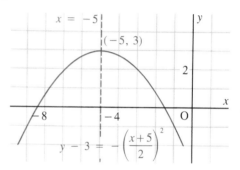

The equations in the above examples are examples of the general equation $Ax^2 + By^2 + 2Gx + 2Fy + C = 0$. Such an equation does not always have a graph. For example, if $A = 3$, $B = 2$, $C = 1$, and $G = F = 0$, the equation becomes $3x^2 + 2y^2 + 1 = 0$ which is not satisfied by any values of x and y since the left side is always greater than or equal to 1. When the graph of the general equation exists, it is a conic with its axes (or axis) parallel to the coordinate axes. The nature of the conic depends only on the quadratic terms, $Ax^2 + By^2$.

Properties of the Equation $Ax^2 + By^2 + 2Gx + 2Fy + C = 0$
We assume that A and B are not both 0.
● If the graph of this equation exists, it is a conic.
● The axes (or axis) of the conic are parallel to the coordinate axes.
● If $AB > 0$, the conic is an ellipse (a circle if $A = B$).
  If $AB < 0$, the conic is a hyperbola.
  If $A = 0$ or $B = 0$, the conic is a parabola.

EXERCISES 3-12

1. Write each equation in general form.
   a) $3(x - 1)^2 + (y + 2)^2 = 9$
   b) $(x + 5)^2 - 2(y - 1)^2 = 10$
   c) $y - 2 = 3(x - 4)^2$
   d) $\dfrac{(x + 2)^2}{9} + \dfrac{(y - 3)^2}{4} = 1$
   e) $\dfrac{(x + 1)^2}{6} - \dfrac{(y + 2)^2}{3} = -1$
   f) $x + 4 = -2(y - 3)^2$

2. Each equation represents a conic. State which represents each conic.
   i) a circle   ii) an ellipse   iii) a hyperbola   iv) a parabola
      a) $9x^2 + 4y^2 - 54x + 16y + 61 = 0$
      b) $2x^2 - 3y^2 - 8x - 6y + 11 = 0$
      c) $y^2 - 4x + 6y - 23 = 0$
      d) $x^2 + y^2 + 4x + 5y = 0$

Ⓑ

3. Given the conic defined by each equation, write the equation in standard form, and then sketch the conic.
   a) $2x^2 + y^2 + 12x - 2y + 15 = 0$
   b) $4x^2 + 9y^2 - 8x + 36y + 4 = 0$
   c) $x^2 - 9y^2 - 4x + 18y - 14 = 0$
   d) $x^2 - 4y^2 - 2x - 3 = 0$
   e) $y^2 - 4x + 8y + 3 = 0$
   f) $x^2 + 2x + 3y + 4 = 0$

4. Describe the graph of each equation.
   a) $x^2 + y^2 - 8x + 6y + 9 = 0$
   b) $x^2 + 4y^2 - 2x + 16y + 13 = 0$
   c) $3x^2 + 4y^2 + 18x - 16y + 31 = 0$
   d) $3x^2 - 2y^2 - 36x + 96 = 0$
   e) $y^2 - 8x - 8y = 0$
   f) $6x^2 + 24x - y + 19 = 0$

5. The diagram shows three overlapping squares.
   a) If the colored region has the same area as the shaded square, what is the relation between x and y?
   b) Graph the relation between x and y.

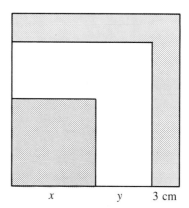

x y 3 cm

6. Find the equation of the locus of a point P which moves such that it is equidistant from the point F(3, 2) and the line defined by $y = 6$.

Ⓒ

7. Find the equation of the locus of a point P which moves such that the sum of its distances from (0, 3) and (8, 3) is 10.

8. Describe the graph of each equation.
   a) $3x^2 + 2y^2 - 6x + 16y + 35 = 0$
   b) $2x^2 + y^2 - 12x - 8y + 36 = 0$
   c) $4x^2 - y^2 + 16x - 4y + 12 = 0$
   d) $x^2 + 2xy + y^2 + 2x + 2y + 1 = 0$

3-13 THE GENERAL QUADRATIC EQUATION IN *x* AND *y*

Up to now in this chapter we have encountered quadratic relations with defining equations such as $4x^2 + 9y^2 = 36$ and $x^2 + 10x + 4y + 13 = 0$, which contain terms in x^2 and/or y^2. Furthermore, the axes of the conics have always been parallel to the coordinate axes.

Observe that none of the equations considered so far has contained an xy term. A conic whose defining equation contains an xy term has axes which are inclined to the coordinate axes. A study of its properties involves trigonometry, and requires an analysis of the effect on the equation of a relation when its graph is rotated about the origin through an angle θ, which is beyond the scope of this book. Hence, in this section, we will simply state some of the results and verify them in particular examples.

A simple example of an equation with an xy term is $xy - 4 = 0$. Three points on the graph of this equation are $(2, 2)$, $(4, 1)$, and $(1, 4)$. As x increases beyond 4, y decreases and becomes closer and closer to 0. Similarly, as y increases beyond 4, x decreases and becomes closer and closer to 0. A similar situation occurs when x and y are both negative. Hence, we can sketch the graph as shown. The graph is a rectangular hyperbola with centre $(0, 0)$ and vertices $(2, 2)$ and $(-2, -2)$. The asymptotes are the x- and y-axes. The line $y = x$ contains the transverse axis, and the line $y = -x$ contains the conjugate axis.

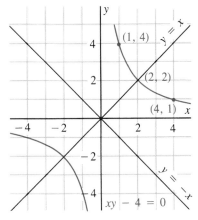

This example suggests that an xy term occurs in the equation of a quadratic relation when the graph is rotated such that the axes (or axis) of the conic are inclined to the coordinate axes. We can verify this in an example such as the following.

Example 1. Find the equation of the locus of a point P which moves such that it is always the same distance from the point F(5,1) as it is from the line defined by $y = x$.

Solution. Let P(x, y) be any point on the locus, and let D be the foot of the perpendicular from P to the line $y = x$. To obtain an expression for the length of PD, let N be the point on the line $y = x$ such that PN is parallel to the x-axis.

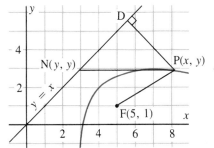

Then $\triangle$PDN is an isosceles right triangle,
and, PN $= \sqrt{2}$ PD,

or, PD $= \dfrac{PN}{\sqrt{2}}$

Since P is any point on the locus,

$$PF = PD$$

$$PF = \dfrac{PN}{\sqrt{2}}$$

$$\sqrt{(x-5)^2 + (y-1)^2} = \dfrac{\sqrt{(x-y)^2 + 0^2}}{\sqrt{2}}$$

Square both sides.

$$x^2 - 10x + 25 + y^2 - 2y + 1 = \dfrac{x^2 - 2xy + y^2}{2}$$

This equation simplifies to $x^2 + 2xy + y^2 - 20x - 4y + 52 = 0$, which is the equation of the locus.

In *Example 1*, the equation $x^2 + 2xy + y^2 - 20x - 4y + 52 = 0$ represents a parabola. Its axis of symmetry is the line through $(5, 1)$ with slope -1. Its equation is $y - 1 = -1(x - 5)$, or $x + y - 6 = 0$. This result provides further evidence that an xy term is introduced when a conic is rotated such that its axes (or axis) are inclined to the coordinate axes. We will assume that this property is true for all quadratic relations, without proof.

The equation in *Example 1* has the form $Ax^2 + 2Hxy + By^2 + 2Gx + 2Fy + C = 0$. This equation is called the *general quadratic equation in x and y*. Such an equation does not always have a graph, but when it does, the nature of the graph depends only on the quadratic terms $Ax^2 + 2Hxy + By^2$. In particular, it depends on the value of the expression $AB - H^2$. The table below gives the value of this expression for the examples in this section and in *Section 3-12*.

Equation	Conic	Value of $AB - H^2$
$16x^2 + 9y^2 - 64x - 18y - 71 = 0$	ellipse	$(16)(9) - 0^2 = 144$
$4x^2 - 9y^2 + 32x + 18y + 91 = 0$	hyperbola	$(4)(-9) - 0^2 = -36$
$x^2 + 10x + 4y + 13 = 0$	parabola	$(1)(0) - 0^2 = 0$
$xy = 0$	hyperbola	$(0)(0) - \left(\frac{1}{2}\right)^2 = -\frac{1}{4}$
$x^2 + 2xy + y^2 - 20x - 4y + 52 = 0$	parabola	$(1)(1) - 1^2 = 0$

Observe that, in these examples, the value of $AB - H^2$ is positive for the ellipse, negative for the hyperbolas, and 0 for the parabolas. This property is true in general.

Properties of the Equation $Ax^2 + 2Hxy + By^2 + 2Gx + 2Fy + C = 0$
We assume that A, B, and C are not all 0.
- If the graph of this equation exists, it is a conic.
- If $H = 0$, the axes (or axis) of the conic are parallel to the coordinate axes.
- If $H \neq 0$, the axes (or axis) are not parallel to the coordinate axes.
- If $AB - H^2 > 0$, the conic is an ellipse.
  If $AB - H^2 < 0$, the conic is a hyperbola.
  If $AB - H^2 = 0$, the conic is a parabola.

EXERCISES 3-13

1. Only one of these equations represents a conic with axes parallel to the coordinate axes. Which equation is this?
   $x^2 - 2xy + y^2 - 6x - 14y + 19 = 0$
   $xy + 2x - 2y + 4 = 0$
   $3x^2 + 2y^2 - 6x + 8y - 1 = 0$
   $3x^2 - 4xy + 16x - 8y + 16 = 0$

2. Only one of these equations represents an ellipse. Which equation is this?
   $7x^2 + 6xy - y^2 - 54x - 14y + 63 = 0$
   $x^2 - 6xy + 9y^2 + 130x + 10y - 575 = 0$
   $4xy + 3y^2 - 8x - 16y + 4 = 0$
   $5x^2 - 4xy + 8y^2 + 2x - 44y + 29 = 0$

3. State which equations could represent each conic.
   i) an ellipse   ii) a hyperbola   iii) a parabola
      a) $9x^2 - 24xy + 16y^2 - 125y + 355 = 0$
      b) $8x^2 + 12xy + 17y^2 - 4x + 22y - 7 = 0$
      c) $x^2 - 16xy - 11y^2 + 135 = 0$
      d) $4x^2 - 36xy + 31y^2 + 28x - 26y - 21 = 0$
      e) $16x^2 + 24xy + 9y^2 - 120x + 160y + 600 = 0$
      f) $41x^2 + 4xy + 44y^2 - 720 = 0$

4. Describe and sketch the graph of each relation.
   a) $xy - 6 = 0$ b) $xy + 6 = 0$
   c) $(x - 4)(y + 3) - 6 = 0$ d) $xy - 3x + 4y - 18 = 0$

5. Find the equation of the locus of a point P which moves such that it is always the same distance from the point F(3,0) as it is from the line defined by $y = x + 5$.

6. The diagram shows three overlapping
squares. The smallest square has sides of
length 5 cm. If the colored region has the
same area as the shaded region, what is the
relation between *x* and *y*?

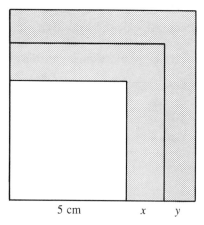

5 cm   *x*   *y*

7. The general quadratic equation can be written as
$Ax^2 + Bxy + Cy^2 + Dx + Ey + F = 0$.
a) In this form, what expression would be used to test if the equation represents
an ellipse, a hyperbola, or a parabola?
b) Discuss the advantages and disadvantages of the two forms of the general
quadratic equation.

8. Find the equation of the locus of a point which moves such that:
a) the sum of its distances from $(1, 1)$ and $(-1, -1)$ is 4
b) the sum of its distances from $(0, 0)$ and $(2, 2)$ is 4.

9. Given any conic with equation $Ax^2 + 2Hxy + By^2 + 2Gx + 2Fy + C = 0$,
prove that the quadratic terms $Ax^2 + 2Hxy + By^2$ do not change if the graph of
the conic is translated.

10. If the graph of a circle was rotated, would an xy term be introduced in its equation?
Explain.

11. Given the equation $Ax^2 + 2Hxy + By^2 + 2Gx + 2Fy + C = 0$, what conditions
must be satisfied if this equation represents:
a) a circle
b) an ellipse with major axis on: i) the x-axis   ii) the y-axis
c) a hyperbola with transverse axis on: i) the x-axis   ii) the y-axis
d) a parabola with: i) a horizontal axis   ii) a vertical axis?

1. Find the equation of the locus of a point P which moves according to each condition. Identify the locus and sketch its graph.
    a) P is always 3 units from $Q(-2,1)$.
    b) The slope of the segment from P to $S(5, -3)$ is $-\frac{3}{4}$.

    c) P is the same distance from $F(3,2)$ as it is from the line $y = -2$.
    d) P is the same distance from $A(2, -5)$ as it is from $B(-6,1)$.

2. Graph each relation and identify the curve.
    a) $\dfrac{x^2}{16} + \dfrac{y^2}{9} = 1$ b) $x^2 = 4y$ c) $x^2 + y^2 = 25$
    d) $x^2 - y^2 = 9$ e) $4x^2 + 4y^2 = 49$ f) $9x^2 - 16y^2 = -144$

3. Determine if the given point is on the given conic. Identify the conic.
    a) $(-2, -20)$; $y = 5x^2$ b) $(-4,7)$; $x^2 + y^2 = 65$
    c) $(-7,2)$; $\dfrac{x^2}{25} - \dfrac{y^2}{4} = 1$ d) $(2, -\sqrt{2})$; $4x^2 + 9y^2 = 36$

4. Find the coordinates of the centre, and the radius of each circle.
    a) $4x^2 + 4y^2 = 25$ b) $x^2 + y^2 - 4x + 6y - 12 = 0$

5. Find the equation of a parabola with vertex $(0,0)$ and axis of symmetry the y-axis if it passes through: a) $(4,2)$ b) $(-4, -24)$.

6. An ellipse has centre $(0,0)$ and major axis on the y-axis. Write the equation of the ellipse if:
    a) the x- and y-intercepts are ± 3 and ± 5 respectively
    b) the major axis is 12 units and the minor axis is 6 units.

7. Find the equation of the hyperbola, centre $(0,0)$, conjugate axis on the y-axis, and:
    a) vertices at $(\pm 4,0)$, and an asymptote defined by $y = 2x$
    b) a transverse axis of 8 units, and a conjugate axis of 14 units.

8. A stone thrown horizontally from a bridge 25 m above the river splashes in the water 40 m from the base of the bridge. If the stone falls in a parabolic path, find its equation.

9. One of the supports in a retractable roof of a sports complex is semi-elliptical. If it is 25 m high and spans 60 m, find its equation.

10. The base of a bridge arch is 80 m wide and 25 m high. Find its equation if the arch is in the shape of a rectangular hyperbola.

11. State what conic each equation could represent.
    a) $x^2 + y^2 + 4x - 10y - 20 = 0$ b) $9x^2 + 16y^2 - 18x + 96y + 9 = 0$
    c) $y^2 - 4y - 6x = 38$ d) $5x^2 - 4y^2 - 30x - 16y + 49 = 0$

Cumulative Review, Chapters 1-3

1. Graph each function. State its domain and range.
   a) $3x - 4y = 12$
   b) $y = 2(x - 3)^2 + 5$
   c) $y = \dfrac{2x - 1}{x}$

2. If $f(x) = 3x - 2$ and $g(x) = x^2 + 3x - 1$, find:
   a) $f(5)$
   b) $g(-2)$
   c) $f(4a)$
   d) $f(x^2 - 1)$
   e) $g(2x - 1)$
   f) $f(g(x))$.

3. Graph each function and its inverse on the same grid. State the domain and range of the inverse. Is the inverse a function?
   a) $f(x) = \dfrac{6 - 3x}{2}$
   b) $g(x) = \dfrac{3x + 2}{x}, \; x \neq 0$

4. Determine the nature of the roots of each equation.
   a) $2x^2 + 7x - 5 = 0$
   b) $4x^2 - 3x + 2 = 0$
   c) $16x^2 - 24x + 9 = 0$

5. Solve each equation.
   a) $x^2 - 5x - 8 = 0$
   b) $2x^2 + 3x + 4 = 0$
   c) $2.5x^2 + 2x - 4.5 = 0$

6. Solve graphically.
   a) $x^2 + 2x - 5 = 0$
   b) $2x^3 + 2x = 0$

7. If $x - 3$ is a factor of each polynomial, find the other factors.
   a) $x^3 - 6x^2 - x + 30$
   b) $4x^3 - x - 12x^2 + 3$
   c) $x^4 - x^3 - 7x^2 + x + 6$

8. Which polynomials have $x + 2$ as a factor? If $x + 2$ is not a factor, find the remainder when the polynomial is divided by $x + 2$.
   a) $x^4 - x^3 - 5x^2 + 7x + 10$
   b) $2x^4 + 4x^3 - x^2 + 2x + 6$

9. Factor completely.
   a) $x^3 + 7x^2 + 7x - 15 = 0$
   b) $x^4 + 2x^3 - 7x^2 - 8x + 12 = 0$

10. List the possible rational roots of each equation.
    a) $x^3 - 5x^2 + 7x - 12 = 0$
    b) $2x^3 - 9x + 3 = 0$

11. Solve each inequality.
    a) $(x + 2)(x + 3)(x - 1) < 0$
    b) $(x^2 - 1)(x^2 - x - 6) \geq 0$

12. Identify the locus of each point P and sketch its graph.
    a) P is the same distance from $A(-3, -5)$ as it is from $B(2,3)$.
    b) P is always 4 units from $Q(-2, -3)$.

13. Find the equation of an ellipse with major axis on the x-axis if:
    a) the x- and y-intercepts are ± 4 and ± 1 respectively
    b) the semi-major axis is 6 units and the minor axis is 8 units.

14. A rectangular hyperbola with centre $O(0,0)$ and vertices on the y-axis passes through $P(-6,8)$. Find the equation of the hyperbola.

4 Analysing Survey Data

John Chan runs a successful restaurant, which is open
for lunch and dinner. He has noticed that more people
seem to be going out for breakfast and wonders
if it would be profitable to open his restaurant for
breakfast. He asks his son Ken to help him find out
how many people in the town eat breakfast out at least
once a week. (See Section 4-7 *Example 1* and Exercises
4-8 *Exercise 10*.)

4-1 OPINION SURVEYS

Hardly a day goes by without someone using data collected from a survey. Every time you listen to the "Top 20" Hit Parade, you are using survey data. The Government relies heavily on survey data for the information needed in the day-to-day running of the country. Whenever you ask someone if he or she liked a particular movie, you are conducting an informal survey. If enough of your friends say that they enjoyed the movie, you might decide to see it yourself.

All over the country, people use survey data to help them make better decisions. The cost of making a bad decision is often great. So decision makers try to gather as much information as possible before deciding on a course of action. It is rarely possible to ask an opinion of the entire population, so they ask a sample of the population. It is surprising that with a sample of about 1000 people we can usually estimate, to within 3 or 4 percent, the information we would have got if we had asked everyone.

We use survey sampling in many areas that affect us all. When you read consumer reports on the latest cars, you are looking at information compiled from the opinions of several reviewers. When looking for a job in another part of the country, you might look at the unemployment figures for different provinces. Statistics Canada uses survey methods to collect this data.

The most visible of all opinion surveys are those published before an election. Professional survey companies charge large amounts to conduct a national survey for political parties. We read and listen to their reports in the press and on radio and television.

Many surveys are conducted to find out what Canadians think about environmental problems. On the next page is part of a report on one survey, published in the Toronto Star in August 1988.

Notice the statement describing the accuracy of this survey. Until 4 or 5 years ago, it was unusual to find such a statement in a survey report. Even now, not many people who read such a statement would understand what it means. By the end of this chapter you will have a better understanding of this statement, and other parts of the report. You will learn much more about the background of opinion surveys:
- How it is possible to achieve errors as low as 4% in a sample of 100 people
- The importance of finding a correct method of selecting the sample
- The ways in which data from surveys can be misinterpreted
- The difficulties that pollsters meet when conducting a survey

Most willing to pay for safe environment

Seventy-seven per cent of Canadians would pay 10 per cent more for a product if it were labelled environmentally safe, according to a poll released today.

And 56 per cent would pay a two-cent tax on a litre of milk or gasoline to help improve the environment, the poll says.

The Angus Reid poll, done exclusively for The Star and Southam News, shows the majority of Canadians are willing to pay to protect the environment because they don't think governments are doing enough.

Eighty-four per cent said they think "governments here in Canada should be doing more," compared with 14 per cent who felt governments are doing enough.

The poll said results suggest significant public despair over attention to the environment.

Sixty-five per cent said the environment "will have to become a bigger problem before enough attention is paid to improve it."

Atlantic Canadians were the strongest advocates of a special tax for the environment, with 66 per cent in favor. Quebec residents were 59 per cent in favor, while support in Ontario was 53 per cent.

A total of 1,501 Canadians were interviewed by telephone between July 25-30.

A sample this size is considered accurate to within 2.5 percentage points 19 times out of 20.

First, it is important to look at reports of survey data. When you work through the Exercises that follow, you will compile a collection of newspaper articles that report survey data. In this way you will see the wide range of subjects that appear in opinion polls.

EXERCISES 4-1

1. Read several magazines and newspapers to find at least 5 articles describing surveys. Look for surveys in which the answers to the questions are YES or NO. Cut out each article, and if possible, paste it on a single piece of paper. Leave room to write your own comments. You will need these cuttings to answer more questions in the Exercises later in the chapter.

2. Make a list of 5 common examples of the use of survey information.

3. Obtain information from Statistics Canada on the monthly unemployment data; in particular, how the data are collected and what the accuracy is.

4. The majority of workers in North America work in what is loosely called the "information industry". Thirty years ago, most workers worked in manufacturing or resource industries. The Neilsen TV ratings is one example of a branch of the information industry which uses survey data on a regular basis. Give 9 more examples of branches of the information industry which routinely use survey data.

4-2 ANSWERING YES AND NO

In this chapter we shall look at survey data collected from YES-NO populations. In a YES-NO population, every member of that population answers a question with a YES or a NO. For example, the answer to the question, "Have you bought a Led Zeppelin record this month?" is either YES or NO. The question, "How many Led Zeppelin records have you bought this year?" is not a YES-NO question.

Sometimes we have to reword a question to make it into a YES-NO question. Here is a question from a survey conducted by a student at A.Y. Jackson Secondary School.

Which of the following best describes your reaction to the statement "I prefer to be taught rather than work independently"?
Strongly Agree ☐   Agree ☐   Don't know ☐   Disagree ☐
Strongly Disagree ☐

We could turn this into a YES-NO question by asking, "Did you respond by answering Agree or Strongly Agree?"

If we could ask every member of a YES-NO population, we would be able to discover the percentage of the population who answered YES to the question. If we found that 70% of the population answered YES, we would call this a 70% YES population.

The main idea of this chapter is that by examining data from samples, it is possible to estimate the percentage of yesses that we would have got by taking a census of the population.

The word *census* indicates the process of asking questions of every member of a population.

EXERCISES 4-2

Ⓐ

1. Explain in your own words the meaning of each term.
   a) sample   b) population   c) census   d) YES-NO population

2. In a survey, students in schools in Nanaimo, North Vancouver, and Chicago answered the following questions. If the students answered a YES-NO question, they are a sample of a YES-NO population. Which questions are YES-NO questions?
   a) What is your sex?   MALE/FEMALE
   b) How much do you spend on a date?
   c) Do you play a sport at least once a week?
   d) Do you have a driver's licence?
   e) How many cigarettes do you smoke per day?
   f) How many classes did you miss last week?

Ⓑ

3. Some questions in *Exercise 2* did not give YES-NO answers. Rewrite these questions so the answer is either YES or NO.

4. For each question that you constructed in *Exercise 3*, complete this sentence. "Using sampling methods, we would be able to estimate the percentage of . . ."

5. You want to survey students in your school to compare the drinking and smoking habits of males and females. Make a list of at least ten YES-NO questions that you might use in such a survey. Include questions on other factors related to students' smoking and drinking habits.

6. a) You have been asked to conduct a survey of residents of your school district concerning their opinions of the public and the private school systems. Make a list of 5 YES-NO questions which might be included in that survey.
   b) Do you think that YES-NO questions are the most appropriate to use in this kind of survey? Give reasons.

4-3 SAMPLES FROM YES-NO POPULATIONS

Our first task is to examine the data we get when we take samples from different populations. We will first look at samples from a 30% YES population.

There are many methods of collecting data on samples from a YES-NO population. We will use a method called *simulation*. To use simulation you will need a table of random digits. In the table on the next page the digits are in groups of 10. Each set of 20 digits represents a sample (size 20) from the population. In the experiment that follows, we will examine 40 samples.

Experiment. Collect 40 samples from a 30% YES population and analyse the results.

Step 1. Make a simulation model.

Each digit in a set of 20 represents a YES or a NO response. For a 30% YES population of digits, we need to choose 3 out of the 10 digits to represent the YES responses. In this case we will choose 1, 2, and 3 to represent the YES responses.

Step 2. Examine the samples.

We obtain the first sample from the first 20 digits in the table.
0659301470 7606649757
This set of 20 digits has two digits, 3 and 1, that represent YES responses. Hence, there are 2 YES responses in this sample.
The second sample 4029900091 5932309464 has 5 YES responses.
We repeat this for the remaining 38 samples.

Random-Digits Table

0659301470	7606649757	0349412385	1580473432
4029900091	5932309464	5955365408	1956618065
0539182950	4961840104	0194593086	2424236952
2215677723	9111180265	3934125583	9082929291
8195811617	6882605939	5927541175	5304794871
8319152521	0595533326	4948984027	1986989903
6111653546	7318169616	1980660628	1201486415
2303088164	2591251198	6082088660	8202845547
6021492141	1346436374	4650446649	2154994865
4974066112	7545165189	6710437842	9217985540
0001932034	8935386532	1902625141	6760258469
5723443903	7940084443	6053474525	8331891205
9637255305	1391403573	6149597660	7281714750
4006907454	0232381400	9231691541	3073046926
4803956090	3584948088	0130667625	4017492891
8854547729	7644801864	2827640643	1544473800
4450033269	1406588780	7014203762	9585762244
8151052159	6091785491	7791529740	4476766259
9637374112	8827867727	5799998684	9064825570
3953699445	0172177846	2345891590	3634248640

Step 3. Make a table to collect the data.

We record the data from each sample using tally marks. Then we can add the tally marks to get the frequency of each kind of sample.

Number of yesses in the sample	Tally	Frequency	Total number of yesses
0		0	0
1	l	1	1
2	llll	4	8
3	llll	4	12
4	ll	2	8
5	∦∦ llll	9	45
6	∦∦ ll	7	42
7	lll	3	21
8	∦∦	5	40
9	lll	3	27
10	ll	2	20
11		0	0
•		•	•
•		•	•
•		•	•
20		0	0
	Total		224

Step 4. Analyse the results.

The samples cluster around 5 or 6 YES responses. This means that these samples occurred most often and that the rest of the samples occur on both sides of these samples. Notice, however, that even though the population had 30% YES responses, $\frac{6}{20}$ was not the sample that occurred most frequently.

We examined a total of 800 digits. Of these digits, 224 represented yesses. Hence, $\frac{224}{800}$, or 28% of the 800 digits represented yesses. This is quite close to the percentage (30%) of yesses in this population.

EXERCISES 4-3

1. The table of random digits has 40 columns with 20 digits in each column. Use each column of digits to represent a sample of size 20 from a 30% YES population. Follow the steps above to make a frequency table showing the distribution of samples from a 30% YES population. Comment on the results.

2. Work in groups of 3 or 4. Use the random-digits table on page 188 to collect data on 100 samples (size 20) for YES-NO populations. Each group should work with one of these YES percentages: 10%, 20%, 30%, ..., 80%, 90%. Repeat the experiment preceding this exercise, using 100 samples. Make a frequency table for each population. Keep these data for use in Exercises 3 and 4.

3. In constructing the frequency tables in *Exercise 2*, you examined 100 samples each of which contained 20 responses. Calculate the total number of YES responses in the 100 samples, and find the percentage of YES responses in the 2000 responses.

4. In *Exercise 3*, would you expect the percentage of yesses in the sample to be exactly the same as the percentage of yesses in your population? If not, why not?

COMPUTER POWER

Generating Data from a YES-NO Population

In the previous section, you used simulation to collect data from different YES-NO populations. The power of the computer makes this an ideal computer application. The following program provides data for samples from a YES-NO population.

You will be asked to enter the size of the sample (maximum 100), the percentage of yesses in the population and the number of samples. The program will display a frequency table of the sample data. The table also shows the likely and unlikely samples (see Section 4-4).

```
VAR
            F : ARRAY[0..101] OF REAL;
            LF : ARRAY[0..101] OF REAL;
            UF : ARRAY[0..101] OF REAL;
            I,SAM,NS,N,S,YE : INTEGER;
            WH,P,R: REAL;
            CH : CHAR;
BEGIN          { GENERATE 100 SAMPLES FROM YES-NO POPULATION }
            CLRSCR;
            WRITE("WHAT IS THE PERCENTAGE OF YESSES IN THE
            POPULATION?");
            READ(P);
            WRITE("WHAT IS THE SIZE OF THE SAMPLE?");
            READ(S);
            WRITE("HOW MANY SAMPLES DO YOU WANT?");
            READ(NS);
            RANDOMIZE;
            FOR I:=0 TO 101 DO BEGIN
                F[I] := 0; LF[I] := 0; UF[I] : = 0;
            END;
            IF(P < 0) THEN P : = 1;
            IF(P > 100) THEN P := 99;
            P := P / 100;
            IF(S < 10) THEN S := 10;
            IF(S > 100) THEN S := 100;
            { GENERATE SAMPLES AND COUNT YESSES }
            FOR SAM := 1 TO NS DO BEGIN
                YE := 0;
                FOR N := 1 TO S DO BEGIN
                    R := RANDOM;
                    IF(R <= P) THEN YE := SUCC(YE);
                END;
                GOTOXY(1,6);
                WRITE("EXAMINING SAMPLE",SAM);
                F[YE] := F[YE]+1;
```

```
END;
WRITELN;
{ GET CUMULATIVE FREQUENCIES TO DETERMINE LIKELY
SAMPLES }
LF[0] := UF[0];
FOR I := 1 TO S DO LF[I] := LF[I-1]+F[I];
UF[S] := F[S]; I := S;
REPEAT
     UF[I-1] := UF[I]+F[I-1];
     I := I - 1;
UNTIL I = 1;
{ DISPLAY THE DATA }
WRITELN;
WRITELN("NUMBER OF            LIKELY");
WRITELN("YESSES IN THE       FREQUENCY OR");
WRITELN("SAMPLE              UNLIKELY");
WRITELN("_____");
WH := 0.05 * NS;
FOR I := 0 TO S DO BEGIN
    IF (UF[I] <> 0) AND (LF[I] <> 0) THEN BEGIN
        WRITE(I,"          ",F[I]:3:3,"        ");
        IF (LF[I] <= WH) OR (UF[I] <= WH) THEN
        WRITELN("UNLIKELY")
        ELSE WRITELN("LIKELY");
    END;
END;
CH := READKEY;
END;
```

QUESTIONS

1. Use this program to answer the questions in *Exercises 4-3*.

2. Compare the frequency table for 1000 samples with the frequency table for 100 samples, when the sample sizes and percentage of yesses in the population remain the same. What differences do you notice?

3. Use this program to help you answer the questions in *Exercises 4-4*.

The Pigeonhole Principle

"The public image of mathematics as both dull and difficult is a gross misconception. This image has prevailed only because people have never encountered mathematics that is both interesting and easy — not so easy it is trivial, but just elusive enough to require a little effort."

Robert Wirtz

Six people are at a party. Prove that either at least three of them are mutual acquaintances or at least three of them are mutual strangers.

Understand the problem
- What do "mutual acquaintances" and "mutual strangers" mean?

Think of a strategy

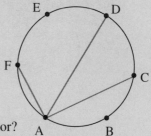

- Represent the six people by points on a circle.
- Join each pair of points. Use a black segment if they know each other, and a blue segment if they do not know each other.
- Can you prove that at least three of the points are joined by line segments of the same color?

Carry out the strategy
- From point A, there are 5 segments, and only 2 possible colors. Hence, at least 3 of the segments must be the same color, say, blue. Suppose that these are AC, AD, and AF.
- Consider $\triangle$CDF. Is it possible to color the sides of this triangle without making a triangle with all three sides the same color?

Look back
- The key to the solution was recognizing that at least 3 of the segments from A must have the same color. This is an example of the pigeonhole principle.

> **The Pigeonhole Principle**
> If more than kn objects are to be placed in n boxes, then at least one box must contain $k + 1$ objects.

- In the above problem, $kn = 4$ (there are 5 segments from A) and $n = 2$ (the colors). Hence $k = 2$, and there must be at least $2 + 1$, or 3 segments from A having the same color.

PROBLEMS

1. How many cards must you draw from a deck of playing cards to be certain that you will have at least two with the same value?

2. Given any 10 different natural numbers, prove that at least two of them leave the same remainder when divided by 9.

3. Prove the following properties of Pascal's triangle.
   a) The sum of the numbers in the nth row is 2^n.
   b) The numbers in any row can always be arranged in two sets with the same sum.

4. This triangle of numbers is a generalization of Pascal's triangle. Instead of starting in the top row with two 1s, it starts with 1 and 2. The numbers in the succeeding rows are then generated in the usual way. Determine the first three numbers in the 50th row.

```
        1    2
      1    3    2
    1    4    5    2
  1    5    9    7    2
1    6   14   16    9    2
```

5. In the diagram, the tangent PT and the chord AB have equal lengths. Prove that B divides AP in the golden ratio.

6. Five points are randomly located in an equilateral triangle with sides 1 unit long. Prove that at least two of the points are no more than 0.5 units apart.

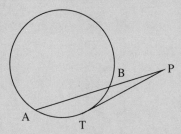

7. Six circles are drawn such that none of them contains the centre of another. Prove that they have no points in common.

8. On a staircase I can go up 1 or 2 steps at a time.
   a) How many different ways can I go up a staircase that has 10 steps?
   b) Describe a method I could use to determine the number of ways I could go up a staircase that has n steps.

9. Kevin wrote 5 letters and wrote the corresponding addresses on 5 envelopes. How many different ways are there of placing all the letters in the wrong envelopes?

4-4 MAKING A SAMPLE CHART

In *Exercises 4-3* you examined the distribution of 100 samples from different YES-NO populations. You may have noticed that frequencies do not always increase towards the mode (the most frequent sample) and then decrease after this. There were probably "hills and valleys". For example, in the frequency table in Step 3 of *Section 4-3*, there were 4 samples with 2 yesses but only 2 samples with 4 yesses. Variations like these occur when the frequency distribution is based on a small number of samples. In the work that follows, the data are obtained from a computer simulation using many more samples.

Using a computer simulation, a group of students collected data from 100 million samples (size 20) from a 30% YES population. The following frequency table shows their data. The frequencies have been rounded to the nearest million.

Number of yesses in the sample	Frequency (millions)
0	0
1	1
2	3
3	7
4	13
5	17
6	20
7	16
8	12
9	7
10	3
11	1
12	1
13	0
14	0
15	0
16	0
17	0
18	0
19	0
20	0

Some of the samples occur frequently. These are the samples that contain between 3 and 9 yesses. Other samples — more than 12 yesses — did not occur at all. The *likely samples* occur in the middle of the distribution. In this chapter we will use the middle 90% of the distribution for the likely samples. The first 5% and last 5% of the distribution are the *unlikely samples*. The frequency table is repeated below showing how to determine the likely and unlikely samples.

	Number of yesses in the sample	Proportion of yesses in the sample	Frequency (millions)	
Unlikely	0	0	0	Total not more than 5
Unlikely	1	0.05	1	Total not more than 5
Unlikely	2	0.10	3	Total not more than 5
	3	0.15	7	
	4	0.20	13	
	5	0.25	17	
	6	0.30	20	
	7	0.35	16	
	8	0.40	12	
	9	0.45	7	
Unlikely	10	0.50	3	Total not more than 5
Unlikely	11	0.55	1	Total not more than 5
Unlikely	12	0.60	1	Total not more than 5
Unlikely	13	0.65	0	Total not more than 5
Unlikely	14	0.70	0	Total not more than 5

Starting at the top of the table, count the frequencies. Stop when the count would go over 5. This occurs at 3 yesses. The 7 samples in this category would put the count above 5. Since this category is 3 yesses out of 20 we express the fraction $\frac{3}{20}$ as a decimal, 0.15. We say that the *proportion* of yesses in the sample is 0.15, and 0.15 is the first of the likely sample proportions.

Repeat the process, starting at the bottom of the table. Stop when you reach the category with 9 yesses (proportion 0.45), since the 7 samples here would put the count over 5.

The likely sample proportions begin at 3 yesses (proportion 0.15) and extend to 9 yesses (proportion 0.45).

We use a *90% boxplot* to summarize this information.

	90% boxplot for samples size 20 from a 30% YES population									
	Proportion of yesses in the sample									

0	0.10	0.20	0.30	0.40	0.50	0.60	0.70	0.80	0.90	1.00

The proportions in the box are the likely proportions. They occur 90% of the time. That is why we call the plot a 90% boxplot. The proportions outside the box are the unlikely proportions. They occur 10% of the time. The whiskers show some of the unlikely proportions. The whiskers stop at the last non-zero frequency, so they extend to 0.05 and to 0.60. Since we rounded the frequencies to the nearest million, the box and the whiskers cover 99% of the sample proportions, because frequencies less than 500 000 would be ignored. Proportions outside the range 0.05 to 0.60 occurred less than 1% of the time, and are ignored.

Here is a summary of the rules for constructing 90% boxplots, starting from a frequency table of the sampling distribution, where the frequencies total 100.

● Examine the frequencies starting from the lower end. Stop at the first proportion for which the frequency is not 0. This proportion marks the beginning of the whisker.

● Count the frequencies. Stop at the proportion in which the number would put the count greater than 5. This proportion marks the beginning of the box.

● Examine the frequencies from the upper end. Stop at the proportion for which the frequency is not 0. This proportion marks the end of the whisker.

● Count the frequencies. Stop at the proportion in which the number would put the count above 5. This proportion marks the end of the box.

On the chart on the next page, you will see the 90% boxplot for a 30% YES population. This is the beginning of our sample chart for samples of size 20. You will complete this chart in Exercise 3.

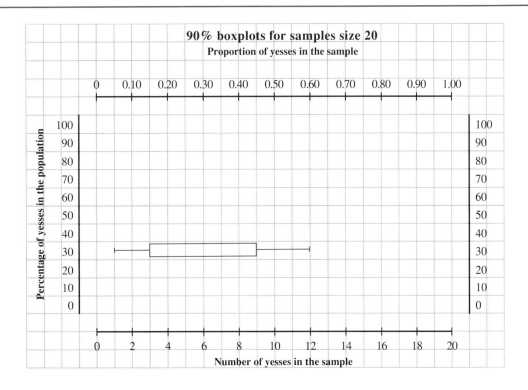

90% boxplots for samples size 20
Proportion of yesses in the sample

EXERCISES 4-4

1. Explain in your own words the meaning of each term.
   a) likely sample
   b) unlikely sample
   c) 90% boxplot
   d) 60% YES population
   e) proportion of yesses in the sample
   f) percentage of yesses in the population

Ⓑ

A computer program was used to calculate the expected frequencies for 100 million samples (size 20) from 9 YES-NO populations. Note that the tables do not include categories for which the frequency is 0. The frequencies have been rounded to the nearest million.

90% YES population

Proportion of yesses	0.70	0.75	0.80	0.85	0.90	0.95	1.0
Frequency	1	3	9	19	29	27	12

80% YES population

Proportion of yesses	0.55	0.60	0.65	0.70	0.75	0.80	0.85	0.90	0.95	1.0
Frequency	1	2	5	11	17	22	21	14	6	1

70% YES population

Proportion of yesses	0.45	0.50	0.55	0.60	0.65	0.70	0.75	0.80	0.85	0.90	0.95
Frequency	1	3	7	12	17	19	18	13	7	3	1

60% YES population

Proportion of yesses	0.30	0.35	0.40	0.45	0.50	0.55	0.60	0.65	0.70	0.75	0.80	0.85
Frequency	1	2	4	7	12	16	18	17	12	7	3	1

50% YES population

Proportion of yesses	0.25	0.30	0.35	0.40	0.45	0.50	0.55	0.60	0.65	0.70	0.75
Frequency	1	4	8	12	16	18	16	12	8	4	1

40% YES population

Proportion of yesses	0.15	0.20	0.25	0.30	0.35	0.40	0.45	0.50	0.55	0.60	0.65	0.70
Frequency	1	3	7	12	17	18	16	12	7	4	2	1

30% YES population

Proportion of yesses	0.05	0.10	0.15	0.20	0.25	0.30	0.35	0.40	0.45	0.50	0.55
Frequency	1	3	7	13	18	19	17	11	7	3	1

20% YES population

Proportion of yesses	0	0.05	0.10	0.15	0.20	0.25	0.30	0.35	0.40	0.45
Frequency	1	6	14	21	22	17	11	5	2	1

10% YES population

Proportion of yesses	0	0.05	0.10	0.15	0.20	0.25	0.30
Frequency	12	27	29	19	9	3	1

2. Use the information on the previous 2 pages. Copy and complete this table showing the likely sample proportions for each population.

Percentage of yesses in the population	Lowest likely proportion	Greatest likely proportion
90		
80		
70		
60		
50		
40		
30	0.15	0.45
20		
10		

3. Work in groups of 3 or 4. Using graph paper, make a copy of the sample chart. Construct 90% boxplots for samples of size 20 for each population listed above. Draw the boxplot on the appropriate line of the sample chart. Make one chart per group.

4. Use the computer program in *COMPUTER POWER* to construct a sample chart for a sample of size 43. Compare your chart with the chart for samples of size 40. Make a list of the differences between the two charts.

4-5 USING A SAMPLE CHART

In *Section 4-4* you learned how to construct sample charts. To construct a more complete sample chart requires a lot of time. So, in the sample chart on page 168 extra boxplots have been added to the one you constructed. This chart shows boxplots for 0% to 100% YES populations at 5% intervals. The charts on pages 189 to 192 allow even greater accuracy. They show the boxplots for the YES percentage of the population every 2%. These charts will be used in the next section.

You can use these charts to solve two kinds of problems.

From population information to sample information

The first kind of problem starts with information about the percentage of yesses in the population. Then you use the chart to obtain information about the samples you might expect to get.

Example 1.   In the June 14th, 1988 issue of *PC WEEK*, there was a news item about a computer program called "LOTTO LOGIC!" The following sentence appeared in the article, which described a system for predicting winning numbers in lotteries like LOTTO 649.

> "The system is based on statistical analysis that shows that 85% of the winning numbers in any lottery have been picked in the last 10 draws."

That statement seems suspicious. So Janice decides to check out the claim. Is it true that all winning lottery numbers are an 85% YES population?

Solution.   The YES-NO question for each winning number is,
"Was this also a winning number in any of the 10 previous draws?"
Janice looks at data from the LOTTO 649 lottery. There are 7 winning numbers (including the bonus number) in each draw. Janice needed 20 numbers for her sample so she looked at the 21 winning numbers in the previous 3 draws. One number was chosen at random and ignored. For each of the 20 winning numbers, Janice looked to see if it was also a winning number in any of the previous 10 draws. She found that 13 of the 20 numbers had also been winning numbers in at least one of the previous 10 draws.

Now she looks at the 90% boxplot (sample size 20) for an 85% YES population.

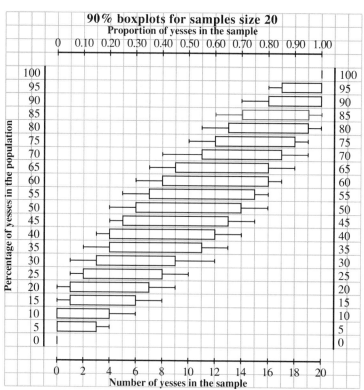

The box extends from 0.70 to 0.95. These are the proportions between which the likely samples occur. But Janice's sample had $\frac{13}{20}$, or 0.65 proportion of yesses. The proportion 0.65 does not lie in this box. So she comes to the conclusion that, based on that particular sample, she cannot agree that 85% of winning lottery numbers have occurred in the previous 10 draws.

Janice realizes that she might, in fact, be wrong in her disagreement. The likely samples make up only 90% of all samples that occur. So she is prepared to be wrong 10% of the time. This is the number of times she would get an unlikely sample from an 85% YES population. Her sample with a 0.65 YES proportion might be one of the unlikely samples from an 85% YES population.

In the situation in *Example 1*, it is not a serious matter to make a wrong decision. However, in a statistical experiment to determine the effectiveness of a new vaccine (like the Salk polio vaccine) it is very important to decide if the vaccine is truly effective. To minimise the risk of making errors, researchers use very large samples. Over 1 million children were involved in the Salk vaccine experiment.

From sample information to population information

The second kind of problem is found in opinion surveys. In this case, you start with some information about the proportion of yesses in a sample. Then you use the chart to deduce information about the YES percentage in the population from which the sample was collected.

This is the most common application of sample charts. The power of the survey technique lies in its ability to use data from a sample to deduce information about the population from which it was taken.

Example 2. A biologist was using survey methods to estimate the size of the squirrel population in a town. He set traps to catch squirrels, which he then released after marking them with a dye. After several days he had marked 40 squirrels. The next day he caught 20 squirrels, 8 of them marked. What is the percentage of marked squirrels in the population at that time?

Solution. The sample has $\frac{8}{20}$, or a 0.40 proportion of yesses, where YES represents a marked squirrel. Put a ruler down the chart on page 170 through a proportion of 0.40. You will see that the edge of the ruler lies in a box if the percentage of yesses in the population is 25%, 30%, 35%, 40%, 45%, 50%, 55% or 60%. The proportion 0.40 is a likely proportion if the percentage of marked squirrels is between 25% and 60%. This means that the percentage of marked squirrels is somewhere between 25% and 60%.

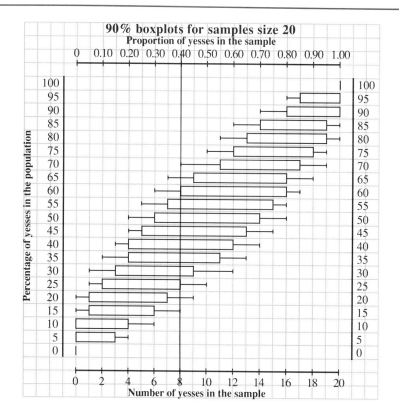

In *Example 2*, we call the range between 25% and 60% a *confidence interval*. The sample that the biologist caught gave him a confidence interval (25% to 60%) for the percentage of marked squirrels in the population. If he repeated this experiment, he would get a different confidence interval for each sample he caught. The sample chart used here was made up from 90% boxplots, hence 9 times out of 10, the confidence interval will contain the correct percentage of marked squirrels. So the confidence intervals that we obtain from charts of 90% boxplots are called 90% *confidence intervals*.

Because the biologist used a sample chart with 90% boxplots, he cannot be certain that every one of the confidence intervals contains the actual percentage of marked squirrels. He can only say that 9 out of 10 confidence intervals will contain the percentage of marked squirrels. In fact, a professional biologist would not be comfortable with a 90% confidence interval. He or she would use 95% boxplots, since this is the usual practice among statisticians. These charts would give wider confidence intervals because the boxes are wider. He would now be able to say that 19 out of 20 confidence intervals will contain the correct percentage of marked squirrels. We would call these *95% confidence intervals*.

EXERCISES 4-5

Ⓐ

1. Use your ruler and the chart on page 170. For the population percentages given below, say if each sample proportion is likely or unlikely. The sample size is 20.

	Percentage of yesses in the population	Proportion (number) of yesses in the sample
a)	80%	0.65 (13)
b)	20%	0.35 (7)
c)	65%	0.80 (16)
d)	65%	0.40 (8)
e)	35%	0.55 (11)
f)	35%	0.70 (14)
g)	15%	0.35 (7)

2. For each sample proportion (sample size 20), give the range of percentage of yesses in the population for which the sample proportion is likely.
   a) 0.20   b) 0.35   c) 0.60   d) 0.70   e) 0.85

3. Copy and complete the table to show the likely sample proportion of yesses for each given percentage of yesses in the population.

	Percentage of yesses in the population	Likely proportion of yesses in the sample (size 20)
	20%	0.05 to 0.35
a)	45%	
b)	60%	
c)	80%	
d)	95%	

4. Copy and complete the table to show the 90% confidence interval for each percentage of yesses in the population from which the sample came.

	Proportion of yesses in the sample	90% confidence interval
	0.15	5% to 30%
a)	0.30	
b)	0.55	
c)	0.60	
d)	0.75	

5. If you had a chart made from 95% boxplots:
   a) would the boxes be longer or shorter than those for 90% boxplots?
   b) would the confidence intervals be longer or shorter than those from charts of 90% boxplots?

Ⓑ

6. A newspaper article said that 40% of the cars on the ferries to Vancouver Island were Japanese cars. If you took samples (size 20) of the cars on a ferry, what are the likely proportions of Japanese cars? (Use the chart of 90% boxplots on page 170.)

7. On a ferry from Nanaimo to Horseshoe Bay in July 1988, a sample of 20 cars included 8 Japanese cars. Find the 90% confidence interval for the percentage of Japanese cars on the ferry.

8. A computer generated 10 samples from a 60% YES population. An x shows a YES response and an o shows a NO response. For each sample, find the corresponding 90% confidence interval. Check to see if the percentage of yesses in the population lies in 9 out of 10 confidence intervals on average.

Sample	Confidence interval	Contains 60%
a) X X O X X O X X X O O X X O X X X X X O	50%–85%	Yes
b) O X X X X O X O X X X X O O O O X X O		
c) O X O O O X X X O O X X X X X X X X O X		
d) O O O X X O X X X O X X X X X O O O X X		
e) O O X O O O O X X O X X X O O X X O		
f) O X X X X X X O X X X X X X X X X O X		
g) O X X O O X X X O X X O X O X O X X X O		
h) O O O X X X O X O X O X O X O X X X O X		
i) X O X X X X O X X X X X X O O X X X O X		
j) X X X X X O X X O X X O O O O O X X X O		

9. Repeat *Exercise 8* for the 10 samples from each of the 75% and 35% YES populations.

a) From a 75% YES population

X X X O X X O X X O X X O X X X X X X
X X O X X X X X X X X X O O X X X X X O
X X X X X O X O X X O O X X O X O X O X X X
X O X X X X X O X X X X O X X X X X O X
X X X O X X X X X X X X X X O X X X X O
O O X X X X X O O X X X O X X X O X X X
O X X X X X O O X X X O X X O X X X X O
X X X X X X O O X X O O X X O X X X X O
O X O X X X X X O X X X O X X O X X O X X X
X X X X O X X O X X X X O X X O O X X O

b) From a 35% YES population

X O X O O O X O O O X X O O O O X O O X
X X O O O X O O O O O X O O O X X O X O
O O X O X O O O O X O X X O O O O O O O
O O O O O O O O O O X O O X O O X O O
X X X O X O O O O O O O X O X O O O X O
X O O O X O O X O O O O X O X O O X X O
O O O O O O X X O X O X O X O X O O X O O
O O O O O O O X X O X X X O O O O O O O
X O O X X O O O O O X O X O O O X O X O
O O O O O X O X O O O O X X X O O O X O

4-6 USING SAMPLE CHARTS FOR DIFFERENT SIZE SAMPLES

You may have noticed that the confidence intervals for samples of size 20 are quite wide. That is, for any given sample, there is a wide range of the percentage of yesses in the population for which the sample is likely. If we increase the size of a sample, then we can obtain more precise information about the percentage of yesses in the population. Look at the two sample charts on pages 189 and 192. These are the charts for samples of size 20 and samples of size 100.

The boxes for samples of size 100 are shorter than those for samples of size 20. There is an inverse relation between the length of the box and the size of the sample (see Exercise 13). Also, the confidence intervals for samples of size 100 are shorter than the confidence intervals for samples of size 20. This is because the boxes themselves are shorter. So, the larger the sample size, the shorter the confidence interval.

One application of larger sample surveys is the capture-recapture method of estimating the size of a wildlife population. Biologists use the confidence interval for the marked percentage in the population to calculate a confidence interval for the number of animals in the population.

Example. In *Example 2*, Section 4-5, we looked at survey data collected by a biologist. After the biologist had marked and released 60 squirrels, he continued to capture squirrels, but released them without marking. He found 25 marked squirrels in a sample of 100 squirrels. Find a 90% confidence interval for the number of squirrels in the town.

Solution. The proportion of marked squirrels in the sample is 0.25. From the chart of 90% boxplots for samples size 100 on page 192, we see that the 90% confidence interval for the percentage of marked squirrels in the town is 18% to 32%.

The biologist knows there are 60 marked squirrels, but he does not know the total number N of the squirrels in the town.

Using the lower estimate 18%:

If 18% of N is 60

then $0.18N = 60$

$$N = \frac{60}{0.18}$$

$$\doteq 333$$

Similarly, using the upper estimate of 32%:

If 32% of N is 60, then $0.32N = 60$

$$N = \frac{60}{0.32}$$

$$\doteq 188$$

The biologist assumes that there are between 188 and 333 squirrels in the town. This is a 90% confidence interval for the number of squirrels in the town.

EXERCISES 4-6

Ⓐ

1. Explain how the size of a sample affects the size of the confidence interval obtained from the sample.

2. Explain the meaning of the term "capture-recapture method".

Ⓑ

In these exercises, use the sample charts of 90% boxplots on pages 189-192.

3. Referring to the *Example*, using a sample size 20, the biologist found that it contained 8 marked squirrels. Assuming there were 40 marked squirrels in the population, calculate a 90% confidence interval for the number of squirrels in the population.

4. Repeat *Exercise 3* for a sample size 80 which contained 32 marked squirrels. Assume that there are 40 marked squirrels in the population.

5. Explain why the confidence interval you obtained in *Exercise 4* is shorter than the one you calculated in *Exercise 3*.

6. Janice investigated 100 numbers from a published list of winning numbers in the LOTTO 649 draw. She found that, out of 100 winning numbers, 72 were also winning numbers in some of the 10 previous draws. Find a 90% confidence interval for the percentage of winning numbers that also occurred in at least one of the 10 previous draws.

7. Copy and complete the table which compares confidence intervals for samples of size 20, 40, and 100. What conclusions can you draw?

	Proportion of yesses in the sample	Confidence interval sample size 20	Confidence interval sample size 40	Confidence interval sample size 100
	0.20	8% to 40%	12% to 32%	14% to 26%
a)	0.35			
b)	0.63			
c)	0.37			
d)	0.88			
e)	0.07			
f)	0.93			

8. One hundred boys and 100 girls answered questions in two surveys. Some of the data are listed below. For each piece of sample data, calculate a 90% confidence interval. Write your answer as a complete sentence; for example, "I am 90% confident that between 15% and 25% of grade 11 and 12 boys missed at least 2 classes last week".
   a) 68 grade 11 and 12 boys said that they spend more than $20 on a date
   b) 44 grade 11 and 12 girls said that they spend more than $20 on a date
   c) 6 grade 11 and 12 boys said that they smoked 10 or more cigarettes per day
   d) 14 grade 11 and 12 girls said that they smoked 10 or more cigarettes per day

9. Look at your answers to *Exercise 8 a)* and *b)*.
   a) Do the confidence intervals overlap?
   b) When the confidence intervals from two samples do not overlap, there are no populations for which both samples are likely samples. Then we say there is a *significant difference* between the two samples. Complete the following sentence for the two samples in *Exercise 8 a)* and *b)*.
      "It seems there is a significant difference in the percentage of grade 11 and 12 boys and girls who ..."

10. Is there a significant difference in the percentage of girls and boys who smoke 10 or more cigarettes per day? (See *Exercise 8 c)* and *d)*.)

11. Thirty students from a grade 12 statistics class went to a shopping mall on a Friday afternoon. They walked around the mall individually. At 2:30, each student counted the number of people he or she could see, recording results until the sample size was 40, 80 or 100. The students also counted the number of students from their class in their samples. Here are the data from three students.

Sample size	40	80	100
Number of students	4	7	8

   a) For each sample, find a 90% confidence interval for the percentage of people in the mall who are students in the class.
   b) Knowing that there are 30 students in the mall, find three 90% confidence intervals for the number of people in the mall.

12. In this question there are one hundred letters. Count the e's in this question and estimate the percentage of e's in English.

Ⓒ

13. a) For a sample with a 0.50 proportion of yesses, find the confidence interval for the percentage of yesses in the population for sample sizes $N = 20, 40, 60, 80,$ and 100. (The confidence interval for $N = 60$ is 40% to 60%.)
   b) Draw a graph, plotting the width W of the confidence interval against the sample size N.
   c) Is the relation between W and N inverse or direct?
   d) Investigate the graphs of W against $\frac{1}{N}$, W against $\frac{1}{N^2}$, and W against $\frac{1}{\sqrt{N}}$ to determine which graph is linear.
   e) Find an equation relating W and N.

14. In an experiment to test for ability in Extra Sensory Perception, a girl was shown 20 photographs of people, none of whom she knew. Below each photograph were 5 telephone numbers, one of which was the phone number of the person in the photograph. The girl had to identify the correct phone number.
   a) What is the likely number of correct phone numbers she would get if she guessed?
   b) If she correctly identified 9 phone numbers, would you think that she had ESP ability?

4-7 LARGE SAMPLE SIZES

If we need more precise information about the percentage of yesses in
a population, we must select a larger sample. People who commission
opinion surveys would not be satisfied with confidence intervals that
are 10 percentage points wide. They need much more precision than that;
that is, much narrower confidence intervals.

In a survey of 100 grade 11 and 12 students, 50% of them said
that they spent more than $16 on a date. From the chart of 90% boxplots
for samples size 100 on page 192, the confidence interval for this sample
is 58% to 42%. The percentage of yesses in the population differs
from the percentage of yesses in the sample by up to 8 percentage
points. We say that the *sampling error* is 8%. The sampling error
measures the accuracy of the survey and it depends on the size of
the sample. Newspaper reports sometimes call this the *margin
of error*. The sample charts that we are using in this chapter are not
suitable for obtaining the greater accuracy available from samples
of one thousand or more. Instead, we will use a formula for the
sampling error. This formula provides the sampling error from which
we can obtain 95% confidence intervals. Note that we use 95%
confidence intervals with larger samples.

If the size of a sample is N, then the sampling error of the percentage
of yesses in the population is approximately $\frac{100}{\sqrt{N}}$. This is quite accurate
for sample sizes greater than 100, if the percentage of yesses in the
population is between 30% and 70%. Outside that range, the sampling
error is less than $\frac{100}{\sqrt{N}}$. So, for a sample of size N, where $N > 100$, the
sampling error of the percentage of yesses in the population is no greater
than $\frac{100}{\sqrt{N}}$.

Example 1.   The students in Ken Chan's class conducted a telephone survey of their
town. They asked 760 people if they had eaten breakfast at a restaurant
or fast food outlet at least once in the past week. One hundred forty-
five people said YES. Find a 95% confidence interval for the percentage
of people in that town who eat breakfast out at least once a week.

Solution.   The proportion of yesses in the sample is $\frac{145}{760}$, or approximately 0.19. So,
the percentages of yesses is 19%. Hence, the sampling error for a sample
size 760 is $\frac{100}{\sqrt{760}}$, or about 3.6%.

The 95% confidence interval is 19% $-$ 3.6% to 19% $+$ 3.6%, or about
15% to 23%, rounding to the nearest percent.

Example 2. Angus Reid conducted a survey in January 1988, of 1500 Canadians. Of those surveyed, 36% said that they felt the New Democratic Party was most likely to provide honest and open government. What is the 95% confidence interval for this survey?

Solution. For a sample of 1500, the sampling error is $\frac{100}{\sqrt{1500}}$, which is about 2.6%. So the confidence interval is from $36\% - 2.6\%$ to $36\% + 2.6\%$, or 33.4% to 38.6%. In a report, the writer would usually round this to 33% to 39%.

Information about the percentage of yesses in a population comes in the form of a confidence interval. In *Example 2*, we have no way of knowing where the percentage of yesses lies in the interval. Just because 36% is in the middle of the interval it does not mean that the percentage of yesses is likely to be near 36%. It could be *any* number in the interval.

Two opinion polls were conducted in June 1988. The Gallup Poll (June 9) reported that 39% of those surveyed supported the Liberal Party. The Angus Reid Poll (June 21) reported that 34% supported the Liberals. Each poll sampled about 1500 people. We have just calculated the sampling error as about 3%. So, all we can say about these two surveys is that in early June, somewhere between 36% and 42% supported the Liberals. Later, somewhere between 31% and 37% supported the Liberals. We have no way of knowing if the Liberal support went up by 1% or down by 11%.

When you read a statement such as "the survey found that 34% . . .", do not assume that the figure of 34% is exact. It isn't. It is a "fuzzy" number. It really represents any number you like between 31% and 37%. When you report on a survey, use a sentence like this.

"From our survey of 1500 people, we learned that somewhere between 31% and 37% of the population would support the Liberal Party if an election were held tomorrow. We are 95% confident of this, realizing that such statements are only correct 19 times out of 20."

Gallup regularly conducts polls across all 10 provinces. When a sample of 1500 people is taken, the number taken from each province is proportional to the population of that province. So there may be only 150 people from Atlantic Canada, which means that the sampling error for opinions from this region might be as high as 9% (see Exercise 10).

EXERCISES 4-7

Ⓑ

1. Examine the survey reports that you assembled in *Exercises 4-1*. For each report, find the size of the sample and calculate the sampling error. Write your answer on the paper on which you pasted the report. The reported sampling error may differ from yours because different sampling methods produce different sizes of the sampling error. The report may use the term margin of error instead of sampling error.

For each survey reported in *Exercises 2* to *6*, calculate the 95% confidence interval using the $\frac{100}{\sqrt{N}}$ approximation. Write each answer as a sentence.

2. Angus Reid conducted a survey in British Columbia, where 33% of the 250 people questioned approved of the performance of the leader of the Federal Progressive Conservative Party.

3. A Gallup poll reported that 27% of Canadians say that unemployment is the country's key problem. The results were based on interviews with 1022 people.

4. In the same poll as *Exercise 3*, 57% of those surveyed in Atlantic Canada said that unemployment is the country's key problem. Ninety people from Atlantic Canada took part in the survey.

5. Fifteen hundred six Canadians were asked if they approved of the decision to grant the CBC a licence for an all-news television channel; 43% of them said YES.

6. Seven hundred twelve secondary school students in Nanaimo, North Vancouver, and Chicago took part in a survey in 1982. They provided the following data.
   a) 30% of the students spent more than $15 on a date
   b) 45% of the students had a part-time job
   c) 11% of the students worked 20 or more hours per week
   d) 16% of the students watched television for more than 20 h per week
   e) 50% of the students spent more hours on school assignments than watching TV
   f) 37% of the students spent more than 10 h a week on school assignments
   g) 17% of the students smoked
   h) 52% of the students had a driver's licence

7. In an experiment to determine the number of salmon in an area, 1000 salmon were tagged by removing their adipose fins. Later in a catch of 800 salmon, 45 were found to have had their adipose fins removed.
   a) Calculate the 95% confidence interval for the number of salmon in that area.
   b) Suggest two reasons, other than statistical uncertainty, why the figures you obtained might be inaccurate.

8. In a poll conducted in February 1989, 1002 Canadians were asked if they supported an elected Senate. Five hundred two said YES and 390 said NO, while the rest did not know. Find a 95% confidence interval for the number of Canadians who agree with the Prime Minister who does not support plans for an elected Senate.

9. At the time that the Canadian Parliament was debating whether to reinstate capital punishment for first-degree murder, a poll showed that 780 in a survey of 1050 Canadians thought that capital punishment should be reinstated.
   a) Find a 95% confidence interval for the percentage of Canadians who think that the Government should reinstate the death penalty for first-degree murder.
   b) Members of Parliament, in a free vote, voted not to reinstate the death penalty at this time. Do you think that Members of Parliament should vote based on the results of opinion surveys? Give reasons.

Ⓒ

10. The following paragraph was written in an article titled "The Pollstergeists" in the April 1988 issue of Saturday Night magazine.

   "… the tiny margins of error (*sampling error*) reported for national samples may be more significant than they look. Sub-samples ("How do Liberals feel about John Turner?", "What do Westerners feel about free trade?") are subject to bigger probabilities of error. A good example was provided by a June 1987 Macleans-Angus Reid poll. Readers were told that Brian Mulroney's approval rating was 50% in Atlantic Canada and only 36% in Ontario. But the small number of Easterners in the sample meant a big error in the comparison. If that margin of error had been reckoned in, there might not have been any difference at all between the two groups — in fact, the approval rating in Ontario could have been 41% and the Atlantic figure only 1 point lower."

   Explain how the author arrived at the figure of 41% and the implied figure of 40% in the last sentence.

4-8 COLLECTING SURVEY DATA — HOW TO CHOOSE A SAMPLING METHOD

Most of the work in this chapter is based on the use of the sample charts of 90% boxplots. A computer program produced these charts based on the laws of probability. One of the assumptions made in these calculations is that every sample of that size that could be drawn from the population has the same chance of being drawn.

It is not always convenient or possible to meet this requirement. So there are now many different ways of collecting samples. Some of the methods used by professional polling organizations are complicated and costly.

It is important to use a method that reduces the risk of getting a *biased sample*. This occurs when non-random methods affect the choice of individuals for the sample. A political organization which mails a large number of replies to a newspaper poll is biasing the sample in favor of the responses it would like to see. Data collected from a "mail-in" survey are biased in favor of those who feel strongly about the subject matter of the poll.

If your sample is biased, then you may get false information about the population. If you conducted a survey on women's rights and your sample of 20 students contained 2 boys, then your results might not reflect the opinions of all students.

Sampling methods are designed to prevent the bias that occurs when a particular group of people is overrepresented in a sample. We will look at some of the more common methods.

Simple random sample

A simple random sample is a sample obtained by a method that fits the requirement stated above; that is, every sample of that size that could be drawn from the population has the same chance of being drawn. The simple random sample is the foundation for all sampling methods. Here is an alternative definition.

> Every member of a population has an equal chance of being selected for the sample, *and* every member is selected independently from each other member.

This leads to the most common method of making sure that a sampling method produces a simple random sample — using a table of random digits.

Suppose you want a sample of 30 students enrolled in a Physical Education course. First you make a list of all the students in that course (the population) and number them. Assume there are 254 students on the list. Using the table of random digits (page 188), collect 30 three-digit numbers, each less than 255. The first three columns of the first ten lines are reproduced here.

An easy way to do this is to work down the columns, picking the first 3 digits in each group of 5 that form a number less than 255. The first such number is 195 (on the 7th line), then comes 064, 208, 230, 111, 082, 005, 042, 215, and so on. The students identified by these numbers would make up the sample.	98299	62016	63936
	83032	90329	**111**13
	46245	**208**25	**082**75
	82755	**230**37	83622
	94943	57301	**005**47
	52348	25591	**042**33
	19537	58635	32489
	66214	31057	80911
	06415	66362	98910
	99596	88661	**215**96

You can see that this procedure is convenient only where the population is relatively small. It would be difficult to use this method to obtain a random sample of the voters in your town, even though there is a list of voters that is readily available. In this situation, you would use a process called multi-stage sampling.

Multi-stage sampling

Suppose you wanted to obtain a sample of 100 of the voters in your town. The voters' list is 200 pages long and there are 50 names on each page. You decide that you will pick 5 names off 20 pages. First you would use a table of random digits to pick a simple random sample of 20 pages using random numbers between 1 and 200. We call this Stage 1. Then for each page, you would pick a simple random sample of 5 names, using random numbers between 1 and 50. We call this Stage 2.

This is, perhaps, the best method of picking a sample of students at your school. Students are usually grouped into divisions (or home rooms) for administration purposes. These division lists could be used as the voters' list was used.

Probability sample

If there is a large variation in the number of students in each division, then it would not be true that each student has the same chance of being chosen. Suppose that each grade 8 division had 20 students and each grade 12 division had 30 students. Then, the probability that a particular grade 8 student is chosen is greater than that for a particular grade 12 student. This is the normal situation in Gallup and other polls. If we know the probability of selecting someone for each group in a multi-stage sampling method, then it is possible to compensate for this error after collecting the data. We call this *probability sampling*. Polling organisations use this method. The details of the compensation calculations are beyond the level of this book.

Stratified random sample

You may want to be sure that a sample is representative of all parts of the population. A simple random sample can sometimes produce samples that do not represent all groups in a population. Suppose that in your school you have the following numbers of students in each grade.

Grade	Number of students
8	300
9	300
10	250
11	200
12	200
	Total 1250

If you wanted a sample of 125 students, then you could collect simple random samples from each grade; 30 students from each of grades 8 and 9, 25 students from grade 11, and 20 students from each of grades 11 and 12. We call this a *stratified random sample*.

Cluster sample

You would use this method if you wanted to conduct a survey of your town using door-to-door interviews. First you get a street map of your town. This usually has a street index. You use a table of random digits to pick a simple random sample of streets; one street for each student in the project. Then each student would pick a simple random sample of houses in that street. It makes it easier to collect the information, if all the houses for a particular student are close together.

Systematic sampling

One way of making sure that a sample is representative of the population is to use systematic sampling. In this method, you put the population in some order then select a random number, say 10, and choose every 10th person for the sample.

You could use this method to sample cars leaving the school parking lot. Post a student at each exit (there may be more than one) of the parking lot and then select every 10th car. This method is also useful in selecting a sample of shoppers in a shopping mall. Select an area that is neutral; that is, not near a particular store. Decide on a time interval long enough to conduct the interview, say 10 min. Then every 10 min, select the next person who crosses the area you have selected.

The main point of any method is that you must set the rules for yourself before you start sampling and then keep to the rules. Otherwise, you may find yourself selecting people who look "easy to talk to". If you are a girl, you may find yourself selecting more females than males, which may introduce bias into the survey.

Bias occurs in a sampling method when factors other than random selection affect the choice of a person for the sample. One method of sampling that often gives very biased samples is convenience sampling.

Convenience sample

We give this name to any sampling method that does not meet the requirements of a simple random sample. An inspector who inspects crates of apples from the Okanagan valley will usually select her sample from the top of the crate. She takes a sample from those members of the population that are conveniently available.

If you sample the students at your school by talking to students in the cafeteria during a particular class, that would be a convenience sample. Similarly, a survey conducted by asking your friends would be using a convenience sample. Such samples are easy to collect, but they will often give biased data.

Self-selected sample
This is the least reliable method of sampling. The data are almost always biased. A well-known example of self-selected sampling involved Ann Landers. She asked her readers to write and tell her if they would have children if they could live their lives over again. Seventy percent of the 10 000 responses said, "No, they would not have children again." This caused consternation in some places. Newsweek commissioned a professional survey, asking the same question. Of the 1200 people questioned, 91% said that they would have children again. One reason that the Ann Landers data were so biased against having children may be connected with the kind of people who read and write to Ann Landers. Often these are people with personal problems, some of which concern parents or children (see Exercise 7).

Another example occurred in the 1972 American presidential election campaign. A local TV station asked viewers if they approved of President Nixon's decision to mine Haiphong Harbour in Vietnam. About 5000 said YES and 1000 said NO. Later, the station found that workers from the Nixon campaign had mailed over 2000 postcards agreeing with the decision. The bias occurred in this example because a large number of pro-Nixon responses had self-selected themselves for the sample. This was a non-random factor that strongly affected the results.

There seems to be very little value in the information obtained from self-selected samples, yet they are a very common part of media activity.

EXERCISES 4-8

1. Describe how you would obtain the following samples of 30 grade 11 students from your school.
   a) Simple random sample
   b) Stratified random sample
   c) Cluster sample
   d) Self-selected sample
   e) Convenience sample

(B)

2. The owner of a sporting goods store in a shopping mall wanted to conduct a market research survey. He thought that he would do this as soon as the mall opened on a Monday morning because he was not very busy then. So he asked the first 100 people who passed his store to answer a brief questionnaire.
   a) What kind of a sample would you call this?
   b) What kind of people would not be represented in this sample?
   c) Would the owner get a sample representative of those who used his store?
   d) How would the data be biased?
   e) What sampling method would you propose to the store owner that might avoid this bias?

3. A student surveyed grade 12 students about some of the factors involved with teenage suicide. She gave the questionnaire to all the students in the four grade 12 courses in which she was a student.
   a) What kind of a sample would you call this?
   b) What students would not be represented in this sample?
   c) What kind of bias might occur with this method?
   d) What sampling method would you propose that might avoid this bias?

4. Which of the following methods would give a simple random sample?
   a) The first 10 students who entered your classroom
   b) The students who were selected by your teacher to answer a question in class
   c) Students whose locker number ends in a randomly-selected digit
   d) The students in your class who walked to school that day
   e) Number the desks 1 to 30. Use a table of random digits to select 10 students.

5. Examine the survey reports that you collected in *Exercises 4-1*. Describe the sampling method used in each survey. Write your answer on the paper on which you pasted the report.

6. In the following examples, decide which groups might be underrepresented using the sampling methods described.
   a) The largest survey ever was conducted in 1936. The Literary Digest conducted a survey of voting preferences in the Roosevelt/Landon American presidential election campaign, using a sample of 2.4 million voters. It used a list of names from telephone directories, automobile owners, club memberships and its own subscription list. The poll predicted Landon would win 53% to 47%. In fact, Roosevelt won 62% to 38%.
   b) Ann Landers asked her readers to write in to say whether they would have children again if they had the opportunity to live their lives over again.
   c) In a survey to discover students' attitudes towards the new Star Trek series, a student asked the teachers of the grade 12 mathematics course to give the questionnaire to every third student on the class lists.
   d) In a survey to discover whether Toronto residents support a bid to hold the 1996 Summer Olympic Games in Toronto, a student surveyed 100 spectators at a Blue Jays baseball game.
   e) A Vancouver sports fan wanted to know how many people regularly watched the Vancouver Canucks on television. She asked 200 spectators at a B.C. Lions football game.
   f) A student conducted an opinion survey about the school's sports activities. He asked students at the end of afternoon school. Seven of the 20 people he asked said that they did not have time to answer his questions. Instead, he asked 7 others who were waiting for a ride home.

7. Give your reasons why the Ann Landers poll (*Exercise 6b*) might give biased results.

8. Describe how you would collect a sample of 100 people from the following populations to participate in a survey of opinions on the public and private school systems.
   a) The parents of students at your school
   b) The parents of all students in your school district
   c) Members of the public who do not have any children in school
   d) All secondary school students in the school district
   e) Members of the legal, medical, architectural and engineering professions working in your school district
   f) Listeners to an open-line radio show
   g) Shoppers at a local shopping mall

9. In *Exercise* 8, which of the samples would not be representative of the entire population in your school district?

10. Assume that you are Ken Chan who has the task of sampling the residents of his town (say 20 000 adults) to determine what percentage of the residents eat breakfast out at least once a week. Write a description of the procedure you would use to obtain a sample of about 700 people. Assume that you have the cooperation of the 25 students in your mathematics class.

4-9 CONDUCTING A SURVEY

One of the most interesting aspects of studying surveys is conducting your own survey. As a final activity in this chapter you should design, conduct, and write a brief report on an opinion survey. The work involved in doing this is reduced if you work with a team of 4 or 5 students. Each student should make up a YES-NO question. Preferably, all the questions on the questionnaire should be on the same theme. Here are some suggestions of ways to avoid some of the problems you may incur.

Wording the questions
It is sometimes very surprising to see how the results differ when you make even small changes to the wording of a question. Your group might like to use the same questionnaire as another group in the class and make *slight* changes to the wording of the questions. Then you could compare the results obtained by the two groups.

A very common problem occurs when you use vague wording. Consider the question, "Do you smoke?" A YES could include students who smoke less than 1 cigarette per month as well as heavy smokers. A more precise question would be, "Did you smoke more than 10 cigarettes last week?"

Try to word each question in such a way that there is a clear YES or NO reply. Then try out the questionnaire on some of your friends. You are not trying to get a simple random sample here. You are just testing the questions to observe any difficulties that may arise that you had not thought about.

Choosing the sampling method
You should take some time planning this phase of the survey. The most important thing to remember is that you must avoid a sample that could give a biased answer. Remember that you are using the sampling method to try to obtain information about a population. You should try to get a simple random sample which is representative of the population in which you are interested. At the same time, the method should not be so complicated that you will spend many hours collecting the data. The aim of this project is that you should learn some of the problems involved in conducting surveys. In this way you will read survey reports with some scepticism and learn to question the validity of survey reports.

You may find that a telephone survey is more comfortable than conducting personal interviews. It is not difficult to collect a simple random sample using telephone numbers. You can either generate random telephone numbers (last 4 digits) or use systematic sampling from the telephone directory. There are problems with each method. The difficulty with the first method is that you may get many "number not in service" messages. Using the second method will prevent you from sampling those people with unlisted telephone numbers.

Administering the questionnaire
If you are working with several other students, you should decide on the exact words you will use when you approach someone for data. If you have ever been interviewed by a professional pollster, you should have noticed that the person read every word from the printed questionnaire, including the introductory remarks. When you compile your questionnaire, you should include *all* the words that you will use. Try to make sure each member of the group uses the same wording.

Writing the report

The report need not be lengthy, but should contain all the relevant information. There is an organization called the American Association for Public Opinion Research. It has a code of ethics which specifies some of the items that should be in a report. These include the answers to the following questions.

- Whose opinions were being surveyed? What was the population in which you were interested?
- What sampling method did you use? You should name the method as well as giving a brief description. It should be clear that you understand elementary survey methods.
- How large was the sample? What was the margin of error for this size of sample? It is better to use a sentence like the one given as an example earlier on page 177. Not many readers will understand a sentence like, "This figure is accurate to 2.8% 19 times out of 20."
- What was the *exact* wording of the questions?
- When and how was the survey administered? Did you use personal interviews, or telephone or mail-in surveys?

Make the report interesting to read. Use a word processor or simple desk-top publishing software. You should try to make people want to read your report. After all, you will have put some effort into compiling this information.

Making it interesting

For the survey, try to find a subject in which you have a strong personal interest. It does not really matter what the subject is as long as *you* find it interesting. Most students have, at some time or other, asked the question, "I wonder how many people . . .". Perhaps now is your opportunity to find out. The more interest you have in the survey, the more enjoyable it will be. Have fun!

Table of Random Digits

```
98299 62016 63936 42696 79412 33464 71626 91585 60512 45640 91504 14845 12356
83032 90329 11113 05030 72392 43564 24524 16443 36221 54893 26696 34281 82327
46245 20825 08275 88425 93739 77577 55718 00139 94440 89650 00680 29357 26169
87255 23037 83622 37490 51432 00083 73365 29632 79251 28412 25570 23097 50924
94943 57301 00547 04263 20935 85062 68603 22225 00080 48185 33139 25929 52365
52348 25591 04233 49508 86629 75577 52033 26456 17744 69916 31212 81012 70161
19537 58635 32489 79669 22784 13984 89615 94563 80549 88900 23192 93300 33493
66214 31057 80911 66007 42808 51823 75535 68873 37082 82744 75279 57057 63554
06415 66362 98910 39960 20965 11177 09433 23013 17323 78169 88913 30061 08361
99596 88661 21596 17513 69241 06641 09689 14563 29364 61651 67431 43471 29622

86558 31875 62192 23105 75275 58219 92246 53591 88908 73287 84285 63717 97433
90867 91666 35703 37257 30915 34229 25276 22933 54664 46204 33299 89129 40748
85068 17481 29329 53598 71516 49554 08753 14697 40096 87862 98301 16453 58627
02019 06674 70505 05516 79450 73774 42109 14206 13459 15851 92143 93455 49132
95122 23288 61670 64127 67185 75648 43277 42771 30663 90033 17542 24737 34300
02996 32054 98680 86553 25829 80882 43614 50183 18783 74654 63453 33855 28926
44234 48229 02558 94375 28724 74621 24345 85393 27376 27644 95517 19474 78433
80565 34758 36903 49513 25699 86653 30049 49562 19420 91420 52455 63980 03159
42989 31477 95475 24134 75397 69272 61904 94867 65333 72819 81794 93813 99743
92589 46721 27515 54218 08632 84504 79120 89415 61201 06450 63606 66274 46331

02240 81310 33497 01527 40858 87432 34188 83233 95127 91802 59499 53488 85799
20559 04464 57017 88591 40628 55186 43742 32273 67707 87911 07268 67230 63421
52874 41406 63374 41177 52216 27449 69470 88660 88081 69409 34617 01409 41270
82576 61832 35422 31330 84594 93327 89555 71439 75225 25619 69794 41035 28062
94713 97139 44270 21271 69439 66009 35865 95403 50113 65683 24451 43244 83159
84275 08194 45171 26506 21629 31029 01232 21545 84595 82470 98995 11079 15121
38341 88829 85103 61685 84981 08660 77671 73521 00304 16942 99491 16744 28304
00755 14648 83899 74765 51164 75375 76336 69073 59391 58938 17171 64942 88432
90575 90437 04719 28597 77252 77595 89877 26074 56756 12767 97203 04674 40438
69233 57412 94995 24667 98627 34108 31918 71374 05922 38404 01519 88149 57264

62825 12099 64288 33836 19246 63962 77023 54186 50249 92586 34410 75926 34129
11076 69454 78625 65783 41060 53270 35340 56453 04130 58385 88768 91546 81119
96145 29069 77788 57184 24303 49355 79212 62632 39065 59954 15997 88301 25120
58084 60014 30152 78117 70892 03738 54847 77704 89057 00508 65819 91880 85745
15452 64240 59950 99098 92683 08628 17308 28641 14340 17549 97771 45409 87344
27103 81698 58223 06951 52844 39332 34522 43644 51488 91803 52201 11900 76717
94809 29832 22884 56830 35332 04551 88725 37115 80527 51566 59491 01644 22299
48756 27521 76857 64597 67302 87677 48915 11504 84115 04166 34320 37382 63488
32658 26792 62341 60390 85585 95824 54161 68833 20440 21411 86863 04533 84508
05380 54390 98936 52443 68213 90935 12609 53768 28777 05975 79677 80074 50395
```

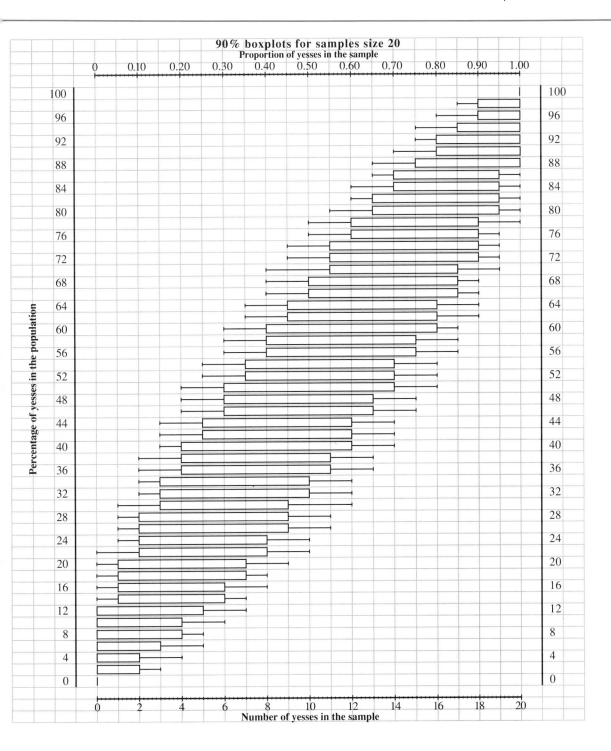

90% boxplots for samples size 20
Proportion of yesses in the sample

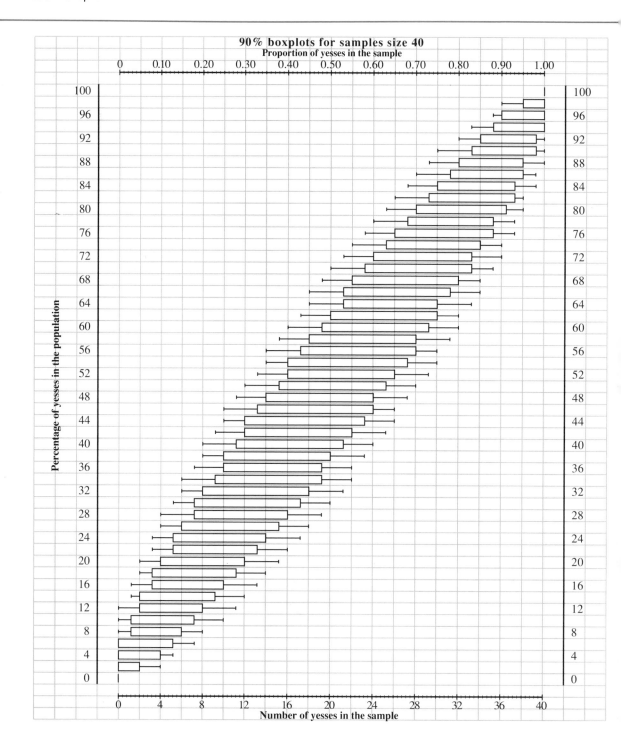

90% boxplots for samples size 40
Proportion of yesses in the sample

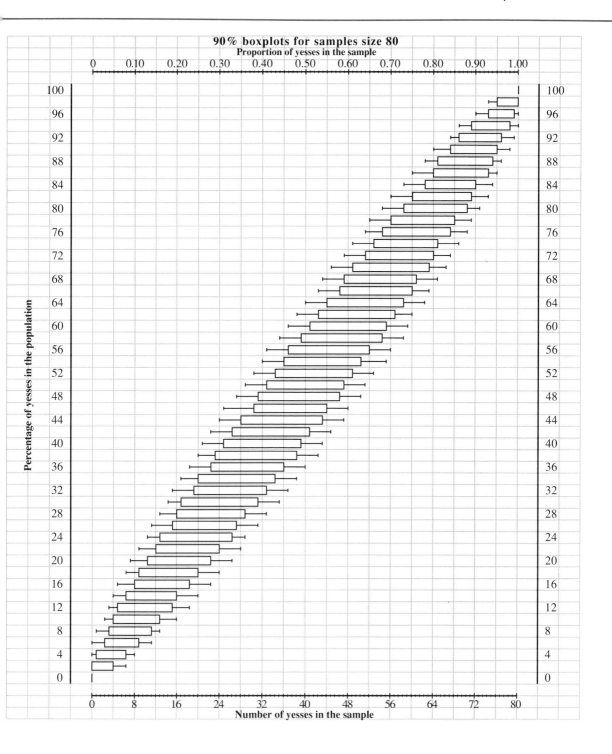

90% boxplots for samples size 80
Proportion of yesses in the sample

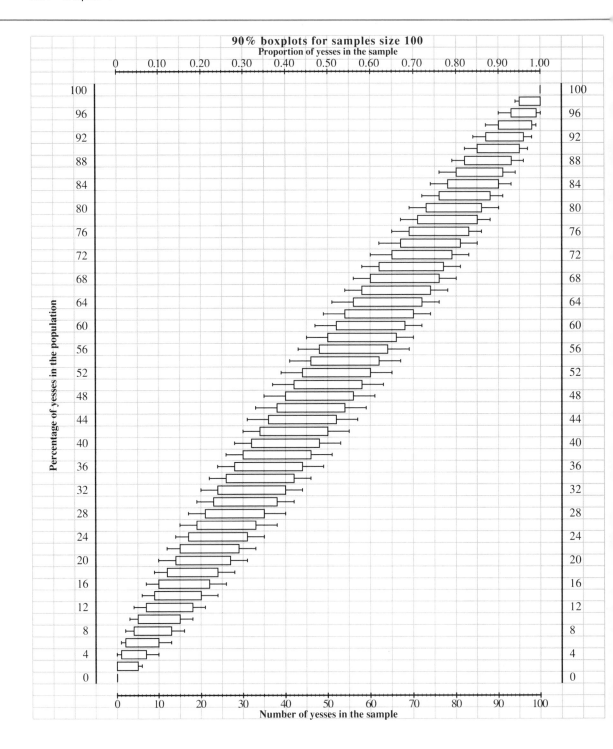

5 Trigonometric Functions

The tides in the Bay of Fundy are among the highest in the world. Suppose you know how high the water is at high tide, and the time of day this occurs, and also how high it is at low tide, and the time it occurs. How can you determine the height of the water at any other time of the day? (See Section 5-13 *Example 1.*)

5-1 INTRODUCTION TO PERIODIC FUNCTIONS

In this chapter we will describe many applications of mathematics involving quantities that change in a regular way. Applications concerned with the sun and human physiology are shown on these pages.

The time of the sunset
In summer, the sun sets later than it does in winter. The graph below shows how the time of the sunset at Ottawa varies during a two-year period. The times are given on a 24 h clock in hours and decimals of hours. For example, on June 21 the sun sets at 20.3 h. This means 20 h and 0.3 × 60 min, or 20 h 18 min.

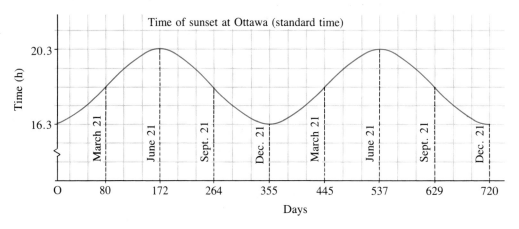

1. a) Estimate the time of the sunset at Ottawa on these dates.
      i)   February 2   ii)   July 25   iii)   October 30
   b) Estimate the dates when the sun sets at these times.
      i)   8 P.M.   ii)   7 P.M.   iii)   6 P.M.   iv)   5 P.M.

2. Suppose similar graphs were drawn for Yellowknife and Mexico City. In what ways would the graphs for these cities differ from the graph above? In what ways would they be similar?

	Approximate time of sunset on			
	March 21	June 21	September 21	December 21
Mexico City	18.8 h	19.3 h	18.6 h	17.9 h
Yellowknife	18.9 h	22.4 h	18.7 h	15.2 h

Sunspots
Sunspots are dark spots that appear from time to time on the surface of the sun. The periodic variation in the number of sunspots has been recorded for hundreds of years. The following graph shows how the number of sunspots varied from 1944 to 1986.

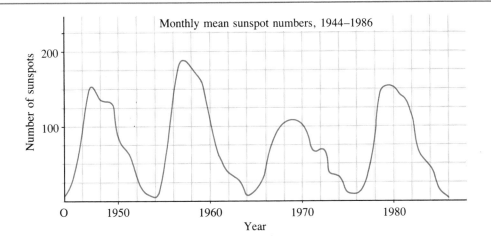

3. The graph shows that sunspot activity increases and decreases at fairly regular intervals. Estimate the number of years, on the average, between the times when there is a maximum number of sunspots.

Lengths of shadows

The graph below shows how the length of the shadow of a 100-m building varies during a three-day period. It is assumed that the sun is directly overhead at noon.

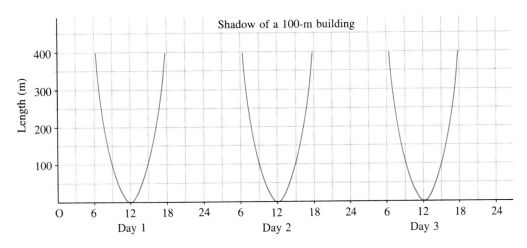

4. a) How long is the shadow at 8 A.M.? at 2 P.M.?
   b) For about how many hours during the day is the shadow longer than 100 m?

5. In many localities the sun is never directly overhead. What change would be needed in the graph if it were drawn for such a locality?

Blood pressure and volume

There are two significant phases to a heart-beat. During the systolic phase, the heart contracts, and pumps blood into the arteries. This phase is marked by a sudden increase in the pressure and a decrease in the volume of blood in the heart. The second phase is the diastolic phase, when the heart relaxes. The pressure decreases and the volume increases as more blood is drawn into the heart from the veins.

Graphs showing how the pressure and volume of blood in the left ventricle of the heart vary during five consecutive heartbeats are shown below. The time scale is the same for both graphs.

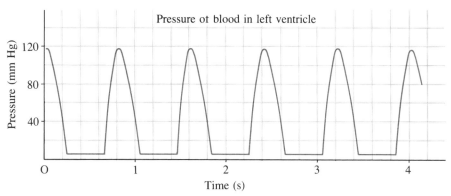

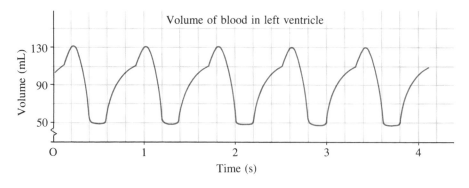

6. During intense physical activity the heart beats faster to satisfy the body's demand for more oxygen. Suppose graphs showing the variation of blood pressure and volume were drawn in this situation. How would the graphs differ from those above? In what ways would they be similar?

Volume of air in the lungs

The volume of air in your lungs is a periodic function of time. This graph shows how the volume of air in the lungs varies during normal breathing.

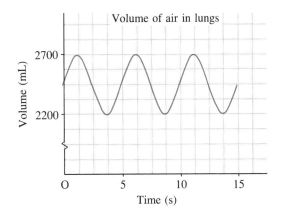

7. According to the graph, how long does it take to inhale and exhale once?

8. When the average person takes a deep breath, about 5000 mL of air can be inhaled. But only about 4000 mL of this air can be exhaled. Suppose that such a breath takes twice as much time as a normal breath. If a graph similar to the one shown were drawn for deep breathing, in what ways would it differ?

Summary

The graphs in this section suggest what is meant by a *periodic function*. The graph of such a function repeats in a regular way. The length of the part that repeats, measured along the horizontal axis, is called the *period* of the function.

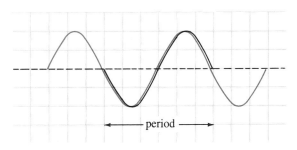

9. All periodic functions have a period. Estimate the period for the functions illustrated above.

10. State the period of this function.

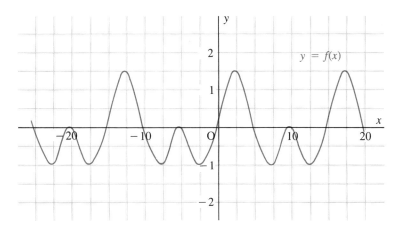

11. One of the examples in this section suggests a periodic function, but it is not a periodic function. Which example is this?

5-2 RADIAN MEASURE

When we construct a circle graph, we assume that the area of a *sector* of a circle is proportional to the *sector angle*. The length of the arc bounding the sector is proportional to the sector angle and is called the *arc length*.

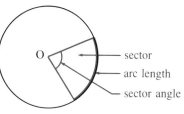

Example 1. Calculate the arc length of a sector of a circle of radius 20 cm if the sector angle is 140°.

Solution. Since the angle subtended at the centre of the circle by the circumference is 360°,

the arc length of the sector shown is $\frac{140}{360}$ of the circumference.

$$\frac{\text{Arc length}}{\text{Circumference}} = \frac{140}{360}$$

The circumference of the circle is $2\pi(20)$, or 40π.

Therefore, arc length $= \frac{140}{360}(40\pi)$

$$\doteq 48.9$$

The arc length is about 49 cm.

Example 1 illustrates the following relationship.

$$\frac{\text{Arc length of a sector}}{\text{Circumference}} = \frac{\text{Sector angle}}{\text{Full-turn angle}}$$

Using this relationship, we can calculate the sector angle that corresponds to a given arc length.

Example 2. Find the measure of the angle, to the nearest tenth of a degree, subtended at the centre of a circle, radius R, by an arc of each length.
   a) R b) $2R$ c) $3R$

Solution. a) Rewrite the proportion above.

$$\frac{\text{Sector angle}}{\text{Full-turn angle}} = \frac{\text{Arc length}}{\text{Circumference}}$$

For an arc length R

$$\frac{\text{Sector angle}}{360°} = \frac{R}{2\pi R}$$

Therefore, sector angle $= \frac{360°}{2\pi}$

$$= \frac{180°}{\pi}$$

$$\doteq 57.3°$$

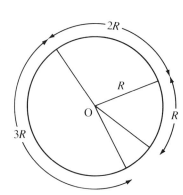

b) Since the sector angle is proportional to the arc length, for an arc length $2R$ the sector angle is twice as large as in part a).

$$\text{Sector angle} = 2\left(\frac{180°}{\pi}\right)$$
$$\doteq 114.6°$$

c) Similarly, for an arc length $3R$

$$\text{Sector angle} = 3\left(\frac{180°}{\pi}\right)$$
$$\doteq 171.9°$$

In *Example 2* we discovered that an angle of $\frac{180°}{\pi}$ (approximately 57°) is subtended at the centre of a circle by an arc of length R, where R is the radius.

Definition: One *radian* is the measure of an angle which is subtended at the centre of a circle by an arc equal in length to the radius of the circle.

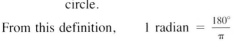

From this definition, 1 radian $= \frac{180°}{\pi}$.

Multiply both sides by π, to get the following result.

$$\boxed{\pi \text{ radians} = 180°}$$

Hence, a full-turn angle, 360°, is equal to 2π radians.

We can use this result to derive a simple relation between the arc length, the radius, and the sector angle measured in radians. Let a represent the arc length which subtends an angle θ radians at the centre of a circle, radius R.

Substitute in this proportion.

$$\frac{\text{Arc length of a sector}}{\text{Circumference}} = \frac{\text{Sector angle}}{\text{Full-turn angle}}$$
$$\frac{a}{2\pi R} = \frac{\theta}{2\pi}$$
$$a = R\theta$$

This formula can be used to find an arc length if the angle it subtends at the centre of the circle is measured in radians.

The arc length a subtended by an angle θ radians in a circle with radius R is given by the formula: $a = R\theta$

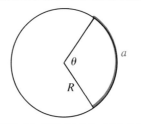

The fact that π radians is equal to 180° can be used to convert from radians to degrees, and vice versa.

Example 3.   Express each angle to 2 decimal places.

  a) 4 radians in degrees   b) 138° in radians

Solution.   a) π radians $= 180°$ b) $180° = \pi$ radians

$$1 \text{ radian} = \frac{180°}{\pi}$$ $$1° = \frac{\pi}{180} \text{ radians}$$

$$4 \text{ radians} = 4\left(\frac{180°}{\pi}\right)$$ $$138° = 138\left(\frac{\pi}{180}\right) \text{ radians}$$

$$\doteq 229.18°$$ $$\doteq 2.41 \text{ radians}$$

Most scientific calculators have keys which enable you to convert from radians to degrees, and vice versa. Read your calculator manual to determine how to make these conversions. Verify the answers in *Example 3*.

Example 4.   A circle has radius 6.5 cm. Calculate the length of an arc of this circle subtended by each angle.

  a) 2.4 radians   b) 75°

Solution.   a) $a = R\theta$

$$a = (6.5)(2.4)$$
$$= 15.6$$

The arc length is 15.6 cm.

  b) To use the formula $a = R\theta$, the angle must be in radians.

$$180° = \pi \text{ radians}$$

$$1° = \frac{\pi}{180} \text{ radians}$$

$$75° = 75\left(\frac{\pi}{180}\right) \text{ radians}$$

$$\doteq 1.309 \text{ radians}$$

Substitute in the formula $a = R\theta$.

$$a = R\theta$$
$$\doteq (6.5)(1.309)$$
$$\doteq 8.5085$$

The arc length is approximately 8.5 cm.

EXERCISES 5-2

1. Convert from degrees to radians. Express the answer in terms of π.

  a) 30°   b) 45°   c) 60°   d) 90°   e) 120°   f) 135°
  g) 150°   h) 180°   i) 210°   j) 225°   k) 240°   l) 270°
  m) 300°   n) 315°   o) 330°   p) 360°   q) 390°   r) 405°

2. Convert from radians to degrees.

   a) $\frac{\pi}{2}$ radians
   b) $\frac{3\pi}{4}$ radians
   c) $-\frac{2\pi}{3}$ radians
   d) $\frac{7\pi}{6}$ radians

   e) $\frac{\pi}{4}$ radians
   f) $-\frac{3\pi}{2}$ radians
   g) $\frac{7\pi}{4}$ radians
   h) 2π radians

   i) $-\frac{5\pi}{3}$ radians
   j) $\frac{5\pi}{4}$ radians
   k) $\frac{\pi}{6}$ radians
   l) $-\frac{11\pi}{6}$ radians

3. Convert from degrees to radians. Give the answers to 2 decimal places.

   a) $100°$
   b) $225°$
   c) $57.3°$
   d) $-125°$
   e) $75x°$
   f) $\frac{60°}{\pi}$

   g) $-65°$
   h) $24.5x°$
   i) $150°$
   j) $30°$
   k) $\frac{180°}{\pi}$
   l) $-90x°$

4. Convert from radians to degrees. Give the answers to 1 decimal place.
   a) 2 radians
   b) -5 radians
   c) 3.2 radians
   d) 1.8 radians
   e) -0.7 radians
   f) 1.4θ radians
   g) 6.7 radians
   h) $-2\pi x$ radians

5. Find the length of the arc which subtends each angle at the centre of a circle of radius 5 cm. Give the answers to 1 decimal place.
   a) 2.0 radians
   b) 3.0 radians
   c) 1.8 radians
   d) 6.1 radians
   e) 4.2 radians
   f) 0.6 radians

6. Find the length of the arc of a circle with radius 12 cm that subtends each sector angle. Give the answers to 1 decimal place where necessary.
   a) $135°$
   b) $75°$
   c) $105°$
   d) $165°$
   e) $240°$
   f) $180°$
   g) $310°$
   h) $200°$

7. Find the arc length to the nearest centimetre of the sector of a circle with radius:
   a) 7 m, if the sector angle is   i) $120°$ ii) $210°$
   b) 90 cm, if the sector angle is   i) $30°$ ii) $225°$
   c) 216 mm, if the sector angle is   i) $135°$ ii) $300°$.

Ⓑ

8. How many radians are there in:
   a) a full turn
   b) a half turn
   c) a quarter turn?

9. Calculate the arc length to the nearest metre of a sector of a circle with radius 6 m if the sector angle is $140°$.

10. Two sectors of the same circle have sector angles of $35°$ and $105°$ respectively. The arc length of the smaller sector is 17 cm. What is the arc length of the larger sector?

11. Write an expression for the measure in radians of the sector angle of a sector, in a circle graph with radius r, which represents $x\%$ of the total area.

12. The Earth travels in a nearly circular
    orbit around the sun. The radius of the
    orbit is about 149 000 000 km.
    a) What is the measure in radians of
       the angle subtended at the sun by the
       positions of the Earth at two differ-
       ent times 24 h apart?
    b) About how far does the Earth travel
       in one day in its orbit around the sun?

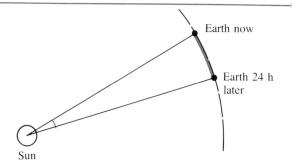

Earth now

Earth 24 h
later

Sun

Ⓒ

13. The *angular velocity* of an object is the angle per unit time through which an object
    rotates about a rotation centre.
    a) What is the angular velocity in radians per second of a car tire of diameter
       64 cm when the car is travelling at 100 km/h?
    b) Write an expression for the angular velocity in radians per second for a car tire
       of diameter d centimetres when the car is travelling at x kilometres per hour?

14. a) Write expressions for the distance
       from A to B:
       i) along the line segment AB
       ii) along the circular arc from A to B.
    b) How many times as long as the
       straight-line distance is the distance
       along the circular arc from A to B?
    c) Write an expression for the area of
       the shaded segment of the circle.
    d) Write an expression for the shortest
       distance from the vertex of the
       right angle to the line segment AB.

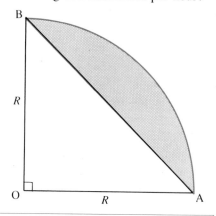

B

R

O   R   A

 INVESTIGATE

A Reason for Introducing Radian Measure

1. The formula $a = R\theta$ for the arc length subtended by an angle θ radians
   in a circle with radius R was derived in this section. Derive a similar formula
   if the measure of the angle is degrees instead of radians. Then compare
   the two formulas.

2. a) Derive a formula for the area of a sector formed by an angle θ radians
      in a circle with radius R.
   b) Derive a similar formula if the measure of the angle is degrees. Then
      compare the two formulas.

3. Suggest an advantage of using radian measure instead of degree measure
   for angles.

5-3 TRIGONOMETRIC FUNCTIONS OF ANGLES IN STANDARD POSITION

Perhaps the simplest example of periodic motion is motion in a circle. To study motion in a circle, we define the standard position of an angle.

Let $P(x,y)$ represent a point which moves around a circle with radius r and centre $(0,0)$. P starts at the point $A(r,0)$ on the x-axis. For any position of P, an angle θ is defined, which represents the amount of rotation about the origin. We say that the angle θ is in *standard position*, where OA is the *initial arm* and OP is the *terminal arm*. If $\theta > 0°$, the rotation is counterclockwise. If $\theta < 0°$, the rotation is clockwise. The measure of the angle may be in degrees or in radians.

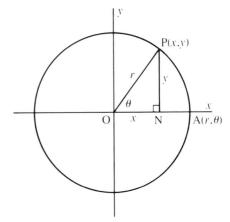

For any position of P on the circle, we define the *primary trigonometric functions* of θ as follows.

$$\sin \theta = \frac{y}{r} \qquad \cos \theta = \frac{x}{r} \qquad \tan \theta = \frac{y}{x} \qquad x \neq 0$$

where $r = \sqrt{x^2 + y^2}$

We can use these definitions to determine the sine, cosine, or tangent of any angle θ in standard position.

Example 1. The point $P(-1,2)$ is on the terminal arm of an angle θ.
    a) Draw a diagram showing θ in standard position.
    b) Calculate the values of $\sin \theta$, $\cos \theta$, and $\tan \theta$ to five decimal places.

Solution.   a)

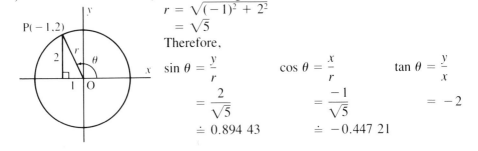

b) From the diagram,
$$r = \sqrt{(-1)^2 + 2^2}$$
$$= \sqrt{5}$$
Therefore,

$$\sin \theta = \frac{y}{r} \qquad\qquad \cos \theta = \frac{x}{r} \qquad\qquad \tan \theta = \frac{y}{x}$$

$$= \frac{2}{\sqrt{5}} \qquad\qquad = \frac{-1}{\sqrt{5}} \qquad\qquad = -2$$

$$\doteq 0.894\ 43 \qquad\qquad \doteq -0.447\ 21$$

In *Example 1*, notice that sin θ is positive, while both cos θ and tan θ are negative. This is because θ is in the second quadrant, where x is negative. The table below summarizes the possible combinations of signs for each function. Since $r = \sqrt{x^2 + y^2}$, its sign is always positive.

	Quadrant I	Quadrant II	Quadrant III	Quadrant IV
Sign of $\sin \theta = \dfrac{y}{r}$	+	+	−	−
Sign of $\cos \theta = \dfrac{x}{r}$	+	−	−	+
Sign of $\tan \theta = \dfrac{y}{x}$	+	−	+	−

We can use a scientific calculator to find the sine, cosine, or tangent of any angle when its measure is given in degrees or radians. When the angle is in radians, it is customary to indicate no unit.

Example 2. Find each value to five decimal places.
   a) tan 125°   b) cos 2.4

Solution. a) First be sure that the calculator is in *degree mode*.
              tan 125° $\doteq$ −1.428 15
           b) Since there is no unit for the angle, the angle is in radians. Be sure that the calculator is in *radian mode*.
              cos 2.4 $\doteq$ −0.737 39

As θ rotates around the circle, past 360° or 2π, the same values of x and y are encountered as before. Hence, in *Example 2*, there are infinitely many other angles which have the same tangent as 125°, or the same cosine as 2.4 radians.

Use your calculator to verify that these expressions are also equal to tan 125°.
tan (125° + 360°), or tan 485°
tan (125° + 720°), or tan 845°
tan (125° − 360°), or tan (−235°)

Use your calculator to verify that these expressions are also equal to cos 2.4.
cos (2.4 + 2π)
cos (2.4 + 4π)
cos (2.4 − 2π)

Conversely, if an equation such as sin θ = 0.75 is given, there are infinitely many values of θ which satisfy the equation. These are called the *roots* of the equation. We are normally interested only in the roots between 0° and 360° (if θ is in degrees) or between 0 and 2π (if θ is in radians).

Example 3. Solve the equation sin θ = 0.85 for θ in radians, to two decimal places, where 0 $\leq$ θ $\leq$ 2π.

Solution. Since sin θ is positive, and sin θ = $\frac{y}{r}$, θ lies in the quadrants in which

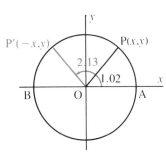

y > 0, namely, Quadrants I and II.
In radian mode, use the inverse sine key
to obtain 1.015 985 3.

Hence, one root is 1.02. Since 1.02 < $\frac{\pi}{2}$,

this root is in Quadrant 1.
To find the root in Quadrant II,
consider the diagram.
P'($-x,y$) is the reflection of P(x,y)
in the y-axis.
By symmetry, $\angle$P'OB = $\angle$POA,
or approximately 1.02
Hence, $\angle$P'OA = π − 1.015 985 3
$\doteq$ 2.125 607 3
To two decimal places, the equation sin θ = 0.85 has two roots between
0 and 2π: θ_1 = 1.02 and θ_2 = 2.13.

In *Example 3*, notice that when the values of the angle are subtracted from π, more than two decimal places are used. This avoids rounding errors.

Example 3 illustrates the following general result.

Property of sine functions
If k is a constant between −1 and +1, the
equation sin θ = k has infinitely many roots.

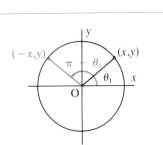

If θ_1 is one root, then another root is:
θ_2 = π − θ_1 (in radians)

All other roots can be found by adding multiples
of 2π to θ_1 or θ_2.

Example 4.   Solve the equation $\sin \theta = -0.428$ in radians, to two decimal places, where $0 \leqslant \theta \leqslant 2\pi$.

Solution.   Since $\sin \theta$ is negative, and $\sin \theta = \frac{y}{r}$, θ lies in the quadrants in which $y < 0$, namely, Quadrants III and IV.
In radian mode, use the inverse sine key to obtain $-0.442\ 278\ 7$.
Hence, one root of the equation is approximately -0.44. Although this is not between 0 and 2π, we can use it to obtain two roots which are between 0 and 2π.
To obtain one root, add 2π: $-0.442\ 278\ 7 + 2\pi \doteq 5.840\ 906\ 6$.
This is the root in Quadrant IV.
To obtain the other root, use the property of sine functions.
Another angle that satisfies the equation is:
$\pi - (-0.442\ 278\ 7) = 3.583\ 871\ 3$.   This is the root in Quadrant III.
To two decimal places, the equation $\sin \theta = -0.428$ has two roots between 0 and 2π: $\theta_1 = 3.58$ and $\theta_2 = 5.84$.
Check these results with your calculator.

Example 5.   Solve the equation $\cos \theta = -0.375$ in radians, to two decimal places, where $0 \leqslant \theta \leqslant 2\pi$.

Solution.   Since $\cos \theta$ is negative, and $\cos \theta = \frac{x}{r}$, θ lies in the quadrants in which $x < 0$, namely, Quadrants II and III.
Use the inverse cosine key to obtain $1.955\ 193\ 1$.
Hence, one root is 1.96, which is in Quadrant II.
To find the root in Quadrant III, consider the diagram. $P'(x, -y)$ is the reflection of $P(x,y)$ in the x-axis. By symmetry, $\angle P'OA = \angle POA$, or approximately 1.96.
Hence, as an angle in standard position,
$\angle P'OA = 2\pi - 1.955\ 193\ 1$
$\qquad\qquad \doteq 4.327\ 992\ 2$
This is the root in Quadrant III.
To two decimal places, the equation $\cos \theta = -0.375$ has two roots between 0 and 2π: $\theta_1 = 1.96$ and $\theta_2 = 4.33$.

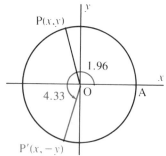

Example 5 illustrates the following general result.

Property of cosine functions
If θ_1 is any value of θ such that $\cos \theta = k$, then another value of θ that satisfies this equation is:
$\theta_2 = 2\pi - \theta_1$ (in radians)
All other roots can be found by adding multiples of 2π to θ_1 or θ_2.

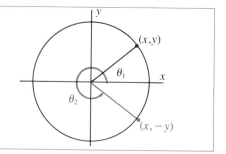

Example 6. Solve the equation $\tan \theta = 1.75$ in radians, to four decimal places, where $0 < \theta < 2\pi$.

Solution. Since $\tan \theta$ is positive, and $\tan \theta = \frac{y}{x}$, θ lies in the quadrants in which

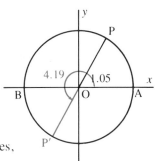

$y > 0$ and $x > 0$, or $y < 0$ and $x < 0$, namely, Quadrants I and III. Use the inverse tangent key to obtain 1.051 650 2. Hence, one root is 1.0517, which is in Quadrant I. To find the root in Quadrant III, consider the diagram. $P'(-x, -y)$ is the reflection of $P(x,y)$ in the origin. By symmetry, $\angle P'OB = \angle POA$, or approximately 1.0517. Hence, as an angle in standard position,

$$\angle P'OA = \pi + 1.051\ 650\ 2$$
$$\doteq 4.193\ 242\ 9$$

This is the root in Quadrant III. To four decimal places, the equation $\tan \theta = 1.75$ has two roots between 0 and 2π: $\theta_1 = 1.0517$ and $\theta_2 = 4.1932$.

Example 6 illustrates the following general result.

Property of tangent functions
If θ_1 is any value of θ such that $\tan \theta = k$, then another value of θ which satisfies this equation is:
$\theta_2 = \pi + \theta_1$ (in radians)
All other roots can be found by adding multiples of π to θ_1.

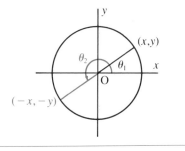

Note: After this section, all angle measures in this book will be in radians, unless stated otherwise.

EXERCISES 5-3

(A)

1. Use a scientific calculator in degree mode. Find each value to 5 decimal places.
   a) $\sin 110°$ b) $\cos 154°$ c) $\tan 103°$ d) $\sin 202°$
   e) $\cos 216°$ f) $\sin 352°$ g) $\tan 337°$ h) $\cos 543°$

2. Use a scientific calculator in radian mode. Find each value to 5 decimal places.
   a) $\sin 0.3$ b) $\cos 0.7$ c) $\tan 1.4$ d) $\sin 1.6$
   e) $\cos 3.2$ f) $\tan 5.05$ g) $\sin 5.93$ h) $\cos 8.57$

3. The point $P(4, -2)$ is on the terminal arm of an angle θ.
   a) Draw a diagram showing θ in standard position.
   b) Calculate $\sin \theta$, $\cos \theta$, and $\tan \theta$ to 5 decimal places.

4. The point P($-2,3$) is on the terminal arm of an angle θ.
   a) Draw a diagram showing θ in standard position.
   b) Calculate sin θ, cos θ, and tan θ to 5 decimal places.

5. Solve for θ in radians to 2 decimal places, if $0 < \theta < 2\pi$.
   a) cos θ = 0.73
   b) tan θ = 0.512
   c) cos θ = 0.165
   d) tan θ = 0.1976
   e) sin θ = 0.3324
   f) cos θ = 0.6215

(B)

6. Each point P is on the terminal arm of an angle θ. Use a diagram to calculate sin θ, cos θ, and tan θ.
   a) P($11,-6$)
   b) P($-5,-1$)
   c) P($-4,2$)
   d) P($-4,-5$)
   e) P($5,-3$)
   f) P($3,8$)
   g) P($0,3$)
   h) P($-4,0$)

7. a) Find sin 135° to 5 decimal places.
   b) Find three other angles which have the same sine as 135°, and verify with a calculator.

8. a) Find tan 5.6 to 5 decimal places.
   b) Find three other angles which have the same tangent as 5.6 radians, and verify with a calculator.

9. Solve for θ to the nearest degree, if $0° < \theta < 360°$.
   a) sin θ = -0.3926
   b) cos θ = -0.7515
   c) tan θ = 0.3125
   d) tan θ = -0.8642
   e) cos θ = -0.4875
   f) sin θ = 0.2425

10. Solve for θ in radians to 2 decimal places, if $0 < \theta < 2\pi$.
    a) tan θ = -0.318
    b) sin θ = -0.525
    c) cos θ = -0.8076
    d) cos θ = 0.2599
    e) tan θ = -0.6741
    f) sin θ = 0.4892

11. Solve for θ:
    a) to the nearest degree, if $0° < \theta < 360°$
    b) in radians to 2 decimal places, if $0 < \theta < 2\pi$.
       i) tan θ = 0.92
       ii) tan θ = -1.425
       iii) tan θ = -2.0217

12. The angle θ is in the first quadrant, and tan θ = $\frac{4}{5}$.
    a) Draw a diagram showing the angle in standard position and a point P on its terminal arm.
    b) Determine possible coordinates for P.
    c) Find the other two primary trigonometric functions of θ.

13. Repeat *Exercise 12* if θ is in the second quadrant, and tan θ = $-\frac{5}{3}$.

14. Repeat *Exercise 12* if θ is in the second quadrant, and sin θ = $\frac{3}{\sqrt{10}}$.

(C)

15. You can use a scientific calculator to find the sine, the cosine, or the tangent of any angle in standard position.
    a) Determine the largest angle your calculator will accept: in degrees; in radians.
    b) Are these two angles equal?

5-4 THE RECIPROCAL TRIGONOMETRIC RATIOS

To this point, we have defined the three primary trigonometric ratios of an angle θ.

$$\sin \theta = \frac{\text{opposite}}{\text{hypotenuse}} \qquad \cos \theta = \frac{\text{adjacent}}{\text{hypotenuse}} \qquad \tan \theta = \frac{\text{opposite}}{\text{adjacent}}$$

The reciprocals of these ratios are respectively called the *cosecant*, *secant*, and *cotangent ratios* and are abbreviated as *csc*, *sec*, and *cot*. These *reciprocal trigonometric ratios* are defined as follows.

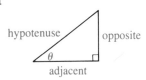

$$\csc \theta = \frac{\text{hypotenuse}}{\text{opposite}} \qquad \sec \theta = \frac{\text{hypotenuse}}{\text{adjacent}} \qquad \cot \theta = \frac{\text{adjacent}}{\text{opposite}}$$

It follows from these definitions that:

$$\csc \theta = \frac{1}{\sin \theta} \qquad \sec \theta = \frac{1}{\cos \theta} \qquad \cot \theta = \frac{1}{\tan \theta}.$$

Since we can readily compute the value of a reciprocal ratio by taking the reciprocal of a primary ratio, most scientific calculators have keys for only the primary trigonometric ratios. For example, to obtain csc 36° on a calculator, we find sin 36° and use the reciprocal key $\boxed{1/x}$.

Example 1. Find the values of the six trigonometric ratios for 47°.

Solution. Use a calculator.

$\sin 47° \doteq 0.731\ 353\ 7$
$\csc 47° \doteq 1.367\ 327\ 5$
$\cos 47° \doteq 0.681\ 998\ 4$
$\sec 47° \doteq 1.466\ 279\ 2$
$\tan 47° \doteq 1.072\ 368\ 7$
$\cot 47° \doteq 0.932\ 515\ 1$

Example 2. Write the six trigonometric ratios for the two acute angles in the right triangle with sides of length 12, 35, and 37 units.

Solution. Let α and β represent the acute angles. From the definition of the trigonometric ratios

$$\sin \alpha = \frac{12}{37} \qquad \cos \alpha = \frac{35}{37} \qquad \tan \alpha = \frac{12}{35}$$

$$\csc \alpha = \frac{37}{12} \qquad \sec \alpha = \frac{37}{35} \qquad \cot \alpha = \frac{35}{12}$$

$$\sin \beta = \frac{35}{37} \qquad \cos \beta = \frac{12}{37} \qquad \tan \beta = \frac{35}{12}$$

$$\csc \beta = \frac{37}{35} \qquad \sec \beta = \frac{37}{12} \qquad \cot \beta = \frac{12}{35}$$

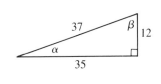

Example 2 not only shows the relationship between the primary and reciprocal ratios, but the diagram suggests a relationship between the trigonometric ratios of two angles which total 90°.

Since $\sin \alpha = \cos \beta = \frac{12}{37}$, and $\beta = 90° - \alpha$

then $\sin \alpha = \cos (90° - \alpha)$

Similarly, $\cos \alpha = \sin (90° - \alpha)$ and $\tan \alpha = \cot (90° - \alpha)$

Just as we can calculate all primary trigonometric ratios given any one primary trigonometric ratio, so also we can calculate all trigonometric ratios given any one trigonometric ratio.

Example 3.   If $\cot \theta = \dfrac{b}{a}$, write expressions for the six trigonometric ratios for θ.

Solution.   Sketch a right triangle with side a opposite θ and side b adjacent θ.

From the Pythagorean Theorem, the hypotenuse has length $\sqrt{a^2 + b^2}$.

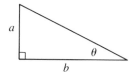

From the definition of the trigonometric ratios

$$\sin \theta = \frac{a}{\sqrt{a^2 + b^2}} \qquad \cos \theta = \frac{b}{\sqrt{a^2 + b^2}} \qquad \tan \theta = \frac{a}{b}$$

$$\csc \theta = \frac{\sqrt{a^2 + b^2}}{a} \qquad \sec \theta = \frac{\sqrt{a^2 + b^2}}{b} \qquad \cot \theta = \frac{b}{a}$$

Example 4.   Find each value of θ to the nearest degree.

a) $\cot \theta = 1.234$ b) $\sec \theta = 2.561$ c) $\csc \theta = 4.032$

Solution.   a) Since $\tan \theta = \dfrac{1}{\cot \theta}$

$$\tan \theta = \frac{1}{1.234}$$
$$\doteq 0.810\ 372\ 8$$
$$\theta \doteq 39°$$

b) Since $\cos \theta = \dfrac{1}{\sec \theta}$

$$\cos \theta = \frac{1}{2.561}$$
$$\doteq 0.390\ 472\ 5$$
$$\theta \doteq 67°$$

c) Since $\sin \theta = \dfrac{1}{\csc \theta}$

$$\sin \theta = \frac{1}{4.032}$$
$$\doteq 0.248\ 015\ 9$$
$$\theta \doteq 14°$$

EXERCISES 5-4

(A)

1. Find the value to 3 decimal places of each trigonometric ratio.
   a) csc 17°   b) cot 29°   c) sec 64°   d) cot 81°   e) sec 57°   f) csc 71°
   g) cot 11°   h) sec 9°   i) cot 53°   j) csc 39°   k) sec 23°   l) csc 84°

2. Find the values to 3 decimal places of the six trigonometric ratios for each angle.
   a) 25°   b) 50°   c) 75°   d) 30°   e) 45°   f) 60°

3. Find each value of θ to the nearest degree, if θ is acute.
   a) csc θ = 1.624   b) cot θ = 0.675   c) sec θ = 1.058   d) cot θ = 0.554
   e) sec θ = 1.325   f) csc θ = 1.305   g) cot θ = 3.732   h) sec θ = 3.628
   i) csc θ = 2.591   j) sec θ = 2.591   k) cot θ = 4.915   l) csc θ = 1.267

(B)

4. Write expressions for the six
   trigonometric ratios of each angle.
   a) ∠A   b) ∠B

5. Match each ratio in the first row with
   an equivalent ratio from the second
   row if ∠A + ∠B = 90°.

   sin A   cos A   tan A   csc A   sec A   cot A
   sin B   cos B   tan B   csc B   sec B   cot B

6. Solve each triangle. Give the answers to 1 decimal place.
   a)   b)   c)

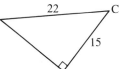
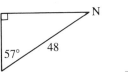
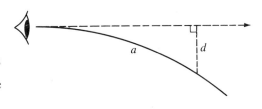

7. Write expressions for the other five trigonometric ratios for each acute angle.

   a) csc $\theta = \dfrac{p}{q}$ b) sec $\phi = \dfrac{x+1}{x-1}$, $x \neq 1$ c) cot $\alpha = \dfrac{2a}{a+1}$, $a \neq -1$

(C)

8. The departure d kilometres of the Earth's surface
   from the line of sight is approximated by this
   formula.

   $d = 6370\left(1 - \cos\left(\dfrac{18a}{637\pi}\right)\right)$ where a kilometres

   is the distance measured along the Earth's surface
   Find the value of d for each given value of a.
   a) 2 km   b) 10 km   c) 50 km   d) 350 km

5-5 FUNCTION VALUES OF SPECIAL ANGLES

This diagram illustrates the angle $\frac{\pi}{4}$ in standard position. If PN is perpendicular to OA, then $\triangle$PON is an isosceles triangle with

$\angle$OPN = $\angle$PON = $\frac{\pi}{4}$.

Let PN = ON = 1
Then, OP = $\sqrt{1^2 + 1^2}$, or $\sqrt{2}$

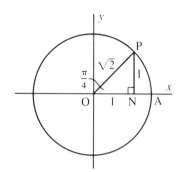

This diagram illustrates the angle $\frac{\pi}{3}$ in standard position. If PN is perpendicular to OA, then $\angle$OPN = $\frac{\pi}{6}$, and $\triangle$OPN is

a $\frac{\pi}{6}, \frac{\pi}{3}, \frac{\pi}{2}$ triangle.

Hence, if OP = 2, then ON = 1, and PN = $\sqrt{3}$.

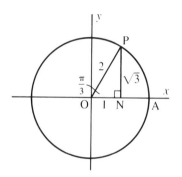

The trigonometric ratios of the angles in the diagrams above can now be calculated. They are shown in the chart below; each angle is in radians.

	sin	cos	tan	csc	sec	cot
$\frac{\pi}{6}$	$\frac{1}{2}$	$\frac{\sqrt{3}}{2}$	$\frac{1}{\sqrt{3}}$	2	$\frac{2}{\sqrt{3}}$	$\sqrt{3}$
$\frac{\pi}{4}$	$\frac{1}{\sqrt{2}}$	$\frac{1}{\sqrt{2}}$	1	$\sqrt{2}$	$\sqrt{2}$	1
$\frac{\pi}{3}$	$\frac{\sqrt{3}}{2}$	$\frac{1}{2}$	$\sqrt{3}$	$\frac{2}{\sqrt{3}}$	2	$\frac{1}{\sqrt{3}}$

The diagrams above can be used to determine the trigonometric ratios for 0 and $\frac{\pi}{2}$.

As OP rotates clockwise, $\angle$PON decreases to 0 radians, OP approaches ON in length, and PN approaches 0.

As OP rotates counterclockwise, $\angle$PON increases to $\frac{\pi}{2}$, PN approaches OP in length, and ON approaches 0.

The trigonometric ratios of 0 radians and $\frac{\pi}{2}$ radians are shown below.

	sin	**cos**	**tan**	**csc**	**sec**	**cot**
0	0	1	0	∞	1	∞
$\dfrac{\pi}{2}$	1	0	∞	1	∞	0

In the previous section, we learned how to find the trigonometric ratios for angles in any quadrant. Recall that the primary ratios, and their reciprocals are all positive in the first quadrant. Only one primary ratio, and its reciprocal are positive in each of the other quadrants.

Example 1. Find the exact values of sin θ, cos θ, and tan θ, for each value of θ.

　　　　a) $\frac{3}{4}\pi$　　　b) $\frac{4}{3}\pi$

Solution. 　a) Since $\angle POA = \frac{3}{4}\pi$, $\angle PON = \pi - \frac{3}{4}\pi$, or $\frac{1}{4}\pi$

$\triangle PON$ is an isosceles right triangle, with sides 1, 1, and $\sqrt{2}$.
　　　In Quadrant II, only the sine ratio is positive.

$$\sin \frac{3}{4}\pi = \frac{1}{\sqrt{2}}$$

$$\cos \frac{3}{4}\pi = -\frac{1}{\sqrt{2}}$$

$$\tan \frac{3}{4}\pi = -1$$

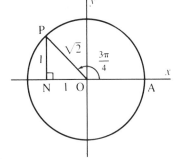

b) Since reflex $\angle POA = \frac{4}{3}\pi$, $\angle PON = \frac{4}{3}\pi - \pi$, or $\frac{\pi}{3}$

$\triangle PON$ is a $\frac{\pi}{6}, \frac{\pi}{3}, \frac{\pi}{2}$ triangle, with sides 1, 2, and $\sqrt{3}$.
　　　In Quadrant III, only the tangent ratio is positive.

$$\sin \frac{4}{3}\pi = -\frac{\sqrt{3}}{2}$$

$$\cos \frac{4}{3}\pi = -\frac{1}{2}$$

$$\tan \frac{4}{3}\pi = \sqrt{3}$$

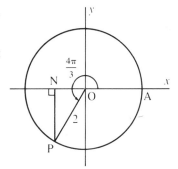

In *Example 1*, each value of $\angle PON$ is called the *reference angle*; that is, the acute angle between OP and the x-axis.

Example 2. Find the exact values of the six trigonometric ratios for each angle.

a) $\dfrac{11\pi}{6}$ b) $\dfrac{3\pi}{2}$

Solution.   a) Since $\angle POA = \dfrac{11\pi}{6}$, the reference

angle $\angle PON = 2\pi - \dfrac{11\pi}{6}$, or $\dfrac{\pi}{6}$

The sides of $\triangle PON$ are 1, 2, and $\sqrt{3}$.

In Quadrant IV, the cosine and secant ratios are positive.

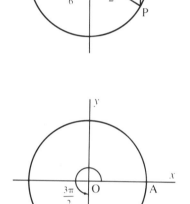

$\sin \dfrac{11\pi}{6} = -\dfrac{1}{2}$ $\qquad$ $\csc \dfrac{11\pi}{6} = -2$

$\cos \dfrac{11\pi}{6} = \dfrac{\sqrt{3}}{2}$ $\qquad$ $\sec \dfrac{11\pi}{6} = \dfrac{2}{\sqrt{3}}$

$\tan \dfrac{11\pi}{6} = -\dfrac{1}{\sqrt{3}}$ $\qquad$ $\cot \dfrac{11\pi}{6} = -\sqrt{3}$

b) For an angle of $\dfrac{3\pi}{2}$, the terminal arm

lies along the negative y-axis.

The "reference angle" is $\dfrac{\pi}{2}$.

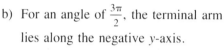

$\sin \dfrac{3\pi}{2} = -1$ $\qquad$ $\csc \dfrac{3\pi}{2} = -1$

$\cos \dfrac{3\pi}{2} = 0$ $\qquad$ $\sec \dfrac{3\pi}{2}$ is undefined

$\tan \dfrac{3\pi}{2}$ is undefined $\qquad$ $\cot \dfrac{3\pi}{2} = 0$

The value of a trigonometric ratio may be raised to a power. For example, $(\sin \theta)^2$ means $(\sin \theta)(\sin \theta)$, and it is written $\sin^2\theta$.

Example 3. Evaluate.   a) $\tan^2 \dfrac{5}{6}\pi$ $\qquad\qquad$ b) $\sec^3 \dfrac{5\pi}{4}$

Solution.   a) $\tan^2 \dfrac{5}{6}\pi = \left(\tan \dfrac{5}{6}\pi\right)^2$ $\qquad\qquad$ b) $\sec^3 \dfrac{5\pi}{4} = \left(\sec \dfrac{5\pi}{4}\right)^3$

$\qquad\qquad\quad = \left(-\dfrac{1}{\sqrt{3}}\right)^2$ $\qquad\qquad\qquad\qquad\qquad = (-\sqrt{2})^3$

$\qquad\qquad\quad = \dfrac{1}{3}$ $\qquad\qquad\qquad\qquad\qquad\qquad\quad = -2\sqrt{2}$

Example 4. If $\cos^2\theta = \dfrac{3}{4}$, find $\sin \theta$ and $\tan \theta$.

Solution.   If $\cos^2\theta = \dfrac{3}{4}$, then $\cos \theta = \pm\dfrac{\sqrt{3}}{2}$

The reference angle is $\dfrac{\pi}{6}$.

For $\cos \theta = \dfrac{\sqrt{3}}{2}$, θ is in Quadrants I or IV.

Hence, $\sin \theta = \pm\frac{1}{2}$ and $\tan \theta = \pm\frac{1}{\sqrt{3}}$

For $\cos \theta = -\frac{\sqrt{3}}{2}$, θ is in Quadrants II or III.

Hence, $\sin \theta = \pm\frac{1}{2}$ and $\tan \theta = \pm\frac{1}{\sqrt{3}}$

EXERCISES 5-5

(A)

1. State the exact value of each ratio.

a) $\sin \frac{\pi}{2}$ b) $\csc \frac{\pi}{3}$ c) $\cos \frac{\pi}{6}$ d) $\tan 0$ e) $\sec \frac{\pi}{3}$ f) $\cot \frac{\pi}{4}$

g) $\csc \frac{\pi}{4}$ h) $\cos \frac{\pi}{4}$ i) $\tan \frac{\pi}{3}$ j) $\sin \frac{\pi}{3}$ k) $\cot \frac{\pi}{2}$ l) $\sec 0$

2. State the exact value of each ratio, where possible.

a) $\sec \frac{3\pi}{4}$ b) $\sin \frac{5\pi}{6}$ c) $\tan \pi$ d) $\cos \frac{7\pi}{3}$ e) $\cot \frac{5\pi}{4}$ f) $\csc 2\pi$

g) $\cos \frac{9\pi}{4}$ h) $\sec \frac{10\pi}{3}$ i) $\csc \frac{8\pi}{3}$ j) $\sin \frac{3\pi}{2}$ k) $\tan \frac{11\pi}{6}$ l) $\cot \frac{7\pi}{3}$

3. Evaluate.

a) $\tan^2 \frac{\pi}{3}$ b) $\csc^2 \frac{5\pi}{6}$ c) $\cos^2 \frac{2\pi}{3}$ d) $\sec^2 \frac{11\pi}{6}$ e) $\sin^3 \frac{7\pi}{4}$ f) $\cot^2 \frac{4\pi}{3}$

(B)

4. Find each value of θ for $0 < \theta < 2\pi$.

a) $\sin \theta = -\frac{1}{2}$ b) $\cos \theta = \frac{1}{\sqrt{2}}$ c) $\tan \theta = -\sqrt{3}$ d) $\csc \theta = 2$

e) $\sec \theta = \sqrt{2}$ f) $\tan \theta = -1$ g) $\sin \theta = \frac{1}{\sqrt{2}}$ h) $\cot \theta = \sqrt{3}$

i) $\cos \theta = -\frac{1}{2}$ j) $\csc \theta = -1$ k) $\sec \theta = -2$ l) $\cot \theta = -\frac{1}{\sqrt{3}}$

5. Find the values of each angle θ if $0 < \theta < 2\pi$.

a) $\sin^2\theta = \frac{1}{2}$ b) $\tan^2\theta = 3$ c) $\sec^2\theta = 2$ d) $\cot^2\theta = \frac{1}{3}$

e) $\csc^2\theta = \frac{4}{3}$ f) $\sec^3\theta = -8$ g) $\sin^3\theta = -\frac{1}{8}$ h) $\tan^2\theta = 1$

6. State the values of the other five trigonometric ratios for each angle θ.

a) $\sin \theta = -\frac{\sqrt{3}}{2}$ b) $\tan \theta = \sqrt{3}$ c) $\sec \theta = -\frac{2}{\sqrt{3}}$

(C)

7. θ is an acute angle defined by a point $P(x, y)$ in the first quadrant. Use x, y, and r to define the six trigonometric ratios of each angle.

a) $\pi + \theta$ b) $2\pi - \theta$

5-6 GRAPHING THE SINE AND COSINE FUNCTIONS

To draw graphs of the functions $y = \sin \theta$ and $y = \cos \theta$, recall their definitions. If $P(x,y)$ is any point on a circle of radius r and centre $(0,0)$, then

$$\sin \theta = \frac{y}{r} \qquad \cos \theta = \frac{x}{r}.$$

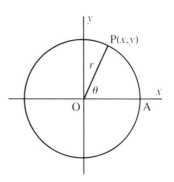

Imagine that P rotates around the circle counterclockwise starting at $A(r,0)$. As θ increases, the values of x and y change periodically. This causes a periodic change in the values of $\sin \theta$ and $\cos \theta$.

Graphing the function $y = \sin \theta$
The function values are independent of the radius of the circle.
Therefore, for convenience, we assume that $r = 2$.
Suppose θ starts at 0 and increases to π. Then $\sin \theta$ changes as follows.

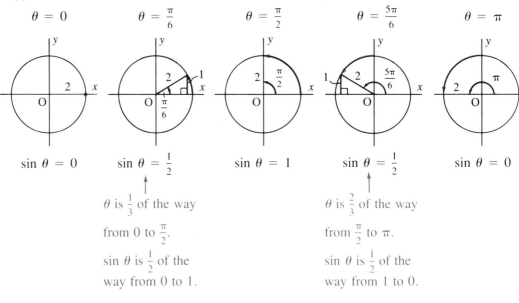

| $\theta = 0$ | $\theta = \dfrac{\pi}{6}$ | $\theta = \dfrac{\pi}{2}$ | $\theta = \dfrac{5\pi}{6}$ | $\theta = \pi$ |

$\sin \theta = 0$ $\qquad \sin \theta = \dfrac{1}{2} \qquad \sin \theta = 1 \qquad \sin \theta = \dfrac{1}{2} \qquad \sin \theta = 0$

θ is $\dfrac{1}{3}$ of the way from 0 to $\dfrac{\pi}{2}$.

$\sin \theta$ is $\dfrac{1}{2}$ of the way from 0 to 1.

θ is $\dfrac{2}{3}$ of the way from $\dfrac{\pi}{2}$ to π.

$\sin \theta$ is $\dfrac{1}{2}$ of the way from 1 to 0.

We use these results to sketch the graph for $0 \le \theta \le \pi$.

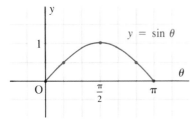

Suppose θ continues from π to 2π. Then $\sin \theta$ changes as follows.

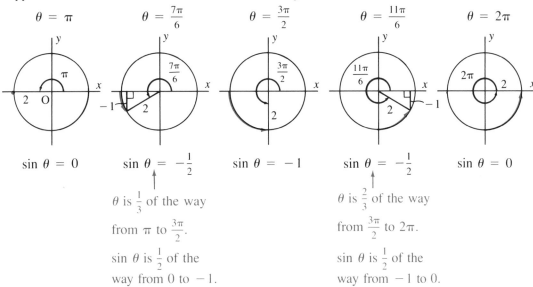

$\theta = \pi$ $\theta = \dfrac{7\pi}{6}$ $\theta = \dfrac{3\pi}{2}$ $\theta = \dfrac{11\pi}{6}$ $\theta = 2\pi$

$\sin \theta = 0$ $\sin \theta = -\dfrac{1}{2}$ $\sin \theta = -1$ $\sin \theta = -\dfrac{1}{2}$ $\sin \theta = 0$

θ is $\dfrac{1}{3}$ of the way from π to $\dfrac{3\pi}{2}$.

$\sin \theta$ is $\dfrac{1}{2}$ of the way from 0 to -1.

θ is $\dfrac{2}{3}$ of the way from $\dfrac{3\pi}{2}$ to 2π.

$\sin \theta$ is $\dfrac{1}{2}$ of the way from -1 to 0.

We use these results to sketch the graph for $\pi \leqslant \theta \leqslant 2\pi$.

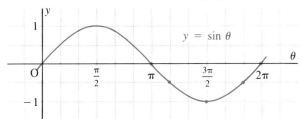

$y = \sin \theta$

As θ continues beyond 2π, P rotates around the circle again, and the same values of $\sin \theta$ are encountered. Hence, the graph can be continued to the right. Similarly, the graph can be continued to the left, corresponding to a rotation in the opposite direction. Hence, the patterns in the graph repeat every 2π in both directions.

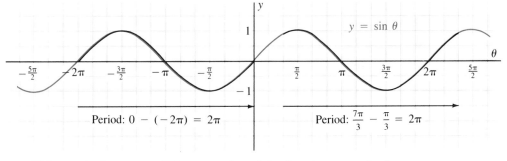

$y = \sin \theta$

Period: $0 - (-2\pi) = 2\pi$ Period: $\dfrac{7\pi}{3} - \dfrac{\pi}{3} = 2\pi$

This graph shows two different cycles of the function $y = \sin \theta$. When θ is in radians, the period of this function is 2π.

A *cycle* of a periodic function is a part of its graph from any point to the first point where the graph starts repeating.

The *period* of a periodic function of θ may be expressed as the difference in the values of θ for the points at the ends of a cycle.

Graphing the function $y = \cos \theta$

We can graph the function $y = \cos \theta$ using the same method as we used to graph the function $y = \sin \theta$. The result is shown below.

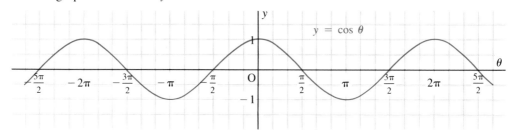

The function $y = \cos \theta$ has a period of 2π. Its graph is congruent to the graph of $y = \sin \theta$, but it is shifted horizontally so that it intersects the y-axis at $(0,1)$ instead of $(0,0)$.

Properties of the function $y = \sin \theta$

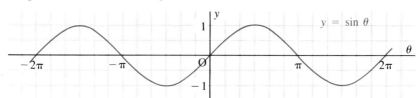

Period: 2π Maximum value of y: 1   Minimum value of y: -1
Domain : θ may represent any angle in standard position
Range: $\{y \mid -1 \leqslant y \leqslant 1\}$
θ-intercepts: ..., $-\pi$, 0, π, 2π, ... y-intercept: 0

Properties of the function $y = \cos \theta$

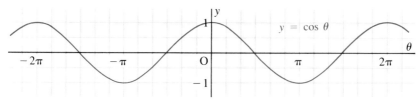

Period: 2π Maximum value of y: 1   Minimum value of y: -1
Domain: θ may represent any angle in standard position
Range: $\{y \mid -1 \leqslant y \leqslant 1\}$

θ-intercepts: ..., $-\dfrac{\pi}{2}, \dfrac{\pi}{2}, \dfrac{3\pi}{2}, \dfrac{5\pi}{2}$, ... y-intercept: 1

These curves are called *sinusoids*, meaning "like sine curves". To use sinusoidal functions in applications involving quantities that change periodically, we must be able to work with them when their maximum and minimum values are different from 1 and −1, and their periods are different from 2π. This involves taking the basic graphs described in this section, and expanding or compressing them in the vertical or horizontal directions, as well as changing their positions relative to the axes. When changes such as these are made to the graphs of these functions, corresponding changes occur in the equations. In the following sections we will investigate how the changes in the equations are related to the changes in the graphs.

EXERCISES 5-6

(A)

1. In the following diagrams, graphs of $y = \sin \theta$ have been started using different scales. Copy each graph on graph paper, and then extend it for the number of cycles indicated.

   a) 2 cycles   b) 2 cycles   c) 1 cycle

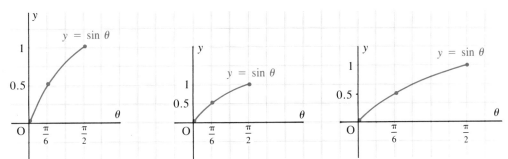

2. **Graphing the function $y = \cos \theta$**

   Let P be a point on the terminal arm of an angle θ in standard position on a circle with radius $r = 2$.

   a) Suppose θ starts at 0 and increases to π. Use diagrams like those on page 216 corresponding to $\theta = 0, \frac{\pi}{3}, \frac{\pi}{2}, \frac{2\pi}{3}$, and π to determine values of $\cos \theta$, and use the results to sketch the graph of $y = \cos \theta$ for $0 \leqslant \theta \leqslant \pi$.

   b) Suppose θ continues from π to 2π. Determine values of $\cos \theta$ for $\theta = \frac{4\pi}{3}, \frac{3\pi}{2}, \frac{5\pi}{3}$, and 2π, and use the results to continue the graph from π to 2π.

   c) Continue the graph of $y = \cos \theta$ for values of θ greater than 2π and less than 0.

3. In the following diagrams, graphs of $y = \cos \theta$ have been started using different scales. Copy each graph on graph paper, and then extend it for the number of cycles indicated.
   a) 2 cycles   b) 2 cycles   c) 4 cycles

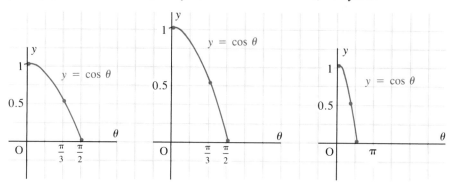

B

4. Without making a table of values, draw graphs of $f(\theta) = \sin \theta$ and $f(\theta) = \cos \theta$ for $-2\pi \leqslant \theta \leqslant 2\pi$.

5. For the graph of $y = \sin \theta$
   a) What is the maximum value of y? For what values of θ does this occur?
   b) What is the minimum value of y? For what values of θ does this occur?
   c) What is the range of the function?
   d) What is the y-intercept?
   e) What are the θ-intercepts?

6. Repeat *Exercise 5* for the graph of $y = \cos \theta$.

7. Compare the graphs of $f(\theta) = \sin \theta$ and $f(\theta) = \cos \theta$. In what ways are they alike? In what ways are they different?

C

8. A function $y = f(x)$ is defined to be *periodic* if there is a number p such that $f(x + p) = f(x)$ for all values of x in the domain. Use this definition to prove that the functions $y = \sin \theta$ and $y = \cos \theta$ are periodic.

9. a) A function $y = f(x)$ is defined to be an *even* function if $f(-x) = f(x)$ for all values of x in the domain. Use this definition to prove that $y = \cos \theta$ is an even function.
   b) A function $y = f(x)$ is defined to be an *odd* function if $f(-x) = -f(x)$ for all values of x in the domain. Use this definition to prove that $y = \sin \theta$ is an odd function.

10. Graph each function.
    a) $y = |\sin \theta|$ b) $y = \sin |\theta|$ c) $y = |\cos \theta|$ d) $y = \cos |\theta|$

INVESTIGATE

Graphing Sinusoids

There is a simple method of sketching the graph of a sinusoidal function without using graph paper. It involves locating nine points on the graph using a rectangle as a guide.

To graph the function $y = \sin \theta$

Step 1. Draw a rectangle divided into 8 congruent sections as shown. Mark the axes, showing their scales. Locate the points which correspond to multiples of $\frac{\pi}{2}$.

Then identify the sections of the rectangle through which the curve will pass. Each section has points marked at the ends of one diagonal.

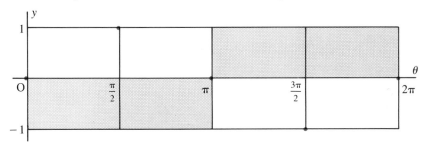

The curve will pass through the unshaded sections.

Step 2. Divide each section into 6 congruent rectangles, as shown. Locate the vertex in each section, which is closest to the point where the graph crosses the θ-axis. Draw a smooth curve through the marked points.

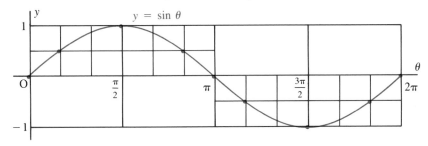

By extending the rectangles to the left or the right, we can sketch additional cycles of $y = \sin \theta$.

1. a) Use the above method to sketch the graph of $f(\theta) = \sin \theta$ for $-2\pi \leq \theta \leq 2\pi$.
   b) Use the method to sketch the graph of $f(\theta) = \cos \theta$ for $-2\pi \leq \theta \leq 2\pi$.

5-7 GRAPHING THE TANGENT FUNCTION

To draw a graph of the tangent function
$f(\theta) = \tan \theta$, recall the definition. If $P(x,y)$
is a point on a circle of radius r and centre

(0,0), then $\tan \theta = \frac{y}{x}$.

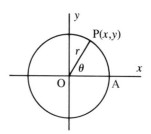

Imagine that P rotates around the circle
counterclockwise, starting at $A(r,0)$. As θ
increases, the values of x and y change
periodically. This causes a periodic change
in the values of $\tan \theta$.

Step 1. Consider values of θ from 0 to $\frac{\pi}{2}$.

When $\theta = 0$, $y = 0$ and $x = r$, so $\tan 0 = \frac{0}{r}$, or 0.

Thus, (0,0) is a point on the graph. As θ increases

from 0 to $\frac{\pi}{4}$, y increases and x decreases.

Hence, $\tan \theta$ increases.

When $\theta = \frac{\pi}{4}$, x and y are equal, so $\tan \frac{\pi}{4} = 1$.

Hence, $\left(\frac{\pi}{4},1\right)$ is a point on the graph. As θ increases

further, $\tan \theta$ continues to increase.

When $\theta = \frac{\pi}{2}$, $y = r$ and $x = 0$. Hence, $\tan \frac{\pi}{2}$ is

undefined. When θ is close to $\frac{\pi}{2}$, $\tan \theta$ is very large.

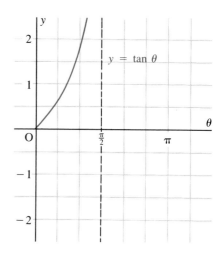

Step 2. Consider values of θ from $\frac{\pi}{2}$ to π.

When θ is close to $\frac{\pi}{2}$, y is very large and positive. But
x is negative, and has a small absolute value. Hence,
$\tan \theta$ is negative and has a very large absolute value.
As θ increases, y decreases and the absolute value of
x increases.
Since $\tan \theta$ is negative, $\tan \theta$ increases.

When $\theta = \frac{3\pi}{4}$, x and y differ only in sign, so

$\tan \frac{3\pi}{4} = -1$. As θ increases further, $\tan \theta$ continues

to increase.

When $\theta = \pi$, $y = 0$ and $x = -r$. Hence,
$\tan \pi = 0$

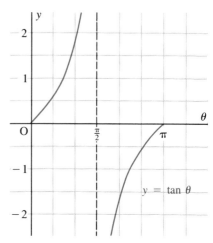

Step 3. This completes one cycle. Other cycles can be graphed similarly.

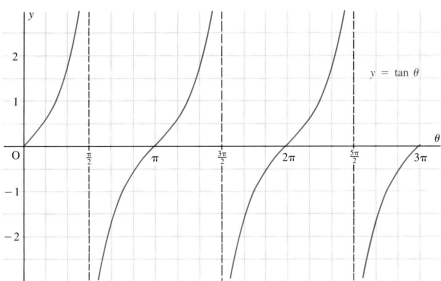

From the graph, we see that the period of the tangent function is π.

The graph of the tangent function illustrates many properties of this function.

Properties of the function $y = \tan \theta$

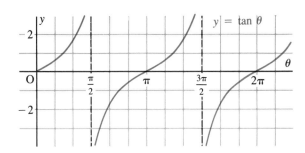

Period: π

Domain: θ may represent any angle in standard position, *except*

$$\ldots -\frac{3\pi}{2}, -\frac{\pi}{2}, \frac{\pi}{2}, \frac{3\pi}{2}, \ldots$$

Range: All real numbers

θ-intercepts: $\ldots -2\pi, -\pi, 0, \pi, 2\pi, \ldots$

y-intercept: 0

EXERCISES 5-7

Ⓐ

1. In the following diagrams, graphs of $y = \tan \theta$ have been started using different scales. Copy each graph on graph paper, and then extend it for at least two cycles.

a)

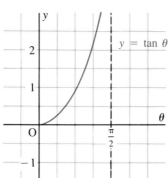

b)

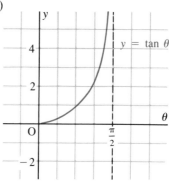

c)

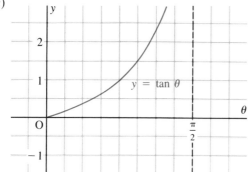

Ⓑ

2. Without making a table of values, draw a graph of $f(\theta) = \tan \theta$ for $-2\pi \leq \theta \leq 2\pi$.

3. For the graph of $y = \tan \theta$
   a) Are there any maximum or minimum values of y? Explain your answer.
   b) What are the domain and the range?
   c) What is the y-intercept?
   d) What are the θ-intercepts?

4. Compare the graph of $f(\theta) = \tan \theta$ with the graphs of $f(\theta) = \sin \theta$ and $f(\theta) = \cos \theta$. In what ways are they alike? In what ways are they different?

Ⓒ

5. Use the definition in Exercise 8, page 220, to prove that the function $f(\theta) = \tan \theta$ is periodic.

6. Is the function $f(\theta) = \tan \theta$ an even function or an odd function? Use the definition in Exercise 9, page 220.

7. Graph each function.
   a) $y = |\tan \theta|$ b) $y = \tan |\theta|$

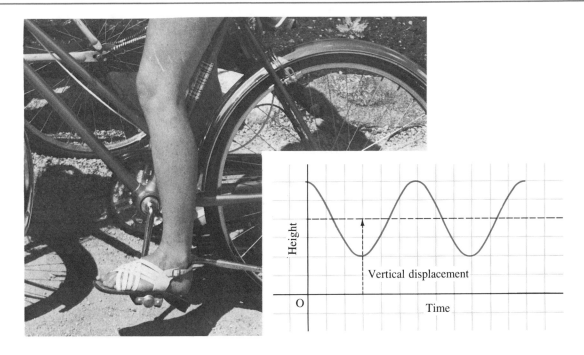

Height

Vertical displacement

O   Time

5-8 VARYING THE VERTICAL DISPLACEMENT AND THE AMPLITUDE OF SINE AND COSINE FUNCTIONS

In this section and the following sections we shall develop a technique for graphing a sinusoidal function without making a table of values.

Varying the Vertical Displacement
As you pedal a bicycle, the heights of the pedals above the ground change periodically. A graph of the height of a pedal against time is a sinusoidal curve with a vertical displacement corresponding to the mean height of the pedal above the ground.

To introduce the vertical displacement of a cosine function, we investigate the effect of q on the graph of $y = \cos \theta + q$. We substitute different values for q, and graph the resulting functions.

If $q = 0$, the equation is $y = \cos \theta$ ... ①

If $q = 1$, the equation is $y = \cos \theta + 1$ ... ②
The y-coordinates of all points on the graph of ② are 1 *greater* than those on the graph of ①. Therefore, the graph of ② is 1 unit *above* the graph of ①. We say that the *vertical displacement* of the function $y = \cos \theta + 1$ is 1.

If $q = -0.5$, the equation is $y = \cos \theta - 0.5$ ... ③
The values of y will all be 0.5 less than those in ①. Therefore, the graph of ③ is 0.5 units *below* the graph of ①. The vertical displacement is -0.5.

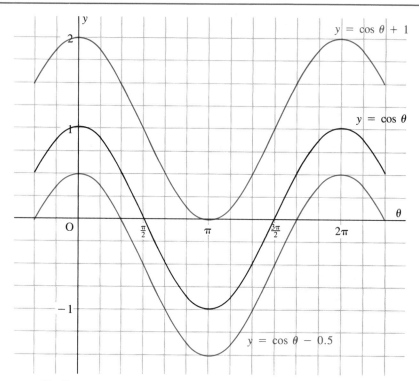

Similar results will be found for other values of q, and for sine functions.

In general, adding a constant to $\sin \theta$ or $\cos \theta$ in the equations of the functions $y = \sin \theta$ or $y = \cos \theta$ causes a vertical translation of the graph. The sign of the constant indicates whether the graph is translated up or down. A positive constant causes a translation up; a negative constant causes a translation down.

The graph of $y = \cos \theta + q$ is related to that of $y = \cos \theta$ by a vertical translation. The vertical displacement is q.

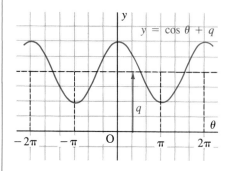

The graph of $y = \sin \theta + q$ is related to that of $y = \sin \theta$ by a vertical translation. The vertical displacement is q.

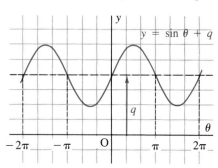

We can draw the graph of an equation in this form without making a table of values.

Example 1. State the vertical displacement for the function $y = \sin\theta + 2$, and draw its graph.

Solution. The vertical displacement is 2.
Draw a graph of $y = \sin\theta$, and then draw its image when translated 2 units up.

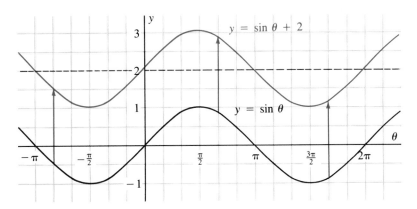

Varying the Amplitude

This graph shows how the top of a building sways in a high wind. The distance the building sways from the centre is called the amplitude of the vibration.

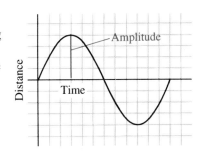

To introduce the amplitude of a sine function, we investigate the effect of a on the graph of $y = a\sin\theta$. We will assume that $a > 0$, since there is no need to consider negative values of a in applications.

If $a = 1$, the equation is $y = \sin\theta$ ... ①
If $a = 2$, the equation is $y = 2\sin\theta$ ... ②
The y-coordinates of all points on the graph of ② are *two times* those on the graph of ①. Therefore, the graph of ② is *expanded* vertically relative to the graph of ①. The factor 2 is called the amplitude of the function.

If $a = \frac{1}{2}$, the equation is $y = \frac{1}{2}\sin\theta$ ... ③
The values of y will all be one-half of those in ①. Therefore, the graph of ③ is *compressed* vertically relative to the graph of ①.

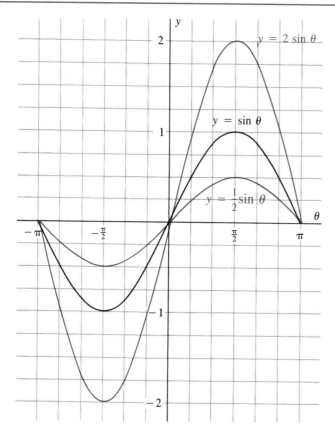

Similar results will be found for other positive values of *a*, and for cosine functions.

In general, multiplying sin θ or cos θ by a positive constant *a* causes a vertical expansion or compression of the graphs of $y = \sin \theta$ or $y = \cos \theta$. That is, for $0 < a < 1$, there is a compression; for $a > 1$, there is an expansion.

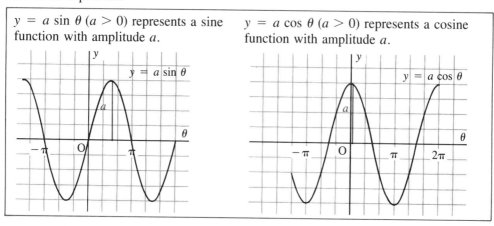

$y = a \sin \theta$ ($a > 0$) represents a sine function with amplitude *a*.

$y = a \cos \theta$ ($a > 0$) represents a cosine function with amplitude *a*.

Since we know that $y = a \sin \theta$ and $y = a \cos \theta$ represent sinusoidal functions with the above properties, we can draw the graph of an equation in this form without making a table of values.

Example 2.   Draw a graph of the function $f(\theta) = 0.75 \cos \theta$, and state its amplitude.

Solution.   Draw a graph of $y = \cos \theta$, then compress it vertically by a factor of 0.75. This means that the y-coordinate of each point on the image is 0.75 times the y-coordinate of the corresponding point on the graph of $y = \cos \theta$.

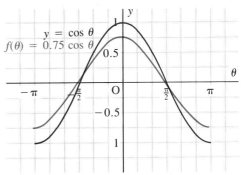

The amplitude of $f(\theta) = 0.75 \cos \theta$ is 0.75.

Vertical displacement and amplitude can be combined in the same function.

Example 3.   Draw a graph of the function $f(\theta) = 2 \sin \theta + 3$ over two cycles.

Solution.   Draw a graph of $y = \sin \theta$, and expand it vertically by a factor of 2. Then translate the image 3 units up.

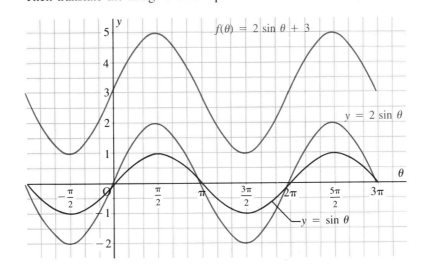

We can use the graph in *Example 3* to derive a definition for the amplitude of a periodic function. In this graph, the maximum value of the function is 5, and the minimum value is 1. The amplitude is one-half the way from the minimum to the maximum, measured in the vertical direction. For this function, the amplitude is $\frac{1}{2}(5 - 1)$, or 2.

If *M* represents the maximum value of a periodic function in any cycle, and *m* represents the minimum value in that cycle, then the *amplitude A* of the function is

$$A = \frac{M - m}{2}$$

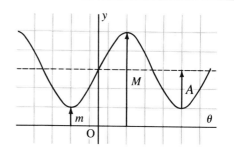

EXERCISES 5-8

Ⓐ

1. a) Graph each set of functions on the same grid for $-\pi \le \theta \le \pi$.
   i) $f(\theta) = \sin \theta$ $f(\theta) = \sin \theta + 1.5$ $f(\theta) = \sin \theta - 2$
   ii) $f(\theta) = \cos \theta$ $f(\theta) = \cos \theta - 3$ $f(\theta) = \cos \theta + 4$

   b) Graph each set of functions on the same grid for $-\pi \le \theta \le \pi$.

   i) $f(\theta) = 2 \cos \theta$ $f(\theta) = \cos \theta$ $f(\theta) = \frac{1}{2} \cos \theta$

   ii) $f(\theta) = 3 \sin \theta$ $f(\theta) = \sin \theta$ $f(\theta) = \frac{1}{4} \sin \theta$

2. Each function graphed below is sinusoidal. Write an equation for each function. State the maximum and minimum values of *y*, and the amplitude.

   a)

   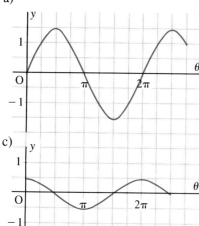

   b)

   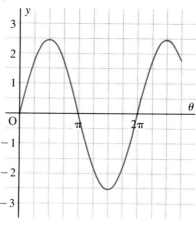

   c)

3. Write an equation to represent each function. State the vertical displacement, the maximum value of *y*, the minimum value of *y*, and the *y*-intercept.

a)

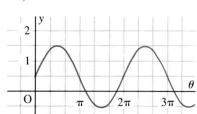

b)

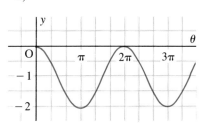

(B)

4. Graph each sinusoidal function over two complete cycles. Determine the maximum and minimum values of the function, and its range.
   a) $y = 5 \sin \theta$
   b) $y = 3 \cos \theta$
   c) $y = 3 \sin \theta + 4$
   d) $f(\theta) = 2 \cos \theta - 3$
   e) $f(\theta) = 4 \sin \theta - 2$
   f) $f(\theta) = \frac{1}{2} \cos \theta + 3$
   g) $f(\theta) = \frac{1}{2} \sin \theta - 1$
   h) $f(\theta) = 2 + 2 \sin \theta$
   i) $f(\theta) = 3 + 3 \cos \theta$

5. Given the function $f(\theta) = a \sin \theta + q$
   a) What is the maximum value of $f(\theta)$? For what values of θ does this occur?
   b) What is the minimum value of $f(\theta)$? For what values of θ does this occur?

6. Repeat *Exercise 5* for the function $g(\theta) = a \cos \theta + q$.

(C)

7. Find the equation of a function of the form $f(\theta) = \sin \theta + p$ whose graph just touches the θ-axis. How many such functions are there?

 INVESTIGATE

Negative values of a in $y = a \sin \theta$ and $y = a \cos \theta$

1. a) Draw graphs of these functions.
      i) $y = -\sin \theta$
      ii) $y = -2 \sin \theta$
      iii) $y = -\frac{1}{2} \sin \theta$
   b) How are the graphs of the functions in part a) related to the graph of the function $y = \sin \theta$?
   c) Draw diagrams to illustrate how the graphs of $y = a \sin \theta$ and $y = a \cos \theta$ are related to the graphs of $y = \sin \theta$ and $y = \cos \theta$ if $a < 0$.
   d) Do negative values of a affect the amplitude? In what way?

2. Graph each function over two cycles, and state the amplitude.
   a) $y = -4 \sin \theta$
   b) $y = -0.2 \sin \theta$
   c) $y = -9 \cos \theta$
   d) $y = -3 \sin \theta + 2$
   e) $y = 4 - 2 \cos \theta$
   f) $y = 5 - 10 \sin \theta$

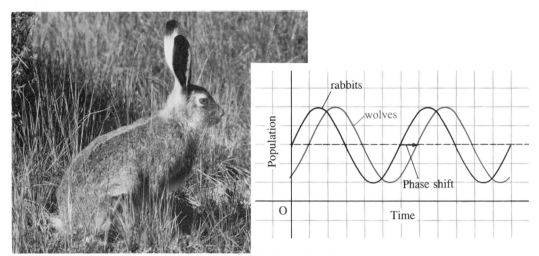

5-9 VARYING THE PHASE SHIFT OF SINE AND COSINE FUNCTIONS

In a certain region the number of rabbits increases and decreases periodically. This variation is caused by wolves which feed on the rabbits. If the number of wolves is small, the rabbits will flourish. But then the number of wolves will increase, since food is easy to find. This, in turn, causes a decrease in the number of rabbits, which causes the number of wolves to decrease, and the cycle begins all over again. The population graph for the wolves is shifted horizontally relative to the population graph for the rabbits.

In $y = \sin \theta$, if θ is replaced with $\theta - p$, we obtain $y = \sin (\theta - p)$. To investigate the effect of this on the graph of the function $y = \sin \theta$, we substitute different values for p, and graph the resulting functions.

If $p = 0$, the equation is $y = \sin \theta$ ...... ①

If $p = \frac{\pi}{2}$, the equation is $y = \sin \left(\theta - \frac{\pi}{2}\right)$ ...... ②

If we were to graph this function using a table of values, we would start with values of θ, subtract $\frac{\pi}{2}$, and then find the sines of the results. To give the same y-coordinates as in ①, the values of θ must be $\frac{\pi}{2}$ units greater than in ①. That is, the θ-coordinates of all points on the graph of ② are $\frac{\pi}{2}$ *greater* than those on the graph of ①. Therefore, the graph of ② is shifted $\frac{\pi}{2}$ units to the *right* relative to the graph of ①.

We say that the phase shift of the function $y = \sin \left(\theta - \frac{\pi}{2}\right)$ is $+\frac{\pi}{2}$.

If $p = -\frac{\pi}{3}$, the equation is $y = \sin\left(\theta + \frac{\pi}{3}\right)$ ...... ③

To give the same y-coordinates as in ①, the values of θ must be $\frac{\pi}{3}$ *less* than those in ①. Therefore, the graph of ③ is shifted $\frac{\pi}{3}$ units to the *left* relative to the graph of ①. The phase shift is $-\frac{\pi}{3}$.

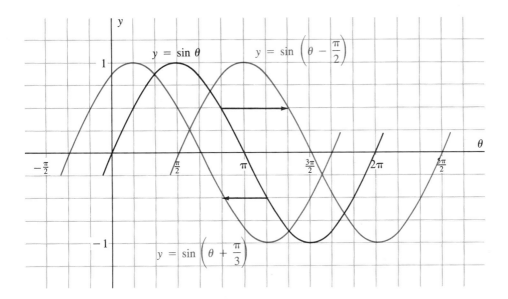

The graph of $y = \sin\left(\theta + \frac{\pi}{3}\right)$ is the image of the graph of $y = \sin \theta$, which has been translated $\frac{\pi}{3}$ to the *left*.

The graph of $y = \sin\left(\theta - \frac{\pi}{2}\right)$ is the image of the graph of $y = \sin \theta$, which has been translated $\frac{\pi}{2}$ to the *right*.

The *phase shift* of a periodic function is the amount by which the graph of the function is translated horizontally with respect to the basic function. A negative phase shift corresponds to a translation to the left. A positive phase shift corresponds to a translation to the right.

Similar results will be found for other values of θ, and for cosine functions. In general, adding a constant to the variable θ in the equations of the functions $y = \sin \theta$ or $y = \cos \theta$ causes a horizontal translation of the graph. A positive constant causes a translation to the left; a negative constant causes a translation to the right.

The graph of $y = \sin(\theta - p)$ is the image of the graph of $y = \sin \theta$ under a horizontal translation of p units.

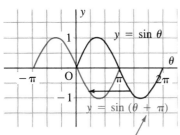

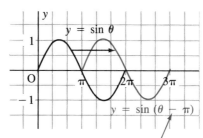

Positive sign, graph moved π units to the *left*

Negative sign, graph moved π units to the *right*

The graph of $y = \cos(\theta - p)$ is the image of the graph of $y = \cos \theta$ under a horizontal translation of p units.

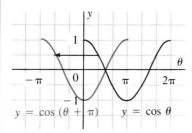

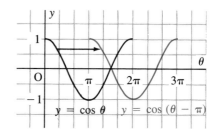

We can draw the graph of an equation in this form without making a table of values.

Example 1. Draw a graph of the function $y = \cos\left(\theta + \frac{2\pi}{3}\right)$ over two cycles, and state its phase shift.

Solution. Draw a graph of $y = \cos \theta$, then translate it $\frac{2\pi}{3}$ units to the left. The phase shift is $-\frac{2\pi}{3}$.

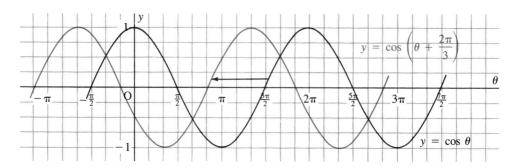

In general, the phase shift of $y = \sin(\theta - p)$ or $y = \cos(\theta - p)$ is the value of θ for which $\theta - p = 0$; that is, p.

Vertical displacement, phase shift, and amplitude are often combined in the same function.

Example 2. Draw a graph of the function $f(\theta) = 3 \sin\left(\theta - \frac{2\pi}{3}\right) + 2$ over two cycles. State the vertical displacement, the phase shift, and the amplitude.

Solution. Draw a graph of $y = \sin\theta$, and expand it vertically by a factor of 3. Then translate the image $\frac{2\pi}{3}$ units to the right and 2 units up.

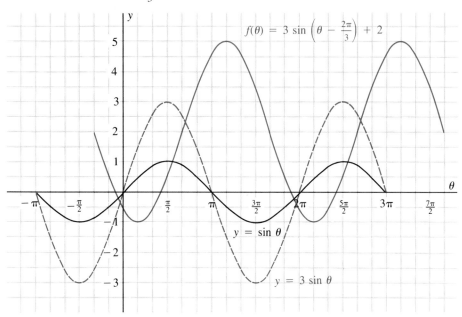

The vertical displacement is 2, the phase shift is $\frac{2\pi}{3}$, and the amplitude is 3.

EXERCISES 5-9

1. a) Graph these functions on the same grid for $-\pi \leqslant \theta \leqslant \pi$.

$$y = \sin\theta \qquad y = \sin\left(\theta - \frac{\pi}{6}\right) \qquad y = \sin\left(\theta - \frac{\pi}{3}\right) \qquad y = \sin\left(\theta + \frac{\pi}{4}\right)$$

b) Graph these functions on the same grid for $-\pi \leqslant \theta \leqslant \pi$.

$$y = \cos\theta \qquad y = \cos\left(\theta + \frac{\pi}{3}\right) \qquad y = \cos\left(\theta - \frac{\pi}{3}\right) \qquad y = \cos\left(\theta - \frac{\pi}{4}\right)$$

2. The function graphed below can be considered as a sine function. Find two possible values for the phase shift. What is the equation of the function for each phase shift?

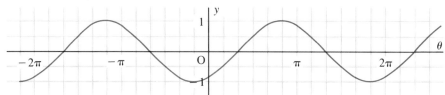

3. The function in *Exercise 2* can also be considered as a cosine function. Find two possible values for the phase shift. What is the equation of the function for each phase shift?

(B)

4. Graph each sinusoidal function over two cycles.

a) $y = \sin\left(\theta - \frac{\pi}{4}\right)$ b) $y = \sin\left(\theta - \frac{4\pi}{3}\right)$ c) $y = 2\sin\left(\theta + \frac{5\pi}{6}\right)$

d) $y = 3\cos\left(\theta - \frac{\pi}{6}\right)$ e) $y = 2\cos\left(\theta + \frac{5\pi}{3}\right)$ f) $y = 5\cos\left(\theta - \frac{7\pi}{6}\right)$

5. Graph each sinusoidal function, and determine its domain and range.

a) $f(\theta) = 2\sin\left(\theta - \frac{\pi}{4}\right) + 3$ b) $g(\theta) = 2\cos\left(\theta - \frac{\pi}{6}\right) + 2$

c) $h(\theta) = 4\cos\left(\theta - \frac{4\pi}{3}\right) - 1$ d) $k(\theta) = 4\sin\left(\theta + \frac{2\pi}{3}\right) - 2$

6. a) Graph the function $f(\theta) = \sin\left(\theta + \frac{\pi}{2}\right)$. What conclusion can you make?

   b) Graph the function $g(\theta) = \cos\left(\theta - \frac{\pi}{2}\right)$. What conclusion can you make?

7. Find values of p for which the graph of $y = \sin(\theta - p)$ coincides with the graph of:
   a) $y = \sin\theta$ b) $y = \cos\theta$.

8. Repeat *Exercise 7* for the function $y = \cos(\theta - p)$.

(C)

9. Given the function $f(\theta) = a\sin(\theta - p) + q$, where $a > 0$
   a) What is the maximum value of $f(\theta)$? For what values of θ does this occur?
   b) What is the minimum value of $f(\theta)$? For what values of θ does this occur?

10. Repeat *Exercise 9* for the function $f(\theta) = a\cos(\theta - p) + q$, where $a > 0$.

11. Find an equation of a function of the form $f(\theta) = \sin(\theta - p) + q$ which has a maximum value of 3 when $\theta = 0$.

12. Find an equation of a function of the form $f(\theta) = \cos(\theta - p) + q$ which has a minimum value of -5 when $\theta = 0$.

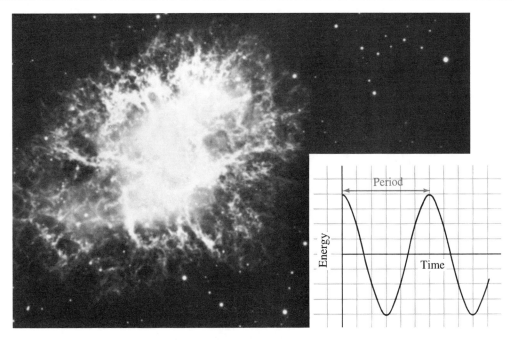

5-10 VARYING THE PERIOD OF SINE AND COSINE FUNCTIONS

In 1968 the scientific world was astonished when two astronomers detected extremely massive stars which spin on their axes in a fraction of a second. Since a pulse of radio energy is sent out on each rotation, these stars are called pulsating stars, or pulsars. One pulsar, in the Crab Nebula, pulses every 0.033 s. This time is called the period.

In $y = \cos \theta$, if θ is replaced with $k\theta$, we obtain $y = \cos k\theta$. To investigate the effect of this on the graph of the function $y = \cos \theta$, we substitute different values for k, and graph the resulting functions. We will assume that k is positive, since there is no need to consider negative values of k in applications.

If $k = 1$, the equation is $y = \cos \theta$ ...... ①
Since one cycle is completed in 2π units along the θ-axis, the period of $y = \cos \theta$ is 2π.

If $k = 2$, the equation is $y = \cos 2\theta$ ...... ②
If we were to graph this function using a table of values, we would start with values of θ, multiply by 2, and then find the cosines of the results. To give the same y-coordinates as in ①, the values of θ must be one-half of those in ①. That is, the θ-coordinates of all points on the graph of ② are *one-half* of those on the graph of ①. Therefore, the graph of ② is *compressed* horizontally relative to the graph of ①. The period of $y = \cos 2\theta$ is π, since one cycle is completed in π units along the θ-axis.

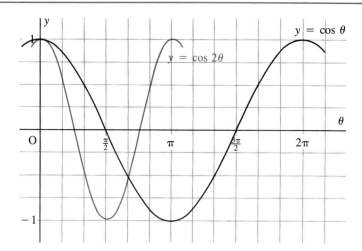

The graph of $y = \cos 2\theta$ is the image of the graph of $y = \cos \theta$ which has been compressed horizontally by a factor of $\frac{1}{2}$.

If $k = \frac{1}{2}$, the equation is $y = \cos \frac{1}{2}\theta$ ...... ③

To give the same y-coordinates as in ①, the values of θ must be *two times* those in ①. Therefore, the graph of ③ is *expanded* horizontally relative to the graph of ①. The period of $y = \cos \frac{1}{2}\theta$ is 4π.

The graph of $y = \cos \frac{1}{2}\theta$ is the image of the graph of $y = \cos \theta$ which has been expanded horizontally by a factor of 2.

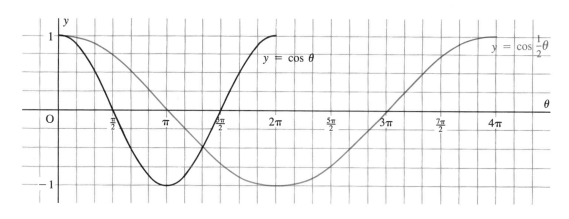

Similar results will be found for other positive values of k, and for sine functions.

In general, multiplying the variable θ in the equations of the functions $y = \cos \theta$ or $y = \sin \theta$ by a positive constant k affects the period and causes a horizontal expansion or compression of its graph. If $0 < k < 1$, there is an expansion; if $k > 1$, there is a compression.

To discover how k is related to the period, we compare the three functions graphed on the previous page with their periods.

Function	Value of k	Period
$y = \cos \theta$	1	2π
$y = \cos 2\theta$	2	π
$y = \cos \frac{1}{2}\theta$	$\frac{1}{2}$	4π

In each case, if we multiply the value of k by the period, the product is 2π.
$(k)(\text{period}) = 2\pi$

$$\text{period} = \frac{2\pi}{k}$$

The graphs of $y = \cos k\theta$ and $y = \sin k\theta$ $(k > 0)$ are related to the graphs of $y = \cos \theta$ and $y = \sin \theta$ by a horizontal expansion or compression. The period of each function is $\frac{2\pi}{k}$.

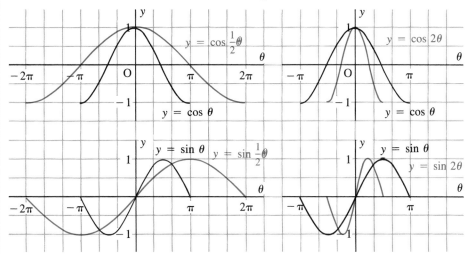

If $0 < k < 1$, there is a horizontal expansion.

If $k > 1$, there is a horizontal compression.

Since we know that $y = \sin k\theta$ and $y = \cos k\theta$ represent sinusoidal functions with the above properties, we can draw the graph of an equation in this form without making a table of values.

Example 1.   Draw a graph of the function $y = \sin 3\theta$ over two cycles, and state its period.

Solution.   Graph $y = \sin \theta$, then compress horizontally by a factor of $\frac{1}{3}$.

If (θ,y) is any point on the graph of $y = \sin \theta$, then $\left(\frac{1}{3}\theta,y\right)$ is the image point on the graph of $y = \sin 3\theta$. For example, the image of $A(2\pi,0)$ is $A'\left(\frac{2\pi}{3},0\right)$.

The period of this function is $\frac{2\pi}{3}$.

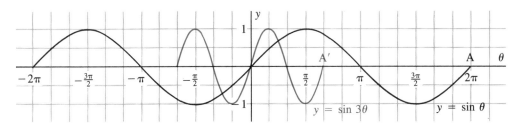

Very often, horizontal expansions or compressions are combined with horizontal translations. The result depends on the order in which these two transformations are applied. With sinusoidal functions we will assume that the expansion or compression is applied first, since there is no need to consider the reverse order in applications.

Suppose the graph of the function $y = \cos \theta$ is compressed horizontally by a factor of $\frac{1}{2}$. To find the equation of the image, replace θ with 2θ. The equation becomes $y = \cos 2\theta$.

Now suppose the resulting graph is translated $\frac{\pi}{3}$ units to the right. To find the image equation after the translation, replace θ with $\left(\theta - \frac{\pi}{3}\right)$.

The equation becomes $y = \cos 2\left(\theta - \frac{\pi}{3}\right)$.

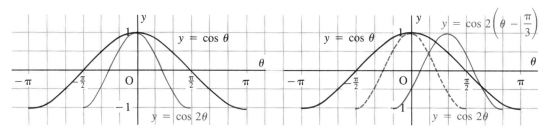

In the above example, the magnitude and direction of the translation give the phase shift. Also, the translation does not affect the period.

The phase shift of $y = \cos 2\left(\theta - \frac{\pi}{3}\right)$ is $\frac{\pi}{3}$. The period of $y = \cos 2\left(\theta - \frac{\pi}{3}\right)$ is $\frac{2\pi}{2}$, or π.

Similar results will be found for other functions.

The graphs of $y = \cos k(\theta - p)$ and $y = \sin k(\theta - p)$ are related to the graphs of $y = \cos \theta$ and $y = \sin \theta$ by a horizontal expansion or compression followed by a horizontal translation. For $y = \cos k(\theta - p)$ and $y = \sin k(\theta - p)$:

● the phase shift is p ● the period is $\dfrac{2\pi}{k}$.

Example 2.   Graph the function $y = 2 \cos 3\left(\theta - \dfrac{\pi}{2}\right)$ over two cycles, and state its amplitude, phase shift, and period.

Solution.   Graph $y = 2 \cos \theta$, then compress horizontally by a factor of $\dfrac{1}{3}$. At this point, the equation of the curve is $y = 2 \cos 3\theta$.

Then translate the image $\dfrac{\pi}{2}$ units to the right.

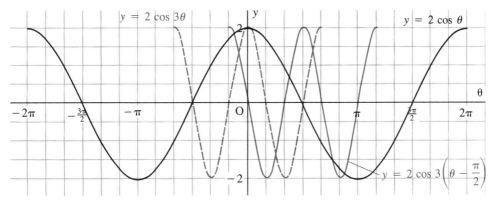

The amplitude of the function is 2.

The phase shift is $\dfrac{\pi}{2}$.

The period is $\dfrac{2\pi}{3}$.

EXERCISES 5-10

1. a) Graph these functions on the same grid for $-\pi \leqslant \theta \leqslant \pi$.

   $y = \sin 2\theta$ $y = \sin \theta$ $y = \sin \dfrac{1}{2}\theta$

   b) Graph these functions on the same grid for $-\pi \leqslant \theta \leqslant \pi$.

   $y = \cos 3\theta$ $y = \cos \theta$ $y = \cos \dfrac{1}{3}\theta$

   c) Describe the effect on the graphs of $y = \sin k\theta$ and $y = \cos k\theta$ as the value of k varies.

2. Each function graphed below is sinusoidal. Write an equation for each function.

a)   b)

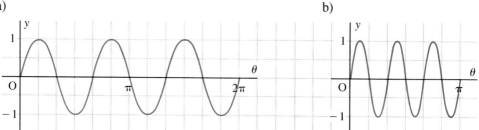

Ⓑ

3. Graph each sinusoidal function, and state its amplitude and period.

a) $y = 2 \sin 2\theta$ b) $y = 3 \sin \frac{1}{2}\theta$ c) $y = 4 \sin 2\theta$

d) $y = 4 \cos \frac{1}{2}\theta$ e) $y = 5 \cos 2\theta$ f) $y = 3 \cos 3\theta$

4. State the amplitude, the period, and the phase shift for each function.

a) $f(\theta) = 5 \cos 3(\theta - \pi)$ b) $f(\theta) = 2 \sin 4\left(\theta + \frac{\pi}{2}\right)$

c) $f(\theta) = 2.5 \sin 6\left(\theta - \frac{2\pi}{3}\right)$ d) $f(\theta) = 0.5 \cos 5\left(\theta + \frac{5\pi}{4}\right)$

5. Graph each function over two cycles, and state its amplitude, period, and phase shift.

a) $y = \sin 2\left(\theta - \frac{\pi}{3}\right)$ b) $y = 2 \cos 3\left(\theta - \frac{\pi}{2}\right)$

c) $y = 4 \cos \frac{1}{2}(\theta + \pi)$ d) $y = 0.5 \sin \frac{1}{2}\left(\theta - \frac{5\pi}{4}\right)$

Ⓒ

6. **Negative values of k in $y = \sin k\theta$ and $y = \cos k\theta$**
   a) Draw graphs of these functions.

   i) $y = \sin(-\theta)$ ii) $y = \sin(-2\theta)$ iii) $y = \sin\left(-\frac{1}{2}\theta\right)$

   b) How are the graphs of the functions in part a) related to the graph of the function $y = \sin \theta$?
   c) Draw diagrams to illustrate how the graphs of $y = \sin k\theta$ and $y = \cos k\theta$ are related to the graphs of $y = \sin \theta$ and $y = \cos \theta$ if $k < 0$.
   d) Do negative values of k affect the period? In what way?

7. Graph each function over two cycles, and state the period.

   a) $y = \sin(-3\theta)$ b) $y = 4 \cos\left(-\frac{1}{2}\theta\right)$ c) $y = 3 \sin(-2\theta) + 3$

8. Compare the graphs of each pair of functions. What conclusions can you make?
   a) $y = \sin \theta$ and $y = \sin(-\theta)$ b) $y = \cos \theta$ and $y = \cos(-\theta)$

THE MATHEMATICAL MIND

Evaluating Trigonometric Functions

To keep pace with progress in navigation and astronomy in the 17th and 18th centuries, mathematicians required increasingly more accurate values of certain functions, including trigonometric functions. Credit goes to the Englishman, Brook Taylor (1685-1731) and the Scotsman, Colin Maclaurin (1698-1746) for showing that under certain conditions a function $f(x)$ can be expressed as an infinite series of powers of x. Two important series are the series for $\sin x$ and $\cos x$, where x is a real number.

$$\sin x = \frac{x}{1!} - \frac{x^3}{3!} + \frac{x^5}{5!} - \frac{x^7}{7!} + \ldots \qquad \cos x = 1 - \frac{x^2}{2!} + \frac{x^4}{4!} - \frac{x^6}{6!} + \ldots$$

The denominators in these series use a special notation called *factorial notation*. The factorial sign ! following a number means the product of all natural numbers up to and including the number. For example, $4! = 4 \times 3 \times 2 \times 1$, or 24

We can regard these series as formulas for calculating values of the trigonometric functions for all real values of x. The formulas are valid only when x is in radians. Hence, to calculate $\cos 60°$, we substitute $\frac{\pi}{3}$ for x in the second formula. Taking the first four terms,

we obtain:

$$\cos \frac{\pi}{3} \doteq 1 - \frac{1}{2}\left(\frac{\pi}{3}\right)^2 + \frac{1}{24}\left(\frac{\pi}{3}\right)^4 - \frac{1}{720}\left(\frac{\pi}{3}\right)^6$$

$$\doteq 1 - 0.548\ 311\ 4 + 0.050\ 107\ 6 - 0.001\ 831\ 6$$

$$\doteq 0.499\ 964\ 6$$

This is very close to the actual value of 0.5. For a more accurate result, additional terms of the series can be used.

QUESTIONS

1. Simplify each factorial.

   a) 3! b) 5! c) 7! d) 8! e) 9! f) 10!

2. Write the first six terms of the series for $\sin x$ and $\cos x$.

3. Use the result of *Question 2* to calculate each value. Check using the $\boxed{\sin}$ or $\boxed{\cos}$ key on your calculator.

   a) $\cos \frac{\pi}{6}$ b) $\sin \frac{\pi}{2}$ c) $\sin \frac{\pi}{5}$ d) $\cos \pi$

4. How many terms of the series are needed to obtain a value of $\cos \frac{\pi}{5}$:

   a) to 2 decimal places b) to 4 decimal places c) to 6 decimal places?

5-11 GRAPHING GENERAL TRIGONOMETRIC FUNCTIONS

When we graph a function, we customarily draw the axes before we draw the curve. Then we make the curve fit the scales on the axes we have already drawn. We have used this method in previous sections of this book. However, with sinusoidal functions, it is easier to draw the curve first and then add the axes later. In other words, we make the axes fit the curve.

For example, consider the function $y = 3 \cos 2\left(\theta - \frac{\pi}{3}\right) + 4$.

We can graph this function as follows.

Step 1. Draw a sinusoidal curve, without axes.

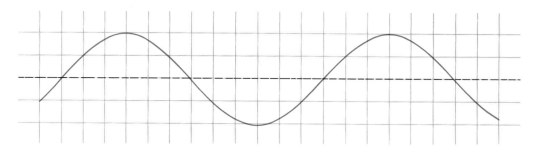

Step 2. Find the phase shift and the period, and use them to establish a horizontal scale.

The phase shift is $\frac{\pi}{3}$, and the period is $\frac{2\pi}{2}$, or π.

Since the function is a cosine function, the phase shift $\frac{\pi}{3}$ is the θ-coordinate of a maximum point. Since the period is π, the θ-coordinate of the next maximum point is $\frac{\pi}{3} + \pi$, or $\frac{4\pi}{3}$. Label these points.

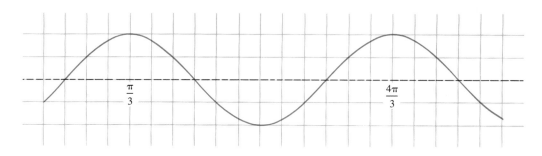

Step 3. Complete the graph by drawing the axes and their scales.
The graph was drawn such that the period corresponds to 12 squares. Therefore, the horizontal scale is:

12 squares correspond to π

4 squares correspond to $\dfrac{\pi}{3}$.

The position of O is 4 squares to the left of the first maximum point. Draw the *y*-axis through this point.

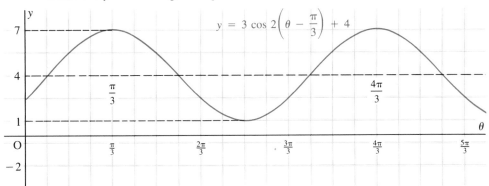

The vertical displacement is 4. Since the amplitude is 3, the maximum value of *y* is 7 and the minimum value is 1. Use these values to mark the vertical scale. Draw the θ-axis and mark its scale.

The method illustrated above may be used to graph any sinusoidal function.

Example 1. Draw a graph of the function $y = 5 \sin 3\left(\theta + \dfrac{\pi}{4}\right) + 3$ over two cycles.

Solution. *Step 1.*

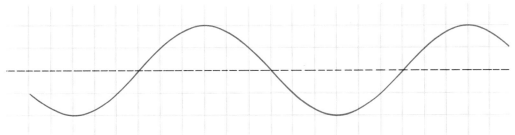

Step 2. The phase shift is $-\dfrac{\pi}{4}$, and the period is $\dfrac{2\pi}{3}$. Since the function is a sine function, the phase shift $-\dfrac{\pi}{4}$ is the θ-coordinate of a point on the axis preceding a maximum point. Then, since the period is $\dfrac{2\pi}{3}$, the θ-coordinate of the next point preceding a maximum point is

$-\dfrac{\pi}{4} + \dfrac{2\pi}{3}$, or $\dfrac{5\pi}{12}$.

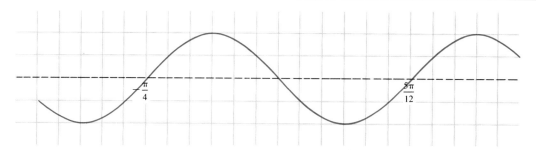

Step 3. The graph was drawn such that the period corresponds to 12 squares. Therefore, the horizontal scale is:

12 squares correspond to $\frac{2\pi}{3}$, so 1 square corresponds to $\frac{\pi}{18}$.

Mark the horizontal scale as shown. The position of O is halfway between $-\frac{\pi}{12}$ and $\frac{\pi}{12}$. Draw the y-axis through this point.

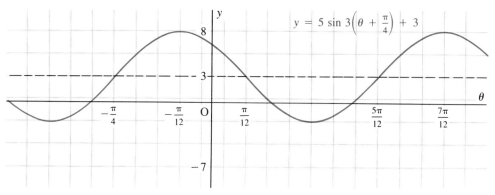

$$y = 5 \sin 3\left(\theta + \frac{\pi}{4}\right) + 3$$

The vertical displacement is 3. Since the amplitude is 5, the maximum value of y is 8 and the minimum value is -2. Use these values to mark the vertical scale.

We can also find an equation of a sinusoidal function from its graph.

Example 2. A sinusoidal function is shown in the graph below.
  a) Determine the vertical displacement and the amplitude.
  b) Determine a possible phase shift, and the period.
  c) Write an equation of the function.

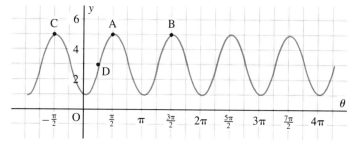

Solution.   a) The vertical displacement is 3.
The amplitude is 2.

b) There are many possible phase shifts, depending on whether we regard the function as a cosine function or a sine function, and on which point is taken to correspond to the phase shift.

    For example, if we consider the function to be a cosine function, the phase shift is the θ-coordinate of any maximum point. Using point A, the phase shift is $\frac{\pi}{2}$.

    The period is the difference in the values of θ for two consecutive maximum points. Using points A and B, the period is $\frac{3\pi}{2} - \frac{\pi}{2}$, or π.

c) An equation of the function is $y = 2 \cos 2\left(\theta - \frac{\pi}{2}\right) + 3$.

In *Example 2*, there are other functions with the same graph.

Using point B and its θ-coordinate $\frac{3\pi}{2}$ as the phase shift: $y = 2 \cos 2\left(\theta - \frac{3\pi}{2}\right) + 3$

Using point C and its θ-coordinate $-\frac{\pi}{2}$ as the phase shift: $y = 2 \cos 2\left(\theta + \frac{\pi}{2}\right) + 3$

Considering the function as a sine function, and using point D and its θ-coordinate $\frac{\pi}{4}$ as the phase shift: $y = 2 \sin 2\left(\theta - \frac{\pi}{4}\right) + 3$

EXERCISES 5-11

(A)

1. For each graph below, state:
    i) the amplitude   ii) the period   iii) a possible phase shift
    iv) the maximum value of y, and the values of θ for which it occurs
    v) the minimum value of y, and the values of θ for which it occurs
    vi) the vertical displacement.
    a)   b)

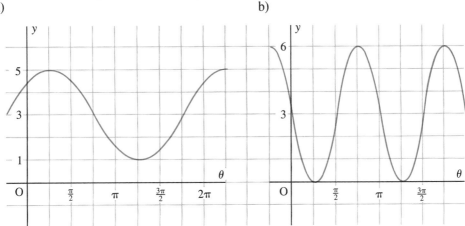

c)

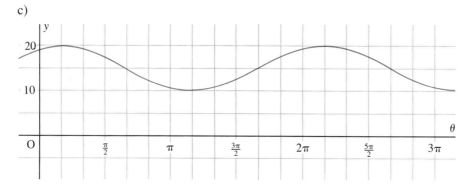

2. Write an equation to represent each function in *Exercise 1*.

Ⓑ

3. Given the function $y = 2 \cos 2\left(\theta - \dfrac{\pi}{3}\right) + 4$

   a) Find the phase shift and the period.
   b) Determine the vertical displacement and the amplitude.
   c) Graph the function by graphing a sinusoidal curve first, and making the axes fit the curve.

4. Given the function $y = 3 \sin 2\left(\theta - \dfrac{\pi}{4}\right) + 3$

   a) Find the phase shift and the period.
   b) Determine the vertical displacement and the amplitude.
   c) Graph the function by graphing a sinusoidal curve first, and making the axes fit the curve.

5. Determine the phase shift and the period for each function. Then graph the function by graphing a sinusoidal curve first, and making the axes fit the curve.

   a) $y = 4 \cos 3\left(\theta - \dfrac{\pi}{2}\right) + 4$ b) $y = 2 \cos 4(\theta + \pi) + 3$

   c) $y = 3 \sin 2\left(\theta + \dfrac{\pi}{6}\right) + 6$ d) $y = 4 \sin 3\left(\theta - \dfrac{\pi}{6}\right) + 2$

6. Graph each function.

   a) $y = \sin 2\left(\theta - \dfrac{\pi}{2}\right)$ b) $y = 2 \sin 3\left(\theta - \dfrac{\pi}{3}\right) + 5$

   c) $y = 3 \cos 2\left(\theta + \dfrac{\pi}{4}\right) + 1$ d) $y = 3 \cos 3\left(\theta - \dfrac{2\pi}{3}\right) + 4$

7. Describe what happens to each graph.

   a) $y = a \sin 2\left(\theta - \dfrac{\pi}{6}\right) + 5$ as a varies

   b) $y = 3 \sin k\left(\theta - \dfrac{\pi}{6}\right) + 5$ as k varies

   c) $y = 3 \sin 2(\theta - p) + 5$ as p varies

   d) $y = 3 \sin 2\left(\theta - \dfrac{\pi}{3}\right) + q$ as q varies

8. Determine the phase shift and the period of each function, and draw the graph.
   a) $y = \sin (2\theta - \pi)$
   b) $y = 2 \cos (3\theta - \pi) + 1$
   c) $y = 2 \cos (3\theta - \pi) + 4$
   d) $y = 5 \sin (4\theta + \pi) - 3$

9. Graph each function.
   a) $y = 2 \sin \left(2\theta + \dfrac{\pi}{3} \right)$
   b) $y = 5 \cos \left(2\theta - \dfrac{\pi}{2} \right)$
   c) $y = 3 \cos \left(2\theta - \dfrac{\pi}{2} \right)$
   d) $y = 5 \sin \left(2\theta + \dfrac{\pi}{3} \right)$

Ⓒ

10. Two of these equations represent the same function. Which two are they?
    a) $y = 3 \sin 2\left(\theta + \dfrac{\pi}{2} \right)$
    b) $y = 3 \cos 2\theta$
    c) $y = 3 \cos 2\left(\theta + \dfrac{\pi}{4} \right)$
    d) $y = 3 \sin 2(\theta + \pi)$

11. Two of these equations represent the same function. Which two are they?
    a) $y = 3 \sin (2\theta + \pi)$
    b) $y = 3 \cos \left(2\theta + \dfrac{\pi}{2} \right)$
    c) $y = 3 \cos 2\theta$
    d) $y = 3 \sin (2\theta + 2\pi)$

12. a) Find three different roots of the equation $2 \cos \left(\theta + \dfrac{\pi}{2} \right) = 0$.
    b) Write a general expression which could be used to represent all the roots of the equation in part a).

13. a) Find three different roots of the equation $3 \sin 2\left(\theta - \dfrac{\pi}{4} \right) = 0$.
    b) Write a general expression which could be used to represent all the roots of the equation in part a).

14. Two students discussed their methods of graphing sinusoidal functions. Their discussion went as follows.
    Kwan: "I always draw the curve first and make the axes fit the curve. That method is very easy."
    Marc: "But then all your graphs are going to look the same, even if they have different amplitudes and different periods."
    Kwan: "Not really. I have two different ways of getting around that problem."
    What methods might Kwan have been using so that her graphs do not all look like they have the same amplitude and the same period?

15. Given the function $y = \cos 2\pi\theta$
    a) Find the phase shift and the period.
    b) Graph the function.

16. Repeat *Exercise 15* for these functions.
    a) $y = \sin 2\pi\theta$
    b) $y = \cos \dfrac{\pi}{2}\theta$
    c) $y = \sin \dfrac{\pi}{2}\theta$

5-12 SCALING THE HORIZONTAL AXIS

In the first section of this chapter several graphs were shown illustrating some examples of sinusoidal functions.

- time of the sunset
- number of sunspots
- lengths of shadows
- blood pressure
- volume of blood in the heart
- volume of air in the lungs

These graphs differ from the trigonometric graphs we studied in the preceding sections in one major way. They show periodic functions without the use of angles.

Up to now the horizontal axis has been scaled in degrees or in radians. These scales are not very useful in applications such as those above, where the horizontal axis is usually marked in time intervals. To use sinusoidal functions in applications we must change their graphs in two ways.

- We will no longer use θ as the variable on the horizontal axis. Instead, we will use t to indicate time. This involves nothing more than changing the letter on the axis and in the equations.
- We will scale the horizontal axis with whole numbers such as 1, 2, 3, or their multiples. We do this by adjusting the period of the functions.

For example, the graphs below show cosine and sine functions with period 1. Their equations can be written in the form $y = \cos kt$ and $y = \sin kt$. Since the period of each function is $\frac{2\pi}{k}$, we can write

$$\frac{2\pi}{k} = 1$$

$$k = 2\pi$$

The equations of the functions are $y = \cos 2\pi t$ and $y = \sin 2\pi t$.

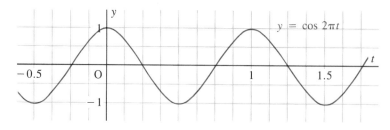

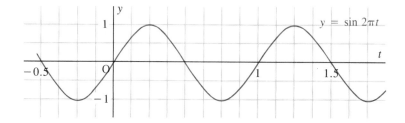

The examples on the previous page show that if π occurs in the equation as a factor of the quantity whose sine or cosine is to be found, then it does not appear on the horizontal axis. The fact that π does not occur on the axis means that it must occur in the equation.

Example 1. a) Find the period of the function $y = \sin \dfrac{2\pi t}{5}$.

b) Graph the function in part a).

Solution. a) The equation is in the form $y = \sin kt$, which has period $\dfrac{2\pi}{k}$.

Since $k = \dfrac{2\pi}{5}$, we see that the period of the function is $\dfrac{2\pi}{\frac{2\pi}{5}}$, or 5.

b) Draw the graph of a sine function with period 5.

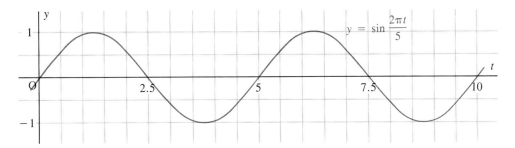

In *Example 1*, notice that the coefficient of t in the equation can be expressed in the form of a fraction, $\dfrac{2\pi}{k}$. When the coefficient is written in this form, the denominator is the period of the function.

$y = \cos \dfrac{2\pi t}{k}$ represents a cosine function with period k.

$y = \sin \dfrac{2\pi t}{k}$ represents a sine function with period k.

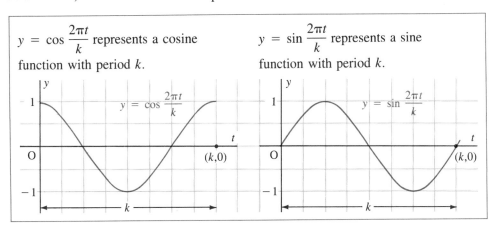

This scaling of the horizontal axis affects only the period, as shown above. It does not affect the vertical displacement, amplitude or how the phase shift is found.

Example 2. Graph the function $y = 3 \sin 2\pi \dfrac{(t - 2)}{4} + 6$.

Solution. *Step 1.* Draw a sinusoidal curve.

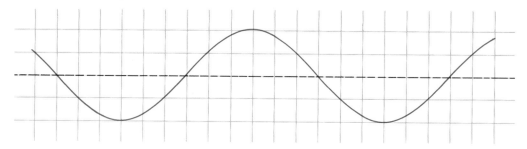

Step 2. Find the phase shift and the period, and use them to establish a horizontal scale.
The phase shift is 2. The period is 4.

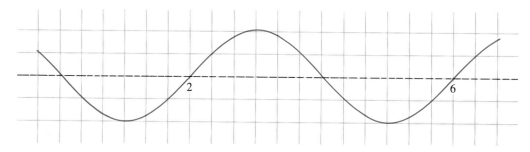

Step 3. Complete the graph by drawing the axes and their scales. We use the fact that the amplitude is 3 and the vertical displacement is 6.

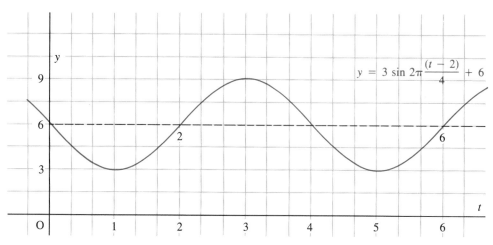

In *Example 2*, the period, amplitude, phase shift, and vertical displacement are all represented by numbers in the equation.

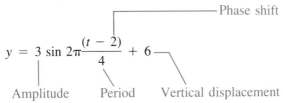

Notice the factor 2π in the equation. This factor must be present for the period to be as indicated. We can use this pattern to write the equation when these data are given or when they can be read from a graph.

Example 3. Write an equation of this sinusoidal function.

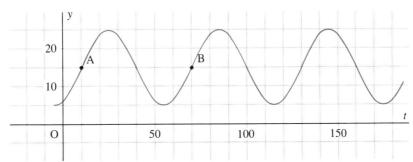

Solution. The vertical displacement is 15.
The amplitude is 10.
For a sine function, the phase shift is the horizontal coordinate of A: 10.
The period is the difference between the horizontal coordinates of A and B: $70 - 10$, or 60.

An equation of the function is $y = 10 \sin 2\pi \dfrac{(t - 10)}{60} + 15$.

In *Example 3*, the function can also be expressed as a cosine function. The only difference is the phase shift. Since the first maximum occurs when $t = 25$, the phase shift is 25. An equation of the function is $y = 10 \cos 2\pi \dfrac{(t - 25)}{60} + 15$. What are other equations for this function?

Example 4. The volume of air in the lungs is a sinusoidal function of time. A graph illustrating this variation for normal breathing is shown on page 197. Write an equation for this function.

Solution. The vertical displacement is 2450 mL. The amplitude is 250 mL. The period is 5 s. If V millilitres represents the volume of air in the lungs at time t seconds, then an equation for the function is:

$$V = 250 \sin \frac{2\pi t}{5} + 2450.$$

EXERCISES 5-12

Ⓐ

1. State the amplitude, period, phase shift, and vertical displacement for each function.

   a) $y = 3 \sin 2\pi\dfrac{(t-1)}{5} + 4$

   b) $y = 2 \cos 2\pi\dfrac{(t-5)}{4} + 6$

2. For each graph, determine the amplitude, period, phase shift, and vertical displacement.

   a)
   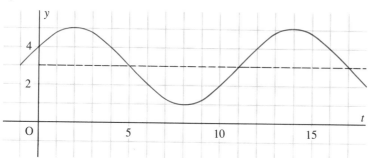

   b)
   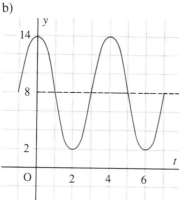

   c)
   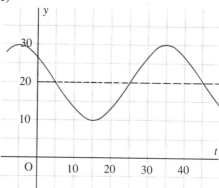

3. Write an equation to represent each function in *Exercise 2*.

4. Write an equation to represent each function.

   a)
   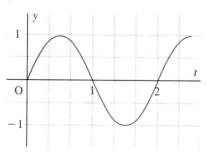

   b)
   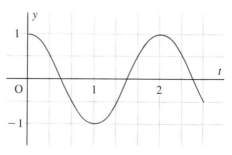

c)

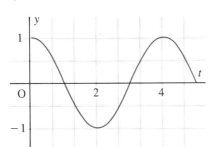

d)

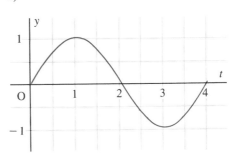

5. Write an equation for a cosine function with the following properties.
   a) amplitude: 5   period: 1   phase shift: 9   vertical displacement: 4
   b) amplitude: 12   period: $\frac{1}{2}$ phase shift: -3 vertical displacement: 1.5
   c) amplitude: 2.4   period: 27   phase shift: 19   vertical displacement: 15.1

Ⓑ

6. Draw a graph of each function.
   a) $y = 2 \cos 2\pi \dfrac{(t - 1)}{3} + 4$ b) $y = 3 \cos 2\pi \dfrac{(t - 4)}{2} + 3$

   c) $y = 2.4 \cos 2\pi \dfrac{(t + 3)}{12} + 3.6$ d) $y = 3.5 \sin 2\pi \dfrac{(t - 8.4)}{9.2} + 10$

7. Draw a graph of each function.
   a) $y = \sin 2\pi t$ b) $y = \sin \dfrac{2\pi t}{3}$

   c) $y = \sin 2\pi(t - 2)$ d) $y = \sin 2\pi \dfrac{(t - 2)}{3}$

   e) $y = \cos 2\pi t$ f) $y = \cos \dfrac{2\pi t}{3}$

   g) $y = \cos 2\pi(t - 2)$ h) $y = \cos 2\pi \dfrac{(t - 2)}{3}$

8. State the maximum and minimum values of y, and the values of t for which they occur, where $-5 \leqslant t \leqslant 5$.
   a) $y = 2 \cos 2\pi \dfrac{(t - 1)}{3} + 3$ b) $y = 4 \sin 2\pi \dfrac{(t + 2)}{5} - 4$

   c) $y = 2 \sin 2\pi \dfrac{(t - 1)}{3} + 6$ d) $y = 5 \cos 2\pi \dfrac{(t + 3)}{6} + 2$

9. Write an equation to represent a sine function with the following properties.
   a) maximum: 23   minimum: 11   period: 5   phase shift: 9
   b) maximum: 17.2   minimum: 8.6   period: 3.9   phase shift: 4.7

10. Write an equation for the volume of air in the lungs during deep breathing, when the variation is from 1000 mL to 5000 mL. Assume that the period is 10 s.

11. The twin towers of the World Trade Center in New York were once the tallest buildings in the world. During a strong wind, the top of each tower swings back and forth as much as 80 cm, with a period of 10 s.
    a) Draw a graph showing the departure of the top of one of the buildings from the normal position as a function of time, for 20 s.
    b) Write an equation for the function in part a).

12. A piston in an engine moves up and down in the cylinder, as shown in the diagram. The height h centimetres of the piston at time t seconds is given by this formula.

    $$h = 20 \sin \frac{2\pi t}{0.05} + 20$$

    a) State the piston's:
        i) maximum height
        ii) minimum height
        iii) period.
    b) If the piston operates for exactly one hour, how many complete cycles does it make?

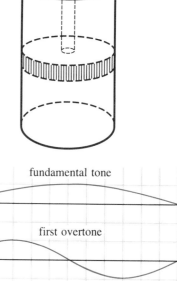

13. The fundamental tone of a guitar string with length L is associated with a sinusoidal function with a period of $2L$.

    The period of the first overtone is $\frac{2L}{2}$;

    the period of the second overtone is $\frac{2L}{3}$;

    and so on.
    a) Assuming that the string is 50 cm long, and that the amplitude of the vibration is 0.5 cm, write the equations of the functions associated with the fundamental tone and the first three overtones.
    b) Draw the graphs of the functions in part a) on the same axes.

fundamental tone

first overtone

second overtone

third overtone

14. Two of these equations represent the same function. Which two are they?

    a) $y = 3 \sin 2\pi \frac{(t-1)}{8} + 2$

    b) $y = 3 \cos 2\pi \frac{(t-5)}{8} + 2$

    c) $y = 3 \sin 2\pi \frac{(t-3)}{8} + 2$

    d) $y = 3 \cos 2\pi \frac{(t+1)}{8} + 2$

5-13 APPLYING GENERAL TRIGONOMETRIC FUNCTIONS

The tides are the periodic rise and fall of the water in the oceans, caused almost entirely by the gravitational attraction of the moon and the sun. An equation expressing the depth of the water as a function of time is extremely complicated, since the distances and relative positions of the moon and sun are constantly changing. However, the depth can be approximated by a sinusoidal function. The amplitude of the function depends on the location, and at any particular location it varies considerably at different times of the year.

   Some of the highest tides in the world occur in the Bay of Fundy, where the Annapolis Tidal Generating Station has been in operation since 1984. The graph below shows how the depth of the water at the station varies during a typical day. Notice that times are given in decimal form using a 24 h clock.

   When we work with sinusoidal functions involving time in hours, a fractional part of an hour must be expressed in decimal form. For example, the period of the tidal motion (below) is 12 h 25 min. Converting to decimal form,

$$12 \text{ h } 25 \text{ min} = \left(12 + \frac{25}{60} \right) \text{ h}$$
$$\doteq 12.4 \text{ h}$$

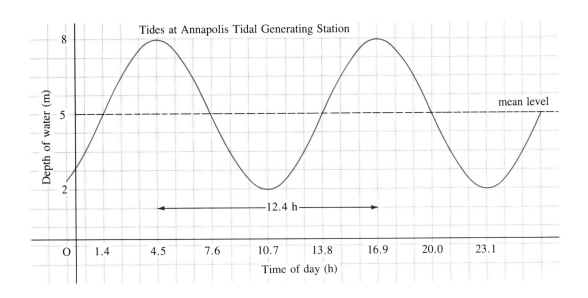

Tides at Annapolis Tidal Generating Station

   We can find the vertical displacement, the phase shift, the period, and the amplitude of the function from the graph, and use these to write an equation of the function.

Since the mean level is 5 m, the vertical displacement is 5 m.

The amplitude is the difference between high tide level and mean level, 3 m.

The first high tide occurs at 4.5 h. If we think of the function as a cosine function, then the phase shift is 4.5 h.

The period is the time between two high tides, 12.4 h.

Therefore, if *h* metres represents the depth, and *t* hours represents the time, an equation of the function is:

$$h = 3 \cos 2\pi \frac{(t - 4.5)}{12.4} + 5 \quad \begin{array}{l}\text{Phase shift} \\ \text{(time at first} \\ \text{high tide)}\end{array}$$

Amplitude   Period   Mean level

We can use this equation to calculate the depth of the water at any time during the day.

Example 1.   Calculate the depth of the water to the nearest tenth of a metre at:

a) 9:30 A.M.   b) 6:45 P.M.

Solution.   Convert the times to decimals of hours, on a 24 h clock.

9:30 A.M = 09.50 h   6:45 P.M. = (12 + 6.75) h
                                              = 18.75 h

a) Substitute *t* = 9.5 in the above equation.

$$h = 3 \cos 2\pi \frac{(t - 4.5)}{12.4} + 5$$

$$= 3 \cos 2\pi \frac{(9.5 - 4.5)}{12.4} + 5$$

Use a scientific calculator in *radian mode* to evaluate this expression.

$h \doteq 2.537\ 709\ 7$

At 9:30 A.M., the depth of the water is approximately 2.5 m.

b) Substitute *t* = 18.75 in the above equation.

$$h = 3 \cos 2\pi \frac{(t - 4.5)}{12.4} + 5$$

$$= 3 \cos 2\pi \frac{(18.75 - 4.5)}{12.4} + 5$$

$\doteq 6.775\ 631$

At 6:45 P.M., the depth of the water is approximately 6.8 m.

If your calculator requires the function key to be pressed first you may need to use the memory or brackets to evaluate expressions such as those in *Example 1*.

The pattern suggested by *Example 1* can be used to solve other problems involving quantities which change periodically. In each case, we use a sinusoidal function to approximate the data. The general pattern in the equation of the function is shown below.

$$y = A \cos 2\pi\frac{(t - S)}{P} + M$$

Phase shift
(value of t at
first maximum)

Amplitude   Period   Mean value or
vertical displacement

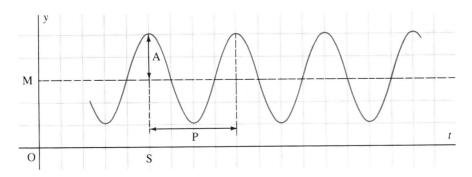

Example 2. A Ferris wheel with a radius of 20 m rotates once every 40 s. Passengers get on at point S, which is 1 m above level ground. Suppose you get on at S and the wheel starts to rotate.
a) Draw a graph showing how your height above the ground varies during the first two cycles.
b) Write an equation which expresses your height as a function of the elapsed time.
c) Calculate your height above the ground after 15 s.

Solution.   a) *Step 1.* Draw a sinusoidal curve.

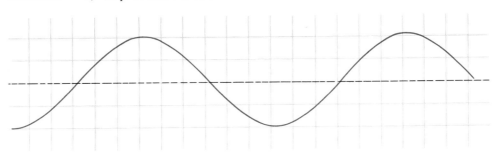

Step 2. Find the phase shift and the period, and use them to establish a horizontal scale.

For a cosine function, the phase shift is the *t*-coordinate of the first maximum, point A. Since you take 20 s to reach A, the phase shift is 20 s. Since the Ferris wheel rotates once every 40 s, the period is 40 s. Hence, the *t*-coordinates of two consecutive maximum points are 20 and 60.

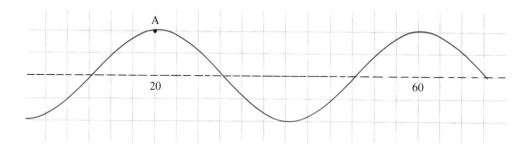

Step 3. Complete the graph by drawing the axes and their scales. The vertical displacement is 21 m, and the amplitude is 20 m. Since the people get on at the bottom, draw the vertical axis as shown.

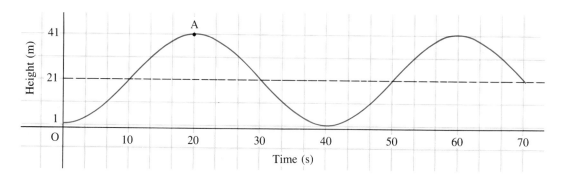

b) An equation which expresses your height as a function of time is:
$$h = 20 \cos 2\pi\frac{(t - 20)}{40} + 21.$$

c) To calculate your height above the ground after 15 s, substitute 15 for *t* in the above equation.
$$h = 20 \cos 2\pi\frac{(t - 20)}{40} + 21$$
$$= 20 \cos 2\pi\frac{(15 - 20)}{40} + 21$$
$$\doteq 35.142\ 136$$
After 15 s you will be about 35 m above the ground.

EXERCISES 5-13

(A)

1. At a seaport, the depth of the water h metres at time t hours during a certain day is given by this formula.

$$h = 1.8 \sin 2\pi \frac{(t - 4.00)}{12.4} + 3.1$$

   a) Calculate the depth of the water at 5 A.M. and at 12 noon.
   b) What is the maximum depth of the water? When does it occur?

2. The equation below gives the depth of the water h metres at an ocean port at any time t hours during a certain day.

$$h = 2.5 \sin 2\pi \frac{(t - 1.5)}{12.4} + 4.3$$

   Calculate the approximate depth of the water at 9:30 A.M.

(B)

3. At an ocean port, the water has a maximum depth of 4 m above the mean level at 8 A.M., and the period is 12.4 h.
   a) Assuming that the relation between the depth of the water and time is a sinusoidal function, write an equation for the depth of the water at any time t.
   b) Find the depth of the water at 10 A.M.

4. Tidal forces are greatest when the Earth, the sun, and the moon are in line. When this occurs at the Annapolis Tidal Generating Station, the water has a maximum depth of 9.6 m at 4:30 A.M. and a minimum depth of 0.4 m 6.2 h later.
   a) Write an equation for the depth of the water at any time t.
   b) Calculate the depth of the water at 9:30 A.M. and at 6:45 P.M.
   c) Compare the results of part b) with *Example 1*.

5. Repeat *Exercise 4* when the tidal forces are weakest. The maximum and minimum depths of the water at this time are 6.4 m and 3.6 m.

6. A certain mass is supported by a spring so that it is at rest 0.5 m above a table top. The mass is pulled down 0.4 m and released at time $t = 0$, creating a periodic up and down motion, called *simple harmonic motion*. It takes 1.2 s for the mass to return to the low position each time.

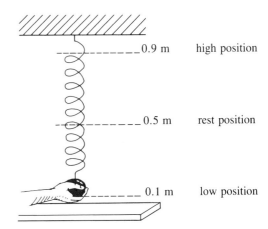

0.9 m   high position

0.5 m   rest position

0.1 m   low position

   a) Draw a graph showing the height of the mass above the table top as a function of time for the first 2.0 s.
   b) Write an equation for the function in part a).
   c) Use your equation to determine the height of the mass above the table top after: i) 0.3 s ii) 0.7 s iii) 1.2 s.

7. A Ferris wheel has a radius of 25 m, and its centre is 26 m above the ground. It rotates once every 50 s. Suppose you get on at the bottom at $t = 0$.
   a) Draw a graph showing how your height above the ground changes during the first two minutes.
   b) Write an equation for the function in part a).
   c) Use your equation to determine how high you will be above the ground after:
      i)   10 s   ii)   20 s   iii)   40 s   iv)   60 s.

8. The pedals of a bicycle are mounted on a bracket whose centre is 29.0 cm above the ground. Each pedal is 16.5 cm from the bracket. Assume that the bicycle is pedalled at the rate of 12 cycles per minute.

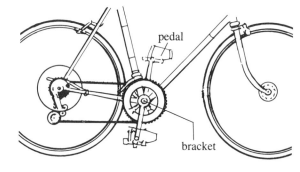

   a) Draw a graph showing the height of a pedal above the ground for the first few cycles. Assume that the pedal starts at the topmost position at $t = 0$.
   b) Write an equation for the function in part a).
   c) Use your equation to determine the height of the pedal after:
      i)   5 s   ii)   12 s   iii)   18 s.

9. The graph shows how the time of the sunset at Edmonton varies during the year.
   a) Write an equation which gives the time of the sunset on the nth day of the year.
   b) Use the equation found in part a) to calculate, to the nearest minute, the time of the sunset on:
      i)   May 10 (day 130)
      ii) June 12 (day 163)
      iii) September 17 (day 260)
      iv) December 2 (day 336).

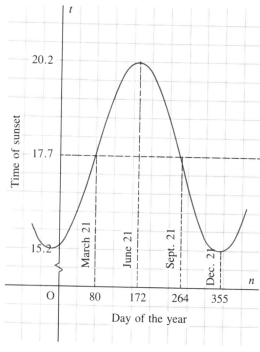

Time of sunset at Edmonton (standard time)

10. A graph showing the time of the sunset at Ottawa was shown on page 194.
    a) Write an equation which can be used to find the time of the sunset at Ottawa on the nth day of the year. (Assume it is not a leap year.)
    b) Use the equation to find the time of the sunset at Ottawa on:
       i)   February 20   ii)   April 14
       iii) July 25   iv)   November 5.

11. At St. John's, the time of the sunrise on the *n*th day of the year is given by this formula.

$$t = 1.89 \sin 2\pi \frac{(n - 80)}{365} + 6.41$$

a) Calculate the time the sun rises on October 20 (day 293).

b) Give one significant reason why the actual time of the sunrise on October 20 may differ somewhat from your answer in part a).

12. On December 21 each year, the sun is closest to the Earth, at approximately 147.2 million kilometres. On June 21 the sun is at its greatest distance, approximately 152.2 million kilometres.

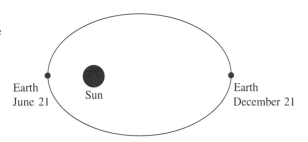

Earth
June 21

Sun

Earth
December 21

a) Express the distance *d* from the Earth to the sun as a sinusoidal function of the number of the day of the year.

b) Use the function to calculate the approximate distance from the Earth to the sun on:

i) March 1   ii) April 30   iii) September 2.

13. a) In *Example 1*, if the calculator is in *degree mode*, what change would have to be made in the equation?

b) Solve *Example 1* using your calculator in degree mode.

14. In the solution of *Example 1*, a cosine function was used. Solve *Example 1* using a sine function.

15. On the *n*th day of the year, the number of hours of daylight at Victoria is given by this formula.

$$h = 3.98 \sin 2\pi \frac{(n - 80)}{365} + 12.16$$

a) About how many hours of daylight should there be today?

b) On what dates should there be about 10 h of daylight?

16. In *Example 1*, calculate to the nearest minute the first time after 4:30 A.M. when the depth of the water is: a) 6.0 m   b) 3.0 m.

 INVESTIGATE

1. From an almanac or newspaper files, determine the approximate time the sun rises and sets in your locality on June 21 and December 21.

2. Determine equations which represent the time the sun rises and sets on the *n*th day of the year.

3. Use the equations to predict the time the sun rises and sets today, and check your results in the newspaper.

Beauty in Mathematics

"I have found a very great number of exceedingly beautiful theorems."

Pierre de Fermat

How can a theorem be beautiful? Consider the Pythagorean Theorem and a right triangle. In *any* right triangle, no matter how large or how small, the lengths of the sides always satisfy $c^2 = a^2 + b^2$. Some would say that's a beautiful theorem.

But there is more. Draw a rectangle and two parallelograms in the spaces between the squares on the Pythagorean diagram.

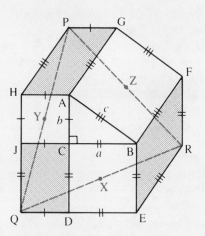

1. Prove that the areas of the shaded rectangle and the two shaded parallelograms are all equal.

2. △PQR is formed by the outer vertices of the rectangle and the parallelograms. Prove that the centres of the squares are the midpoints of the sides of △PQR.

3. Prove that the area of △PQR is $(a + b)^2$.

Think of a strategy and carry it out
- What other segments in the diagram have lengths represented by *a* or *b*?
- Can you construct other segments with these lengths?
- Try to use this information to solve each problem.

Look back
- Prove that XY, YZ, and ZX divide △PQR into four congruent triangles.
- If △ABC is isosceles, what is the ratio of the areas of △PQR and △ABC?
- Prove that the area of △PQR is never less than 8 times the area of △ABC.
- If you think that these results are rather "neat", that's what Pascal meant when he wrote that some theorems are beautiful.

PROBLEMS

Ⓑ

1. Let B be any point on the parabola $y^2 = 4px$, and let A be the fixed point $(-2a^2, 0)$. Find the equation of the locus of the midpoint of AB.

2. Calculate the perpendicular distance from the point P(5, 4) to the line $4x - 3y + 12 = 0$.

3. Given the line $Ax + By + C = 0$ and the point $P(x_1, y_1)$, determine an expression for the perpendicular distance from the point to the line.

4. Find, to the nearest degree, the measures of the angles of the triangle formed by the lines $5x - 2y - 13 = 0$, $3x + 2y - 11 = 0$, $x - 2y + 7 = 0$.

Ⓒ

5. Prove that one root of the equation $ax^2 + bx + c = 0$ is double the other if and only if $2b^2 - 9ac = 0$.

6. In $\triangle ABC$, the bisector of $\angle A$ intersects BC at D. Prove that $\dfrac{BD}{DC} = \dfrac{BA}{AC}$.

7. a) D is any point on side BC of $\triangle ABC$. If m, n, and d are as defined on the diagram, prove that $mb^2 + nc^2 = a(mn + d^2)$.
   b) Determine whether the result of part a) holds for points D on line BC, but not between B and C.
   c) Express d in terms of a, b, and c only, if AD is:
      i) the median from A to BC
      ii) the bisector of $\angle A$
      iii) the altitude from A to BC.

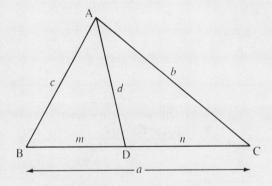

8. Points P, Q, R, and S are the midpoints of the sides of square ABCD. Find the ratio of the area of the shaded square to the area of square ABCD.

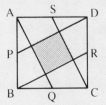

Ⓓ

9. In $\triangle ABC$, the bisectors of $\angle B$ and $\angle C$ meet AC and AB at M and N respectively. If segments BM and CN have the same length, prove that $\triangle ABC$ is isosceles.

Review Exercises

1. Convert from radians to degrees. Give the answers to 1 decimal place where necessary.
   a) $\frac{\pi}{3}$ radians
   b) $-\frac{7\pi}{4}$ radians
   c) $\frac{5\pi}{6}$ radians
   d) 4.7 radians

2. Convert from degrees to radians. Give the answers to 2 decimal places where necessary.
   a) $135°$
   b) $270°$
   c) $330°$
   d) $-47°$

3. Calculate the arc length to the nearest centimetre of a sector of a circle with radius 9 cm if the sector angle is $220°$.

4. Each point P is on the terminal arm of angle θ. Find $\sin \theta$, $\cos \theta$, and $\tan \theta$ to 3 decimal places.
   a) P(4,9)
   b) P(8, -15)
   c) P(-4,7)
   d) P(-6, -5)

5. Find each value of θ in *Exercise 4*:
   i)   in degrees to 1 decimal place
   ii) in radians to 3 decimal places.

6. Solve for θ to the nearest degree, $0° \leqslant \theta \leqslant 360°$.
   a) $\sin \theta = 0.7295$
   b) $\cos \theta = -0.3862$
   c) $\tan \theta = -5.1730$

7. Solve for θ in radians to 2 decimal places, $0 \leqslant \theta \leqslant 2\pi$.
   a) $\cos \theta = 0.2681$
   b) $\tan \theta = 1.0744$
   c) $\sin \theta = -0.4683$

8. Given θ is an acute angle, find expressions for the other five trigonometric ratios.
   a) $\sin \theta = \frac{a}{b}$
   b) $\tan \theta = \frac{p}{p + q}$
   c) $\sec \theta = \frac{2m - 1}{m + 3}$

9. State the exact values of the six trigonometric ratios of each angle.
   a) $\frac{5\pi}{6}$
   b) $\frac{\pi}{3}$
   c) $\frac{7\pi}{4}$
   d) $\frac{4\pi}{3}$
   e) $\frac{11\pi}{6}$

10. Draw graphs of $y = \sin \theta$ and $y = \cos \theta$ for $-2\pi \leqslant \theta \leqslant 2\pi$. For each graph
    a) State the maximum value of y, and the values of θ for which it occurs.
    b) State the minimum value of y, and the values of θ for which it occurs.
    c) State the θ- and y-intercepts.

11. Find the amplitude, the period, the phase shift, and the vertical displacement for each function.
    a) $y = 3 \sin 2\left(\theta - \frac{\pi}{4}\right) - 4$
    b) $y = 2 \cos 5\left(\theta + \frac{\pi}{3}\right) + 1$

12. Sketch the graphs of each set of functions on the same grid for $-2\pi \leqslant \theta \leqslant 2\pi$.
    a) $y = \sin \theta$ $y = 3 \sin \theta$ $y = 3 \sin \theta + 2$
    b) $y = \frac{1}{2} \cos \theta$ $y = \frac{1}{2} \cos\left(\theta + \frac{\pi}{3}\right)$ $y = \frac{1}{2} \cos\left(\theta + \frac{\pi}{3}\right) + 2$

13. Sketch the graph of each function.
    a) $y = \frac{1}{2} \sin 2\pi \frac{(t + 1)}{2} - 3$
    b) $y = 3 \sin 2\pi \frac{(t - 2)}{4} + 3$

6 Trigonometric Identities and Equations

Suppose you have an equation which expresses the depth of water as a trigonometric function of the time on a particular day. How can you determine the time if the depth is given? (See Section 6-5 *Example 4.*)

6-1 PYTHAGOREAN, RECIPROCAL, AND QUOTIENT IDENTITIES

Let $P(x,y)$ be any point on a circle of radius r, corresponding to an angle θ in standard position. Recall that the six trigonometric functions are defined as follows.

$$\sin \theta = \frac{y}{r} \qquad\qquad \cos \theta = \frac{x}{r} \qquad\qquad \tan \theta = \frac{y}{x}, x \neq 0$$

$$\csc \theta = \frac{r}{y}, y \neq 0 \qquad \sec \theta = \frac{r}{x}, x \neq 0 \qquad \cot \theta = \frac{x}{y}, y \neq 0$$

where $r = \sqrt{x^2 + y^2}$

These definitions apply for any angle θ in any quadrant.

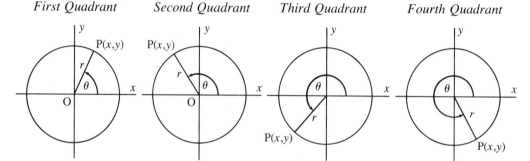

First Quadrant   *Second Quadrant*   *Third Quadrant*   *Fourth Quadrant*

Since the definitions involve only three quantities x, y, and r, and since $r^2 = x^2 + y^2$, the trigonometric functions are related in a wide variety of different ways. For example, the following identities are direct consequences of the definitions.

Reciprocal Identities

$$\csc \theta = \frac{1}{\sin \theta} \qquad \sec \theta = \frac{1}{\cos \theta} \qquad \cot \theta = \frac{1}{\tan \theta}$$

Quotient Identities

$$\frac{\sin \theta}{\cos \theta} = \tan \theta \qquad \frac{\cos \theta}{\sin \theta} = \cot \theta$$

Equations such as those above are called *identities*. They are satisfied for all values of the variable for which they are defined. The reciprocal and quotient identities can be used to prove other identities, such as those in the following example.

Example 1. Prove each identity.

a) $\sec \theta (1 + \cos \theta) = 1 + \sec \theta$

b) $\sec \theta = \tan \theta \csc \theta$

Solution.   a) $\sec \theta (1 + \cos \theta) = 1 + \sec \theta$

Left side	Reason
$\sec \theta (1 + \cos \theta)$	
$= \sec \theta + \sec \theta \cos \theta$	Expanding
$= \sec \theta + 1$	Reciprocal identity
$=$ Right side	

Since the left side simplifies to the right side, the identity is correct.

b) $\sec \theta = \tan \theta \csc \theta$

Left side	Reason
$\sec \theta$	
$= \dfrac{1}{\cos \theta}$	Reciprocal identity

Right side	Reason
$\tan \theta \csc \theta$	
$= \dfrac{\sin \theta}{\cos \theta} \times \dfrac{1}{\sin \theta}$	Quotient and reciprocal identities
$= \dfrac{1}{\cos \theta}$	

Since both sides simplify to the same expression, the identity is correct.

Observe the methods used in *Example 1* to prove the identities. We use the reciprocal and quotient identities, along with algebraic simplification, to show that one side of the identity is equal to the other side, or that both sides of the identity are equal to the same expression.

The reciprocal and quotient identities are rather like theorems in geometry, because they are used to prove other identities.

Another useful set of identities is called the *Pythagorean identities* because the identities are established by applying the Pythagorean Theorem to $\triangle$PON in the diagram shown.

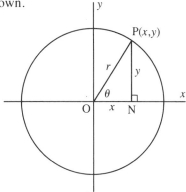

$x^2 + y^2 = r^2$

Divide both sides by r^2.

$\dfrac{x^2}{r^2} + \dfrac{y^2}{r^2} = 1$

$(\cos \theta)^2 + (\sin \theta)^2 = 1$

An expression such as $(\cos \theta)^2$ occurs so frequently that it is abbreviated as $\cos^2\theta$. Similarly, $(\sin \theta)^2$ is written as $\sin^2\theta$. Hence, we obtain the identity

$\cos^2\theta + \sin^2\theta = 1.$

We can obtain two additional Pythagorean identities from the equation $x^2 + y^2 = r^2$.

Divide both sides by x^2.

$$1 + \frac{y^2}{x^2} = \frac{r^2}{x^2}$$

$$1 + (\tan \theta)^2 = (\sec \theta)^2$$

$$1 + \tan^2\theta = \sec^2\theta$$

Divide both sides by y^2.

$$\frac{x^2}{y^2} + 1 = \frac{r^2}{y^2}$$

$$(\cot \theta)^2 + 1 = (\csc \theta)^2$$

$$\cot^2\theta + 1 = \csc^2\theta$$

Pythagorean Identities

$$\sin^2\theta + \cos^2\theta = 1 \qquad 1 + \tan^2\theta = \sec^2\theta \qquad 1 + \cot^2\theta = \csc^2\theta$$

Example 2. Prove the identity $1 - \cos^2\theta = \cos^2\theta \tan^2\theta$.

Solution.

Left side	Reason
$1 - \cos^2\theta$	
$= \sin^2\theta$	Pythagorean identity

Right side	Reason
$\cos^2\theta \tan^2\theta$	
$= \cos^2\theta \times \dfrac{\sin^2\theta}{\cos^2\theta}$	Quotient identity
$= \sin^2\theta$	

Since both sides simplify to the same expression, the identity is correct.

Example 3. a) Prove the identity $\dfrac{\sin \theta}{1 + \cos \theta} = \dfrac{1 - \cos \theta}{\sin \theta}$.

b) Predict a similar identity for the expression $\dfrac{\cos \theta}{1 + \sin \theta}$, and prove that it is correct.

Solution. a)

Left side	Reason
$\dfrac{\sin \theta}{1 + \cos \theta}$	
$= \dfrac{\sin \theta}{1 + \cos \theta} \times \dfrac{1 - \cos \theta}{1 - \cos \theta}$	Multiplying by 1
$= \dfrac{\sin \theta(1 - \cos \theta)}{1 - \cos^2\theta}$	
$= \dfrac{\sin \theta(1 - \cos \theta)}{\sin^2\theta}$	Pythagorean identity
$= \dfrac{1 - \cos \theta}{\sin \theta}$	Dividing numerator and denominator by $\sin \theta$
$=$ Right side	

Since the left side simplifies to the right side, the identity is correct.

b) The pattern of the terms $\sin \theta$ and $\cos \theta$ in part a) suggests that a similar identity might be:

$$\frac{\cos \theta}{1 + \sin \theta} = \frac{1 - \sin \theta}{\cos \theta}.$$

We can prove this identity in a similar way.

Another way to prove this identity (and the one in part a)) is to start with the Pythagorean identity $\sin^2\theta + \cos^2\theta = 1$ and perform the same operation to both sides. That is, we may write

$$\sin^2\theta + \cos^2\theta = 1$$
$$\cos^2\theta = 1 - \sin^2\theta$$
$$\cos^2\theta = (1 - \sin \theta)(1 + \sin \theta)$$

Hence, $\quad \dfrac{\cos \theta}{1 + \sin \theta} = \dfrac{1 - \sin \theta}{\cos \theta}$

EXERCISES 6-1

Ⓐ

1. Prove each identity.
   a) $\tan \theta \cos \theta = \sin \theta$
   b) $\cot \theta \sec \theta = \csc \theta$
   c) $\sin \theta \cot \theta = \cos \theta$
   d) $\tan \theta \csc \theta = \sec \theta$
   e) $\sin \theta = \dfrac{\tan \theta}{\sec \theta}$
   f) $\dfrac{\cot \theta}{\csc \theta} = \cos \theta$

2. Prove each identity.
   a) $\csc \theta (1 + \sin \theta) = 1 + \csc \theta$
   b) $\sin \theta (1 + \csc \theta) = 1 + \sin \theta$
   c) $\cos \theta (\sec \theta - 1) = 1 - \cos \theta$
   d) $\sin \theta \sec \theta \cot \theta = 1$
   e) $\dfrac{1 - \tan \theta}{1 - \cot \theta} = - \tan \theta$
   f) $\cot \theta = \dfrac{1 + \cot \theta}{1 + \tan \theta}$

Ⓑ

3. Prove each identity.
   a) $\sin \theta \tan \theta + \sec \theta = \dfrac{\sin^2\theta + 1}{\cos \theta}$
   b) $\dfrac{1 + \cos \theta}{1 - \cos \theta} = \dfrac{1 + \sec \theta}{\sec \theta - 1}$
   c) $\dfrac{1 + \sin \theta}{1 - \sin \theta} = \dfrac{\csc \theta + 1}{\csc \theta - 1}$
   d) $\dfrac{1 + \tan \theta}{1 + \cot \theta} = \dfrac{1 - \tan \theta}{\cot \theta - 1}$
   e) $\dfrac{1 + \sin \theta}{1 + \csc \theta} = \sin \theta$
   f) $\dfrac{\sin \theta + \tan \theta}{\cos \theta + 1} = \tan \theta$

4. Prove each identity.
   a) $\sin^2\theta \cot^2\theta = 1 - \sin^2\theta$
   b) $\csc^2\theta - 1 = \csc^2\theta \cos^2\theta$
   c) $\sin^2\theta = \dfrac{\tan^2\theta}{1 + \tan^2\theta}$
   d) $\dfrac{\sin \theta + \cos \theta \cot \theta}{\cot \theta} = \sec \theta$
   e) $\sin \theta \cos \theta \tan \theta = 1 - \cos^2\theta$
   f) $\dfrac{\cos \theta}{1 + \sin \theta} + \dfrac{\cos \theta}{1 - \sin \theta} = 2 \sec \theta$

5. a) Prove this identity. $\dfrac{\sin\theta + \cos\theta}{\csc\theta + \sec\theta} = \sin\theta\cos\theta$

   b) Predict a similar identity for the expression $\dfrac{\sin\theta + \tan\theta}{\csc\theta + \cot\theta}$, and prove that it is correct.

   c) Establish another identity like those in parts a) and b).

6. a) Prove this identity. $\dfrac{\tan\theta}{\sec\theta + 1} = \dfrac{\sec\theta - 1}{\tan\theta}$

   b) Predict a similar identity for the expression $\dfrac{\cot\theta}{\csc\theta + 1}$, and prove that it is correct.

7. a) Prove this identity. $\dfrac{1}{1 + \sin\theta} + \dfrac{1}{1 - \sin\theta} = 2\sec^2\theta$

   b) Establish a similar identity for this expression. $\dfrac{1}{1 + \cos\theta} + \dfrac{1}{1 - \cos\theta}$

8. a) Prove this identity. $\tan^2\theta\,(1 + \cot^2\theta) = \sec^2\theta$
   b) Predict a similar identity for the expression $\cot^2\theta\,(1 + \tan^2\theta)$, and prove that it is correct.

9. a) Prove each identity.
      i) $(1 - \cos^2\theta)(1 + \tan^2\theta) = \tan^2\theta$ ii) $(1 - \sin^2\theta)(1 + \cot^2\theta) = \cot^2\theta$
   b) Establish another identity like those in part a).

10. Prove each identity.
    a) $\tan\theta + \cot\theta = \sec\theta\csc\theta$ b) $\sec^2\theta + \csc^2\theta = \sec^2\theta\csc^2\theta$
    c) $\sec^2\theta + \csc^2\theta = (\tan\theta + \cot\theta)^2$ d) $\sin^2\theta = \cos\theta\,(\sec\theta - \cos\theta)$

11. Let P be any point on the unit circle, and construct the tangent to the circle at P. Let the tangent intersect the x-axis at A and the y-axis at B.
    a) Show that:
       i) $PN = \sin\theta$ ii) $ON = \cos\theta$
       iii) $OB = \csc\theta$ iv) $OA = \sec\theta$
       v) $AP = \tan\theta$ vi) $BP = \cot\theta$.
    b) Use the results of part a) and similar triangles on the diagram to illustrate these identities.
       i) $1 + \tan^2\theta = \sec^2\theta$
       ii) $\sin^2\theta = \cos\theta\,(\sec\theta - \cos\theta)$
       iii) $\tan\theta\cot\theta = 1$
    c) What other identities can you find that can be illustrated by this diagram?

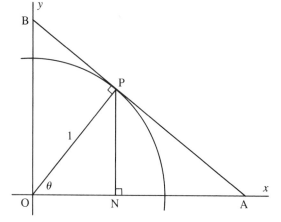

Ⓒ

12. In *Exercise 7*, identities for $\dfrac{1}{1 + f(x)} + \dfrac{1}{1 - f(x)}$, where $f(x) = \sin x$ and
$f(x) = \cos x$, were established. Establish similar identities where $f(x)$ represents each of the other four trigonometric functions.

13. Establish an identity which involves all six trigonometric functions.

14. Prove each identity.

a) $\dfrac{1}{1 + \cos \theta} = \csc^2\theta - \dfrac{\cot \theta}{\sin \theta}$

b) $\tan \theta + \tan^3\theta = \dfrac{\sec^2\theta}{\cot \theta}$

c) $\dfrac{1 + \csc \theta}{\cot \theta} - \sec \theta = \tan \theta$

d) $\dfrac{(1 - \cos^2\theta)(\sec^2\theta - 1)}{\cos^2\theta} = \tan^4\theta$

15. Let $P(x,y)$ be any point on a circle of radius r, corresponding to an angle θ in standard position. Let A and C be the points shown on the diagram.

a) Express the lengths AP and CP as functions of r and θ.

b) Check the results of part a) when $\theta = 0, \dfrac{\pi}{2}, \pi,$ and $\dfrac{3\pi}{2}$.

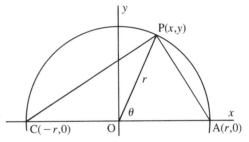

16. Solve for x. $\sin x - \tan x = 0, 0 \leqslant x \leqslant 2\pi$

17. Prove that the following expressions are *not* identities.

a) $\sin 2\theta = 2 \sin \theta$ b) $\cos 2\theta = 2 \cos \theta$ c) $\tan 2\theta = 2 \tan \theta$

 INVESTIGATE

Identities for $\sin 2\theta$, $\cos 2\theta$, and $\tan 2\theta$ can be established using the diagram of the unit circle shown. Since $\triangle ONP$ is a right triangle with hypotenuse 1 unit, then $ON = \cos 2\theta$ and $PN = \sin 2\theta$. Similarly, since $\triangle MCO$ is a right triangle with hypotenuse 1 unit, then $CM = \cos \theta$ and $MO = \sin \theta$.

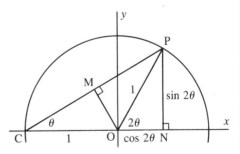

1. If $\angle MCO = \theta$, explain why $\angle PON = 2\theta$.

2. Write two different expressions for the length of CP. Use the results to establish an identity for $\cos 2\theta$ in terms of $\cos \theta$.

3. Use the results of *Question 2* to establish identities for $\sin 2\theta$ and $\tan 2\theta$ in terms of functions of θ.

6-2 ODD-EVEN, RELATED-ANGLE, AND COFUNCTION IDENTITIES

In addition to the reciprocal, quotient, and Pythagorean identities, and identities that can be derived from them, there are many other identities relating the trigonometric functions.

Odd-Even Identities

Let $P(x, y)$ be any point which is on a circle with radius r, and on the terminal arm of an angle θ. Then,

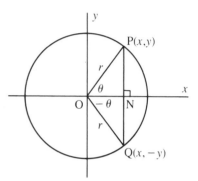

$$\sin \theta = \frac{y}{r} \dots \text{①} \qquad \cos \theta = \frac{x}{r} \dots \text{②}$$

Let $Q(x, -y)$ be the other point on the circle with the same x-coordinate as P. Then, by the SAS congruence theorem, $\triangle QON \cong \triangle PON$. Since the triangles are congruent, $\angle QON = \angle PON$. Therefore, Q is on the terminal arm of an angle $-\theta$. Hence, by definition,

$$\sin (-\theta) = \frac{-y}{r} \dots \text{③} \qquad \cos (-\theta) = \frac{x}{r} \dots \text{④}$$

Comparing ① and ③, we obtain the identity
$\sin (-\theta) = -\sin \theta$.
Comparing ② and ④, we obtain $\cos (-\theta) = \cos \theta$.

These identities are called *odd-even identities*, because they are similar to a property of powers: if n is a natural number, then $(-x)^n = -x^n$ if n is odd, and $(-x)^n = x^n$ if n is even. Odd-even identities for the other trigonometric functions can be proved in the same way.

Odd-Even Identities

$\sin (-\theta) = -\sin \theta$	$\cos (-\theta) = \cos \theta$	$\tan (-\theta) = -\tan \theta$
$\csc (-\theta) = -\csc \theta$	$\sec (-\theta) = \sec \theta$	$\cot (-\theta) = -\cot \theta$

The identities $\cos (-\theta) = \cos \theta$ and $\sin (-\theta) = -\sin \theta$ can be seen on the graphs of the cosine and sine functions.

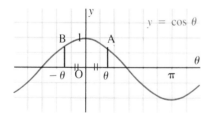

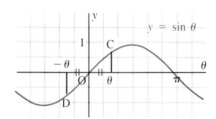

cos θ is the y-coordinate of A.
cos $(-\theta)$ is the y-coordinate of B.
Since these y-coordinates are equal,
$\cos (-\theta) = \cos \theta$.

sin θ is the y-coordinate of C.
sin $(-\theta)$ is the y-coordinate of D.
Since these y-coordinates are equal in absolute value, but have opposite signs,
$\sin (-\theta) = -\sin \theta$.

Related-Angle Identities

Let $Q(-x, y)$ be the reflection of P in the y-axis. Then, Q is on the terminal arm of an angle in standard position equal to $\pi - \theta$. We apply the definitions of the trigonometric functions to Q.

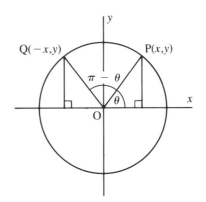

$$\sin (\pi - \theta) = \frac{y}{r} \dots ⑤$$

$$\cos (\pi - \theta) = -\frac{x}{r} \dots ⑥$$

Comparing ① and ⑤, we obtain
$$\sin (\pi - \theta) = \sin \theta$$
Comparing ② and ⑥, we obtain
$$\cos (\pi - \theta) = -\cos \theta$$

These identities are called *related-angle identities*.

Similar identities relating the other trigonometric functions can be proved in the same way.

Related-Angle Identities

$\sin (\pi - \theta) = \sin \theta$	$\csc (\pi - \theta) = \csc \theta$
$\cos (\pi - \theta) = -\cos \theta$	$\sec (\pi - \theta) = -\sec \theta$
$\tan (\pi - \theta) = -\tan \theta$	$\cot (\pi - \theta) = -\cot \theta$

These identities can be seen on graphs.

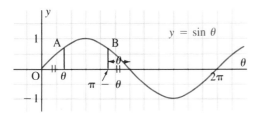

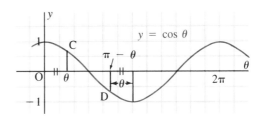

sin θ is the y-coordinate of A.
sin $(\pi - \theta)$ is the y-coordinate of B.
Since these y-coordinates are equal,
$\sin (\pi - \theta) = \sin \theta$.

cos θ is the y-coordinate of C.
cos $(\pi - \theta)$ is the y-coordinate of D.
Since these y-coordinates are equal in absolute value, but have opposite signs,
$\cos (\pi - \theta) = -\cos \theta$

Cofunction Identities

Let $Q(y,x)$ be the reflection of P in the line $y = x$. Then, Q is on the terminal arm of an angle in standard position equal to $\frac{\pi}{2} - \theta$. We apply the definitions of the trigonometric functions to Q.

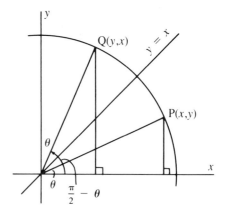

$$\sin\left(\frac{\pi}{2} - \theta\right) = \frac{x}{r} \dots \text{⑦}$$

$$\cos\left(\frac{\pi}{2} - \theta\right) = \frac{y}{r} \dots \text{⑧}$$

Comparing ② and ⑦, we obtain

$$\sin\left(\frac{\pi}{2} - \theta\right) = \cos\theta.$$

Comparing ① and ⑧, we obtain

$$\cos\left(\frac{\pi}{2} - \theta\right) = \sin\theta.$$

These identities are called *cofunction identities* because they involve complementary angles and the *co*sine and sine functions. They state that:
- the *co*sine of an angle is equal to the sine of the *co*mplementary angle.
- the sine of an angle is equal to the *co*sine of the *co*mplementary angle.

Similar identities relating the other trigonometric functions can be proved in the same way.

Cofunction Identities

$$\sin\left(\frac{\pi}{2} - \theta\right) = \cos\theta \qquad \csc\left(\frac{\pi}{2} - \theta\right) = \sec\theta$$

$$\cos\left(\frac{\pi}{2} - \theta\right) = \sin\theta \qquad \sec\left(\frac{\pi}{2} - \theta\right) = \csc\theta$$

$$\tan\left(\frac{\pi}{2} - \theta\right) = \cot\theta \qquad \cot\left(\frac{\pi}{2} - \theta\right) = \tan\theta$$

The cofunction identities can be seen on graphs. For example, on the graph (below left), $\cos\theta$ is the y-coordinate of A. On the other graph, $\sin\left(\frac{\pi}{2} - \theta\right)$ is the y-coordinate of B. Since these y-coordinates are equal, $\sin\left(\frac{\pi}{2} - \theta\right) = \cos\theta.$

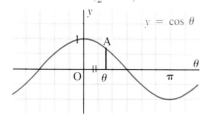

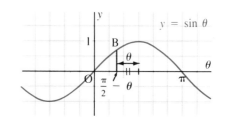

Example 1. Simplify. a) $\cos\left(-\frac{\pi}{3}\right)$ b) $\sin\left(-\frac{\pi}{4}\right)$

Solution. a) $\cos\left(-\frac{\pi}{3}\right) = \cos\frac{\pi}{3}$ b) $\sin\left(-\frac{\pi}{4}\right) = -\sin\frac{\pi}{4}$

$$= \frac{1}{2}$$ $$= -\frac{1}{\sqrt{2}}$$

Example 2. Simplify. a) $\sin\frac{5\pi}{6}$ b) $\cos\frac{3\pi}{4}$

Solution. a) $\sin\frac{5\pi}{6} = \sin\left(\pi - \frac{\pi}{6}\right)$ b) $\cos\frac{3\pi}{4} = \cos\left(\pi - \frac{\pi}{4}\right)$

$$= \sin\frac{\pi}{6}$$ $$= -\cos\frac{\pi}{4}$$

$$= \frac{1}{2}$$ $$= -\frac{1}{\sqrt{2}}$$

Example 3. Use your calculator to check.

a) $\cos 2.4 = -\cos(\pi - 2.4)$ b) $\sin 1.5 = \cos\left(\frac{\pi}{2} - 1.5\right)$

Solution. Be sure the calculator is in radian mode.
a) $\cos 2.4 \doteq -0.737\ 393\ 7$ and $\cos(\pi - 2.4) \doteq 0.737\ 393\ 7$
b) $\sin 1.5 \doteq 0.997\ 495$ and $\cos\left(\frac{\pi}{2} - 1.5\right) \doteq 0.997\ 495$

The identities established in this section are special cases of more general identities involving trigonometric functions of the sum or the difference of two angles. These identities will be developed in the next section.

EXERCISES 6-2

(A)

1. Simplify.

   a) $\sin\left(-\frac{\pi}{6}\right)$ b) $\cos\left(-\frac{\pi}{4}\right)$ c) $\sin\left(-\frac{\pi}{2}\right)$ d) $\cos(-\pi)$

   e) $\cos\frac{5\pi}{6}$ f) $\sin\frac{3\pi}{4}$ g) $\sin\frac{2\pi}{3}$ h) $\cos\frac{2\pi}{3}$

2. Use your calculator to check that:
   a) $\sin 1 = \sin(\pi - 1)$ b) $\cos 1 = -\cos(\pi - 1)$
   c) $\cos 0.8 = -\cos(\pi - 0.8)$ d) $\sin 1 = \cos\left(\frac{\pi}{2} - 1\right)$
   e) $\cos 1 = \sin\left(\frac{\pi}{2} - 1\right)$ f) $\sin 0.8 = \cos\left(\frac{\pi}{2} - 0.8\right)$

(B)

3. Simplify.

a) $\tan \left(-\dfrac{\pi}{3}\right)$ b) $\sec \left(-\dfrac{\pi}{4}\right)$ c) $\csc \left(-\dfrac{\pi}{6}\right)$ d) $\cot \left(-\dfrac{\pi}{3}\right)$

e) $\tan \dfrac{5\pi}{6}$ f) $\cot \dfrac{3\pi}{4}$ g) $\csc \dfrac{2\pi}{3}$ h) $\sec \dfrac{5\pi}{6}$

4. On the graph, the y-coordinates of A and B are equal; the y-coordinates of C and B are equal in absolute value but opposite in sign. State the corresponding identities.

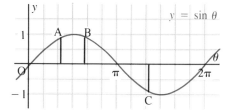

5. a) Related-angle identities for the sine and the cosine functions were developed on page 275. Establish the related-angle identities for the other four trigonometric functions.
   b) Cofunction identities for the sine and cosine functions were developed on page 276. Establish the cofunction identities for the other four trigonometric functions.

6. In the identity $\sin \left(\dfrac{\pi}{2} - \theta\right) = \cos \theta$, substitute $\dfrac{\pi}{2} - \theta$ for θ and simplify the result. What do you notice?

(C)

7. a) Prove each identity.

   i) $\sin \left(\dfrac{\pi}{2} + \theta\right) = \sin \left(\dfrac{\pi}{2} - \theta\right)$ ii) $\cos \left(\dfrac{\pi}{2} + \theta\right) = -\cos \left(\dfrac{\pi}{2} - \theta\right)$

   b) Establish similar identities involving π, $\dfrac{3\pi}{2}$, and 2π.

 I N V E S T I G A T E

Relations Among the Identities

A variety of other identities can be obtained from the related-angle identities and the cofunction identities, by substitution. For example, in *Exercise 6* the expression $\dfrac{\pi}{2} - \theta$ was substituted for θ in one of the cofunction identities.

This substitution can be made in any of the identities of this section. Similarly, other expressions such as $-\theta$ and $\pi + \theta$ can also be substituted for θ in the identities.

1. Investigate the effect of substituting expressions such as those above in the identities of this section. Look for patterns in the results, and classify the results in some way.

6-3 SUM AND DIFFERENCE IDENTITIES

In mathematics we often combine the operation of evaluating a function with the operations of addition or subtraction. These operations frequently give different results if they are carried out in different orders.

For example:

1. Triple a sum
   $3(a + b)$

   The sum of the numbers tripled
   $3a + 3b$

2. The square of a sum
   $(a + b)^2$

   The sum of the squares
   $a^2 + b^2$

3. The square root of a sum
   $\sqrt{a + b}$

   The sum of the square roots
   $\sqrt{a} + \sqrt{b}$

4. The reciprocal of a sum
   $\dfrac{1}{a + b}$

   The sum of the reciprocals
   $\dfrac{1}{a} + \dfrac{1}{b}$

5. The sine of a sum
   $\sin (\alpha + \beta)$

   The sum of the sines
   $\sin \alpha + \sin \beta$

6. The cosine of a sum
   $\cos (\alpha + \beta)$

   The sum of the cosines
   $\cos \alpha + \cos \beta$

The first pair of expressions are equal for all values of the variables. That is, we can write $3(a + b) = 3a + 3b$. We say that the operation of multiplication is *distributive* over addition.

   In general, function operations are not distributive over addition. For example, the next three pairs of expressions above are not equal.

$$(a + b)^2 \neq a^2 + b^2; \quad \sqrt{a + b} \neq \sqrt{a} + \sqrt{b}; \quad \text{and } \frac{1}{a + b} \neq \frac{1}{a} + \frac{1}{b}$$

We can show that $\cos (\alpha + \beta) \neq \cos \alpha + \cos \beta$ by using a counter-example. Suppose $\alpha = \dfrac{\pi}{6}$ and $\beta = \dfrac{\pi}{3}$.

Then $\cos (\alpha + \beta) = \cos \left(\dfrac{\pi}{6} + \dfrac{\pi}{3} \right)$ but $\cos \alpha + \cos \beta = \cos \dfrac{\pi}{6} + \cos \dfrac{\pi}{3}$

$$= \cos \frac{\pi}{2} \qquad\qquad\qquad = \frac{\sqrt{3}}{2} + \frac{1}{2}$$

$$= 0 \qquad\qquad\qquad\qquad \neq 0$$

Therefore, $\cos \left(\dfrac{\pi}{6} + \dfrac{\pi}{3} \right) \neq \cos \dfrac{\pi}{6} + \cos \dfrac{\pi}{3}$

Hence, $\cos (\alpha + \beta) \neq \cos \alpha + \cos \beta$

Similarly, $\sin (\alpha + \beta) \neq \sin \alpha + \sin \beta$

   Therefore, in general, the operation of evaluating a sine or a cosine is not distributive over addition or subtraction. Hence, we now consider the problem of finding expressions for $\cos (\alpha + \beta)$ and $\sin (\alpha + \beta)$. To do this, we must use the definitions of the trigonometric functions as given in *Section 5-3*.

The trigonometric functions were defined using a circle with radius r. If the circle is a unit circle, then $r = 1$, and an important special case of the definitions results. Let $P(x, y)$ represent any point on a unit circle. Then P is on the terminal arm of an angle θ in standard position. By definition,

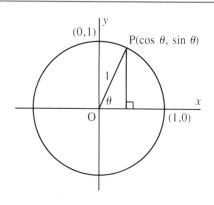

$$\sin \theta = \frac{y}{r} \qquad \cos \theta = \frac{x}{r}$$
$$= \frac{y}{1} \qquad\qquad = \frac{x}{1}$$
$$= y \qquad\qquad = x$$

Hence, $x = \cos \theta$ and $y = \sin \theta$. That is, the coordinates of P are $(\cos \theta, \sin \theta)$. Hence, the coordinates of any point P on a unit circle can be represented by $(\cos \theta, \sin \theta)$, where θ is the angle in standard position corresponding to P. We can use this property to derive identities for $\cos (\alpha - \beta)$ and $\sin (\alpha - \beta)$.

Deriving Identities for cos ($\alpha - \beta$) and sin ($\alpha - \beta$)

Let $A(\cos \alpha, \sin \alpha)$ and $B(\cos \beta, \sin \beta)$ be points on a unit circle, where α and β are the angles in standard position corresponding to A and B, respectively. Let C be on the circle such that OC is perpendicular to OB. Since the slopes of OC and OB are negative reciprocals, the coordinates of C may be represented by $(-\sin \beta, \cos \beta)$.

Rotate quadrilateral OBAC clockwise about the origin through angle β. Then B coincides with E(1, 0), C coincides with F(0, 1), and A coincides with D, where $\angle DOE = \alpha - \beta$. Hence, the coordinates of D are $(\cos (\alpha - \beta), \sin (\alpha - \beta))$.

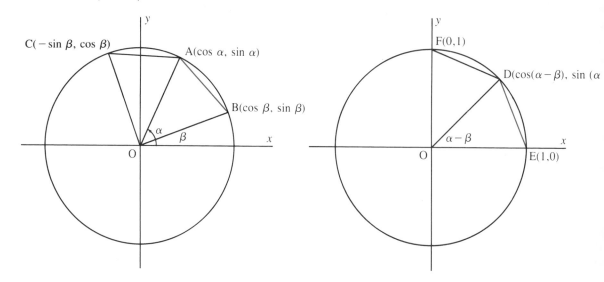

Since $\angle AOB = \angle DOE$, $\triangle AOB \cong \triangle DOE$.
Since the triangles are congruent,
$$AB = DE$$
$$\sqrt{(\cos \alpha - \cos \beta)^2 + (\sin \alpha - \sin \beta)^2} = \sqrt{(\cos (\alpha - \beta) - 1)^2 + (\sin (\alpha - \beta) - 0)^2}$$
Square both sides to eliminate the radicals.
$$(\cos \alpha - \cos \beta)^2 + (\sin \alpha - \sin \beta)^2 = (\cos (\alpha - \beta) - 1)^2 + \sin^2(\alpha - \beta)$$
Expand the binomial squares and use the Pythagorean identity.
$$\cos^2\alpha - 2 \cos \alpha \cos \beta + \cos^2\beta + \sin^2\alpha - 2 \sin \alpha \sin \beta + \sin^2\beta$$
$$= \cos^2(\alpha - \beta) - 2 \cos (\alpha - \beta) + 1 + \sin^2(\alpha - \beta)$$
$$(\cos^2\alpha + \sin^2\alpha) + (\cos^2\beta + \sin^2\beta) - 2 (\cos \alpha \cos \beta + \sin \alpha \sin \beta)$$
$$= (\cos^2(\alpha - \beta) + \sin^2(\alpha - \beta)) + 1 - 2 \cos (\alpha - \beta)$$
$$2 - 2(\cos \alpha \cos \beta + \sin \alpha \sin \beta) = 2 - 2 \cos (\alpha - \beta)$$

$$\text{Hence, } \cos (\alpha - \beta) = \cos \alpha \cos \beta + \sin \alpha \sin \beta \ldots \text{①}$$

Similarly, using $AC = DF$, we can derive the following identity for $\sin (\alpha - \beta)$.

$$\sin (\alpha - \beta) = \sin \alpha \cos \beta - \cos \alpha \sin \beta \ldots \text{②}$$

Equations ① and ② are the identities for $\cos (\alpha - \beta)$ and $\sin (\alpha - \beta)$ we have been seeking.

Example 1. Use a calculator to verify identities ① and ② for $\alpha = 1.2$ and $\beta = 0.9$.

Solution. Substitute $\alpha = 1.2$ and $\beta = 0.9$ into each identity.
Using identity ①:
$$\cos (1.2 - 0.9) = \cos 1.2 \cos 0.9 + \sin 1.2 \sin 0.9$$
or $\quad \cos 0.3 = \cos 1.2 \cos 0.9 + \sin 1.2 \sin 0.9$
Be sure the calculator is in radian mode.
Both sides of this equation are equal to approximately 0.955 336 5.

Using identity ②:
$$\sin (1.2 - 0.9) = \sin 1.2 \cos 0.9 - \cos 1.2 \sin 0.9$$
or $\quad \sin 0.3 = \sin 1.2 \cos 0.9 - \cos 1.2 \sin 0.9$
Both sides of this equation are equal to approximately 0.295 520 2.

Deriving Identities for $\cos (\alpha + \beta)$ and $\sin (\alpha + \beta)$
It is possible to obtain identities for $\cos (\alpha + \beta)$ and $\sin (\alpha + \beta)$ using diagrams similar to those on page 280. However, it is simpler to apply the odd-even identities to the identities ① and ② we already have.
We can do this because the sum of two angles can also be expressed as a difference. That is, $\alpha + \beta = \alpha - (-\beta)$. Hence, we can write:
$$\cos (\alpha + \beta) = \cos (\alpha - (-\beta))$$
$$= \cos \alpha \cos (-\beta) + \sin \alpha \sin (-\beta)$$
$$= \cos \alpha \cos \beta - \sin \alpha \sin \beta$$
Similarly, we can obtain $\sin (\alpha + \beta) = \sin \alpha \cos \beta + \cos \alpha \sin \beta$.

Sum and Difference Identities

$$\sin (\alpha + \beta) = \sin \alpha \cos \beta + \cos \alpha \sin \beta$$
$$\sin (\alpha - \beta) = \sin \alpha \cos \beta - \cos \alpha \sin \beta$$

$$\cos (\alpha + \beta) = \cos \alpha \cos \beta - \sin \alpha \sin \beta$$
$$\cos (\alpha - \beta) = \cos \alpha \cos \beta + \sin \alpha \sin \beta$$

We can use the sum and difference identities to find expressions for the sine or cosine of an angle obtained by adding or subtracting multiples of $\frac{\pi}{6}$ or $\frac{\pi}{4}$. For example, since $\frac{5\pi}{12} = \frac{\pi}{4} + \frac{\pi}{6}$, we can find an expression for $\sin \frac{5\pi}{12}$ without using a calculator.

Example 2. Find an exact expression for $\sin \frac{5\pi}{12}$, and check with a calculator.

Solution. $\sin \frac{5\pi}{12} = \sin \left(\frac{\pi}{4} + \frac{\pi}{6} \right)$

$$= \sin \frac{\pi}{4} \cos \frac{\pi}{6} + \cos \frac{\pi}{4} \sin \frac{\pi}{6}$$

$$= \frac{1}{\sqrt{2}} \left(\frac{\sqrt{3}}{2} \right) + \frac{1}{\sqrt{2}} \left(\frac{1}{2} \right)$$

$$= \frac{\sqrt{3} + 1}{2\sqrt{2}}$$

Both sides of this equation are equal to approximately 0.965 925 8.

We can use the sum and difference identities to prove the cofunction identities, and many other related identities.

Example 3. Prove each identity.

a) $\cos \left(\frac{\pi}{2} + \theta \right) = - \sin \theta$ b) $\sin (\pi - \theta) = \sin \theta$

Solution. a) $\cos \left(\frac{\pi}{2} + \theta \right) = \cos \frac{\pi}{2} \cos \theta - \sin \frac{\pi}{2} \sin \theta$

$$= (0)\cos \theta - (1)\sin \theta$$
$$= - \sin \theta$$

b) $\sin (\pi - \theta) = \sin \pi \cos \theta - \cos \pi \sin \theta$

$$= (0) \cos \theta - (-1)\sin \theta$$
$$= \sin \theta$$

To use the sum and difference identities, we must know both the sine and the cosine of the two angles involved in the expression.

Example 4. Given $\cos \theta = \frac{3}{5}$, where θ is in Quadrant I, evaluate $\cos \left(\theta + \frac{\pi}{6} \right)$.

Solution. The two angles are θ and $\frac{\pi}{6}$. Hence, we need to know the sine and the cosine of each angle.

We know that $\sin \frac{\pi}{6} = \frac{1}{2}$ and $\cos \frac{\pi}{6} = \frac{\sqrt{3}}{2}$.

The value of $\cos \theta$ is given, and we can obtain the value of $\sin \theta$ from a diagram.

Since θ is in Quadrant I, let $P(x,y)$ be a point in the first quadrant. Compare the general value of $\cos \theta = \frac{x}{r}$ with the given value of $\cos \theta = \frac{3}{5}$. Hence, $x = 3$ and $r = 5$.

Then, from the Pythagorean theorem,
$$r^2 = x^2 + y^2$$
$$25 = 9 + y^2$$
$$y = \pm 4$$

Since P is in Quadrant I, $y = 4$

Hence, $\sin \theta = \frac{4}{5}$

$$\cos \left(\theta + \frac{\pi}{6} \right) = \cos \theta \cos \frac{\pi}{6} - \sin \theta \sin \frac{\pi}{6}$$

$$= \frac{3}{5}\left(\frac{\sqrt{3}}{2} \right) - \frac{4}{5}\left(\frac{1}{2} \right)$$

$$= \frac{3\sqrt{3} - 4}{10}$$

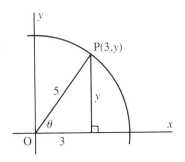

EXERCISES 6-3

1. Use a calculator to verify the sum and difference identities for $\alpha = 2.2$ and $\beta = 1.4$.

2. Expand and simplify each expression.

   a) $\sin \left(\frac{\pi}{6} + \frac{\pi}{3} \right)$ b) $\cos \left(\frac{\pi}{4} + \frac{\pi}{4} \right)$ c) $\sin \left(\frac{\pi}{3} - \frac{\pi}{6} \right)$ d) $\cos \left(\frac{\pi}{2} - \frac{\pi}{6} \right)$

3. Evaluate $\cos \frac{2\pi}{3}$ by expanding and simplifying each expression.

   a) $\cos \left(\frac{\pi}{3} + \frac{\pi}{3} \right)$ b) $\cos \left(\frac{\pi}{2} + \frac{\pi}{6} \right)$ c) $\cos \left(\pi - \frac{\pi}{3} \right)$

4. Evaluate $\sin \frac{3\pi}{4}$ by expanding and simplifying each expression.

   a) $\sin \left(\frac{\pi}{2} + \frac{\pi}{4} \right)$ b) $\sin \left(\pi - \frac{\pi}{4} \right)$

5. a) Use the fact that $\frac{\pi}{12} = \frac{\pi}{3} - \frac{\pi}{4}$ to prove that $\sin \frac{\pi}{12} = \frac{\sqrt{3} - 1}{2\sqrt{2}}$.

   b) Find a similar expression for $\cos \frac{\pi}{12}$.

   c) Check the results in parts a) and b) with a calculator.

6. Find an exact expression for each sine or cosine.

   a) $\cos \frac{7\pi}{12}$ b) $\sin \frac{11\pi}{12}$ c) $\cos \frac{5\pi}{12}$ d) $\sin \frac{5\pi}{12}$

7. Show that the cofunction identities provide counterexamples to prove that $\cos(\alpha - \beta) \neq \cos\alpha - \cos\beta$ and $\sin(\alpha - \beta) \neq \sin\alpha - \sin\beta$.

8. Prove each identity.

   a) $\sin\left(\frac{\pi}{2} + \theta\right) = \cos\theta$ b) $\cos(\pi + \theta) = -\cos\theta$

   c) $\cos\left(\frac{3\pi}{2} + \theta\right) = \sin\theta$ d) $\sin\left(\frac{3\pi}{2} - \theta\right) = -\cos\theta$

9. Simplify each expression.

   a) $\cos(\pi - \theta)$ b) $\sin\left(\frac{\pi}{2} - \theta\right)$ c) $\sin(\pi - x)$ d) $\cos\left(x - \frac{\pi}{2}\right)$

10. Given $\sin\theta = \frac{4}{5}$, where θ is in Quadrant I, evaluate each expression.

    a) $\sin\left(\theta + \frac{\pi}{6}\right)$ b) $\sin\left(\theta + \frac{\pi}{4}\right)$ c) $\cos\left(\theta - \frac{\pi}{3}\right)$

11. Given $\cos\theta = -\frac{2}{3}$, where θ is in Quadrant II, evaluate each expression.

    a) $\sin\left(\theta + \frac{\pi}{6}\right)$ b) $\cos\left(\theta + \frac{\pi}{3}\right)$ c) $\cos\left(\theta - \frac{\pi}{4}\right)$

12. Given $\sin\theta = 0.75$, where $\frac{\pi}{2} < \theta < \pi$, evaluate each expression.

    a) $\sin\left(\theta + \frac{\pi}{3}\right)$ b) $\cos\left(\theta - \frac{\pi}{6}\right)$ c) $\cos\left(\theta + \frac{\pi}{4}\right)$

13. a) Prove that $\sin\left(\frac{\pi}{4} + \theta\right) + \sin\left(\frac{\pi}{4} - \theta\right) = \sqrt{2}\cos\theta$.

    b) Find a similar expression for:

       i) $\sin\left(\frac{\pi}{6} + \theta\right) + \sin\left(\frac{\pi}{6} - \theta\right)$ ii) $\sin\left(\frac{\pi}{3} + \theta\right) + \sin\left(\frac{\pi}{3} - \theta\right)$.

    c) State a general result suggested by parts a) and b), and prove it.

14. Given that $\sin\alpha = \frac{3}{5}$ and $\cos\beta = \frac{5}{13}$, where both α and β are in Quadrant I, evaluate each expression.

    a) $\cos(\alpha + \beta)$ b) $\cos(\alpha - \beta)$ c) $\sin(\alpha + \beta)$ d) $\sin(\alpha - \beta)$

15. Given that $\cos\alpha = -\frac{4}{5}$ and $\sin\beta = \frac{2}{3}$, where both α and β are in Quadrant II, evaluate each expression.

    a) $\cos(\alpha + \beta)$ b) $\cos(\alpha - \beta)$ c) $\sin(\alpha + \beta)$ d) $\sin(\alpha - \beta)$

Ⓒ

16. Determine whether or not there are any values of α and β such that:

    a) $\sin(\alpha + \beta) = \sin\alpha + \sin\beta$ b) $\cos(\alpha + \beta) = \cos\alpha + \cos\beta$
    c) $\tan(\alpha + \beta) = \tan\alpha + \tan\beta$.

17. Derive the identity $\sin(\alpha - \beta) = \sin\alpha\cos\beta - \cos\alpha\sin\beta$ in two ways.

    a) using the diagram on page 280
    b) using the identity for $\cos(\alpha + \beta)$ and a cofunction identity

6-4 DOUBLE-ANGLE IDENTITIES

In *Section 6-3* we developed identities for the sine and cosine of the sum of two angles.

$$\sin (\alpha + \beta) = \sin \alpha \cos \beta + \cos \alpha \sin \beta$$
$$\cos (\alpha + \beta) = \cos \alpha \cos \beta - \sin \alpha \sin \beta$$

If the two angles α and β are equal, then these identities reduce to identities for $\sin 2\alpha$ and $\cos 2\alpha$.

$$\begin{aligned}
\sin 2\alpha &= \sin (\alpha + \alpha) \\
&= \sin \alpha \cos \alpha + \cos \alpha \sin \alpha \\
&= 2 \sin \alpha \cos \alpha
\end{aligned}
\qquad
\begin{aligned}
\cos 2\alpha &= \cos (\alpha + \alpha) \\
&= \cos \alpha \cos \alpha - \sin \alpha \sin \alpha \\
&= \cos^2\alpha - \sin^2\alpha \quad \dots \text{①}
\end{aligned}$$

We can use the Pythagorean identity $\sin^2\alpha + \cos^2\alpha = 1$ to express the identity for $\cos 2\alpha$ in two other forms.

Since $\sin^2\alpha + \cos^2\alpha = 1$, then
$$\sin^2\alpha = 1 - \cos^2\alpha$$
Substitute this expression in ①
$$\begin{aligned}
\cos 2\alpha &= \cos^2\alpha - \sin^2\alpha \\
&= \cos^2\alpha - (1 - \cos^2\alpha) \\
&= 2 \cos^2\alpha - 1
\end{aligned}$$

Since $\sin^2\alpha + \cos^2\alpha = 1$, then
$$\cos^2\alpha = 1 - \sin^2\alpha$$
Substitute this expression in ①
$$\begin{aligned}
\cos 2\alpha &= \cos^2\alpha - \sin^2\alpha \\
&= (1 - \sin^2\alpha) - \sin^2\alpha \\
&= 1 - 2 \sin^2\alpha
\end{aligned}$$

Double-Angle Identities

$$\sin 2\alpha = 2 \sin \alpha \cos \alpha \qquad \begin{aligned} \cos 2\alpha &= \cos^2\alpha - \sin^2\alpha \\ &= 2 \cos^2\alpha - 1 \\ &= 1 - 2 \sin^2\alpha \end{aligned}$$

Example 1. Use a calculator to verify that $\sin 1.2 = 2 \sin 0.6 \cos 0.6$.

Solution. Both sides of the equation are equal to approximately $0.932\ 039\ 1$.

Example 2. If $\cos \theta = -\dfrac{1}{3}$, and $\dfrac{\pi}{2} < \theta < \pi$, evaluate each expression.

a) $\sin 2\theta$ \qquad\qquad b) $\cos 2\theta$ \qquad\qquad c) $\tan 2\theta$

Solution. To find the values of these expressions, we need the value of $\sin \theta$ in addition to the given value of $\cos \theta$.

Since $\dfrac{\pi}{2} < \theta < \pi$, the point P lies in the second quadrant where $x < 0$ and $y > 0$.

Compare the general value of $\cos \theta = \dfrac{x}{r}$

with the given value of $-\dfrac{1}{3}$.

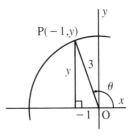

The x-coordinate of P is -1 and $r = 3$.

Since $r^2 = x^2 + y^2$
$$9 = 1 + y^2$$
$$y = \sqrt{8} \qquad \text{(since } y > 0\text{)}$$

Hence, $\sin \theta = \dfrac{y}{r}$

$$= \dfrac{\sqrt{8}}{3}$$

a) $\sin 2\theta = 2 \sin \theta \cos \theta$

$$= 2 \left(\dfrac{\sqrt{8}}{3} \right) \left(-\dfrac{1}{3} \right)$$

$$= -\dfrac{2\sqrt{8}}{9}$$

b) We can find $\cos 2\theta$ using the Pythagorean identity,
or any of the three identities for $\cos 2\theta$. For example,
$\cos 2\theta = 2 \cos^2 \theta - 1$

$$= 2 \left(-\dfrac{1}{3} \right)^2 - 1$$

$$= -\dfrac{7}{9}$$

c) To find $\tan 2\theta$ we use the quotient identity.

$$\tan 2\theta = \dfrac{\sin 2\theta}{\cos 2\theta}$$

$$= \dfrac{-\dfrac{2\sqrt{8}}{9}}{-\dfrac{7}{9}}$$

$$= \dfrac{2\sqrt{8}}{7}$$

The patterns in the double-angle identities can be used to simplify
certain trigonometric expressions.

Example 3.   Write each expression in terms of a single trigonometric function.

a) $2 \sin 0.45 \cos 0.45$ b) $\cos^2 5 - \sin^2 5$

Solution.   a) $2 \sin 0.45 \cos 0.45$

This expression can be obtained by substituting 0.45 for α in
the right side of the identity $\sin 2\alpha = 2 \sin \alpha \cos \alpha$. Hence, we
substitute 0.45 for α in the left side of the identity. Therefore,
$2 \sin 0.45 \cos 0.45 = \sin 0.90$

b) $\cos^2 5 - \sin^2 5$

Similarly, by substituting 5 for α in the identity
$\cos 2\alpha = \cos^2 \alpha - \sin^2 \alpha$, we obtain $\cos^2 5 - \sin^2 5 = \cos 10$.

Example 4. Prove the identity $\dfrac{1 + \cos 2\theta}{\sin 2\theta} = \cot \theta$.

Solution. In the left side, we use the double-angle identities for $\sin 2\theta$ and $\cos 2\theta$. There are three expressions we could substitute for $\cos 2\theta$. We choose the one which eliminates the 1 from the numerator.

Left side	Reason
$\dfrac{1 + \cos 2\theta}{\sin 2\theta}$	
$= \dfrac{1 + (2\cos^2\theta - 1)}{2\sin\theta\cos\theta}$	Double-angle identities
$= \dfrac{2\cos^2\theta}{2\sin\theta\cos\theta}$	
$= \dfrac{\cos\theta}{\sin\theta}$	Dividing numerator and denominator by $2\cos\theta$
$= \cot\theta$	Reciprocal identity
$= $ Right side	

Since the left side simplifies to the right side, the identity is correct.

In *Example 4*, the expression $\dfrac{1 + \cos 2\theta}{\sin 2\theta}$ on the left side is not defined for values of θ such that $\sin 2\theta = 0$. Hence, the identity holds for all values of θ except those for which $\sin 2\theta = 0$.

EXERCISES 6-4

1. Use a calculator to verify the double-angle identities for $\alpha = 0.45$.

2. Use a calculator to verify the double-angle identities for $\alpha = 5$.

3. Write each expression in terms of a single trigonometric function.
   a) $2\sin 0.6\cos 0.6$ b) $2\sin 3\cos 3$ c) $2\sin 2\cos 2$
   d) $\cos^2 0.45 - \sin^2 0.45$ e) $2\cos^2 5 - 1$ f) $1 - 2\sin^2 3$

4. Write each expression in terms of a single trigonometric function.
   a) $2\sin\dfrac{\pi}{6}\cos\dfrac{\pi}{6}$ b) $\cos^2\dfrac{\pi}{10} - \sin^2\dfrac{\pi}{10}$ c) $2\cos^2 0.5 - 1$

5. Given that $\sin\dfrac{\pi}{3} = \dfrac{\sqrt{3}}{2}$ and $\cos\dfrac{\pi}{3} = \dfrac{1}{2}$, use the double-angle identities to determine the values of $\sin\dfrac{2\pi}{3}$ and $\cos\dfrac{2\pi}{3}$.

6. Given that $\sin\dfrac{\pi}{4} = \dfrac{1}{\sqrt{2}}$ and $\cos\dfrac{\pi}{4} = \dfrac{1}{\sqrt{2}}$, use the double-angle identities to determine the values of $\sin\dfrac{\pi}{2}$ and $\cos\dfrac{\pi}{2}$.

(B)

7. The identity $\cos 2\theta = 2 \cos^2\theta - 1$ was used to prove the identity in *Example 4*. Prove the identity using one of the other identities for $\cos 2\theta$.

8. If $\sin \theta = \frac{1}{3}$, and θ is in Quadrant I, evaluate each expression.

   a) $\sin 2\theta$ b) $\cos 2\theta$ c) $\tan 2\theta$

9. A value of θ is defined. Evaluate the expressions $\sin 2\theta$, $\cos 2\theta$, and $\tan 2\theta$.

   a) $\cos \theta = -\frac{1}{2}$, and θ is in Quadrant II

   b) $\sin \theta = -\frac{2}{3}$, and θ is in Quadrant III

   c) $\tan \theta = 0.75$ and $\pi < \theta < \frac{3\pi}{2}$

10. Prove each identity.

   a) $1 + \sin 2\theta = (\sin \theta + \cos \theta)^2$ b) $\sin 2\theta = 2 \cot \theta \sin^2\theta$

   c) $\cos 2\theta = \dfrac{1 - \tan^2\theta}{1 + \tan^2\theta}$ d) $\sec^2\theta = \dfrac{2}{1 + \cos 2\theta}$

11. a) Show that the expression $\dfrac{1 - \cos 2\theta}{2}$ is equivalent to $\sin^2\theta$.

   b) Find a similar expression equivalent to $\cos^2\theta$. Try to do this in more than one way.

12. Show that the expression $\dfrac{\sin^2\theta + \cos^2\theta}{\sin^2\theta - \cos^2\theta}$ is equivalent to $-\sec 2\theta$, provided that $\sin^2\theta \neq \cos^2\theta$.

13. a) Show that the expression $\dfrac{(\sin \theta + \cos \theta)^2}{\sin 2\theta}$ is equivalent to the expression $\csc 2\theta + 1$, provided that $\sin 2\theta \neq 0$.

   b) Find a similar expression equivalent to $\csc 2\theta - 1$.

14. In *Example 4*, an identity for $\dfrac{1 + \cos 2\theta}{\sin 2\theta}$ was proved. Establish similar identities for each expression.

   a) $\dfrac{1 - \cos 2\theta}{\sin 2\theta}$ b) $\dfrac{\sin 2\theta}{1 + \cos 2\theta}$ c) $\dfrac{\sin 2\theta}{1 - \cos 2\theta}$

15. a) If $\sin \theta + \cos \theta = \frac{1}{2}$, find the value of $\sin 2\theta$.

   b) Check the result of part a) with your calculator.

(C)

16. a) Sketch the graphs of the functions $y = \sin 2\theta$ and $y = 2 \sin \theta$.
   b) Use the graphs to explain why $\sin 2\theta \neq 2 \sin \theta$.
   c) Are there any values of θ such that $\sin 2\theta$ is equal to $2 \sin \theta$?

17. Repeat *Exercise 16* using the cosine function.

6-5 SOLVING TRIGONOMETRIC EQUATIONS

In *Section 5-3*, we solved equations such as $\sin \theta = 0.75$ and $\cos \theta = -0.275$ for θ. These equations are examples of trigonometric equations.

An equation involving one or more trigonometric functions of a variable is called a *trigonometric equation*.

These are trigonometric equations.	There are *not* trigonometric equations.
$2 \sin 2x - \cos x = 0$	$4x - 2 \sin 4.5 = 3$
$x + \tan x = 1$	$x^2 + \cos \pi = 0$

Since trigonometric functions are periodic, a trigonometric equation usually has infinitely many roots. Sometimes, only the roots in a particular domain are required.

Example 1. Solve the equation $3 \cos^2\theta + \cos \theta - 1 = 0$ for θ, to two decimal places, where $0 \le \theta < 2\pi$.

Solution. $3 \cos^2\theta + \cos \theta - 1 = 0$ is a quadratic equation in $\cos \theta$.
Use the quadratic formula.

$$\cos \theta = \frac{-b \pm \sqrt{b^2 - 4ac}}{2a} \qquad \begin{array}{l} a = 3 \\ b = 1 \\ c = -1 \end{array}$$

$$= \frac{-1 \pm \sqrt{1^2 - 4(3)(-1)}}{2(3)}$$

$$= \frac{-1 \pm \sqrt{13}}{6}$$

$$\doteq 0.434\ 258\ 5 \text{ or } -0.767\ 591\ 9$$

When $\cos \theta \doteq 0.434\ 258\ 5$
$$\theta \doteq 1.121\ 581\ 3,$$
which is one root of the equation
By the property of cosine functions in *Section 5-3*, another root is
$2\pi - 1.121\ 581\ 3 = 5.161\ 604$.
When $\cos \theta \doteq -0.767\ 591\ 9$
$$\theta \doteq 2.445\ 871\ 8,$$
which is a root of the equation
Another root is $2\pi - 2.445\ 871\ 8 = 3.837\ 313\ 5$.
Hence, the given equation has four roots between 0 and 2π. To two decimal places, these roots are 1.12, 2.45, 3.84, and 5.16.

In *Example 1*, notice that when the values of θ are subtracted from 2π, more than two decimal places are used. This avoids rounding errors. For example, if the root 2.445 871 8 had been rounded to two decimal places as 2.45 and then subtracted from 2π, the result would have been 3.83. This value is not correct to two decimal places.

In *Example 1*, only one trigonometric function was present in the equation. Other equations contain two or more trigonometric functions.

Example 2. Solve the equation $2 \sin x = 3 + 2 \csc x$ over the domain $0 \leq x < 2\pi$.

Solution. Since the sine and cosecant functions are reciprocal functions, we can write $\csc x$ in terms of $\sin x$.

$$2 \sin x = 3 + 2 \csc x$$

$$2 \sin x = 3 + \frac{2}{\sin x}$$

Multiply both sides by $\sin x$.

$$2 \sin^2 x - 3 \sin x - 2 = 0$$

$$(2 \sin x + 1)(\sin x - 2) = 0$$

Either $2 \sin x + 1 = 0$ or $\sin x - 2 = 0$

$\qquad\qquad \sin x = -0.5$ $\sin x = 2$

One value of x satisfying this   There are no real values of

equation is $x = -\dfrac{\pi}{6}$. x satisfying this equation.

The root $x = -\dfrac{\pi}{6}$ is not in the domain. By the property of sine functions

in *Section 5-3*, a root in the domain is $\pi - \left(-\dfrac{\pi}{6}\right)$, or $\dfrac{7\pi}{6}$. Since the sine

function has period 2π, another root in the domain is $-\dfrac{\pi}{6} + 2\pi$, or $\dfrac{11\pi}{6}$.

Hence, for $0 \leq x < 2\pi$, the equation has two roots: $\dfrac{7\pi}{6}$ and $\dfrac{11\pi}{6}$.

No general methods exist for solving trigonometric equations, but the strategy used in *Example 2* is often helpful. The given equation involved both the sine and the cosecant function. We used a trigonometric identity to reduce the equation to one involving only the sine function, which we solved using algebraic methods.

Example 3. Solve over the real numbers. $4 \sin x \cos x - 1 = 0$

Solution. A product of the form $\sin x \cos x$ occurs in the double-angle identity $\sin 2\theta = 2 \sin \theta \cos \theta$. Hence, we write the equation as follows.

$$2 (2 \sin x \cos x) - 1 = 0$$

$$2 \sin 2x - 1 = 0$$

$$\sin 2x = 0.5 \ldots \textcircled{1}$$

Since $\sin \dfrac{\pi}{6} = 0.5$, one value is   By the property of sine functions, another value is

$2x = \dfrac{\pi}{6}$ $2x = \pi - \dfrac{\pi}{6}$

$x = \dfrac{\pi}{12}$ $x = \dfrac{5\pi}{12}$

These are two roots of the equation. Since the function in equation $\textcircled{1}$ is periodic with period π, we can find infinitely many other roots by adding multiples of the period to these roots.

There are infinitely many roots   And, there are infinitely many of the form   roots of the form

$x = \dfrac{\pi}{12} + n\pi$, where $n \in$ I. $x = \dfrac{5\pi}{12} + n\pi$, where $n \in$ I.

In *Example 3*, the expressions $\frac{\pi}{12} + n\pi$ and $\frac{5\pi}{12} + n\pi$ form what is called the *general solution* of the equation. Particular solutions can be obtained by substituting integers for n. For example, if $n = 2$, we obtain the roots $\frac{25\pi}{12}$ and $\frac{29\pi}{12}$. You can check that these are correct by substituting them for x into the left side of the original equation and using your calculator.

In *Section 5-13* we expressed the depth of the water at Annapolis Tidal Generating Station as a function of the time on a particular day, by the equation $h = 3 \cos 2\pi \dfrac{(t - 4.5)}{12.4} + 5$. We used this equation to calculate the depth at different times. The graph of this function is repeated below.

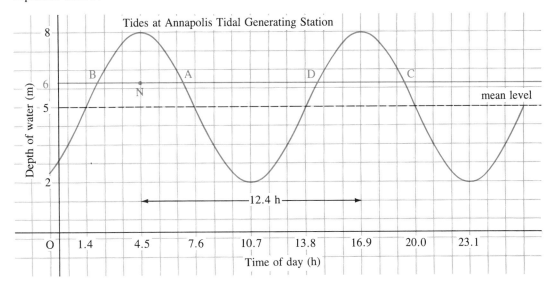

Tides at Annapolis Tidal Generating Station

We now ask the inverse question — if we know the depth of the water, how can we calculate the time? For example, if the depth is 6.0 m, we would write this equation.

$$3 \cos 2\pi \frac{(t - 4.5)}{12.4} + 5 = 6$$

This is an example of a trigonometric equation with the variable t. We can see from the graph that this equation has more than one solution. That is, the times when the water is 6.0 m deep are represented by the points A, B, C, and D. This is what we should expect, because the water will be 6.0 m deep at different times during the day.

Example 4. a) Calculate, to the nearest minute, one of the times when the water is 6.0 m deep on the day represented by the graph.

b) Calculate the other times on the same day when the water is 6.0 m deep.

Solution. a) $3 \cos 2\pi \dfrac{(t - 4.5)}{12.4} + 5 = 6$

$$3 \cos 2\pi \dfrac{(t - 4.5)}{12.4} = 1$$

$$\cos 2\pi \dfrac{(t - 4.5)}{12.4} = \dfrac{1}{3}$$

To solve this equation, we must find a number whose cosine is $\dfrac{1}{3}$.

Since the cosine function is periodic, there are infinitely many numbers with this property. Using a calculator, one of these numbers is approximately 1.230 959 4.

Hence, we can write

$$2\pi \dfrac{(t - 4.5)}{12.4} \doteq 1.230\ 959\ 4$$

To solve this equation for t, we multiply both sides by 12.4, then divide both sides by 2π, and finally add 4.5 to both sides. We do these steps with the calculator and get 6.929 324 6. This is one root of the equation.

To convert to minutes, multiply the fractional part by 60 and get 55.759 477. Hence, to the nearest minute, the water was 6 m deep at 6:56 A.M.

b) The time found in part a) is represented by point A on the graph. The other times when the water is 6 m deep are represented by B, C, and D.

To calculate the t-coordinate of B, we use the fact that the segments AN and BN have the same length.

Since 6.929 324 6 − 4.5 = 2.429 324 6, the t-coordinate of B is 4.5 − 2.429 324 6, or 2.070 675 4. As before, we convert to minutes by multiplying the fractional part by 60. The water was 6 m deep at 2:04 A.M.

To calculate the t-coordinates of C and D, we add the period to the t-coordinates of A and B. The results are:

Point C: $t = 6.929\ 324\ 6 + 12.4$

$\qquad = 19.329\ 324\ 6$

The corresponding time is 19:20, or 7:20 P.M.

Point D:

$t = 2.070\ 675\ 4 + 12.4$

$\ = 14.470\ 675\ 4$

The corresponding time is 14:28, or 2:28 P.M.

Hence, during the day represented by the graph, the water was 6.0 m deep at 2:04 A.M., 6:56 A.M., 2:28 P.M., and 7:20 P.M.

EXERCISES 6-5

Ⓑ

1. Solve for θ to 2 decimal places, $0 \leqslant \theta < 2\pi$.
   a) $2 \sin^2\theta - 3 \sin \theta + 1 = 0$ b) $2 \cos^2\theta + 5 \cos \theta - 3 = 0$
   c) $2 \tan^2\theta = 3 \tan \theta - 1$ d) $3 \tan^2\theta = 2 \tan \theta + 4$

2. Solve for x to 2 decimal places, $0 \leqslant x < 2\pi$.
   a) $2 \cos^2 x + \cos x - 1 = 0$ b) $3 \sin^2 x + \sin x - 1 = 0$

   c) $4 \cos x = 6 \sec x - 5$ d) $\sec x - 7 \cos x = \dfrac{5}{6}$

3. Solve over the domain $0 \leqslant x < 2\pi$.
   a) $2 \cos x = 7 - 3 \sec x$ b) $\csc x = 2 \sin x + 1$
   c) $2 \sin x \cos x + 1 = 0$ d) $\cos^2 x - \sin^2 x = 1$

4. Solve over the real numbers.
   a) $4 \sin x \cos x + 1 = 0$ b) $4 \sin 2x \cos 2x + 1 = 0$
   c) $\dfrac{\sin x + 1}{\csc x} = 3$ d) $4 \tan x + \cot x = 5$

5. At a seaport, the depth of the water h metres at time t hours during a certain day is given by this formula.
$$h = 2.4 \cos 2\pi \frac{(t - 5.00)}{12.4} + 4.2$$
   Calculate, to the nearest minute, at least two different times during this day when the water is 5.0 m deep.

6. a) On the same grid, draw the graphs of $y = \cos x$ and $y = \cos 2x$ over the domain $0 \leqslant x < 2\pi$. Then use the graph to determine the roots of the equation $\cos x + \cos 2x = 0$ over this domain.
   b) Give an algebraic solution of the equation in part a).
   c) Repeat parts a) and b) for the sine function.

Ⓒ

7. A carpenter makes the triangular frame-work shown, in which AC = 2000 mm, BC = 1000 mm, and $\angle$ACB = 90°. The framework is reinforced by segments BD and DE, where DE $\perp$ AB. If the total length of material to be used for the segments BD and DE is 1875 mm, calculate $\angle$DBC to the nearest degree.

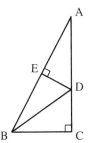

8. Write an example of a trigonometric equation, with domain the set of real numbers, that has:
   a) no real roots b) only one real root c) exactly three real roots.

9. Determine the root of each equation as accurately as you can, where $0 \leqslant \theta < \dfrac{\pi}{2}$.
   a) $\sin \theta = \theta$ b) $\cos \theta = \theta$ c) $\tan \theta = \theta$

The Golden Ratio

"Geometry has two great treasures: one is the theorem of Pythagoras; the other, the division of a line segment into extreme and mean ratio. The first we may compare to a measure of gold; the second we may name a precious jewel."

Johannes Kepler

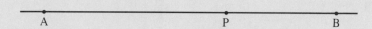

Given any line segment AB, there is a point P which divides the segment into two parts such that the length of the longer part is to the length of the shorter part as the length of the entire segment is to the length of the longer part. That is, $\dfrac{AP}{PB} = \dfrac{AB}{AP}$. This is what Kepler meant by "division . . . into extreme and mean ratio". The ratio is now known as the *golden ratio*.

The golden ratio occurs frequently and unexpectedly in a wide variety of problems. The problems below and in the problems section provide only a glimpse of this variety.

Problem 1. Find the numerical value of the golden ratio.

Understand the problem
- How can a ratio have a numerical value?

Think of a strategy and carry it out
- On the diagram above, let AP = x and PB = 1.
- Use the definition of the golden ratio to write an equation in x, then solve the equation.
- The golden ratio is the positive root of this equation.

Look back
- Did you get the equation $x^2 - x - 1 = 0$?
- Did you obtain the root $\dfrac{1 + \sqrt{5}}{2}$? This is the golden ratio expressed as a real number.
- Why is the golden ratio the positive root rather than the negative root?
- Use a calculator to express the golden ratio in decimal form.

Problem 2. Prove that the diagonals of a regular pentagon divide each other in the golden ratio.

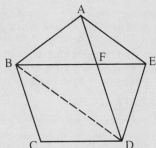

Understand the problem
- What is a regular pentagon?
- Do all the diagonals have the same length?

Think of a strategy
- Since the pentagon is regular, what properties would certain angles and segments have in a diagram like the one above?
- Could you prove these properties?
- There is no loss of generality in letting the sides of the pentagon have length 1. Hence, let the diagonals have length x.
- Write what is required to prove about point F and the diagonal BE. Are some of the segments involved sides of triangles?
- What kind of triangles might they be?

Carry out the strategy
- BF and FE are sides of $\triangle$BFD and $\triangle$EFA. Use properties of a regular pentagon to prove that these triangles are similar.
- Then use the result to prove that F divides BE in the same ratio that a diagonal bears to a side.
- Is this true about every diagonal and every side?
- Complete the proof that F divides BE in the golden ratio.

Look back
- Did you obtain the equation $x^2 - x - 1 = 0$?
- Does F divide DA in the golden ratio?
- What is the ratio of a diagonal to a side?
- Why is there no loss of generality in assuming that the sides of the pentagon have length 1?

PROBLEMS

Ⓑ

1. Prove each identity.
   a) $\sin 3\theta = 3 \sin \theta - 4 \sin^3\theta$ b) $\cos 3\theta = 4 \cos^3\theta - 3 \cos \theta$

2. The function $z(n)$ is defined as the number of zeros at the end of $n!$. For example, since $5! = 120$, which ends in one zero, then $z(5) = 1$.
   a) Determine.   i) $z(10)$ ii) $z(20)$ iii) $z(30)$
   b) Is it possible to find a value of n such that $z(n) = 5$?
   c) Given any natural number n, describe a method you could use to determine the value of $z(n)$.

3. If $\triangle ABC$ is a right triangle, prove that
   $\sin^2 A + \sin^2 B + \sin^2 C = 2(\cos^2 A + \cos^2 B + \cos^2 C)$.

4. Prove that $\cos 36° = \dfrac{\sqrt{5} + 1}{4}$ and $\cos 72° = \dfrac{\sqrt{5} - 1}{4}$.

5. Find the equations of the lines with slope $\dfrac{3}{4}$ that are 2 units from the point P(5, −1).

Ⓒ

6. Find the equations of two parallel lines passing through A(0, 2) and B(0, 7) which are 3 units apart.

7. Triangle ABC has vertices A(4, 9), B(1, 2), and C(9, 6). Find the area of $\triangle ABC$.

8. T is any point on a circle with centre C. P is a point on the tangent at T such that PT = 2CT. With centre P a second circle is drawn tangent to the given circle to intersect PT at N.
   a) Prove that N divides PT in the golden ratio.
   b) Use the result of part a) to construct a regular pentagon with one side PN.

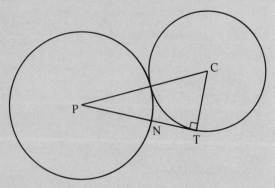

Ⓓ

9. In $\triangle ABC$, $\angle B = 90°$, and the ratio of the sides is AB : BC : CA = 3 : 4 : 5. O is the point of intersection of BC and the bisector of $\angle A$. With centre O and radius OB, a circle is drawn to intersect AO at P and Q. Prove that P divides QA in the golden ratio.

1. Prove each identity.
   a) $\sec \theta (1 + \sin \theta) = \tan \theta (1 + \csc \theta)$
   b) $\csc \theta - \dfrac{\cot \theta}{\sec \theta} = \sin \theta$

   c) $\cos^2\theta = \sin \theta (\csc \theta - \sin \theta)$
   d) $\sec^2\theta - 1 = (\sin \theta \sec \theta)^2$

2. Prove each identity.
   a) $\cos^2\theta = \dfrac{\cot^2\theta}{1 + \dfrac{1}{\tan^2\theta}}$
   b) $\dfrac{\sin \theta}{1 - \cos \theta} + \dfrac{\sin \theta}{1 + \cos \theta} = 2 \csc \theta$

   c) $\sin \theta \cot^2\theta + \cos \theta \tan^2\theta = \dfrac{\sin^3\theta + \cos^3\theta}{\sin \theta \cos \theta}$
   d) $\dfrac{\tan^2\theta + 1}{\cot^2\theta + 1} = \dfrac{1 - \cos^2\theta}{\cos^2\theta}$

3. Simplify.
   a) $\sin \left(-\dfrac{\pi}{3}\right)$
   b) $\sec \left(-\dfrac{\pi}{4}\right)$
   c) $\tan \left(-\dfrac{2\pi}{3}\right)$
   d) $\cos \left(-\dfrac{5\pi}{6}\right)$

4. Expand and simplify.
   a) $\cos \left(\dfrac{\pi}{6} + \dfrac{\pi}{4}\right)$
   b) $\cos \left(\dfrac{3\pi}{4} - \dfrac{\pi}{3}\right)$
   c) $\sin \left(\dfrac{\pi}{2} + \dfrac{\pi}{6}\right)$
   d) $\sin \left(\dfrac{5\pi}{6} - \dfrac{\pi}{6}\right)$

5. Find an exact expression for each trigonometric ratio.
   a) $\sin \dfrac{\pi}{12}$
   b) $\cos \dfrac{13\pi}{12}$
   c) $\cos \dfrac{7\pi}{12}$
   d) $\sin \dfrac{23\pi}{12}$

6. Given $\cos \theta = -\dfrac{2}{5}$ and θ is in Quadrant II, evaluate:

   a) $\sin \left(\theta + \dfrac{\pi}{6}\right)$
   b) $\cos \left(\theta - \dfrac{\pi}{4}\right)$.

7. If $\sin \alpha = \dfrac{3}{4}$ and $\cos \beta = -\dfrac{3}{5}$, where α and β are in Quadrant II, evaluate:
   a) $\cos (\alpha + \beta)$
   b) $\cos (\alpha - \beta)$
   c) $\sin (\alpha + \beta)$
   d) $\sin (\alpha - \beta)$.

8. Write each expression as a single trigonometric ratio.
   a) $\cos^2 \dfrac{\pi}{6} - \sin^2 \dfrac{\pi}{6}$
   b) $2 \sin 0.8 \cos 0.8$
   c) $2 \cos^2 0.35 - 1$

9. If $\sin \theta = \dfrac{1}{4}$ and θ is in Quadrant II, evaluate:
   a) $\sin 2\theta$
   b) $\cos 2\theta$
   c) $\tan 2\theta$.

10. Prove each identity.
    a) $\dfrac{(\sin \theta + \cos \theta)^2}{\sin 2\theta} = 1 + \csc 2\theta$
    b) $\dfrac{\sin 2\theta}{1 - \cos 2\theta} = \dfrac{1}{\tan \theta}$

    c) $2 \cos^2\theta - 1 = \cos^4\theta - \dfrac{1}{\csc^4\theta}$
    d) $\dfrac{\cos 2\theta}{\sin 2\theta + 1} = \dfrac{1 - \tan \theta}{1 + \tan \theta}$

11. Solve for θ to 2 decimal places, where $0 < \theta < 2\pi$.
    a) $8 \sin^2\theta - 6 \sin \theta + 1 = 0$
    b) $3 \cos^2\theta = 4 \cos \theta + 4$
    c) $\sin 2\theta + \cos \theta = 0$
    d) $3 \cos^2\theta - 3 \sin^2\theta + 2 = 0$

1. Convert from radians to degrees. Give each answer to 2 decimal places where necessary.

   a) $\frac{3\pi}{4}$ b) $-\frac{7\pi}{6}$ c) 2.7 radians   d) $-\frac{11\pi}{3}$

2. Convert from degrees to radians. Give each answer to 2 decimal places where necessary.

   a) $210°$ b) $-225°$ c) $147°$ d) $270°$

3. Each point P is on the terminal arm of an angle θ.
   a) Find $\sin \theta$, $\cos \theta$, and $\tan \theta$.
      i) P(3,1)   ii) P($-5, -2$)   iii) P(6, -4)
   b) Find each value of θ in degrees to 1 decimal place.

4. Solve for θ in radians to 2 decimal places, if $0 \leqslant \theta \leqslant 2\pi$.
   a) $\sin \theta = 0.7642$ b) $\tan \theta = -1.4950$ c) $\sec \theta = 1.1541$

5. If θ is an acute angle, find expressions for the other 5 trigonometric ratios.

   a) $\sin \theta = \dfrac{a}{b - c}$ b) $\cot \theta = \dfrac{2p}{q}$

6. State the amplitude, period, phase shift, and vertical displacement for each function.

   a) $y = 2 \sin 3\left(\theta - \dfrac{\pi}{6}\right)$ b) $y = \frac{1}{2}\cos\left(2\theta + \dfrac{\pi}{2}\right) - 1$

7. Prove each identity.
   a) $\sin^4\theta - \cos^4\theta = 2\sin^2\theta - 1$
   b) $\dfrac{\csc \theta}{\sec^2\theta} = \csc \theta - \sin \theta$
   c) $\dfrac{\sin \theta + \tan \theta}{1 + \cos \theta} = \tan \theta$
   d) $\dfrac{\cos \theta}{1 - \sin \theta} + \dfrac{\cos \theta}{1 + \sin \theta} = 2 \sec \theta$

8. Expand and simplify.

   a) $\sin\left(\dfrac{\pi}{6} + \dfrac{\pi}{4}\right)$ b) $\cos\left(\dfrac{\pi}{3} - \dfrac{\pi}{4}\right)$ c) $\tan\left(\dfrac{\pi}{3} + \dfrac{\pi}{4}\right)$

9. If $\sin \alpha = \frac{2}{3}$ and $\cos \beta = -\frac{1}{4}$, where α and β are in Quadrant II, evaluate:

   a) $\cos(\alpha + \beta)$ b) $\sin(\alpha - \beta)$
   c) $\cos 2\alpha$ d) $\cos(\alpha - \beta)$.

10. Solve for θ to 2 decimal places where necessary, if $0 \leqslant \theta \leqslant 2\pi$.
    a) $6\sin^2\theta + \sin \theta - 2 = 0$ b) $12\cos^2\theta = 13\cos \theta - 3$

7 Exponential and Logarithmic Functions

In 1947 an investor bought Van Gogh's painting *Irises* for $84 000. In 1987 she sold it for $49 million. What annual rate of interest corresponds to an investment of $84 000 which grows to $49 million in 40 years? (See Section 7-10 *Example 2.*)

7-1 INTRODUCTION TO EXPONENTIAL FUNCTIONS

Exponents were originally introduced into mathematics as a shorthand for repeated multiplication. Repeated multiplication occurs frequently in applications involving growth and decay.

Compound Interest

Compound interest provides a simple example of *exponential growth*. Suppose you make a long-term investment of $500 at a fixed interest rate of 8% per annum compounded annually. We can calculate the value of your investment at the end of each year.

Value in dollars of the investment after

year 1: $500(1.08) = 540$
year 2: $500(1.08)(1.08) = 500(1.08)^2$, or 583.20
year 3: $500(1.08)(1.08)(1.08) = 500(1.08)^3$, or 629.86

$\qquad \cdot \qquad\qquad \cdot$
$\qquad \cdot \qquad\qquad \cdot$
$\qquad \cdot \qquad\qquad \cdot$

year n: $500(1.08)^n$

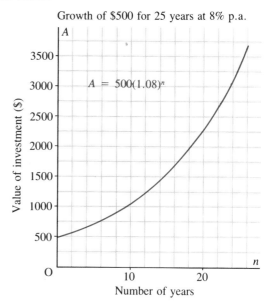

Growth of $500 for 25 years at 8% p.a.

Hence, the value of an investment A dollars can be expressed as a function of the number of years n by this equation.

$$A = 500(1.08)^n$$

In this equation, n is a natural number since it indicates how many factors of 1.08 there are in the expression. Using values of n from 1 to 25, we obtain values of A and draw the graph shown. The fact that we can draw a smooth curve through the plotted points on the graph suggests that an expression such as $(1.08)^n$ can be defined for values of n that are not natural numbers. We will see how to do this in the next section.

Growth of Populations

In 1987 the world population reached 5 billion, and was increasing at the rate of approximately 1.6% per year. If we assume that this rate of growth is maintained, we can write an equation expressing the predicted population P billion as a function of the number of years n since 1987.

$$P \doteq 5(1.016)^n$$

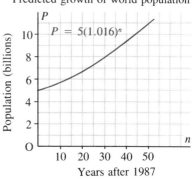

Predicted growth of world population

The graph on the facing page shows this equation plotted for values of n from 0 to 50 corresponding to the years from 1987 to 2037. In this equation, n is also a natural number, but since the graph represents as many as 50 values of n, the graph is drawn as a smooth curve.

A Bouncing Ball

A bouncing ball provides a simple example of *exponential decay*. In this picture, on each bounce the ball rises to 70% of the height from which it fell. Suppose that the ball originally fell from a height of 2.00 m. We can calculate the height to which the ball rises on each successive bounce.

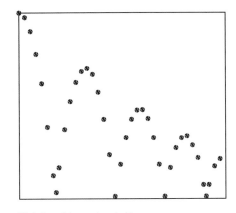

Height in metres of the ball after

bounce 1: $2.00(0.7) = 1.4$

bounce 2: $2.00(0.7)(0.7) = 2.0(0.7)^2$, or 0.98

bounce 3: $2.00(0.7)(0.7)(0.7) = 2.0(0.7)^3$, or 0.69

.   .
.   .
.   .

bounce n: $2.00(0.7)^n$

Hence, the height h metres can be expressed as a function of the number of bounces n by this equation.

$$h = 2.00(0.7)^n$$

The graph shows the values of n for $0 \le n \le 10$. Since it is not meaningful to have a fractional number of bounces, the points are not joined by a smooth curve.

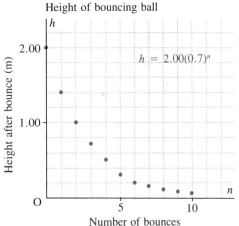

Height of bouncing ball

Light Penetration Under Water

For every metre a diver descends below the surface, the light intensity is reduced by 2.5%. Hence, the percent P of surface light present can be expressed as a function of the depth d metres by this equation.

$$P = 100(1 - 0.025)^d$$
$$\text{or} \quad P = 100(0.975)^d$$

The graph shows P as a function of d for $0 \le d \le 100$. Although d is understood to represent a natural number in the expression above, we have drawn a smooth curve to indicate light intensity at all depths to 100 m, including those depths that are not whole numbers of metres.

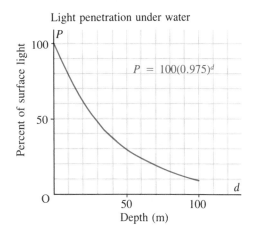

Light penetration under water

In each of the above equations, the variable in the expression on the right side appears in an exponent. Functions whose defining equation have this property are called exponential functions.

> An *exponential function* has an equation which can be written in the form $f(x) = ca^x$, where c and a are constants, and $a > 0$.

Note the following properties of the variable x, and the constants a and c.

● In this section, x is understood to represent a natural number, since it represents the number of times the constant a occurs as a factor. This restriction will be removed in the next section.

● Since all the applications of exponential functions are ones in which the base is positive, we will assume that $a > 0$.

● The constant c is any real number, though in most applications we shall encounter this number is usually positive also.

In the following example an exponential function is defined by a statement describing how variables are related.

Example.   In favorable breeding conditions, a colony of insects can multiply 10-fold every 3 weeks. If there are now 500 insects in the colony, express the number of insects N as a function of the elapsed time w weeks.

Solution.   "Multiply 10-fold every 3 weeks" means that every time 3 weeks elapse, there are 10 times as many insects as before.

Number of insects after:

3 weeks: $500(10)$ Each exponent is $\frac{1}{3}$ of
6 weeks: $500(10)^2$
9 weeks: $500(10)^3$ the number of weeks.

.   .
.   .
.   .

w weeks: $500(10)^{\frac{w}{3}}$

Hence, $N(w) = 500(10)^{\frac{w}{3}}$

EXERCISES 7-1

Note: Exercises 1 to 8 refer to the above examples.

Ⓑ

1. Use the graph on page 300 to estimate how many years it takes, at 8%, for the original investment:
   a) to double in value   b) to triple in value.

2. Describe how the graph would differ if:
   a) the interest rate were
      i) greater than 8%   ii) less than 8%;
   b) the original investment were
      i) greater than $500   ii) less than $500.

3. Use the graph on page 300 to estimate the number of years required for the population of the world to double.

4. Describe how the population graph would differ for a country such as:
   a) Mexico which has a growth rate of approximately 3.5%
   b) Japan which has a growth rate of approximately 1.1%.

5. Use the graph on page 301 to estimate how many bounces are needed before the ball bounces to only 10% of the original height from which it was dropped.

6. Describe how both the graph and the equation on page 301 would differ for a ball which is:
   a) more resilient, and bounces higher than the one shown
   b) less resilient, and does not bounce as high as the one shown.

7. Use the graph on page 301 to estimate the depth where the light intensity is only 50% of that at the surface.

8. The depth to which light penetrates under water depends on the color of the light. The graph was drawn for yellow light. How would the graph differ for:
   a) red light which penetrates about 20% as far as yellow light
   b) blue light which penetrates about 4 times as far as yellow light?

9. At current growth rates, the population of Mexico is doubling about every 20 years. The population in 1985 was 80 million. Write an expression for the population P million as an exponential function of the time n years since 1985.

10. There are now 300 insects in a colony. The population of the colony doubles every 5 days. Express the population P of the colony as an exponential function of the elapsed time d days.

11. Several layers of glass are stacked together, as shown. Each layer reduces the light passing through it by 5%. Write an expression for the percent P of light that passes through n panes of glass.

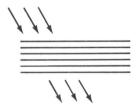

12. Most cars have a plastic container which holds fluid for cleaning the windshield. Throughout the winter, a motorist used 100% pure solvent in the container. One day in the spring, when the container was half full of solvent, she topped up the container with water. From then on throughout the summer, whenever the container was half full, she topped it up with water. Write an equation that expresses the concentration C of the solvent in the container as an exponential function of the number of times n it was topped up with water.

7-2 THE LAWS OF EXPONENTS

By counting the bacteria in a culture, scientists can learn how bacteria grow under controlled conditions. The growth of a certain bacteria is shown in the table. The number of bacteria doubles every hour, over several hours. The number of bacteria N is an exponential function of the time t hours. We can represent this function by the equation

$N(t) = 1000(2)^t$ ... ①

with the graph shown below.

Time t hours	Number of bacteria N
-3	125
-2	250
-1	500
0	1 000
1	2 000
2	4 000
3	8 000
4	16 000

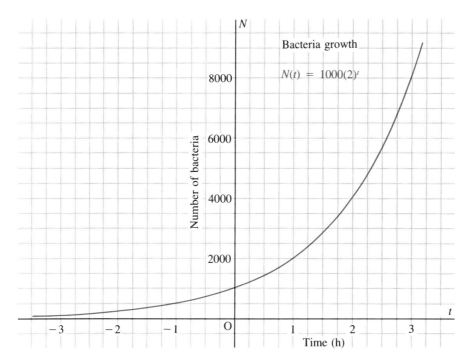

We can use the following definitions to approximate the number of bacteria at any time.

Definition of Integral and Rational Exponents

$a^0 = 1$ where $a \neq 0$ $\qquad$ $a^{-n} = \dfrac{1}{a^n}$ where $n \in N$, $a \neq 0$

$a^{\frac{m}{n}} = (\sqrt[n]{a})^m$ $\quad$ and $\quad$ $a^{-\frac{m}{n}} = \dfrac{1}{a^{\frac{m}{n}}} = \dfrac{1}{(\sqrt[n]{a})^m}$ where $m, n \in N$, $a > 0$

Example 1. How many bacteria are in the culture when:

a) $t = 0$ h   b) $t = -2$ h   c) $t = \frac{1}{2}$ h   d) $t = 1$ h 40 min?

Solution. Substitute each value of t into equation ①.

a) $N(0) = 1000(2)^0$
$= 1000(1)$
$= 1000$

b) $N(-2) = 1000(2)^{-2}$
$= 1000\left(\frac{1}{2^2}\right)$
$= 250$

c) $N\left(\frac{1}{2}\right) = 1000(2)^{\frac{1}{2}}$
$= 1000\sqrt{2}$
$\doteq 1414$

d) 1 h 40 min $= 1\frac{2}{3}$ h, or $\frac{5}{3}$ h
$N\left(\frac{5}{3}\right) = 1000(2)^{\frac{5}{3}}$
$= 1000(\sqrt[3]{2})^5$
$\doteq 3175$

Example 2. Evaluate each expression without using a calculator.

a) $(0.75)^{-2}$ b) $9^{1.5}$ c) $8^{-\frac{2}{3}}$

Solution. a) $(0.75)^{-2} = \left(\frac{3}{4}\right)^{-2}$

$= \dfrac{1}{\left(\frac{3}{4}\right)^2}$

$= \dfrac{16}{9}$

b) $9^{1.5} = 9^{\frac{3}{2}}$
$= (\sqrt{9})^3$
$= 27$

c) $8^{-\frac{2}{3}} = \dfrac{1}{8^{\frac{2}{3}}}$

$= \dfrac{1}{(\sqrt[3]{8})^2}$

$= \dfrac{1}{4}$

The definition of a positive integral exponent, as indicating repeated multiplication, leads to the five exponent laws shown below. It can be shown that the definitions of integral and rational exponents are consistent with these laws. In fact, the definition of an exponent and the laws of exponents can even be extended to include irrational exponents such as π and $\sqrt{2}$.

Laws of Exponents for Real Exponents
If m and n are any real numbers, then
1. $a^m \times a^n = a^{m+n}$
2. $\dfrac{a^m}{a^n} = a^{m-n}$ $(a \neq 0)$
3. $(a^m)^n = a^{mn}$
4. $(ab)^n = a^n b^n$
5. $\left(\dfrac{a}{b}\right)^n = \dfrac{a^n}{b^n}$ $(b \neq 0)$

The laws of exponents are useful for simplifying expressions involving exponents.

Example 3. Simplify each expression.

a) $\dfrac{a^2b^{-1}}{a^{-3}b}$ b) $\left(\dfrac{a^{\frac{1}{2}}}{b^{-2}}\right)^{\frac{2}{3}}$ c) $\left(\dfrac{x}{y^2}\right)^{\frac{1}{2}}(xy^2)^{-\frac{1}{2}}$

Solution.   a) $\dfrac{a^2b^{-1}}{a^{-3}b} = a^{2-(-3)}b^{-1-1}$ b) $\left(\dfrac{a^{\frac{1}{2}}}{b^{-2}}\right)^{\frac{2}{3}} = (a^{\frac{1}{2}}b^2)^{\frac{2}{3}}$

$= a^5b^{-2}$, or $\dfrac{a^5}{b^2}$ $= a^{\frac{1}{3}}b^{\frac{4}{3}}$

c) $\left(\dfrac{x}{y^2}\right)^{\frac{1}{2}}(xy^2)^{-\frac{1}{2}} = (xy^{-2})^{\frac{1}{2}}(xy^2)^{-\frac{1}{2}}$

$= x^{\frac{1}{2}}y^{-1}x^{-\frac{1}{2}}y^{-1}$
$= x^0y^{-2}$
$= \dfrac{1}{y^2}$

Example 4. If $x = 4$ and $y = \dfrac{1}{9}$, evaluate this expression. $(x^2y^{-\frac{1}{2}})^{-2}(x^{-3}y)^{-\frac{1}{2}}$

Solution.   Simplify the expression before substituting.
$(x^2y^{-\frac{1}{2}})^{-2}(x^{-3}y)^{-\frac{1}{2}} = (x^{-4}y^1)(x^{\frac{3}{2}}y^{-\frac{1}{2}})$
$= x^{-\frac{5}{2}}y^{\frac{1}{2}}$

Substitute. $= 4^{-\frac{5}{2}}\left(\dfrac{1}{9}\right)^{\frac{1}{2}}$

$= \dfrac{1}{(\sqrt{4})^5}\left(\dfrac{1}{3}\right)$

$= \left(\dfrac{1}{32}\right)\left(\dfrac{1}{3}\right)$

$= \dfrac{1}{96}$

Example 5. a) Evaluate $3.2^{2.57}$ to the nearest thousandth.
b) Explain the meaning of the result.

Solution.   a) Using the $\boxed{y^x}$ key on a calculator, we obtain
$3.2^{2.57} \doteq 19.872$
b) To explain the meaning of the result, write the exponent 2.57 in fractional form.
$2.57 = \dfrac{257}{100}$
Hence, $3.2^{2.57} = 3.2^{\frac{257}{100}}$
$= (\sqrt[100]{3.2})^{257}$
Hence, $(\sqrt[100]{3.2})^{257} \doteq 19.872$

EXERCISES 7-2

Ⓐ

1. Evaluate.

a) 7^0 b) 5^{-1} c) $\left(\dfrac{2}{5}\right)^3$ d) 2^{-3} e) 4^{-2} f) $\left(\dfrac{4}{9}\right)^0$

g) $\left(\dfrac{1}{2}\right)^{-2}$ h) $\left(\dfrac{3}{2}\right)^{-4}$ i) 8^{-2} j) $\left(\dfrac{5}{3}\right)^{-2}$ k) 3^4 l) $\left(\dfrac{3}{4}\right)^{-3}$

2. Evaluate.

a) $27^{\frac{1}{3}}$ b) 3^{-2} c) $(0.4)^{-1}$ d) $25^{\frac{1}{2}}$ e) $(0.008)^{-\frac{1}{3}}$ f) $16^{-\frac{1}{4}}$

g) 10^{-3} h) $64^{\frac{1}{6}}$ i) $\left(\dfrac{25}{49}\right)^{-\frac{1}{2}}$ j) $81^{-\frac{1}{2}}$ k) $(0.125)^{-\frac{1}{3}}$ l) $32^{\frac{1}{5}}$

3. Evaluate.

a) $36^{-\frac{3}{2}}$ b) $27^{\frac{2}{3}}$ c) $(0.125)^{-\frac{2}{3}}$ d) $16^{-\frac{5}{4}}$ e) $9^{\frac{5}{2}}$ f) $(2.25)^{\frac{3}{2}}$

g) $(0.6)^{-3}$ h) $100^{-\frac{3}{2}}$ i) $\left(\dfrac{8}{125}\right)^{\frac{2}{3}}$ j) $(0.36)^{-\frac{3}{2}}$ k) $64^{\frac{5}{6}}$ l) $81^{-\frac{3}{4}}$

4. Evaluate.

a) $4^{2.5}$ b) $25^{-1.5}$ c) $81^{-1.25}$ d) $400^{1.5}$

e) $32^{0.6}$ f) $\left(\dfrac{1}{16}\right)^{-0.75}$ g) $\left(\dfrac{27}{49}\right)^0$ h) $(6.25)^{-2.5}$

i) $(0.0625)^{-\frac{1}{4}}$ j) $\left(\dfrac{32}{243}\right)^{0.8}$ k) $\left(\dfrac{9}{4}\right)^{-1.5}$ l) $(5.25)^0$

5. Evaluate to the nearest thousandth.

a) $2.1^{1.6}$ b) $3.7^{2.14}$ c) $7.4^{0.85}$ d) $16^{0.75}$ e) $4.5^{3.19}$ f) $1.9^{1.9}$
g) $1.4^{-2.2}$ h) $2.8^{-1.7}$ i) $4.65^{2.75}$ j) $0.52^{-3.61}$ k) $3.82^{-1.44}$ l) $1.75^{-0.64}$

6. Simplify.

a) $m^2 \times m^{-8}$ b) $\dfrac{x^{-4}}{x^{-9}}$ c) $-15a^{-3} \times 3a^{10}$

d) $\dfrac{42s^4}{-3s^{-11}}$ e) $-3m^4 \times 12m^{-6} \times \dfrac{1}{4}m^7$ f) $\dfrac{(16n^{-2})(12n^{-3})}{15n^{-6}}$

7. Simplify.

a) $x^{\frac{2}{3}} \times x^{-\frac{5}{3}}$ b) $\dfrac{s^{-\frac{3}{4}}}{s^{-\frac{1}{2}}}$ c) $\dfrac{-12m^{-\frac{8}{5}}}{4m^{\frac{2}{5}}}$

d) $\dfrac{18a^{\frac{2}{5}}}{-6a^{-\frac{1}{5}}}$ e) $n^{\frac{3}{4}} \times n^{-\frac{3}{5}} \times n^{\frac{2}{3}}$ f) $\dfrac{-5x^{-\frac{1}{2}} \times 8x^{-\frac{3}{4}}}{10x^{-2}}$

Ⓑ

8. Simplify.

a) $3^2 - 16^{\frac{1}{2}}$

b) $2^5 - 5^2$

c) $3^{-2} + 2^{-3}$

d) $2^{-4} - 4^{-2}$

e) $3^3 - \left(\dfrac{1}{2}\right)^{-4}$

f) $12^0 - 4^{-\frac{1}{2}}$

g) $(8^{\frac{2}{3}})(16^{\frac{3}{2}})$

h) $4^{\frac{1}{2}} + \left(\dfrac{1}{2}\right)^4$

i) $\left(\dfrac{4}{9}\right)^{-\frac{3}{2}} \div \left(\dfrac{16}{25}\right)^{-\frac{1}{2}}$

9. A colony of insects doubles in size every 6 days. If there are now 2000 insects in the colony, how many
a) will there be in: i) 12 days   ii) 21 days   iii) 3 days;
b) were there: i) 6 days ago   ii) 3 days ago   iii) 10 days ago?

10. During the twentieth century, the population of Canada has been growing at the rate of approximately 1.85% per annum. The population in 1981 was 24.3 million.
a) Write an equation representing the population P million as a function of the time t years relative to 1981.
b) Use this equation to approximate the population in 1971.

11. In 1940, a large computer could perform about 100 operations per second. Since then, the speed of computers has multiplied 10-fold about every 7 years.
a) Express the number of operations per second N as an exponential function of the time t years since 1940.
b) About how many operations per second could computers perform in 1986?

12. Simplify.

a) $\dfrac{-28a^2b^{-5}}{4a^{-7}b^3}$

b) $4m^{-3}n^9 \times 5m^{-4}n^{-6}$

c) $\dfrac{12x^{-2}y^4 \times 15x^7y^{-11}}{20x^{-4}y^5}$

d) $\dfrac{6a^3b^{-7}c^0 \times 18a^{-5}b^2}{-9a^{-5}b^{-1}c^4}$

e) $\dfrac{(14m^{-3}n)(-15m^4n^{-2})}{-21mn^{-5}}$

f) $\dfrac{(24x^3z^{-4})(-35x^{-7}z^3)}{(-8x^5z^0)(-14x^{-5}z^{-6})}$

13. Simplify.

a) $\dfrac{-12a^{-\frac{1}{3}}b}{3a^{-\frac{1}{3}}b^{\frac{2}{3}}}$

b) $\dfrac{-25m^{\frac{3}{4}}n^{-\frac{1}{2}}}{-10m^{-\frac{1}{4}}n^{\frac{1}{3}}}$

c) $\left(\dfrac{x^{\frac{2}{3}}}{y^{-\frac{1}{2}}}\right)^{\frac{6}{5}}$

d) $\left(\dfrac{a^2}{b^{\frac{1}{3}}}\right)^{\frac{3}{4}}(a^2b^{-1})^{-3}$

e) $\left(\dfrac{m^{\frac{3}{4}}n^{\frac{4}{3}}}{m^2}\right)^{\frac{2}{3}}$

f) $\dfrac{(a^{-5}b^3)^{\frac{1}{2}}}{a^{-\frac{2}{3}}b^{-\frac{1}{2}}}$

14. Simplify.

a) $\dfrac{-21m^{\frac{5}{6}}n^{-\frac{1}{3}}}{7m^{\frac{1}{2}}n^{\frac{1}{6}}}$

b) $-7a^{\frac{2}{3}}b^{-\frac{1}{2}} \times 6a^{-\frac{1}{2}}b^{\frac{2}{3}}$

c) $\dfrac{-8x^{-\frac{4}{3}}y^{\frac{1}{2}} \times 6x^{-\frac{3}{4}}y^{-\frac{2}{3}}}{24x^{-\frac{5}{6}}y^{-\frac{1}{6}}}$

d) $\dfrac{(9a^{-\frac{1}{3}}b^{-\frac{4}{5}}c^{-\frac{4}{5}})(-4a^{-\frac{1}{2}}b^{\frac{3}{5}}c^0)}{-18a^{\frac{1}{6}}b^{-\frac{1}{2}}c^{-\frac{1}{3}}}$

e) $\dfrac{(13a^{-\frac{3}{4}}c^{-\frac{1}{2}})(-6a^{-\frac{1}{2}}c^{-\frac{3}{2}})}{(-21c^{\frac{1}{4}})(-39a^{-\frac{3}{2}}c^{\frac{3}{4}})}$

f) $\dfrac{(25x^{\frac{1}{4}}z^{\frac{1}{2}})(-16x^{-\frac{3}{4}}z^{\frac{3}{2}})}{(-6x^{-\frac{1}{4}}z^{-\frac{1}{2}})(-15x^{\frac{3}{2}}z^{\frac{3}{4}})}$

15. If $a = \dfrac{1}{8}$ and $b = 4$, evaluate each expression.

   a) $a^{-1}b^{\frac{1}{2}}$
   b) $(a^{-2}b^{\frac{1}{2}})(a^{\frac{1}{3}}b^{\frac{1}{2}})^{-1}$
   c) $(a^{\frac{4}{3}}b^{-\frac{3}{2}})^3(a^{-2}b^{\frac{5}{2}})$
   d) $(a^{\frac{2}{3}}b^{-2})^2(a^{-\frac{2}{3}}b^{-1})^{-3}$

16. If $x = \dfrac{4}{9}$ and $y = 27$, evaluate each expression.

   a) $-x^2y^{\frac{2}{3}}$
   b) $(3x^{-1}y^{\frac{1}{3}})(-4x^{\frac{3}{2}})^{-2}$
   c) $\dfrac{6x^{-\frac{3}{2}}y^{-\frac{2}{3}}}{16x^{-\frac{5}{2}}y^{-\frac{4}{3}}}$
   d) $\dfrac{-16x^{-\frac{5}{2}}y^{\frac{4}{3}}}{-9x^{-\frac{1}{2}}y^{-\frac{1}{3}}}$

17. If $x = 2a^4$, $y = a^3$, and $z = \dfrac{1}{2}a^2$, write each expression as an exponential function
   of a.
   a) $(xyz)^{\frac{1}{2}}$
   b) $xy^{-2}z^{-1}$
   c) $(3x^2yz)^3$

18. If $p = 3x$, $q = \dfrac{2}{3}x^2$, and $r = x^5$, write each expression as an exponential function
   of x.
   a) p^2qr
   b) $p^{-1}q^2r^{-3}$
   c) $(9p^{-2}q^2r^{-1})^{-1}$

19. Simplify.

   a) $\dfrac{(x^{2a})(x^{-5a})}{x^{-3a}}$
   b) $\dfrac{(s^{2n})(s^{-n})}{(s^{-3n})(s^{-4n})}$
   c) $\dfrac{(a^{x-1})(a^{x+1})}{a^{2x-1}}$

   d) $\dfrac{(m^{-ac})(m^{-ab})}{m^{-bc}}$
   e) $\dfrac{(x^{-3})^a(x^a)^2}{x^{a-2}}$
   f) $\dfrac{(a^{2x-y})(a^{x-y})}{(3a^{x+y})^2}$

   g) $\dfrac{(x^{\frac{a}{4}})(x^{-\frac{a}{3}})}{x^{\frac{a}{12}}}$
   h) $\dfrac{(m^{-\frac{n}{2}})(n^{-\frac{m}{4}})}{(m^{\frac{n}{3}})(n^{\frac{m}{2}})}$
   i) $\dfrac{(a^{-\frac{x}{2}})^3(a^{-\frac{x}{3}})^4}{(a^{\frac{x}{4}})^2}$

Ⓒ

20. Use your calculator to evaluate to the nearest thousandth.
   a) 3^{π}
   b) π^{π}
   c) $10^{\sqrt{2}}$
   d) $(\sqrt{2})^{\sqrt{3}}$
   e) $4^{-\pi}$
   f) $7^{-\sqrt{2}}$
   g) $2^{\sqrt{\pi}}$
   h) $2^{\sqrt{2}} + 2^{-\sqrt{2}}$

21. a) Evaluate each power.
   i) 2^2
   ii) $(0.5)^2$
   iii) 2^{-2}
   iv) $(0.5)^{-2}$
   v) $4^{\frac{1}{2}}$
   vi) $(0.25)^{\frac{1}{2}}$
   vii) $4^{-\frac{1}{2}}$
   viii) $(0.25)^{-\frac{1}{2}}$
   b) Using the results of part a) as a guide, make a conjecture about how you can
      tell, given the values of x and y ($y > 0$), if:
      i) $y^x > 1$
      ii) $0 < y^x < 1$.

22. Write as a single power.
   a) $3(5)^{\frac{1}{3}} + 2(5)^{\frac{1}{3}}$
   b) $(2^x)^2 + 2^{2x}$
   c) $3(4)^x + 2^{2x}$

 PROBLEM SOLVING

Look for a Pattern

"One cannot escape the feeling that these mathematical formulas have an independent existence and an intelligence of their own, that they are wiser than we are, wiser even than their discoverers, that we get more out of them than was originally put into them."

Heinrich Hertz

Find a function $f(x)$ such that $f(x + 2) = 9f(x)$ for all values of x.

Understand the problem
- What does $f(x + 2)$ mean?
- What does $9f(x)$ mean?

Think of a strategy
- The left side involves addition, and the right side involves multiplication. What kinds of functions relate addition and multiplication?
- The numbers in the given equation are 2 and 9. What kind of natural number is 9? How might this be related to the 2?
- What kind of function might $f(x)$ be?

Carry out the strategy
- The function $f(x)$ might be an exponential function.
- Let $f(x) = a^x$, where x is a constant to be determined.
- If $f(x) = a^x$, then what does $f(x + 2)$ equal? What does $9f(x)$ equal?
- Since $f(x + 2) = 9f(x)$, can you find the value of a?
- What is the function $f(x)$?

Look back
- For the function $f(x)$ you found, check that $f(x + 2) = 9f(x)$.
- Is the function $f(x)$ unique?
- Write similar relations involving $f(x + 3), f(x + 4), ..., f(x + n)$.
- Find a function $f(x)$ such that $f(x + n) = kf(x)$ for all values of x.

PROBLEMS

Ⓑ

1. Triangle ABC is an equilateral triangle with sides 6 cm long. Calculate the area of the shaded square, to the nearest hundredth of a square centimetre.

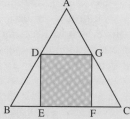

2. The natural number 64 is both a perfect square (since $64 = 8^2$) and a perfect cube (since $64 = 4^3$).
   a) Find other natural numbers which are both perfect squares and perfect cubes.
   b) Find a natural number which is a perfect square, a perfect cube, and a perfect fourth power.

3. Three cylindrical logs with radius 10 cm are piled as shown. Determine the distance from the top of the pile to the ground.

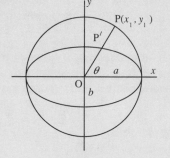

4. Find the equations of the lines which are parallel to the line $3x - 4y + 12 = 0$, and 2 units from it.

Ⓒ

5. If the sides of a triangle are in the ratio $3 : 4 : 5$, the triangle is right-angled. Find out something about a triangle whose sides are in the ratio $4 : 5 : 6$, and prove your result.

6. The double factorial symbol !! is defined as follows.
   $n!! = n(n - 2)(n - 4) \ldots 5 \times 3 \times 1$ if n is odd
   $\qquad n(n - 2)(n - 4) \ldots 6 \times 4 \times 2$ if n is even
   a) Simplify $n!!(n - 1)!!$ b) Prove that $(2n)!! = 2^n(n!)$
   c) Find a similar expression for $(2n - 1)!!$

7. The ellipse $b^2x^2 + a^2y^2 = a^2b^2$ is inscribed in the circle $x^2 + y^2 = a^2$. $P(x_1, y_1)$ is any point on the circle, forming an angle θ with the major axis. If P' is the corresponding point on the ellipse, determine the ratio $\dfrac{OP'}{OP}$ in terms of a, b, and θ.

Ⓓ

8. Prove that it is impossible to fill a rectangular box completely with cubes no two of which are congruent.

MATHEMATICS AROUND US

The Loudness of Sounds

The range of sounds detectable by the human ear is enormous. A rock group can be *10 trillion* times as loud as a leaf rustling in a breeze. The loudness of sounds is measured in units called *decibels* (dB).

> Every increase of 10 dB corresponds to a 10-fold increase in loudness.

For example, the increase from the hum of a refrigerator to an air conditioner is 20 dB. This is 2 increases of 10 dB, so the increase in loudness is $(10)^2$, or 100. Hence, an air conditioner is 100 times as loud as a refrigerator.

QUESTIONS

1. a) How many times as loud as conversational speech is a chain saw?
   b) How many times as loud as a quiet whisper is a chain saw?

2. Let L_1 and L_2 represent the loudnesses of sounds of S_1 decibels and S_2 decibels respectively. Show that
$$\frac{L_2}{L_1} = 10^{0.1(S_2 - S_1)}$$
   Use this equation in the questions below.

3. How many times as loud as:
   a) an air conditioner is a heavy truck
   b) a refrigerator hum is average street traffic
   c) average street traffic is a jet at 100 m?

4. It was once reported that the loudness level of a heavy snore is 69 dB. How many times is this as loud as:
   a) conversational speech
   b) a quiet whisper?

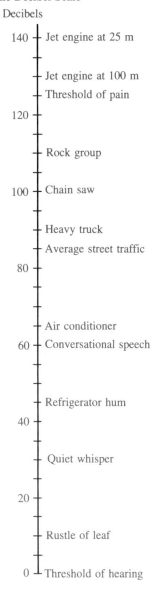

The Decibel Scale

Decibels

140 — Jet engine at 25 m

— Jet engine at 100 m
— Threshold of pain

120 —

— Rock group

100 — Chain saw

— Heavy truck
— Average street traffic

80 —

— Air conditioner
60 — Conversational speech

— Refrigerator hum
40 —

— Quiet whisper

20 —

— Rustle of leaf

0 — Threshold of hearing

Composers use these symbols to indicate the levels of loudness for playing their music.

pp   pianissimo (very soft)
p   piano (soft)
mp   mezzopiano (moderately soft)
mf   mezzoforte (moderately loud)
f   forte (loud)
ff   fortissimo (very loud)

But do performers actually play in such a way that the differences between six levels of loudness can be detected? It has been determined that, during a performance, the level of loudness must change by at least 5 dB before most people can detect it. Several musicians were asked to play their instruments at each of the six loudness levels indicated above. The difference in loudness between the softest notes and the loudest notes was measured. These are the results.

Bassoon 10 dB   Flute 20 dB   Trumpet 36 dB   Clarinet 45 dB

5. a) For which instruments could the six loudness levels have been detected?
   b) At how many levels of loudness could each instrument have been played?

6. The use of earplugs can reduce the noise level by as much as 25 dB. How many times less intense would a sound be if earplugs were worn?

7. In a noise reduction study, the noise caused by a train was compared at two locations A and B. It was found that the forest reduced high frequency sounds by as much as 20 dB, but low frequency sounds were reduced by 4 dB or less. By what factor did the forest reduce:
   a) high frequency sounds
   b) low frequency sounds?

8. A person's hearing can be permanently damaged by listening to very loud sounds for prolonged periods of time. An 8 h exposure to a 90 dB sound is considered acceptable. For every 5 dB increase in loudness, the acceptable exposure time is reduced by one-half.
   a) Derive an equation expressing the acceptable exposure time t hours as an exponential function of the loudness level d decibels.
   b) What is the acceptable exposure time for:
      i) a rock group playing at 100 dB?   ii) a jet engine at 130 dB? 140 dB?

7-3 GRAPHING EXPONENTIAL FUNCTIONS

Some of the properties of exponential functions that we have studied can be illustrated on a graph. For example, we can graph the function $f(x) = 2^x$ using a table of values.

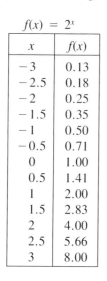

$f(x) = 2^x$

x	$f(x)$
-3	0.13
-2.5	0.18
-2	0.25
-1.5	0.35
-1	0.50
-0.5	0.71
0	1.00
0.5	1.41
1	2.00
1.5	2.83
2	4.00
2.5	5.66
3	8.00

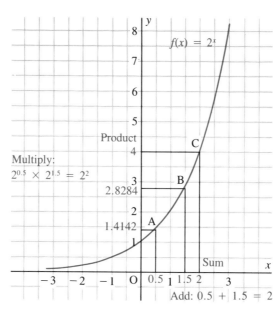

We can use the graph to illustrate the following properties of the function $f(x) = 2^x$.

Vertical intercept

$f(0) = 2^0$
     $= 1$

The vertical intercept is 1.

Horizontal intercept

Let $f(x) = 0$.
Then $2^x = 0$
This equation has no real solution since $2^x > 0$ for all real values of x. Hence, there is no horizontal intercept.

Domain

Since we can define 2^x for all real values of x, the domain is the set of all real numbers.

Range

Since there is a value of x for all positive real values of 2^x, the range is the set of all positive real numbers.

Law of Exponents

Select any two points on the curve, such as $A(0.5, 2^{0.5})$ and $B(1.5, 2^{1.5})$.

Add their x-coordinates.

$0.5 + 1.5 = 2$

Multiply their y-coordinates.

$(2^{0.5})(2^{1.5}) = 2^2$

The results are the coordinates of another point $C(2, 2^2)$ on the graph. Is this true for any two points on the graph?

We can graph other exponential functions using tables of values, but it is more efficient to sketch the graphs by considering how they are related to the graph of $f(x) = 2^x$, which we have already drawn.

Example 1. Sketch these functions on the same grid.

a) $f(x) = 2^x$ b) $g(x) = 1.5^x$ c) $h(x) = 1^x$ d) $k(x) = 0.5^x$

Solution. All four graphs pass through the point $(0,1)$.

a) The graph of $f(x) = 2^x$ is shown.

b) If $x > 0$, then $1.5^x < 2^x$. Hence, in the first quadrant, the graph of $g(x) = 1.5^x$ lies below that of $f(x) = 2^x$. To judge how far below, use a test point. Substitute $x = 2$ into 1.5^x to get 2.25. Hence, the point $(2, 2.25)$ lies on the graph.

Conversely, if $x < 0$, then $1.5^x > 2^x$. Hence, in the second quadrant, the graph of $g(x) = 1.5^x$ lies above that of $f(x) = 2^x$. To judge how far above, use a test point. Substitute $x = -2$ into 1.5^x to get approximately 0.44. Hence, $(-2, 0.44)$ lies on the graph.

c) Since $1^x = 1$ for all values of x, the graph of $h(x) = 1^x$ is a horizontal line 1 unit above the x-axis.

d) If $x > 0$, 0.5^x is less than 1. Also, as x increases, 0.5^x becomes closer and closer to 0. If $x < 0$, 0.5^x becomes larger and larger, without limit.

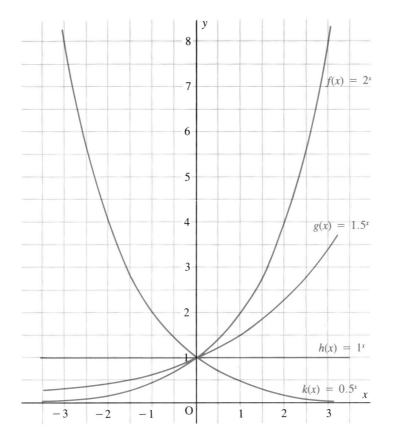

Example 1 illustrates properties of the graph of the exponential function $f(x) = a^x$.

**Properties of the graph of
the function $f(x) = a^x$**
Vertical intercept: 1
Horizontal intercept: none
Domain: all real numbers
Range: all positive real numbers

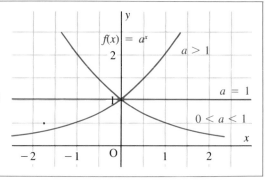

Example 2.   Prove that if (x_1, y_1) and (x_2, y_2) are points on the graph of $f(x) = a^x$,
then $(x_1 + x_2, y_1y_2)$ is also a point on the graph.

Solution.   Since (x_1, y_1) is on the graph of $f(x) = a^x$, its coordinates satisfy the
equation $y = a^x$.
Hence, $y_1 = a^{x_1}$ . . . ①
Similarly, $y_2 = a^{x_2}$ . . . ②
Multiply equations ① and ②, and use the law of exponents.
$$y_1y_2 = (a^{x_1})(a^{x_2})$$
$$= a^{x_1 + x_2}$$
Hence, the coordinates of the point $(x_1 + x_2, y_1y_2)$ also satisfy the equation
$y = a^x$. That is, $(x_1 + x_2, y_1y_2)$ is also a point on the graph of $f(x) = a^x$.

The result of *Example 2* is a
consequence of the law of exponents
for multiplication. Adding the
horizontal coordinates of points on
the graph of $f(x) = a^x$ corresponds
to multiplying their vertical
coordinates.

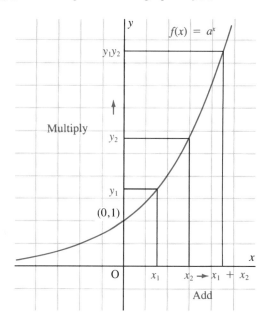

EXERCISES 7-3

1. Identify the graph which best represents each function.

   a) $f(x) = 3^x$ b) $g(x) = 10^x$ c) $h(x) = \left(\dfrac{3}{4}\right)^x$ d) $k(x) = \left(\dfrac{1}{4}\right)^x$

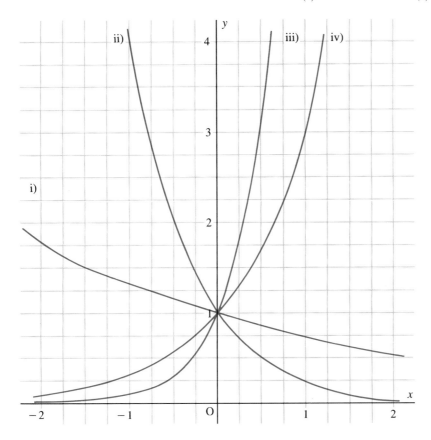

2. Describe how the graph of $f(x) = a^x$ varies as a varies.

3. a) Make tables of values and graph these functions on the same grid.

   $f_1(x) = 3^x$ for $-2 \leqslant x \leqslant 2$ $f_2(x) = \left(\dfrac{1}{3}\right)^x$ for $-2 \leqslant x \leqslant 2$

   b) On the same grid as in part a), sketch the graph of each function.

   $f_1(x) = 4^x$ $g_1(x) = 2^x$ $f_2(x) = \left(\dfrac{1}{2}\right)^x$ $g_2(x) = \left(\dfrac{1}{4}\right)^x$

4. Draw the graphs of these functions on the same grid.

   $f_1(x) = 2^x$ $g_1(x) = 5^x$ $h_1(x) = 10^x$

   $f_2(x) = \left(\dfrac{1}{2}\right)^x$ $g_2(x) = \left(\dfrac{1}{5}\right)^x$ $h_2(x) = \left(\dfrac{1}{10}\right)^x$

5. Find each value of a if the graph of $f(x) = a^x$ passes through each point.
   a) A(3, 216)   b) B(5, 32)   c) C(3, 512)   d) D(4, 256)
   e) E(-2, 64)   f) F$\left(-3, \dfrac{1}{216}\right)$ g) G(3, 343)   h) H$\left(\dfrac{1}{3}, 3\right)$

6. Prove that if $f(x) = a^x$, then $f(x)f(y) = f(x + y)$.

7. a) Prove that if (x_1, y_1) and (x_2, y_2) are two points on the graph of $f(x) = a^x$, then both $(x_1 + x_2, y_1y_2)$ and $\left(x_1 - x_2, \dfrac{y_1}{y_2}\right)$ are points on the graph.
   b) Prove that if (x_1, y_1) is a point on the graph of $f(x) = a^x$, then both $(2x_1, y_1{}^2)$ and $\left(-x_1, \dfrac{1}{y_1}\right)$ are points on the graph.

8. a) Graph the function $f(x) = 2^x$.
   b) On the same grid as in part a), sketch the graph of each function.
      i) $y = f(x) - 1$ ii) $y = f(x - 1)$ iii) $y = f(x + 1)$
      iv) $y = f(0.5x)$ v) $y = f(2x)$ vi) $y = f(-x)$

Ⓒ

9. If $a > 0$, for what values of a and x is each statement true?
   a) $a^x = 1$ b) $a^x > 1$ c) $0 < a^x < 1$

10. a) Graph the function $f(x) = 2^x$ for $-3 \le x \le 3$.
    b) By expressing 5 as a power of 2, show that the graph of $g(x) = 5^x$ is a horizontal compression of the graph of $f(x) = 2^x$.
    c) Similarly, show that the graph of $h(x) = 1.5^x$ is a horizontal expansion of the graph of $f(x) = 2^x$.
    d) Use the results of parts b) and c) to graph the functions $g(x) = 5^x$ and $h(x) = 1.5^x$ on the same grid as in part a).

11. Explain why the graphs of all exponential functions can be regarded as transformations of the graph of $f(x) = 2^x$.

12. Graph each function.
    a) $f(x) = 2^{|x|}$ b) $f(x) = x(2^x)$ c) $f(x) = x^x$

INVESTIGATE

The ⬚log⬚ key on a Calculator

Find out what the ⬚log⬚ key on your calculator does. Try a wide variety of numbers such as those below. Look for patterns in the results.

● Numbers selected at random, for example, 3, 65, 239, 4772
● Powers of 10; for example, 10, 100, 1000, 10 000, 1, 0.1, 0.01, 0.001
● Multiples of 10; for example, 20, 200, 2000, 30, 300, 3000
● Zero and negative numbers; for example, 0, -2, -3, -10

Write a report of your findings.

THE MATHEMATICAL MIND

Doubling the Cube

It is said that around 427 B.C. in ancient Greece, a plague was responsible for the death of more than a quarter of the Athenian population. A special delegation was sent to the oracle of Apollo at Delos to inquire how the plague should be averted. The oracle instructed that they must double the size of Apollo's cubical altar. The Athenians thought that they could do this by doubling each dimension of the altar, but in doing so, they were not able to curb the plague. Since each dimension was doubled, they had in fact multiplied the volume of the altar by $2 \times 2 \times 2$, or 8.

According to the legend, this faulty mathematics on the part of the Athenians led the Greek geometers to study the problem of doubling the volume of a given cube while keeping its cubic shape. The first progress in the solution of this problem was given by Hippocrates. He reduced the problem to that of constructing lengths x and y such that $\frac{r}{x} = \frac{x}{y} = \frac{y}{2r}$, where r is the given length of an edge of the cubical altar. From these equations he deduced that $x^3 = 2r^3$. Hence, x is the edge length of a cube having twice the volume of the cube with edge length r.

For 2000 years mathematicians tried to construct a segment of length x using straightedge and compasses, but none succeeded. This construction was proved to be impossible by the mathematicians of the nineteenth century.

QUESTIONS

1. a) Show that $x^3 = 2r^3$ can be deduced from the equations
   $$\frac{r}{x} = \frac{x}{y} = \frac{y}{2r}.$$
   b) Solve the equation for x.
   c) Find a similar equation for y, and solve it.

2. In his attempt to solve the problem of doubling the cube, Plato used this diagram. Show that if the figure were constructed such that DE $= r$ and CE $= 2r$, then BE would be the segment whose length is the edge length of the cubical altar to be constructed.

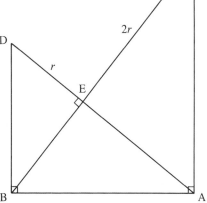

MATHEMATICS AROUND US

Carbon Dating

In 1950 the Nobel Prize in chemistry went to Dr. W.F. Libby who had developed a method of dating organic matter, known as *carbon dating*. All living matter contains traces of radioactive carbon-14. When an organism dies, the carbon-14 decays with a halflife of about 5760 years. Hence, the age of an ancient specimen can be determined by measuring the radioactivity of the carbon-14 it contains, and comparing it with that of living matter. The table shows the percent remaining at various times after an organism dies.

Time		Percent
Halflives n	**Years** t	**remaining** P
0	0	100
1	5 760	50
2	11 520	25
3	17 280	12.5
4	23 040	6.25
5	28 800	3.125

The percent P remaining after n halflives have elapsed is expressed as a function of n by the equation $P = 100(0.5)^n$. Since $t = 5760n$, we can write this equation in terms of t.

$$P = 100(0.5)^{\frac{t}{5760}}$$

We can use this equation to approximate the age of a specimen if we know the radioactivity of its carbon-14 relative to living matter.

QUESTIONS

1. The Dead Sea Scrolls are about 2000 years old. What percent radioactivity should be expected from a sample taken from the Dead Sea Scrolls?

2. Charred remains found in Lascaux Cave in France are about 15.3% radioactive. About how old might the famous paintings in this cave be?

3. Determine the approximate age of each specimen, given its radioactivity relative to living matter.
   a) charred bread found at Pompeii   79.6%
   b) wood in First Dynasty tombs   68.9%
   c) charcoal found at Stonehenge   62.0%
   d) specimen from the end of the last ice age 24.0%
   e) skin of a Siberian mammoth   2.2%

4. Illustrate the above results on a graph.

7-4 COMMON LOGARITHMS

In *Exercises 7-1* we encountered problems such as these.

In how many years will an investment of $500 double in value at 8% per annum compounded annually?

The answer to this question is the solution of this equation.

$$1000 = 500(1.08)^n$$
or $(1.08)^n = 2$

At what depth under water is the light level 50% of the light level at the surface?

The answer to this question is the solution of this equation.

$$50 = 100(0.975)^d$$
or $(0.975)^d = 0.5$

In these equations the variable appears in an exponent. Such equations are called *exponential equations*, and they can be solved to any degree of accuracy by systematic trial. However, exponential equations occur so frequently in applications that mathematicians have developed a more direct method of solution. This method involves logarithms. After defining a logarithm and introducing some of its properties, we will show how the above equations can be solved using logarithms.

In the preceding investigation you may have discovered that the $\boxed{\text{log}}$ key of a calculator gives exponents for powers of 10.

Using a calculator: log 100 = 2
2 is the exponent that 100 has when it is expressed as a power of 10.
Since $100 = 10^2$
we write log 100 = 2

Using a calculator: log 0.001 = -3
-3 is the exponent that 0.001 has when it is expressed as a power of 10.
Since $0.001 = 10^{-3}$
we write log 0.001 = -3

These logarithms are called *common logarithms* since they are the exponents of numbers written as powers with base 10. In a later section we will study logarithms with bases other than 10.

Definition of a Logarithm
- log x is the exponent that x would have if it were written as a power with base 10.
- log $x = y$ means that $x = 10^y$.

Since $10^y > 0$ for all real values of y, then $x > 0$. Hence, log x is defined as a real number only when $x > 0$.

Example 1. Use the definition of a logarithm to evaluate each expression.
  a) log 100 000   b) log 0.01   c) log $\sqrt{10}$ d) log 1

Solution. a) Since $100\,000 = 10^5$, then log 100 000 = 5
  b) Since $0.01 = 10^{-2}$, then log 0.01 = -2
  c) Since $\sqrt{10} = 10^{0.5}$, then log $\sqrt{10}$ = 0.5
  d) Since $1 = 10^0$, then log 1 = 0

The answers in *Example 1* can be checked with a calculator.

We can use the $\boxed{\log}$ key of a calculator to find approximations to the logarithm of any positive number. Hence, we can write any positive number as a power of 10.

Example 2.   Use your calculator to evaluate each logarithm. Then write the result in exponential form.

a) log 7   b) log 500   c) log 0.4

Solution.   a) $\log 7 \doteq 0.845\ 098$
                    This means that $10^{0.845098} \doteq 7$
                 b) $\log 500 \doteq 2.698\ 97$
                    This means that $10^{2.69897} \doteq 500$
                 c) $\log 0.4 \doteq -0.397\ 94$
                    This means that $10^{-0.39794} \doteq 0.4$

The results in *Example 2* can be checked using the $\boxed{10^x}$ or $\boxed{y^x}$ keys.

Since $\log x$ is defined as a real number only when $x > 0$, you will get an error message if you attempt to find the logarithm of 0, or of a negative number.

$\log 0 = y$ means $10^y = 0$, which is impossible.

$\log (-2) = y$ means $10^y = -2$, which is impossible.

Example 3.   Simplify each expression.

a) $\log 10^x$ b) $10^{\log x}$

Solution.   a) $\log 10^x$ is the exponent that 10^x would have if it were written as a power of 10. But, 10^x *is* written as a power of 10, and has exponent x. Hence, $\log 10^x = x$
                 b) $10^{\log x}$ is 10 raised to the exponent that x would have if x were written as a power of 10. Hence, $10^{\log x} = x$

Example 3 shows that taking a common logarithm of a number and raising the number to a power of 10 are inverse operations, just as squaring a number and taking the square root of the number are inverse operations. If your calculator has a $\boxed{10^x}$ key, you can illustrate this by using the $\boxed{10^x}$ and $\boxed{\log}$ keys in succession in either order. For example, $\log\left(10^{4.5}\right) = 4.5$ and $10^{\log 4.5} = 4.5$

Summary
- A logarithm is an exponent.
- $\log x = y$ means that $x = 10^y, x > 0$.
- $\log x$ is defined only when $x > 0$.
- $\log 10^x = x$ and $10^{\log x} = x$

EXERCISES 7-4

(A)

1. Use the definition to evaluate each logarithm.
   a) log 100
   b) log 1000
   c) log 1 000 000
   d) log 10
   e) log 0.1
   f) log 0.001
   g) log 1
   h) log $\sqrt[3]{10}$
   i) log 10^5
   j) log $10^{\frac{1}{5}}$
   k) log $10^{\frac{2}{3}}$
   l) log 10^n

2. Use your calculator to evaluate each logarithm to 4 decimal places. Then write each result in exponential form, and check it with the calculator.
   a) log 5
   b) log 18
   c) log 62.4
   d) log 4877
   e) log 0.25
   f) log 0.8
   g) log 0.02
   h) log 0.006

3. In 1987, the Canadian astronomer Ian Shelton discovered a supernova, or exploding star, from an observatory in Chile. State the common logarithm of each number.
   a) The supernova was more than 100 000 light years, or 10^{20} m, from the Earth.
   b) At its brightest, a supernova is about 10^9 times as bright as a star like the sun.
   c) Throughout recorded history only about 10 supernovas have been visible to the unaided eye.

4. On a single optical disk, an amount of data equivalent to all the text appearing in 15 years of daily newspapers can be recorded. State the common logarithm of each number.
   a) More than 10^{12} bytes of data are recorded on each disk.
   b) To avoid errors, a laser beam is focused within 10^{-7} m of dead centre for each pit on the surface of the disk.
   c) The error rate for a typical disk is 10^{-12}.

(B)

5. Write in exponential form.
   a) log 10 000 = 4
   b) log 10 = 1
   c) log 0.01 = −2

6. Write in logarithmic form.
   a) $10^3 = 1000$
   b) $10^0 = 1$
   c) $10^{-3} = 0.001$

7. One centillion is defined as the 100th power of 1 000 000. What is the common logarithm of one centillion?

8. Solve each equation.
   a) log x = 2
   b) log x = 5
   c) log x = −3
   d) log x = 0
   e) log x = 1
   f) log log x = 1

9. Simplify each expression.
   a) log 10^4
   b) log 10^5
   c) log 10^{-3}
   d) $10^{\log 100}$
   e) $10^{\log 20}$
   f) $10^{\log 0.2}$

10. a) Use your calculator to evaluate each logarithm.
    i) log 2
    ii) log 20
    iii) log 200
    iv) log 2000
    v) log 0.2
    vi) log 0.02
    vii) log 0.002
    viii) log 0.0002
    b) Account for the pattern in the results.

7-5 THE LAWS OF LOGARITHMS (BASE 10)

A logarithm is an exponent. Hence, it should be possible to write the laws of exponents in logarithmic form.

Consider an example of the law of exponents for multiplication, such as $10^2 \times 10^3 = 10^5$. Since $\log 10^2 = 2$, $\log 10^3 = 3$, and $\log 10^5 = 5$, we can write this equation as:
$\log 10^2 + \log 10^3 = \log 10^5$
or $\qquad \log 10^5 = \log 10^2 + \log 10^3$

This example suggests that a possible law of logarithms for multiplication might be $\log xy = \log x + \log y$. This equation states that the exponent that xy would have if it were expressed as a power of 10 is equal to the sum of the exponents that x and y would have if they were expressed as powers of 10.

Theorem   **Law of Logarithms for Multiplication (Base 10)**

If x and y are any positive real numbers, then $\log xy = \log x + \log y$

Given: Two real numbers x and y
Required to Prove: $\log xy = \log x + \log y$
Proof: Let $\log x = M$ and $\log y = N$
$$x = 10^M \qquad y = 10^N$$
Hence, $xy = (10^M)(10^N)$
$$= 10^{M+N}$$
Therefore, $\log xy = \log (10^{M+N})$
$$= M + N$$
$$= \log x + \log y$$

Corollary   **Law of Logarithms for Division (Base 10)**

If x and y are any positive real numbers, then $\log \left(\dfrac{x}{y} \right) = \log x - \log y$

Example 1.   Write $\log 6$ as:
        a) a sum of two logarithms   b) a difference of two logarithms.

Solution.   a) Since $6 = 2 \times 3$, then by the law of logarithms for multiplication,
           $\log 6 = \log 2 + \log 3$
        b) Since $6 = 12 \div 2$, then by the law of logarithms for division,
           $\log 6 = \log 12 - \log 2$

In *Example 1*, $\log 6$ can be expressed as a sum or a difference of logarithms in infinitely many other ways, such as:
$\log 6 = \log 1.5 + \log 4 \qquad \log 6 = \log 18 - \log 3$
$\log 6 = \log 10 + \log 0.6 \qquad \log 6 = \log 60 - \log 10$
Check these results with your calculator.

Example 2. Write each expression as a single logarithm.

    a) $\log 5 + \log 4$ b) $\log 21 - \log 3$

Solution.   a) $\log 5 + \log 4 = \log (5 \times 4)$ b) $\log 21 - \log 3 = \log \left(\frac{21}{3}\right)$

$$= \log 20 \qquad\qquad\qquad\qquad\qquad = \log 7$$

Example 3. Given that $\log 5 \doteq 0.698\ 97$, find an approximation for each logarithm.

    a) $\log 50$ b) $\log 500$ c) $\log 0.5$ d) $\log 0.05$

Solution.   a) $\log 50 = \log 10 + \log 5$ b) $\log 500 = \log 100 + \log 5$

$$\doteq 1 + 0.698\ 97 \qquad\qquad\qquad \doteq 2 + 0.698\ 97$$
$$\doteq 1.698\ 97 \qquad\qquad\qquad\quad\ \doteq 2.698\ 97$$

     c) $\log 0.5 = \log 5 - \log 10$ d) $\log 0.05 = \log 5 - \log 100$

$$\doteq 0.698\ 97 - 1 \qquad\qquad\qquad \doteq 0.698\ 97 - 2$$
$$\doteq -0.301\ 03 \qquad\qquad\qquad\quad\ \doteq -1.301\ 03$$

Check the results of *Examples 2* and *3* with your calculator.

The law of logarithms for products may be applied when the factors are equal. For example, if $x = y$, then the law:

$$\log xy = \log x + \log y \quad \text{may be written}$$
$$\log (x)(x) = \log x + \log x$$

or $\qquad \log (x^2) = 2 \log x$

This example suggests that a possible law of logarithms for powers might be $\log (x^n) = n \log x$. This equation states that the exponent that x^n would have if it were expressed as a power of 10 is n times the exponent that x would have if it were expressed as a power of 10.

Theorem   **Law of Logarithms for Powers (Base 10)**

If x and n are real numbers, and $x > 0$, then $\log (x^n) = n \log x$

Given: Two real numbers x and n, where $x > 0$
Required to Prove: $\log (x^n) = n \log x$
Proof: Let $\log x = M$

$$x = 10^M$$

Hence, $x^n = (10^M)^n$

$$= 10^{nM}$$

Therefore, $\log (x^n) = \log (10^{nM})$

$$= nM$$
$$= n \log x$$

Corollary   **Law of Logarithms for Roots (Base 10)**

If x and n are real numbers, and $x > 0$, then $\log \sqrt[n]{x} = \frac{1}{n} \log x$

Example 4.   a) Write log 125 as a product of a whole number and a logarithm.
b) Write 4 log 3 as a single logarithm.

Solution.   a) Since $125 = 5^3$, then $\log 125 = \log (5^3)$
$$= 3 \log 5$$
b) $4 \log 3 = \log (3^4)$, or log 81

Example 5.   Given that $\log 2 \doteq 0.301\ 03$, find an approximation for each logarithm.

a) log 8   b) $\log \sqrt[3]{2}$

Solution.   a) $\log 8 = \log (2^3)$ b) $\log \sqrt[3]{2} = \log (2^{\frac{1}{3}})$
$$= 3 \log 2$$
$$\doteq 3(0.301\ 03)$$
$$\doteq 0.903\ 09$$

$$= \frac{1}{3} \log 2$$

$$\doteq \frac{1}{3}(0.301\ 03)$$

$$\doteq 0.100\ 34$$

Check the results of *Examples 4* and *5* with your calculator.

Laws of Logarithms (Base 10)

- Multiplication $\log xy = \log x + \log y$ $x, y > 0$
- Division $\log \left(\frac{x}{y}\right) = \log x - \log y$ $x, y > 0$
- Powers $\log (x^n) = n \log x$ $x > 0$
- Roots $\log \sqrt[n]{x} = \frac{1}{n} \log x$ $x > 0$

These laws are the laws of exponents (with base 10) restated in logarithmic form.

Example 6.   Write in terms of log a and log b.

a) $\log (100ab^2)$ b) $\log \left(\frac{a^2}{\sqrt{b}}\right)$

Solution.   a) $\log (100ab^2) = \log 100 + \log a + \log (b^2)$
$$= 2 + \log a + 2 \log b$$
b) $\log \left(\frac{a^2}{\sqrt{b}}\right) = \log (a^2) - \log (\sqrt{b})$

$$= 2 \log a - \frac{1}{2} \log b$$

Example 7.   Write as a single logarithm.

a) $\log a + \log b - \log c$ b) $\log a + 3 \log b - \frac{1}{2} \log c$

Solution.   a) $\log a + \log b - \log c = \log ab - \log c$
$$= \log \left(\frac{ab}{c}\right)$$
b) $\log a + 3 \log b - \frac{1}{2} \log c = \log a + \log (b^3) - \log \sqrt{c}$

$$= \log \left(\frac{ab^3}{\sqrt{c}}\right)$$

An important application of the laws of logarithms is to the problem of expressing any positive number as a power of any other positive number (except 1).

Example 8. Express 19 as a power of 2 and check with a calculator.

Solution.   Let $19 = 2^x$

Take the logarithm of each side.

$$\log 19 = \log (2^x)$$
$$\log 19 = x \log 2$$

Hence, $x = \dfrac{\log 19}{\log 2}$

$\doteq 4.247\ 927\ 5$

Therefore, $19 \doteq 2^{4.2479275}$

To check, use the $\boxed{y^x}$ key on your calculator.

EXERCISES 7-5

Ⓐ

1. Write as a single logarithm, and check with your calculator.
   a) log 6 + log 7   b) log 24 − log 6   c) log 3 + log 8
   d) log 35 − log 5   e) log 12 + log 7   f) log 1 − log 2
   g) log 5 + log 8 − log 4   h) log 6 + log 3 + log 5
   i) log 12 − log 4 + log 7   j) log 7 + log 8 − log 2

2. Write as a sum of logarithms, and check with your calculator.
   a) log 10   b) log 21   c) log 28   d) log 36
   e) log 9   f) log 44   g) log 57   h) log 121

3. Write as a difference of logarithms, and check with your calculator.
   a) log 5   b) log 8   c) log 12   d) log 13
   e) log 10   f) log 21   g) log 17   h) log 40

4. Write as a product of a whole number and a logarithm, and check with your calculator.
   a) log 9   b) log 25   c) log 8   d) log 27
   e) log 1000   f) log 32   g) log 343   h) log 128

5. Write as a single logarithm, and check with your calculator.
   a) 2 log 6   b) 3 log 4   c) 2 log 9   d) 2 log 7
   e) 5 log 3   f) 4 log 2   g) 3 log 6   h) 5 log 10

Ⓑ

6. Given log 3 $\doteq$ 0.477 12, find an approximation for each logarithm.
   a) log 30   b) log 3000   c) log 0.3   d) log 0.003
   e) log 9   f) log 81   g) log $\sqrt{3}$ h) log $\sqrt[5]{3}$

7. Given that log 5 $\doteq$ 0.698 97, find an approximation for each logarithm.
   a) log 625   b) log $\sqrt[3]{5}$ c) log 0.2   d) log 0.04

8. If log 70 $\doteq$ 1.8451, find an approximation for each logarithm.
   a) log 7
   b) log 700
   c) log 0.07
   d) log 0.7
   e) log 700 000
   f) log 0.007

9. Write in terms of log a and log b.
   a) log $(1000ab)$
   b) log (a^2b)
   c) log $(a\sqrt{b})$
   d) log $\left(\dfrac{a}{b^2}\right)$
   e) log $\left(\dfrac{\sqrt{a}}{b}\right)$
   f) log $\left(\dfrac{\sqrt[3]{a}}{b^2}\right)$

10. Write each expression in terms of log x.
    a) log $(10x^2)$
    b) log $\sqrt{x}$
    c) log $\sqrt{10x}$
    d) log $\sqrt{10x}$
    e) log $10\sqrt{x}$

11. Write as a single logarithm.
    a) log x + log y − log z
    b) log m − (log n + log p)
    c) log a + log b − log c − log d
    d) log a + log $(a + b)$ − log $(a − b)$

12. Write as a single logarithm.
    a) 2 log a + 5 log b
    b) 3 log x + $\frac{1}{2}$ log y
    c) 2 log m + log n − 5 log p
    d) $\frac{1}{2}$ log x − 2 log y − log z
    e) 3 log a + $\frac{1}{2}$ log b − $\frac{5}{4}$ log c
    f) 10 log a − 3 log b + $\frac{1}{2}$ log c − log d

13. Write as a single logarithm. For what values of the variable is each expression not defined?
    a) log $(x + 3)$ − log $(x − 1)$
    b) log $(2x − 7)$ − log $(x + 3)$
    c) −log $(a − 2)$ + log $(a + 2)$
    d) log $(8a + 15)$ − log $(2a + 3)$

14. If log 2 = x and log 3 = y, write each logarithm as an expression in x and y.
    a) log 6
    b) log 1.5
    c) log 60
    d) log 12
    e) log 18
    f) log 36
    g) log 3.6
    h) log $\left(\dfrac{1}{6}\right)$

15. Express.
    a) 7 as a power of 3
    b) 5 as a power of 2
    c) 29 as a power of 2
    d) 77 as a power of 8
    e) 3 as a power of 0.5
    f) 0.45 as a power of 6

16. Solve to the nearest thousandth.
    a) $2^x = 11$
    b) $3^x = 17$
    c) $6^x = 5$
    d) $5^{x-1} = 9$
    e) $2^{x+3} = 6$
    f) $5^{1+x} = 2^{1-x}$

17. Solve.
    a) $3^x = 2$
    b) $4^x = 5$
    c) $7^{-x} = 3$
    d) $3^{1-x} = 5$
    e) $\left(\dfrac{1}{8}\right)^x = 25$
    f) $5^{3x} = 41$

18. x and y are two positive numbers. How are $\log x$ and $\log y$ related if:
    a) $y = 10x$ b) $y = \dfrac{1}{x}$ c) $y = x^2$
    d) $y = \sqrt{x}$ e) $y = 10\sqrt{x}$ f) $y = \sqrt{10x}$?

Ⓒ

19. Prove each identity, and state the value(s) of x for which the identity is true.
    a) $\log (x - 1) + \log (x - 2) = \log (x^2 - 3x + 2)$
    b) $\log x + \log (x + 3) = \log (x^2 + 3x)$
    c) $\log (x - 5) + \log (x + 5) = \log (x^2 - 25)$

20. Solve and check.
    a) $\log (x + 2) + \log (x - 1) = 1$
    b) $\log (3x + 2) + \log (x - 1) = 2$
    c) $2 \log (x - 1) = 2 + \log 100$

21. Express y as a function of x. What is the domain?
    a) $\log 3 + \log y = \log (x + 2) - \log x$
    b) $\log y - 2 + \log x - \log (x + 1) = 0$
    c) $\log 4y = x + \log 4$

22. The table shows some large prime numbers that were discovered using computers. How many digits does each prime number have?

	Prime Number	Year	Computer
a)	$2^{11213} - 1$	1963	ILLIAC-II
b)	$2^{21701} - 1$	1978	CDC-CYBER-174
c)	$2^{132049} - 1$	1983	CRAY-1
d)	$2^{216091} - 1$	1985	CRAY-1

23. In 1938, the physicist Sir Arthur Eddington calculated that the number of particles in the universe is 33×2^{259}. He called this number the *cosmical number*.
    a) Write the cosmical number in scientific notation.
    b) How many digits are there in this number?

24. If n is a natural number, find the least value of n such that:
    a) $1.1^n > 10^9$ b) $1.01^n > 10^9$ c) $1.001^n > 10^9$
    d) 1.001^n exceeds the capacity of your calculator's display.

25. Let N be any positive number, no matter how large. Prove that no matter how small the positive number x is, it is always possible to find a value of n such that $(1 + x)^n > N$.

MATHEMATICS AROUND US

Orders of Magnitude

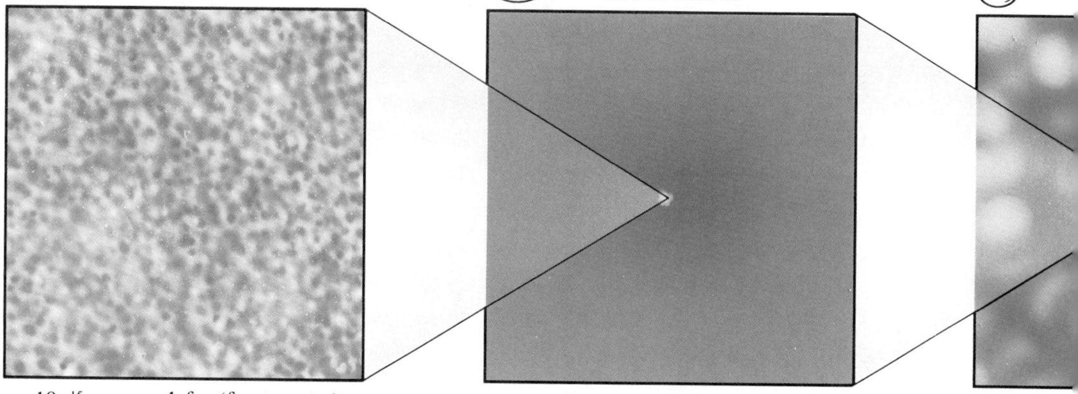

(−15) Proton in carbon nucleus

10^{-15} m   1 fm (femtometre)

(−12) Carbon nucleus

10^{-12} m   1 pm (picometre)

(−9)

10^{-9} m

Scientists have always wanted to extend our range of observation of the world around us, from the microscopic scale to the astronomic scale. What might we see if we could take an imaginary journey along a straight line beginning at the nucleus of an atom and ending at the farthermost reaches of outer space?

The first illustration shows part of the nucleus of a carbon atom. As we get farther and farther away, greater and greater distances are brought into view. The steps we take in this journey are not regular steps, but rather, each step is 1000 times as great as the previous one.

Hence, the dimensions of each illustration represent a distance 1000 times as long as the one before it. And, each illustration shows a 1000× enlargement of a small portion at the centre of the next one. Although it can be seen in only the first illustration, the nucleus of the carbon atom where we started the journey is at the centre of all of them.

The journey covers four pages in this book. Study the illustrations on all four pages before you begin the questions.

QUESTIONS

1. Notice the circled number in the upper left corner of each illustration.
   a) How is this number related to the distance represented by the illustration?
   b) As you move from one illustration to the next, compare the change in the circled number with the change in the distance represented by the illustration.

2. A factor of 10 is called one *order of magnitude*. Hence, a factor of 100, or 10 × 10, represents two orders of magnitude. How many orders of magnitude are represented by the change from:
   a) any illustration to the next
   b) the first illustration to the last?

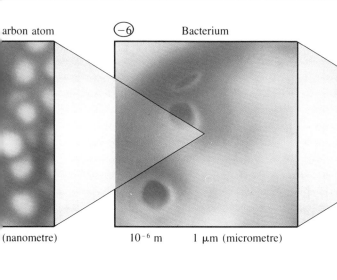

arbon atom $\widehat{-6}$ Bacterium $\widehat{-3}$ Skin pore

(nanometre) 10^{-6} m   1 μm (micrometre) 10^{-3} 1 mm

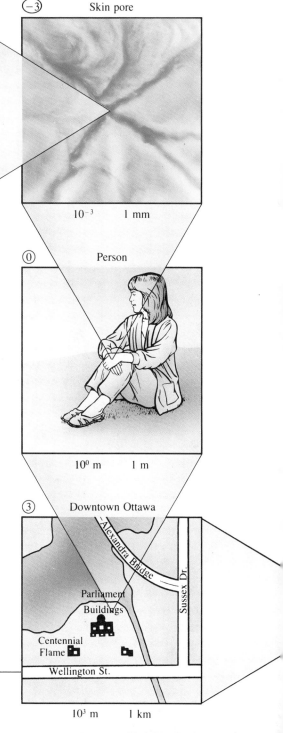

$\widehat{0}$ Person

10^{0} m   1 m

$\widehat{3}$ Downtown Ottawa

Alexandra Bridge

Sussex Dr.

Parliament Buildings

Centennial Flame

Wellington St.

10^{3} m   1 km

3. Two common units of length are the Ångstrom unit (used for measuring atoms) and the fermi (used for measuring nuclear particles).

1 Ångstrom unit	10^{-10} m
1 fermi	10^{-15} m

a) How many orders of magnitude is the Ångstrom unit greater than the fermi?

b) Name two other units of length that differ by the same order of magnitude.

4. The double-helix strands of a DNA molecule are approximately 2×10^{-9} m apart. If the twisted molecule were stretched out, its length would be 7 orders of magnitude greater. How long is the molecule?

5. What common interval of time is approximately 4 orders of magnitude longer than one minute?

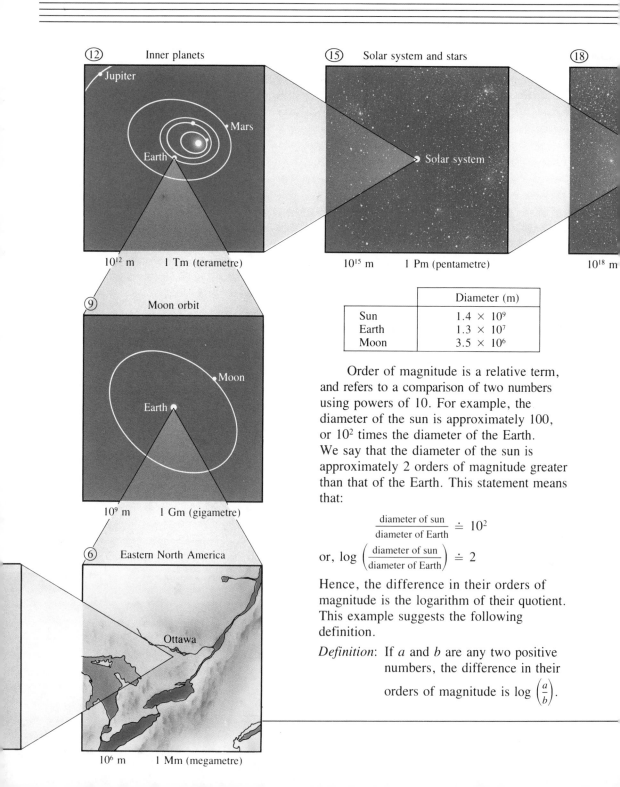

⑫ Inner planets

Jupiter

Mars

Earth

10^{12} m   1 Tm (terametre)

⑮ Solar system and stars

Solar system

10^{15} m   1 Pm (pentametre)

⑱

10^{18} m

⑨ Moon orbit

Moon

Earth

10^{9} m   1 Gm (gigametre)

⑥ Eastern North America

Ottawa

10^{6} m   1 Mm (megametre)

	Diameter (m)
Sun	1.4×10^{9}
Earth	1.3×10^{7}
Moon	3.5×10^{6}

Order of magnitude is a relative term, and refers to a comparison of two numbers using powers of 10. For example, the diameter of the sun is approximately 100, or 10^2 times the diameter of the Earth. We say that the diameter of the sun is approximately 2 orders of magnitude greater than that of the Earth. This statement means that:

$$\frac{\text{diameter of sun}}{\text{diameter of Earth}} \doteq 10^2$$

or, $\log \left(\dfrac{\text{diameter of sun}}{\text{diameter of Earth}} \right) \doteq 2$

Hence, the difference in their orders of magnitude is the logarithm of their quotient. This example suggests the following definition.

Definition: If a and b are any two positive numbers, the difference in their orders of magnitude is $\log \left(\dfrac{a}{b} \right)$.

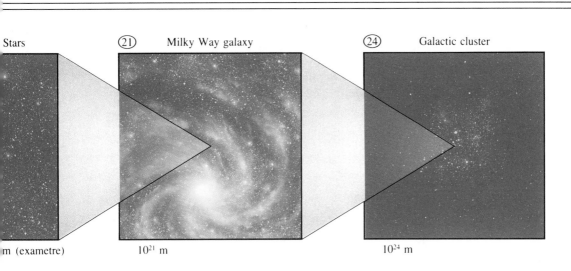

Stars   ㉑   Milky Way galaxy   ㉔   Galactic cluster

m (exametre) 10^{21} m 10^{24} m

6. Show that the diameter of the sun is approximately 2.6 orders of magnitude greater than that of the moon.

7. Two common units of length are the astronomical unit (used for measuring planetary distances) and the light year (used for measuring stellar and galactic distances).

| 1 astronomical unit | 1.5×10^{11} m |
| 1 light year | 9.5×10^{15} m |

How many orders of magnitude is the light year greater than the astronomical unit?

8. The planets Neptune and Pluto are approximately 5×10^{12} m from the Earth. How many orders of magnitude greater than this are these distances?
   a) The nearest star, Proxima Centauri, 4×10^{18} m from Earth
   b) The centre of the Milky Way Galaxy, 6.7×10^{20} m from Earth
   c) A chain of galaxies 7×10^{24} m from Earth

9. In 1989, the space probe *Voyager II* will photograph the planet Neptune, about 5×10^{12} m from the Earth. The *Space Telescope* will be able to examine objects 13.4 orders of magnitude farther than this. What is the limit of observation of the Space Telescope?

10. The limit of the known universe is about 2.3 orders of magnitude greater than the distance represented by the last illustration above. How many metres is this?

11. Now that we have finished our journey from the nucleus of the carbon atom to outer space, suppose we reverse our direction and take the return trip back to the nucleus of the carbon atom where we started. What percent of the remaining distance would we cover from one illustration to the next?

7-6 INTRODUCTION TO LOGARITHMIC FUNCTIONS

Many examples of exponential functions were given in the previous sections of this chapter. Associated with each of these functions there is a corresponding function whose equation we can obtain by solving for the variable in the exponent.

Growth of Populations

In 1987 the world population reached 5 billion. At the time, the population was increasing at the rate of approximately 1.6% per year. If the rate of growth remains constant, then the population P billion is expressed as an exponential function of the number of years n relative to 1987 by this equation.

$$P = 5(1.016)^n \ldots \text{①}$$

Suppose we ask in how many years will the population reach P billion? We express the number of years n as a function of P by solving equation ① for n. Hence, we take the logarithm of each side.

$$\log P = \log 5 + n \log 1.016$$

Solve for n.

$$n \log 1.016 = \log P - \log 5$$

$$n = \frac{\log \left(\dfrac{P}{5}\right)}{\log 1.016}$$

The coefficient of the expression on the right side is $\dfrac{1}{\log 1.016}$, or about 145.

Hence, the equation for n becomes

$$n \doteq 145 \log \left(\frac{P}{5}\right) \ldots \text{②}$$

Equation ② expresses the number of years n as a logarithmic function of the population P. The graph shows the values of n for $3 \leqslant P \leqslant 10$.
Compare this graph with the one on page 300.

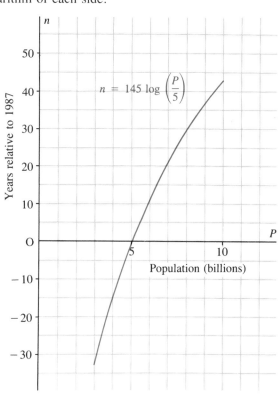

$$n = 145 \log \left(\frac{P}{5}\right)$$

Years relative to 1987

Population (billions)

In this example, notice that n is not defined if P is 0, or if P is negative. This is reasonable, since the population P must be a positive number. Hence, the domain of the function is the set of positive integers.

Light Penetration Under Water

For every metre a diver descends below the surface, the light intensity
is reduced by 2.5%. The percent P of surface light present is expressed
as an exponential function of the depth d metres by this equation.
$$P = 100(0.975)^d \ldots \text{①}$$
Suppose we ask at what depth is the light intensity $P\%$? We express d
as a function of P by solving equation ① for d. Take the logarithm
of each side.

$\log P = \log 100 + d \log 0.975$

Solve for d.

$$d = \frac{\log\left(\frac{P}{100}\right)}{\log 0.975}$$

$$d \doteq -90.9 \log\left(\frac{P}{100}\right) \ldots \text{②}$$

Equation ② expresses the depth d metres
as a logarithmic function of the light intensity
P. The graph shows the values of d for
$0 < P \leqslant 100$. Compare this graph with the
one on page 301.

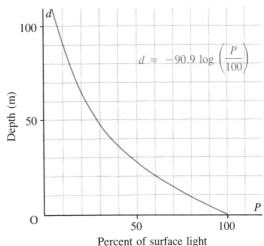

In the final equations of the above examples, the expression on the
right side involves the logarithm of the variable. Functions whose
defining equation have this property are called logarithmic functions.

> A *logarithmic function* has an equation which can be written in the
> form $f(x) = k \log x$, where k is a constant, and $x > 0$.

Example. Given the exponential function $f(x) = 10^x$

    a) Determine the inverse function $f^{-1}(x)$.

    b) Graph $f(x)$ and $f^{-1}(x)$ on the same grid.

Solution. a) Recall that to obtain the inverse of a function from its equation, we
interchange x and y in the equation and solve for y. Hence, to find the
inverse of $f(x) = 10^x$:

Step 1. Let $y = 10^x$, then interchange x and y. $x = 10^y$

Step 2. Solve for y. $y = \log x$

Hence, the inverse of the exponential function $f(x) = 10^x$ is the
logarithmic function $f^{-1}(x) = \log x$.

b) We graph $f(x) = 10^x$ using a table of values. Recall that we can graph the inverse by reflecting the graph of $y = 10^x$ in the line $y = x$. This is equivalent to interchanging the ordered pairs in the table of values for $y = f(x)$.

$f(x) = 10^x$

x	y
-2	0.01
-1.5	0.03
-1	0.10
-0.5	0.32
-0.2	0.63
0	1.00
0.1	1.26
0.2	1.58
0.3	2.00

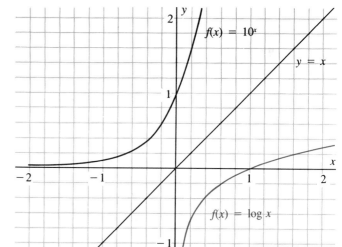

Recall that in *Section 7-4* we observed that taking a common logarithm of a number and raising the number to a power of 10 are inverse operations. This is consistent with the above *Example*, which shows that the logarithmic function $y = \log x$ can be defined as the inverse of the exponential function $y = 10^x$.

EXERCISES 7-6

(A)

1. Solve each equation for x, thus expressing x as a logarithmic function of y.
   a) $y = 5(2)^x$
   b) $y = 1.3(10)^x$
   c) $y = 8.2(1.03)^x$
   d) $y = 6.4\left(\frac{1}{2}\right)^x$
   e) $y = 3.5(2.7)^x$
   f) $y = 2.75\left(\frac{2}{3}\right)^x$

(B)

2. An investment of $500 at 8% per annum compounded annually grows to A dollars in n years. In Section 7-1, page 300, we showed that an equation expressing the amount A dollars as an exponential function of the time n years is $A = 500(1.08)^n$.
   a) Solve this equation for n, thus expressing n as a logarithmic function of A.
   b) Calculate the value of n for each value of A and interpret the result.
      i) $A = 1250$ ii) $A = 350$

c) Graph the function in part a) for $0 < A \leqslant 1250$. Compare your graph with the one on page 300.

d) State the domain and the range of the function.

3. A ball is dropped from a height of 2.00 m. On each bounce the ball rises to 70% of the height from which it fell. In Section 7-1, page 301, we showed that an equation expressing the bounce height h metres as an exponential function of the number of bounces n is $h = 2.00(0.7)^n$.

   a) Solve this equation for n, thus expressing n as a logarithmic function of h.

   b) Calculate the value of n for each value of h and interpret the result.

      i) 0.7 m   ii) 0.12 m

   c) Graph the function in part a) for $0 < h \leqslant 2.00$. Compare your graph with the one on page 301.

   d) What is the range of the function?

4. a) The population of the town of Elmira was 6800 in 1987. If the population is growing at the rate of 1.8% per annum, write an equation expressing the population P as a function of n, the number of years relative to 1987.

   b) Solve this equation for n.

   c) Find the value of n if P is: i) 9200   ii) 5500.

   d) Graph the functions in parts a) and b). How are these functions related?

5. On bright sunny days, the amount of bromine in a municipal swimming pool decreases by 10% each hour. If there was 145 g of bromine in the pool at noon on a sunny day, when would the pool contain: a) 102 g   b) 85 g   c) 200 g?

6. Given the exponential function $f(x) = 3^x$, graph $y = f(x)$ and $y = f^{-1}(x)$ on the same grid.

7. Graph each function and its inverse on the same grid.

   a) $f(x) = 2^x$

   b) $g(x) = \left(\dfrac{2}{3}\right)^x$

I N V E S T I G A T E

At the beginning of this section, the equation $n \doteq 145 \log\left(\dfrac{P}{5}\right)$ was derived to represent the number of years for the world population to grow to P billion, assuming a constant growth rate of 1.6% per year. Notice that the coefficient 145 is the reciprocal of the logarithm of the base of the corresponding exponential function; that is, $\dfrac{1}{\log 1.016} \doteq 145$. This suggests that the form of the equation of the logarithmic function will be simpler if the base of the corresponding exponential function is 10, for then that coefficient will be 1, since $\log 10 = 1$.

   Investigate whether this is true by first changing the base of the corresponding exponential function, $P = 5(1.016)^n$, to base 10, and then solving for n to obtain the corresponding logarithmic function.

7-7 DEFINING AND GRAPHING LOGARITHMIC FUNCTIONS

In the *Example* of the preceding section we saw that the logarithmic function $y = \log x$ can be defined as the inverse of the exponential function $y = 10^x$. This suggests that other logarithmic functions can be defined as inverses of exponential functions with bases other than 10. In fact, for each choice of base for the exponential function $g(x) = a^x$, $a > 0$, there is an associated logarithmic function. Hence, we define the function $f(x) = \log_a x$, $a > 0$, as follows.

> The logarithmic function $f(x) = \log_a x$ $(a > 0, a \neq 1)$ is the inverse of the exponential function $g(x) = a^x$.

We say, "$f(x)$ equals log to the base a of x".

Recall that we can graph the inverse of any function by reflecting its graph in the line $y = x$. This is equivalent to interchanging the ordered pairs in the table of values of the function. For example, the graph below shows the function $g(x) = 2^x$ and its inverse $g^{-1}(x) = \log_2 x$. Compare this graph with the one on page 336.

$g(x) = 2^x$

x	y
-3	0.13
-2	0.25
-1	0.50
-0.5	0.71
0	1.00
0.5	1.41
1	2.00
1.5	2.83
2	4.00

$g^{-1}(x) = \log_2 x$

x	y
0.13	-3
0.25	-2
0.50	-1
0.71	-0.5
1.00	0
1.41	0.5
2.00	1
2.83	1.5
4.00	2

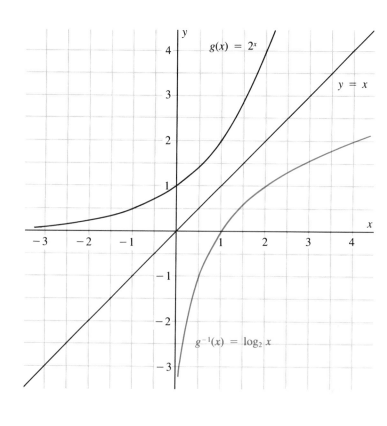

The graph illustrates the following properties of the function $g^{-1}(x) = \log_2 x$. These properties are consequences of the corresponding properties of $y = 2^x$.

Vertical intercept

There is no vertical intercept since the function $g(x) = 2^x$ has no horizontal intercept.

Horizontal intercept

The horizontal intercept is 1, since the vertical intercept of $g(x) = 2^x$ is 1. Hence, $\log_2 1 = 0$

Domain

The domain of $g^{-1}(x) = \log_2 x$ is the set of positive real numbers, since this is the range of $g(x) = 2^x$.

Range

The range of $g^{-1}(x) = \log_2 x$ is the set of all real numbers, since this is the domain of $g(x) = 2^x$.

If any exponential function is given, we can sketch its graph. The graph of the inverse is then the graph of the corresponding logarithmic function.

Example 1. a) Sketch the graph of the exponential function $f(x) = \left(\frac{1}{3}\right)^x$.

b) Sketch the graph of the inverse of the function in part a) on the same grid.

c) Write the equation of the inverse function.

Solution. a) $f(x) = \left(\frac{1}{3}\right)^x$

When x is very large and positive, $f(x)$ is very small and positive.

$f(0) = 1$

When x is negative and has a large absolute value, $f(x)$ is very large.

b) Reflect $y = \left(\frac{1}{3}\right)^x$ in the line $y = x$. The image is $y = \log_{\frac{1}{3}} x$.

c) The equation of the inverse function is $f^{-1}(x) = \log_{\frac{1}{3}} x$.

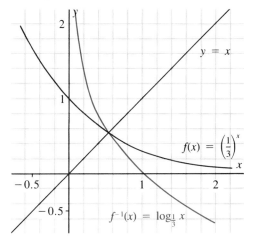

The graphs in the above examples illustrate properties of the logarithmic function $f(x) = \log_a x$.

**Properties of the graph of the
function** $f(x) = \log_a x$
Vertical intercept: none
Horizontal intercept: 1
Domain: all positive real numbers
Range: all real numbers

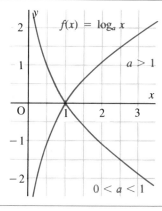

Example 2.   Prove that if (x_1, y_1) and (x_2, y_2) are points on the graph of
$f(x) = \log_a x$, then $(x_1 x_2, y_1 + y_2)$ is also a point on the graph.

Solution.   Since (x_1, y_1) is on the graph of $f(x) = \log_a x$, its coordinates satisfy the
equation $y = \log_a x$.
Hence, $y_1 = \log_a x_1$ . . . ①
Similarly, $y_2 = \log_a x_2$ . . . ②
Add equations ① and ②, and use the law of logarithms.
$$y_1 + y_2 = \log_a x_1 + \log_a x_2$$
$$= \log_a (x_1 x_2)$$
Hence, the coordinates of the point $(x_1 x_2, y_1 + y_2)$ also satisfy the equation
$y = \log_a x$. That is, $(x_1 x_2, y_1 + y_2)$ is also a point on the graph of
$f(x) = \log_a x$.

The result of *Example 2* is a
consequence of the law of
logarithms for multiplication.
Multiplying the horizontal
coordinates of points on the
graph of $f(x) = \log_a x$ corresponds
to adding their vertical coordinates.
Compare this example with
Example 2, page 316.

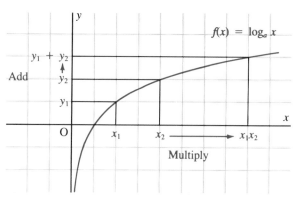

EXERCISES 7-7

Ⓐ

1. Write the inverse of each exponential function.
   a) $f(x) = 10^x$
   b) $g(x) = 3^x$
   c) $h(x) = 7^x$
   d) $f(x) = (0.4)^x$
   e) $g(x) = \left(\dfrac{3}{2}\right)^x$
   f) $h(x) = 15^x$

2. Write the inverse of each logarithmic function.
   a) $f(x) = \log x$ b) $g(x) = \log_2 x$ c) $h(x) = \log_6 x$
   d) $f(x) = \log_{\frac{1}{2}} x$ e) $g(x) = \log_{\frac{5}{4}} x$ f) $h(x) = \log_{21} x$

3. Copy each graph and sketch the graph of the inverse of the given function on the same grid. Then write the equation of the inverse function.
   a)   b)

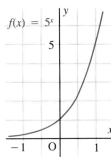
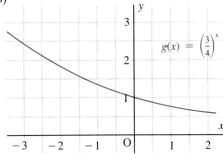

4. a) Sketch the graph of the exponential function $f(x) = 3^x$.
   b) Sketch the graph of the inverse of the function in part a) on the same grid.
   c) Write the equation of the inverse function.

5. Repeat *Exercise 4*, starting with the function $g(x) = \left(\frac{1}{2}\right)^x$

6. Graph each function.
   a) $f(x) = \log_4 x$ b) $g(x) = \log_6 x$ c) $h(x) = \log_{\frac{1}{2}} x$

   d) $f(x) = \log_{0.8} x$ e) $g(x) = \log_{1.5} x$ f) $h(x) = \log_{\frac{2}{5}} x$

7. Prove that if $f(x) = \log_a x$, then $f(xy) = f(x) + f(y)$.

8. a) Prove that if (x_1, y_1) and (x_2, y_2) are two points on the graph of $y = \log_a x$,
      then $\left(\dfrac{x_1}{x_2}, y_1 - y_2\right)$ is also a point on the graph.
   b) Prove that if (x_1, y_1) is a point on the graph of $y = \log_a x$, then $(x_1^2, 2y_1)$ and
      $\left(\dfrac{1}{x_1}, -y_1\right)$ are also points on the graph.

9. In *Example 1*, the graphs of $f(x) = \left(\frac{1}{3}\right)^x$, $f^{-1}(x) = \log_{\frac{1}{3}} x$, and $y = x$ are shown.
   Determine the coordinates of their point of intersection to 3 decimal places.

10. Given the function $f(x) = a^x$ and its inverse $f^{-1}(x) = \log_a x$, where $a > 0$
    a) For what values of a do the graphs of $y = f(x)$ and $y = f^{-1}(x)$ intersect?
    b) Find out as much as you can about the point of intersection of the graphs in part a).

7-8 LOGARITHMS AS EXPONENTS

Recall that to find the inverse of a function from its equation, we interchange x and y in the equation and solve for y. Hence, to find the inverse of $y = a^x$:

Step 1. Interchange x and y. $x = a^y \ldots$ ①

Step 2. Solve for y. We can do this using common logarithms, but it is preferable to use the definition on page 338. According to the definition, the inverse is
$y = \log_a x \ldots$ ②

Hence, this is the equation that results when equation ① is solved for y. Comparing equations ① and ②, we see that

$$\underset{\text{base} \quad \text{exponent}}{\log_a x = y} \quad \text{means that} \quad x = a^y, x > 0.$$

Hence, $\log_a x$ is an exponent. It is the exponent that x would have if it were written in power form with base a $(a > 0, a \neq 1)$. If the base is omitted, it is understood to be base 10.

Example 1.   Evaluate each logarithm.

   a) $\log_5 25$ b) $\log_7 \sqrt{7}$ c) $\log_{\frac{1}{3}} 9$ d) $\log_a a$

Solution.   a) Since $25 = 5^2$, then $\log_5 25 = 2$

   b) Since $\sqrt{7} = 7^{\frac{1}{2}}$, then $\log_7 \sqrt{7} = \frac{1}{2}$

   c) Write 9 as a power of $\frac{1}{3}$. Since $\left(\frac{1}{3}\right)^2 = \frac{1}{9}$, then $\left(\frac{1}{3}\right)^{-2} = 9$

   Hence, $\log_{\frac{1}{3}} 9 = -2$

   d) Since $a = a^1$, then $\log_a a = 1$

Since any positive number can be expressed as a power of any other positive number (except 1), we can find approximations to the logarithm of any positive number to any positive base (except 1).

Example 2.   Find $\log_5 9$ to the nearest thousandth.

Solution.   To find $\log_5 9$ means to find the exponent that 9 would have if it were expressed as a power of 5.
Let $9 = 5^x$
Take the logarithm of each side to base 10.
$\log 9 = \log (5^x)$
$\log 9 = x \log 5$
$$x = \frac{\log 9}{\log 5}$$
$\doteq 1.365\ 212\ 4$
To the nearest thousandth, $9 \doteq 5^{1.365}$
Therefore, $\log_5 9 \doteq 1.365$

Example 3. Simplify each expression.

 a) $\log_a a^x$

 b) $a^{\log_a x}$

Solution. a) $\log_a a^x$ is the exponent that a^x would have if it were written as a power of a. This exponent is x. Hence, $\log_a a^x = x$

 b) $a^{\log_a x}$ is a raised to the exponent that x would have if x were written as a power of a. Hence, $a^{\log_a x} = x$

Summary

- $\log_a x = y$ means that $x = a^y$, where $a > 0$, $a \neq 1$, and $x > 0$
- $\log_a a^x = x$ and $a^{\log_a x} = x$
- $\log_a a = 1$

Example 4. Write each expression in exponential form.

 a) $\log_2 16 = 4$

 b) $\log_2 0.5 = -1$

Solution. a) $\log_2 16 = 4$

 b) $\log_2 0.5 = -1$

 $16 = 2^4$

 $0.5 = 2^{-1}$

Example 5. Write each expression in logarithmic form.

 a) $3^5 = 243$

 b) $a^b = c$

Solution. a) $3^5 = 243$

 b) $a^b = c$

 $5 = \log_3 243$

 $b = \log_a c$

EXERCISES 7-8

Ⓐ

1. Write in exponential form.

 a) $\log_2 8 = 3$

 b) $\log_2 32 = 5$

 c) $\log_2 \left(\dfrac{1}{4}\right) = -2$

 d) $\log_5 625 = 4$

 e) $\log_3 9 = 2$

 f) $\log_9 3 = \dfrac{1}{2}$

2. Evaluate each logarithm.

 a) $\log_2 16$

 b) $\log_2 4$

 c) $\log_3 27$

 d) $\log_5 25$

 e) $\log_5 \left(\dfrac{1}{5}\right)$

 f) $\log_7 7$

 g) $\log_3 1$

 h) $\log_3 3^4$

3. In geography, sediments are classified by particle size, as shown.
 a) Write the logarithm to base 2 of each number.
 b) Write the logarithm to base 4 of each number.

Type of sediment	Size (mm)
Boulder	256
Cobble	64
Pebble	4
Granule	2
Sand	$\dfrac{1}{16}$
Silt	$\dfrac{1}{256}$

(B)

4. Evaluate each logarithm.

a) $\log_5 \sqrt{5}$ b) $\log_{\frac{1}{2}}\left(\frac{1}{16}\right)$ c) $\log_{\frac{3}{2}}\left(\frac{9}{4}\right)$ d) $\log_{\sqrt{3}} 9$

e) $\log_{\frac{1}{2}} 8$ f) $\log_{\frac{2}{5}}\left(\frac{25}{4}\right)$ g) $\log_3 (\sqrt{3})^3$ h) $\log_{\sqrt{5}} 125$

5. Evaluate each logarithm to the nearest thousandth.

a) $\log_3 5$ b) $\log_7 4$ c) $\log_2 50$ d) $\log_5 12$ e) $\log_4 27$ f) $\log_{16} 8$

6. Write in logarithmic form.

a) $6^2 = 36$ b) $4^{-2} = \frac{1}{16}$ c) $3^5 = 243$

d) $7^3 = 343$ e) $8^{\frac{1}{3}} = 2$ f) $2^0 = 1$

g) $5^{-2} = 0.04$ h) $4^{-\frac{1}{2}} = \frac{1}{2}$ i) $\left(\frac{1}{2}\right)^2 = \frac{1}{4}$

j) $\left(\frac{2}{3}\right)^{-1} = \frac{3}{2}$ k) $\left(\frac{1}{9}\right)^2 = \frac{1}{81}$ l) $x^y = z$

7. Write in exponential form.

a) $\log_{20} 400 = 2$ b) $\log_7 \left(\frac{1}{49}\right) = -2$ c) $\log_8 4 = \frac{2}{3}$

d) $\log_6 36^2 = 4$ e) $\log_{0.5} 8 = -3$ f) $\log_r s = t$

8. Solve for x.

a) $x = \log_5 25$ b) $\log_4 1 = x$ c) $\log_x 16 = 2$

d) $\log_x 3 = \frac{1}{2}$ e) $\log_2 x = 3$ f) $\log_3 x = 4$

9. Solve for x.

a) $\log_2 x = 9$ b) $\log_2 x = -2$ c) $\log_3 \left(\frac{1}{3}\right) = x$

d) $\log_{\sqrt{2}} 32 = x$ e) $\log_x 16 = -2$ f) $\log_x 125 = -3$

10. If $\log_8 3 = x$ and $\log_4 7 = y$, find an expression in terms of x and y for:
a) $\log_2 21$ b) $\log_2 63$.

11. Given that $f(x) = x - \log_2 x$ and $g(x) = 2^x$, find: a) $f(g(x))$ b) $g(f(x))$.

12. If a telephone network is designed to carry N telephone calls simultaneously, then the number of switches needed per call must be at least $\log_2 N$. If the network can carry 10 000 calls simultaneously, how many switches would be needed:
a) for one call   b) for 10 000 simultaneous calls?

(C)

13. a) Evaluate each logarithm. i) $\log_2 8$ and $\log_8 2$ ii) $\log_5 25$ and $\log_{25} 5$
b) On the basis of the results of part a), make a conjecture about how $\log_a b$ and $\log_b a$ are related, where a, $b > 0$. Prove your conjecture.

14. Let a and b be any two positive numbers. Prove that for all positive values of x, $\log_b x$ is directly proportional to $\log_a x$.

MATHEMATICS AROUND US

The Logarithmic Spiral

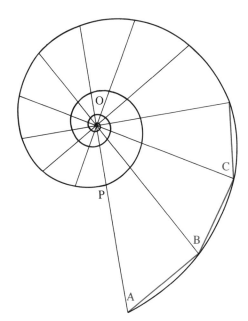

Some living creatures exhibit exponential growth in their dimensions.
A well-known example is the chambered nautilus of the Indian
and Pacific Oceans. As it grows, the shell extends continuously,
generating a natural spiral.

QUESTIONS

1. The diagram shows a series of equally-spaced radii drawn from the centre of
   the spiral. The radii are spaced every 30°.
   a) Measure and record the length of each radius, starting with OP and pro-
      ceeding clockwise around the spiral.
   b) Verify that the length of the radius L centimetres satisfies the equation
      $L = 1.5(1.0034)^\theta$, where θ degrees is the angle of rotation measured
      clockwise starting at OP.

2. a) Measure the angles represented by A, B, C, . . ., on the diagram.
   b) Prove that if the length of the radius is an exponential function of the angle
      of rotation, then the angles A, B, C, . . ., are all equal.

3. a) Suggest why the spiral is called a *logarithmic spiral*.
   b) The spiral is also referred to as an *equiangular spiral*. Suggest why.

7-9 THE LAWS OF LOGARITHMS (BASE *a*)

In *Section 7-5* we developed the laws of logarithms for logarithms with base 10. The restriction to base 10 is not necessary, and the laws can be extended to logarithms with any positive base (except 1).

For example, an equation such as $2^3 \times 2^4 = 2^7$ can be written in logarithmic form as $\log_2 8 + \log_2 16 = \log_2 128$. This equation states that the sum of the exponents that 8 and 16 have when expressed as powers of 2 is equal to the exponent that 128 has when expressed as a power of 2.

Theorem   Law of Logarithms for Multiplication (Base *a*)
If x and y are positive real numbers, then
$$\log_a xy = \log_a x + \log_a y \qquad a > 0, a \neq 1$$

Given: Two positive real numbers x and y
Required to Prove: $\log_a xy = \log_a x + \log_a y \qquad a > 0, a \neq 1$
Proof: Let $\log_a x = M$ and $\log_a y = N$
$$x = a^M \qquad\qquad y = a^N$$
Hence, $xy = (a^M)(a^N)$
$$= a^{M+N}$$
Therefore, $\log_a xy = \log_a (a^{M+N})$
$$= M + N$$
$$= \log_a x + \log_a y$$

Corollary   Law of Logarithms for Division (Base *a*)
If x and y are positive real numbers, then
$$\log_a \left(\frac{x}{y}\right) = \log_a x - \log_a y \qquad a > 0, a \neq 1$$

Example 1.   Write $\log_2 15$ as:
   a) a sum of two logarithms   b) a difference of two logarithms.

Solution.   a) Since $15 = 5 \times 3$, then $\log_2 15 = \log_2 5 + \log_2 3$
   b) Since $15 = 30 \div 2$, then $\log_2 15 = \log_2 30 - \log_2 2$

What other answers can you find for *Example 1*?

Example 2.   Write each expression as a single logarithm and simplify it.
   a) $\log_3 6 + \log_3 1.5$ b) $\log_5 50 - \log_5 0.4$

Solution.   a) $\log_3 6 + \log_3 1.5 = \log_3 (6 \times 1.5)$
$$= \log_3 9$$
$$= 2$$

   b) $\log_5 50 - \log_5 0.4 = \log_5 \left(\frac{50}{0.4}\right)$
$$= \log_5 125$$
$$= 3$$

> **Theorem   Law of Logarithms for Powers (Base *a*)**
> If x and n are real numbers, and $x > 0$, then
> $$\log_a (x^n) = n \log_a x \qquad a > 0, a \neq 1$$

Given: Two real numbers x and n, where $x > 0$
Required to Prove: $\log_a (x^n) = n \log_a x$
Proof: Let $\log_a x = M$

$$x = a^M$$

Hence, $x^n = (a^M)^n$

$$= a^{nM}$$

Therefore, $\log_a (x^n) = \log_a (a^{nM})$

$$= nM$$
$$= n \log_a x$$

> **Corollary   Law of Logarithms for Roots (Base *a*)**
> If x and n are real numbers, and $x > 0$, then
> $$\log_a \sqrt[n]{x} = \frac{1}{n} \log_a x \qquad a > 0, a \neq 1$$

Example 3.   a) Write $\log_5 16$ as a product of a whole number and a logarithm.

b) Write as a single logarithm.   i) $2 \log_6 5$ ii) $\frac{1}{3} \log_4 125$

Solution.   a) Since $16 = 2^4$, then $\log_5 16 = \log_5 (2^4)$
$$= 4 \log_5 2$$

b)   i) $2 \log_6 5 = \log_6 (5^2)$
$$= \log_6 25$$

ii) $\frac{1}{3} \log_4 125 = \log_4 (\sqrt[3]{125})$
$$= \log_4 5$$

Example 4.   Given that $\log_2 7 \doteq 2.8074$, find an approximation for each logarithm.

a) $\log_2 14$ b) $\log_2 49$ c) $\log_2 \left(\frac{4}{7}\right)$ d) $\log_2 \sqrt[3]{7}$

Solution.   a) $\log_2 14 = \log_2 (7 \times 2)$ b) $\log_2 49 = \log_2 (7^2)$
$$= \log_2 7 + \log_2 2 \qquad\qquad = 2 \log_2 7$$
$$\doteq 2.8074 + 1 \qquad\qquad\quad \doteq 2(2.8074)$$
$$\doteq 3.8074 \qquad\qquad\qquad\quad \doteq 5.6148$$

c) $\log_2 \left(\frac{4}{7}\right) = \log_2 4 - \log_2 7$ d) $\log_2 \sqrt[3]{7} = \frac{1}{3} \log_2 7$
$$\doteq 2 - 2.8074 \qquad\qquad\qquad\quad \doteq \frac{1}{3} (2.8074)$$
$$\doteq -0.8074 \qquad\qquad\qquad\qquad\quad \doteq 0.9358$$

> **Laws of Logarithms (Base a)** $a > 0, a \neq 1$
> - Multiplication $\log_a xy = \log_a x + \log_a y$ $x, y > 0$
> - Division $\log_a \left(\dfrac{x}{y}\right) = \log_a x - \log_a y$ $x, y > 0$
> - Powers $\log_a (x^n) = n \log_a x$ $x > 0$
> - Roots $\log_a \sqrt[n]{x} = \dfrac{1}{n} \log_a x$ $x > 0$

We can solve equations involving logarithms by using the laws of logarithms and the definition of a logarithm.

Example 5.   Solve each equation, and check.

a) $2 \log x = \log 8 + \log 2$ b) $\log_8 (2 - x) + \log_8 (4 - x) = 1$

Solution.   a) $2 \log x = \log 8 + \log 2$
$$\log x^2 = \log 16$$
Hence, $x^2 = 16$
$$x = \pm 4$$

To check, substitute each value of x into the original equation.
When $x = 4$,
L.S. $= 2 \log 4$ R.S. $= \log 8 + \log 2$
$ = \log 16$ $ = \log 16$
4 is a root.
When $x = -4$, the left side is not defined since $\log x$ is defined only when $x > 0$. Hence, -4 is an extraneous root.

b) $\log_8 (2 - x) + \log_8 (4 - x) = 1$
Simplify the left side using the law of logarithms for multiplication.
$$\log_8 (2 - x)(4 - x) = 1$$
Use the definition of a logarithm.
$$(2 - x)(4 - x) = 8^1$$
$$8 - 6x + x^2 = 8$$
$$-6x + x^2 = 0$$
$$x = 0 \text{ or } x = 6$$
When $x = 0$,
L.S. $= \log_8 2 + \log_8 4$ R.S. $= 1$
$ = \log_8 8$
$ = 1$
0 is a root.
When $x = 6$, the left side is not defined. Hence, 6 is an extraneous root.

In *Example 5b* we may ask, if 6 is an extraneous root, then where did it come from? The key to the answer is the quadratic equation $(2 - x)(4 - x) = 8$ which occurred in the solution. This equation may also be written as $(x - 2)(x - 4) = 8$ without changing the two roots. But then the associated logarithmic equation would be $\log_8 (x - 2) + \log_8 (x - 4) = 1$. Hence, if this equation were solved using the method of *Example 5b* the same two roots 0 and 6 would result, but this time 6 would be the root and 0 would be extraneous.

EXERCISES 7-9

Ⓐ

1. Write each expression as a single logarithm, and simplify it.
   a) $\log_6 9 + \log_6 4$ b) $\log_5 15 - \log_5 3$ c) $\log_4 2 + \log_4 32$
   d) $\log_2 48 - \log_2 6$ e) $\log_3 54 - \log_3 2$ f) $\log_3 9 + \log_3 9$

2. Write as a sum of logarithms.
   a) $\log_3 20$ b) $\log_7 45$ c) $\log_5 90$ d) $\log_{12} 6$ e) $\log_8 75$ f) $\log_{20} 39$

3. Write as a difference of logarithms.
   a) $\log_4 11$ b) $\log_3 12$ c) $\log_9 5$ d) $\log_6 7$ e) $\log_{11} 21$ f) $\log_2 13$

4. Write each expression as a single logarithm and simplify it.
   a) $\log_6 4 + \log_6 3 + \log_6 3$ b) $\log_4 8 + \log_4 6 + \log_4 \left(\frac{4}{3}\right)$
   c) $\log_3 18 + \log_3 5 - \log_3 10$ d) $\log_2 20 - \log_2 5 + \log_2 8$

5. Simplify.
   a) $\log_2 (8 \times 16)$ b) $\log_3 (27 \times 81)$ c) $\log_5 (625 \times 25)$
   d) $\log_2 \left(\frac{32}{4}\right)$ e) $\log_3 \left(\frac{27}{3}\right)$ f) $\log_5 \left(\frac{125}{25}\right)$

6. Write each logarithm as a product of a whole number and a logarithm.
   a) $\log_3 8$ b) $\log_5 36$ c) $\log_2 27$ d) $\log_6 32$ e) $\log_{12} 81$ f) $\log_4 125$

7. Write as a single logarithm.
   a) $3 \log_2 5$ b) $2 \log_7 4$ c) $6 \log_3 8$ d) $5 \log_{12} 4$ e) $15 \log_2 3$

Ⓑ

8. Write as a single logarithm and simplify it.
   a) $\log_4 48 + \log_4 \left(\frac{2}{3}\right) + \log_4 8$ b) $\log_8 24 + \log_8 4 - \log_8 3$
   c) $\log_9 36 + \log_9 18 - \log_9 24$ d) $\log_4 20 - \log_4 5 + \log_4 8$
   e) $\log_3 \sqrt{45} - \log_3 \sqrt{5}$ f) $\log_2 \sqrt{5} - \log_2 \sqrt{40}$
   g) $\log_5 \sqrt{10} + \log_5 \sqrt{\frac{25}{2}}$ h) $\log_4 \sqrt{40} + \log_4 \sqrt{48} - \log_4 \sqrt{15}$

9. Given $\log_2 5 \doteq 2.3219$, find an approximation for each logarithm.
   a) $\log_2 20$ b) $\log_2 25$ c) $\log_2 2.5$ d) $\log_2 \sqrt{5}$

10. Simplify.

   a) $\log_2 24 - \log_2 \left(\frac{3}{4}\right)$

   b) $\log_2 20 + \log_2 0.4$

   c) $\log_8 48 + \log_8 4 - \log_8 3$

   d) $\log_{21} 7 + \log_{21} 9 + \log_{21} \left(\frac{1}{3}\right)$

11. Given $\log_3 10 \doteq 2.0959$, find an approximation for each logarithm.

   a) $\log_3 1000$

   b) $\log_3 30$

   c) $\log_3 \sqrt{0.3}$

   d) $\log_3 \left(\frac{100}{9}\right)$

12. Express y as a function of x. What is the domain?
   a) $\log_2 xy = 3 \log_2 x$
   b) $\log_5 y = 2 \log_5 (x + 1) + \log_5 (x - 1)$
   c) $\log_3 (y - 3) = 1 + 2 \log_3 (x + 3)$

13. Use your calculator to evaluate each expression.
   a)   i) $\log_2 3000$ ii) $\log_2 300$ iii) $\log_2 30$ iv) $\log_2 3$
        v) $\log_2 0.3$ vi) $\log_2 0.03$ vii) $\log_2 0.003$ viii) $\log_2 0.0003$
   b) Can you find a pattern in the results of part a)? Account for the pattern.

14. If $\log_3 2 = x$, simplify each logarithm.
   a) $\log_3 8$

   b) $\log_3 24$

   c) $\log_3 \sqrt{2}$

   d) $\log_3 6\sqrt{2}$

15. If $\log_2 5 = x$, simplify each logarithm.

   a) $\log_2 20$

   b) $\log_2 100$

   c) $\log_2 10\sqrt{5}$

   d) $\log_2 \left(\frac{\sqrt[3]{5}}{2}\right)$

16. Given that $\log_2 x = 5$, evaluate each logarithm.

   a) $\log_2 2x$

   b) $\log_2 \left(\frac{x}{2}\right)$

   c) $\log_2 (x^2)$

   d) $\log_2 (4x^2)$

17. Given that $\log_3 x = 2$ and $\log_3 y = 5$, evaluate each logarithm.

   a) $\log_3 xy$

   b) $\log_3 (9x^2y)$

   c) $\log_3 \left(\frac{3x^2}{y}\right)$

   d) $\log_3 (27x^{-2}y)$

18. Solve and check.
   a) $2 \log x = \log 32 + \log 2$
   b) $2 \log x = \log 3 + \log 27$
   c) $\log_4 (x + 2) + \log_4 (x - 1) = 1$
   d) $\log_2 (x - 5) + \log_2 (x - 2) = 2$
   e) $\log_2 x + \log_2 (x + 2) = 3$
   f) $\log_6 (x - 1) + \log_6 (x + 4) = 2$

19. Solve and check.
   a) $2 \log m + 3 \log m = 10$
   b) $\log_3 x^2 - \log_3 2x = 2$
   c) $\log_3 s + \log_3 (s - 2) = 1$
   d) $\log (x - 2) + \log (x + 1) = 1$
   e) $\log_7 (x + 4) + \log_7 (x - 2) = 1$
   f) $\log_2 (2m + 4) - \log_2 (m - 1) = 3$

Ⓒ

20. Solve each equation to the nearest thousandth.
   a) $\log_2 x + \log_4 x = 5$
   b) $\log_5 x + \log_{10} x = 5$

21. a) Show that: i) $\dfrac{1}{\log_3 10} + \dfrac{1}{\log_4 10} = \dfrac{1}{\log_{12} 10}$ ii) $\dfrac{1}{\log_3 x} + \dfrac{1}{\log_4 x} = \dfrac{1}{\log_{12} x}$.
   b) Using the results of part a) as a guide, state a general result and prove it.

7-10 APPLICATIONS OF EXPONENTIAL AND LOGARITHMIC FUNCTIONS: PART ONE

Exponential functions have defining equations of the form $y = ca^x$. In many applied problems, we are given three of the quantities c, a, x, and y, and are required to calculate the fourth quantity.

Compound Interest

Example 1. What amount of money would grow to $1000 in 5 years if it is invested at 9% per annum compounded annually?

Solution. Let the amount of money be P dollars. Then,
$$P(1.09)^5 = 1000$$
$$P = \frac{1000}{(1.09)^5}$$
$$= 1000(1.09)^{-5}$$
$$\doteq 649.93$$

Hence, $649.93 would grow to $1000 in 5 years at 9% per annum.

Solving an equation of the form $y = ca^x$ for the base a amounts to taking a root of both sides. We illustrate this in the next example.

Example 2. In 1947 an investor bought Van Gogh's painting *Irises* for $84 000. In 1987 she sold it for $49 million. What annual rate of interest corresponds to an investment of $84 000 which grows to $49 million in 40 years?

Solution. Let i represent the rate of interest. Then,
$$84\ 000(1 + i)^{40} = 49\ 000\ 000$$
$$(1 + i)^{40} = \frac{49\ 000}{84}$$

Take the 40th root of each side.
$$1 + i = \left(\frac{49\ 000}{84}\right)^{\frac{1}{40}}$$
$$1 + i \doteq 1.173$$
$$i \doteq 0.173$$

The annual rate of interest is approximately 17.3%.

Example 3. Suppose you invest $500 at 8% per annum compounded annually. How many years would it take for your investment to double?

Solution. Let n represent the number of years. Then,
$$500(1.08)^n = 1000$$
$$(1.08)^n = 2$$

Take the logarithm of each side (base 10).
$$n \log 1.08 = \log 2$$
$$n = \frac{\log 2}{\log 1.08}$$
$$\doteq 9.0$$

Hence, $500 earning interest at 8% per annum will double in approximately 9 years.

In many applications of exponential functions it is necessary to solve an equation of the form $y = ca^x$ for the exponent x. This was illustrated in *Example 3*.

Light Penetration

Example 4. For every metre a diver descends below the water surface, the light intensity is reduced by 2.5%. At what depth is the light intensity only 50% of that at the surface?

Solution. Let d metres represent the required depth.

Then, $\qquad 50 = 100(0.975)^d$

$\qquad\qquad (0.975)^d = 0.5$

Take the logarithm of each side (base 10).

$d \log 0.975 = \log 0.5$

$$d = \frac{\log 0.5}{\log 0.975}$$

$$\doteq 27.4$$

The light intensity is only 50% of that at the surface at a depth of approximately 27 m.

Nuclear Fallout

Exponential functions occur in the study of nuclear fallout. This refers to the contamination of the atmosphere and the ground from radioactive particles released in a nuclear accident or explosion. The harmful effects arise when these particles decay into other particles and release radiation. Each radioactive substance decays with a characteristic *halflife*. This is the time required for one-half of the material to decay.

Example 5. In a nuclear test explosion, some strontium-90 is released. This substance has a halflife of 28 years.
   a) Draw a graph showing the percent of strontium-90 remaining up to 140 years.
   b) Express the percent P of strontium-90 remaining as a function of:
      i) the number of halflives elapsed, n
      ii) the number of years elapsed, t.
   c) What percent of strontium-90 remains after 50 years?

Solution. a) Make a table of values for time intervals of 1 halflife. Plot the percent remaining against the time in years.

Halflives (n)	0	1	2	3	4	5
Years (t)	0	28	56	84	112	140
Percent remaining (P)	100	50	25	12.5	6.25	3.13

b) i) After each half life, the percent remaining is halved. Hence, the percent remaining after n half lives have elapsed is:

$$P = 100\left(\frac{1}{2}\right)^n \quad \ldots \text{①}$$

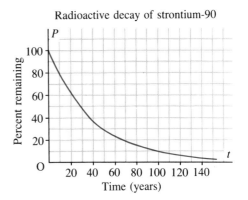

Radioactive decay of strontium-90

ii) Since $t = 28n$, we can write equation ① in terms of t.

Substitute $\frac{t}{28}$ for n.

$$P = 100\left(\frac{1}{2}\right)^{\frac{t}{28}} \quad \ldots \text{②}$$

c) Substitute 50 for t in equation ②.

$$P = 100\left(\frac{1}{2}\right)^{\frac{50}{28}}$$

$$\doteq 29.003\ 235$$

Hence, about 29% of the strontium-90 remains after 50 years.

Example 6. In April 1986 there was a major nuclear accident at the Chernobyl power plant in the Soviet Union. The atmosphere was contaminated with quantities of radioactive iodine-131, which has a half life of 8.1 days. How long did it take for the level of radiation to reduce to 1% of the level immediately after the accident?

Solution. Let P represent the percent of the original radiation that was present after t days. Then, since the halflife is 8.1 days,

$$P = 100\left(\frac{1}{2}\right)^{\frac{t}{8.1}}$$

Substitute 1 for P and solve for t by taking the logarithm of each side.

$$1 = 100(0.5)^{\frac{t}{8.1}}$$

$$\log 1 = \log 100 + \frac{t}{8.1}\log 0.5$$

$$0 = 2 + \frac{t}{8.1}\log 0.5$$

$$t = -\frac{16.2}{\log 0.5}$$

$$\doteq 54$$

It took about 54 days for the level of radiation to reduce to 1% of the level immediately after the accident.

EXERCISES 7-10

Compound Interest

1. How much should you invest at 7% per annum compounded annually so that $5000 will be available in 4 years?

2. The 50¢ Bluenose is one of Canada's most famous postage stamps. In 1930 it could be bought at the post office for 50¢. In 1987 a superb copy was sold at an auction for $500. What annual rate of interest corresponds to an investment of 50¢ in 1930 which grows to $500 in 1987?

3. In 1626, Manhattan Island was sold for $24. If that money had been invested at 8% per annum compounded annually, what would it have amounted to today?

4. Suppose you invest $200 at 9% per annum compounded annually. How many years would it take for your investment to grow to $500?

5. Mary invests $2500 at 11% per annum compounded annually. How many years will it take for her investment to double in value?

Light Penetration

6. For every metre a diver descends under water, the intensity of three colors of light is reduced as shown.
   a) For each color, write an equation which expresses the percent P of surface light as a function of the depth d metres.

Color	Percent Reduction per metre
Red	35%
Green	5%
Blue	2.5%

   b) For each color, determine the depth at which about half the light has disappeared.
   c) Let us agree that, for all practical purposes, the light has disappeared when the intensity is only 1% of that at the surface. At what depth would this occur for each color?

7. Several layers of glass are stacked together. Each layer reduces the light passing through it by 5%.
   a) What percent of light passes through 10 layers of glass?
   b) How many layers of glass are needed to reduce the intensity to only 1% of the original light?

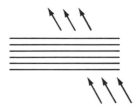

Growth of Populations

8. The town of Springfield is growing at a rate of 6.5% per annum. How many people are there in Springfield now, if there will be 15 000 in 4.5 years?

9. In 1950 the world population was approximately 2.5 billion. The population doubled to 5 billion in 1987. What was the average annual growth rate of the world population from 1950 to 1987?

10. A culture has 750 bacteria. The number of bacteria doubles every 5 h. How many bacteria are in the culture after 12 h?

11. A colony of bees increases by 25% every three months. How many bees should Raiman start with if he wishes to have 10 000 bees in 18 months?

12. If the population of a colony of bacteria doubles every 30 min, how long would it take for the population to triple?

13. Prove that if the growth rate is constant, the time required for a population to double is independent of the population size.

Nuclear Fallout

14. When strontium-90 decays, the percent P remaining is expressed as a function of the time t years by the equation $P \doteq 100(2)^{-0.0357t}$. How long is it until the percent remaining is: a) 10% b) 1%?

15. The halflives of two products of a nuclear explosion are shown. For each substance
    a) Draw a graph showing the percent remaining during the first five halflives.

Substance	Halflife
Iodine-131	8.1 days
Cesium-144	282 days

   b) Express the percent remaining as a function of:
      i) the number of halflives elapsed, n ii) the number of days elapsed, t.
   c) What percent of the substance remains after:
      i) one week   ii) 30 days   iii) one year?
   d) How long is it until the percent remaining of each substance is:
      i) 10%   ii) 0.1%?

16. Another product of a nuclear explosion is plutonium-239, which has a halflife of 24 000 years. What percent of plutonium-239 remains after:
    a) 100 years   b) 1000 years   c) 10 000 years   d) 100 000 years?

17. Polonium-210 is a radioactive element with a halflife of 20 weeks. From a sample of 25 g, how much would remain after:
    a) 30 weeks   b) 14 weeks   c) 1 year   d) 511 days?

Other Applications

18. Jacques bought a new car for $15 000. Each year the value of the car depreciates to 70% of its value the previous year. In how many years will the car be worth only $500?

19. A pan of water is brought to a boil and then removed from the heat. Every 5 min thereafter the difference between the temperature of the water and room temperature is reduced by 50%.
    a) Room temperature is 20°C. Express the temperature of the water as a function of the time since it was removed from the heat.
    b) How many minutes does it take for the temperature of the water to reach 30°C?

20. A cup of coffee contains approximately 100 mg of caffeine. When you drink the coffee, the caffeine is absorbed into the bloodstream, and is eventually metabolized by the body. Every 5 h the amount of caffeine in the bloodstream is reduced by 50%.
    a) Write an equation which expresses the amount of caffeine c milligrams in the bloodstream as an exponential function of the elapsed time t hours since drinking one cup of coffee.
    b) How many hours does it take for the amount of caffeine to be reduced to:
       i) 10 mg   ii) 1 mg?

21. In a steel mill, red-hot slabs of steel are pressed many times between heavy rollers. The drawings show two stages in rolling a slab.

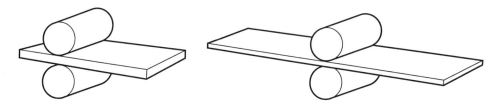

    A slab is 2.00 m long and 0.120 m thick. On each pass through the rollers, its length increases by 20%.
    a) Write the equation which expresses the length L metres of the slab as an exponential function of the number of passes n through the rollers.
    b) How many passes are needed to increase the length of the slab to 50 m?

22. a) For the slab in *Exercise 21*, by what factor does the thickness of the slab decrease on each pass through the rollers? Assume the width is constant.
    b) Write an equation which expresses the thickness t metres of the slab as an exponential function of the number of passes n through the rollers.
    c) How many passes are needed to reduce the thickness of the slab to 0.001 m?
    d) How long would the slab be when its thickness is 0.001 m?

Ⓒ

23. The total amount of arable land in the world is about 3.2×10^9 ha. At current population rates, about 0.4 ha of land is required to grow food for each person in the world.
    a) Assuming a 1987 world population of 5 billion and a constant growth rate of 1.5%, determine the year when the demand for arable land exceeds the supply.
    b) Compare the effect of each comment on the result of part a).
       i) doubling the productivity of the land so that only 0.2 ha is required to grow food for each person
       ii) reducing the growth rate by one-half, to 0.75%
       iii) doubling the productivity of the land *and* reducing the growth rate by 50%

7-11 APPLICATIONS OF EXPONENTIAL AND LOGARITHMIC FUNCTIONS: PART TWO

Growth of Populations
Occasionally we see statements such as this, in magazines and newspapers.

In favorable breeding conditions, the population of a swarm of desert locusts can multiply 10-fold in 20 days.

This information is not sufficient to calculate the population of a swarm of locusts, since an initial population figure is not given. But we can still use the statement to compare the populations of a swarm at two different times.

Example 1.   Use the information above to compare the population of a swarm of locusts after 30 days with its population after 20 days.

Solution.   Let P_0 represent the population of a swarm at $t = 0$. Then we can use the fact that the population is multiplied 10-fold in 20 days to express the population P as an exponential function of the time t days.

$$P = P_0(10)^{\frac{t}{20}}$$
$$\text{or} \qquad P = P_0(10)^{0.05t} \quad \ldots \text{①}$$

Let P_{20} and P_{30} represent the populations after 20 and 30 days, respectively. Then, using equation ①, we obtain

$$P_{20} = P_0(10)^{0.05(20)}$$
$$= P_0(10) \quad \ldots \text{②}$$
$$P_{30} = P_0(10)^{0.05(30)}$$
$$= P_0(10)^{1.5} \quad \ldots \text{③}$$

Since we do not know the value of P_0, we cannot calculate P_{20} or P_{30}. But we can find their ratio by dividing equation ③ by equation ②.

$$\frac{P_{30}}{P_{20}} = \frac{P_0(10)^{1.5}}{P_0(10)}$$
$$= 10^{0.5}$$
$$\doteq 3.162\ 277\ 7$$

A swarm is about 3.2 times as large after 30 days as it was after 20 days.

Calculations such as those in *Example 1* are used in many applications of exponential and logarithmic functions.

Earthquakes
A scale for comparing the intensities of earthquakes was devised by Charles Richter about 50 years ago. The intensity of an earthquake is measured by the amount of ground motion as recorded on a seismometer.

When we use the Richter scale, we do not need to know the actual intensities, or seismometer readings. The scale is used simply to compare the intensities of two earthquakes using the following rule.

> Each increase of 1 unit in magnitude on the Richter scale represents a 10-fold increase in intensity as measured on a seismometer.

Consider, for example, the Italy earthquake of 1976 which had a magnitude of 6.5 on the Richter scale. Notice that the Guatemala earthquake the same year had a magnitude of 7.5, which is exactly 1 unit greater. This means that the second earthquake was *10 times* as intense as the first. Similarly, the Alaska earthquake in 1964 was 10 × 10, or *100 times* as intense as the 1976 Italy earthquake, and 10 × 10 × 10, or *1000 times* as intense as the 1983 earthquake in Colombia. But, how do we compare the intensities of earthquakes such as the Alaska earthquake in 1964 and the Turkey earthquake in 1966, whose magnitudes do not differ by a whole number?

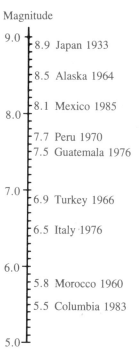

The Richter Scale

Magnitude

9.0 — 8.9 Japan 1933

8.5 Alaska 1964

8.0 — 8.1 Mexico 1985

7.7 Peru 1970
7.5 Guatemala 1976

7.0 — 6.9 Turkey 1966

6.5 Italy 1976

6.0 — 5.8 Morocco 1960

5.5 Columbia 1983

5.0 —

Example 2. Use the information above to compare the intensity of the 1964 Alaska earthquake with the intensity of the 1966 Turkey earthquake.

Solution. Let I_0 represent the intensity of an earthquake with a magnitude of 0 on the Richter scale. Then we can use the fact that the intensity is multiplied 10-fold for each increase in 1 unit of magnitude to express the intensity I as an exponential function of the magnitude M.

$$I = I_0(10)^M \quad \ldots \text{①}$$

Let I_A and I_T represent the intensities of the Alaska and Turkey earthquakes, respectively. Then, using equation ①, we obtain

$$I_A = I_0(10)^{8.5} \quad \ldots \text{②}$$
$$I_T = I_0(10)^{6.9} \quad \ldots \text{③}$$

Since we do not know the value of I_0, we cannot calculate I_A or I_T. But we can find their ratio by dividing equation ② by equation ③.

$$\frac{I_A}{I_T} = \frac{I_0(10)^{8.5}}{I_0(10)^{6.9}}$$
$$= 10^{8.5-6.9}$$
$$= 10^{1.6}$$
$$\doteq 39.810\ 717$$

The Alaska earthquake was about 40 times as intense as the Turkey earthquake.

Acid Rain

Acid rain has become a major environmental problem. The acidity of rainwater is measured on a special scale called a *pH scale*. Each 1 unit decrease in pH represents a 10-fold *increase* in acidity. For example, the pH of vinegar is 2 units less than that of tomatoes. Hence, vinegar is 10^2, or 100 times more acidic than tomatoes.

Let A represent the acid content of a substance with a pH of P. Then, since each increase of 1 unit in P represents a 10-fold decrease in A,

$$A = A_0(0.1)^P \ldots \text{①}$$

where A_0 represents the acid content of a substance with pH 0.
To express P as a function of A, solve equation ① for P.

$$\log A = \log A_0 + P \log 0.1$$
$$P \log 0.1 = \log A - \log A_0$$

$$P = \frac{\log \left(\frac{A}{A_0}\right)}{\log 0.1}$$

or $\quad P = -\log \left(\frac{A}{A_0}\right) \ldots \text{②}$

Equation ② expresses the pH of a substance as a logarithmic function of its acid content.

In the equation for pH, $P = -\log \left(\frac{A}{A_0}\right)$, notice that the value of A_0 is not given. Despite this, we can still use this equation to obtain useful information. This involves a comparison of the acid content, or pH of two substances.

Example 3. A lake in the Muskoka region of Ontario has a pH of 4.0. How many times as acidic as clean rain water, which has a pH of 5.6, is the water in this lake?

Solution. Use the equation developed above. $P = -\log \left(\frac{A}{A_0}\right)$

Let P_1 and A_1 represent the pH and acid content of clean rain water, and let P_2 and A_2 represent the pH and acid content of the lake. Then,

$$P_1 = -\log \left(\frac{A_1}{A_0}\right)$$
$$P_2 = -\log \left(\frac{A_2}{A_0}\right)$$

Subtract and then use the law of logarithms for division.

$$P_1 - P_2 = -\log \left(\frac{A_1}{A_0}\right) + \log \left(\frac{A_2}{A_0}\right)$$
$$= \log \left(\frac{A_2}{A_0}\right) - \log \left(\frac{A_1}{A_0}\right)$$
$$= \log \left(\frac{A_2}{A_1}\right)$$

Substitute 5.6 for P_1 and 4.0 for P_2.

$$5.6 - 4.0 = \log \left(\frac{A_2}{A_1} \right)$$

$$1.6 = \log \left(\frac{A_2}{A_1} \right)$$

By the definition of a logarithm

$$\frac{A_2}{A_1} = 10^{1.6}$$

$$\doteq 39.8$$

Hence, the lake is about 40 times as acidic as clean rain water.

EXERCISES 7-11

Growth of Populations

1. The population of a swarm of insects can multiply 5-fold in 4 weeks. Let P_0 represent the population at time $t = 0$.
   a) Write expressions to represent the population after:
      i) 4 weeks   ii) 6 weeks.
   b) How many times as great is the population after 6 weeks as it was after 4 weeks?

2. The population of a nest of ants can multiply 3-fold in 5 weeks. After 8 weeks, how many times as great is the population as it was after 5 weeks?

3. The population of a colony of bacteria can double in 25 min. After one hour, how many times as great is the population as it was after 25 min?

Earthquakes

4. On July 26, 1986, an earthquake with magnitude 5.5 hit California. The next day a second earthquake with magnitude 6.2 hit the same region. How many times as intense as the first earthquake was the second earthquake?

5. In 1985/86, three earthquakes hit Mexico City. How many times as intense as:
   a) the second earthquake was the first
   b) the third earthquake was the second
   c) the third earthquake was the first?

Mexico City Earthquakes	
Date	Magnitude
Sept. 19, 1985	8.1
Sept. 21, 1985	7.5
April 30, 1986	7.0

6. It has been observed that for every decrease of 1 unit in magnitude, earthquakes are about 6 or 7 times as frequent. In a given year, how should the number of earthquakes with magnitudes between 4.0 and 4.9 compare with the number of earthquakes with magnitudes between:
   a) 5.0 and 5.9   b) 6.0 and 6.9   c) 7.0 and 7.9?

Acid Rain

7. Between 1956 and 1976 the annual average pH of precipitation at Sault Ste. Marie, Ontario, dropped from 5.6 to 4.3. How many times as acidic as the precipitation in 1956 was the precipitation in 1976?

8. In the spring, the pH of a stream dropped from 6.5 to 5.5 during a 3-week period in April.
   a) How many times as acidic did the stream become?
   b) Why would this happen in April?
   c) The mean pH of Lake Huron is 8.2. How many times as acidic was the stream:
   i) before the 3-week period   ii) after the 3-week period?

9. When the pH of the water in a lake falls below 4.7, nearly all species of fish in the lake are deformed or killed. How many times as acidic as clean rainwater, which has a pH of 5.6, is such a lake?

Ⓒ

Other Applications

10. If the temperature is constant, the pressure of the Earth's atmosphere decreases by 5% for every 300 m increase in altitude.
    a) Let P_1 and P_2 represent the pressures at altitudes h_1 and h_2 respectively. Derive an equation which expresses the ratio $\dfrac{P_2}{P_1}$ as an exponential function of the difference in altitudes $h_2 - h_1$.
    b) A jet gains 1000 m in altitude. By what percent did the atmospheric pressure decrease?

11. One of the most remarkable technological trends ever recorded is the growth of the number of components on a silicon chip. Since 1970, the number of components on each chip has quadrupled every three years. It is expected that this level should persist until the early 1990s.
    a) Let N_1 and N_2 represent the numbers of components on a chip in the years t_1 and t_2 respectively. Derive an equation which expresses the ratio $\dfrac{N_2}{N_1}$ as an exponential function of the time difference $t_2 - t_1$.
    b) How did the number of components on a chip in 1985 compare with the number in: i) 1980   ii) 1975   iii) 1970?

 INVESTIGATE

The $\boxed{\text{ln}}$ key on a Calculator

Your calculator should have a key marked $\boxed{\text{ln}}$. This key calculates logarithms of numbers to a base different from 10. Find the base of these logarithms as accurately as you can.

THE MATHEMATICAL MIND

Natural Logarithms

Logarithms were introduced into mathematics almost four hundred years ago by the Scotsman, John Napier. The invention was enthusiastically hailed throughout Europe as a great breakthrough in computation. This was because logarithms can be used to reduce multiplication and division to the simpler operations of addition and subtraction. For example, the law of logarithms, $\log xy = \log x + \log y$, can be applied to multiply two numbers x and y by adding their logarithms. In the past, extensive tables of logarithms were prepared for this purpose. Of course, modern technology has rendered this method of computation obsolete.

Originally, Napier's logarithms had a certain base which was different from 10. These logarithms are called *natural logarithms*.

You can evaluate natural logarithms using the ⌐ln⌐ key on your calculator. For example, key in: 3 ⌐ln⌐ to display 1.0986123. We write ln 3 ≐ 1.098 612 3, and we say "lawn 3 is approximately 1.098 612 3". To explain what this means, we need to know the base of the logarithms. The base of the natural logarithms is always represented by the letter e.

You can use your calculator to find the value of e. Key in: 1 ⌐e^x⌐ or 1 ⌐INV⌐ ⌐ln⌐ to display 2.7182818. Hence, $e ≐ 2.718\ 281\ 8$

Therefore, ln 3 ≐ 1.098 612 3 means that $e^{1.0986123} ≐ 3$, where $e ≐ 2.718\ 281\ 8$.

Natural logarithms are a particular case of logarithms to base a, which were studied earlier in this chapter. Hence, natural logarithms have all the properties of logarithms to base a. This means that we can use natural logarithms to solve problems like those solved earlier.

For example, to solve the equation $e^x = 3.5$ for x, take the natural logarithm of both sides, and write $x \ln e = \ln 3.5$. Since $\ln e = 1$, then $x = \ln 3.5$. Key in: 3.5 ⌐ln⌐ to display 1.2527630. Hence, $x ≐ 1.252\ 763$.

QUESTIONS

1. Use your calculator to evaluate each logarithm. Then write the result in exponential form and check with the calculator.
   a) ln 2   b) ln 4   c) ln 30   d) ln 100
   e) ln 8750   f) ln 0.5   g) ln 0.1   h) ln 0.000 44

2. Solve for x.
   a) $e^x = 5$ b) $e^x = 15$ c) $e^x = 53.9$ d) $e^x = 266$
   e) $e^x = 1$ f) $e^x = 0.25$ g) $e^x = 0.092$ h) $e^x = 0.0003$

3. Solve for x.
   a) $\ln x = 1$ b) $\ln x = 1.6$ c) $\ln x = 3$ d) $\ln x = 4.5$
   e) $\ln x = 0.33$ f) $\ln x = -1$ g) $\ln x = -1.4$ h) $\ln x = -2.2$

4. Write as a single logarithm, and check with your calculator.
   a) $\ln 5 + \ln 3$ b) $\ln 2 + \ln 10$ c) $2 \ln 6$

   d) $\ln 18 - \ln 2$ e) $\ln 21 - \ln 3$ f) $\frac{1}{2} \ln 25$

5. a) Simplify each expression.
      i) $\ln e$ ii) $\ln e^2$ iii) $\ln e^{-3}$ iv) $\ln e^{0.2}$
   b) Based on the results of part a), state a general result.

6. About 200 years ago, at age 15, Carl Friedrich Gauss noticed that the number

   of primes less than a given natural number n can be approximated by $\dfrac{n}{\ln n}$.

   Use this expression to approximate the number of primes less than:
   a) 10   b) 100   c) 1000   d) 10^6 e) 10^9.

7. Although it has never been proved, mathematicians have observed that the number of twin primes less than a given number n is approximately equal to

   $\dfrac{2n}{(\ln n)^2}$. Use this result to approximate the number of twin primes less than:
   a) 10   b) 100   c) 1000   d) 10^6 e) 10^9.

8. It has been proved that the average spacing of the prime numbers near a given natural number n is approximately equal to $\ln n$. For example, the six prime numbers closest to 50, and the successive differences between them are:

   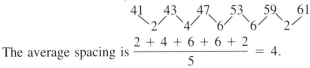

   The average spacing is $\dfrac{2 + 4 + 6 + 6 + 2}{5} = 4$.

   a) Find ln 50, and compare it with the above result.
   b) Check that the average spacing of the six primes closest to:
      i) 100 is approximately ln 100   ii) 150 is approximately ln 150.

MATHEMATICS AROUND US

Applications of Natural Logarithms

In the applications of exponential and logarithmic functions studied in *Sections 7-10* and *7-11*, many different bases were used. For example, in compound interest applications the base depended on the interest rate. In other applications we used bases 2, $\frac{1}{2}$, and 10. It would simplify matters to use the same base every time, and mathematicians have found that there is an advantage to using base e.

For example, consider population growth. In 1987 the world population reached 5 billion, and was increasing at about 1.6% per annum. Hence, an equation expressing the population P billion as a function of time t years relative to 1987 is

$$P = 5(1.016)^t \ldots ①$$

Let's investigate what would happen if we express this equation with base e instead of base 10. To do this, we must write 1.016 as a power of e.

Let $1.016 = e^k$. Then, by definition, $k = \ln 1.016$
Key in: 1.016 $\boxed{\ln}$ to display 0.0158733
To two significant figures, $k \doteq 0.016$
Hence, $1.016 \doteq e^{0.016}$, and equation $①$ can be written as follows.

$$P = 5e^{0.016t}$$

Initial   Growth rate
population

Look at that! The constant in the exponent is 0.016, which is the growth rate. We now see an advantage of using base e. When an exponential function is expressed with base e, the constant in the exponent is the rate of growth. e is the only number with this property. Hence, it is the natural base to use in problems involving exponential growth and decay.

There is another advantage. Notice that the value of k obtained was not exactly 0.016. This slight discrepancy is caused by the way in which e is defined in higher mathematics. The definition assumes that the population grows continuously, and that the new members are not added all at once at the end of the year. In this case, the growth rate is called *instantaneous*. In the above example, the instantaneous rate of growth is 0.015 873 3, whereas the annual rate is 0.016. In some applications the difference may not be significant. Since a rigorous development of instantaneous rates of growth requires calculus, we will ignore its effect.

Example 1. In 1986 the population of Canada was 25.5 million, and was growing at the rate of approximately 1.0% per annum.
  a) Write an equation for the population P million after t years.
  b) Assuming that the growth rate remains constant, use the equation to determine:
    i) the predicted population in the year 2000
    ii) the number of years required for the population to reach 40 million.

Solution. a) The equation is $P = 25.5e^{0.01t}$.
  b) i) The year 2000 is 14 years later than 1986. Hence, substitute 14 for t.
$$P = 25.5e^{0.01(14)}$$
$$= 25.5e^{0.14}$$
$$\doteq 29.331\ 982$$
The population will be approximately 29.3 million in the year 2000.
    ii) Substitute 40 for P.
$$40 = 25.5e^{0.01t}$$
To solve for t, take the natural logarithm of each side.
$$\ln 40 = \ln 25.5 + 0.01t$$
$$t = \frac{\ln 40 - \ln 25.5}{0.01}$$
$$\doteq 45.020\ 100$$
The population will reach 40 million 45 years after 1986, or in the year 2031.

Example 2. In 1987 the world population reached 5 billion. According to United Nations forecasts, the population will reach 6.1 billion in the year 2001. Calculate the average annual rate of growth from 1987 to 2001.

Solution. Let $P = P_0 e^{kt}$
Substitute 5 for P_0, 6.1 for P, and 14 for t.
$$6.1 = 5e^{14k}$$
Take the natural logarithm of each side.
$$\ln 6.1 = \ln 5 + 14k$$
$$k = \frac{\ln 6.1 - \ln 5}{14}$$
$$\doteq 0.014\ 203\ 6$$
Hence, the average annual rate of growth is about 1.42%.

The conventions of writing log x to mean the logarithm to base 10 of x, and ln x to mean the logarithm to base e of x are by no means universal. In higher mathematics, natural logarithms are usually the only logarithms that are used, and log x often refers to the natural logarithm of x. Also, many computer languages use LOG(X) for the natural logarithm function.

QUESTIONS

1. Each equation represents the population P million of a country t years after 1985. State the 1985 population and the growth rate for each country.
   a) Italy $P = 57e^{0.007t}$
   b) Kenya $P = 20e^{0.030t}$
   c) Costa Rica $P = 2.6e^{0.038t}$

2. In 1985 the population of India was 770 million, and was growing at approximately 1.6% per annum.
   a) Write an equation for the population P million after t years, using an exponential function with base e.
   b) Assuming that the growth rate is constant, determine:
      i) the predicted population in 1995
      ii) when the population will reach 1 billion
      iii) when the population was 500 million.

3. When uranium-238 decays, the percent P remaining after t years is given by the equation $P = 100e^{-1.53 \times 10^{-10}t}$.
   a) What percent remains after 10 million years?
   b) Determine the halflife of uranium-238.

4. The altitude of an aircraft can be determined by measuring the air pressure. In the stratosphere (between 12 000 m and 30 000 m) the pressure P kilopascals is expressed as an exponential function of the altitude h metres by the equation $P = 130e^{-0.000155h}$.
   a) What is the altitude if the pressure is 8.5 kPa;   2.5 kPa?
   b) What is the pressure at an altitude of 20 000 m?
   c) Solve the equation for h to obtain an equation expressing the altitude as a logarithmic function of the pressure.

5. A rule of thumb which is used to approximate the time required for an investment to double in value is to divide 70 by the interest rate. For example, if the interest rate is 8%, then an investment will double in approximately $\frac{70}{8}$, or 9 years. Explain why the rule of thumb works.

1. Evaluate.

a) $8^{-\frac{2}{3}}$
b) $27^{\frac{1}{3}}$
c) $32^{\frac{3}{5}}$
d) $\left(\dfrac{1}{125}\right)^{-\frac{2}{3}}$

e) $(2.25)^{1.5}$
f) $\left(\dfrac{16}{81}\right)^{-0.75}$
g) $(0.0144)^0$
h) $(0.0016)^{1.25}$

2. A bacteria culture doubles in size every 8 h. If there are now 1000 bacteria in the culture, how many:
a) will there be in   i) 16 h   ii) 44 h
b) were there   i) 24 h ago   ii) 1.5 days ago?

3. Simplify.

a) $\dfrac{-15x^{-3}y^2 \times 8x^5y^3}{-24x^{-1}y^7}$

b) $\dfrac{18m^2n^{-5} \times (-5m^{-4}n^2)}{-15m^3n^{-4} \times 12m^{-7}n^0}$

c) $(2a^2b)^{-3}(5ab^{-2})^2$

d) $(x^{\frac{1}{2}}y^{-\frac{2}{3}})^3 \times \left(\dfrac{3}{5}x^{-\frac{3}{4}}y^{\frac{1}{3}}\right)^2$

e) $\dfrac{21a^{-\frac{3}{4}}b^{\frac{2}{3}}}{-35a^{-\frac{1}{2}}b}$

f) $\dfrac{6m^{\frac{1}{4}}n^{-\frac{1}{3}} \times 35m^{-\frac{3}{4}}n^{\frac{1}{2}}}{14m^{\frac{1}{2}}n^{\frac{5}{6}} \times 10m^{\frac{3}{2}}n^{-\frac{1}{2}}}$

4. Simplify.

a) $\dfrac{(x^{3a})(x^{-5a})}{x^{-2a}}$

b) $\dfrac{(m^{3x+y})(2m^{x-2y})}{(3m^{-2x+3y})}$

c) $\dfrac{(a^{\frac{x}{4}})(b^{\frac{2x}{3}})^3}{(a^{\frac{3x}{2}})^{-\frac{1}{2}}(b^{\frac{3x}{4}})^2}$

5. How much must be invested at 7.5% interest compounded annually, so that there will be $5600 in 12 years?

6. There are 5400 red ants in a particular colony. If there were 1200 ants in the colony 8 months ago, what is the monthly rate of growth?

7. A diamond ring worth $12 500 increases in value by 12% per year. In how many years will it be worth $50 000?

8. Write in exponential form.

a) $\log 1000 = 3$
b) $\log \sqrt{10} = \dfrac{1}{2}$
c) $\log_3 81 = 4$

9. Write in logarithmic form.
a) $10^4 = 10\ 000$
b) $10^{-3} = 0.001$
c) $5^4 = 625$

10. Solve for x.
a) $\log x = 2$
b) $\log x = -5$
c) $\log_x 64 = 2$
d) $\log_3 x = 3$
e) $\log_5 0.04 = x$
f) $\log_2 x = 5$

11. Write in terms of $\log x$ and $\log y$.
a) $\log (xy^2)$
b) $\log (x\sqrt{y})$
c) $\log (10x^3y^2)$

d) $\log (\sqrt[3]{xy^2})$
e) $\log \left(\dfrac{x}{\sqrt{y}}\right)$
f) $\log \left(\dfrac{x^2}{\sqrt[3]{y}}\right)$

12. Write as a single logarithm.
    a) $\log x + \log y - \log z$
    b) $2 \log x - \log y$
    c) $3 \log x + 5 \log y$
    d) $\dfrac{1}{2} \log x + 3 \log y$
    e) $\log (2x - 3) + \log (y + 5)$
    f) $3 \log (x + y) - \log (x - y)$

13. Express.
    a) 8 as a power of 3
    b) 24 as a power of 6
    c) 12 as a power of 1.3
    d) 0.78 as a power of 2

14. Solve for x. Give the answers to 4 decimal places.
    a) $5^x = 9$
    b) $14^x = 8$
    c) $3^{2x-1} = 25$
    d) $4^{5-x} = 45$
    e) $7^{3-x} = 4$
    f) $8^{5x-2} = 69$
    g) $2^{1-x} = 9^{x+1}$
    h) $5^{3x+1} = 12^{x+4}$

15. Evaluate.

    a) $\log 10\ 000$
    b) $\log_2 16$
    c) $\log_3 243$
    d) $\log_2 \left(\dfrac{1}{8}\right)$

    e) $\log_{\frac{1}{3}} 27$
    f) $\log_{\sqrt{2}} 32$
    g) $\log_5 0.008$
    h) $\log_7 343$

16. Solve and check.
    a) $3 \log x = \log 512 - \log 8$
    b) $\log_2 x + \log_2 (x - 3) = 2$
    c) $\log_{\sqrt{2}} (x - 2) + \log_{\sqrt{2}} (x + 1) = 4$
    d) $\log_6 (x + 3) + \log_6 (x - 2) = 1$

17. Graph each function and its inverse on the same grid.
    a) $y = 3^x$
    b) $y = \log_5 x$
    c) $y = \log_{\frac{1}{3}} x$

18. The halflife of a radioactive substance is 23 days. How long is it until the percent remaining is:
    a) 10%
    b) 3%   ?

19. a) An air filter loses about 0.3% of its effectiveness each day. What is its effectiveness after 145 days as a percent of its initial effectiveness?
    b) The filter should be replaced when its effectiveness has decreased to 20% of its initial value. After how long should it be replaced?

20. In 1951 the UNIVAC computer performed approximately 1000 arithmetic operations per second. Since then, the speed of computers has doubled, on the average, about every 2 years.
    a) Express the number of operations per second N as an exponential function of the time n years since 1951.
    b) Predict when computers will be able to perform a billion operations per second. What assumption are you making?

21. On each bounce a ball rises to 70% of the height from which it fell. Let us agree that, for all practical purposes, the ball stops bouncing when the height to which it rises is only 0.1% of the height from which it was dropped originally. How many bounces will this take?

8 Sequences and Series

The Olympic Games are held every four years. The dates form an arithmetic sequence. Were they held the year you were born? (See Section 8-2 *Example 4*.)

8-1 WHAT IS A SEQUENCE?

"Sequence" and "series" are two words which are often used interchangeably in everyday language. In mathematics, however, they have precise and different meanings. We shall consider sequence first, and series in a later section.

In a sequence, the order in which the events or numbers occur is important. Here are some examples of sequences.

In football, the quarterback uses a sequence of audible signals which informs and directs his team but confuses the defensive team. One such sequence might be:

Red 5 29 6 Blue 4 14 2 Green 3 21 5

This tells player 4 to use play 14 and carry the ball through hole 2.

A computer program is a sequence of instructions. You will find several programs in this text.

IQ tests sometimes contain problems in which a sequence of letters, numbers, or geometric figures is given. The problem is to discover the pattern. Can you determine the next diagram?

In mathematics, many sequences involve numbers. These numbers are called the *terms* of the sequence. Frequently, there is a pattern that is used to write the terms of the sequence.

Example 1. Describe each pattern, and predict the next term.
a) 3, 7, 11, 15, . . .   b) 2, 6, 18, 54, . . .   c) 1, 1, 2, 3, 5, 8, . . .

Solution. a) 3, 7, 11, 15, . . .
Add 4 to the preceding term. The next term is 19.
b) 2, 6, 18, 54, . . .
Multiply the preceding term by 3. The next term is 162.
c) 1, 1, 2, 3, 5, 8, . . .
Add the two preceding terms. The next term is 13.

Several sequences may begin with the same three or four terms. It is therefore necessary, when describing a sequence, to list enough terms to show the pattern which generates the succeeding terms.

The symbols, t_1, t_2, t_3, . . . are used to represent the terms of a sequence. Thus for the sequence of square numbers: 1, 4, 9, 16, . . .

$t_1 = 1$, or 1^2 $t_2 = 4$, or 2^2 $t_3 = 9$, or 3^2 $t_4 = 16$, or 4^2

The *general term* is n^2; that is, $t_n = n^2$

In many sequences, the formula for the general term can be used to generate the terms of the sequence.

Example 2. Write the first four terms and the 10th term for the sequence defined by $t_n = \dfrac{n}{n + 1}$.

Solution. Substitute 1, 2, 3, 4, and 10 for n in the formula for t_n.

$$t_1 = \frac{1}{1 + 1}, \text{ or } \frac{1}{2} \qquad t_2 = \frac{2}{2 + 1}, \text{ or } \frac{2}{3} \qquad t_3 = \frac{3}{3 + 1}, \text{ or } \frac{3}{4}$$

$$t_4 = \frac{4}{4 + 1}, \text{ or } \frac{4}{5} \qquad t_{10} = \frac{10}{10 + 1}, \text{ or } \frac{10}{11}$$

The sequence is: $\dfrac{1}{2}, \dfrac{2}{3}, \dfrac{3}{4}, \dfrac{4}{5}, \ldots, \dfrac{10}{11}, \ldots$

When a few terms of a sequence are given, a formula for the general term can sometimes be found.

Example 3. Describe each sequence and write an expression for the general term t_n.
      a) 101, 102, 103, 104, . . .   b) 2, 4, 6, 8, . . .
      c) 6, 11, 16, 21, 26, . . .   d) 3, 9, 27, 81, . . .
      e) 0, 3, 8, 15, 24, . . .

Solution. a) 101, 102, 103, 104, . . .
         The sequence is the positive integers greater than 100.
         $t_n = 100 + n$
      b) 2, 4, 6, 8, . . .
         The sequence is the even numbers. $t_n = 2n$
      c) 6, 11, 16, 21, 26, . . .
         The sequence is the multiples of 5 increased by 1. $t_n = 5n + 1$
      d) 3, 9, 27, 81, . . .
         The sequence is the powers of 3. $t_n = 3^n$
      e) 0, 3, 8, 15, 24, . . .
         The sequence is the square numbers decreased by 1. $t_n = n^2 - 1$

EXERCISES 8-1

(A)

1. Explain how a sequence is involved in each operation.
    a) Opening a combination lock   b) Dialing a telephone number
    c) Starting a car   d) Writing a computer program
    e) Baking a cake   f) Finding a word in a dictionary

2. What are the next three letters in each sequence?
   a) A C E G I . . .   b) A B D G . . .   c) A B C B D B E B . . .

3. Describe each pattern and predict the next 3 terms.
   a) 2, 4, 6, 8, . . .   b) 1, 3, 9, 27, . . .   c) 5, 10, 15, 20, . . .
   d) 1, 2, 4, 7, 11, . . .   e) 16, 8, 4, 2, . . .   f) 2, 5, 8, 11, . . .

Ⓑ

4. The general term of a sequence is given. Write the first 5 terms.
   a) $t_n = 2n$ b) $t_n = 10 + n$ c) $t_n = 3n$
   d) $t_n = 2^n$ e) $t_n = 10 - n$ f) $t_n = n$

5. Describe each sequence and write an expression for its general term t_n.
   a) 1, 3, 5, 7, 9, . . .   b) 5, 10, 15, 20, 25, . . .
   c) 4, 9, 14, 19, 24, . . .   d) 10, 100, 1000, 10 000, . . .

6. The general term of a sequence is given. Write the first 5 terms.
   a) $t_n = 3n - 2$ b) $t_n = 2^n - 1$ c) $t_n = 21 - 3n$
   d) $t_n = 2n + 5$ e) $t_n = \dfrac{n}{3n + 1}$ f) $t_n = 3 - \dfrac{1}{n}$

7. Find the indicated terms in each sequence.
   a) $t_n = 10 + 2n$, t_7 and t_{12} b) $t_n = 6n + 5$, t_2 and t_8
   c) $t_n = n^2 - 5$, t_4 and t_9 d) $t_n = (-2)^n$, t_2 and t_5

8. Which of the general terms listed is the general term for each sequence?
   i) $t_n = 5n - 1$ ii) $t_n = 22 - 2n$ iii) $t_n = 10^{n-1}$
   iv) $t_n = 2n - 20$ v) $t_n = 4n - 3$ vi) $t_n = 2(4^{n-1})$
   a) 1, 5, 9, 13, . . .   b) 20, 18, 16, 14, . . .
   c) 2, 8, 32, 128, . . .   d) 1, 10, 100, 1000, . . .

9. Find an expression for the general term of each sequence.
   a) 2, 4, 6, 8, 10, . . .   b) 5, 7, 9, 11, 13, . . .
   c) −3, −1, 1, 3, 5, . . .   d) 2, 4, 8, 16, 32, . . .
   e) 1, 3, 7, 15, 31, . . .   f) 16, 13, 10, 7, 4, . . .
   g) $1, \dfrac{2}{3}, \dfrac{3}{5}, \dfrac{4}{7}, \dfrac{5}{9}, \ldots$ h) $\dfrac{1}{2}, \dfrac{2}{3}, \dfrac{3}{4}, \dfrac{4}{5}, \dfrac{5}{6}, \ldots$

10. Create as many different patterns as you can that start with 1, 2, 3, . . .

Ⓒ

11. Is each statement a correct definition of a sequence of numbers?
    a) A sequence is a set of numbers.
    b) A sequence is a set of numbers written in a definite order.
    c) A sequence is a function with domain the real numbers.
    d) A sequence is a function with domain the positive integers.

12. Write the next 2 terms of each sequence.
    a) Power functions: $f(x) = x^2$, $f(x) = x^3$, $f(x) = x^4$, . . .
    b) Polynomial functions: $f(x) = ax + b$, $f(x) = ax^2 + bx + c$,
       $f(x) = ax^3 + bx^2 + cx + d$, . . .

13. The least number of diagonals needed to divide a sequence of regular polygons into triangles forms a sequence.
    a) List the next three terms of the sequence shown for the number of diagonals.
    b) Find a formula for the general term.

Regular Polygon	Number of		Angle
	sides	diagonals	
Equilateral triangle	3	0	60°
Square	4	1	90°
Pentagon	5	2	108°

14. The angle measures in a sequence of regular polygons also form a sequence.
    a) List the next three terms of the sequence shown in *Exercise 13*.
    b) Find a formula for the general term.

15. The diagram shows a system of one-way streets.
    a) How many different routes are there from A:
       i) to B   ii) to C   iii) to D   iv) to E?
    b) Explain how you could find the number of routes if there were more squares in the diagram.

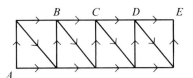

INVESTIGATE

These sequences all start with the same 3 terms. What is the pattern in each sequence?
a) 2, 3, 5, 7, 11, 13, . . .   b) 2, 3, 5, 8, 12, 17, . . .
c) 2, 3, 5, 8, 13, 21, . . .   d) 2, 3, 5, 10, 20, 40, . . .
e) 2, 3, 5, 6, 7, 8, 10, . . .   f) 2, 3, 5, 14, 69, 965, . . .

INVESTIGATE

The first 6 terms of this sequence are prime; the next term is not. Find other sequences like this. Write a report of your findings.
7,   37,   337,   3337,   33 337,   333 337,   3 333 337, . . .

8-2 ARITHMETIC SEQUENCES

Throughout recorded history, comets have been associated with significant events such as famine, plague, and floods. In 1705, the English astronomer, Edmund Halley, noticed striking similarities in the records of major comets which had appeared in 1531, 1607, and 1682. He noticed also that these dates were almost the same number of years apart.

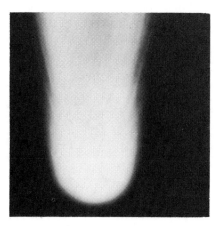

1531   1607   1682

76 years   75 years

Halley concluded that the three appearances represented return visits of the same comet, which was in an extremely elongated orbit around the sun. He predicted it would return in 1758. The comet, now known as Halley's comet, returned in 1759, and records have since been found for every appearance of the comet since 239 B.C.

If it were not for the gravitational influence of the planets, the comet would always reappear every 77 years.

1531   1608   1685   1762 . . .

+ 77   + 77   + 77

The sequence of numbers 1531, 1608, 1685, 1762, . . . is an example of an *arithmetic sequence*. Each successive term is formed by adding the same number, 77. In an arithmetic sequence, the difference between consecutive terms is a constant. This constant is called the *common difference*.

These are arithmetic sequences:

3, 7, 11, 15, . . .	common difference 4
9, 4, -1, -6, . . .	common difference -5
1, 1.25, 1.5, 1.75, 2, . . .	common difference 0.25
a, $a + d$, $a + 2d$, $a + 3d$, . . .	common difference d

If the first term and the common difference of an arithmetic sequence are known, any other term can be found.

Example 1. In the arithmetic sequence 2, 5, 8, . . ., find each term.
  a) t_5 b) t_{20} c) t_n

Solution. By inspection, the common difference is 3.
  a) t_5 can be found by extending the sequence two more terms.

   2, 5, 8, 11, 14
   t_5 is 14.

t_5 can also be found by adding 4 differences to the first term:

$2 + 3 + 3 + 3 + 3 = 14$

The number of differences is
1 less than the term number.

b) To find t_{20}, add 19 differences to the first term.

$$t_{20} = 2 + (19)3$$
$$= 2 + 57$$
$$= 59$$

c) An expression for t_n can be found by adding $(n - 1)$ differences to the first term.

$$t_n = 2 + (n - 1)3$$
$$= 2 + 3n - 3$$
$$= 3n - 1$$

The general arithmetic sequence has the first term represented by a and the common difference by d. The first few terms are shown here.

$$t_1 = a$$
$$t_2 = a + d$$
$$t_3 = a + 2d$$
$$t_4 = a + 3d$$

$$\cdot \qquad \cdot$$
$$\cdot \qquad \cdot$$
$$\cdot \qquad \cdot$$

$$t_n = a + (n - 1)d$$

The general term of an arithmetic sequence is given by:
$t_n = a + (n - 1)d$,
where a is the first term, n is the number of the term, and d is the common difference.

Example 2. Given the arithmetic sequence 8, 14, 20, 26, . . .
a) Find the 20th term. b) Which term is 236?

Solution. By inspection, the common difference is 6.
Use the formula. $t_n = a + (n - 1)d$
a) $t_{20} = 8 + (20 - 1)6$
$\qquad = 8 + (19)6$
$\qquad = 122$
The 20th term is 122.
b) $236 = 8 + (n - 1)6$
$\qquad = 2 + 6n$
$\quad 6n = 234$
$\quad\ n = 39$
236 is the 39th term of the sequence.

Given the position of any two terms of an arithmetic sequence, the first term and the common difference can be found.

Example 3. In an arithmetic sequence, the third term is 8 and the tenth term is 4.5. Find the sequence.

Solution. Let the first term be a and the common difference d.

Since the third term is 8: $8 = a + 2d$ . . . ①

Since the tenth term is 4.5: $4.5 = a + 9d$ . . . ②

Solve equations ① and ② to find a and d.

Subtract ② from ①. $3.5 = -7d$

$d = -0.5$

Substitute -0.5 for d in ①. $8 = a + 2(-0.5)$

$a = 9$

The first term is 9 and the common difference is -0.5.
The sequence is 9, 8.5, 8, 7.5, . . .

Example 4. The Olympic Games are held every four years. The dates form an arithmetic sequence. Were they held the year you were born?

Solution. The Olympic Games were held in Seoul, Korea, in 1988. Write the sequence 1988, 1984, 1980, 1976, . . . as far as necessary to determine if they were held in the year you were born.

EXERCISES 8-2

(A)

1. Is each sequence arithmetic? If it is, what is the common difference?
   a) 3, 5, 9, 15, 23, . . .
   b) $-4, -1, 2, 5, 8, 11, . . .$
   c) 2, 1, 0, $-1, -2, . . .$
   d) $1, \frac{1}{2}, \frac{1}{3}, \frac{1}{4}, . . .$
   e) 4, 4, 4, 4, 4, . . .
   f) 3, 11, 19, 27, 35, . . .

2. State the common difference and list the next 3 terms of each arithmetic sequence.
   a) 1, 4, 7, 10, . . .
   b) $-5, -1, 3, 7, . . .$
   c) 16, 14, 12, 10, . . .
   d) $-2, -8, -14, -20, . . .$
   e) 2, 7, 12, 17, . . .
   f) 6, 3, 0, $-3, . . .$

3. Write the first 5 terms of each arithmetic sequence with the given values of a and d.
   a) $a = 2, d = 3$
   b) $a = 7, d = 4$
   c) $a = -1, d = -3$
   d) $a = 12, d = -4$
   e) $a = -8, d = 5$
   f) $a = 25, d = -5$

(B)

4. In the arithmetic sequence 3, 5, 7, 9, . . ., find each term.
   a) t_8
   b) t_{25}
   c) t_n

5. In the arithmetic sequence 11, 8, 5, 2, . . ., find each term.
   a) t_6
   b) t_{20}
   c) t_n

6. The disappearance of the dinosaurs about 65 million years ago is one of the great mysteries of science. Scientists have recently found that mass extinctions of the Earth's creatures are separated by periods of roughly 26 million years.
   a) About when did other mass extinctions occur?
   b) If the theory is correct, estimate when the next mass extinction should occur.

7. The years in which the Olympic Games are held form an arithmetic sequence. The sequence since 1968 is 1968, 1972, 1976, 1980, 1984, 1988, . . .
   a) Will the Olympic Games be held: i) in 1998   ii) in 2000?
   b) The modern Olympics began in 1896. Explain why the 1988 Olympics, in Seoul, is referred to as the XXIV Olympiad.

8. Which of the general terms listed is the general term of each arithmetic sequence?
   i) $t_n = 3 + 2n$ ii) $t_n = 2 + 3n$ iii) $t_n = 1 + 4n$
   iv) $t_n = 20 - 3n$ v) $t_n = 12 - 2n$ vi) $t_n = 1 + 3n$
       a) 5, 8, 11, 14, . . .   b) 17, 14, 11, 8, . . .
       c) 5, 7, 9, 11, . . .   d) 10, 8, 6, 4, . . .

9. Write the first 5 terms of each arithmetic sequence defined by the given terms.
   a) $t_1 = 3$, $t_2 = 10$ b) $t_1 = -3$, $t_2 = 1$ c) $t_n = 2n + 3$
   d) $t_n = -5n + 21$ e) $t_n = -7 + 3n$ f) $t_n = -4n - 6$

10. For the arithmetic sequence 2, 5, 8, 11, 14, . . ., find:
    a) t_{24} and t_{35} b) which term is 152.

11. For the arithmetic sequence -8, -3, 2, 7, . . ., find:
    a) t_{17} and t_{43} b) which term is 322.

12. For each arithmetic sequence, write a formula for t_n and use it to find each indicated term.
    a) 1, 5, 9, 13, . . ., t_{17} b) 3, 6, 9, 12, . . ., t_{21}
    c) -4, 1, 6, 11, . . ., t_{13} d) 41, 35, 29, 23, . . ., t_{18}
    e) -2, -5, -8, -11, . . ., t_{10} f) 9, 1, -7, -15, . . ., t_{46}

13. In an arithmetic sequence, the third term is 11 and the eighth term is 46. Find the first 2 terms of the sequence.

14. The 10th term of an arithmetic sequence is 39. If the first term is 3, find the next 3 terms.

15. The 8th term of an arithmetic sequence is 45. If the common difference is -6, find the first 3 terms.

16. In an arithmetic sequence, the 11th term is 53 and the sum of the 5th and 7th terms is 56. Find the first 3 terms of the sequence.

17. The sum of the first 2 terms of an arithmetic sequence is 15, and the sum of the next 2 terms is 43. Find the first 3 terms of the sequence.

18. How many terms are in each sequence?
    a) 2, 6, 10, . . ., 94   b) -9, -4, 1, . . ., 171
    c) 4, 15, 26, . . ., 213   d) 18, 13, 8, . . ., -102

19. Find the missing terms in each arithmetic sequence.
    a) $-, 9, 16, -, -$
    b) $-, -, 8, 2, -$
    c) $12, -, 22, -, -$
    d) $3, -, -, 24, -$
    e) $-, 4, -, -, -8$
    f) $15, -, -, -, -21$

20. If $5 + x, 8$, and $1 + 2x$ are consecutive terms in an arithmetic sequence, find x.

21. If $2x + y + 3, 4x - y - 2$, and $x + 5y - 8$ are consecutive terms in an arithmetic sequence, find the relation between x and y.

22. Every appearance of Halley's comet has been recorded since 239 B.C. How many times has it been recorded?

Ⓒ

23. The sum of the first three terms of an arithmetic sequence is 12. The sum of their squares is 66. Find the fourth term.

24. Find an expression for the general term of each sequence. Is the sequence arithmetic?
    a) $1 \times 1, 3 \times 4, 5 \times 7, 7 \times 10, \ldots$
    b) $2 \times 3, 4 \times 6, 6 \times 9, 8 \times 12, \ldots$
    c) $\dfrac{1}{3}, \dfrac{2}{5}, \dfrac{3}{7}, \dfrac{4}{9}, \ldots$
    d) $\dfrac{1 \times 3}{2 \times 4}, \dfrac{3 \times 5}{4 \times 6}, \dfrac{5 \times 7}{6 \times 8}, \dfrac{7 \times 9}{8 \times 10}, \ldots$

25. The diagram shows a pattern of positive integers in five columns. If the pattern is continued, in which columns will these numbers appear?
    a) 49   b) 117
    c) 301   d) 8725

Columns				
1	**2**	**3**	**4**	**5**
1		2		3
	5		4	
6		7		8
	10		9	
11		12		13
			14	

26. The diagram shows a pattern of positive integers in four rows. If the pattern is continued:
    a) what are the first ten numbers in row 3
    b) in which row will these numbers appear?
       i) 75   ii)   93
       iii) 259   iv) 3267

Rows					
1	1	8	9	16	17
2	2	7	10	15	18
3	3	6	11	14	
4	4	5	12	13	

 INVESTIGATE

Find, if possible, three or more perfect squares in arithmetic sequence.

COMPUTER POWER

Prime Sequences

Prime numbers have always interested mathematicians. This interest has increased in recent years because many investigations can now be carried out with a computer. One of these investigations concerns prime numbers which are in arithmetic sequence; 11, 17, 23, 29 is an example. In this sequence, $a = 11$ and $d = 6$

In 1983, Paul A. Pritchard of Cornell University programmed a computer to find, in its free time, long arithmetic sequences of prime numbers. After about a month, the longest sequence the computer had found was one with 18 terms. The first term of this sequence is 107 928 278 317 and the common difference is 9 922 782 870. At the time, this was the longest known arithmetic sequence of primes.

1. Using primes less than 100, find some that are in arithmetic sequence.

2. The following program can be used to find primes in arithmetic sequence.

```
LABEL 140,150,200;
VAR
   CH : CHAR;
   A,D : REAL;
   I : INTEGER;
BEGIN  { PRIME SEQUENCES }
       REPEAT
          WRITELN('WHAT IS THE FIRST NUMBER? ');
          READ(A); WRITELN;
          WRITELN('WHAT IS THE COMMON DIFFERENCE? ');
          READ(D); WRITELN;
          IF A = 3 THEN BEGIN
             WRITELN(A:5:0);
             A := A + D;
          END;
```

```
140:    IF (A > 2) AND ((A / 2.0) = TRUNC(A / 2.0)) THEN GOTO
        200;
        {IF (A / 2.0) = INT(A / 2.0) THEN GOTO 200;}
        I := 3;
150:    IF ABS(A / I - TRUNC(A / I)) < 0.0000001 THEN GOTO
        200;
        I := I + 2;
        IF I < TRUNC(SQRT(A)) THEN GOTO 150;
        WRITELN(A:5:0);
        A := A + D;
        GOTO 140;
200:    WRITELN(A:5:0,' IS COMPOSITE');
        WRITELN('PRESS S TO STOP, C TO CONTINUE');
        CH := READKEY;
      UNTIL CH = CHR(83);
END.
```

   a) Run the program several times and try to find sequences with 6 or more terms.
   b) What is the longest arithmetic sequence of primes you can find?

3. The first term of an arithmetic sequence of 7 primes is less than 10. Find the sequence if its common difference is a multiple of 30 and less than 200.

4. Primes which differ by 2, such as 29 and 31, are called twin primes.
   a) Find two arithmetic sequences of twin primes in primes less than 100.
   b) Two long arithmetic sequences of twin primes have first terms less than 50 and common differences that are multiples of 210. Find the sequences.

The next two questions concern the arithmetic sequence of 18 primes
found by the computer in Paul Pritchard's investigation.

5. Find the last prime in the longest known arithmetic sequence of primes.

6. Express the common difference 9 922 782 870 as a product of prime factors. Do the same with the suggested differences given above. The results may suggest possible differences to use in your search for long arithmetic sequences of primes.

8-3 GEOMETRIC SEQUENCES

More potatoes are grown on Prince Edward Island than in any other province of Canada. The industry is so large that an entire farm is devoted to producing the seed potatoes for the other farms in the province.

Part of the eye of a potato is allowed to grow and is then cut to produce six more. When this is done again and again, the number of potato plants increases according to this pattern.

$$1, \quad 6, \quad 36, \quad 216, \quad 1296, \quad 7776, \quad 46\,656, \quad 279\,936, \ldots$$
$$\times 6 \quad \times 6 \quad \times 6 \quad \times 6 \quad \times 6 \quad \times 6 \quad \times 6$$

This sequence of numbers is an example of a *geometric sequence*. Each successive term is formed by multiplying by the same number, 6. In a geometric sequence, the ratio of consecutive terms is a constant. This constant is called the *common ratio*.

These are geometric sequences.

$2, 10, 50, 250, \ldots$	common ratio 5
$12, 6, 3, 1.5, 0.75, \ldots$	common ratio $\frac{1}{2}$
$3, -12, 48, -192, \ldots$	common ratio -4
$a, ar, ar^2, ar^3, \ldots$	common ratio r

Each successive term is formed by multiplying by the same number, the common ratio.

If the first term and the common ratio of a geometric sequence are known, any other term can be found.

Example 1. In the geometric sequence 5, 15, 45, . . ., find each term.
   a) t_5 b) t_{10} c) t_n

Solution. By inspection, the common ratio is 3.
   a) t_5 can be found by extending the sequence.
   5, 15, 45, 135, 405, . . .
   t_5 is 405.
   t_5 can also be found by multiplying the first term successively by 3, four times.

   $5 \times 3 \times 3 \times 3 \times 3 = 405$ —— The number of factors is 1 less than the term number.

   b) Similarly, t_{10} is found by multiplying the first term successively by 3, nine times.
   $$5 \times 3 \times 3 \times \ldots \times 3 = 5(3)^9$$
   $$= 98\,415$$

c) An expression for t_n can be found by multiplying the first term successively by $(n - 1)$ factors of 3.
$$t_n = 5(3)^{n-1}$$

The general geometric sequence has its first term represented by a and the common ratio by r. The first few terms are shown here.

$$t_1 = a$$
$$t_2 = ar$$
$$t_3 = ar^2$$
$$t_4 = ar^3$$

$$\vdots \qquad \vdots$$

$$t_n = ar^{n-1}$$

The general term of a geometric sequence is given by:
$$t_n = ar^{n-1},$$
where a is the first term, n is the number of the term, and r is the common ratio.

Example 2.   Given the geometric sequence 3, 6, 12, 24, . . .,
  a) Find the 14th term.   b) Which term is 384?

Solution.   Use the formula. $t_n = ar^{n-1}$
  a) $t_{14} = 3(2)^{13}$ $a = 3$
        $= 3(8192)$ $r = 2$
        $= 24\ 576$ $n = 14$
  The 14th term is 24 576.
  b) $384 = 3(2)^{n-1}$ $a = 3$
     $128 = 2^{n-1}$ $r = 2$
     Since $128 = 2^7$, $t_n = 384$
       $n - 1 = 7$
          $n = 8$
  384 is the 8th term of the sequence.

If any two terms of a geometric sequence are known, the first term and the common ratio can be found.

Example 3.   In a geometric sequence, the 3rd term is 20 and the 6th term is -540. Find the first six terms.

Solution.   Let the first term be a and the common ratio be r.
  Since the 3rd term is 20: $ar^2 = 20$ . . . ①
  Since the 6th term is -540: $ar^5 = -540$ . . . ②
  To solve this system, divide each side of equation ② by the corresponding side of equation ①.

$$\frac{ar^5}{ar^2} = \frac{-540}{20}$$
$$r^3 = -27$$
$$r = -3$$

Substitute -3 for r in ①. $\quad a(-3)^2 = 20$
$$a = \frac{20}{9}$$

The first term is $\frac{20}{9}$ and the common ratio is -3.

The first six terms of the sequence are $\frac{20}{9}$, $-\frac{20}{3}$, 20, -60, 180, -540.

If a, x, and b are in geometric sequence, then x is the *geometric mean* of a and b.

Example 4. Between 4 and 324, insert:
   a) one geometric mean   b) three geometric means.

Solution. a) Let the geometric mean be x. Then 4, x, and 324 are in geometric sequence.
   Hence, $\frac{x}{4} = \frac{324}{x}$
   $$x^2 = 324(4)$$
   $$= 1296$$
   $$x = \pm 36$$
   The geometric mean of 4 and 324 is 36 or -36.

   b) We need two additional geometric means, y and z, such that 4, y, ± 36, z, 324 form a geometric sequence. But there are no real values of y and z for which 4, y, -36, z, 324 form a geometric sequence. Hence, we consider the sequence 4, y, 36, z, 324.
   Then $\frac{y}{4} = \frac{36}{y}$ and $\frac{z}{36} = \frac{324}{z}$
   $$y = \pm 12 \qquad z = \pm 108$$

   Hence, the three geometric means are 12, 36, 108 or -12, 36, -108.

EXERCISES 8-3

Ⓐ

1. Is each sequence geometric? If it is, what is the common ratio?
   a) 1, 2, 4, 8, 16, . . .   b) 2, 4, 6, 10, 16, . . .
   c) 4, -2, 1, $-\frac{1}{2}$, $\frac{1}{4}$, . . .   d) 0.6, 0.06, 0.006, . . .
   e) -3, 2, 7, 12, 17, . . .   f) 1, $-\frac{1}{3}$, $\frac{1}{9}$, $-\frac{1}{27}$, . . .

2. State the common ratio and list the next 3 terms of each geometric sequence.

   a) 1, 3, 9, 27, . . .

   b) 5, − 15, 45, − 135, . . .

   c) 3, 6, 12, 24, . . .

   d) $6, 2, \frac{2}{3}, \frac{2}{9}, . . .$

   e) $36, 9, \frac{9}{4}, \frac{9}{16}, . . .$

   f) $\frac{1}{2}, -2, 8, -32, . . .$

3. Write the first 5 terms of each geometric sequence with the given values of *a* and *r*.

   a) $a = 2, r = 3$

   b) $a = 5, r = 2$

   c) $a = 3, r = -5$

   d) $a = 60, r = \frac{1}{2}$

   e) $a = -4, r = -2$

   f) $a = 8, r = 3$

Ⓑ

4. In the geometric sequence 3, 6, 12, ..., find each term.

   a) t_6

   b) t_{11}

   c) t_n

5. Which of the general terms listed is the general term for each geometric sequence?

   i) $5(2)^{n-1}$

   ii) $2(5)^{n-1}$

   iii) $3(3)^{n-1}$

   iv) $3(-4)^{n-1}$

   v) $4(-3)^{n-1}$

   vi) $5(3)^{n-1}$

   a) 2, 10, 50, . . .

   b) 3, − 12, 48, . . .

   c) 3, 9, 27, . . .

   d) 5, 15, 45, . . .

6. Is each sequence geometric?

   a) Camera shutter speeds (seconds): $1, \frac{1}{2}, \frac{1}{4}, \frac{1}{8}, \frac{1}{15}, \frac{1}{30}, \frac{1}{60}, . . .$

   b) Frequencies of a piano's A notes in hertz (cycles per second):
      27.5, 55, 110, 220, 440, 880, 1760, 3520

   c)

Type of sediment	Grain size (mm)
Very fine sand	$\frac{1}{16} - \frac{1}{8}$
Fine sand	$\frac{1}{8} - \frac{1}{4}$
Medium sand	$\frac{1}{4} - \frac{1}{2}$
Coarse sand	$\frac{1}{2} - 1$
Very coarse sand	1 − 2
Granules	2 − 4
Pebbles	4 − 64
Cobbles	64 − 256

d) The electromagnetic spectrum

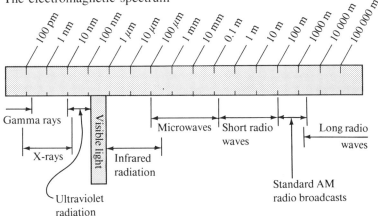

7. Find a geometric mean for each pair of numbers.
   a) 3, 48
   b) 4, 64
   c) 5, 80
   d) 2, 1250

8. Insert three geometric means between each pair of numbers in *Exercise 7.*

9. Write the first 5 terms of each geometric sequence defined by the given terms.
   a) $t_1 = 2, t_2 = -6$
   b) $t_1 = 20, t_2 = 10$
   c) $t_n = 3(2)^{n-1}$
   d) $t_n = 7(3)^{n-1}$
   e) $t_n = \frac{1}{8}(4)^{n-1}$
   f) $t_n = -2(-5)^{n-1}$

10. For each geometric sequence, write a formula for t_n and use it to find each indicated term.
    a) 2, 4, 8, 16, . . . , t_{10}
    b) 5, 10, 20, 40, . . . , t_{13}
    c) $-3, 15, -75, 375, \ldots, t_8$
    d) $12, 6, 3, \frac{3}{2}, \ldots, t_{12}$
    e) $6, -2, \frac{2}{3}, -\frac{2}{9}, \ldots, t_9$
    f) 3, 18, 108, 648, . . . , t_7

11. For the geometric sequence 3, 12, 48, 192, . . ., find:
    a) the 9th term
    b) which term is 12 288.

12. Find the first 5 terms of the geometric sequence with the 3rd term 18 and the 7th term 1458.

13. Find the first 4 terms of the geometric sequence with the 5th term 1536 and the 10th term 48.

14. Find the missing terms in each geometric sequence.
    a) 4, _, 16, _
    b) 2, 12, _, _
    c) 3, _, 12, _
    d) _, 5, _, 125
    e) _, _, 2, 1
    f) 3, _, _, 375

15. In a geometric sequence, $t_3 = 20$ and $t_6 = 1280$; find the first 2 terms of the sequence.

16. In a geometric sequence, $t_1 = 2$ and $t_5 = 162$; find the common ratio and the terms between t_1 and t_5.

17. Write the geometric sequence formed if, between 2 and 1458:
    a) two geometric means are inserted   b) five geometric means are inserted.

18. How many terms are in each sequence?

    a) 2, 6, 18, . . ., 486

    b) $12, 4, \frac{4}{3}, \ldots, \frac{4}{729}$

    c) 3, 6, 12, . . ., 3072

    d) $64, 32, 16, \ldots, \frac{1}{256}$

19. If $x - 3$, $x + 1$, and $4x - 2$ are consecutive terms in a geometric sequence, find x.

20. If $m + 2$, $m + 4$, and $2m + 11$ are consecutive terms in a geometric sequence, find m.

21. The population of a city is 16 million and is increasing at about 4% per year. Show that the yearly populations form a geometric sequence and predict the population in 10 years.

Ⓒ

22. The arithmetic mean of two numbers is 65. The geometric mean of the same two numbers is 25. Find the numbers.

23. The sum of the first 2 terms of a geometric sequence is 3. The sum of the next 2 terms is $\frac{4}{3}$. Find the first 4 terms of the sequence.

24. In a geometric sequence, $t_3 + t_4 = 36$, and $t_4 + t_5 = 108$; find the first 5 terms of the sequence.

25. In a geometric sequence, $t_1 + t_2 + t_3 = 3$, and $t_3 + t_4 + t_5 = 12$; find the first 5 terms of the sequence.

26. Show that the arithmetic mean of two numbers is always greater than the geometric mean of those two numbers.

27. A geometric sequence has positive terms. The sum of the first 3 terms of a geometric sequence is 13. The sum of the reciprocals of the first 3 terms is $\frac{13}{9}$. Find the first 3 terms of the sequence.

28. The aperture markings on a camera lens are:
    1.4   2   2.8   4   5.6   8   11   16   22
    They form a geometric sequence but the numbers have been rounded for convenience. Determine the common ratio as accurately as possible.

29. The following sequences start with the same two terms.
    Arithmetic sequence: 3, 12, 21, . . . ①
    Geometric sequence: 3, 12, 48 . . . ②
    a) Show that t_3 of ② is the same as t_6 of ①.
    b) Which term in ① is the same as t_4 in ②?
    c) Show that every term in the geometric sequence is also a term in the arithmetic sequence.

8-4 RECURSIVE DEFINITION OF A SEQUENCE

In the arithmetic sequence 5, 7, 9, 11, . . ., the first term is 5 and every term after the first is 2 greater than the preceding term. Hence, the sequence is defined by these two equations: $t_1 = 5$, $t_n = t_{n-1} + 2$, $n > 1$. Such a definition of a sequence is called a *recursive definition*.

Example 1. Write the first four terms of the sequence defined by
$t_1 = 3$, $t_n = 2t_{n-1} + 1$, $n > 1$.

Solution.
$t_1 = 3$ $\quad$ $t_2 = 2t_1 + 1$ $\quad$ $t_3 = 2t_2 + 1$ $\quad$ $t_4 = 2t_3 + 1$
$\qquad\qquad\qquad = 2(3) + 1$ $\qquad = 2(7) + 1$ $\qquad = 2(15) + 1$
$\qquad\qquad\qquad = 7$ $\qquad\qquad = 15$ $\qquad\qquad = 31$

The first four terms are 3, 7, 15, 31.

Example 2. Write a recursive definition for the geometric sequence 2, 6, 18, . . .

Solution. The first term is 2. Each term after the first is obtained by multiplying the preceding term by 3. Hence, the recursive definition is
$t_1 = 2$, $t_n = 3t_{n-1}$, $n > 1$.

A recursive definition consists of two parts. The first part specifies the first term(s). The second part indicates how each term is calculated from preceding term(s).

EXERCISES 8-4

1. Write the first 4 terms of each sequence.
   a) $t_1 = 5$, $t_n = t_{n-1} - 3$, $n > 1$
   b) $t_1 = \frac{1}{2}$, $t_n = 2t_{n-1}$, $n > 1$
   c) $t_1 = -2$, $t_n = 1 - t_{n-1}$, $n > 1$
   d) $t_1 = 1$, $t_n = 10t_{n-1} + 1$, $n > 1$
   e) $t_1 = 1$, $t_2 = 2$, $t_n = t_{n-1} + t_{n-2}$, $n > 2$

(B)

2. Write a recursive definition for each sequence.
   a) 1, 6, 11, 16, . . .
   b) -2, 6, -18, 54, . . .
   c) 1, 3, 7, 15, . . .
   d) 1, 4, 9, 16, . . .
   e) 1, 1, 2, 3, 5, 8, 13, . . .
   f) 1, 2, 3, 6, 11, 20, . . .

3. Show that the recursive definition of a sequence is not necessarily unique. That is, give an example of two different recursive definitions which describe the same sequence.

8-5 WHAT IS A SERIES?

In mathematics, sequences and series have separate and distinct meanings. The following examples illustrate how they differ.

These are sequences.	These are series.
1, 2, 3, 4, 5, . . .	$1 + 2 + 3 + 4 + 5 + . . .$
2, 4, 8, 16, 32, . . .	$2 + 4 + 8 + 16 + 32 + . . .$
1, 0.1, 0.01, 0.001, . . .	$1 + 0.1 + 0.01 + 0.001 + . . .$
$1, \frac{1}{2}, \frac{1}{3}, \frac{1}{4}, \frac{1}{5}, . . .$	$1 + \frac{1}{2} + \frac{1}{3} + \frac{1}{4} + \frac{1}{5} + . . .$

A series is obtained from a sequence by writing addition signs between the terms to indicate that the terms are to be added. A *series* is the indicated sum of the terms of a sequence.

The symbols $S_1, S_2, S_3, . . ., S_n$ are used to represent the sums of the terms of a series. S_3 means the sum of the first three terms and S_n denotes the sum of the first n terms. We can sometimes find an expression for the first n terms of a series by looking for a pattern.

Example 1. Find a possible expression for the sum of the first n terms of the series of odd numbers $1 + 3 + 5 + . . . + (2n - 1)$.

Solution. Evaluate $S_1, S_2, S_3, . . .$

The first term, S_1:	1, or 1^2
Sum of first two terms, S_2:	$1 + 3 = 4$, or 2^2
Sum of first three terms, S_3:	$1 + 3 + 5 = 9$, or 3^2
Sum of first four terms, S_4:	$1 + 3 + 5 + 7 = 16$, or 4^2

The resulting numbers are all perfect squares. This pattern suggests that a possible expression for the sum of the first n terms is $S_n = n^2$.

In *Example 1*, the expression is called ''possible'' because there is no guarantee that the pattern of perfect squares will continue to hold if more than four terms of the series are added.

In the same example, the values of S_3 and S_4 could have been found with fewer additions. For example, S_4 is the sum of the first three terms and the fourth term.

$$S_4 = S_3 + t_4$$
$$= 9 + 7$$
$$= 16$$

If an expression for the sum of the first n terms of a series is known, the series can easily be found.

Example 2. Given $S_n = 4n^2 + n$

        a) Find the first four terms of the series.

        b) Find the nth term of the series.

Solution.   a) Substitute 1, 2, 3, 4, in turn, in $S_n = 4n^2 + n$ to find the values of
S_1, S_2, S_3, and S_4.

$S_1 = 4(1)^2 + 1$, or 5

$t_1 = 5$

$S_2 = 4(2)^2 + 2$, or 18

Since $5 + t_2 = 18$, $t_2 = 18 - 5$, or 13

$S_3 = 4(3)^2 + 3$, or 39

Since $18 + t_3 = 39$, $t_3 = 39 - 18$, or 21

$S_4 = 4(4)^2 + 4$, or 68

Since $39 + t_4 = 68$, $t_4 = 68 - 39$, or 29

The first four terms of the series are $5 + 13 + 21 + 29$.

    b) The terms of the series appear to form an arithmetic sequence with
first term 5 and common difference 8. Therefore, the nth term is

$$t_n = a + (n - 1)d$$
$$= 5 + (n - 1)8$$
$$= 8n - 3$$

In *Example 2b*, the general term can also be found by subtracting
the sum of $(n - 1)$ terms from the sum of n terms.

$$t_n = S_n - S_{n-1}$$

$$= [4n^2 + n] - [4(n - 1)^2 + (n - 1)]$$

$$= [4n^2 + n] - [4n^2 - 8n + 4 + n - 1]$$

$$= 8n - 3$$

$t_1 + t_2 + t_3 + \ldots t_{n-1} + t_n$

$\leftarrow S_{n-1} \longrightarrow$

$\leftarrow S_n \longrightarrow$

In any series
- The general term is the difference between the sum of the
first n terms and the sum of the first $(n - 1)$ terms.
$$t_n = S_n - S_{n-1} \quad (n > 1)$$
- The first term is the same as S_1. $t_1 = S_1$

Example 3. Given $\dfrac{1}{1 \times 3} + \dfrac{1}{3 \times 5} + \dfrac{1}{5 \times 7} + \dfrac{1}{7 \times 9} + \ldots + \dfrac{1}{(2n - 1)(2n + 1)}$

    a) Find S_1, S_2, and S_3 for this series, and from the pattern predict S_4.

    b) Find a possible expression for S_n.

Solution.   a) $S_1 = \dfrac{1}{3}$ $S_3 = S_2 + \dfrac{1}{35}$

$S_2 = \dfrac{1}{3} + \dfrac{1}{15}$ $= \dfrac{2}{5} + \dfrac{1}{35}$

$\quad = \dfrac{5 + 1}{15}$ $= \dfrac{14 + 1}{35}$

$\quad = \dfrac{6}{15}$, or $\dfrac{2}{5}$ $= \dfrac{15}{35}$, or $\dfrac{3}{7}$

Since the sums are $\frac{1}{3}, \frac{2}{5}, \frac{3}{7}, \ldots,$ S_4 might be $\frac{4}{9}$.

b) A possible expression for S_n is $S_n = \dfrac{n}{2n + 1}$.

The above method of finding an expression for the sum of the first n terms of a series applies only when we can see a pattern in the values of $S_1, S_2, S_3, S_4, \ldots$. If no pattern can be seen, an expression for S_n must be found by other methods. Some of these will be presented in the following sections.

EXERCISES 8-5

(A)

1. Write the series corresponding to each sequence.
   a) 2, 6, 10, 14, 18, . . .
   b) 9, 3, 1, $\frac{1}{3}, \frac{1}{9}, \ldots$

2. State whether each list is a sequence or series.
   a) 2, 6, 18, 54, . . .
   b) 1 + 3 + 5 + 7
   c) 3 + 6 + 12 + 24 + . . .
   d) 3 + 6 + 9 + 12 + . . .
   e) 12, 7, 2, −3, −8, . . .
   f) −2 + 3 + 1 + 4 + 5 + . . .

(B)

3. The sum of the first 4 terms of a series is 24. Find the 4th term if the sum of the first 3 terms is:
   a) 20
   b) 10
   c) 8
   d) 30.

4. For a given series, $S_4 = 36$; find t_5 if S_5 equals:
   a) 40
   b) 60
   c) 76
   d) 30.

5. Find the first 5 terms of each series for which:
   a) $S_n = 3n$
   b) $S_n = 2n^2 - n$
   c) $S_n = n^2 - 3n$
   d) $S_n = 5n - 2$
   e) $S_n = n^2 + 2n$
   f) $S_n = 15 - 2n^2$.

6. Which of the expressions for S_n is the sum of the first n terms of each series?
   i) $S_n = 2n^2 - n$
   ii) $S_n = n^2 + 4n$
   iii) $S_n = n^2 + 2n$
   iv) $S_n = n^2 - 4n$
   v) $S_n = 2n^2 + n$
   a) 3 + 5 + 7 + 9 + 11 + . . .
   b) 1 + 5 + 9 + 13 + 17 + . . .
   c) 3 + 7 + 11 + 15 + 19 + . . .
   d) −3 − 1 + 1 + 3 + 5 + . . .

7. A formula for the sum of the first n terms of each series is given. Find S_{n-1} and t_n.
   a) $S_n = n^2 + n$
   b) $S_n = 3n^2 - 5n$
   c) $S_n = 2^n - 1$
   d) $S_n = 2n^2 - 3n$
   e) $S_n = 2(3^n - 1)$
   f) $S_n = n^2 - 4n$

8. For a certain series, $S_n = an$, where a is a constant. Find the first 4 terms of the series.

9. Which of the expressions for S_n is the sum of the first n terms of each series?

   i) $S_n = \dfrac{n}{6n + 4}$

   ii) $S_n = n^2(n + 1)$

   iii) $S_n = \dfrac{n(n + 1)(n + 2)(n + 3)}{4}$

   iv) $S_n = 2^n - 1$

   v) $S_n = \dfrac{n(n + 1)(n + 2)}{3}$

   vi) $S_n = (n - 1)2^n + 1$

       a) $1 \times 2 + 2 \times 3 + 3 \times 4 + \ldots + n(n + 1)$

       b) $1 \times 2 \times 3 + 2 \times 3 \times 4 + 3 \times 4 \times 5 + \ldots + n(n + 1)(n + 2)$

       c) $1 \times 1 + 2 \times 2 + 3 \times 2^2 + 4 \times 2^3 + \ldots + n(2)^{n-1}$

       d) $\dfrac{1}{2 \times 5} + \dfrac{1}{5 \times 8} + \dfrac{1}{8 \times 11} + \ldots + \dfrac{1}{(3n - 1)(3n + 2)}$

10. Find a possible expression for the sum of the first n terms of each series.

    a) $-1 + 1 + 3 + 5 + 7 + \ldots$

    b) $1 + 2 + 4 + 8 + 16 + \ldots$

    c) $1 + \dfrac{1}{2} + \dfrac{1}{4} + \dfrac{1}{8} + \dfrac{1}{16} + \ldots$

    d) $1 + 7 + 19 + 37 + 61 + 91 + \ldots$

11. a) Find S_n if t_n is equal to: i) $2n + 1$ ii) $2n + 3$ iii) $2n + 5$.

    b) Using the results of part a), predict S_n if $t_n = 2n + 7$. Show that your prediction is correct.

12. Show that only two terms of this sequence are perfect squares.

    $1, \quad 1 + (1 \times 2), \quad 1 + (1 \times 2) + (1 \times 2 \times 3),$

    $1 + (1 \times 2) + (1 \times 2 \times 3) + (1 \times 2 \times 3 \times 4)$

INVESTIGATE

Proving Series Expressions

In *Example 1* of Section 8-5, we found that a possible expression for the sum of the first n terms of the series $1 + 3 + 5 + 7 + \ldots + (2n - 1)$ is $S_n = n^2$. We can show that this expression is correct by evaluating $S_n - S_{n-1}$. It should simplify to the expression for the general term of the series.

$$S_n - S_{n-1} = n^2 - (n - 1)^2$$
$$= n^2 - (n^2 - 2n + 1)$$

That is, $S_n - S_{n-1} = 2n - 1 \ldots$ ①

This equation is correct for all integral values of $n > 1$.

We now know these facts about the possible formula $S_n = n^2$.

When $n = 1$ $S_1 = 1$ All terms on the
When $n = 2$, ① becomes: $S_2 - S_1 = 3$ left side add
When $n = 3$, ① becomes: $S_3 - S_2 = 5$ to 0 except the
When $n = 4$, ① becomes: $S_4 - S_3 = 7$ one term, S_n.

$$\vdots \qquad\qquad \vdots$$

For any value of n: $S_n - S_{n-1} = 2n - 1$

Add: $S_n = 1 + 3 + 5 + \ldots + (2n - 1)$

That is, S_n is the sum of the first n terms of the series.

This suggests a method of showing that a possible formula for the sum of the first n terms of a series is correct.

If S_n is a possible formula for the sum of the first n terms of a series, it is the correct formula if both these conditions are satisfied.
- S_1 is the first term.
- $S_n - S_{n-1}$ is equal to the general term.

---

1. Given the series $2 + 7 + 19 + 37 + \ldots + (3n^2 - 3n + 1)$; show that $S_n = n^3 + 1$.

2. Given the series $1 \times 4 + 2 \times 7 + 3 \times 10 + \ldots + n(3n + 1)$; show that $S_n = n(n + 1)^2$.

3. Determine a possible expression for the sum of the first n terms of each series, and show that the expression is correct.
   a) $2 + 4 + 6 + \ldots + 2n$
   b) $1 + 2 + 4 + 8 + \ldots + 2^{n-1}$
   c) $\dfrac{1}{1 \times 2} + \dfrac{1}{2 \times 3} + \dfrac{1}{3 \times 4} + \ldots + \dfrac{1}{n(n + 1)}$
   d) $\dfrac{1}{1 \times 4} + \dfrac{1}{4 \times 7} + \dfrac{1}{7 \times 10} + \ldots + \dfrac{1}{(3n - 2)(3n + 1)}$

4. Given $1^2 + 2^2 + 3^2 + \ldots + n^2$; show that $S_n = \dfrac{n(n + 1)(2n + 1)}{6}$.

5. Given $1^3 + 2^3 + 3^3 + \ldots + n^3$; show that $S_n = \dfrac{n^2(n + 1)^2}{4}$.

8-6 ARITHMETIC SERIES

Each of two summer jobs is for 3 months, or 12 weeks.

Job A pays $400 per month with a $100 raise each month.

Job B pays $100 per week with a $5 raise each week.

Which is the better-paying job?

Job A. Total salary for 3 months, in dollars, is $400 + 500 + 600 = 1500$

Job B. Payments, in dollars, are $100, 105, 110, \ldots, t_{12}$
This is an arithmetic sequence with t_{12} representing the last payment.
$t_{12} = t_1 + (n - 1)d$, where n is the number of payments, and d is the weekly increase.
$t_{12} = 100 + (11)5$
$\quad\; = 155$
Total salary for job B is $\$100 + \$105 + \$110 + \ldots + \$155$

This expression is an example of an *arithmetic series* because it indicates that the terms of an arithmetic sequence are to be added. Instead of adding the twelve numbers, the sum can be found as follows.
Let S represent the sum of the series.
$S = 100 + 105 + 110 + \ldots + 145 + 150 + 155 \ldots ①$
Write the series in reverse order.
$S = 155 + 150 + 145 + \ldots + 110 + 105 + 100 \ldots ②$
Add ① and ②.
$2S = 255 + 255 + 255 + \ldots + 255 + 255 + 255$
$\quad\;\; = 12 \times 255 \quad$ (since there are 12 terms)
$\quad\;\; = 3060$
$\;\; S = 1530$
Job B pays a total of $1530. It is the better-paying job.

This method can be used to find the sum of any number of terms of an arithmetic series. The formulas for t_n can be used with both sequences and series.

Example 1. Find the sum of the first 25 terms of the arithmetic series
$2 + 9 + 16 + 25 + \ldots$

Solution. Find the 25th term using $t_n = a + (n - 1)d$ $a = 2$

$$t_{25} = 2 + (24)7 \qquad d = 7$$
$$= 170 \qquad n = 25$$

Let S represent the sum of the series.

Then	$S =$	$2 + \ 9 + \ 16 + \ldots + 170$
Reversing:	$S =$	$170 + 163 + 156 + \ldots + \ 2$
Adding:	$2S =$	$172 + 172 + 172 + \ldots + 172$

Since there are 25 terms,
$$2S = 25(172)$$
$$S = \frac{25(172)}{2}$$
$$= 2150$$
The sum of the first 25 terms of the series is 2150.

The method of *Example 1* can be used to find a formula for the sum of the first n terms of the general arithmetic series, using l to represent the last term $a + (n - 1)d$.

$$S_n = a \qquad + a + d \ + a + 2d + \ldots + l - d \ + l$$
$$S_n = l \qquad + l - d \ + l - 2d + \ldots + a + d \ + a$$
$$2S_n = (a + l) + (a + l) + (a + l) + \ldots + (a + l) + (a + l)$$
Since there are n terms on the right side,
$$2S_n = n(a + l)$$
$$S_n = \frac{n}{2}(a + l), \text{ or } S_n = \frac{n}{2}[2a + (n - 1)d]$$

For the general arithmetic series
$$a + a + d + a + 2d + \ldots + a + (n - 1)d$$
the sum of the first n terms is
$$S_n = \frac{n}{2}(a + l) \qquad \text{where } l = a + (n - 1)d$$
$$\text{or } S_n = \frac{n}{2}[2a + (n - 1)d]$$

Example 2. Find the sum of the first 50 terms of the arithmetic series
$$3 + 4.5 + 6 + 7.5 + \ldots.$$

Solution. Use the formula $S_n = \dfrac{n}{2}[2a + (n - 1)d]$

$a = 3$
$d = 1.5$
$n = 50$

$$S_{50} = \dfrac{50}{2}[2(3) + (50 - 1)1.5]$$
$$= 25[6 + (49)1.5]$$
$$= 25(79.5)$$
$$= 1987.5$$

The sum of the first 50 terms is 1987.5.

Example 3. Find the sum of the arithmetic series $6 + 10 + 14 + \ldots + 50$.

Solution. The number of terms must be found before a formula for S_n can be used.
Let 50 be the nth term.

Use $t_n = a + (n - 1)d$ $a = 6$
$50 = 6 + (n - 1)4$ $d = 4$
$4n = 48$ $t_n = 50$
$n = 12$

There are 12 terms in the series.

To find the sum of the series, use $S_n = \dfrac{n}{2}[2a + (n - 1)d]$

$S_{12} = 6[12 + (11)4]$ $a = 6$
$= 6[12 + 44]$ $d = 4$
$= 6(56)$ $n = 12$
$= 336$

The sum of the series is 336.

EXERCISES 8-6

1. Find the sum of the first ten terms of each arithmetic series.
   a) $3 + 7 + 11 + \ldots$ b) $5 + 12 + 19 + \ldots$
   c) $2 + 8 + 14 + \ldots$ d) $45 + 39 + 33 + \ldots$
   e) $6 + 18 + 30 + \ldots$ f) $21 + 15 + 9 + \ldots$

2. Find the sum of each arithmetic series.
   a) $3 + 12 + 21 + 30 + 39 + 48 + 57 + 66$
   b) $6 + 13 + 20 + 27 + 34 + 41 + 48 + 55 + 62 + 69$
   c) $13 + 19 + 25 + 31 + 37 + 43 + 49 + 55 + 61 + 67 + 73 + 79$
   d) $19 + 31 + 43 + 55 + 67 + 79 + 91 + 103 + 115 + 127 + 139 + 151$

3. For the arithmetic series $6 + 8 + 10 + 12 + \ldots$, find:
   a) the 50th term   b) the sum of the first 50 terms.

4. For the arithmetic series $44 + 41 + 38 + 35 + \ldots$, find the sum of the first:
   a) 15 terms   b) 30 terms   c) 60 terms.

5. Which of the expressions for S_n is the sum of the first n terms of each arithmetic series?

   i) $S_n = \dfrac{3n^2 + 5n}{2}$ ii) $S_n = 2n^2$ iii) $S_n = 3n^2 + 2n$

   iv) $S_n = 5n^2 - 2n$ v) $S_n = 2n^2 + 5n$ vi) $S_n = \dfrac{3n^2 + n}{2}$

   a) $2 + 6 + 10 + \ldots$ b) $2 + 5 + 8 + \ldots$
   c) $7 + 11 + 15 + \ldots$ d) $5 + 11 + 17 + \ldots$

6. For the three summer months (12 weeks), Job A pays $325 per month with a monthly raise of $100. Job B pays $50 per week with a weekly raise of $10. Which is the better-paying job?

7. In a supermarket, cans of apple juice are displayed in a pyramid containing 12, 11, 10, . . ., 5 cans. How many cans are displayed?

8. *Tasty Treats* finds that its profit from the sale of ice cream increases by $5 per week during the 15-week summer season. If the profit for the first week is $30, find the profit for the season.

9. Find the sum of each arithmetic series.
   a) $2 + 7 + 12 + \ldots + 92$ b) $4 + 11 + 18 + \ldots + 88$
   c) $3 + 5.5 + 8 + \ldots + 133$ d) $20 + 14 + 8 + \ldots + (-70)$

10. The sum of the first 5 terms of an arithmetic series is 85 and the sum of the first 6 terms is 123. Write the first 3 terms of the series.

11. The sum of the first 9 terms of an arithmetic series is 162 and the sum of the first 12 terms is 288. Write the first 3 terms of the series.

12. The 5th term of an arithmetic series is 16 and the sum of the first 10 terms is 145. Write the first 3 terms of the series.

13. In an arithmetic series, $t_1 = 6$ and $S_9 = 108$; find the common difference and the sum of the first 20 terms.

14. Write the first 3 terms of the arithmetic series with $S_{10} = 210$ and $S_{20} = 820$.

15. If $S_n = -441$ for the series $19 + 15 + 11 + \ldots + t_n$, find n.

16. Find an expression for the sum of:
    a) the first n even integers   b) the first n odd integers.

17. Given $3 + 7 + 11 + 15 + \ldots$
    a) Find.   i) t_{20} and t_n ii) S_{20} and S_n
    b) How many terms:
       i) are less than 500   ii) have a sum less than 500?

18. For each arithmetic series, find S_n if t_n is equal to each value.
    a) $5 + (n - 1)2$ b) $-8 + (n - 1)6$ c) $4n + 1$
    d) $5n - 2$ e) $12 - 3n$ f) $7n + 4$

ⓒ

19. a) Verify each statement.
    b) Use the pattern to write the next line.
    c) If the pattern continues, what is the first number on the *n*th line?
    d) Show that the sum of the numbers on the *n*th line is n^3.

$$1 = 1^3$$
$$3 + 5 = 2^3$$
$$7 + 9 + 11 = 3^3$$
$$13 + 15 + 17 + 19 = 4^3$$

20. a) Verify each statement.
    b) What is the first number on the *n*th line?
    c) What is the sum of the numbers on the *n*th line?
    d) What is the general term of the sequence 1, 5, 15, 34, 65, . . .?

$$1 = 1$$
$$2 + 3 = 5$$
$$4 + 5 + 6 = 15$$
$$7 + 8 + 9 + 10 = 34$$
$$11 + 12 + 13 + 14 + 15 = 65$$

 INVESTIGATE

$$17 + 2 = 19$$
$$19 + 4 = 23$$
$$23 + 6 = 29$$
$$29 + 8 = 37$$
$$37 + 10 = 47$$
$$47 + 12 = 59$$
.
.
.

How long does this list continue to give primes?
Find other lists like this.

 **INVESTIGATE**

How many letters are in this snowball sentence?
I do not know where family doctors acquired illegibly perplexing handwriting; nevertheless, extraordinary pharmaceutical intellectuality, counterbalancing indecipherability, transcendentalizes intercommunications' incomprehensibleness.
Create your own snowball sentence.
Create a reverse snowball sentence.

8-7 GEOMETRIC SERIES

A favorite pastime of some people is to construct their family tree. Some families have succeeded in tracing their roots as far back as ten generations. If you go back through ten generations, how many ancestors will you find that you have?

Every person has 2 parents, 4 grandparents, 8 great-grandparents, and so on. The number of ancestors through ten generations is:

$$2 + 4 + 8 + 16 + 32 + 64 + 128 + 256 + 512 + 1024$$

Let S represent the sum of this series.

$$S = 2 + 4 + 8 + \ldots + 512 + 1024 \qquad \ldots ①$$

Multiply by the common ratio 2.

$$\text{Then } 2S = \underline{\quad 4 + 8 + \ldots + 512 + 1024 + 2048} \ldots ②$$
$$S = -2 \qquad\qquad\qquad\qquad + 2048 \quad \text{Subtracting } ① \text{ from } ②$$
$$= 2046$$

The sum of the first ten terms of the series is 2046. Going back through ten generations, each person has 2046 ancestors.

In the above example, the expression for S is a *geometric series* because it indicates that the terms of a geometric sequence are to be added.

The above method can be used to find the sum of any number of terms of a geometric series.

Example 1. Find the sum of the first 9 terms of the geometric series
$$2 + 6 + 18 + 54 + \ldots.$$

Solution. Find t_9 using $t_n = ar^{n-1}$
$$t_9 = 2(3)^8 \qquad a = 2$$
$$= 2(6561) \qquad r = 3$$
$$= 13\ 122 \qquad n = 9$$

Let S represent the sum of the series.
$$S = 2 + 6 + 18 + \ldots + 13\ 122 \qquad \ldots ①$$
Multiply by the common ratio 3.
$$\text{Then } 3S = \underline{\quad 6 + 18 + \ldots + 13\ 122 + 39\ 366} \ldots ②$$
$$2S = -2 \qquad\qquad\qquad + 39\ 366$$
$$= 39\ 364 \qquad \text{Subtracting } ① \text{ from } ②$$
$$S = 19\ 682$$

The sum of the first 9 terms of the series is 19 682.

The method of *Example 1* can be used to find a formula for the sum of the first n terms of the general geometric series.

Let $S_n = a + ar + ar^2 + \ldots + ar^{n-1}$ $\ldots$ ①
Multiply ① by r.
$\quad rS_n = \quad ar + ar^2 + \ldots + ar^{n-1} + ar^n \ldots$ ②
Subtract ① from ②.
$rS_n - S_n = -a + ar^n$
$S_n(r - 1) = a(r^n - 1)$
$\qquad S_n = \dfrac{a(r^n - 1)}{r - 1}$

For the general geometric series $a + ar + ar^2 + \ldots + ar^{n-1}$,

the sum of the first n terms is $S_n = \dfrac{a(r^n - 1)}{r - 1}, \quad r \neq 1$

Example 2. Find the sum of the first seven terms of each geometric series.
$\quad$ a) $5 + 10 + 20 + 40 + \ldots$
$\quad$ b) $12 + 6 + 3 + 1.5 + \ldots$
$\quad$ c) $100 - 50 + 25 - 12.5 + \ldots$

Solution. $\quad$ Use the formula $S_n = \dfrac{a(r^n - 1)}{r - 1}$

$\quad$ a) $5 + 10 + 20 + 40 + \ldots$

$\qquad S_7 = \dfrac{5(2^7 - 1)}{2 - 1}$ $\qquad a = 5$
$\qquad\qquad\qquad\qquad\qquad r = 2$
$\qquad\quad = 5(128 - 1)$ $\qquad n = 7$
$\qquad\quad = 5(127)$
$\qquad\quad = 635$

$\quad$ The sum of the first seven terms is 635.

$\quad$ b) $12 + 6 + 3 + 1.5 + \ldots$

$\qquad S_7 = \dfrac{12[(0.5)^7 - 1]}{0.5 - 1}$ $\qquad a = 12$
$\qquad\qquad\qquad\qquad\qquad\quad r = 0.5$
$\qquad\quad = -24(0.007\ 812\ 5 - 1)$ $\quad n = 7$
$\qquad\quad = -24(-0.992\ 187\ 5)$
$\qquad\quad = 23.8125$

$\quad$ The sum of the first seven terms is 23.8125.

$\quad$ c) $100 - 50 + 25 - 12.5 + \ldots$

$\qquad S_7 = \dfrac{100[(-0.5)^7 - 1]}{-0.5 - 1}$ $\qquad a = 100$
$\qquad\qquad\qquad\qquad\qquad\qquad r = -0.5$
$\qquad\quad = 67.1875$ $\qquad\qquad\qquad n = 7$

$\quad$ The sum of the first seven terms is 67.1875.

If the numerator and the denominator of the right side of the formula $S_n = \dfrac{a(r^n - 1)}{r - 1}$ are both multiplied by -1, we obtain $S_n = \dfrac{a(1 - r^n)}{1 - r}$.
This form is more convenient to use when $|r| < 1$, as in *Example 2b)* and *c)*.

When a calculator is used to find the value of S_n for some series, certain values of n and r may lead to a decimal approximation for the sum. This is usually sufficient for most purposes.

EXERCISES 8-7

1. Using the method of *Example 1*, find the sum of each geometric series.
   a) $1 + 2 + 4 + 8 + 16 + 32$ b) $3 + 9 + 27 + 81 + 243 + 729$
   c) $2 + 8 + 32 + 128 + 512$ d) $40 + 20 + 10 + 5 + 2.5$

2. Use the formula for S_n to find the sum of the first 5 terms of each geometric series.
   a) $2 + 10 + 50 + \ldots$ b) $4 + 12 + 36 + \ldots$
   c) $3 + 6 + 12 + \ldots$ d) $24 + 12 + 6 + \ldots$
   e) $5 + 15 + 45 + \ldots$ f) $80 + 40 + 20 + \ldots$

3. Which of the expressions for S_n is the sum of the first n terms of each geometric series?

   i) $S_n = \dfrac{2(1 - 6^n)}{3}$ ii) $S_n = -(1 - 4^n)$ iii) $S_n = \dfrac{5(3^n - 1)}{2}$

   iv) $S_n = \dfrac{2(1 - 6^n)}{-5}$ v) $S_n = 4(2^n - 1)$ vi) $S_n = 6(2^n - 1)$

   a) $2 + 12 + 72 + \ldots$ b) $6 + 12 + 24 + \ldots$
   c) $3 + 12 + 48 + \ldots$ d) $4 + 8 + 16 + \ldots$

4. For the geometric series $6 + 3 + 1.5 + 0.75 + \ldots$, find:
   a) the 7th term   b) the sum of the first 7 terms.

5. For the geometric series $6 + 18 + 54 + \ldots$, find:
   a) the 6th term   b) the sum of the first 6 terms.

6. a) How many ancestors does a person have in:
      i) 12 generations   ii) 15 generations?
   b) Write a formula for the number of ancestors a person has in n generations.

7. A doctor prescribes 200 mg of medication on the first day of treatment. The dosage is halved on each successive day for one week. To the nearest milligram, what is the total amount of medication administered?

8. Sixty-four players are entered in a tennis tournament. When a player loses a match, he or she drops out; the winners go on to the next round. What is the total number of matches that must be played before a winner is decided?

9. If you are paid $0.01 on the first day, $0.02 on the second day, $0.04 on the third day, $0.08 on the fourth day, and so on, how much money would you have at the end of a 30-day month?

10. Find the sum of each geometric series.

   a) $2 + 6 + 18 + \ldots + 1458$

   b) $1 + 5 + 25 + \ldots + 3125$

   c) $48 + 24 + 12 + \ldots + \frac{3}{8}$

   d) $\frac{1}{3} + 1 + 3 + \ldots + 6561$

   e) $5 + 20 + 80 + \ldots + 20\,480$

   f) $32 + 16 + 8 + \ldots + \frac{1}{8}$

11. How many generations must a person go back to have at least 1000 ancestors?

12. The sum of the first two terms of a geometric series is 12 and the sum of the first 3 terms is 62. Find the first 3 terms of the series.

13. In a geometric series, $t_1 = 3$ and $S_3 = 21$; find the common ratio and the sum of the first 7 terms.

14. The second term of a geometric series is 15 and the sum of the first 3 terms is 93. Find the first 3 terms of the series.

15. Find S_n for a series with t_n equal to each value.

   a) $2(3)^{n-1}$

   b) $5(2)^{n-1}$

   c) $3(4)^{n-1}$

   d) 2^{n+1}

Ⓒ

16. Show that for the series $1 + \frac{1}{2} + \frac{1}{4} + \frac{1}{8} + \ldots$, S_n is never greater than 2.

17. Find the sum of the factors of 2^{10}.

 INVESTIGATE

Is it possible to find 3 numbers that form an arithmetic series and a geometric series?

THE MATHEMATICAL MIND

Population and Food

Thomas R. Malthus was a man of many talents. A mathematics graduate of Cambridge University, he was also a minister of the Church of England and a professor of history and political economy. In 1798, he published his famous ''Essay on the Principle of Population As It Affects the Future Improvement of Society''.

In this essay, Malthus set forth his theory that the rate of increase of the world's population was fast exceeding the development of food supplies. He reasoned that the population, if left unchecked, doubles about every 25 years, or increases geometrically. But the food supply increases, at best, only arithmetically. Thus, sooner or later, there will be widespread starvation unless a limit is placed on the population.

Malthus' essay provoked considerable controversy because it offended those who believed that society would eventually be perfect; they thought a time would come when suffering, crime, disease, and war would be eliminated. Malthus held the opposite view, and felt that the basic structure of society would always remain unchanged. Although his essay was written almost 200 years ago, the truth of his theory is even more evident today than in his time. Here is an excerpt from Malthus' essay:

> ''Taking the whole earth. . . . and, supposing the present population to equal a thousand millions, the human species would increase [every 25 years] as the numbers 1, 2, 4, 8, 16, 32, 64, 128, 256, and subsistence as 1, 2, 3, 4, 5, 6, 7, 8, 9. In two centuries the population would be to the means of subsistence as 256 to 9; in three centuries 4096 to 13; and in two thousand years the difference would be almost incalculable.''

QUESTIONS

1. Use Malthus' figures to predict the ratio of population to food supply after:
   a) four centuries   b) five centuries.

2. If Malthus' reasoning and figures were correct, the world population today would be about 256 billion.
   a) Give reasons why this is far in excess of the present world population.
   b) Does this negate the essential validity of his theory?

3. Use a calculator to find the ''almost incalculable'' figures for the ratio of population to food supply after two thousand years.

8-8 INFINITE GEOMETRIC SERIES

In the 4th century B.C. the Greek philosopher Zeno of Elea made certain statements concerning motion that have come to be known as Zeno's paradoxes. A paradox is a statement that appears to be absurd, yet its explanation seems logical.

In Zeno's *racecourse paradox*, he argued that a runner can never reach the end of a racecourse! For example, consider a racecourse 100 m long, represented by segment AB. Let us assume that the runner can run at a uniform rate of 10 m/s.

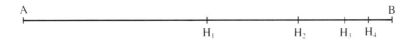

Zeno argued as follows:
The runner must reach the halfway point, H_1. This takes 5 s.
Then the runner must reach H_2, halfway between H_1 and B. This takes 2.5 s.
Then the runner must reach H_3, halfway between H_2 and B. This takes 1.25 s.
Then the runner must reach H_4, the next halfway point. This takes 0.625 s.
And so on . . .
There are infinitely many steps like this, and each will take a certain time. Since the total time is the sum of infinitely many times, the runner will never reach point B.

Yet common experience tells us that the runner does reach point B. At 10 m/s, this will take only 10 s. But it took mathematicians and philosophers almost two thousand years to find the flaw in the reasoning.

The times to reach the various halfway points are terms of a geometric series with first term 5 and common ratio 0.5.

$$5 + 2.5 + 1.25 + 0.625 + \ldots$$

Since there is always a next term, this is an example of an *infinite geometric series*. The time to reach each halfway point is the sum of a corresponding number of terms of this series.
Time to reach H_1: $S_1 = 5$
Time to reach H_2: $S_2 = 7.5$
Time to reach H_3: $S_3 = 8.75$
Time to reach H_4: $S_4 = 9.375$

Time to reach H_{10}: $S_{10} = 9.990\ 234\ 375$

Time to reach H_{20}: $S_{20} \doteq 9.999\ 990\ 463$

Notice that as n gets larger, S_n gets closer and closer to 10. By adding enough terms of the series we can make the sum as close to 10 as we like. Hence, we say that the sum of the infinite series is 10, and we write:
$$5 + 2.5 + 1.25 + 0.625 + \ldots = 10$$

The error in Zeno's argument is his statement that the sum of an infinite number of times is infinite. We have just shown that this particular sum is not infinite.

We can apply the above analysis to an infinite geometric series with first term a and common ratio r.
$$a + ar + ar^2 + ar^3 + \ldots + ar^{n-1} + \ldots$$
For this series,
$$S_1 = a$$
$$S_2 = a + ar$$
$$S_3 = a + ar + ar^2$$
$$S_4 = a + ar + ar^2 + ar^3$$

$$S_n = a + ar + ar^2 + ar^3 + \ldots + ar^{n-1}$$

But $S_n = \dfrac{a(r^n - 1)}{r - 1}$, provided that $r \neq 1$

$$= \left(\frac{ar^n}{r - 1}\right) - \left(\frac{a}{r - 1}\right)$$

If $|r| < 1$, then r^n becomes smaller and smaller as n increases. We can make r^n as small as we please by taking a sufficiently large value of n. Hence, if $|r| < 1$, the sum of the infinite geometric series is

$$S = 0 - \left(\frac{a}{r - 1}\right)$$

$$= \frac{a}{1 - r}$$

The sum of the infinite geometric series
$$a + ar + ar^2 + \ldots + ar^{n-1} + \ldots$$
is $S = \dfrac{a}{1 - r}$, provided that $|r| < 1$.

Example 1.   Which infinite geometric series has a sum? What is the sum?

   a) $4 - 6 + 9 - 13.5 + \ldots$

   b) $6 + 2 + \dfrac{2}{3} + \dfrac{2}{9} + \ldots$

Solution.   a) $4 - 6 + 9 - 13.5 + \ldots$
      For this series, $a = 4$ and $r = -1.5$; since $|r| > 1$, this series has no sum.

b) $6 + 2 + \frac{2}{3} + \frac{2}{9} + \ldots$

For this series, $a = 6$ and $r = \frac{1}{3}$; since $|r| < 1$, this series does have a sum. Use the formula.

$$S = \frac{a}{1 - r}$$

$$= \frac{6}{1 - \frac{1}{3}}$$

$$= \frac{6}{\frac{2}{3}}$$

$$= 9$$

The sum of the series is 9.

Example 2. Express the repeating decimal $2.\overline{37}$ as a rational number in the form $\frac{m}{n}$.

Solution. $2.\overline{37} = 2 + 0.37 + 0.0037 + 0.000\,037 + \ldots$
$= 2 + 0.37 + 0.37(0.01) + 0.37(0.0001) + \ldots$
The terms after the first term form an infinite geometric series with first term 0.37 and common ratio 0.01. Using the above formula with $a = 0.37$ and $r = 0.01$, we obtain

$$2.\overline{37} = 2 + \frac{0.37}{1 - 0.01}$$

$$= 2 + \frac{0.37}{0.99}$$

$$= 2 + \frac{37}{99}$$

$$= \frac{235}{99}$$

EXERCISES 8-8

Ⓐ

1. Which infinite geometric series have a sum? What is the sum?
   a) $8 + 4 + 2 + 1 + \ldots$ b) $27 + 18 + 12 + 8 + \ldots$
   c) $3 + 7 + 11 + 15 + \ldots$ d) $50 - 40 + 32 - 25.6 + \ldots$
   e) $2 + 6 + 18 + 54 + \ldots$ f) $-16 + 12 - 9 + 6.75 - \ldots$

Ⓑ

2. Find the sum of each infinite geometric series.
   a) $60 + 30 + 15 + 7.5 + \ldots$ b) $5 + 2.5 + 1.25 + 0.625 + \ldots$
   c) $20 - 15 + 11.25 - 8.4375 + \ldots$ d) $8 + 2 + \frac{1}{2} + \frac{1}{8} + \ldots$

3. Express each repeating decimal as an infinite series. Then find the sum of the series, and use it to express the number in the form $\frac{m}{n}$.

   a) $2.\overline{3}$ b) $3.\overline{18}$ c) $1.\overline{521}$ d) $6.0\overline{85}$

4. The general term of an infinite geometric series is given. Determine the sum of the series, if it exists.

   a) $12\left(\frac{2}{3}\right)^{n-1}$ b) $32\left(\frac{3}{8}\right)^{n-1}$ c) $9\left(\frac{3}{2}\right)^{n-1}$ d) $8\left(-\frac{5}{6}\right)^{n-1}$

5. The sum of an infinite geometric series is 63 and the first term is 21. Find the common ratio.

6. The sum of an infinite geometric series is $\frac{24}{7}$ and the common ratio is $-\frac{3}{4}$. Find the first term.

7. a) Find the sum of the series $12 - 6 + 3 - 1.5 + \ldots$
   b) Find the difference between the sum of the series in part a) and the sum of the first eight terms of the series.

8. A ball is dropped from a height of 2 m to a floor. On each bounce the ball rises to 50% of the height from which it fell. Calculate the total distance the ball travels before coming to rest.

9. Repeat *Exercise 8* if the ball rises to 70% of the height from which it fell on each bounce.

10. The midpoints of a square with sides 1 m long are joined to form another square. Then the midpoints of the sides of the second square are joined to form a third square. This process is continued indefinitely to form an infinite set of smaller and smaller squares converging on the centre of the original square. Determine the total length of the segments forming the sides of all the squares.

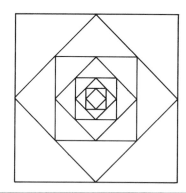

Ⓒ

11. Determine the values of x such that each series has a sum.

   a) $1 + x + x^2 + x^3 + \ldots$ b) $1 + \frac{1}{2}x + \frac{1}{4}x^2 + \frac{1}{8}x^3 + \ldots$

   c) $1 - \frac{1}{3}x^2 + \frac{1}{9}x^4 - \frac{1}{27}x^6 + \ldots$ d) $\frac{1}{x} + \frac{1}{x^2} + \frac{1}{x^3} + \ldots$

THE MATHEMATICAL MIND

Infinity

The concept of infinity has intrigued mathematicians and non-mathematicians alike for centuries.

Infinity in Language

Great fleas have little fleas upon
   their backs to bit 'em
And little fleas have lesser fleas,
   and so *ad infinitum*,
And the great fleas themselves, in turn,
   have greater fleas to go on,
While these again have greater still,
   and greater still, and so on.

        A. de Morgan

I could be bounded in a nutshell and
count myself a king of infinite space.

        William Shakespeare

The notion of infinity is our greatest
friend; it is also the greatest enemy of
our peace of mind.

        James Pierpont

Infinity in Art

Circle Limit III
By Maurits Escher

Infinity in Mathematics

About two hundred years ago mathematicians noticed some strange results when they began to work with infinite quantities. Here is a small sample of some of the difficulties they encountered. Some of the world's greatest mathematicians were surprised by results such as these, and it was many years before the concept of infinity was understood.

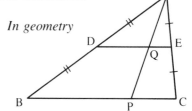

In arithmetic

Natural numbers: 1, 2, 3, 4, . . .

Even numbers: 2, 4, 6, 8, . . .

Since the natural numbers include both odd and even numbers, there appear to be twice as many natural numbers as even numbers. But the natural numbers can be paired with the even numbers as shown above. This suggests that there are the same number of even numbers as natural numbers!

In geometry

D and E are midpoints of two sides of △ABC. Since BC is twice as long as DE, it contains twice as many points as DE. But any point P on BC can be paired with a corresponding point Q on DE by joining PA. This suggests that DE contains the same number of points as BC!

Examples like the two above convinced mathematicians that when they deal with infinite sets, they need to define what is meant by the "number" of quantities in those sets.

In arithmetic

$$\frac{1}{3} = 0.333\ 333\ .\ .\ .\ ,\ \text{or}\ 0.\overline{3}$$

$$\frac{2}{3} = 0.666\ 666\ .\ .\ .\ ,\ \text{or}\ 0.\overline{6}$$

Add. $\overline{1} = \overline{0.999\ 999}$ . . . , or $0.\overline{9}$

But 0.999 999 . . . is never exactly equal to 1; no matter how many 9s we take, this expression will always be less than 1. How can a quantity that is less than 1 be equal to 1? The answer is that we can make 0.999 999 . . . as close to 1 as we like by taking enough 9s. This is what we mean when we write $1 = 0.999\ 999$ . . ., or $0.\overline{9}$.

In algebra

Consider the infinite series

$1 + 2 + 4 + 8 + 16 + \ .\ .\ .$

Let $S = 1 + 2 + 4 + 8 + 16 + \ .\ .\ .$

$S = 1 + 2(1 + 2 + 4 + 8 + 16 + \ .\ .\ .)$

$S = 1 + 2S$

Hence, $S = -1$

But, how can a series of infinitely many positive terms have a sum of -1? The answer, of course, is that it can't. Yet, the algebra above appears correct. Hence, mathematicians began to realize that they cannot assume that familiar algebraic operations can always be performed with infinite quantities.

QUESTIONS

1. Consider the quotation by A. de Morgan. What does de Morgan mean by "ad infinitum?"

2. In his quotation, A. de Morgan describes the infinitely large and the infinitely small. How does Escher's print, Circle Limit III, illustrate the infinitely large and the infinitely small?

3. This quotation appeared in Readers' Digest magazine some years ago.

   "High up in the North, in the land called Svetjod, there stands a rock. It is a thousand miles long and a thousand miles high. Once every thousand years a little bird comes to sharpen its beak. When the rock has thus been worn away, then a single day of eternity will have gone by."

   According to this quotation, how long is a "single day of eternity"? Make any assumptions that seem reasonable.

4. Here is another example of an infinite series that can lead to absurd results.
   Let $S = 1 - 1 + 1 - 1 + 1 - 1 + \ldots$
   $S = (1 - 1) + (1 - 1) + (1 - 1) + \ldots$
   $S = 0 + 0 + 0 + \ldots$
   $S = 0$
   Assuming that the rules of algebra apply, demonstrate that:
   a) $S = 0.5$ b) $S = 1$.

In *Question 4*, and the series on the previous page, one reason for the absurd results is that the sum S does not exist. But there are other examples of series for which the corresponding sum S *does* exist, and yet similar contradictory results can be obtained!

5. Here is a "proof" of the formula for the sum of an infinite geometric series.
   Let $S = a + ar + ar^2 + ar^3 + \ldots$
   $S = a + r(a + ar + ar^2 + \ldots)$
   $S = a + rS$
   $S(1 - r) = a$
   $$S = \frac{a}{1 - r} \quad \text{(if } r \neq 1\text{)}$$
   Although this "proof" leads to the correct formula, it is not a valid proof of the formula. Explain the error.

8-9 SIGMA NOTATION FOR A SERIES

There is a special notation that is used to represent a series. For example, the arithmetic series with 6 terms, $1 + 4 + 7 + 10 + 13 + 16$, has general term $t_n = a + (n - 1)d$

$$= 1 + (n - 1)3$$
$$= 3n - 2$$

Each term in the series can be expressed in this form.

$t_1 = 3(1) - 2 \qquad t_2 = 3(2) - 2 \qquad t_3 = 3(3) - 2$
$t_4 = 3(4) - 2 \qquad t_5 = 3(5) - 2 \qquad t_6 = 3(6) - 2$

The series is the sum of all the terms. This is abbreviated to:

The sum of . . . $\longrightarrow \displaystyle\sum_{k=1}^{6} (3k - 2) \longleftarrow$ . . . all numbers of the form $3k - 2$ . . .

. . . for values of k from 1 to 6.

The symbol Σ is the capital Greek letter *sigma*, which corresponds to S, the first letter of Sum. When Σ is used as shown, it is called *sigma notation*. In sigma notation, k is often used as the variable under the Σ sign and in the expression following it. Although any letter can be used for this purpose, n should be avoided because n usually represents the number of terms in a series.

Example 1. Write the series corresponding to $\displaystyle\sum_{j=1}^{3} (j^2 + 2j + 5)$.

Solution. Substitute values from 1 to 3, in turn, for j in the expression $j^2 + 2j + 5$ and add the results.

$$\sum_{j=1}^{3} (j^2 + 2j + 5)$$
$$= [1^2 + 2(1) + 5] + [2^2 + 2(2) + 5] + [3^2 + 2(3) + 5]$$
$$= 8 + 13 + 20$$

Example 2. Write each series using sigma notation.
a) $3 + 9 + 15 + 21 + 27$ \qquad b) $5 + 10 + 20 + 40 + 80 + 160$

Solution. a) $3 + 9 + 15 + 21 + 27$
This is an arithmetic series with $a = 3$ and $d = 6$.
The general term is $\quad t_n = a + (n - 1)d$
$$= 3 + (n - 1)6$$
$$= 6n - 3$$

Since there are 5 terms, the series can be written $\displaystyle\sum_{k=1}^{5} (6k - 3)$.

b) 5 + 10 + 20 + 40 + 80 + 160

This is a geometric series with $a = 5$ and $r = 2$.

The general terms is $t_n = ar^{n-1}$
$$= 5(2)^{n-1}$$

Since there are 6 terms, the series can be written $\sum\limits_{k=1}^{6} 5(2)^{k-1}$.

The formulas for the sums of an arithmetic series or a geometric series can sometimes be used to simplify expressions involving sigma notation.

Example 3.   Simplify.   a) $\sum\limits_{i=1}^{20} (3i + 1)$ b) $\sum\limits_{k=1}^{7} 2^k$ c) $\sum\limits_{k=1}^{\infty} \left(\frac{1}{2}\right)^{k-4}$

Solution.   a) $\sum\limits_{i=1}^{20} (3i + 1) = 4 + 7 + 10 + \ldots + 61$

This is an arithmetic series with $a = 4$, $d = 3$, $n = 20$.

The sum of the series is $S_n = \frac{n}{2}(a + l)$

$$S_{20} = \frac{20}{2}(4 + 61)$$
$$= 10(65)$$
$$= 650$$

Therefore, $\sum\limits_{i=1}^{20} (3i + 1) = 650$

b) $\sum\limits_{k=1}^{7} 2^k = 2 + 2^2 + 2^3 + \ldots + 2^7$

This is a geometric series with $a = 2$, $r = 2$, $n = 7$.

The sum of the series is $S_n = \frac{a(r^n - 1)}{r - 1}$

$$S_7 = \frac{2(2^7 - 1)}{2 - 1}$$
$$= 2(2^7 - 1)$$
$$= 2(127)$$
$$= 254$$

Therefore, $\sum\limits_{k=1}^{7} 2^k = 254$

c) $\sum\limits_{k=1}^{\infty} \left(\frac{1}{2}\right)^{k-4} = 8 + 4 + 2 + \cdots$

This is an infinite geometric series with $a = 8$ and $r = \frac{1}{2}$.

The sum of the series is $\quad S = \dfrac{a}{1-r}$

$$= \dfrac{8}{1 - \dfrac{1}{2}}$$

$$= 16$$

Therefore, $\displaystyle\sum_{k=1}^{\infty} \left(\dfrac{1}{2}\right)^{k-4} = 16$

When sigma notation is used to represent an infinite series, both notations $\displaystyle\sum_{k=1}^{\infty}$ and $\displaystyle\sum_{k}$ can be used.

EXERCISES 8-9

(A)

1. Write the series corresponding to each expression.

   a) $\displaystyle\sum_{k=1}^{5} (k + 3)$

   b) $\displaystyle\sum_{j=1}^{4} (4j + 1)$

   c) $\displaystyle\sum_{m=1}^{6} 2m$

   d) $\displaystyle\sum_{j=1}^{5} (3j - 8)$

   e) $\displaystyle\sum_{i=1}^{\infty} \left(\dfrac{1}{3}\right)^{i-2}$

   f) $\displaystyle\sum_{k=1}^{4} (5k - 12)$

2. Write each series using sigma notation.

   a) $2 + 5 + 8 + 11 + \ldots + 20$

   b) $3 + 5 + 7 + 9 + 11 + 13$

   c) $5 + 1 + \dfrac{1}{5} + \dfrac{1}{25} + \ldots$

   d) $24 + 18 + 12 + 6$

(B)

3. Which of the expressions in sigma notation is correct for each series?

   i) $\displaystyle\sum_{k=1}^{5} (3k + 1)$

   ii) $\displaystyle\sum_{k=1}^{5} (2k - 3)$

   iii) $\displaystyle\sum_{k=1}^{5} (3k - 2)$

   iv) $\displaystyle\sum_{k=1}^{5} (2k + 3)$

   v) $\displaystyle\sum_{k=1}^{5} (3 - 2k)$

   vi) $\displaystyle\sum_{k=1}^{5} (5k - 1)$

   a) $5 + 7 + 9 + 11 + 13$

   b) $-1 + 1 + 3 + 5 + 7$

   c) $1 + 4 + 7 + 10 + 13$

   d) $4 + 9 + 14 + 19 + 24$

4. Simplify.

   a) $\displaystyle\sum_{k=1}^{12} (2k + 3)$

   b) $\displaystyle\sum_{j=1}^{8} (j - 2)$

   c) $\displaystyle\sum_{k=1}^{10} (4k - 1)$

5. Simplify.

   a) $\displaystyle\sum_{i=1}^{7} 3(2)^i$

   b) $\displaystyle\sum_{k=1}^{6} 2^{k+1}$

   c) $\displaystyle\sum_{i=1}^{6} 3^i$

6. Write the series corresponding to each expression.

a) $\displaystyle\sum_{j=1}^{5} (j^2 - 2j)$

b) $\displaystyle\sum_{i=1}^{7} (i^2 + 3)$

c) $\displaystyle\sum_{k=1}^{4} (3k^2 + 2k - 5)$

d) $\displaystyle\sum_{m=1}^{6} (2m^2 - 5m)$

e) $\displaystyle\sum_{k=1}^{5} (3k - k^2)$

f) $\displaystyle\sum_{i=1}^{7} (i^2 + 5i - 2)$

7. Write each series using sigma notation.
a) $2 + 5 + 8 + \ldots + (3n - 1)$ b) $18 + 13 + 8 + \ldots$
c) $3 + 9 + 15 + \ldots + 93$ d) $2 + 6 + 10 + \ldots + 46$
e) $2 + 6 + 18 + \ldots$ f) $3 + 6 + 12 + \ldots + 768$

8. Write the series corresponding to each expression.

a) $\displaystyle\sum_{k=1}^{4} a^k$

b) $\displaystyle\sum_{k=1}^{4} ka^k$

c) $\displaystyle\sum_{k=1}^{4} ak^k$

d) $\displaystyle\sum_{k=1}^{4} (-ak)^k$

9. Write each series using sigma notation.
a) $3 + 6 + 9 + 12 + 15$ b) $2 + 4 + 8 + 16 + 32 + 64$

c) $1 + \dfrac{1}{2} + \dfrac{1}{3} + \dfrac{1}{4} + \dfrac{1}{5}$ d) $-3 + 6 - 12 + 24 - 48$

10. Simplify.

a) $\displaystyle\sum_{j=3}^{15} (3j - 1)$

b) $\displaystyle\sum_{k=2}^{11} (2k + 5)$

c) $\displaystyle\sum_{i=4}^{14} (4i - 3)$

11. Simplify.

a) $\displaystyle\sum_{i=2}^{6} 2^{i-1}$

b) $\displaystyle\sum_{j=3}^{7} 2^{2j-3}$

c) $\displaystyle\sum_{k=1}^{5} 2^{1-k}$

12. Write each series using sigma notation.
a) $1 + 2 + 3 + 4 + \ldots + n$ b) $1 + 4 + 9 + 16 + \ldots$
c) $1 + 4 + 27 + 256 + \ldots + n^n$ d) $3 + 6 + 12 + \ldots + 3(2)^{n-1}$

13. Find the sum of the series $\displaystyle\sum_{i=1}^{n} (-)^i$ if:

a) n is odd b) n is even.

Ⓒ

14. Write each series using sigma notation.
a) $a + a + d + a + 2d + a + 3d + \ldots + a + (n - 1)d$
b) $a + ar + ar^2 + ar^3 + \ldots + ar^{n-1}$

 INVESTIGATE

Π, the capital Greek letter P, is the first letter of *Product*. Make up some examples to show what pi notation would mean.

COMPUTER POWER

The Snowflake Curve and Fractal Geometry

About a hundred years ago, mathematicians devised some strange curves
to serve as counterexamples to disprove certain intuitive ideas about
geometry. For example, we might think that a figure cannot have an
infinite perimeter. But in 1906, Helge von Koch came up with a curve
to show that it can! To visualize this curve, we construct a sequence
of polygons $S_1, S_2, S_3, \ldots$ as follows.

S_1 is an equilateral
triangle.

To obtain S_2, construct
an equilateral triangle on
each side of S_1 and
remove the base.

S_3 is obtained from S_2 in
the same way as S_2 is
obtained from S_1.

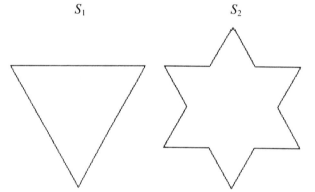

S_1 S_2 S_3

Continue in the same way to obtain the other polygons of the sequence.

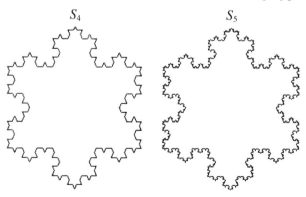

S_4 S_5

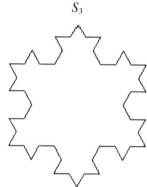

It can be proved that these polygons come closer and closer to a
certain limiting curve, called the *snowflake curve*.

QUESTIONS

1. Assume that the equilateral triangle S_1 has sides 3 cm long.
   a) Calculate the perimeters of the five polygons shown.
   b) Calculate the areas of the five polygons.
   c) Calculate the area of the region enclosed by the snowflake curve, and explain why this region has an infinite perimeter.

2. Write recursive definitions for the sequence of:
   a) polygons S_1, S_2, S_3, . . .   b) perimeters P_1, P_2, P_3, . . .
   c) areas A_1, A_2, A_3, . . .

Some computer languages are well suited for displaying figures defined recursively on the screen. The two LOGO procedures below define a command called SNOWFLAKE. (On some computers it may be necessary to replace SETPOS in the second line with SETXY:)

```
TO SNOWFLAKE :X
CS PU SETPOS [-90 52] RT 90 PD
MAKE "SIZE 180
MAKE "N 5 - :X
MAKE "X 1
REPEAT :N [MAKE "X :X * 3]
REPEAT 3 [DRAW :SIZE :X RT 120]
END

TO DRAW :SIZE :X
IF :SIZE < :X [FD :SIZE STOP]
DRAW :SIZE / 3 :X LT 60
DRAW :SIZE / 3 :X RT 120
DRAW :SIZE / 3 :X LT 60
DRAW :SIZE / 3 :X
END
```

3. If you have a computer with LOGO, experiment with the SNOWFLAKE command. For example, to display the polygon S_3 on the screen, type SNOWFLAKE 3. Try to get the best example you can within the limitations of your computer screen.

   The snowflake curve is one of several weird curves that were introduced early in the 20th century. Another curve passes through every point inside a square! Still another intersects itself at every one of its points! At the time, these curves were dismissed by mathematicians as little more than pathological curiosities. No one would have thought that 70 years later they would be an important part of a new kind of geometry called *fractal geometry*.

Fractal geometry was introduced in 1977 by Benoit B. Mandelbrot for the purpose of modelling natural phenomena that are irregular (or crinkled) over several different size scales. Examples include coastlines, the surface of the lungs, the network of arteries and veins in the body, the branching structure of plants, the thermal agitation of molecules in a fluid (Brownian motion), sponges, and even the rings of Saturn.

Fractal geometry deals with novel kinds of curves and surfaces with a fractional dimension! For example, the snowflake curve is not two-dimensional because it does not include the points inside it. And, it is not one-dimensional either because it zigzags infinitely often. We can find the dimension of the snowflake curve as follows.

A key feature of the snowflake curve is its self-similarity. This means that parts of it are similar to larger copies of themselves. For example, the two parts shown are similar. The larger part is a $3\times$ enlargement of the smaller, and 4 copies of the smaller part are needed to make the enlargement.

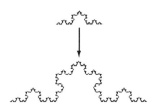

Consider what happens with simpler self-similar figures such as a line segment, a square, or a cube.

- In *1 dimension*, to make a $3\times$ enlargement of a line segment, we used 3^1, or 3 copies.

- In *2 dimensions*, to make a $3\times$ enlargement of a square, we need 3^2, or 9 copies.

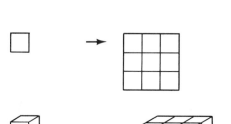

- In *3 dimensions*, to make a $3\times$ enlargement of a cube, we need 3^3, or 27 copies.

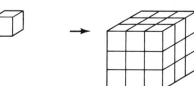

Observe that, in each case, the number of copies needed to make the enlargement is a power of the scale factor, and the exponent is the number of dimensions.

4. Let x represent the dimension of the snowflake curve. Use the above observation to write an exponential equation in x. Solve the equation to obtain the dimension of the snowflake curve.

Fractal geometry is a new and complicated branch of geometry that is accessible only with computers. Computers are needed to handle the enormous computations involved in recursive processes, and to display the intricate results. The example below provides one small glimpse of this new world. It is a set of points that is studied in fractal geometry.

5. Examine the illustration carefully.
   a) Describe as many patterns in it as you can find.
   b) Find as many examples of self-similarity as you can.

8-10 THE PRINCIPLE OF MATHEMATICAL INDUCTION

Several problem-solving strategies were developed in earlier grades. In this section we introduce a new strategy that is useful for many kinds of problems, such as this one:

Prove that the sum of the first n terms of the series

$$\frac{1}{1 \cdot 2} + \frac{1}{2 \cdot 3} + \frac{1}{3 \cdot 4} + \dots + \frac{1}{n(n + 1)} \text{ is } \frac{n}{n + 1} \text{ for all } n \in \mathrm{N}.$$

(The dots in the above expression indicate multiplication.)
In trying to solve this problem, it is natural to verify the result for a few values of n.

When $n = 1, S_1 = \dfrac{1}{2}$

When $n = 2, S_2 = \dfrac{1}{2} + \dfrac{1}{6} = \dfrac{3}{6} + \dfrac{1}{6} = \dfrac{4}{6} = \dfrac{2}{3}$

When $n = 3, S_3 = \dfrac{1}{2} + \dfrac{1}{6} + \dfrac{1}{12} = \dfrac{6}{12} + \dfrac{2}{12} + \dfrac{1}{12} = \dfrac{9}{12} = \dfrac{3}{4}$

We can continue and add the first 4 terms to determine S_4. A more efficient method is to use the fact that we already know the sum of the first 3 terms:

When $n = 4, S_4 = S_3 + \dfrac{1}{4 \cdot 5}$

$$= \dfrac{3}{4} + \dfrac{1}{20}$$

$$= \dfrac{16}{20}$$

$$= \dfrac{4}{5}$$

Since we now know the sum of the first 4 terms, we can determine S_5 in the same way. We can extend these calculations as far as we please to verify the result for any value of n. But we cannot do this for all values of n. A proof for all values of n requires that the above calculations be generalized. We can do this as follows.

Suppose we have already proved that $S_k = \dfrac{k}{k + 1}$ for some value of k. Then we can prove that the result is true for the next value of k:

$$S_{k+1} = S_k + \frac{1}{(k + 1)(k + 2)}$$

$$= \frac{k}{k + 1} + \frac{1}{(k + 1)(k + 2)}$$

$$= \frac{k}{k + 1} \times \frac{k + 2}{k + 2} + \frac{1}{(k + 1)(k + 2)}$$

$$= \frac{k(k + 2) + 1}{(k + 1)(k + 2)}$$

$$= \frac{k^2 + 2k + 1}{(k + 1)(k + 2)}$$

$$= \frac{(k + 1)^2}{(k + 1)(k + 2)}$$

$$= \frac{k + 1}{k + 2}$$

When $k = 4$ these calculations reduce to those above. When $k = 5$ they prove that $S_5 = \frac{5}{6}$. When $k = 6$, they prove that $S_6 = \frac{6}{7}$, and so on. Since we can continue this reasoning for all natural numbers, we have proved our result. That is, $S_n = \frac{n}{n + 1}$ for all $n \in$ N. The method we used to prove this is called the *Principle of Mathematical Induction*.

Principle of Mathematical Induction

A result involving natural numbers is true for all natural numbers if *both* of the following are true.
1. The result is true when $n = 1$.
2. *If* the result is true when $n = k$, *then* it is true for $n = k + 1$.

Example 1. Use the Principle of Mathematical Induction to prove that
$3 + 7 + 11 + \ldots + (4n - 1) = 2n^2 + n$ for all $n \in$ N.

Solution. *Step 1. Check that the result is true when $n = 1$.*
When $n = 1$, $S_1 = 3$, and $2(1)^2 + 1 = 3$
Therefore, the result is true when $n = 1$.

Step 2. Given that the result is true when $n = k$, prove that it is true when $n = k + 1$.
Given: $S_k = 2k^2 + k$
Required to prove: $S_{k+1} = 2(k + 1)^2 + (k + 1)$
$$= 2(k^2 + 2k + 1) + (k + 1)$$
$$= 2k^2 + 5k + 3$$

Proof: $S_{k+1} = S_k + t_{k+1}$
$$= [2k^2 + k] + [4(k + 1) - 1]$$
$$= 2k^2 + k + 4k + 3$$
$$= 2k^2 + 5k + 3$$
Hence, if $S_k = 2k^2 + k$, then $S_{k+1} = 2(k + 1)^2 + (k + 1)$

Therefore, $S_n = 2n^2 + n$ for all $n \in$ N, by the Principle of Mathematical Induction.

Example 2. Prove that $3 + 6 + 12 + 24 + \ldots + 3(2^{n-1}) = 3(2^n - 1)$ for all $n \in N$.

Solution. Use the Principle of Mathematical Induction.

Step 1. When $n = 1$, $S_1 = 3$, and $3(2^n - 1) = 3(2^1 - 1) = 3$
Therefore, the result is true when $n = 1$.

Step 2. Given: $S_k = 3(2^k - 1)$
Required to prove: $S_{k+1} = 3(2^{k+1} - 1)$
Proof: $S_{k+1} = S_k + t_{k+1}$
$= 3(2^k - 1) + 3(2^k)$
$= 3(2^k) + 3(2^k) - 3$
$= 3(2 \times 2^k - 1)$
$= 3(2^{k+1} - 1)$
Hence, if $S_k = 3(2^k - 1)$, then $S_{k+1} = 3(2^{k+1} - 1)$
Therefore, $S_n = 3(2^n - 1)$ for all $n \in N$, by the Principle of Mathematical Induction.

In the preceding examples, the formula to be proved was given in the statement of the problem. In the next example, the formula is not given.

Example 3. Establish a formula for the sum of the first n terms of this series.
$$\frac{1}{1\cdot3} + \frac{1}{3\cdot5} + \frac{1}{5\cdot7} + \ldots + \frac{1}{(2n-1)(2n+1)}.$$

Solution. Since no formula is given we might discover it by looking for a pattern.
$$S_1 = \frac{1}{3}$$
$$S_2 = \frac{1}{3} + \frac{1}{15} = \frac{6}{15} = \frac{2}{5}$$
$$S_3 = S_2 + \frac{1}{35} = \frac{2}{5} + \frac{1}{35} = \frac{15}{35} = \frac{3}{7}$$

From these examples, it appears as though $S_n = \frac{n}{2n+1}$.

We now prove this using the Principle of Mathematical Induction.
Step 1. The result is true when $n = 1$, as shown above.

Step 2. Given: $S_k = \frac{k}{2k+1}$
Required to prove: $S_{k+1} = \frac{k+1}{2(k+1)+1}$
$= \frac{k+1}{2k+3}$

Proof: $S_{k+1} = S_k + t_{k+1}$
$= \frac{k}{2k+1} + \frac{1}{(2k+1)(2k+3)}$
$= \frac{k}{2k+1} \times \frac{2k+3}{2k+3} + \frac{1}{(2k+1)(2k+3)}$

$$= \frac{2k^2 + 3k + 1}{(2k + 1)(2k + 3)}$$

$$= \frac{(2k + 1)(k + 1)}{(2k + 1)(2k + 3)}$$

$$= \frac{k + 1}{2k + 3}$$

Hence, if $S_k = \dfrac{k}{2k + 1}$, then $S_{k+1} = \dfrac{k + 1}{2(k + 1) + 1}$.

Therefore, $S_n = \dfrac{n}{2n + 1}$ for all $n \in$ N, by the Principle of Mathematical Induction.

When we guessed the formula in the solution of *Example 3*, we used a method of reasoning called *induction*, and we proved the formula using *mathematical induction*. The following quotation from "How to Solve It" by George Polya explains the difference between induction and mathematical induction.

> *Induction* is the process of discovering general laws by the observation and combination of particular instances. It is used in all sciences and in mathematics. *Mathematical induction* is used in mathematics alone to prove theorems of a certain kind. It is rather unfortunate that their names are similar because there is very little logical connection between the two processes. There is, however, some practical connection; we often use both methods together.

This was done in the above example. The result to be proved was *discovered* by induction and *proved* by mathematical induction. To use mathematical induction we must know what assertion is to be proved. It may come from any source, and it does not matter what the source is. In many cases, as in the above, the source is induction—the assertion is found experimentally.

Mathematical induction is a very powerful method of proof, but it can only be used to solve certain kinds of problems:
- The statement to be proved must involve natural numbers.
- The statement to be proved must be known in advance. We cannot use mathematical induction to make discoveries.

Up to now, all the examples we have used to illustrate mathematical induction have involved series. However, this method can be used in a variety of other problems. The essential requirement is that the problem involve natural numbers.

Example 4. Prove that $n^3 + 2n$ is divisible by 3 for all $n \in$ N.

Solution. Use the Principle of Mathematical Induction.

Step 1. When $n = 1$, $n^3 + 2n = 1^3 + 2(1) = 3$, which is divisible by 3.

Therefore, the result is true when $n = 1$.

Step 2. Given: $k^3 + 2k$ is divisible by 3.
Required to prove: $(k + 1)^3 + 2(k + 1)$ is divisible by 3.
Proof: $(k + 1)^3 + 2(k + 1)$
$= (k + 1)(k^2 + 2k + 1) + 2k + 2$
$= k^3 + 2k^2 + k + k^2 + 2k + 1 + 2k + 2$
$= (k^3 + 2k) + 3k^2 + 3k + 3$
$= (k^3 + 2k) + 3(k^2 + k + 1) \ldots ①$
The first expression is divisible by 3. (Given)
The second expression is divisible by 3.
Therefore, expression ① is divisible by 3.
Hence, if $k^3 + 2k$ is divisible by 3, then
$(k + 1)^3 + 2(k + 1)$ is also divisible by 3.
Therefore, $n^3 + 2n$ is divisible by 3 for all $n \in N$, by the Principle of
Mathematical Induction.

EXERCISES 8-10

(A)

1. In each expression below the variable k represents a natural number. Substitute $k + 1$ for k and simplify the result.
   a) $\dfrac{k}{k + 1}$ b) $\dfrac{k}{2k + 1}$ c) $\dfrac{k + 1}{k - 1}$ d) $\dfrac{2k - 1}{3k - 1}$ e) $\frac{1}{2}k(k + 1)$
   f) $\frac{1}{3}k(k + 1)(k + 2)$ g) $(k - 1)(k + 1)$ h) $\frac{1}{2}k(2k - 1)(2k + 1)$

(B)

2. Prove, using the Principle of Mathematical Induction.
   a) $1 + 3 + 5 + \ldots + (2n - 1) = n^2$
   b) $2 + 4 + 6 + \ldots + 2n = n(n + 1)$
   c) $1 + 2 + 4 + 8 + \ldots + 2^{n-1} = 2^n - 1$
   d) $1 + \dfrac{1}{2} + \dfrac{1}{4} + \dfrac{1}{8} + \ldots + \dfrac{1}{2^{n-1}} = 2 - \dfrac{1}{2^{n-1}}$

3. Prove by mathematical induction.
   a) $\displaystyle\sum_{k=1}^{n} k = \frac{1}{2}n(n + 1)$ b) $\displaystyle\sum_{k=1}^{n} k^2 = \frac{1}{6}n(n + 1)(2n + 1)$
   c) $\displaystyle\sum_{k=1}^{n} k^3 = \left[\frac{1}{2}n(n + 1)\right]^2$

4. Prove by mathematical induction.
   a) $1 \cdot 2 + 2 \cdot 3 + 3 \cdot 4 + \ldots + n(n + 1) = \frac{1}{3}n(n + 1)(n + 2)$
   b) $1 \cdot 1 + 2 \cdot 2 + 3 \cdot 4 + 4 \cdot 8 + \ldots + n(2^{n-1}) = 1 + (n - 1)2^n$

5. Prove by mathematical induction.
   a) $1 \cdot 3 + 2 \cdot 4 + 3 \cdot 5 + \ldots + n(n + 2) = \frac{1}{6}n(n + 1)(2n + 7)$
   b) $1 \cdot 3 + 2 \cdot 5 + 3 \cdot 7 + \ldots + n(2n + 1) = \frac{1}{6}n(n + 1)(4n + 5)$
   c) $1 \cdot 2 \cdot 3 + 2 \cdot 3 \cdot 4 + 3 \cdot 4 \cdot 5 + \ldots + n(n + 1)(n + 2) = \frac{1}{4}n(n + 1)(n + 2)(n + 3)$

6. Establish a formula for each series.
   a) $\displaystyle\sum_{k=1}^{n} \frac{1}{(2k - 1)(2k + 1)}$ b) $\displaystyle\sum_{k=1}^{n} \frac{1}{(3k - 2)(3k + 1)}$ c) $\displaystyle\sum_{k=1}^{n} \frac{1}{(4k - 3)(4k + 1)}$

7. Establish a formula for the sum $1 + 2 \cdot 2! + 3 \cdot 3! + 4 \cdot 4! + \ldots + n \cdot n!$.

8. Prove by mathematical induction.
   a) $\dfrac{1}{1 \cdot 2 \cdot 3} + \dfrac{1}{2 \cdot 3 \cdot 4} + \dfrac{1}{3 \cdot 4 \cdot 5} + \ldots + \dfrac{1}{n(n + 1)(n + 2)} = \dfrac{n(n + 3)}{4(n + 1)(n + 2)}$
   b) $\dfrac{1}{1 \cdot 2} + \dfrac{2}{1 \cdot 2 \cdot 3} + \dfrac{3}{1 \cdot 2 \cdot 3 \cdot 4} + \ldots + \dfrac{n}{(n + 1)!} = 1 - \dfrac{1}{(n + 1)!}$

9. Prove each statement by mathematical induction, where $n \in$ N.
   a) $n(n + 1)(n + 2)$ is always divisible by 6.
   b) $n(n + 1)(n + 2)(n + 3)$ is always divisible by 24.
   c) $x^{2n-1} + y^{2n-1}$ is divisible by $x + y$.

10. Prove each statement by mathematical induction for the values of n shown, $n \in$ N.
    a) $2^n < n!$ for $n = 4, 5, 6, \ldots$ b) $2^n < 3^{n-1}$ for $n \geqslant 2$.
    c) $(1 + x)^n \geqslant 1 + nx$, where $x \in$ R
    d) If $0 \leqslant x < y$, then $x^n < y^n$, where $x, y \in$ R.

11. Prove that a regular polygon with n sides has $\frac{1}{2}n(n - 3)$ diagonals.

Ⓒ

12. Prove by mathematical induction.
    a) $a + (a + d) + (a + 2d) + \ldots + [a + (n - 1)d] = \dfrac{n}{2}[2a + (n - 1)d]$
    b) $a + ar + ar^2 + \ldots + ar^{n-1} = \dfrac{a(1 - r^n)}{1 - r}$, where $r \neq 1$

13. Establish a formula for each product.
    a) $(1 + 1)\left(1 + \dfrac{1}{2}\right)\left(1 + \dfrac{1}{3}\right)\left(1 + \dfrac{1}{4}\right) \ldots \left(1 + \dfrac{1}{n}\right)$
    b) $\left(1 - \dfrac{1}{2}\right)\left(1 - \dfrac{1}{3}\right)\left(1 - \dfrac{1}{4}\right) \ldots \left(1 - \dfrac{1}{n}\right)$
    c) $\left(1 - \dfrac{1}{4}\right)\left(1 - \dfrac{1}{9}\right)\left(1 - \dfrac{1}{16}\right) \ldots \left(1 - \dfrac{1}{n^2}\right)$

14. Prove that $(\cos \theta + i \sin \theta)^n = \cos n\theta + i \sin n\theta$, where $i^2 = -1$ and $n \in$ N.

PROBLEM SOLVING

Creative Problem Posing

"For both problem solving and the teaching of problem solving, Polya's advice is most appropriate — practice, practice, practice."

Linda J. DeGuire

What happens if the constants in the equation $Ax + By + C = 0$ are in arithmetic sequence?

Think of a strategy and carry it out

- Write an example of an equation in which the constants are in arithmetic sequence.
- Write another equation like it, and then solve the system formed by the two equations.
- Repeat with another pair of equations.
- Compare your results with those of other students. What do you notice?

OR

- Write an example of an equation in which the constants are in arithmetic sequence.
- Draw the graph of the equation.
- Write some other equations like it and draw their graphs on the same grid.
- Compare your results with those of other students. What do you notice?

Look back

- Can you prove your results?
- Would it matter if the equation were written in the form $Ax + By = C$?
- Write a report of your discoveries.

The quotation below is taken from an essay entitled, "How Much Mathematics Can There Be?".

"All experience so far seems to show that there are two inexhaustible sources of new mathematical questions. One source is the development of science and technology, which makes ever new demands on mathematics for assistance. The other source is mathematics itself. As it becomes more elaborate and complex, each new, completed result becomes the potential starting point for several new investigations. Each pair of seemingly unrelated mathematical specialties pose an implicit challenge: to find a fruitful connection between them."

The last sentence of the quotation, and the above example, suggest that one method of posing problems in mathematics is to try to find connections between apparently unrelated topics. This can often be done by matching or linking certain constants or numbers that occur in the two topics.

For example, in the problem about linear equations and arithmetic sequences we matched the coefficients in the equation with the terms of an arithmetic sequence.

Many topics in mathematics can be linked in this way to create problems to investigate. To assist with this, the table below is useful. For example, cell A links the topics which suggested the problem discussed above. Each cell links two different topics and represents a potential source of problems for investigation.

| Consecutive numbers |
| Perfect squares |
| Prime numbers |
| Coordinates of a point |
| Sides of a triangle |
| Angles of a triangle |
| Line $y = mx + b$ |
| Line $Ax + By + C = 0$ |
| Parabola $y = ax^2 + bx + c$ |
| $ax^2 + bx + c = 0$ |
| Arithmetic sequence |
| Geometric sequence |

A

Choose one or more of the cells. Create problems based on the topics linked by each cell, and then solve the problems.

PROBLEMS

Ⓑ

1. Find an expression for the sum of the squares of the terms of the finite arithmetic series $a + (a + d) + (a + 2d) + \ldots + [a + (n - 1) d]$.

2. Write the numbers from 1 to 9 in the spaces such that a correct addition of two 3-digit numbers is illustrated, and consecutive digits are in adjacent spaces.

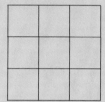

3. Sketch the curve $y = 2 \sin x \, |\cos x|$.

4. A card 12 cm long and 6 cm wide is cut along a diagonal to form two congruent triangles. Then, the triangles are arranged as shown. Find the area of the region where the triangles overlap.

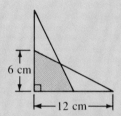

Ⓒ

5. Prove that there is no infinite arithmetic sequence of natural numbers whose terms are all prime numbers, except for the trivial case when the common difference is 0.

6. In pentagon ABCDE, all five sides have the same length. If O is the midpoint of AB, and $\angle EOC = 90°$, determine the measures of $\angle BCD$ and $\angle AED$.

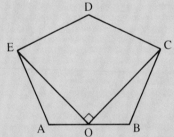

7. a) Prove that x, y, and z are consecutive terms of a geometric sequence if, and only if, $(x^2 + y^2)(y^2 + z^2) = (xy + yz)^2$.

   b) Determine whether or not a similar result holds for four consecutive terms of a geometric sequence.

8. Calculate the coordinates of all the points on the ellipse defined by $4x^2 + 9y^2 = 36$ which are twice as far from one vertex as from the other vertex.

Ⓓ

9. In $\triangle ABC$, $AB = AC$, and $\angle A = 20°$. M is a point on AB such that $\angle MCB = 50°$, and N is a point on AC such that $\angle NBC = 60°$. Calculate $\angle BNM$.

1. Write the first 4 terms of each sequence defined by the given term.
   a) $t_n = 3n + 1$ b) $t_n = (n - 1)^2$
   c) $t_n = 5n^2 - 2n$ d) $t_n = \dfrac{n - 2}{n + 1}$

2. Find the indicated terms of each sequence.
   a) $t_n = 3 + 5n$, t_4 and t_{11} b) $t_n = 2^n - 3$, t_5 and t_{10}
   c) $t_n = \dfrac{n}{3n - 1}$, t_3 and t_8 d) $t_n = 10 - 2^{n-1}$, t_4 and t_7

3. Write the first 4 terms of each sequence with the given values of a and d or r.
   a) $a = 2$, $d = 7$ b) $a = 1$, $r = 3$
   c) $a = 21$, $d = -4$ d) $a = -2$, $r = 5$

4. Classify each sequence as arithmetic or geometric, and find the value of d or r.

   a) $13, 9, 5, 1, \ldots$ b) $\dfrac{1}{4}, \dfrac{1}{2}, 1, 2, \ldots$
   c) $18, -9, 4.5, -2.25, \ldots$ d) $5, 13, 21, 29, \ldots$

5. Find an expression for the general term of each sequence.
   a) $2, 6, 10, 14, \ldots$ b) $2, 6, 18, 54, \ldots$
   c) $1, 8, 27, 64, \ldots$ d) $\dfrac{3}{2}, \dfrac{8}{3}, \dfrac{15}{4}, \dfrac{24}{5}, \ldots$

6. Find an expression for the general term of each sequence.
   a) $2, 9, 16, 23, \ldots$ b) $2, 8, 32, 128, \ldots$
   c) $1, 5, 25, 125, \ldots$ d) $19, 14, 9, 4, \ldots$

7. Find x and y if $2, 8, x, y$ are consecutive terms of:
   a) an arithmetic sequence   b) a geometric sequence.

8. Find t_5 in the sequence $5, 2, \ldots$, if the sequence is:
   a) arithmetic   b) geometric.

9. In the arithmetic sequence $5, 9, 13, 17, \ldots$, find each term.
   a) t_7 b) t_{20} c) t_n

10. Find the 10th and nth terms of the sequence $25, 23.5, 22, 20.5, \ldots$

11. In the sequence $4, 12, 36, 108, \ldots$, find: a) t_7 b) t_{15} c) t_n.

12. Find the 6th and the nth terms of the sequence $2, 12, 72, 432, \ldots$

13. How many terms are in each sequence?
    a) $1, 4, 16, \ldots, 4096$ b) $9, 13, 17, \ldots, 121$
    c) $35, 29, 23, \ldots, -91$ d) $27, 9, 3, \ldots, \dfrac{1}{243}$

14. How many multiples of 12 are there from 36 to 252 inclusive?

15. Find the middle term of the sequence $3, 8, 13, 18, \ldots, 303$.

16. In an arithmetic sequence, the third term is 19 and the fifteenth term is -17. Find the first 3 terms of the sequence.

17. In a geometric sequence, the third term is 50 and the sixth term is 6250. Find the first 3 terms of the sequence.

18. In an arithmetic sequence, $t_4 + t_5 + t_6 = 300$, and $t_{15} + t_{16} + t_{17} = 201$; find t_{18}.

19. In a geometric sequence, $t_1 + t_2 + t_3 = 21$, and $t_4 + t_5 + t_6 = 168$; find the first 3 terms of the sequence.

20. Write the first 4 terms of each sequence.
   a) $t_1 = 1, t_n = 3t_{n-1} + 4, n > 1$ b) $t_1 = -0.5, t_n = -4t_{n-1}, n > 1$

21. Classify each series as arithmetic, geometric, or other.
   a) $1 + 7 + 13 + 19 + \ldots$ b) $1 + 4 + 9 + 16 + \ldots$
   c) $1 + 3 + 9 + 27 + \ldots$ d) $64 + 32 + 16 + 8 + \ldots$
   e) $21 + 13 + 5 + (-3) + \ldots$ f) $\frac{1}{2} + \frac{2}{3} + \frac{3}{4} + \frac{4}{5} + \ldots$

22. The sum of the first 3 terms of a series is 32. Find the fourth term if the sum of the first 4 terms is:
   a) 40   b) 55   c) 25.

23. Write the first 4 terms of the series for which:
   a) $S_n = 2n$ b) $S_n = n^2 + 2n$ c) $S_n = 3n + 1$ d) $S_n = 2n^2 - n$.

24. Find S_5 and S_n for each series.
   a) $2 + 5 + 8 + \ldots$ b) $12 + 5 + (-2) + \ldots$ c) $6 + 10 + 14 + \ldots$
   d) $5 + 10 + 20 + \ldots$ e) $12 + 6 + 3 + \ldots$ f) $2 + 6 + 18 + \ldots$

25. For the series $-3 + 1 + 5 + 9 + \ldots$, find: a) t_{10} b) S_{16}.

26. For the series $1 + 2 + 4 + 8 + \ldots$, find: a) t_8 b) S_{21}.

27. How many terms of the series $1 + 3 + 5 + 7 + \ldots$ add to 144?

28. How many terms of the series $3 + 6 + 12 + 24 + \ldots$ add to 765?

29. In an arithmetic series, if the fifth term is 74 and the twelfth term is 116, find:
   a) the first 3 terms of the series   b) the sum of the first 30 terms.

30. In a geometric series, $t_3 = 18$ and $t_6 = 486$; find:
   a) the first 3 terms of the series   b) S_{17}.

31. Find the sum of the first 15 terms of an arithmetic series if the middle term is 92.

32. Find the sum of each infinite geometric series.
   a) $40 + 20 + 10 + 5 + \ldots$ b) $-30 + 20 - \frac{40}{3} + \frac{80}{9} - \ldots$

33. Simplify.
   a) $\sum_{i=1}^{6} (4i + 3)$ b) $\sum_{i=2}^{10} (-3i + 5)$ c) $\sum_{j=3}^{7} 2^{2-j}$

9 Statistics

An extensive study of 10 000 adult males throughout the world reveals that the height H of the adult male is normally distributed with mean 175 cm and standard deviation 6.5 cm. What percent of the adult male population is shorter than 190 cm? (See Section 9-7 *Example 2*.)

9-1 INTERPRETING AND DISPLAYING DATA

In this "Information Age" we are confronted daily with tables of data, graphs, and statements which require careful interpretation and critical analysis.

Omega Oil Company Has Windfall Profits Up 1000% Over Last Year

Information behind the headline

Omega Oil Company Profit per $100 invested

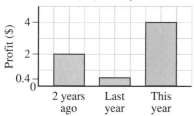

Analysis
- What was Omega's profit as a percent of investment last year? this year?
- Is the headline correct?
- Is the headline misleading? Explain.

Interest Rate Increases Continue To Decline

Information behind the headline

Bank of Canada rate in recent weeks

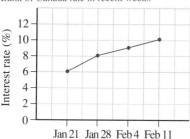

Analysis
- What was the Bank of Canada rate increase as a fraction of the previous rate from:
  Jan. 21 to Jan. 28?
  Jan. 28 to Feb. 4?
  Feb. 4 to Feb. 11?
- Is the headline correct?
- Is the headline misleading? Explain.

The Average Canadian Is More Likely To Die From Heart Disease

Information behind the headline

Major causes of death among Canadians

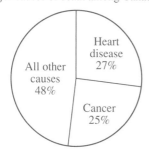

Analysis
- Additional information for the province of Quebec shows that the percents of deaths in that province for heart disease and cancer are respectively 25.7% and 26%. Is a person from Quebec more likely to die of heart disease or cancer?
- Is the headline correct? Does it apply to all Canadians?

Our Immigration Practices Discriminate Against Males

Information behind the headline

Age-Sex Distribution Per 1000
Immigrants

Age range in years	Males	Females
0–9	57	53
10–19	80	76
20–29	142	156
30–39	88	89
40–49	35	41
50–59	29	44
60 and over	45	65
Total	476	524

Analysis
- Are more female immigrants admitted than male immigrants?
- Is the headline misleading? Explain.
- Are girls younger than 10 victims of discrimination?

The foregoing examples demonstrate how headlines can be misleading. Sometimes the headlines are intentionally worded to promote controversy and consequently sell more newspapers. In other cases, headlines are misleading because they attempt to summarize complex information. Since the human mind cannot easily extract patterns and trends from large amounts of numerical information, mathematicians have devised graphs, tabular formats, and data displays from which patterns can be more readily observed. Some of these devices are used in the following example.

There are exactly 100 people living in the Santa Maria Towers condominium. The printout below presents the ages of these people by family groupings.

20 20	29 28 5 1	68 70	89	48 46 19 14 12	68 38 36 17 15 10
38 32 12 10	82 58 46	73 47 47 5 2	36 34	42 16	40 38 14 14
53 52	67 64	46 43 21 17 15	27	50 46	24 24	44 36	61 57	37	32
29 26 4	66 65 62	30 26 8 3	49 48	23 22 2	59 40 19 16 9
37 34 9 7 2	92	67 63	46 41 15 14 10	41 38	87 82	23 23 2

We shall explore devices for presenting the data above, so that answers to questions such as these can be determined.

a) How many 14-year-olds live in Santa Maria Towers?
b) What is the most common age of the residents at Santa Maria Towers?
c) How many residents are between 20 and 30 years of age?
d) What is the age of the oldest resident? the youngest resident?
e) What percent of the residents are over 60 years of age?

It is convenient to group the ages in decades. We list them in increasing order within each decade.

1   2   2   2   2   3   4   5   5   7   8   9   9
10 10 10 12 12 14 14 14 14 15 15 15 16 16 17 17 19 19
20 20 21 22 23 23 23 24 24 26 26 27 28 29 29
30 32 32 34 34 36 36 36 37 37 38 38 38 38
40 40 41 41 42 43 44 46 46 46 46 46 47 47 48 48 49
50 52 53 57 58 59
61 62 63 64 65 66 67 67 68 68
70 73
82 82 87 89
92

Rather than repeat the tens digit in each decade, we can simplify the array of numbers above to form a *stem-and-leaf plot*. The tens digit is the "stem" and the units digit forms a "leaf" of each number

d) The youngest resident is 1 year old.

Tens digit	Units digits
0	1 2 2 2 2 3 4 5 5 7 8 9 9
1	0 0 0 2 2 4 4 4 4 5 5 5 6 6 7 7 9 9
2	0 0 1 2 3 3 3 4 4 6 6 7 8 9 9
3	0 2 2 4 4 6 6 6 7 7 8 8 8 8
4	0 0 1 1 2 3 4 6 6 6 6 6 7 7 8 8 9
5	0 2 3 7 8 9
6	1 2 3 4 5 6 7 7 8 8
7	0 3
8	2 2 7 9
9	2

a) There are four 14-year-olds living in Santa Maria Towers.

c) There are 15 residents between 20 and 30 years of age.

b) The most common age is 46 years. There are five people of this age.

e) There are 17 out of the 100 residents who are over 60. That is, 17% of the residents are over 60 years of age.

d) The oldest resident is 92 years old.

For a stem-and-leaf plot, it is not necessary to write the units digits in order. We do so to facilitate finding the number that occurs most frequently. Also, it is not necessary to work only in decades for a stem-and-leaf plot.

The data in the stem-and-leaf plot can be summarized by recording the *number* of residents in each decade (or class) rather than the actual ages of these residents. A graph showing the number of people in each class is called a *histogram*.

Class	Frequency
0– 9 years	13
10–19 years	18
20–29 years	15
30–39 years	14
40–49 years	17
50–59 years	6
60–69 years	10
70–79 years	2
80–89 years	4
90–99 years	1
Total	100

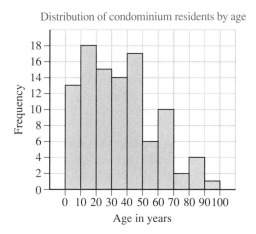

Distribution of condominium residents by age

The graph does not begin at zero; this is to leave room for the final segment in the frequency polygon. The histogram is a visual display of the stem-and-leaf plot. In fact, the outline of the histogram could be obtained by rotating the stem-and-leaf plot counterclockwise 90°. However, the histogram gives only the number of people in each class, and not their specific ages.

When we represent data in a histogram, we lose some information but we gain a visual sense of how the data are distributed across the classes. Hence, if our only data were that given in the histogram, we would be able to answer questions c) and e) above, but not questions a), b), and d).

Sometimes it is the *shape* of a histogram that is most important in displaying how a set of data is distributed. In such a case we join the midpoints of the bars of the histogram to form a *frequency polygon*.

The broken-line graph in color is the frequency polygon showing the distribution of the ages of the residents.

Observe that line segments are drawn from the midpoints of the first and last histogram bars to the horizontal axis so that the broken-line graph together with the horizontal axis forms a polygon.

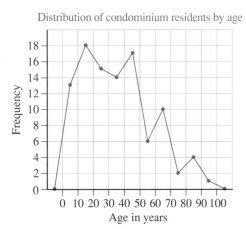

Distribution of condominium residents by age

The frequency polygon illustrates the peaks and valleys more obviously than the histogram does.

EXERCISES 9-1

Ⓐ

1. Discuss each statement. What information would be needed to verify or refute each headline?
   a) "Fewer students are choosing science courses at universities"
   b) "AIDS virus has reached epidemic proportions"
   c) "Canadian students are not as well trained in mathematics as Japanese students are"
   d) "Job discrimination against women is on the increase"
   e) "Most Canadians will suffer some form of mental disorder in their lifetimes"
   f) "By the year 2000, two out of three Canadians will be unemployed"

2. This bar graph, taken from the Second International Mathematics Study, shows the average class sizes for senior high school classes in the various nations. The countries are listed in order of student achievement from high (Hong Kong) to low (Hungary). Use the graph to help you answer these questions.
   a) What was the size of the average Ontario senior mathematics class?
   b) What two countries had the largest class size? the smallest class size?
   c) Does there seem to be a relationship between class size and student achievement?

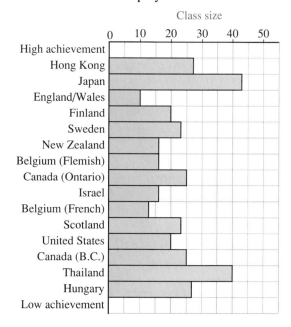

3. These circle graphs present data collected on the attitudes of American students in grades 8 and 12 in response to the statement, "I am looking forward to taking more math." Use the graphs to answer these questions.
   a) i) Estimate the percent of grade 8 students who are looking forward to taking more math.
      ii) Estimate the percent who are undecided.
   b) Answer part a) for grade 12 students.
   c) Explain how the attitudes of students to the survey question above changed between grades 8 and 12.

I am looking forward to taking more mathematics

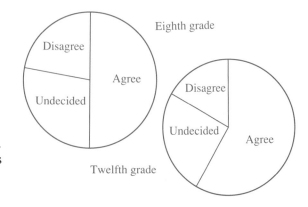

Ⓑ

4. The double histogram shows the distribution of Canadians by age as of June 1, 1985.

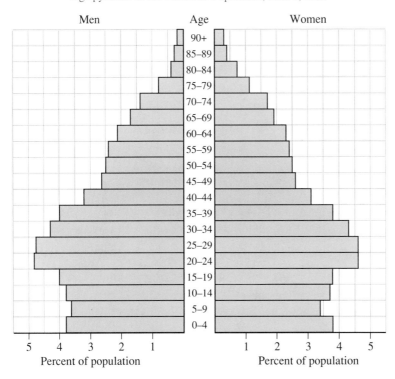

Age pyramid of the Canadian Population, June 1, 1985

Use the histogram to answer these questions.

a) What percent of Canadians were between ages 5 and 9? 10 and 14? 15 and 19?

b) What percent of Canadians were school age; that is, between 5 and 19 as of June 1, 1985?

c) What percent of Canadians were under 5 years? over 64?

d) In what age classes were most Canadians in 1985?

5. The table gives the number of families out of 1000 Canadian families surveyed, and the numbers of children.

a) Show this information on a bar graph.

b) Use your bar graph to sketch the corresponding frequency polygon.

c) What number of children was most common?

Number of children	Number of families
0	103
1	148
2	405
3	251
4	71
5	16
6	5
7+	1

6. The table shows the percent of single
   Canadian males (15 years or older) in
   each age class.
   a) Use these data to construct a
      histogram.
   b) Sketch the corresponding frequency
      polygon on your histogram.

Age in years	Percent
15–19	31.6
20–24	32.4
25–29	16.0
30–34	6.3
35–39	4.8
40–44	2.0
45–49	1.5
50 and over	5.4

7. A public opinion survey indicated that
   people would probably vote as shown
   in the table. Illustrate this information
   with a circle graph.

Party	Number of people
Conservative	275
Liberal	225
New Democrat	375
Other	50
Undecided	325

8. The masses in kilograms of 30 students in a grade 9 class are given below.
   48   52   47   46   50   56   61   54   45   42   49   50   41   47   44
   49   48   43   58   39   43   48   54   38   48   48   35   49   60   53
   a) Display these data in a stem-and-leaf plot.
   b) Construct a histogram to show the distribution of the masses of the students, in
      intervals of 5 kg.
   c) Sketch a frequency polygon on your histogram.
   d) In what interval do the masses of the students seem to cluster?

9. Use the data in *Exercise 6* to construct a circle graph which shows the percent of
   all single Canadian males (15 years and older) in age classes A, B, and C where
   A denotes all single males aged 15 to 19, B denotes all single males aged 20 to 39,
   and C denotes all single males aged 40 and older.

10. The table shows the percent of Canadian
    males in each age class who are single.
    a) Use these data to construct a
       histogram.
    b) Sketch the corresponding frequency
       polygon on your histogram.
    c) The percents in the table of *Exercise
       6* total 100%. Why do the percents
       in this table not total 100%?
    d) Explain the difference between the
       "percent of single Canadian males
       between 20 and 24 years" and the
       "percent of Canadian males between
       20 and 24 years who are single".

Age in years	Percent
15–19	99.7
20–24	85.0
25–29	42.1
30–34	18.0
35–39	10.6
40–44	7.7
45–49	6.9
50 +	28.4

9-2 MEASURES OF CENTRAL TENDENCY

In the previous section we studied the age distribution of the 100 residents of Santa Maria Towers condominium. These data were summarized in a stem-and-leaf plot to provide ready answers to certain types of questions. However, a different kind of data graph might be more appropriate for answering the following questions.

In what age interval are:
a) the youngest 10% of the residents?
b) the youngest 25% of the residents?
c) the youngest 50% of the residents?
d) the oldest 25% of the residents?
e) the oldest 10% of the residents?

To answer these questions we write the ages of the 100 residents in 10 rows of 10 from youngest to oldest.

a) The ages of the youngest 10% of the residents are in row 1.

1	2	2	2	2	3	4	5	5	7
8	9	9	10	10	10	12	12	14	14
14	14	15	15	15	16	16	17	17	19
19	20	20	21	22	23	23	23	24	24
26	26	27	28	29	29	30	32	32	34
34	36	36	36	37	37	38	38	38	38
40	40	41	41	42	43	44	46	46	46
46	46	47	47	48	48	49	50	52	53
57	58	59	61	62	63	64	65	66	67
67	68	68	70	73	82	82	87	89	92

b) The youngest 25% of the residents are between 1 and 16 years of age.

c) The ages of the youngest 50% of the residents are in the first 5 rows.

d) The oldest 25% of the residents are between 48 and 92 years of age.

e) The ages of the oldest 10% of the residents are in row 10.

The youngest 10% of the residents have ages displayed in the first row of the array above. The youngest 10% have ages ranging from 1 to 7 years of age.

Since 10% of the residents are below 8 years of age, we say that 8 is the *10th percentile* (denoted P_{10}) of the age distribution.

Similarly, 16, 34, 48, and 67 are the 25th, 50th, 75th, and 90th percentiles respectively. In general, we define a percentile as follows:

Definition: The xth percentile P_x of a distribution is the number below which $x\%$ of the values fall.

One device for summarizing and presenting such data is the *box-and-whisker* plot shown below. The box contains the middle 50% and the whiskers contain the middle 80%.

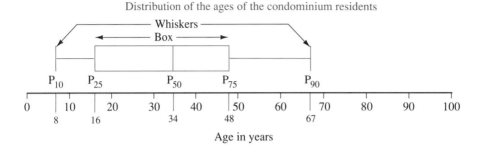

Distribution of the ages of the condominium residents

Age in years

From this box-and-whisker plot we can read the following information.
- The youngest 10% of the residents are younger than 8 years.
- The youngest 25% of the residents are younger than 16 years.
- Half of the residents are younger than 34 years.
- The oldest 25% of the residents are 48 years or older.
- The oldest 10% of the residents are 67 years or older.

In summary, the middle 50% of the residents are between 16 and 48 years of age (that is, within the box) and the middle 80% are between 8 and 67 (that is, within the whiskers).

Some percentiles are used so frequently that they are given special names. Since P_{25} and P_{75} are respectively the values below which $\frac{1}{4}$ and $\frac{3}{4}$ of the numbers lie, they are called the *first quartile* and *third quartile* respectively. The second quartile P_{50} is called the *median*.

Definition: The *median* of a set of n numbers arranged in order of magnitude is the middle number when n is odd or the value midway between the two middle numbers when n is even.

Since the median is the "middle" value in a set of data, it represents an average or representative value for the data. However, the number which occurs most often in a set of data is called the mode.

Definition: The *mode* of a set of numbers is that value which occurs with greatest frequency.

In the discussion above, the most frequently occurring age was 46 years. We say that the mode of the age distribution is 46. We observe in the box-and-whisker plot above that the mode is almost at P_{75}, hence 46 years of age is not representative, because nearly 70% of the people are below 46 years of age.

A third kind of average is represented by the mean.

Definition: If $x_1, x_2, \ldots, x_n$ denotes a set of n numbers, then the *arithmetic mean* of this set of numbers is denoted by $\overline{x}$. We say, ''x bar''.

$$\overline{x} = \frac{\displaystyle\sum_{i=1}^{n} x_i}{n}$$

The mean, the median, and the mode are called the measures of central tendency.

Example 1. a) Calculate the arithmetic mean of the ages of the residents in the Santa Maria Towers condominium.

b) Determine which is the best measure of the average age of a condominium resident: the mean, the median or the mode.

Solution. a) To determine the mean, we could enter the 100 ages into a calculator and then divide by 100. Another method is to use the stem-and-leaf plot and add up the tens and ones separately.

Tens digit	Units digits
0	1 2 2 2 2 3 4 5 5 7 8 9 9
1	0 0 0 2 2 4 4 4 4 5 5 5 6 6 7 7 9 9
2	0 0 1 2 3 3 3 4 4 6 6 7 8 9 9
3	0 2 2 4 4 6 6 6 7 7 8 8 8 8
4	0 0 1 1 2 3 4 6 6 6 6 6 7 7 8 8 9
5	0 2 3 7 8 9
6	1 2 3 4 5 6 7 7 8 8
7	0 3
8	2 2 7 9
9	2

- Multiply each of the numbers 10, 20, 30, ... , 90 by the frequency of ages in that decade, and add.
  $10(18) + 20(15) + 30(14) + 40(17) + 50(6) + 60(10) + 70(2) + 80(4) + 90 = 3030$
- Add the units digits.
  $1 + 2 + 2 + 2 + \ldots + 2 + 2 + 7 + 9 + 2 = 464$
- Add the results of the first two steps. $3030 + 464 = 3494$
- Divide by 100. $\dfrac{3494}{100} = 34.94$

The mean age of the residents of the condominium is 34.94 years.

b) For the residents of the condominium the average ages are: mode, 46 years; median, 34 years; mean, 34.94 years.

As noted previously, the mode is not representative of the ages of the residents. The mean and the median are so close in value that both measures are equally representative of the ages of the residents.

Note, in *Example 1*, that if the 10 oldest residents had been over 100 years of age, these large ages would have made the mean much larger and much less appropriate as a measure of the average age.

Example 2. These data were recorded from the measures of the heights (to the nearest centimetre) of 36 female students in a senior grade of secondary school. Estimate the mean height from this data.

Height (cm)	Frequency
145–149	2
150–154	1
155–159	1
160–164	3
165–169	4
170–174	6
175–179	8
180–184	5
185–189	4
190–194	2

Solution. Since the table gives grouped data instead of actual heights, we cannot calculate the mean height.

We can, however, calculate the approximate mean by assuming that all the heights in each class are at the midpoint height. That is, we assume that the person in the class of 155–159 has a height of 157 cm and that the 3 people in the class of 160–164 all have height 162 cm.

Multiply the midpoint height in each class by the frequency, and add the results.

147(2) + 152(1) + 157(1) + 162(3) + 167(4) + 172(6) + 177(8) + 182(5) + 187(4) + 192(2) = 6247

Divide by 36. $\frac{6247}{36} \doteq 173.5$

The mean height is about 174 cm.

EXERCISES 9-2

Ⓐ

1. Discuss the measure of central tendency which would best describe each of the following "averages".
   a) the average salary of a hockey player
   b) the dress size worn by most women
   c) the average speed of a car during a trip
   d) the income tax rate for the average Canadian
   e) the average distance between the Earth and the sun
   f) the average lifetime of a television picture tube

2. a) For each set of integers find the mean, the median, and the mode.
      $R = \{0, 1, 2, 3, 4, 5, 6, 7, 8, 9, 10\}$
      $S = \{0, 1, 1, 2, 2, 2, 3, 3, 3, 3, 4, 4, 4, 4, 4\}$
      $T = \{0, 0, 0, 0, 0, 5, 5, 5, 5, 40\}$

b) Are the mean, the median, and the mode of a set of numbers always members of that set? Explain your answer.

3. A student scored the following percents on a set of examinations: 83, 95, 87, 94, 86, and 86.
   a) What is her mean score?
   b) What must she score on her seventh examination to obtain a 90% average?
   c) Can she score a 95% average on the seven examinations? Explain.

4. When the heights of all the grade 12 students were plotted on a graph, it was found that the graph had a hump at 165 cm and a hump at 177 cm. Explain why we could expect this distribution to be clustered around two modes.

5. Lesley is told that she placed in the 98th percentile among all students taking a mathematics aptitude test.
   a) Explain what that means.
   b) If 15 000 Canadian students took that test, about how many students scored lower than Lesley?

(B)

6. Create a set of numbers with a mean of 5, a median of 6, and a mode of 7.

7. The following data give the lifetimes of 56 electronic components, in months.

34	56	37	28	51	64	28	37	46	51	39	28	38	49
37	48	53	29	27	35	48	50	68	27	36	34	35	54
48	45	39	38	36	44	35	39	37	40	33	39	42	48
40	46	49	38	39	48	56	59	27	60	36	33	31	25

   a) Display this data on a stem-and-leaf plot.
   b) Find the mean, the median, and the mode lifetimes.
   c) Find the 25th percentile and the 75th percentile.
   d) Find P_{10} and P_{90}.
   e) Construct a box-and-whisker plot of the lifetimes of the electronic components.

8. The ages of all the guests at a family reunion are given in this stem-and-leaf plot.

Tens digit	Units digit
0	1 3 3 6 8 8 9 9 9
1	0 0 2 3 4 6 7
2	4 5 6 6 7 8
3	0 0 2 3 5 5 8 9 9
4	1 1 2 5 7 7 9
5	0 2 2 3 6 6 7 8
6	0 1 5 5 7 8 8
7	1 1 2 8
8	0 2 3

   a) What is the median age of the people?
   b) Calculate the mean age.
   c) Find P_{10}, P_{25}, P_{75}, and P_{90}.
   d) Display the age distribution on a box-and-whisker plot.

9. a) Draw a histogram for the data in *Exercise 8*. Use the class intervals 0–9, ...
   10–19, 20–29, ...
   b) Using only the data in your histogram, calculate the mean age.
   c) Compare the mean age calculated in *Exercise 8* with the mean age calculated
   in part b). How close are the two results?
   d) What distribution of data would lead to a large difference between the mean
   calculated from exact data and the mean calculated from a histogram?

10. The Second International Mathematics Study included a survey of the number of
    hours per week of mathematics homework assigned by grade 8 and grade 12 teachers
    throughout the United States. The results of that survey were presented in these
    box-and-whisker plots.

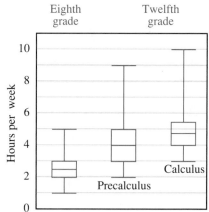

   The ends of the box are located at P_{25} and
   P_{75}. That is, the box contains the middle
   50% of all teachers surveyed. The whiskers
   contain the middle 90% of all teachers
   surveyed (not the middle 80% as in the
   plots previously studied).
   a) What percentile is represented by the
   end of each whisker?
   b) What is the median number of hours of
   mathematics homework assigned by
   grade 8 teachers? precalculus teachers?
   calculus teachers?
   c) What percent of the calculus teachers
   assigned 10 or more hours of homework per week in calculus?
   d) What percent of grade 8 teachers assigned less than 2 h of mathematics homework per week? less than 1 h per week?

11. In university, a student's final grades in mathematics, physics, chemistry, English,
    philosophy, and music were respectively 86, 76, 90, 72, 81, and 70. If the
    respective credits assigned to these courses are 7, 6, 4, 4, 2, and 1 find the students's
    grade average.

Ⓒ
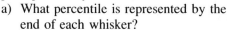

12. Let $x_1, x_2, x_3, \ldots, x_n$ denote n measurements. Let $\bar{x}$ denote the mean value of these
    measurements, and let d_i be defined by $d_i = x_i - \bar{x}$. Use the properties of the
    notation, and the definition of the mean to prove that $\displaystyle\sum_{i=1}^{n} d_i = 0$.

13. A variable can take any one of the values in the set S where S is defined by
    $S = \{x_1, x_2, \ldots, x_n\}$. Let $f(x_i)$ denote the number of times the variable takes the
    value x_i on a set on N measurements.

    a) Prove that $\displaystyle\sum_{i=1}^{n} f(x_i) = N.$ b) Prove that $\bar{x} = \dfrac{\displaystyle\sum_{i=1}^{n} x_i f(x_i)}{N}.$

9-3 MEASURES OF DISPERSION

In the previous section, we studied measures of central tendency; that is, single numbers (such as the mean) calculated to represent the "typical" or "average" number in a set of data. When we summarize data in this way, we lose information. For example, knowing that the mean lifetime of a particular brand of battery is 5.6 years does not tell us what proportion of these batteries will last less than 1 year. To measure the extent to which given data differ from the mean, statisticians have developed various measures of dispersion.

The lifetimes of 30 brand X batteries and 30 brand Y batteries are presented in the tables below.

Measured lifetimes of 30 brand X batteries (in years)					
5.0	7.2	6.8	4.6	4.5	6.1
6.3	5.4	4.8	6.8	5.9	4.7
4.0	5.2	8.0	6.2	7.4	4.9
5.6	9.2	3.2	3.0	4.2	5.8
6.5	5.7	4.9	6.0	4.5	5.6

Measured lifetimes of 30 brand Y batteries (in years)					
5.3	6.2	4.9	5.8	5.5	4.6
5.9	3.2	6.5	5.9	4.9	6.4
5.7	5.3	4.8	5.6	6.7	5.5
4.8	5.9	4.8	5.6	6.1	7.4
5.7	6.7	5.8	5.2	5.5	5.8

Mean brand X battery lifetime is 5.6 years. Mean brand Y battery lifetime is 5.6 years.

Which brand of battery is more reliable?

The short answer to this question is that it depends on which batteries are chosen from each brand. For any randomly-chosen brand Y battery, we can find brand X batteries with longer or shorter lives. Since both batteries have a mean lifetime of 5.6 years, we might ask, "Which randomly-selected battery, brand X or brand Y, is more likely to have a lifetime of about 5.6 years?"

Range

One way to measure dispersion; that is, the extent to which data cluster around the mean, is to calculate the *range*. The range is the difference between the largest and smallest numbers in a set of data.

Lifetimes of brand X batteries
Largest value is 9.2.
Smallest value is 3.0.
Range = 9.2 − 3.0
      = 6.2

Lifetimes of brand Y batteries
Largest value is 7.4.
Smallest value is 3.2.
Range = 7.4 − 3.2
      = 4.2

A comparison of these two brands shows that brand X lifetimes are more widely dispersed than brand Y.

The histograms below show the difference in distributions for the lifetimes of the two brands of batteries.

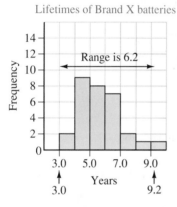

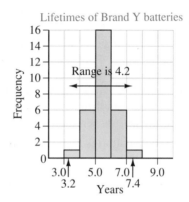

The range indicates how far the extreme values deviate from the mean. It may be, however, that a set of data has a few aberrant values which deviate substantially from the mean but the remaining values cluster tightly around the mean. In such a case the range would suggest that the data were quite widely dispersed when in fact the contrary were true.

Mean Deviation

To obtain a more reliable measure of dispersion we can calculate the absolute value of the difference between each value and the mean as shown in the following example.

Example 1. a) Calculate the absolute value of the deviation from the mean for each of the lifetimes of the 30 brand X batteries.
   b) Find the mean value of the deviations found in part a).

Solution. a) The tables below show the measured lifetimes x_i and the absolute value of the deviation $|x_i - \bar{x}|$, where $\bar{x} = 5.6$.

Lifetime, x_i	Deviation from the mean $|x_i - \bar{x}|$	Lifetime, x_i	Deviation from the mean $|x_i - \bar{x}|$
5.0	0.6	6.2	0.6
7.2	1.6	7.4	1.8
6.8	1.2	4.9	0.7
4.6	1.0	5.6	0
4.5	1.1	9.2	3.6
6.1	0.5	3.2	2.4
6.3	0.7	3.0	2.6
5.4	0.2	4.2	1.4
4.8	0.8	5.8	0.2
6.8	1.2	6.5	0.9
5.9	0.3	5.7	0.1
4.7	0.9	4.9	0.7
4.0	1.6	6.0	0.4
5.2	0.4	4.5	1.1
8.0	2.4	5.6	0

   b) The mean value of the deviations is found by adding them together and dividing by 30.

$$\frac{0.6 + 1.6 + 1.2 + 1.0 + \ldots + 0.4 + 1.1. + 0}{30} = \frac{31}{30}$$
$$\doteq 1.03$$

The mean value of the deviations from 5.6, is about 1.03.

The mean value of the deviations is called the *mean deviation*. In general, the mean deviation of a set of data $\{x_1, x_2, x_3, \ldots, x_n\}$ is given by

$$\frac{\sum\limits_{i=1}^{n} |x_i - \bar{x}|}{n},$$ where $\bar{x}$ is the mean for the set of data.

The calculation in *Example 1* indicates that the mean deviation of the brand X lifetimes from the mean lifetime is about 1.03. If a similar calculation is performed for the brand Y lifetimes, the mean deviation is found to be $0.5\overline{6}$. That is, although brand X and brand Y batteries have the same mean life, brand Y batteries on average deviate less from the mean lifetime than brand X batteries do, and in this sense are more reliable.

Standard Deviation

Another more common measure of dispersion involves the squares of the deviations from the mean and is therefore more sensitive to extreme values in the data. This measure is called the *standard deviation*, σ. We say "sigma". (σ is the lower case of Σ in the Greek alphabet.)

If $(x_1, \ldots, x_n)$ are the values in a set of data, then the standard deviation of the set of data is given by

$$\sigma = \sqrt{\frac{(x_1 - \bar{x})^2 + (x_2 - \bar{x})^2 + \ldots + (x_n - \bar{x})^2}{n}}$$

or using sigma notation,

$$\sigma = \sqrt{\frac{\sum_{i=1}^{n} (x_i - \bar{x})^2}{n}}, \text{ where } \bar{x} = \frac{\sum_{i=1}^{n} x_i}{n}$$

Data which are distributed close to the mean value $\bar{x}$ will have small values for $(x_i - \bar{x})^2$ and therefore a small standard deviation. However, data which are dispersed widely will have large values of $(x_i - \bar{x})^2$ and will have a large standard deviation.

Some scientific calculators have special keys which enable you to obtain the standard deviation of a set of data directly by entering only the data $x_1, x_2, \ldots, x_n$. However, when calculating standard deviation without such an aid, it is necessary to calculate $(x_i - \bar{x})^2$ for each value in the set of data. The following formula is more convenient for calculating standard deviation.

$$\sigma = \sqrt{\frac{\sum_{i=1}^{n} x_i^2}{n} - \bar{x}^2}$$

The following example illustrates the use of this formula.

Example 2. Calculate the standard deviation of the lifetimes for:

a) brand X batteries   b) brand Y batteries.

Comment on the results.

Solution. a) For brand X batteries

$$\sum_{i=1}^{30} x_i^2 = 5.0^2 + 7.2^2 + \ldots + 5.6^2$$
$$= 993.86$$

$$\sigma = \sqrt{\dfrac{\displaystyle\sum_{i=1}^{30} x_i^2}{30} - \bar{x}^2}$$

$$= \sqrt{\dfrac{993.86}{30} - (5.6)^2}$$

$$\doteq 1.33$$

b) For brand Y batteries

$$\sum_{i=1}^{30} x_i^2 = 5.3^2 + 6.2^2 + \ldots + 5.8^2$$

$$= 958.96$$

$$\sigma = \sqrt{\dfrac{958.96}{30} - (5.6)^2}$$

$$\doteq 0.78$$

The lifetimes of brand Y batteries are clustered more closely to the mean than the lifetimes of brand X batteries are.

EXERCISES 9-3

1. Explain the meaning of ''dispersion''.

2. The heights in centimetres of the 10 players on the school basketball team are 193, 189, 196, 178, 183, 198, 204, 190, 209, and 200. What is the range in heights?

3. Discuss which measure of dispersion would be most useful in determining each variation.
   a) The change in the value of a stock over a 1-year period
   b) The fluctuation in the temperature during the day
   c) The variation of IQ in a class of students
   d) The average amount by which steel bars in a shipment differ in diameter from a prescribed value
   e) The likelihood that an electronic component will have a lifetime within the advertised limits.
   Explain the reason(s) for each choice.

4. Brand A picture tubes have a mean life of 7 years and a standard deviation of 24 months. Brand B picture tubes have a mean life of 7 years and a standard deviation of 10 months. For which brand of picture tube is a lifetime of about 7 years a more reasonable estimate?

5. Let S denote the set of integers from 0 to 10 inclusive.
   a) What is the mean value of the members of S?
   b) What is the mean deviation?
   c) What is the standard deviation of the members of S?

6. Let V and W denote two sets of 9 measurements.
   V = {0, 1, 2, 3, 4, 5, 6, 7, 8} and W = {0, 4, 4, 4, 4, 4, 4, 4, 8}
   a) What is the mean value of each set of numbers?
   b) Which set has the greater dispersion?
   c) What is the range in each set?
   d) Compare the mean deviation of the numbers in each set.
   e) Compare the standard deviation of the numbers in each set.

(B)

7. In a steel mill, the standard deviation for an order of steel sheets must not exceed
   0.0003 mm. A random selection of measurements from three orders results in
   these thicknesses in millimetres.
   i)   1.9, 2.0, 2.0, 1.8, 2.1, 2.1, 2.2, 1.9
   ii) 1.8, 2.0, 2.1, 1.9, 1.8, 2.1, 2.3, 1.8, 1.7, 2.2
   iii) 2.1, 2.4, 2.0, 1.8, 1.7, 2.1, 1.9, 1.9, 2.3, 1.6
   For each sample find:
   a) the mean   b) the range
   c) the mean deviation   d) the standard deviation.
   Which samples pass the quality control standard?

8. For the data in *Exercise 2* calculate:
   a) the mean   b) the mean deviation   c) the standard deviation.

9. Let X = {0, 1, 2, 3, 6, 8, 9, 11}.

   a) If the members of X are denoted by $x_1, x_2, x_3, \ldots, x_n$, calculate $\displaystyle\sum_{i=1}^{n} (x_i - \bar{x})^2$.

   b) Calculate $\displaystyle\sum_{i=1}^{n} x_i^2 - n\bar{x}^2$.

   Compare the expressions calculated in parts a) and b), and verify that they
   are equal.

10. The masses in kilograms of the boys on the school football team are given below.
    85 92 77 85 94 115 105 98 96 111
    94 87 71 92 86 104 118 97 89 104
    a) Calculate the mean mass.

    b) Calculate the standard deviation using $\sigma = \sqrt{\dfrac{\displaystyle\sum_{i=1}^{n}(x_i - \bar{x})^2}{n}}$.

    c) Calculate the standard deviation using $\sigma = \sqrt{\dfrac{\displaystyle\sum_{i=1}^{n} x_i^2}{n} - \bar{x}^2}$.

d) Which formula is more convenient for calculating the standard deviation of these data?

e) i) The player with the mass of 111 kg was injured and left the team for the season. Calculate the mean mass of the remaining 19 players to one decimal place.

   ii) Use the two formulas to calculate the standard deviation of the masses of the remaining 19 players. Which formula is more convenient for calculating the standard deviation of these data?

11. A sample of 20 bags of potato chips produced by the Crispy Chips Company were found to have these masses in grams.
    80   85   88   92   76   85   94   76   78   80
    84   88   75   78   77   68   70   72   80   74
    A sample of 20 bags of potato chips produced by the Special Spuds Company were found to have these masses in grams.
    85   96   90   69   78   77   79   82   80   81
    76   78   81   77   80   75   79   76   81   80
    a) Calculate the mean and the range for each brand of chips.
    b) Which brand has the smaller standard deviation?

12. Discuss which of the frequency polygons displays data with:
    a) the greatest range   b) the greatest standard deviation?
    i)   ii)   iii)

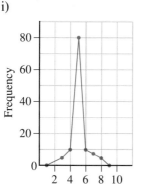 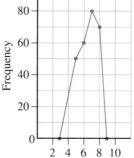 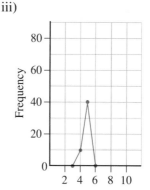

Ⓒ

13. Prove that the sum $\sum\limits_{i=1}^{n} (x_i - b)^2$ assumes its smallest value when b is the mean of the values x_i for $i = 1$ to n.

14. A variable can take any of the values $x_1, x_2, \ldots, x_n$. Let $f(x_i)$ denote the number of times the variable takes the value of x_i in a set of N observations. Prove that the standard deviation of the set of data is given by this formula.

$$\sigma = \sqrt{\frac{\sum\limits_{i=1}^{n} (x_i - \bar{x})^2 f(x_i)}{N}}$$

PROBLEM SOLVING

Introduce Another Expression

"A mathematician, like a poet or painter, is a maker of patterns. If his patterns are more permanent than theirs, it is because they are made with ideas ... A mathematician ... has no material to work with but ideas, and so his patterns are likely to last longer."

G. H. Hardy

When solving problems it sometimes helps to introduce another expression that was not present originally. We do this when we use the method of completing the square. This strategy is helpful in other kinds of problems also.

Prove the identity $\cos \theta \cos 2\theta \cos 4\theta \cos 8\theta \cos 16\theta = \dfrac{\sin 32\theta}{32 \sin \theta}$

Think of a strategy
- The solution will probably involve the double-angle formulas.
- There are three formulas for $\cos 2\theta$. We can use any of these to obtain similar formulas for $\cos 4\theta$, $\cos 8\theta$, and $\cos 16\theta$. We could substitute the results in the left side, but the expression would become very complicated because the expressions are polynomials which would have to be multiplied.
- Since the right side involves sines, we might need the formula $\sin 2\theta = 2 \sin \theta \cos \theta$.
- Notice that if we *multiply* the left side by $\sin \theta$, the first two factors become $\sin \theta \cos \theta$, which occurs in the formula for $\sin 2\theta$.

Carry out the strategy
- Multiply the left side by $\sin \theta$, and use the formula $\sin 2\theta = 2 \sin \theta \cos \theta$ to simplify the result. What happens to the 2 on the right side of the formula?
- Simplify the resulting expression as much as possible.
- Does it simplify to the expression on the right side above?
- Since we multiplied the left side by $\sin \theta$, we must divide by $\sin \theta$ at some point. Does this make the expression simplify to the expression on the right side?

Look back
- Can the identity be generalized to n factors on the left side?
- Is there a similar identity with sines on the left and cosines on the right?

PROBLEMS

Ⓑ

1. For any function $f(x)$, we define $f^2(x) = [f(x)]^2$. Find a function $f(x)$ such that $f^2(x) = f(2x)$ and $f(2) = 2$.

2. Simplify the expression $\left(1 + \frac{1}{2}\right)\left(1 + \frac{1}{4}\right)\left(1 + \frac{1}{16}\right)\left(1 + \frac{1}{256}\right)$.

3. The function $d(n)$ is defined as the number of digits in $n!$. For example, since $5! = 120$, which has 3 digits, then $d(5) = 3$.
   a) Use your calculator to determine: i) $d(7)$ ii) $d(20)$.
   b) Determine whether or not it is always possible to find a value of n such that $d(n) = n$.

Ⓒ

4. Find a real root of the equation $2^{3x} + 2^x - 30 = 0$.

5. Prove that $\dfrac{1}{\log_2 x} + \dfrac{1}{\log_3 x} + \dots + \dfrac{1}{\log_n x} = \dfrac{1}{\log_{n!} x}$.

6. Prove that $1 \times 1! + 2 \times 2! + 3 \times 3! + \dots + n \times n! = (n + 1)! - 1$.

7. $P(x, y)$ is any point on the terminal arm of an angle θ in standard position. If P also lies on a circle with radius r, express the shaded area in terms of:
   a) r and θ only
   b) x and y only.

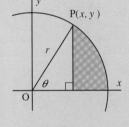

8. Find the value of:
   a) $\sin^2 1° + \sin^2 2° + \sin^2 3° + \dots + \sin^2 90°$
   b) $\sin^2 1° + \sin^2 2° + \sin^2 3° + \dots + \sin^2 360°$.

9. A triangle is uniquely determined by one side and two angles. Prove that the area A of any $\triangle PQR$ is given by this formula.
   $$A = \frac{p^2 \sin Q \sin R}{2 \sin (Q + R)}$$

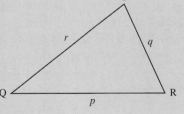

Ⓓ

10. $\triangle PQR$ has sides of length p, q, and r. Prove that $p^2 + q^2 + r^2 \geqslant 4\sqrt{3}A$, where A is the area of the triangle.

9-4 SCATTERPLOTS AND CORRELATION

To determine whether there was a relationship between the marks that her students received on an examination and the number of hours of study and preparation, Ms. Bates recorded the data below.

Hours of Study	Exam Mark
14	68
19	80
11	54
4	46
9	85
13	79
8	62
18	96
12	72
15	87
11	65
7	53
10	58
16	74
25	93
21	80
12	67
16	65
20	78
9	63
6	57
10	69
8	91
16	82
12	74

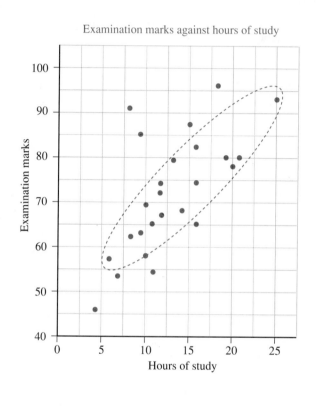

Examination marks against hours of study

For each student, each ordered pair was plotted as a point on a grid. The diagram obtained by plotting ordered pairs associated with corresponding values of two variables is called a *scatterplot*.

Ms. Bates observed that most of the points in her scatterplot could be contained in a thin ellipse with major axis having positive slope. If all the points were located on this major axis, we would say that the examination marks were directly proportional to the hours of study. However, since the points merely cluster around the major axis of this ellipse, we say that the examination marks are *correlated* with the hours of study.

When two variables are correlated so that the scatterplot reveals a clustering around a line of positive slope, we say the variables are *positively correlated*. When the scatterplot reveals a clustering around a line of negative slope we say the variables are *negatively correlated*. The diagrams below show five types of scatterplots.

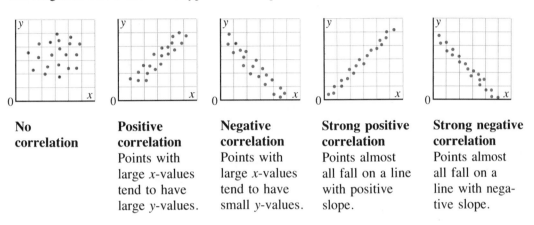

No correlation	**Positive correlation**	**Negative correlation**	**Strong positive correlation**	**Strong negative correlation**
	Points with large *x*-values tend to have large *y*-values.	Points with large *x*-values tend to have small *y*-values.	Points almost all fall on a line with positive slope.	Points almost all fall on a line with negative slope.

Though scatterplots are useful for determining whether or not two variables are correlated, a more precise measure of correlation is required to determine the extent to which two variables are correlated. To this purpose, statisticians sought a mathematical expression that could be used to measure the deviation from a straight line of the points (*x*,*y*) in a scatterplot.

To create an expression to measure correlation, we need a *correlation coefficient* between variables *x* and *y* such that:

If large deviations of *x* from $\overline{x}$ are associated with large deviations of *y* from $\overline{y}$, then the absolute value of the correlation coefficient is large indicating a strong correlation between *x* and *y*.

If we consider the product $(x_i - \overline{x})(y_i - \overline{y})$ for any point (x_i, y_i) in a scatterplot, we observe that this satisfies the condition above. That is, the product is largest (in absolute value) when both the *x* and the *y* deviations are large. To obtain a measure of the correlation for all the points in the scatterplot, we would average these products for all *n* points in the scatterplot, using this expression.

$$\frac{\sum\limits_{i=1}^{n} (x_i - \overline{x})(y_i - \overline{y})}{n}$$

To standardize the measure of correlation and make it independent of the scale used in measuring *x* and *y*, we divide the expression above by σ_x and σ_y, respectively the standard deviations of variables *x* and *y*.

Hence, we define the *Pearson correlation coefficient* ρ (we say, "row") by this expression.

$$\rho = \frac{\sum\limits_{i=1}^{n} (x_i - \bar{x})(y_i - \bar{y})}{\sqrt{\sum\limits_{i=1}^{n} (x_i - \bar{x})^2 \sum\limits_{i=1}^{n} (y_i - \bar{y})^2}} \quad \text{...} \; \text{①}$$

When $\rho = 1$, the variables are perfectly correlated; that is, points (x_i, y_i) all lie on a straight line with positive slope. When $\rho = -1$, the variables are perfectly correlated in the negative sense; that is, points (x_i, y_i) all lie on a straight line with negative slope. Values of ρ close to 0 indicate that there is little or no correlation between x and y. If $\rho = 0.1$ or 0.2, there is a visible correlation; if ρ is greater than 0.5, there is a strong correlation.

The expression above for ρ is not the most convenient form for calculation. The following formula for ρ is more useful for evaluating ρ on a scientific calculator. (Some calculators require only that you enter the values of x_i and y_i, and they calculate automatically the value of ρ. It is not important how you calculate ρ so long as you understand how to interpret its significance.)

$$\rho = \frac{\sum\limits_{i=1}^{n} x_i y_i - n\bar{x}\bar{y}}{\sqrt{\left(\sum\limits_{i=1}^{n} x_i^2 - n\bar{x}^2\right)\left(\sum\limits_{i=1}^{n} y_i^2 - n\bar{y}^2\right)}} \quad \text{...} \; \text{②}$$

Example.   Calculate the Pearson correlation coefficient between the hours of study and the examination marks for the students in Ms. Bates' class.

Solution.   Using a calculator, the data from the table, and equation ② above, we find:

$$\sum_{i=1}^{25} x_i y_i = 24\;221$$

$$\bar{x} = 12.88$$
$$\bar{y} = 71.92$$

$$\sum_{i=1}^{25} x_i^2 = 4774$$

$$\sum_{i=1}^{25} y_i^2 = 133\;516$$

so, $\rho = \dfrac{24\;221 - 25(12.88)(71.92)}{\sqrt{(4774 - 25(12.88)^2)(133\;516 - 25(71.92)^2)}}$

$\doteq 0.65$

In the *Example*, a correlation of 0.65 reveals that there is a strong correlation between the number of hours of study and the final examination marks. This does not mean that long hours of study guarantee high examination marks or that high marks are possible only with long hours of study, but it does confirm a strong relationship. Naturally, this correlation is different for different tests and for different classes of students.

EXERCISES 9-4

Ⓐ

1. Explain what we mean when we say that two variables are:
   a) correlated   b) uncorrelated.

2. If ρ denotes the Pearson correlation coefficient between the variables x and y, explain how you would interpret each statement.
   a) $\rho = 1$ b) $\rho = 0$ c) $\rho = -1$ d) $\rho = -0.8$

3. Each scatterplot shows various points (x,y) where x and y represent different variables. For each diagram indicate whether x and y are uncorrelated, positively correlated or negatively correlated. If x and y are correlated, indicate whether the correlation is weak or strong.

a)   b)   c)   d)

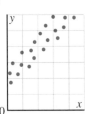   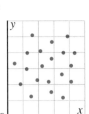   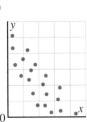   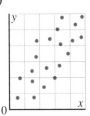

4. Draw a scatterplot and calculate each value of ρ.

a)
x	y
1	2
2	3
3	4
4	5
5	6

b)
x	y
1	2
2	4
3	4
4	4
5	6

c)
x	y
1	2
2	5
3	4
4	3
5	6

d)
x	y
1	6
2	5
3	4
4	3
5	2

e)
x	y
1	5
2	3
3	3
4	3
5	1

f)
x	y
1	6
2	2
3	4
4	2
5	6

Describe the correlation in each case.

5. A recent study indicated that there was a high positive correlation between the socio-economic status of students and their learning ability. Can we deduce from this study that a high socio-economic environment tends to increase learning ability? Explain your answer.

6. Draw a scatterplot and calculate the Pearson correlation coefficient in each case.

a)
Grade placement-reading	4 6 5 4 5 5 6
Grade placement-mathematics	5 4 5 3 3 4 4

b)
Days absent	10 12 8 6 10 14
Average mark	65 60 70 75 70 50

c)
Height (m)	1.6 1.5 1.7 1.5 1.6 1.7
Mass (kg)	50 55 80 45 70 60

7. To support her hypothesis that crime does not pay, a sociologist recorded the net assets of 1000 habitual criminals and 1000 honest citizens. She found there was a strong negative correlation between criminal behaviour and net assets; that is, life-long criminals tended to have very little accumulated wealth. Do her data show that crime does not pay?

(B)

8. The table shows corresponding values for the four variables w, x, y, and z.

w	1	3	5	7	10	12	15	17
x	26	3	5	17	3	12	10	10
y	24	21	19	16	14	12	10	7
z	56	58	60	62	65	68	70	73

Consider the sets of variables two at a time. Name one or more pairs of variables which appear, on the basis of this limited data, to be:
a) positively correlated
b) negatively correlated
c) strongly correlated
d) uncorrelated.

9. For the data in *Exercise 8*, draw a scatterplot for each pair of variables.
   a) w, z b) x, y c) w, y d) y, z
   Do your scatterplots support your answers to *Exercise 8*?

10. For the data in *Exercise 8*, calculate the Pearson correlation coefficient for:
    a) w and z b) y and z c) w and y.

11. If the Pearson correlation coefficient between x and y is 0.65, and between x and z is -0.90, is x more closely related to y or to z?

12. Find the Pearson correlation coefficient for each set of data. Explain why the values differ.

a)

Name	Intelligence test A	Intelligence test B
Ann	90	93
Bob	105	101
Carol	115	110
Don	93	97
Eve	102	108
Fred	97	92
Jerry	105	99

b)

Name	English mark	Mathematics mark
Ann	62	75
Bob	70	60
Carol	84	90
Don	68	80
Eve	92	81
Fred	65	60
Jerry	77	65

Ⓒ

13. For a particular set of data the standard deviation of x is 5, and of y is 4. What is the largest possible value of $\sum_{i=1}^{n} (x_i - \bar{x})(y_i - \bar{y})$?

14. We may conjecture that the sum of the natural numbers from 1 to n is a quadratic function of n of the form $F(n) = an^2 + bn + c$.
   a) Use the identity $F(n) - F(n-1) = n$, and facts such as $F(0) = 0$ and $F(1) = 1$ to find the values of the constants a, b, and c.
   b) Prove that $\sum_{k=1}^{n} k = \dfrac{n(n+1)}{2}$.

15. Since the sum of the natural numbers from 1 to n is a quadratic function of n, it is reasonable to conjecture that the sum of the squares of the natural numbers from 1 to n is a cubic function of the form $f(n) = an^3 + bn^2 + cn + d$, where a, b, c, and d are rational numbers.
   a) Use the identity $f(n) - f(n-1) = n^2$, and facts such as $f(0) = 0$ and $f(1) = 1$ to find the values of a, b, c, and d.
   b) Prove that $\sum_{k=1}^{n} k^2 = \dfrac{n(n+1)(2n+1)}{6}$.

16. Prove that if $y = 3x + 1$, then the Pearson correlation coefficient between x and y is 1.

9-5 LINE OF BEST FIT

If a variable y were perfectly correlated with a variable x, then y would be a linear function of x. That is, we could find the value of y corresponding to any given value of x. In other words, the equation of the line containing the ordered pair (x, y) could be used as a predictor of y for any given value of x.

However, when x and y are correlated but have correlation coefficient $\rho < 1$, the points (x, y) do not lie on a line but merely cluster around one or more straight lines.

In this section, we shall use a formula for the equation of the particular line which is the "best fit" for a set of data. Recall the scatterplot in which we plotted each student's examination mark against the number of hours of study for the examination. The *line of best fit* is that particular line for which the sum of the squares of the deviations is a minimum. The deviation of a point from the line is the vertical distance from the point to the line. The vertical line segments show the deviations.

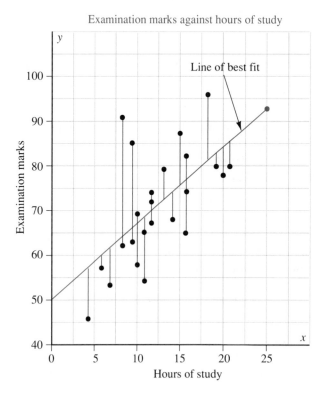

Examination marks against hours of study

The equation of the line of best fit has the form $y = mx + b$, where the slope m is given by

$$m = \frac{\sum\limits_{i=1}^{n} x_i y_i - n\bar{x}\bar{y}}{\sum\limits_{i=1}^{n} x_i^2 - n\bar{x}^2}$$

and the y-intercept $b = \bar{y} - m\bar{x}$.
The derivations of these formulas are complicated, and beyond the scope of this text.

Example. For the data on the hours of study and examination marks for the students in Ms. Bates' class:

a) Find the equation of the line of best fit.
b) Use this equation to predict the examination mark of a student who studies for 15 h.

Solution. a) From the *Example* in Section 9-4,

$$\sum_{i=1}^{n} x_i y_i = 24\ 221$$

$$\bar{x} = 12.88$$

$$\sum_{i=1}^{n} x_i^2 = 4774$$

$$\bar{y} = 71.92$$

Use the formula for the line of best fit.

$$m = \frac{\sum\limits_{i=1}^{n} x_i y_i - n\bar{x}\bar{y}}{\sum\limits_{i=1}^{n} x_i^2 - n\bar{x}^2}$$

$$m = \frac{24\ 221 - 25(12.88)(71.92)}{4774 - 25(12.88)^2}$$

$$\doteq 1.70$$

Use the formula for the y-intercept.
$$b = \bar{y} - m\bar{x}$$
$$\doteq 71.92 - 1.70(12.88)$$
$$\doteq 50$$

The equation of the line of best fit is $y = 1.7x + 50$
b) When $x = 15$, $y = 1.70(15) + 50$
$$= 75.5$$

The line of best fit predicts an examination mark of about 75 or 76 for a student who studies 15 h.

EXERCISES 9-5

Ⓐ

1. Complete the following statement. "The line of best fit for a set of points is the line which minimizes . . .

2. For each scatterplot, estimate the slope of the line of best fit.

a)
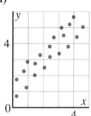

b)
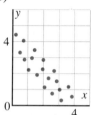

c)
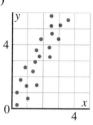

3. If $y = 2x - 7$ is the equation of the line of best fit relating variables x and y, what is the predicted value of y corresponding to $x = 9$?

Ⓑ

4. The table shows the marks in mathematics and physics for 10 students.

   a) Calculate the correlation coefficient between mathematics and physics marks.

   b) Find the equation of the line of best fit, for the physics marks plotted on the y-axis.

   c) Use the equation of the line of best fit to estimate the physics mark corresponding to a mark of 87 in mathematics.

Mathematics	Physics
92	96
81	80
58	66
72	80
75	86
69	67
57	69
88	88
92	84
97	99

5. The graph shows the population of Canada every 10 years from 1941 to 1981.

   a) Using this limited data, calculate the equation of the line of best fit.

   b) Use your line to predict the population of Canada in 1991 and 2001.

   c) Calculate the average population growth per year using the line.

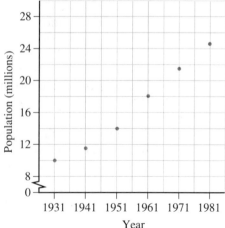

Population of Canada, 1931-1981

9-6 STATISTICAL INFERENCE: SAMPLING

To this point we have studied ways of representing, displaying, and analysing data pertaining to populations. However, most of the important applications of statistics use those statistical techniques which enable us to draw inferences about an entire population based upon data from relatively small random samples.

The need for sampling techniques arises out of several constraints associated with gathering data on an entire population.

- Sometimes a population is so vast that it is difficult or impossible to collect data on every member of the population.

- In experiments which determine the expected lifetime of an electronic component or the stress limits of a manufactured part, the experiment must run until the component fails. Performing the experiment on the entire supply of such components would serve no purpose but to obliterate the supply.

- When information about a population is needed in a limited time, it is more expedient to collect data from a random sample and draw inferences about the population, than to attempt to collect data on the entire population.

- It is usually much less expensive to collect data from a random sample than from an entire population.

When a sample is truly representative of the population from which it is drawn, the inferences made about the population are likely to be valid. For example, the Nielsen ratings which rank the popularity of television shows across this continent are determined by a survey which samples fewer than one home in 10 000; that is, less than 0.01% of the entire population! Gallup polls assess the political preferences of the entire Canadian electorate by surveying fewer than 2000 people!

It is critically important that the sampling process be purely random in that all members of the population share an equal chance of being selected. Furthermore, it is essential that the sample be sufficiently large to decrease the likelihood that the sample data differ significantly from the corresponding population data. In the case of the battery lifetimes studied in a previous section, it is clear that a sample of 3 batteries chosen randomly would be more likely to have a mean lifetime substantially different from the population, than would a sample of 20 batteries. Furthermore, the fact that the lifetimes of the brand Y batteries had a smaller standard deviation than the lifetimes of the brand X batteries indicates that the lifetimes of the brand Y batteries are less disperse. This means that a smaller sample of brand Y batteries than brand X batteries would be needed to make estimates of the same precision about both populations.

The mean, and the standard deviation of a population P are usually denoted by the Greek letters μ (we say, "mew") and σ respectively.

$$\mu = \frac{\sum\limits_{i=1}^{N} z_i}{N} \quad \text{and} \quad \sigma = \sqrt{\frac{\sum\limits_{i=1}^{N} (z_i - \mu)^2}{N}}$$

where $P = \{z_i \mid i = 1, 2, 3, ..., N\}$

When not all the values z_i are known, we cannot calculate μ and σ. To obtain estimates of μ and σ, we take a random sample S of population P where $S = \{x_i \mid i = 1, 2, ..., n\}$ and $n < N$.

To estimate μ, we use $\bar{x}$ where $\bar{x} = \dfrac{\sum\limits_{i=1}^{n} x_i}{n}$.

That is, the mean of the sample is used as an estimate of the mean of the population. Similarly, it would seem logical to use as an estimate of the standard deviation of the population, the standard deviation for the sample. The expression for this is given below.

$$\sqrt{\frac{\sum\limits_{i=1}^{n} (x_i - \mu)^2}{n}}$$

However, this expression cannot be calculated since the true value of μ is unknown. If we replace μ in the expression above by $\bar{x}$, then the expression takes on a different value because $\bar{x}$ is not usually equal to μ. It can be shown that, on average, the expression above is best approximated by this expression.

$$\sqrt{\frac{\sum\limits_{i=1}^{n} (x_i - \bar{x})^2}{n - 1}}$$

Recall from Section 9-3 that the expression

$$\sqrt{\frac{\sum\limits_{i=1}^{n} (x_i - \bar{x})^2}{n}} \quad \text{can be written} \quad \sqrt{\frac{\sum\limits_{i=1}^{n} x_i^2}{n} - \bar{x}^2} \quad \text{or} \quad \sqrt{\frac{\sum\limits_{i=1}^{n} x_i^2 - n\bar{x}^2}{n}}.$$

Hence the expression

$$\sqrt{\frac{\sum\limits_{i=1}^{n} (x_i - \bar{x})^2}{n - 1}} \quad \text{can be written} \quad \sqrt{\frac{\sum\limits_{i=1}^{n} x_i^2 - n\bar{x}^2}{n - 1}}.$$

Therefore, the standard deviation for the sample is given by

$$s = \sqrt{\dfrac{\sum\limits_{i=1}^{n} x_i^2 - n\bar{x}^2}{n-1}}.$$

The sample standard deviation s is used as an estimate of the population standard deviation σ. Note that the definitions of the sample and the population standard deviations differ in that the denominator of s is $\sqrt{n-1}$ while the denominator of σ is $\sqrt{N}$.

Example 1. The stem-and-leaf plot gives the measured lifetimes for a sample of 40 Perma-glow light bulbs. Estimate the mean, and the standard deviation of the lifetimes of all Perma-glow light bulbs using only the data from this sample.

Stem-and-leaf plot for lifetimes in months

Tens digit	Units digit
0	0 8 9
1	1 3 6 8
2	2 2 3 5 6 7 9 9
3	0 0 1 2 2 5 6 7 7 8
4	0 1 1 2 3 5 5
5	0 0 1 2 6 6
6	2 5

Solution. For an estimate of μ, the mean, we use $\bar{x} = \dfrac{\sum\limits_{i=1}^{n} x_i}{n}$. We first add the lifetimes of the bulbs in the sample.

The sum of the tens digits of all 40 lifetimes is:
$$10(4) + 20(8) + 30(10) + 40(7) + 50(6) + 60(2) = 1200$$
The sum of the ones digits of all 40 lifetimes is 155.

$$\sum_{i=1}^{n} x_i = 1200 + 155$$
$$= 1355$$

Therefore, $\bar{x} = \dfrac{1355}{40}$
$$= 33.875$$

The mean lifetime of the Perma-glow light bulbs is about 34 months.

To obtain s, we use $s = \sqrt{\dfrac{\sum\limits_{i=1}^{n} x_i^2 - n\bar{x}^2}{n-1}}$

Using a calculator, we obtain $\sum_{i=1}^{n} x_i^2 = 55\ 007$ and $\bar{x}^2 \doteq 1147.52$

Then, $s = \sqrt{\dfrac{55\ 007 - 40(1147.52)}{39}}$

$\doteq 15.3$

That is, the standard deviation of the lifetimes of Perma-glow light bulbs is about 15 months.

If we plot the frequency polygon for the lifetimes of the 40 Perma-glow bulbs using the data from *Example 1*, we obtain the diagram below left.

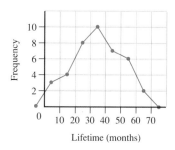
Lifetime (months)

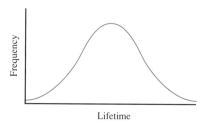
Lifetime

If the lifetimes of several thousand Perma-glow bulbs were measured and the corresponding frequency polygon were plotted, it would resemble the continuous curve on the right. This famous "bell-shaped" curve is the frequency curve for what is called a *normal distribution*. It has been found that human characteristics such as height, mass, intelligence, and abilities of various kinds as well as most characteristics of manufactured products have frequency polygons which closely approximate the frequency curve of the normal distribution. For this reason, the properties of the normal distribution have been studied in significant detail. Here are some of these properties.

- The normal distribution is symmetric about the vertical line $x = \mu$, where μ is the mean of the population. That is, the percent of observed values a units greater than the mean will be the same as the percent a units less than the mean.

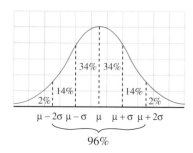

- About 68% of all measured values of a normally-distributed variable lie between $\mu - \sigma$ and $\mu + \sigma$; that is, within one standard deviation from the mean.

- About 96% of all measured values of a normally-distributed variable lie between $\mu - 2\sigma$ and $\mu + 2\sigma$; that is, within two standard deviations from the mean.

- About 99.74% of all measured values of a normally-distributed variable lie between $\mu - 3\sigma$ and $\mu + 3\sigma$.

The next example shows how we can draw inferences about a population on the assumption that it is normally distributed; that is, on the assumption that its frequency polygon closely approaches the shape of a normal distribution curve.

Example 2. Assuming that the lifetimes of the Perma-glow light bulbs are normally distributed, use the data in *Example 1* to answer each question.
  a) What percent of the light bulbs would have lifetimes which are less than 34 months?
  b) What are the lifetimes of light bulbs which lie within:
    i) one standard deviation from the mean
    ii) two standard deviations from the mean?
  c) Approximately how many light bulbs in a random sample of 10 000 would have lifetimes less than 4 months?

Solution. We are assuming that the lifetimes of the Perma-glow bulbs have a normal distribution; that is, a frequency polygon resembling closely the normal-distribution curve. From *Example 1*, the mean and the standard deviation of the entire population of bulbs are respectively 34 months and 15 months.
  a) Since the normal distribution is symmetric about the mean and since the mean is 34, then there is the same proportion of lifetimes which are greater than 34 as there are less than 34. That is, 50% of the bulbs have lifetimes less than 34 months.
  b) i) About 68% of the measured lifetimes lie within one standard deviation from the mean.
        So, 68% of the lifetimes lie within $(34 - 15)$ months, or 19 months; and $(34 + 15)$ months, or 49 months.
        Hence, light bulbs which lie within one standard deviation from the mean have lifetimes between 19 months and 49 months.
    ii) About 96% of the measured lifetimes lie within two standard deviations from the mean.
        So, 96% of the lifetimes lie within $[34 - 2(15)]$ months, or 4 months; and $[34 + 2(15)]$ months, or 64 months.
        Hence, light bulbs which lie within two standard deviations from the mean have lifetimes between 4 months and 64 months.
  c) Since 96% of the lifetimes lie within 4 months and 64 months; by symmetry, 2% of the light bulbs will have lifetimes less than 4 months (and 2% will have lifetimes greater than 64 months).
     2% of 10 000 = 200
     About 200 light bulbs have lifetimes less than 4 months.

EXERCISES 9-6

1. State 3 reasons why it might be more appropriate to gather information from a sample of a population rather than gathering information from the entire population.

2. A business magazine conducts a poll of the political party preferred by each of its subscribers. It uses the results of this survey to forecast the results of the next election. Can this poll be relied upon to produce an accurate forecast? Discuss.

3. To determine what percent of grade 12 students in her school were planning to attend university after graduation, Melissa surveyed several of her friends. Will Melissa's data provide her with a reasonable estimate? Discuss.

4. To determine the mean salary of computer programmers across Canada, Computer Personnel Incorporated recorded the salaries of 100 computer programmers in each province. These 1000 salaries were then added together and the total divided by 1000 to obtain the mean salary. Will this procedure yield a good estimate of the mean salary of a computer programmer in Canada? Discuss.

5. Describe how you would collect data to determine what fraction of the cars driven in your town or city are domestic and what fraction are imported.

6. How does the formula for calculating the standard deviation of a population differ from the formula for estimating the standard deviation of a sample of that population?

7. Human intelligence, as measured on the Wechsler IQ scale, is normally distributed with a mean of 100 and a standard deviation of 15. What percent of people have IQs which are:
   a) between 100 and 115
   b) between 85 and 115
   c) between 100 and 130
   d) less than 70?

8. Use the information in *Exercise 7*.
   a) At what percentile in intelligence is a person who scores:
      i) 130 on a Wechsler IQ test
      ii) 100 on a Wechsler IQ test?
   b) An IQ of 145 or greater is considered to indicate a genius. What percent of Canadians are geniuses?
   c) If the population of Canada were about 28 000 000, estimate the number of Canadians with a genius IQ.

Ⓑ

9. A sample of 24 Everstrong car mufflers, under similar climatic conditions, are found to have the following lifetimes in months.

31   35   29   36   42   45   28   26   38   37   35   39
46   37   40   32   48   35   39   41   29   36   43   47

a) Estimate the mean lifetime of Everstrong car mufflers under similar climatic conditions.

b) Estimate the standard deviation in the lifetimes of Everstrong car mufflers.

10. The stem-and-leaf plot gives the measured diameters in millimetres of a random sample of 20 steel rods.

a) Estimate the mean diameter of the steel rods in the entire shipment.

b) Estimate the standard deviation in the diameters of the steel rods.

Millimetres	Tenths of a millimetre
6	5 7 8 9 9
7	0 1 2 3 3 4 4 6 7 8
8	0 0 1 1 2

11. Use the data in *Exercise 10* and assume that the diameters of the steel rods are normally distributed.

a) What percent of the steel rods have a diameter less than the mean diameter?

b) What percent of the steel rods have a diameter which deviates from the mean diameter by less than 1 standard deviation?

c) Between what two measurements are the diameters of 68% of the steel rods?

12. The strength of a female athlete as measured by the Universal Test of Physical Strength is normally distributed with a mean of 50 and a standard deviation of 10.

a) What fraction of female athletes achieve a score over 60 on this test?

b) What fraction of female athletes score less than 70 on this test?

c) In what interval do the middle 96% of the female athletes score?

d) Give the percentile ranking corresponding to a score of:
   i) 80   ii) 50   iii) 20.

13. When intelligence is measured on the Stanford-Binet scale, the mean is 100 and the standard deviation is 16. What score on the Stanford-Binet scale corresponds to a score of 130 on the Wechsler scale? (See *Exercise 7*.)

Ⓒ

14. If *x* denotes a variable which is normally distributed with mean μ and standard deviation σ, then z is a normally distributed variable where $z = \dfrac{x - \mu}{\sigma}$. Prove that z has a mean of 0 and a standard deviation of 1.

9-7 THE STANDARD NORMAL DISTRIBUTION

In the previous section we noted that measurements of human characteristics such as height, mass, and intelligence are found to have a normal
distribution. For example, a histogram showing the frequencies of various heights in Canada's adult male population would have the properties of the bell curve described in the previous section. Suppose we know
that the heights of adult males in Canada have a normal distribution with
a mean of 175 cm and a standard deviation of 6.5 cm. How could we
determine the percentile corresponding to a height of 190 cm? How
could we determine what height would correspond to P_{90}?

The notation $N(\mu, \sigma)$ is used to denote the normal distribution with
mean μ and standard deviation σ. The diagram (below left) shows that
there is not one, but an infinite family of graphs of the normal distribution, one for each value of $N(\mu, \sigma)$.

To answer the questions above, we would need a graph of
$N(175, 6.5)$. To avoid having to draw this, we look for a relationship
between the graph of $N(\mu, \sigma)$ for any particular value of μ and σ, and
the graph of a particular normal distribution.

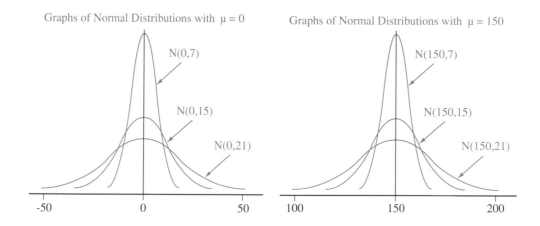

We observe in the diagram (above left) that as the standard deviation
decreases, the graph of the corresponding normal distribution becomes
narrower and taller, crowding most of its area around the mean, or
central value.

Furthermore, the graph of $N(\mu, \sigma)$ can be mapped onto the graph
$N(\mu + 150, \sigma)$ (above right) by a horizontal translation of 150; that
is, by increasing all values of the variable by 150. Hence, the graph of
any normal distribution can be transformed into the graph of another
normal distribution by a suitable linear transformation.

We say that if the values of a variable X have a normal distribution $N(150, 7)$, then the variable Z defined by $Z = \dfrac{X - 150}{7}$ has values which have a normal distribution $N(0, 1)$. This discussion is generalized as a theorem.

Theorem

If the values of a variable X have a normal distribution $N(\mu, \sigma)$, then the variable Z defined by $Z = \dfrac{X - \mu}{\sigma}$ has values which have a normal distribution $N(0, 1)$.

Definition: The variable Z which takes values that have a normal distribution $N(0, 1)$ is said to have a *standard normal distribution* or *Z-distribution.*

Scores on tests of aptitude, ability, achievement or IQ which have a mean of 0 and standard deviation of 1 are called *Z-scores.*

It follows from the theorem above that any normal distribution $N(\mu, \sigma)$ can be transformed by the equation into the standard normal distribution $N(0, 1)$. Therefore, it is necessary only to have a table of values referring to $N(0, 1)$ to obtain information about $N(\mu, \sigma)$. There is a table which gives this information on page 470. The values in the table are probabilities. The table gives the probability that a value, chosen at random from a standard normal distribution, lies between 0 and a, where $a \leqslant 3.49$.

Look at the table on page 470. The first column gives the chosen value to one decimal place, the first line gives the second decimal place.

For example, to find the probability that a randomly-chosen value X lies between 0 and 1.85, move down the left column to 1.8 and along that line until you reach the entry in the column headed 0.05, which is 0.4678. Hence, the probability that a number chosen at random from a standard normal distribution lies between 0 and 1.85 is 0.4678.

This seems reasonable, since a standard normal distribution $N(0, 1)$ has a mean of 0 and a standard deviation of 1. Hence, about 96% of the values lie between -2 and 2; or about 48% (probability of 0.48) lie between 0 and 2.

If we consider the area under a standard normal distribution curve to be 1, then the value 0.4678 corresponds to the shaded area under this curve.

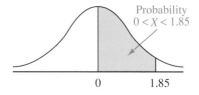

	Area Under a Standard Normal Distribution Curve N(0,1) Between 0 and *a*									
a	0.00	0.01	0.02	0.03	0.04	0.05	0.06	0.07	0.08	0.09
0.0	0.0000	0.0040	0.0080	0.0120	0.0160	0.0199	0.0239	0.0279	0.0319	0.0359
0.1	0.0398	0.0438	0.0478	0.0517	0.0557	0.0596	0.0636	0.0675	0.0714	0.0753
0.2	0.0793	0.0832	0.0871	0.0910	0.0948	0.0987	0.1026	0.1064	0.1103	0.1141
0.3	0.1179	0.1217	0.1255	0.1293	0.1331	0.1368	0.1406	0.1443	0.1480	0.1517
0.4	0.1554	0.1591	0.1628	0.1664	0.1700	0.1736	0.1772	0.1808	0.1844	0.1879
0.5	0.1915	0.1950	0.1985	0.2019	0.2054	0.2088	0.2123	0.2157	0.2190	0.2224
0.6	0.2257	0.2291	0.2324	0.2357	0.2389	0.2422	0.2454	0.2486	0.2517	0.2549
0.7	0.2580	0.2611	0.2642	0.2673	0.2704	0.2734	0.2764	0.2794	0.2823	0.2852
0.8	0.2881	0.2910	0.2939	0.2967	0.2995	0.3023	0.3051	0.3078	0.3106	0.3133
0.9	0.3159	0.3186	0.3212	0.3238	0.3264	0.3289	0.3315	0.3340	0.3365	0.3389
1.0	0.3413	0.3438	0.3461	0.3485	0.3508	0.3531	0.3554	0.3577	0.3599	0.3621
1.1	0.3643	0.3665	0.3686	0.3708	0.3729	0.3749	0.3770	0.3790	0.3810	0.3830
1.2	0.3849	0.3869	0.3888	0.3907	0.3925	0.3944	0.3962	0.3980	0.3997	0.4015
1.3	0.4032	0.4049	0.4066	0.4082	0.4099	0.4115	0.4131	0.4147	0.4162	0.4177
1.4	0.4192	0.4207	0.4222	0.4236	0.4251	0.4265	0.4279	0.4292	0.4306	0.4319
1.5	0.4332	0.4345	0.4357	0.4370	0.4382	0.4394	0.4406	0.4418	0.4429	0.4441
1.6	0.4452	0.4463	0.4474	0.4484	0.4495	0.4505	0.4515	0.4525	0.4535	0.4545
1.7	0.4554	0.4564	0.4573	0.4582	0.4591	0.4599	0.4608	0.4616	0.4625	0.4633
1.8	0.4641	0.4649	0.4656	0.4664	0.4671	0.4678	0.4686	0.4693	0.4699	0.4706
1.9	0.4713	0.4719	0.4726	0.4732	0.4738	0.4744	0.4750	0.4756	0.4761	0.4767
2.0	0.4772	0.4778	0.4783	0.4788	0.4793	0.4798	0.4803	0.4808	0.4812	0.4817
2.1	0.4821	0.4826	0.4830	0.4834	0.4838	0.4842	0.4846	0.4850	0.4854	0.4857
2.2	0.4861	0.4864	0.4868	0.4871	0.4875	0.4878	0.4881	0.4884	0.4887	0.4890
2.3	0.4893	0.4896	0.4898	0.4901	0.4904	0.4906	0.4909	0.4911	0.4913	0.4916
2.4	0.4918	0.4920	0.4922	0.4925	0.4927	0.4929	0.4931	0.4932	0.4934	0.4936
2.5	0.4938	0.4940	0.4941	0.4943	0.4945	0.4946	0.4948	0.4949	0.4951	0.4952
2.6	0.4953	0.4955	0.4956	0.4957	0.4959	0.4960	0.4961	0.4962	0.4963	0.4964
2.7	0.4965	0.4966	0.4967	0.4968	0.4969	0.4970	0.4971	0.4972	0.4973	0.4974
2.8	0.4974	0.4975	0.4976	0.4977	0.4977	0.4978	0.4979	0.4979	0.4980	0.4981
2.9	0.4981	0.4982	0.4982	0.4983	0.4984	0.4984	0.4985	0.4985	0.4986	0.4986
3.0	0.4987	0.4987	0.4987	0.4988	0.4988	0.4989	0.4989	0.4989	0.4990	0.4990
3.1	0.4990	0.4991	0.4991	0.4991	0.4992	0.4992	0.4992	0.4992	0.4993	0.4993
3.2	0.4993	0.4993	0.4994	0.4994	0.4994	0.4994	0.4994	0.4995	0.4995	0.4995
3.3	0.4995	0.4995	0.4995	0.4996	0.4996	0.4996	0.4996	0.4996	0.4996	0.4997
3.4	0.4997	0.4997	0.4997	0.4997	0.4997	0.4997	0.4997	0.4997	0.4997	0.4998

Example 1. A variable X has a standard normal distribution. What is the probability that a randomly-selected value is:
a) greater than 1.85
b) less than 1.85
c) between -1.85 and 1.85
d) less than -1.85 or greater than 1.85?
Illustrate each probability as a shaded area under the standard normal distribution curve.

Solution.

a) We know that the probability that the value is less than 1.85 is 0.4678. Since the curve of $N(0, 1)$ is symmetric about the mean value $X = 0$, half of its area lies to the right of $X = 0$.
So, the probability that $X \geq 0$ is 0.5. The probability that $X > 1.85$ is $0.5000 - 0.4678$, or 0.0322.

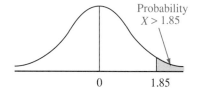

b) The probability that $X < 1.85$ is
$$1 - (\text{probability } X > 1.85)$$
$$= 1 - 0.0322$$
$$= 0.9678$$

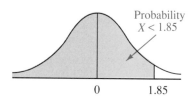

c) The probability that $-1.85 < X < 1.85$ is
$(\text{probability } X < 1.85) - (\text{probability } X < -1.85)$
$$= 0.9678 - 0.0322$$
$$= 0.9356$$

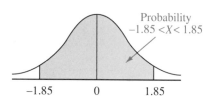

d) The probability that $X < -1.85$ or $X > 1.85$
$$= 1 - (\text{probability} - 1.85 < X < 1.85)$$
$$= 1 - 0.9356$$
$$= 0.0644$$

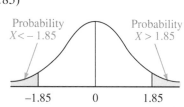

The usefulness of the theorem is evident in the following examples.

Example 2. An extensive study of 10 000 adult males throughout the world reveals that the height H of the adult male is normally distributed with mean 175 cm and standard deviation 6.5 cm.

a) What percent of the adult male population is shorter than 190 cm?
b) What percent of the adult male population is between 170 cm and 190 cm tall?
c) What height corresponds to the 90th percentile of the population?

Solution. To use the table, we must transform the variable H to a standard normal distribution. It follows from the theorem that the variable Z, defined by

$Z = \dfrac{H - 175}{6.5}$, has a standard normal distribution.

a) We want to find the percent of the adult male population for which H is less than 190 cm.

That is, we want to find the probability that $H < 190$ for a randomly-selected adult male.

This is the same as the probability that $Z < \dfrac{190 - 175}{6.5}$, or $Z < 2.31$.

Since Z has a standard normal distribution, we can use the table on page 470.

The probability that Z is between 0 and 2.31 is 0.4896.

Therefore, the probability that $Z < 2.31$ is $0.5000 + 0.4896$, or 0.9896.

That is, the probability that $H < 190$ for a randomly selected adult male is 0.9896.

In other words, 98.96% of the adult male population is shorter than 190 cm.

b) The probability that $H < 170$ is the same as the probability that

$Z < \dfrac{170 - 175}{6.5}$, or $Z < -0.77$.

From the symmetry of the standard normal distribution

The probability that $Z < -0.77 = $ probability $Z > 0.77$

$\qquad\qquad\qquad\qquad = 0.5000 - (\text{probability } 0 \leqslant Z < 0.77)$

$\qquad\qquad\qquad\qquad = 0.5000 - 0.2794$

$\qquad\qquad\qquad\qquad = 0.2206$

Probability that $170 < H < 190$

$= $ Probability that $H < 190 - (\text{Probability that } H < 170)$

$= 0.9896 - 0.2206$

$= 0.7690$

That is, 76.90% of the adult male population is between 170 cm and 190 cm tall.

c) Recall that P_{90} is the number below which 90% of the values fall.
We must find the value a such that the probability that $H < a$ is 0.90.
First we look in our table of values of N(0, 1) for the value closest to
the probability $0.9 - 0.5$, or 0.4.
We observe the closest value is 0.3997 which corresponds to the
probability that $0 < Z < 1.28$.
Therefore, the probability that $Z < 1.28$ is about $0.5000 + 0.3997$,
or 0.8997.
The variable Z takes the value 1.28 when H takes the value
$175 + 6.5(1.28)$, or 183.32.
That is, the 90th percentile of the population corresponds to a height
of about 183 cm.

Example 3. The IQ scores of Canadians on the Wechsler test of intelligence are
normally distributed with a mean of 100 and a standard deviation of
15. The Canadian test of General Learning Ability, when administered
to a large number of Canadian grade 8 students, yielded normally-
distributed scores with a mean of 8.0 and a standard deviation of 1.9.
Amanda scored 110 on the Wechsler test of intelligence and 12.4 on
the Learning-Ability test. Find the percentile in which each of Amanda's
scores lies. Is Amanda's learning ability commensurate with her IQ?

Solution. A score of 110 on the IQ test corresponds to a Z-score of $\dfrac{110 - 100}{15}$, or
0.67.
A score of 12.4 on the Learning Ability test corresponds to a Z-score of
$\dfrac{12.4 - 8.0}{1.9}$, or 2.32.
Use the table on page 470 to find the percentile corresponding to 0.67.
Move down the left column to 0.6 and along to the column headed 0.07,
to reach 0.2486.
This corresponds to the probability $0 < Z < 0.67$.
Therefore, the probability that $Z < 0.67$ is $0.5000 + 0.2486$, or 0.7486.
Hence, 0.67 corresponds to P_{75}.
Similarly, from the table, the Z-score of 2.32 corresponds to a probability
of $0.5000 + 0.4898$, or 0.9898.
Hence, 2.32 corresponds to P_{99}.

Since 0.67 corresponds to P_{75} and 2.32 corresponds to P_{99}, Amanda is
substantially higher on the Learning Ability test than on the IQ test.
The two scores are not commensurate and suggest that either the tests
measure different aptitudes or Amanda had a bad day when she wrote the
IQ test.

Example 3 demonstrates the value of the standard normal distribution in comparing percentiles of different normal distributions. Similar procedures can be used to determine whether a child of given height and mass is overweight by comparing the percentile ranks of her height and her mass. A height at the fifth percentile and a mass in the 95th percentile would suggest a condition of obesity.

Consider the area under a normal distribution curve with mean μ.

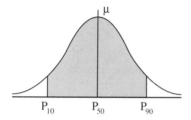

By symmetry, the area between P_{90} and P_{50} is equal to the area between P_{50} and P_{10}.

That is, $P_{90} - P_{50} = P_{50} - P_{10}$
$$P_{90} + P_{10} = 2P_{50}$$

This expression can be generalized.

$$P_x + P_{100 - x} = 2\mu$$

The proof of this equation is left as an exercise. (See Exercise 16.) The expression above can be used to find percentiles whose values are too small to be determined from the table.

EXERCISES 9-7

1. Explain what it means to say the values of X have a normal distribution N(13, 4).

2. If variable X has a normal distribution N(13, 4), describe the distribution of Z, where $Z = \dfrac{X - 13}{4}$.

3. The Stanford-Binet IQ scores of Canadians are normally distributed with a mean of 100 and a standard deviation of 16. What percent of Canadians have (according to this test):
   a) an IQ less than 100   b) an IQ less than 116
   c) an IQ greater than 116   d) an IQ between 84 and 116?

4. The variable X has a distribution N(0, 1). What is the distribution of the variable Y when:
   a) $Y = 3X$ b) $Y = 3X + 2$?

5. X is a normally-distributed variable. Explain how the probability that $X > a$ can be computed from the table of values for $N(0, 1)$ when:
   a) $a > 0$ b) $a < 0$.

6. The heights of adult American males are normally distributed with $\mu = 68.5$ inches and $\sigma = 2.6$ inches.
   a) If H denotes the height of an adult American male in centimetres, is H normally distributed? Why?
   b) What are the mean and the standard deviation of H?

(B)

7. What property of the graph of $N(\mu, \sigma)$ guarantees that its median is equal to its mean?

8. Find the area under the graph of the standard normal distribution Z corresponding to:
   a) $Z < 1.00$ b) $Z > 2.00$ c) $1.00 < Z < 2.00$
   d) $Z < 0$ e) $Z < -1.50$ f) $Z > -1.50$

9. T has distribution $N(50, 10)$. Find the area under the graph of T corresponding to:
   a) $T < 60$ b) $T < 40$ c) $T > 60$
   d) $40 < T < 60$ e) $T > 70$ f) $T < 30$.

10. For the standard normal distribution $N(0, 1)$ find:
    a) P_{90} b) P_{25} c) P_{75} d) P_{10} e) P_{30} f) P_{80}.

11. For the Stanford-Binet IQ test scores with distribution $N(100, 16)$ find:
    a) P_{90} b) P_{25} c) P_{75} d) P_{30} e) P_{80} f) P_{10}.

12. If the scores on a test are converted to Z-scores, does the shape of the distribution change? Explain.

13. If the IQ scores of Canadians are normally distributed with mean 100 and standard deviation 16, how many of Canada's 28 000 000 people would you expect to have IQs above 140?

14. A student scored 103 on a test with mean 117 and standard deviation 12. She scored -0.2 on a test with mean 0 and standard deviation 2. On what test did the student have the better performance?

15. The manufacturer of Perma-glow bulbs finds that the lifetimes of the bulbs are normally distributed with a mean of 87 h and a standard deviation of 7.8 h. The manufacturer guarantees that the bulbs will last at least x hours. What value of x will ensure that only about 5% will fail before x hours?

(C)

16. a) Prove that for the normal distribution $N(\mu, \sigma)$, $P_x + P_{100 - x} = 2\mu$, where P_x is the xth percentile.
    b) Deduce that for $N(0, 1)$ the equation in part a) reduces to $P_x = -P_{100 - x}$.

17. Let X be a variable with distribution $N(0, 1)$. Let Y be a variable defined by $Y = bx + c$. Prove that the distribution of Y is $N(c, b)$.

9-8 CONFIDENCE INTERVALS FOR NORMAL DISTRIBUTIONS

Most people would answer Ian's question by saying, "It will take you about one hour". However, Ian's mother has provided much more information. From the properties of the normal distribution we could draw several conclusions (as shown in the table below) from the professor's answer.

Property of the Normal Distribution	Information Implicit in the Professor's Answer
• The normal distribution is symmetric about the vertical line $x = \mu$, where μ is the population mean.	• The mean travel time to the university is about 58 min with an equal probability of being a few minutes shorter or longer than 58 min.
• About 68% of the measured values of a normally-distributed variable lie within one standard deviation from the mean.	• On about 68% of the days (roughly two-thirds), the travel time will lie in the interval 58 ± 10 min. That is, the travel time will be between 48 min and 68 min on about 68% of the days.
• About 96% of the measured values of a normally-distributed variable lie within two standard deviations from the mean.	• On about 96% of the days, the travel time will lie in the interval 58 ± 20 min. That is, the travel time will be between 38 min and 78 min on about 96% of the days.

The table above demonstrates that we can use the properties of the normal distribution to find the likelihood that a normally-distributed variable on any particular occasion will assume a value in a particular interval. A box-and-whisker plot is useful for displaying such an interval.

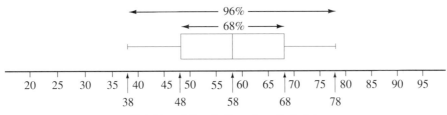

Total travel time to the university (min)

This plot shows that on any randomly-chosen day, the probability that the travel time is between 48 min and 68 min is about 0.68, or 68%. The probability that the travel time is between 38 min and 78 min is about 0.96, or 96%. In only 4% of the cases can we expect travel times outside the interval from 38 min to 78 min.

Example 1. Susan recorded the travel time to school on the school bus almost every day for an entire year. She discovered that the travel times corresponded closely to a normal distribution with a mean of 46 min and a standard deviation of 7 min. Draw a box-and-whisker plot, with the whiskers showing the middle 95%, and the box showing the middle 50%. Find the interval (centred at the mean) which contains an observed travel time:
a) 50% of the time   b) 95% of the time.

Solution. Let T denote the travel time for the bus.
Then, T has a normal distribution with mean $\mu = 46$ and standard deviation $\sigma = 7$.

Use $Z = \dfrac{T - \mu}{\sigma}$

$\qquad = \dfrac{T - 46}{7}$

Rearrange. $T = 46 + 7Z$
Then, Z has a standard normal distribution.
To construct the box-and-whisker plot we must find the percentiles $P_{2.5}$, P_{25}, P_{75}, and $P_{97.5}$ for Z, and consequently T.

We use the table of values for the standard normal distribution curve $N(0, 1)$.
For $P_{97.5}$, we think 0.975, and look for the value closest to 0.975 − 0.500, or 0.475. This is 1.96.
For P_{75}, we think 0.75, and look for the value closest to 0.75 − 0.50, or 0.25. This is about 0.67.
To find the corresponding percentiles for T, we substitute these percentiles for Z into the equation $T = 46 + 7Z$.

For T: $P_{97.5} = 46 + 7(1.96)$ $\qquad P_{75} = 46 + 7(0.67)$
$\qquad\qquad = 59.72$ $\qquad\qquad\qquad\quad = 50.69$
$\qquad\qquad \doteq 60$ $\qquad\qquad\qquad\qquad \doteq 51$

For $P_{2.5}$ and P_{25}, we use the formula from Section 9-7.
$$P_x + P_{100 - x} = 2\mu, \text{ or } P_x = 2\mu - P_{100 - x}$$
For *T*: $P_{2.5} = 2(46) - 59.72 \qquad P_{25} = 2(46) - 50.69$
$$\qquad\qquad = 32.28 \qquad\qquad\qquad = 41.31$$
$$\qquad\qquad \doteq 32 \qquad\qquad\qquad\quad \doteq 41$$

Using these percentiles we construct the box-and-whisker plot.
a) An observed travel time will lie in the interval 41 min to 51 min 50% of the time.
b) An observed travel time will lie in the interval 32 min to 60 min 95% of the time.

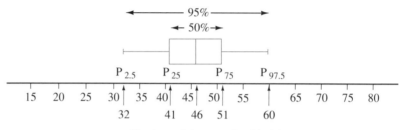

Total travel time to school (min)

Example 1 shows how we can find the likelihood of an observation or measurement occurring within a particular interval if the measured values have a normal distribution with a known mean and a standard deviation. Conversely, we can use the fact that the measured values are normally distributed to draw inferences about the mean or standard deviation. The following example illustrates this idea.

Example 2. On two random occasions, Susan's brother Sean rode the same school bus as Susan and recorded the travel times to the school as 63 min and 71 min. Does Sean have reasonable grounds to doubt Susan's assertion that the travel time is normally distributed with a mean of 46 min and a standard deviation of 7 min?

Solution. The box-and-whisker plot in *Example 1* shows that the observations of 63 min and 71 min are both outside the box and the whiskers. The probability that a single observation will occur outside the box and whiskers is 5%, or 0.05. The probability that two observations will occur outside the box and whiskers is $0.05 \times 0.05 = 0.0025$, or one chance in 400! Unless Sean happened to travel on the bus during conditions such as snow days or road construction, he has good reason to doubt Susan's assertion.

The techniques of *Examples 1* and *2* can be formalized as follows. If X is a variable which has a normal distribution with mean μ and standard deviation σ, then the interval defined by

$$P_{2.5} \leq X \leq P_{97.5} \ldots \text{①}$$

will contain 95% of all observations, or measurements of X.
To find $P_{2.5}$ and $P_{97.5}$ for this distribution, we observe that the variable Z defined by

$$Z = \frac{X - \mu}{\sigma} \ldots \text{②}$$

has a standard normal distribution.
From the tables of $N(0, 1)$, we find that the 2.5th percentile for Z is -1.960 and the 97.5th percentile is $Z = 1.960$. For the corresponding percentiles for X, substitute into the equation $X = \mu + \sigma Z$.

$$P_{2.5} = \mu - 1.96\sigma \quad \text{and} \quad P_{97.5} = \mu + 1.96\sigma \ldots \text{③}$$

Substitute from ③ into ①.

$$\mu - 1.96\sigma \leq X \leq \mu + 1.96\sigma \ldots \text{④}$$

95% of all observations, or measurements of X will fall in this interval. That is, expression ④ may be written as follows.

$$\text{Prob}(\mu - 1.96\sigma \leq X \leq \mu + 1.96\sigma) = 0.95 \ldots \text{⑤}$$

We say, "The probability that a random observation of X lies in the interval between $\mu - 1.96\sigma$ and $\mu + 1.96\sigma$, is 0.95".
We can rewrite the inequality

$$\mu - 1.96\sigma \leq X \text{ as } \mu \leq X + 1.96\sigma \ldots \text{⑥}$$

and

$$\mu + 1.96\sigma \geq X \text{ as } \mu \geq X - 1.96\sigma \ldots \text{⑦}$$

Inequalities ⑥ and ⑦ can be combined into this inequality.

$$X - 1.96\sigma \leq \mu \leq X + 1.96\sigma \ldots \text{⑧}$$

Since inequalities ④ and ⑧ are equivalent, statement ⑤ may be written as follows.

$$\boxed{\text{Prob } (X - 1.96\sigma \leq \mu \leq X + 1.96\sigma) = 0.95}$$

This interval is called a *95% confidence interval for* μ because it asserts that if a random observation of X is made, the true value of μ will be contained in that interval 95% of the time. Confidence intervals are very important in the study of statistical hypothesis testing because they help us test, by sampling, the hypothesis that some parameter (such as μ) of a population has a given value.

Example 3.   a) Find a 95% confidence interval for the mean time for Susan's bus trip.

b) One trip is measured and found to take 59 min. Is this, to a 95% level of confidence, consistent with the hypothesis that the mean travel time is 46 min? (Assume the standard deviation is known to be 7 min.)

Solution.   a) Substituting $X = 59$ and $\sigma = 7$ into the expression above, we obtain the 95% confidence interval for μ.

Prob $(59 - 1.96(7) \leqslant \mu \leqslant 59 + 1.96(7)) = 0.95$
that is, Prob $(45.28 \leqslant \mu \leqslant 72.72) = 0.95$

b) Since μ was assumed to be 46 min and since 46 lies between 45.28 and 72.72, then the observation is consistent (to a 95% level of confidence) with the hypothesis that $\mu = 46$.

EXERCISES 9-8

(A)

1. Explain the meaning of P_{10} and P_{75} for a normally-distributed variable X.

2. Use the table of values on page 470 to find these percentiles for $N(0, 1)$.
   a) P_{50} b) P_{75} c) P_{90} d) P_{40}

3. For the distribution $N(0, 1)$, explain why $P_x = -P_{100 - x}$.

4. Explain the meaning of a 95% confidence interval for the mean of a normal distribution.

5. Between what two percentiles are all the values in the box of a box-and-whisker plot?

(B)

6. Find these percentiles for $N(25, 6)$.
   a) P_5 b) P_{25} c) P_{50} d) P_{75}

7. At the beginning of this section, Ian's mother asserted that the travel time to the university is normally distributed with a mean of 58 min and a standard deviation of 10 min.
   a) Is there, in practice, a lower limit to the travel time?
   b) Is there an upper limit to the travel time?
   c) Is the probability that the travel time will be about 30 min less than the mean, the same as the probability that the travel time will be 30 min greater than the mean?
   d) Could the measure of travel time be symmetric about the line $\mu = 58$?
   e) Could the travel time be a "perfect" normal distribution?

8. A variable Y has a distribution $N(16, 4)$. Find the interval centred around $Y = 16$ that will contain 90% of all observations of Y.

9. A study completed in 1976 revealed that the heights in centimetres of North American women have the distribution $N(163, 5.8)$. Find the interval centred around the mean which will contain 95% of all measured heights.

10. Find a 95% confidence interval for the mean μ of a normally distributed variable X with a standard deviation of 9, if one single observation of X reveals that $X = 28.6$.

11. The lifetime in seconds of a particular type of firecracker has a distribution $N(\mu, 10)$ where μ is unknown. The measurement of one firecracker reveals a lifetime of 23 s. Find a 95% confidence interval for μ, the mean lifetime.

Ⓒ

12. a) Derive a formula, similar to that for a 95% confidence interval, for the 99% confidence interval for μ for a variable X with distribution $N(\mu, \sigma)$.
    b) Use your formula to find a 99% confidence interval for μ in *Exercise 9*.

13. Prove that if X has the distribution $N(\mu, \sigma)$, then:
    a) the variable $Y = X - \mu$ has distribution $N(0, \sigma)$
    b) the variable $Z = \dfrac{X - \mu}{\sigma}$ has distribution $N(0, 1)$.

14. Let $\{x_1, x_2, \dots x_n\}$ denote a sample of size n, and let S_x denote the sample variance, defined by

$$S_x^2 = \frac{n \sum_{i=1}^{n} x_i^2 - \left(\sum_{i=1}^{n} x_i \right)^2}{n(n-1)}.$$

Prove that if $Z_i = \dfrac{x_i - \overline{x}}{S_x}$, then $\sum_{i=1}^{n} Z_i^2 = n - 1$.

Review Exercises

1. On an examination, a class of 30 students scored these marks out of 100.

   82 67 53 75 41 86 68 75 81 98 54 34 65 73 71
   43 78 72 69 72 75 64 88 73 72 67 74 80 77 70

   a) Display these data on a stem-and-leaf plot.
   b) What was the lowest mark? the highest mark?
   c) What mark was most frequently obtained?
   d) What percent of the marks were below 70? above 80?
   e) What was the 15th highest mark?
   f) What mark places a student in the top half of the class? the top quarter?
   g) Construct a histogram to display this distribution of marks.

2. A company pays its secretarial staff according to a category placement related to educational qualifications and experience. The hourly rates of pay and the number of secretaries in each category are given in the table.

   a) Calculate the mean hourly rate.
   b) What is the median hourly rate?
   c) How many secretaries in category I must be promoted to category II to raise the mean hourly rate to $12.00?

Category	Hourly rate	Number
I	$9.50	14
II	$12.00	9
III	$13.50	7
IV	$15.00	5

3. The table shows the ranks of the top 10 countries in mathematics achievement in the Second International Mathematics Study, and the average size of a senior mathematics class in each country.

   a) Calculate the Pearson correlation coefficient between rank and class size.
   b) On the basis of these data, does there appear to be a relationship between class size and student achievement?

Rank	Class Size
1	27
2	43
3	10
4	20
5	23
6	16
7	16
8	25
9	16
10	13

4. The scatterplot displays the number of chin-ups completed by each of 12 members of the football team, and the corresponding mass of each player.
   a) Calculate the correlation coefficient between the number of chin-ups and the body mass.
   b) Calculate the equation of the line of best fit and use it to predict how many chin-ups could be expected from a player of body mass 100 kg.

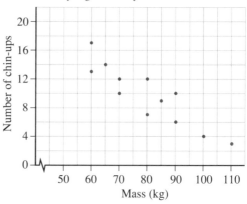

Chin-ups against body mass

To win the LOTTO 649, a person must correctly choose 6 numbers from 49 numbers. In how many ways can this be done? (See Section 10-5, *Example 2*.)

10-1 THE FUNDAMENTAL COUNTING PRINCIPLE

At a very early age we learned how to count. If asked, "How many students are shown in this picture?", we simply matched the students with the counting numbers: 1, 2, 3, . . .

This simple counting procedure can be very time consuming. For example, a customer is told that a certain car dealership sells 8 different models of cars, and each model is available in 5 different colors. To find out how many different cars are available, the customer does not have to count every model in each color. She knows that:

There are 8 ways to select the model.

For each of these ways, there are 5 ways to select the color.

The total number of different cars is $\boxed{8} \times \boxed{5}$, or 40.

model   color

Example 1. *Complete Computers* has a sale on 4 different computers, 2 monitors, 2 disk drives, and 3 printers. How many different complete computer systems are available at the sale price?

Solution.

There are 4 computers.	For each computer, there are 2 monitors.	For each monitor, there are 2 disk drives.	For each disk drive, there are 3 printers.
$\boxed{4}$ $\times$	$\boxed{2}$ $\times$	$\boxed{2}$ $\times$	$\boxed{3}$

The number of different systems is $4 \times 2 \times 2 \times 3$, or 48.

Certain counting problems can be solved by drawing a tree diagram.

Example 2. A 2-digit number is formed using the digits 1, 3, and 5. Draw a tree diagram that illustrates the possible numbers.

Solution. For each first digit chosen, there are 2 possibilities for the second digit.

First digit	*Second digit*	*Possible numbers*
1	3	13
	5	15
3	1	31
	5	35
5	1	51
	3	53

There are six possible numbers, which are listed in the third column.

The counting in these examples illustrates the following principle.

> **The Fundamental Counting Principle**
> If one item can be selected in *m* ways, and for each of these selections a second item can be selected in *n* ways, then there are *mn* ways of selecting the two items.

Example 3. How many even 2-digit whole numbers are there?

Solution. The first, or tens digit can be picked in 9 ways, since 0 cannot be the first digit. For each of these selections, the second, or units digit can be picked from the even digits (0, 2, 4, 6, 8) in 5 ways. There are 9×5, or 45 even 2-digit numbers.

Example 4. How many 2-digit whole numbers can be formed using the digits: 0, 1, 2, 4, 6, 7, 8, 9 if:
    a) repetitions are allowed   b) repetitions are not allowed?

Solution. The tens digit can be chosen in 7 ways.
    a) If repetitions are allowed, the units digit can be chosen in 8 ways. Hence, there are 7×8, or 56 whole numbers.
    b) If repetitions are not allowed, the units digit can be chosen in 7 ways. Hence, there are 7×7, or 49 whole numbers.

EXERCISES 10-1

1. Draw a tree diagram to illustrate the possible outcomes.
   a) Two coins are tossed one after another
   b) Three coins are tossed one after another

2. *Snack Shack* serves: egg or ham sandwiches; coffee, soft drink or milk; and donuts or pie for dessert. Draw a tree diagram to illustrate the possible meals if one item is chosen from each category.

3. Four different books are displayed on a shelf. Illustrate their possible arrangements with a tree diagram.

4. Bill has 3 sweaters and 4 pairs of slacks. In how many ways can he select an outfit?

5. Alisha has 5 blouses, 4 skirts, and 4 sweaters in her wardrobe. In how many ways can she select an outfit, assuming she wears three items at once?

6. How many odd 2-digit numbers are there?

7. How many even 2-digit numbers can be made using the digits 1, 2, 3, 4, 5, 6, 7, 8 if:
   a) repetitions are not allowed   b) repetitions are allowed?

8. Using the digits 1, 3, 5, 7, 9, and no repetitions, how many:
   a) 3-digit numbers can be formed   b) 4-digit numbers can be formed?

9. There are 7 horses in one race and 6 in another. For a person placing a bet, in how many ways can the winners of the two races be chosen?

Ⓑ

10. There are 8 horses in a race. In how many ways can the win, place, and show horses be selected?

11. An ice cream parlor features 64 flavors and 20 toppings, in 3 sizes. How many different sundaes can be made?

12. How many different 7-digit telephone numbers can be made using the digits from 0 to 9, if the first digit may not be 0 or 1?

13. A sports club with 30 members wishes to pick a president, vice-president, secretary, and treasurer. Assuming that no person can hold two offices, in how many ways can the selections be made?

14. How many different licence plates can be made if a plate consists of:
    a) three different letters followed by two different digits
    b) three letters followed by two numbers, not necessarily different
    c) three consecutive letters and three consecutive numbers?

15. The final score in a soccer game is 4-3. How many different half-time scores are possible?

16. A "count" in baseball is an ordered pair indicating the numbers of balls and strikes to the batter. For example, "2 and 1" means 2 balls and 1 strike. How many different counts are possible?

17. The dial on a standard 3-number combination lock contains markings to represent the numbers from 0 to 59. How many combinations are possible if no number can be used twice?

18. a) How many 3-digit numbers have digits that are all different?
    b) How many 4-digit numbers have digits that are all different?
    c) How many 5-digit numbers have digits that are all different?

Ⓒ

19. A Bingo card has 5 columns, each with 5 spaces. The first column contains numbers from 1 to 15; the second column contains numbers from 16 to 30; the third column has its centre square shaded and contains numbers from 31 to 45; the fourth and fifth columns contain numbers from 46 to 60, and 61 to 75 respectively.

B	I	N	G	O
3	23	44	50	73
11	18	40	46	64
9	17		55	65
6	29	31	47	69
2	20	36	51	70

   a) How many different Bingo cards can be printed?
   b) If the population of Canada were to count these cards at the rate of 1 per second, how long would it take?
   c) If the cards were printed on paper 1 mm thick, how high would the stack of all possible cards be?

10-2 PERMUTATIONS

Many student lockers are secured with a
3-number combination lock. Knowing the
correct 3 numbers is not sufficient to open
the lock. The numbers must be used in the
correct sequence; that is, the order of the
numbers is important.

An arrangement of a set of objects is called a *permutation*. The
order of the objects is important.

Example 1. How many permutations can be formed using the letters of the word
MATE?

Solution. Each letter must be placed in one of the four boxes shown.

☐ ☐ ☐ ☐

For the first box, there are 4 choices. So, there are 3 choices for the
second box, 2 choices for the third box, and 1 "choice" for the last box.

4 3 2 1

Hence, there are 4 × 3 × 2 × 1, or 24 permutations of the letters in
MATE.

Some of the permutations in *Example 1* form words, for example,
MEAT, TEAM, and TAME. Other permutations do not form words,
for example, ATME, MTEA, and EMTA.

Example 2. How many permutations are there of the letters in the word COMPUTER?

Solution. Each letter can be placed in one of the eight boxes in the ways shown.

8 7 6 5 4 3 2 1

Hence, there are 8 × 7 × 6 × 5 × 4 × 3 × 2 × 1, or 40 320
permutations.

The product in the solution to *Example 2* can be written more simply
using *factorial notation*.
That is, 8 × 7 × 6 × 5 × 4 × 3 × 2 × 1 = 8! We say, "Eight factorial."
Factorial notation can be applied to any whole number. For example:

1! = 1
2! = 2 × 1
3! = 3 × 2 × 1
5! = 5 × 4 × 3 × 2 × 1

In general, $n! = n(n - 1)(n - 2)(n - 3) \times \ldots \times 3 \times 2 \times 1$

Example 3. Simplify. a) 6! b) $\dfrac{11!}{7!}$ c) $\dfrac{n!}{(n-2)!}$

Solution. a) For 6!, use a calculator. Key in: 6 $\boxed{n!}$ to display 720

b) $\dfrac{11!}{7!} = \dfrac{11 \times 10 \times 9 \times 8 \times 7!}{7!}$

$= 7920$

Using a calculator, key in: 11 $\boxed{n!}$ $\boxed{\div}$ 7 $\boxed{n!}$ $\boxed{=}$ to display 7920

c) $\dfrac{n!}{(n-2)!} = \dfrac{n(n-1)(n-2)!}{(n-2)!}$

$= n^2 - n$

Example 4. How many 3-letter permutations can be formed from the letters of PROVINCE?

Solution. Each letter can be placed in one of the three boxes in the ways shown.

$\boxed{8}$ $\boxed{7}$ $\boxed{6}$

Hence, there are $8 \times 7 \times 6$, or 336 permutations of 3 letters.

In *Example 4*, we found the number of permutations of 8 objects taken 3 at a time. This is denoted $_8P_3$.

That is, $_8P_3 = 8 \times 7 \times 6$ Multiply and divide by 5!

$= \dfrac{8 \times 7 \times 6 \times 5!}{5!}$

$= \dfrac{8!}{5!}$, or $\dfrac{8!}{(8-3)!}$

In general, the number of permutations of n objects taken r at a time is given by:

$$_nP_r = \frac{n!}{(n-r)!}$$

Recall that in the solutions to *Examples 1* and *2*, we arranged all the available objects. That is, the number of permutations of 4 objects taken 4 at a time is $_4P_4$, or 4!; and the number of permutations of 8 objects taken 8 at a time is $_8P_8$, or 8!.

In general, the number of permutations of n objects taken n at a time is $_nP_n = n!$

An interesting result occurs if we substitute n for r in the formula $_nP_r = \dfrac{n!}{(n-r)!}$.

That is, $_nP_n = \dfrac{n!}{(n-n)!}$

$= \dfrac{n!}{0!}$

But we know that $_nP_n = n!$

Hence, we define $0! = 1$.

Example 5. In a certain country, motor-cycle licence plates consist of 2 different letters followed by 3 different digits. How many different plates are possible?

Solution. From 26 letters, we can take 2 in $_{26}P_2$ ways.
For each of these ways, from 10 digits we can take 3 in $_{10}P_3$ ways.
Hence, the total number of licence plates is

$$_{26}P_2 \times {}_{10}P_3 = \frac{26!}{(26-2)!} \times \frac{10!}{(10-3)!}$$
$$= 468\ 000$$

EXERCISES 10-2

Ⓐ

1. Simplify.
   a) 5! b) 7! c) 10! d) 14!
   e) $\dfrac{6!}{3!}$ f) $\dfrac{9!}{5!}$ g) $\dfrac{12!}{6!} \times \dfrac{10!}{4!}$ h) $\dfrac{20!}{15!} \times \dfrac{14!}{7!}$

2. How many permutations are there of the letters in each word?
   a) FRY b) FISH c) FIRST

3. In how many ways can the letters of each word be arranged?
   a) FLOAT b) SAILOR c) HARMONY d) INSURABLE

4. A bowl contains an apple, a peach, a pear, a banana, an apricot, a plum, and an orange. In how many ways can the fruit be distributed among 7 children?

5. Marie has a model train with the following equipment in addition to the engine and caboose: tank car, flat car, box car, refrigerator car, and stock car. In how many ways can she arrange the five cars between the engine and the caboose?

6. In how many ways can each set of books be arranged on a shelf?
   a) 4 different mathematics texts b) 6 different science texts

7. In how many ways can 15 freight cars be arranged on a siding?

Ⓑ

8. Find the value of each expression for $n = 5$.
   a) $n!$ b) $(n + 1)!$ c) $n! + 1$ d) $(n - 1)!$

9. Write each expression without its factorial symbol.
   a) $\dfrac{(n + 2)!}{n!}$ b) $\dfrac{(n - 3)!}{n!}$ c) $\dfrac{(n + 4)!}{(n + 2)!}$ d) $\dfrac{(2n)!}{(2n - 3)!}$

10. Find the value of each expression.
   a) $_6P_3$ b) $_{10}P_6$ c) $_{24}P_{20}$ d) $_{16}P_9$

11. A football team has 6 basic plays. How many arrangements of 3 different plays could be called?

12. A map of the four western provinces is to be colored using a different color for each province. How many different ways are possible if there are 9 colors available?

13. Using the letters of the word PRODUCT, how many:
    a) 3-letter arrangements can be made
    b) 4-letter arrangements can be made
    c) 5-letter arrangements can be made?

14. How many 5-letter arrangements can be formed from the letters of each word?
    a) STUMP   b) CABINET   c) TOWNSHIP

15. There are seven empty seats on a bus and four people enter. In how many ways can they be seated?

16. In the United States, a postal code consists of five digits. In Canada, a postal code consists of a letter, a digit, a letter, a digit, a letter, and a digit. How many different postal codes are possible in each country?

17. How many different ways are there of reading each word vertically?

a)		b)		c)		d)	
	B		HHHH		C		E
	AA		OOO		AA		DD
	NNN		LL		LLL		MMM
	FFFF		I		GGGG		OOOO
	FFFFF		DD		AAA		NNNNN
			AAA		RR		TTTTT
			YYYY		Y		OOOOOOO
							NNNNNNNN

Ⓒ

18. To open a combination lock, three numbers from 0 to 59 must be used in the correct order. How many different combinations must a student try in each case?
    a) The three numbers are known, but their order has been forgotten.
    b) One number and the order have been forgotten.
    c) Two numbers and the order have been forgotten.
    d) Three numbers have been forgotten.

19. Solve for n.
    a) $_nP_2 = 72$ b) $_6P_n = 30$ c) $_7P_n = {}_{15}P_2$
    d) $_nP_n = {}_6P_3$ e) $_{2n}P_3 = 2(_nP_4)$

20. How many 3-letter arrangements can be formed from fifteen consonants and five vowels, if a vowel must be in the middle?

21. a) How many different signals of 4 flags can be formed using any number of flags in 4 colors?
    b) How many different signals of up to 4 flags can be formed using any number of flags in 4 colors?

22. If each number were evaluated, how many zeros would occur on the right?
    a) 22!   b) 55!

10-3 PERMUTATIONS INVOLVING RESTRICTIONS

Often, restrictions are placed on the ways in which objects are to be arranged. When this occurs, the restrictions should be dealt with first.

Example 1. Find the number of permutations of the letters in the word COLUMBIA if:
    a) there are no restrictions
    b) the first letter must be C
    c) the last two letters must be vowels
    d) the letters O and M must be together.

Solution.
    a) There are 8!, or 40 320 permutations.
    b) Since the first letter is C, there are 7 other letters to be arranged. This can be done in 7!, or 5040 ways.
    c) The last two letters are vowels. Pick these first. There are 4 vowels from which 2 are picked. This can be done in 4×3, or 12 ways. The 6 remaining letters can be arranged 6! ways. Hence, there are $12 \times 6!$, or 8640 permutations.
    d) Since O and M must be together, they are considered as one letter. Then, there are 7 letters, which can be arranged 7! ways. For each of these ways, the O and M can be arranged 2 ways. Hence, there are $7! \times 2$, or 10 080 permutations.

Example 2. In how many ways can 5 girls and 4 boys be arranged on a bench, if no two people of the same sex can sit together?

Solution. Arrange the 4 boys first. This can be done in 4! ways. Then arrange the 5 girls between the boys (3 places) or at the ends of the bench (2 places). So, there are 5 places in which to arrange 5 girls. This can be done 5! ways. Hence, the total number of permutations is $4! \times 5!$, or 2880.

EXERCISES 10-3

1. In how many ways can the letters of the word PICTURE be arranged if:
    a) there are no restrictions
    b) the first letter must be T?

2. In how many ways can the letters of the word PETUNIA be arranged if:
    a) the first two letters must be vowels
    b) the last two letters must be vowels?

3. In how many ways can the letters of the word STAPLER be arranged if:
    a) the vowels must be together
    b) the letters STP must be together in any order?

4. In how many ways can the letters of the word FORTUNES be arranged if:
    a) the vowels must be together
    b) the vowels must not be together?

5. In how many ways can the letters of the word PERSON be arranged:
   a) with no restrictions
   b) if the letters E, R, and O are separated by other letters
   c) if the letters P and N are adjacent
   d) if the last letter is a consonant
   e) if the vowels must be at the end?

6. In how many ways can the digits 1, 2, 3, 4, 5, 6, 7, 8, 9 be arranged if no two odd numbers are together?

7. In how many ways can 5 girls and 4 boys be arranged on a bench, if no two girls can sit together?

8. In how many ways can 4 different colored petunias and 7 different colored begonias be planted in a row, if the petunias must be together?

ⓒ

9. In how many ways can the letters of the word LINEAR be arranged if:
   a) the position of the vowels is not changed
   b) the order of the vowels is not changed?

10. How many numbers greater than 30 000 can be made from these digits?
    a) 3, 4, 5, 6, 7   b) 2, 3, 4, 5, 6, 7   c) 1, 2, 3, 4, 5, 6

11. In how many ways can the digits in *Exercise 6* be arranged if no two even numbers are together?

INVESTIGATE

The book ''Cent Mille Milliards de Pommes'' consists of 10 sonnets written in French. Each sonnet was sliced into 14 strips, one for each line. The strips could be flipped so that a sonnet could be created using any one of the 10 available strips for each line. It is said that so many sonnets are possible that you could probably read a sonnet that no one has ever read before, or will ever read again. Check the validity of this statement.

INVESTIGATE

1. Locate the factorial key on your calculator. What is the largest number you can enter without:
   a) getting an answer in scientific notation
   b) getting an error message?
2. Locate the $_nP_r$ and $_nC_r$ keys on your calculator. By entering various numbers, investigate how these symbols are related.

10-4 PERMUTATIONS INVOLVING REPETITIONS, AND OBJECTS IN A CIRCLE

Permutations Involving Repetitions

In the previous section, the letters, numbers, and objects in each set were all different. That is not always the case.

Consider the permutations of the word FUEL.

FUEL	FLUE	UEFL	EFUL	ELFU	LUFE
FULE	FLEU	UELF	EFLU	ELUF	LUEF
FEUL	UFEL	ULFE	EUFL	LFUE	LEFU
FELU	UFLE	ULEF	EULF	LFEU	LEUF

There are $_4P_4$, or 24 permutations.

If we change the E in FUEL to an L, we get the word FULL. If we change the Es to Ls in the list of permutations, the 24 different arrangements become 12 matching pairs of arrangements.

FULL	FLUL	ULFL	LFUL	LLFU	LUFL
FULL	FLLU	ULLF	LFLU	LLUF	LULF
FLUL	UFLL	ULFL	LUFL	LFUL	LLFU
FLLU	UFLL	ULLF	LULF	LFLU	LLUF

That is, arrangements like FUEL and FULE both become FULL. There are $\frac{1}{2}$ as many permutations of FULL as there are of FUEL.

Hence, the number of permutations of FULL is $\frac{4!}{2}$, or 12.

If we change the F and E in FUEL to L, we get the word LULL. If we change the Fs and Es to Ls in the first list of permutations, the 24 different arrangements become 4 matching sets of 6 arrangements.

LULL	LLUL	ULLL	LLUL	LLLU	LULL
LULL	LLLU	ULLL	LLLU	LLUL	LULL
LLUL	ULLL	ULLL	LULL	LLUL	LLLU
LLLU	ULLL	ULLL	LULL	LLLU	LLUL

That is, words like FUEL, FULE, EUFL, and LUFE all become LULL.

There are $\frac{1}{6}$, or $\frac{1}{3!}$ as many permutations of LULL as there are of FUEL.

Hence, the number of permutations of LULL is $\frac{4!}{3!}$, or 4.

Notice the pattern of this example.

When a letter occurs twice in a word, the number of permutations is $\frac{1}{2!}$ of what it would be if the letters were all different.

When a letter occurs 3 times in a word, the number of permutations is $\frac{1}{3!}$ of what it would be if the letters were all different.

Example 1.   Find the numbers of permutations of the letters in the word MINIMUM.

Solution.   If the 7 letters were all different, there would be 7! permutations. Since there are 2 Is and 3 Ms, the number of permutations is $\dfrac{7!}{2!3!}$, or 420.

> In general, the number of permutations of n objects taken n at a time, if there are a alike of one kind, b alike of another kind, c alike of a third kind, and so on, is
>
> $$\dfrac{n!}{a!b!c!}$$

Permutations of Objects in a Circle

Consider the arrangements of 4 people around a circular table. For a given permutation, a rotation of each person clockwise or counterclockwise does not change the permutation.

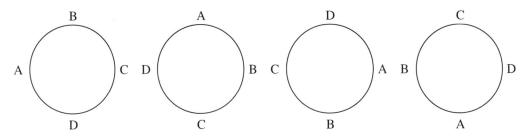

The seating arrangements illustrated above are equivalent permutations.

To find the number of permutations, fix one person and find the number of permutations of the other people with respect to that person. That is, for 4 people, fix 1 person and the other 3 people can be arranged 3!, or 6 ways. Hence, 4 people at a circular table can be arranged 6 ways.

Example 2.   At a wedding reception the guests are seated in groups of 8 at circular tables. How many permutations are there for each table?

Solution.   Fix the position of one person. Then, the other 7 people can be arranged 7!, or 5040 ways.

Hence, there are 5040 permutations for each table.

Consider the arrangements of objects in a circle, when the circle can be flipped, or reflected. For example, there are two different car keys, a house key, and an identification tag on a key ring. In how many ways can they be arranged?

Since the keys move freely on the ring, this is a circular arrangement of 4 objects. Hence, there are 3!, or 6 ways of arranging them. Here is an example of two of those ways.

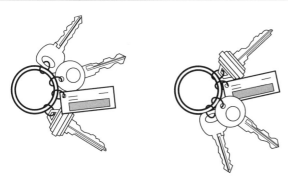

However, if the ring on the right is flipped, or reflected:

the arrangement matches that on the left.

Since each arrangement can be reflected to match another arrangement, the total number of different arrangements is $\frac{6}{2}$, or 3.

Example 3. In how many ways can 10 different wooden beads be arranged on a string, to form a necklace?

Solution. Since this is a circular arrangement, the 10 beads can be arranged 9! ways. But the necklace can be reflected. Hence, the number of arrangements is $\frac{9!}{2}$, or 181 440.

EXERCISES 10-4

1. Simplify.

   a) $\dfrac{5!}{2!2!}$ b) $\dfrac{8!}{3!2!}$ c) $\dfrac{12!}{3!3!2!}$ d) $\dfrac{10!}{2!2!4!}$

   e) $\dfrac{9!}{3 4!2!3!}$ f) $\dfrac{11!}{3!3!2!}$ g) $\dfrac{13!}{3!3!5!}$ h) $\dfrac{14!}{3!6!2!3!}$

2. Find the number of permutations of all the letters in each word.

   a) CALGARY   b) SASKATOON   c) VICTORIA
   d) LETHBRIDGE   e) EDMONTON   f) MINNEWONKA
   g) ASSINIBOINE   h) SASKATCHEWAN

Ⓑ

3. How many 9-digit numbers containing two 1s, three 2s, and four 3s can be formed?

4. How many different signals can be constructed by making a vertical display of eight flags if there are three blue flags, three white flags, and two red flags?

5. In how many ways can 4 red, 2 blue, and 3 green marbles be distributed among 9 children, if each child is to receive one marble?

6. In how many ways can quintuplets sit around a circular table?

7. In how many ways can 6 students be arranged in a circle?

8. A monument is surrounded by ten provincial flags. How many different circular arrangements are possible?

9. A crown and anchor wheel has 42 different symbols arranged in a circle. In how many different ways can this be done?

10. In how many ways can:
    a) 3 different keys be arranged on a key ring
    b) 7 different keys be arranged on a key ring?

11. a) How many different numbers greater than 100 000 can be made from the digits 1, 3, 3, 3, 4, and 5?
    b) How many numbers in part a) are even?

12. Eight different bells are attached to the circumference of a tambourine. If the two sides of the tambourine are identical, in how many ways can the bells be attached?

13. In how many ways can the letters of the word CARRIER be arranged if:
    a) the first letter is R
    b) the first two letters are RR
    c) the first three letters are RRR
    d) the first letter is R, and the next letter is not R
    e) the first two letters are RR, and the next letter is not R?

14. Mum, Dad, and their six children (3 boys and 3 girls) are to be seated at a circular table. In how many ways can this be done if Mum and Dad sit next to each other, and males and females sit in alternating positions?

Ⓒ

15. A person can travel north or west. How many possible routes are there from one place in a city to another place which is:
    a) 3 blocks north and 2 blocks west   b) 5 blocks north and 4 blocks west?

16. Four married couples sit at a circular table. In how many different ways can they be seated if:
    a) men and women alternate
    b) each husband and wife must sit next to each other
    c) each husband must sit opposite his wife?

10-5 COMBINATIONS

Frequently, situations arise where a set of objects must be chosen from a larger set. For example, a mathematics examination consists of 8 questions, and students are required to attempt five. In this situation, the order in which the questions are chosen is not important.

A selection of objects from a set is called a *combination*. The order in which the objects are chosen is not important.

Consider the mathematics examination mentioned above. A set of 5 questions is a combination. Each combination can be arranged 5! ways. Hence, there are 5! more permutations than there are combinations. That is, the number of combinations $= \dfrac{\text{the number of permutations}}{5!}$.

We know that the number of permutations of 5 questions chosen from 8 is $_8P_5$. Hence, the number of combinations is $\dfrac{_8P_5}{5!} = \dfrac{8!}{3!5!}$, or 56. This means that 56 different examination papers are possible.

The number of combinations of 8 objects taken 5 at a time, without regard for order, is written as $_8C_5$. We say, "Eight choose five". This may be denoted by $\dbinom{8}{5}$.

In general, the number of combinations of n objects taken r at a time, without regard for order, is given by

$$_nC_r = \frac{n!}{(n-r)!r!}.$$

Example 1. Ali, Benje, Carmel, Donna, and Evan are nominated to sit on a committee of 3 people. How many different committees can be chosen?

Solution. A committee of 3 people is a combination. The number of committees is the number of combinations of 5 people taken 3 at a time. That is,

$$_5C_3 = \frac{5!}{2!3!}$$
$$= 10$$

Ten different committees can be chosen.

Example 2. To win the LOTTO 649, a person must correctly choose 6 numbers from 1 to 49. How many combinations are possible?

Solution. The number of combinations of 49 numbers taken 6 at a time is:

$$\binom{49}{6} = \frac{49!}{43!6!}$$

Use a calculator. Key in: 49 $\boxed{n!}$ $\boxed{\div}$ 43 $\boxed{n!}$ $\boxed{\div}$ 6 $\boxed{n!}$ $\boxed{=}$ to display 13983816

There are nearly 14 million combinations for the LOTTO 649.

Example 3. A standard deck of 52 playing cards consists of four suits (spades, hearts, diamonds, and clubs) of thirteen cards each. How many different:
a) 5-card hands can be formed
b) 5-card red hands can be formed
c) 5-card red hands or 5-card black hands can be formed
d) 5-card hands can be formed with at least three black cards?

Solution. a) The number of combinations of 5 cards chosen from 52 cards is

$$\binom{52}{5} = \frac{52!}{47!5!}, \text{ or } 2\ 598\ 960.$$

b) There are two red suits (hearts and diamonds) and a total of 26 red cards. The number of combinations of 5 cards chosen from 26 is

$$\binom{26}{5} = \frac{26!}{21!5!}, \text{ or } 65\ 780.$$

c) There are two black suits (spades and clubs) and 65 780 possible 5-card black hands. The total number of 5-card red or black hands is 65 780 + 65 780 = 131 560.

d) If at least three cards must be black there are several possibilities.
- three black and two red cards
  The black cards can be chosen in $\binom{26}{3}$ ways and the red cards can be chosen in $\binom{26}{2}$ ways.
  Total combinations $= \binom{26}{3} \times \binom{26}{2}$, or 845 000

- four black and one red card
  The black cards can be chosen in $\binom{26}{4}$ ways and the red card can be chosen in $\binom{26}{1}$ ways.
  Total combinations $= \binom{26}{4} \times \binom{26}{1}$, or 388 700

- five black cards
  They can be chosen in $\binom{26}{5}$, or 65 780 ways.

  The total number of hands is
  845 000 + 388 700 + 65 780 = 1 299 480.

EXERCISES 10-5

Ⓐ

1. Simplify.

   a) $\binom{5}{2}$
   b) $_6C_3$
   c) $_8C_5$
   d) $\binom{12}{5}$

   e) $\binom{15}{9}$
   f) $_{16}C_6$
   g) $\binom{7}{4} \times \binom{5}{3}$
   h) $_{12}C_4 \times _6C_3$

2. How many 2-member committees can be chosen from 7 people?

3. How many 3-letter combinations can be formed from the letters of VECTORS?

4. How many different 20-question examinations can be formed from a test bank containing 30 questions?

5. In how many ways can
   a) 8 numbers be chosen from 20 numbers
   b) 12 numbers be chosen from 20 numbers?

Ⓑ

6. For a standard deck of 52 playing cards, how many 5-card hands can be formed in which:
   a) there are aces or face cards only
   b) there are spades only
   c) there are only cards numbered 2, 3, 4, . . . 10
   d) there are red face cards only?

7. In how many ways can a Snow Carnival committee of 7 people be selected from 6 boys and 8 girls if:
   a) there are no restrictions
   b) there are exactly 3 boys on the committee
   c) there are exactly 2 girls on the committee?

8. Six boys and six girls were nominated for a homecoming celebration at a local school. In how many ways can a king, a queen, and a court of 2 students be selected from those nominated?

9. In how many ways can a 6-member committee be formed from 10 people, if 2 particular people must be on the committee?

10. In how many ways can 4 or more students be selected from 8 students?

11. From a standard deck of cards, the 12 face cards are removed. From these face cards, 3 are chosen. How many combinations are possible which have at least two red cards?

12. From a standard deck of playing cards, how many different 5-card hands can be formed with:
    a) exactly 3 black cards
    b) at most one black card
    c) at least 3 red cards?

13. How many straight lines are determined by 8 points, no 3 of which are collinear?

14. How many quadrilaterals are formed by the vertices of an octagon?

15. Seven points lie on a circle. How many triangles can be constructed having any three of these points as vertices?

16. Twenty points, no 3 of which are collinear, lie in a plane. Using these points, how many:
    a) straight lines can be drawn
    b) triangles can be drawn
    c) quadrilaterals can be drawn
    d) pentagons can be drawn?

17. How many diagonals has each polygon?
    a) hexagon   b) dodecagon   c) 20-sided polygon

Ⓒ

18. There are 12 boys and 12 girls in the drama club. In how many ways can a committee of 6 be selected if:
    a) there must be at least 2 boys and 2 girls
    b) there must be at least 1 boy?

19. If a committee of 4 is selected from 12 people, what fraction of the committees include two specified people?

20. In a students' council election, there are 4 candidates for president, 4 for secretary, and 3 for treasurer. Each student may vote for at least one of the positions. In how many ways can a ballot be marked?

21. In how many ways can 3 numbers be chosen from 1, 2, 3, . . ., 10, so that no two of the 3 numbers are consecutive?

22. Show that the product of:
    a) four consecutive numbers is always divisible by 4!
    b) r consecutive numbers is always divisible by r!

23. Find the number of 5-letter combinations of the letters of the word SUBTRACT.

24. Find the number of combinations of the letters of the word DIVIDE, taken 4 at a time.

25. How many 6-letter combinations are there of the letters of the word MULTIPLICATION?

26. In how many ways can you choose letters from each word?
    a) FLOOR   b) ADDEND   c) MATHEMATICS

27. How many factors of each number are there, not including the number itself and 1?
    a) 360   b) 3780

10-6 APPLICATIONS OF COMBINATORICS TO PROBABILITY

The counting techniques involving permutations and combinations are part of a branch of mathematics called *combinatorics*. These techniques are important in helping us enumerate favorable and possible outcomes in probability experiments and thereby calculate theoretical probabilities. Sometimes we can calculate probabilities using either permutations or combinations. Both methods are equivalent, as shown in the following example.

Example 1. Two cards are picked at random from a deck of 52 regular playing cards. What is the probability that they are both aces?

Solution. *Using combinations*

The number of ways of choosing two aces from the four aces is $_4C_2$.
The number of ways of choosing two cards from 52 cards is $_{52}C_2$.
The probability of choosing 2 aces in a selection of 2 cards from 52 is

$$
\begin{aligned}
P(2 \text{ aces}) &= \frac{_4C_2}{_{52}C_2} \\
&= \frac{\frac{4!}{2!2!}}{\frac{52!}{50!2!}} \\
&= \frac{4!50!}{2!52!} \\
&= \frac{1}{221}
\end{aligned}
$$

Using permutations

The first ace can be selected in 4 ways. For each choice, the second ace can be selected in 3 ways. There are $_4P_2$ ways (with regard to order) of selecting two aces.
There are $_{52}P_2$ ways (with regard to order) of choosing two cards.
The probability of choosing 2 aces in a selection of 2 cards from 52 is

$$
\begin{aligned}
P(2 \text{ aces}) &= \frac{_4P_2}{_{52}P_2} \\
&= \frac{\frac{4!}{2!}}{\frac{52!}{50!}} \\
&= \frac{4!50!}{52!2!} \\
&= \frac{1}{221}
\end{aligned}
$$

The next examples show that for some questions, permutations provide a more convenient method for calculating probabilities while for others, combinations are more appropriate.

Example 2.   Three prizes are to be awarded in a raffle in which 750 people hold one ticket each.
   a) What is the probability that Mr. Adams, Mr. Becker, and Mr. Chiu respectively win first, second, and third prizes?
   b) What is the probability that Mr. Adams, Mr. Becker, and Mr. Chiu are the three prize winners (though not necessarily in that order)?

Solution.   a) The number of ways of selecting first, second, and third prize winners from 750 ticket holders is $_{750}P_3$.

   Therefore, the probability of a particular selection of the first, second, and third prize winners is

$$\frac{1}{_{750}P_3} = \frac{747!}{750!}$$

$$= \frac{1}{420\ 189\ 000}$$

   b) The number of ways of choosing 3 winners from 750 people, without regard to order is, $_{750}C_3$.

   Therefore, the probability that Mr. Adams, Mr. Becker, and Mr. Chiu are all winners is

$$\frac{1}{_{750}C_3} = \frac{(747!)(3!)}{750!}$$

$$= \frac{1}{70\ 031\ 500}$$

Example 3.   A committee has six women and four men. A subcommittee of four is to be selected by lot. What is the probability that the subcommittee will consist of:
   a) four women   b) two men and two women?

Solution.   a) There are $_{10}C_4$ ways of selecting a subcommittee of 4 from 10 people. There are $_6C_4$ ways of selecting a subcommittee of 4 women from 6 women.

   Therefore, the probability that the subcommittee consists of 4 women is

$$\frac{_6C_4}{_{10}C_4} = \frac{\frac{6!}{4!2!}}{\frac{10!}{6!4!}}$$

$$= \frac{(6!)^2}{(10!)(2!)}$$

$$= \frac{1}{14}$$

b) The number of ways of choosing 2 men from 4 is $_4C_2$.
The number of ways of choosing 2 women from 6 is $_6C_2$.
The number of ways of choosing a subcommittee of two men and two women is $_4C_2 \times _6C_2$.
Therefore, the probability that the subcommittee consists of two men and two women is

$$\frac{_4C_2 \times _6C_2}{_{10}C_4} = \frac{\frac{4!}{2!2!} \times \frac{6!}{4!2!}}{\frac{10!}{6!4!}}$$

$$= \frac{(6!)^2 4!}{10!(2!)^3}$$

$$= \frac{3}{7}$$

Example 3a) could have been solved from first principles without counting combinations. Imagine that the names of all the committee members (6 women and 4 men) were written on pieces of paper. We can reason as follows:

The probability that the first paper drawn names a woman is $\frac{6}{10}$.

This leaves 9 pieces of paper of which 5 contain women's names.

The probability that the next piece of paper drawn names a woman is $\frac{5}{9}$.

Similarly, the probability that the third piece of paper names a woman is $\frac{4}{8}$,

and the probability that the fourth piece of paper names a woman is $\frac{3}{7}$.

The probability that all four of these events will occur is:

$$\left(\frac{6}{10}\right)\left(\frac{5}{9}\right)\left(\frac{4}{8}\right)\left(\frac{3}{7}\right) = \frac{1}{14}$$

The analysis above illustrates how the counting principle can be extended to apply to probability situations.

> If the probability of one event occurring is r and the probability of another event occurring is s, then the probability of both events occurring is rs.

This principle can be applied to the calculation of probabilities of several events provided the events are independent. That is, the occurrence of each event is not influenced by the occurrence of the other events. For example, the outcomes H and T on successive tosses of a coin are independent outcomes because the outcome on any toss does not affect the outcome on a successive toss. However, the outcomes (or events) H and T on the single toss of a coin are dependent because the occurrence of either outcome prevents the occurrence of the other outcome.

EXERCISES 10-6

Ⓐ

1. Three pieces of paper bear the letters C, T, and A. What is the probability that if all the pieces of paper are selected, they will be selected in the order C, A, T?

2. Three students' names are selected at random out of 4 students nominated to serve on the student council. The nominated students are represented by the letters A, B, C, and D. What is the probability that the student council will consist of students A, B, and C?

3. On two successive tosses of a fair coin, what is the probability that:
   a) both tosses yield heads   b) there is one head and one tail?

4. There is a random selection of the members to fill three executive positions on a fund-raising committee. The combined probability that the president will be Ms. Kim, the vice-president Mr. Singh, and the secretary Dr. Achebe is $\frac{1}{720}$. What is the probability that all three people will be selected for the executive, though not necessarily in those positions?

5. Two dice are rolled. What is the probability that they total 11?

6. There are 7 males in a group of 10 people from which two people are chosen by lot. What is the probability that both people are female?

7. A probability experiment has two possible outcomes denoted A and B. Are A and B independent events? Explain.

8. What is the probability that two cards drawn from a standard deck of 52 cards will both be hearts?

Ⓑ

9. If both sexes are equally probable, what is the probability that a family of four children has exactly three boys?

10. Two balls are drawn randomly from a bag containing 5 red balls and 7 white balls. What is the probability that both balls are white?

11. Eight men enter a doubles tennis tournament in which partners are selected by lot. What is the probability that two brothers, Sean and Kevin, will be selected as partners?

12. The school computer club contains 6 girls and 4 boys. If two co-captains are chosen by lot, what is the probability that the co-captains are:
    a) both girls   b) both boys   c) one girl and one boy?

13. Two different cards are selected from a standard deck of 52 cards. What is the probability that the cards are:
    a) both red
    b) both face cards (that is, Jack, Queen, or King)
    c) both clubs?

14. How many paths are there which tra-
verse exactly three edges of a cube and
which join a given pair of diagonally
opposite vertices such as P and Q?

15. Two cards are drawn from a standard deck of 52 cards with replacement after each
draw. Find the probability that:
a) both are spades
b) the first is a heart and the second is a club
c) both are black

16. If both sexes are equally probable, calculate the following probabilities for a family
of three children.
a) the first is male and the next two are females   b) at least one is female

17. Two cards are selected without replacement from a standard deck of 52 cards. What
is the probability that:
a) at least one of the cards is black
b) the first card selected is either red or a face card?

18. In a recent international test, 67% of the students answered Item 1 correctly,
53% answered Item 2 correctly, and 30% answered both items correctly. What
is the probability that a randomly-selected test paper gives the correct answer to at
least one of the first two items?

19. A pizzeria offers 8 different ingredients on its pizza. Andy chooses 3 different
ingredients from the 8 by drawing the names from a hat. What is the probability
that Andy chooses either mushrooms or pepperoni or both among his three
ingredients?

©

20. In a bin of used golf balls, 30% of the golf balls are yellow and the remainder are
white. Three balls are selected, and each one is replaced before the next one is
drawn. What is the probability that at least two of three balls are yellow?

21. A probability experiment has three possible outcomes denoted, X, Y, and Z. Let
XY denote the event in which outcome X is followed by outcome Y on successive
trials of the experiment. If the probabilities of outcomes X, Y, and Z are unchanged
for successive trials of the experiment, is it true that $P(XY) = P(X)P(Y)$? Explain
your answer.

22. The letters in the word PROBABILITY are rearranged randomly by computer.
What is the probability that the new arrangement contains the sequence BAB?

23. Write an equation which relates $_nC_r$ and $_nP_r$ and explain the relationship between
these two expressions.

10-7 THE BINOMIAL THEOREM AND PASCAL'S TRIANGLE

A square parking lot measures p metres on all sides. It is to be enlarged by increasing the length of each side by q metres. What is the area of the enlarged parking lot, and by how much has it increased?

The diagram shows how the new area, $(p + q)^2$, can be calculated from the original area, p^2.

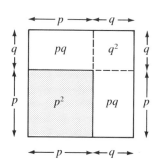

$$(p + q)^2 = \underset{\substack{\uparrow \\ \text{original} \\ \text{area}}}{p^2} + \underset{\substack{\text{increase in} \\ \text{area}}}{\underbrace{2pq + q^2}}$$
$$\underset{\text{new area}}{\uparrow}$$

A cubic carton measures p metres along all its edges. If all dimensions of the carton are increased by q metres, what is the capacity of the enlarged carton? By how much has the capacity increased?

The diagram shows how the new capacity, $(p + q)^3$, can be calculated from the original capacity, p^3.

We can multiply $(p + q)^2$ by $(p + q)$ to calculate $(p + q)^3$.

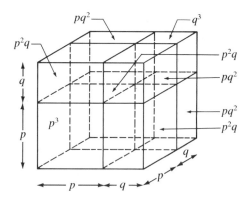

$$
\begin{array}{r}
p^2 + 2pq + q^2 \\
\times \quad (p + q) \\
\hline
p^2q + 2pq^2 + q^3 \\
p^3 + 2p^2q + pq^2 \\
\hline
p^3 + 3p^2q + 3pq^2 + q^3
\end{array}
$$

That is,

$$(p + q)^3 = \underset{\substack{\uparrow \\ \text{original} \\ \text{capacity}}}{p^3} + \underset{\text{increase in capacity}}{\underbrace{3p^2q + 3pq^2 + q^3}}$$
$$\underset{\substack{\text{new} \\ \text{capacity}}}{\uparrow}$$

In general, we may ask, "What are the terms of the expansion of $(p + q)^n$, where n is a positive integer?" The equation that expresses $(p + q)^n$ as a sum of terms of the form $p^a q^b$ (where $a \leqslant n$, $b \leqslant n$) is called the *Binomial Theorem*.

To derive the Binomial Theorem for integral values of n, we write the expansions of $(p + q)^n$ for $n = 0, 1, 2, 3$, and 4.

$(p + q)^0 = 1$

$(p + q)^1 = p + q$

$(p + q)^2 = p^2 + 2pq + q^2$

$(p + q)^3 = p^3 + 3p^2q + 3pq^2 + q^3$

$(p + q)^4 = p^4 + 4p^3q + 6p^2q^2 + 4pq^3 + q^4$

When we examine the exponents of each expression, we discover that:

● the sum of the exponents of p and q in any term is equal to the power to which the binomial is raised

● as we move from term to term in a particular expansion, the exponents of p decrease by 1 while the exponents of q increase by 1.

Furthermore, we observe that the coefficients of the successive expressions form a mathematical pattern.

$(p + q)^0 = \qquad\qquad\qquad\mathbf{1}$

$(p + q)^1 = \qquad\qquad\quad \mathbf{1}p + \mathbf{1}q$

$(p + q)^2 = \qquad\qquad \mathbf{1}p^2 + \mathbf{2}pq + \mathbf{1}q^2$

$(p + q)^3 = \qquad \mathbf{1}p^3 + \mathbf{3}p^2q + \mathbf{3}pq^2 + \mathbf{1}q^3$

$(p + q)^4 = \mathbf{1}p^4 + \mathbf{4}p^3q + \mathbf{6}p^2q^2 + \mathbf{4}pq^3 + \mathbf{1}q^4$

This pattern of coefficients obtained from the expansion of $(p + q)^n$, for $n = 0, 1, 2, 3, \ldots$, is called *Pascal's Triangle*. Notice that every entry in the triangle can be obtained by adding the two adjacent entries in the row above.

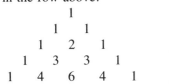

Consider the terms in the 4th row to derive the terms in the 5th row.

We can use Pascal's Triangle and the pattern of exponents when expanding whole number powers of binomials.

Example 1.   Use Pascal's Triangle to expand $(p + q)^5$.

Solution.   We know from the pattern of exponents described above that $(p + q)^5$ is a sum of terms of the form p^aq^b, where $a + b = 5$. That is,

$(p + q)^5 = \square p^5 + \square p^4q + \square p^3q^2 + \square p^2q^3 + \square pq^4 + \square q^5$

The symbol $\square$ represents the unknown coefficients. We use Pascal's Triangle to determine the unknown coefficients. We write the first 5 rows of Pascal's Triangle, then add the coefficients in pairs in the 5th row to derive the coefficients in the 6th row.

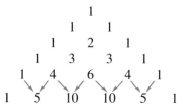

Therefore, the expansion of $(p + q)^5$ is
$$p^5 + 5p^4q + 10p^3q^2 + 10p^2q^3 + 5pq^4 + q^5$$
(This assumes that the pattern discovered above is true for $n = 5$.)

Example 2. Expand and then simplify $(2y - 3)^4$.

Solution. We can think of $(2y - 3)^4$ as $[2y + (-3)]^4$ and use the expansion of $(p + q)^4$.
$$(p + q)^4 = p^4 + 4p^3q + 6p^2q^2 + 4pq^3 + q^4$$
Thus,
$$\begin{aligned}(2y - 3)^4 &= (2y)^4 + 4(2y)^3(-3) + 6(2y)^2(-3)^2 + 4(2y)(-3)^3 + (-3)^4\\ &= 16y^4 + 4(8y^3)(-3) + 6(4y^2)(9) + 4(2y)(-27) + 81\\ &= 16y^4 - 96y^3 + 216y^2 - 216y + 81\end{aligned}$$
Notice in the first line of the expansion, we replace the p and q in our pattern by the entire quantities $(2y)$ and (-3), and use the coefficients 1, 4, 6, 4, 1 from the 5th row of Pascal's Triangle.

Throughout history, many famous mathematicians have worked on developing and proving the Binomial Theorem. Around 300 B.C., Euclid knew the result when $n = 2$, but the statement of the theorem, with any rational number as the exponent, is usually attributed to the English physicist and mathematician, Sir Isaac Newton. In 1676, Newton wrote out the expansion, without proof, in a letter to Henry Oldenburg, the secretary of the British Royal Society. The proof that the Binomial Theorem holds for any complex number exponent was finally produced by a Norwegian mathematician, Niels Henrik Abel, who published his proof in 1826, only three years before his premature death at the age of 27.

EXERCISES 10-7

Ⓐ

1. Write the missing numbers in Pascal's Triangle on the right.

2. Use your answers from *Exercise 1* to expand $(x + y)^7$.

3. Write the value of n for which each term is a term in the expansion of $(p + q)^n$.
   a) p^7q^2 b) p^4q^4 c) p^2q^5
   d) p^7q e) p^8q^8

```
            1
          1   1
        1   2   1
      1   3   3   1
    1   4   6   4   1
  1   5  10  10   5   1
1   6  __  __  __   6   1
1  __  __  __  __  __  __  1
```

4. Write an expression in terms of powers of a and b for the difference between the areas of a square with sides of length a and a square with sides of length $a - b$, where $a > b$.

5. Write the missing exponent in each term of the expansion of $(p + q)^{12}$.
   a) $p^3 q^{\Box}$ b) $p^{\Box} q^7$ c) $pq^{\Box}$ d) $p^{\Box} q$ e) $p^{12} q^{\Box}$

Ⓑ

6. Calculate 101^2 by writing it as $(100 + 1)^2$ and expanding.

7. a) Copy and complete the multiplication table on the right.
   b) Total all the numbers in the table to find the grand sum.
   c) Compare the grand sum with the value of 87^2. Explain the result.

×	80	7
80		
7		
Grand sum		

8. Calculate 101^3 by writing it as the cube of a binomial and expanding.

9. Use Pascal's Triangle to expand $(m + n)^8$.

10. Expand and simplify. $(p + q)^5 - (p - q)^5$

11. Expand.
    a) $(x + 2y)^3$ b) $(a - 1)^3$ c) $(a + 2b)^4$ d) $(2a - 1)^4$

12. Derive the expansion of $(x + y)^2$ by factoring $(x + y)^2 - x^2$ as a difference of squares.

13. The volume V of a sphere in terms of its radius r is given by the formula $V = \frac{4}{3}\pi r^3$. By how much does the volume of a balloon of radius R centimetres increase when its radius is increased by r centimetres? Write your answer as a sum of terms involving powers of R and r.

Ⓒ

14. We consider the Earth as a sphere with radius R.
    a) Suppose a cable were wrapped tightly around the surface of the Earth to circumscribe it at the equator. By how much would we need to increase the length of the cable so it would circumscribe the Earth at a height of 1 m?
    b) Suppose that the Earth is to be enclosed in a spherical glass bubble at a height of 10 km above its surface. Write an expression for the ratio of the volume of the glass bubble to the volume of the Earth. Write the ratio in terms of powers of R^{-1}.

15. One dollar invested at 18% compounded annually grows to a value of $(1.18)^n$ after n years.
    a) What is the value of a one-dollar investment after:
       i) 10 years   ii) 20 years?
    b) Write an expression for the value of a $1000 investment after 3 years if it is invested at a rate of interest of I% per annum.
    c) Express your answer in part b) as a polynomial in I.

10-8 THE BINOMIAL THEOREM FOR POSITIVE INTEGRAL EXPONENTS

In the previous section, we used Pascal's Triangle to investigate the Binomial Theorem in special cases.

To derive the formula for raising a binomial to an exponent, we must examine the process of multiplying binomials in general. Consider the following expansions.

- $(p_1 + q_1)(p_2 + q_2) = p_1p_2 + p_1q_2 + q_1p_2 + q_1q_2$
  Notice that there are 2×2, or 4 terms, and each term consists of two variables — one selected from each set of brackets. The selections are made up of zero qs and two ps, or one q and one p, or two qs and zero ps.

- $(p_1 + q_1)(p_2 + q_2)(p_3 + q_3)$
  $= p_1p_2p_3 + p_1p_2q_3 + p_1q_2p_3 + p_1q_2q_3 + q_1p_2p_3 + q_1p_2q_3 +$
  $\quad q_1q_2p_3 + q_1q_2q_3$
  Notice that there are $2 \times 2 \times 2$, or 8 terms, and each term consists of three variables — one being selected from each set of brackets. The selections are made up of zero qs and three ps, or one q and two ps, or two qs and one p, or three qs and zero ps.

- $(p_1 + q_1)(p_2 + q_2)(p_3 + q_3)(p_4 + q_4)$
  This expansion is too long to write out in full, but it would have $2 \times 2 \times 2 \times 2$, or 16 terms, with each term consisting of four variables — one selected from each set of brackets. The selections are made up of zero qs and four ps, or one q and three ps, or two qs and two ps, or three qs and one p, or four qs and zero ps. For example, here are all the terms which contain three qs and one p.
  $p_1q_2q_3q_4, \quad q_1p_2q_3q_4, \quad q_1q_2p_3q_4, \quad q_1q_2q_3p_4$
  If the subscripts were removed, making the ps and the qs indistinguishable, these 4 terms would each simplify to pq^3. So, in the expansion of $(p + q)^4$, the term with three qs and one p would be $4pq^3$.
  The coefficient 4 may be *calculated* by selecting a q from three of the brackets. (Selecting the qs automatically determines the bracket from which the p is obtained.)
  The selection of $3q$s can be made in ${}_4C_3$ ways.

$${}_4C_3 = \frac{4!}{3!1!}, \text{ or } 4$$

The other coefficients in the expansion of $(p + q)^4$ are generated similarly.

Term Containing	*Coefficient*
$0q$s and $4p$s	${}_4C_0 = 1$
$1q$ and $3p$s	${}_4C_1 = 4$
$2q$s and $2p$s	${}_4C_2 = 6$
$3q$s and $1p$	${}_4C_3 = 4$
$4q$s and $0p$s	${}_4C_4 = 1$

Thus, $(p + q)^4 = p^4 + 4p^3q + 6p^2q^2 + 4pq^3 + q^4$

Relating the coefficients to the theory of selections enables us to raise a binomial to *any* positive integral exponent.

In general,
$$(p + q)^n = {}_nC_0p^n + {}_nC_1p^{n-1}q + {}_nC_2p^{n-2}q^2 + {}_nC_3p^{n-3}q^3 +$$
$$\ldots + {}_nC_kp^{n-k}q^k + \ldots + {}_nC_nq^n, \text{ where } n \in I, n \geqslant 0$$

The term, ${}_nC_kp^{n-k}q^k$, is called the *general term* of the expansion since, by letting $k = 0, 1, 2, 3, \ldots, n$, we can construct any term of the series. It should be noted that ${}_nC_kp^{n-k}q^k$ is the $(k + 1)$th term in the expansion.

Example 1.   Find the 4th term in the expansion of $(2a - b)^{10}$.

Solution.   The 4th term of the expansion is generated by substituting $k = 3$ in the general term.

$$t_4 = {}_{10}C_3(2a)^{10-3}(-b)^3$$
$$= \frac{10 \times 9 \times 8}{3!}(2^7a^7(-1)^3b^3)$$
$$= -15\ 360a^7b^3$$

Example 2.   In the expansion of $\left(\dfrac{1}{x^2} - x\right)^{18}$, find the term independent of x.

Solution.   The general term is ${}_{18}C_k\left(\dfrac{1}{x^2}\right)^{18-k} \times (-x)^k$, or $(-1)^k{}_{18}C_kx^{3k-36}$.

The term of the expansion independent of x is the term containing x^0.
That is, $3k - 36 = 0$
$$k = 12$$
Therefore, the required term is $(-1)^{12}{}_{18}C_{12}$, or 18 564.

We often use an alternative form of the theorem, in which the coefficients are expanded.

$${}_nC_0 = 1$$
$${}_nC_1 = n$$
$${}_nC_2 = \frac{n(n - 1)}{2!}$$
$${}_nC_3 = \frac{n(n - 1)(n - 2)}{3!}$$

.
.
.

$${}_nC_n = 1$$

Thus, the alternative form is:

$$(p + q)^n = p^n + np^{n-1}q + \frac{n(n - 1)}{2!}p^{n-2}q^2 + \frac{n(n - 1)(n - 2)}{3!}p^{n-3}q^3 + \ldots + q^n.$$

EXERCISES 10-8

Ⓐ

1. Write the expansion of each expression.
   a) $(a + b)^3$　　　b) $(x - y)^4$　　　c) $(x + y)^5$　　　d) $(x - 1)^7$

2. a) How many terms are there in $(x + y)^9$?
   b) Is there a middle term in $(x + y)^9$?
   c) Under what conditions does $(x + y)^n$ have a middle term?

3. Explain why the terms $p^a q^b$ and $p^b q^a$ in the expansion of $(p + q)^{a+b}$ have the same coefficient.

4. Expand $(x - y)^{14}$ and $(x + y)^{14}$. What do you notice?

Ⓑ

5. Write the first 3 terms in the expansion of $(c + d)^{10}$.

6. Write the last 3 terms in the expansion of $(s - t)^{10}$.

7. Expand $(a + b)^7$ and $(2a + 2b)^7$. What do you notice?

8. Expand each expression.
   a) $(x + y)^6 + (x - y)^6$　　　　　b) $(x + y)^6 - (x - y)^6$

9. Expand and then simplify each binomial.

   a) $(2a + b)^5$　　　　b) $(x^2 - 1)^6$　　　　c) $\left(1 - \dfrac{1}{x}\right)^7$

10. Find and simplify the first 3 terms in the expansion of each binomial.

    a) $(p + q)^{30}$　　　　b) $(a^2 + 1)^{20}$　　　　c) $\left(2x - \dfrac{y}{2}\right)^{10}$

11. Find and simplify the indicated term in each expansion.
    a) t_4 in $(x - 5)^{13}$　　　　　b) t_{10} in $(1 - 2a)^{12}$

12. Without expanding the binomial, find:

    a) the term involving x^7 in the expansion of $\left(x^2 + \dfrac{2}{x}\right)^8$

    b) the term independent of p in the expansion of $\left(p^3 + \dfrac{1}{p}\right)^{12}$

    c) the middle term in the expansion of $\left(\dfrac{a}{b} + \dfrac{b}{a}\right)^6$.

Ⓒ

13. We have established that the entries in Pascal's Triangle are values of $_nC_r$.
    a) In Pascal's Triangle, find the sum of:
       i) the 3rd row　　　ii) the 10th row　　　iii) the kth row.
    b) Use subsets to prove your answer to part a) iii).

14. a) Expand $(x + y)^6$.
    b) Prove that $_6C_0 - {_6C_1} + {_6C_2} - {_6C_3} + {_6C_4} - {_6C_5} + {_6C_6} = 0$, by substituting $x = 1$ and $y = -1$ in the expansion of $(x + y)^6$.
    c) Derive an expression for $_nC_0 + {_nC_1} + {_nC_2} + \ldots + {_nC_r} + \ldots + {_nC_{n-1}} + {_nC_n}$ by substituting $a = b = 1$ in the expansion formula for $(x + y)^n$.

15. A multiple-choice test has 8 questions. Each question has 4 choices.
    a) What is the probability that a random guess yields the correct answer to a question?
    b) What is the probability that a student guesses the correct answers to the first two questions, and incorrect answers to the rest?
    c) What is the probability that a student guesses the correct answers to the last two questions, and incorrect answers to the rest?
    d) What is the probability that a student guesses the correct answers to exactly two questions?
    e) What is the probability that a student guesses the correct answers to exactly three questions?
    f) Write an expression for the probability that a student guesses the correct answers to exactly r questions.
    g) Compare your answer in part f) to the $(r + 1)$th term in the expansion of $(p + q)^8$, where $p = \frac{3}{4}$ and $q = \frac{1}{4}$.

INVESTIGATE

Pascal's Triangle and Combinations

1. Pascal's Triangle is symmetric, since numbers equidistant from the ends of each row are equal.
   a) Evaluate $\binom{8}{3}$ and $\binom{8}{5}$.

   b) Prove algebraically that $\binom{n}{r} = \binom{n}{n - r}$.

2. a) Evaluate $\binom{8}{3}$ and $\binom{7}{3} + \binom{7}{2}$.

   b) Explain why the number of ways of selecting 3 items from a set of 8 items should be the same as the number of ways of selecting 3 items from a set of 7 items *plus* the number of ways of selecting 2 items from a set of 7 items.

   c) Prove algebraically that $\binom{n}{r} = \binom{n - 1}{r} + \binom{n - 1}{r - 1}$.

 **PROBLEM SOLVING**

Extend the Problem

"(No) problem whatever is completely exhausted. There remains always something to do; with sufficient study and penetration, we can improve any solution, and, in any case, we can always improve our understanding of the solution."

George Polya

George Polya, a former professor of mathematics at Stanford University, gained worldwide recognition for his skills as a teacher. Polya is suggesting that when we have solved a problem, we may also think of related problems. These may often be obtained by generalizing some condition of the problem, or changing some part of the problem to make a new problem. For example, some of the ways in which the Pythagorean Theorem can be extended are given below.

The Pythagorean Theorem states that the areas of the squares constructed on the sides of a right triangle are related:

area of the   sum of the areas of
square on the $=$ the squares on the
hypotenuse   other two sides

$$a^2 = b^2 + c^2$$

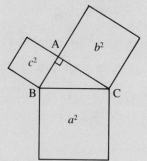

> **First extension**
> The lengths of the sides of a right triangle satisfy the equation $x^2 + y^2 = z^2$. Find integral values of x, y, and z which satisfy this equation. These are called *Pythagorean triples*.

Second extension

Can you find integral values of x, y, and z which satisfy equations such as these?

$$x^2 + y^2 + z^2 = w^2 \qquad x^3 + y^3 + z^3 = w^3$$
$$x^2 + y^2 = z^2 + w^2 \qquad x^3 + y^3 = z^3 + w^3$$
$$x^{-1} + y^{-1} = z^{-1} \qquad x^{\frac{1}{2}} + y^{\frac{1}{2}} = z^{\frac{1}{2}}$$

Third extension

The Pythagorean Theorem can be used to find the distance between any two points in the plane. How could you find the distance between any two points in three dimensions?

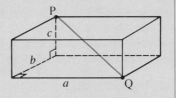

Fourth extension

The Pythagorean Theorem relates the lengths of the sides of any right triangle. If $\triangle ABC$ is not a right triangle, how are the lengths of its sides related?

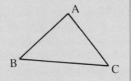

Fifth extension

If figures other than squares are constructed on the sides of a right triangle, does the area relation still hold for these figures?

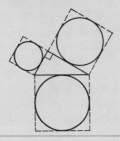
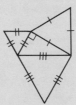
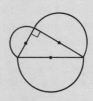

PROBLEMS

Ⓑ

1. The Earth's equatorial diameter is 12 756 km. The polar diameter is about 0.33% less than this. What is the polar diameter?

2. Given any three natural numbers, prove that at least two of them have a sum which is even.

3. Let k be a positive rational number. Prove that $k + \dfrac{1}{k}$ is a natural number if, and only if, $k = 1$.

4. A square with sides of length s is given. A regular octagon is formed by cutting off four corner isosceles triangles as shown. Express x as a function of s.

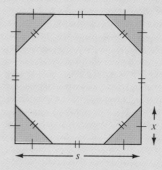

5. An equilateral triangle with sides of length s is divided into three regions with equal areas by two segments of lengths x and y parallel to one of the sides. Find equations expressing x and y as functions of s.

Ⓒ

6. Determine if it is possible to find two prime numbers p and q such that $pq + 1$ is a perfect square. If it is possible, find out as much as you can about primes which have this property.

7. Two vertices of an equilateral triangle are A(1, 8) and B(5, 2). Find the possible coordinates of the third vertex.

8. Four quarter circles are inscribed in a square with sides of 6 cm using the vertices as centres. Calculate the areas of the regions x, y, and z.

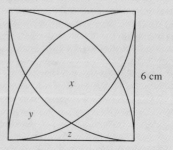

Ⓓ

9. A triangle is inscribed in a circle, and P is any point on the circle. Prove that the distance from P to the farthest vertex of the triangle is equal to the sum of its distances to the other two vertices if, and only if, the triangle is equilateral.

1. The menu in a restaurant offers the following choices.
   Appetizer
     soup; salad
   Entree
     fish; steak; pork roast
   Dessert
     ice cream; pie
   If a complete dinner consists of one choice from each group, in how many different ways can you choose a complete dinner? Draw a tree diagram.

2. Tammy can select an outfit from 3 pairs of pants, 4 tops, and 2 pairs of shoes. How many different choices of outfits are there?

3. A particular make of automobile is available in 5 colors, 3 kinds of upholstery, and 4 option packages. How many cars would a dealer have to keep in stock, to be able to show the complete line to prospective customers?

4. There are 8 different history texts, 6 different science texts, and 3 different mathematics texts on a bookshelf. In how many ways can you choose 3 books, one of each kind?

5. In baseball, a battery consists of the pitcher and the catcher. If a team has 7 pitchers and 3 catchers, how many different batteries can be formed?

6. A room has 5 doors. In how many ways is it possible to enter by one door and leave by another?

7. An ant walks from one corner of a cube to the corner diagonally opposite. If he can walk along the edges of the cube only, how many paths can he follow?

8. How many different arrangements are there of the five letters A, B, C, D, and E?

9. In a certain province, automobile licence plate numbers consist of three letters, followed by three digits, with repetitions allowed. To avoid the possibility that the three letters form words, it was decided not to use vowels (A, E, I, O, U, Y). How many different licence plates are possible?

10. In how many ways can the letters of the word PRODUCT be arranged:
    a) if there are no restrictions
    b) if a vowel must come first
    c) if the vowels must occupy their present positions
    d) if PR must remain together in that order
    e) if PR must remain together in either order?

11. A "family ring" contains the birth stone of each child in the family. These stones are placed in a row on the ring. In how many ways can the ring be made for a family of 4 children all born in different months?

12. If two bills are drawn from a one, two, five, and ten dollar bill, determine how many sums of money can be formed with the two bills.

13. In how many ways can ten theatre tickets be placed in two envelopes if there are four tickets in one envelope and six in the other?

Cumulative Review, Chapters 7-10

1. If a principal P dollars is invested in an account which pays $r\%$ interest per annum compounded semi-annually, then the amount A dollars in the account after n years is given by this formula.

$$A = P\left(1 + \frac{r}{200}\right)^{2n}$$

Find the amount of each investment.
   a) $1000 at 8% compounded semi-annually for 3 years
   b) $5000 at 9.5% compounded semi-annually for 6 years
   c) $4250 at 12.5% compounded semi-annually for 7.5 years

2. Evaluate.
   a) $9^{\frac{3}{2}}$ b) $64^{\frac{1}{3}}$ c) $125^{-\frac{2}{3}}$ d) $(2.75)^0$

3. Simplify.
   a) $\dfrac{12x^3y^{-2} \times 5x^{-7}y^5}{15xy^{-3}}$ b) $\dfrac{-18m^{-4}n^{-2} \times 15m^2n^{-7}}{-10m^2n^{-3} \times 6m^9n^{-4}}$

4. Evaluate to the nearest thousandth.
   a) $5.7^{3.1}$ b) $12.8^{-1.7}$ c) $127^{0.68}$ d) $\log 68$
   e) $\log_8 256$ f) $\log_{\sqrt{5}} 0.04$ g) $\log_{2.3} 17.6$ h) $\log_{0.4} 2.13$

5. Solve.
   a) $\log x = -2$ b) $\log_x 27 = \frac{3}{2}$ c) $\log_4 x = \frac{7}{2}$
   d) $3^x = 12$ e) $5^{x+3} = 83$ f) $7^{x-3} = 3^{x+1}$

6. Express as a single logarithm.
   a) $\log 12 + \log 8 - \log 16$
   b) $\log_4 (x + 5) + \log_4 (2x - 3) - \log_4 (x + 4)$

7. If $\log 12 = x$ and $\log 4 = y$, write each logarithm in terms of x and y.

   a) $\log 3$ b) $\log 0.75$ c) $\log 480$ d) $\log\left(\dfrac{16}{3}\right)$

8. If $\log 11 \doteq 1.0414$, find an approximation for each logarithm.

   a) $\log 121$ b) $\log \sqrt{11}$ c) $\log 110$ d) $\log\left(\dfrac{1}{11}\right)$

9. Solve and check.
   a) $\log_3 x + \log_3 (x + 24) = 4$
   b) $\log_{\sqrt{7}} (x + 4) + \log_{\sqrt{7}} (x - 2) = 2$

10. Classify each sequence as arithmetic or geometric, and find the value of d or r.
    a) $2, 6, 18, 54, \ldots$ b) $3, 7, 11, 15, \ldots$
    c) $15, 9, 3, -3, \ldots$ d) $45, 30, 20, \dfrac{40}{3}, \ldots$

11. Write the first 4 terms of the sequence defined by each expression.

    a) $t_n = 5n - 2$ b) $t_n = 2n^2 - 3n$ c) $t_n = \dfrac{n + 2}{2n - 1}$

    d) $t_n = 3 + 2^{n-1}$ e) $a = -4, d = -2$ f) $a = -16, r = -\dfrac{1}{2}$

12. Write an expression for the general term of each sequence.
    a) $-5, 3, 11, 19, \ldots$ b) $3, 15, 75, 375, \ldots$
    c) $25, 18, 11, 4, \ldots$ d) $48, 36, 27, \dfrac{81}{4}$

13. Find: i) t_5 ii) t_{11} iii) t_n for each sequence.
    a) $5, 15, 45, 135, \ldots$ b) $56, 45, 34, 23, \ldots$
    c) $3, 15, 27, 39, \ldots$ d) $40, 20, 10, 5, \ldots$

14. Find x and y if $3, x, 27, y$ are consecutive terms of:
    a) an arithmetic sequence   b) a geometric sequence.

15. Find how many terms there are in each sequence.
    a) $2, 10, 50, \ldots, 781\ 250$ b) $3, 11, 19, \ldots, 171$
    c) $172, 164, 156, \ldots, -124$ d) $729, 243, 81, \ldots, \dfrac{1}{729}$

16. Find the first 4 terms of each sequence.
    a) $t_1 = 2, t_n = 2t_{n-1} + 3, n > 1$ b) $t_1 = 12, t_n = \dfrac{1}{2}t_{n-1} + 4$

17. Find S_6 and S_n for each series.
    a) $-5 + 1 + 7 + 13 + \ldots$ b) $2 + 4 + 8 + 16 + \ldots$
    c) $27 - 9 + 3 - 1 + \ldots$ d) $42 + 31 + 20 + 9 + \ldots$

18. Find the sum of each infinite geometric series.
    a) $24 + 12 + 6 + 3 + \ldots$ b) $72 + 48 + 32 + \dfrac{64}{3} + \ldots$

19. How many terms of the series $-24 - 15 - 6 + 3 + \ldots$ add to 3696?

20. Simplify.
    a) $\displaystyle\sum_{i=1}^{6} (2i + 3)$ b) $\displaystyle\sum_{n=1}^{8} (10 - 2n)$ c) $\displaystyle\sum_{k=1}^{7} (3 + 2^{k-1})$

21. The masses in kilograms of the players on a senior football team are as shown.

75	93	93	62	103	83	82	86	88	67	63
72	97	97	78	85	73	91	92	84	95	94
68	76	101	83	98	83	65	79	79	70	73
80	83									

   a) Display these data on a stem-and-leaf diagram.
   b) Calculate the mean, the median, and the mode.
   c) What are the range, the mean deviation, and the standard deviation, to 1 decimal place?
   d) Find P_{25} and P_{75}.
   e) Construct a histogram to display the distribution of the masses.
   f) Construct a box-and-whisker plot of the masses.

22. The table shows the marks in English and History for 10 students.

English	85	72	77	82	80	90	93	91	75	87
History	82	68	75	81	77	89	90	86	72	83

   a) Calculate the Pearson correlation coefficient between English and History marks, to 2 decimal places.
   b) Find the equation of the line of best fit if the History marks are plotted on the y-axis.
   c) Use this equation to estimate a History mark corresponding to an English mark of 79.

23. In Sergio's closet there are 3 suits, 7 shirts, and 4 ties. In how many different ways can he select an outfit?

24. In how many ways can the letters of each word be arranged?
   a) PENCIL   b) CLASSES   c) MISSISSIPPI

25. In how many ways can the letters in each word in *Exercise 24* be arranged if the vowels must be first?

26. In how many ways can a house key, 2 different car keys, and 5 different school keys be arranged on a key ring?

27. From a standard deck of 52 playing cards, how many 5-card hands can be formed in which:
   a) there are only Jacks, Queens, Kings, and Aces
   b) there are only red cards
   c) there are only clubs?

28. How many triangles can be formed by joining the vertices of an octagon?

29. Two cards are to be drawn at random from a set of cards numbered 1, 2, 3, …, 10. What is the probability that the two numbers are:
   a) prime   b) larger than 5?

30. Use Pascal's Triangle to expand $(x + y)^7$.

Answers

Chapter 1

Exercises 1-1, page 6

1. a) Function
2. a) Domain: February to October; range, about 75.5¢ to 80.2¢
   b) Domain: 0 km to 50 km; range: 20°C to 29°C
3. a), c) Functions
4. a) R; R b) R; $\{y \mid y \geq 0, y \in R\}$
   c) $\{x \mid x \geq -1, x \in R\}$; $\{y \mid y \geq 0, y \in R\}$
   d), f) Not functions e) R; $\{y \mid y > 0, y \in R\}$
5. a), b) R; R
   c) $\{x \mid x \leq 1, x \in R\}$; $\{y \mid y \geq 0, y \in R\}$
   d) $\{x \mid x \neq 0, x \in R\}$; $\{y \mid y \neq 0, y \in R\}$
   e) $\{x \mid x \neq \pm 1, x \in R\}$; $\{y \mid y \neq 0, y \in R\}$
   f) $\{x \mid x \neq \pm 2, x \in R\}$;
   $\{y \mid y \leq 0 \text{ or } y > 1, y \in R\}$
6. a)   b)

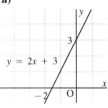

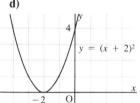

   c)   d)

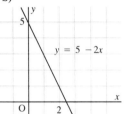

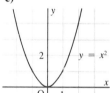

   e)   f)

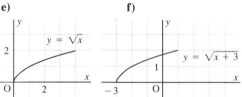

7. a) i) 100 kPa ii) 85 kPa iii) 80 kPa
   iv) 40 kPa v) 28 kPa b) 6.5 km
   c) Domain: 0 km to 14 km;
   range: 23 kPa to 100 kPa
8. a) 560 km, 360 km, 272 km, 240 km
   b) Domain: 0.025 m² to 0.6 m²;
   range: 28 km/h to 100 km/h

c) Domain would not change; the highest and lowest values of the range would increase.

9. a)   b)

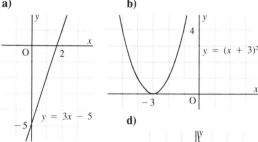

   c)   d)

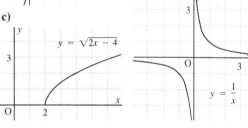

   e)   f)

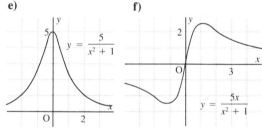

10. a) Hammer-fist strike i) 2.5 m/s, 5 m/s
    ii) 12 m/s Forward karate punch
    i) 3.8 m/s, 5.1 m/s ii) 6.8 m/s
    b) Speed decreases because it's after the punch; speed increasing before the strike.

Exercises 1-2, page 11

1. a) 4 b) 7 c) 3 d) 4 e) 7 f) 12
2. a) −1 b) 5 c) 11 d) 1 e) −11 f) 2
3. a) −17, 18, −4.5 b) 4, 11, −4.75
   c) 6, 20, −0.25
4. a) −3, 2, −2 b) 4, −2, −1
5. a) 30 b) 24 c) 0 d) 10 e) 2 f) 1.25
6. a) −5 b) −8 c) −20 d) −6
   e) −50 f) −8

7. a) i) 1 **ii)** 2 **iii)** 3 **b) i)** 9 **ii)** 90 **iii)** 900

8. a) $2a + 1$ **b)** $6a + 1$ **c)** $3 + 2y$
d) $2x + 3$ **e)** $3 - y$ **f)** $1 + y$
g) $4 - z$ **h)** $6 - 2x$ **i)** $4x + 2$
j) $15 - 5n$ **k)** $-6x - 3$ **l)** $2a - 6$

9. a) R; R **b)** R; $\{y \mid y \geq 0, y \in R\}$

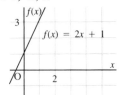 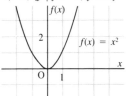

c) $\{x \mid x \geq 0; x \in R\}$; $\{y \mid y \geq 0, y \in R\}$

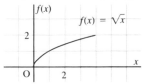

10. a) -4 **b)** -7 **c)** 8 **d)** 6 **e)** 6 **f)** 3

11. a) $\dfrac{2x + 1}{2x - 1}, x \neq \dfrac{1}{2}$ **b)** $\dfrac{x - 1}{x + 1}, x \neq -1$

c) $\dfrac{1 + x}{1 - x}, x \neq 1$ **d)** $\dfrac{1 + x}{1 - x}, x \neq 1$

e) $\dfrac{x + 2}{x}, x \neq 0$ **f)** $\dfrac{-x}{x - 2}, x \neq 2$

g) $\dfrac{x + 1}{x}, x \neq 0$ **h)** $\dfrac{x - 1}{x}, x \neq 0$

12. a) $\frac{2}{3}$ **b)** -2 **c)** 2 **d)** 1 **e)** $\frac{1}{4}$

13. a) $\frac{5}{3}$ **b)** 2 **c)** $\frac{1}{3}$ **d)** 0 **e)** No solution

14. a) i) 6 **ii)** 14 **iii)** 14
b) i) 1, 10, 100, 1000, etc.
ii) 2, 11, 20, 200, 101, 110, etc.
c) i), ii) Infinite number

16. a) i) 0 **ii)** 2 **iii)** 1 **iv)** 2 **b) i)** 30 **ii)** 210

17. b) i) 4, 6, 8, 10, 12, etc. **ii)** 3, 5, 7, 9, etc.

18. a) i) 1, 4, 9, 16 **ii)** 1, 4, 9, 16 **b)** $f(x) = x^2$

20. Answers may vary; for example, 2^x, 2^y

Mathematics Around Us, page 13

1. 4.5, 18 **2.** 4 km

3. The graph would be stretched vertically by a factor of 4.

Exercises 1-3, page 16

1. a) 7 **b)** 22 **c)** 10 **d)** 21

2. $6x + 4; 6x + 3$

3. a) 5 **b)** 10 **c)** 4 **d)** 17

4. $2x^2 + 2; 4x^2 + 1$

5. a) $-6x + 19; -6x - 3$
b) $4x^2 + 14x + 6; 2x^2 + 10x + 1$
c) $32x^2 - 100x + 78; -8x^2 + 12x + 3$

6. a) $3x^2 + 12x + 11; 3x^2 + 1$
b) $12x^2 - 12x + 2; 3 - 6x^2$
c) $3x^4 - 1; 9x^4 - 6x^2 + 1$
d) $3x^4 + 6x^3 + 3x^2 - 1; 9x^4 - 3x^2$
e) $12x^4 - 36x^3 + 27x^2 - 1; 18x^4 - 21x^2 + 5$
f) $\dfrac{3}{x^2} - 1; \dfrac{1}{3x^2 - 1}$

7. $A = \dfrac{\pi d^2}{4}$ **8.** $\dfrac{\pi d^3}{6}$

9. a) -11 **b)** -8 **c)** 5 **d)** 16

10. a) $1 - 6x$ **b)** $4 - 6x$ **c)** $4x - 3$
d) $9x - 2$

11. a) 4 **b)** 30 **c)** -1 **d)** 0

12. a) $4 - x - x^2$ **b)** $20 - 9x + x^2$ **c)** x
d) $x^4 + 2x^3 + 2x^2 + x$

13. a) $\sqrt{4 - 2x}; 4 - 2\sqrt{x}; \sqrt[4]{x}; 4x - 4$
b) $\sqrt{2 + 6x}; 1 + 3\sqrt{2x}; \sqrt{2\sqrt{2x}}; 9x + 4$
c) $\dfrac{x^2 - 1}{x^2}; \dfrac{x^2}{(x + 1)^2} - 1; \dfrac{x}{2x + 1}; x^4 - 2x^2$
d) $2^{3x-4}; 3(2^x) - 4; 2^{2x}; 9x - 16$

14. $A = \dfrac{P^2}{16}$ **15.** $A = \dfrac{d^2}{2}$ **17. b)** No

18. $T = 0.05t + 20$ **19. a)** $0, -6$ **b)** -1

20. a) $f(k(x))$ **b)** $g(e(x))$ **c)** $f(e(x))$
d) $k(e(x))$ or $e(k(x))$

21. Answers may vary; for example,
a) $f(x) = x^2; g(x) = x^3 + 1; f(g(x))$
b) $f(x) = x^2 + 3x + 4; g(x) = x - 4; f(g(x))$
c) $f(x) = \sqrt{x}; g(x) = 3x - 2; f(g(x))$
d) $f(x) = \dfrac{1}{x}; g(x) = x + 3; f(g(x))$

22. a) $\sqrt{x} - 3$ **b)** $\{x \mid x \geq 0, x \in R\}$
c) $\{y \mid y \geq -3, y \in R\}$ **d)** $\sqrt{x - 3}$
e) $\{x \mid x \geq 3, x \in R\}$ **f)** $\{y \mid y \geq 0, y \in R\}$

23. a) x **b)** R **c)** R **d)** $\sqrt{x^2}$
e) R **f)** $\{y \mid y \geq 0, y \in R\}$

24. a) $\dfrac{x - 1}{x}, x \neq 0$ **b)** $\dfrac{1}{x}, x \neq 0$

25. a) i) $4x + 3$ **ii)** $8x + 7$ **iii)** $16x + 15$
b) i) $32x + 31$ **ii)** $2^n x + 2^n - 1$

26. a) i) $\dfrac{x}{2x+1}$, $x \neq -\dfrac{1}{2}$ **ii)** $\dfrac{x}{3x+1}$, $x \neq -\dfrac{1}{3}$

iii) $\dfrac{x}{4x+1}$, $x \neq -\dfrac{1}{4}$

b) i) $\dfrac{x}{5x+1}$, $x \neq -\dfrac{1}{5}$ **ii)** $\dfrac{x}{nx+1}$, $x \neq -\dfrac{1}{n}$

27. $d(a-1) = b(c-1)$

Exercises 1-4, page 24

1. a), b) Yes **c)** No

2. a) $y = \dfrac{x-5}{2}$, yes **b)** $y = \pm\sqrt{\dfrac{4+x}{3}}$, no

c) $y = \dfrac{10-2x}{5}$, yes **d)** $y = \pm\dfrac{\sqrt{x+1}}{2}$, no

e) $f^{-1}(x) = \dfrac{3}{1-x}$, yes **f)** $f^{-1}(x) = \dfrac{4x-3}{2}$, yes

3. a)   **b)**

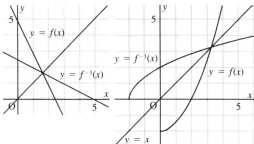

c)   **d)**

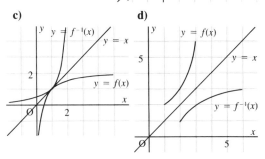

4. a) $f^{-1}(x) = \dfrac{x-3}{2}$; R; R

b) $y = \pm\sqrt{\dfrac{x+3}{2}}$; not a function

c) $h^{-1}(x) = \dfrac{1}{x} - 1$; $\{x \mid x \neq 0, x \in R\}$;
$\{y \mid y \neq -1, y \in R\}$
d) $y = -1 \pm\sqrt{x}$; not a function
e) $g^{-1}(x) = \dfrac{1}{x-1}$; $\{x \mid x \neq 1, x \in R\}$;
$\{y \mid y \neq 0, y \in R\}$
f) $y = x^2 + 2$; $\{x \mid x \geq 0, x \in R\}$;
$\{y \mid y \geq 2, y \in R\}$

5. Answers may vary. Typical answers are:
a) $y = x^2 - 2$, $x \geq 0$

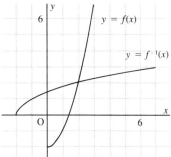

b) $y = 2(x+1)^2 - 3$, $x \geq -1$

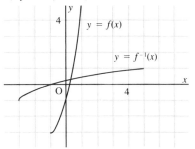

c) $y = -x^2 + 5$, $x \geq 0$

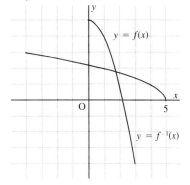

d) $y = -\frac{1}{2}x^2 + 2, x \geqslant 0$

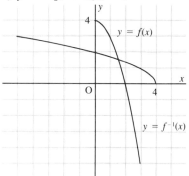

e) $y = (x - 1)^2 - 1, x \geqslant 1$

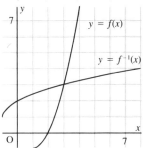

f) $y = -(x - 3)^2 + 4, x \geqslant 3$

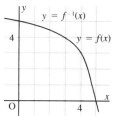

6. a) $f^{-1}(x) = \dfrac{x - 1}{x}, x \neq 0$

b) $f^{-1}(x) = \dfrac{2x + 2}{1 - x}, x \neq 1$

c) $y = \pm\sqrt{\dfrac{4x}{x - 2}}, x \neq 2$

d) $y = \pm\sqrt{\dfrac{1 - 4x}{3x}}, x \neq 0$

7. a) Yes **b)** No **c)** Yes **d)** Yes

8. a) $\dfrac{x - 5}{2}$ **b)** x **c)** x

9. a) $\dfrac{1 + x}{1 - x}$ **b)** x **c)** x **10.** The line $y = x$

12. Yes, except $y = k$, whose inverse is $x = k$, which is not a function.

13. Yes, the inverse of the inverse is the original function.

14. a) $x \geqslant -1$ or $x \leqslant -1$ **b)** $x \geqslant 0$ or $x \leqslant 0$

c) $x \geqslant -\frac{3}{2}$ or $x \leqslant -\frac{3}{2}$

Exercises 1-5, page 29

1. a) ± 2.74 **b)** ± 5.66 **c)** ± 2.24
  d) ± 6.93 **e)** ± 2.26 **f)** ± 3.92

2. a) $2, 7$ **b)** $5, -3$ **c)** $3, 11$ **d)** $-4, -8$
  e) $2, -9$ **f)** $-6, -9$

3. a) $-2, -3$ **b)** $0, 4$ **c)** $\frac{1}{2}, -3$ **d)** $-\frac{2}{3}, 1$
  e) $-\frac{1}{3}, \frac{3}{2}$ **f)** 2

4. a)

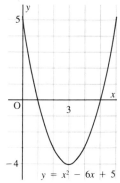

b)

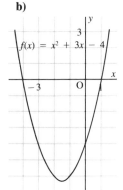

c)

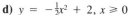

d)

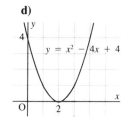

e) f)

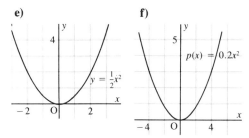

5. a) $\frac{2}{3}$, 1 **b)** $-\frac{1}{5}$, -1 **c)** $\frac{3 \pm \sqrt{11}}{2}$ **d)** 3

e) $\frac{13 \pm \sqrt{89}}{4}$ **f)** $-\frac{1}{2}$, $\frac{3}{2}$

6. a) $\frac{-7 \pm \sqrt{97}}{2}$ **b)** $4 \pm \sqrt{2}$ **c)** $\frac{-5 \pm \sqrt{13}}{6}$

d) $\frac{5}{4}$, 1 **e), f)** No real roots

7. a) $\frac{-5 \pm \sqrt{15}}{2}$ **b)** $-\frac{3}{2}$, $-\frac{7}{2}$ **c)** $-\frac{5}{2}$

8. a) $(x-3)(x-7) = 0$ **b)** $(x+4)(x-9) = 0$

c) $(x-\frac{2}{3})(x+5) = 0$

9. Answers may vary.
a) $f(x) = (x-4)(x+1)$; $g(x) = 2(x-4)(x+1)$
b) $f(x) = (x+3)(x-2)$; $g(x) = 2(x+3)(x-2)$
c) $f(x) = (x-\frac{3}{5})(x+\frac{4}{3})$; $g(x) = 15(x-\frac{3}{5})(x+\frac{4}{3})$

10. a) $f(x) = \frac{8}{3}(x-1)(x-3)$ **b)** $f(x) = \frac{4}{3}(x-1)(x-3)$

11. a) $f(x) = 2(x+1)(x-1)$
b) $f(x) = -(x+1)(x-1)$
c) $f(x) = 4(x+1)(x-1)$

12. a) $s = \sqrt{\dfrac{d}{0.05}}$ **b) i)** 4.5 m/s **ii)** 6.3 m/s

iii) 10.0 m/s **c) i)** Increased by a factor $\sqrt{2}$
ii) Increased by a factor $\sqrt{3}$

13. a) 629.757 184 3 or -635.157 184 3
b) 3461.401 917 or -3466.801 917

14. a) 1 **b)** 73 **c)** -39 **d)** 0 **e)** 121
f) -68

15. a) a, b, and e **b)** d **c)** c and f

16. a) $(3\sqrt{5} - 3)$ cm **b)** $(27\sqrt{5} - 45)$ cm²

17. a), b), d) 2 different real roots
e) 2 equal real roots **c), f)** no real roots

18. a) -1, 0.2 **b)** $\frac{4 \pm \sqrt{6}}{2}$ **c)** $\frac{-5 \pm \sqrt{13}}{6}$

d) No real roots **e)** 2, $\frac{2}{3}$ **f)** No real roots

19. a) $-4 \pm \sqrt{15}$ **b)** -0.8, -1 **c)** $-\frac{2}{3}$
d) $8 \pm \sqrt{102}$

20. a) 5, -3.5 **b)** $\frac{1 \pm \sqrt{217}}{4}$ **c)** $\frac{11 \pm \sqrt{185}}{2}$

d) 0.8, 2

21. $4\sqrt{3}$

22. 3 cm, 5 cm; two different triangles can be drawn from the given information

23. $4\sqrt{3}$ cm

24. No **25. b)** $\frac{2n + 1}{n}$

Problem Solving, page 35

1. a) $1 + \sqrt{5}$

2. Answers will vary. Two answers are $5 = 9 - 4$ and $20 = 36 - 16$. All odd numbers, and all even numbers which are divisible by 4 can be expressed as the difference of two squares.

3. $\frac{37}{64}$

5. $5x + 12y - 13 = 0$

6. 2^{97}

7. 733

8. $4x - 6y + 5 = 0$

9. $\left(\dfrac{x_1(1 - m^2) + 2m(y_1 - b)}{1 + m^2}, \dfrac{y_1(m^2 - 1) + 2(mx_1 + b)}{1 + m^2}\right)$

Exercises 1-6, page 39

1. a) $\sqrt{5}i$ **b)** $7i$ **c)** $2 - 3i$ **d)** $-3 + 8i$
e) $13 - i$ **f)** $33 - 56i$

5. a) $\pm 2i$ **b)** $\pm 3i$ **c)** $\pm 5i$ **d)** $\pm 2\sqrt{3}i$
e) $\pm 3\sqrt{2}i$ **f)** $1 \pm i$

6. a) $10 + 6i$ **b)** 34 **c)** $7 - 4i$ **d)** $43 - 18i$
e) $8 - 16i$ **f)** $-60 - 63i$

7. a) $\frac{-3 \pm \sqrt{11}i}{2}$ **b)** $2 \pm i$ **c)** $\frac{-1 \pm \sqrt{7}i}{2}$

d) $1 \pm \sqrt{2}i$ **e)** $\frac{5 \pm \sqrt{3}i}{2}$ **f)** $\frac{-3 \pm \sqrt{7}i}{4}$

8. a) $\frac{2 \pm \sqrt{2}i}{3}$ **b)** $\frac{1 \pm \sqrt{5}i}{3}$ **c)** $\frac{-\sqrt{2}}{2}$

d) $1 \pm 2i$ **e)** $\frac{2 \pm \sqrt{10}i}{7}$ **f)** $-2 \pm \sqrt{11}$

9. $1 + i, 1 - i$

Investigate, page 39

$-\frac{1}{5} + \frac{8}{5}i$

Yes, provided the divisor is not 0.

Review Exercises, page 40

1. a) R; R

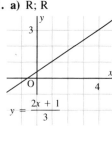

$y = \frac{2x + 1}{3}$

b) R; $\{y \mid y \geqslant -3, y \in R\}$

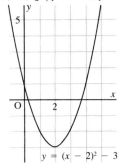

$y = (x - 2)^2 - 3$

c) $\{x \mid x \geqslant 0, x \in R\}$; $\{y \mid y \geqslant 1, y \in R\}$

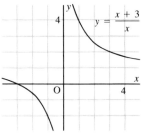

$y = \frac{x + 3}{x}$

2. a) -17 **b)** $10a - 2$ **c)** $5x + 3$
d) $15n - 12$

3. a) -2 **b)** -2 **c)** $1 - 6x^2$ **d)** $x^2 - 6$
e) $19 - 6x - 3x^2$ **f)** $9x^2 - 30x + 19$
g) $x^2 - 4x + 3$ **h)** $x^2 + 5x - 9$

4. a) $\frac{1}{2}, 2$ **b)** $-\frac{3}{2}, 4$ **c)** $-\frac{3}{4}, 2$

5. a) 2   **b)** $\frac{a + 2}{a - 2}, a \neq 2$ **c)** $\frac{3x - 1}{x - 1}, x \neq 1$

d) $\frac{x + 1}{x - 1}, x \neq 1$

6. a) 11   **b)** -9 **c)** 35   **d)** -7
e) $6x - 1$ **f)** $\frac{2x - 3}{3}$ **g)** $\frac{2x - 7}{3}$

h) $\frac{3x + 3}{2}$

7. a) $2x^2 - 6x + 9$ **b)** $4x^2 + 14x + 12$
c) $4x + 15$ **d)** $x^4 - 6x^3 + 10x^2 - 3x$
e) $\frac{x^2 - 3x - 3}{2}$ **f)** $\frac{x^2 - 16x + 63}{4}$
g) x **h)** $\frac{x - 15}{4}$

8. a) $y = -3x + 7$, yes
b) $y = \pm\sqrt{\frac{5x + 1}{2}}$, no

c) $y = \frac{2x + 1}{x - 3}$, yes

9. a) R; R; yes   **b)** $\{x \mid x \geqslant 3, x \in R\}$; R; no

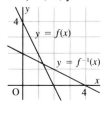

$y = f(x)$

$y = f^{-1}(x)$

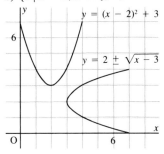

$y = (x - 2)^2 + 3$

$y = 2 \pm \sqrt{x - 3}$

c) $\{x \mid x \geqslant -2, x \in R\}$; $\{y \mid y \geqslant -1, y \in R\}$; yes

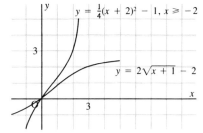

$y = \frac{1}{4}(x + 2)^2 - 1, x \geqslant -2$

$y = 2\sqrt{x + 1} - 2$

10. a) $-1.5, 4$ **b)** $-2.5, 0.5$ **c)** $-4, -\frac{2}{3}$

11. a) No real roots   **b)** 2 different real roots
c) 2 equal real roots

12. a) $\frac{6 \pm \sqrt{6}}{6}$ **b)** $\frac{-3 \pm \sqrt{177}}{14}$

13. a) $-9 + 6i$ **b)** 13   **c)** $28 - 21i$

14. a) $\frac{1 \pm \sqrt{11}i}{2}$ **b)** $\frac{7 \pm \sqrt{35}i}{6}$ **c)** $\frac{-3 \pm \sqrt{23}i}{4}$

Chapter 2

Exercises 2-1, page 44

1. a) 1.7 **b)** 2.3 **c)** −2.7, −1.1, 0.5, 3.3
d) −2.9, −1.4, 0, 1.4, 2.9
2. a) 0, ± 3.2   **b)** −3.6, 2

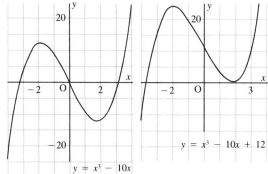

$y = x^3 - 10x$

$y = x^3 - 10x + 12$

c) −2, −1.5, 3.7   **d)** 4

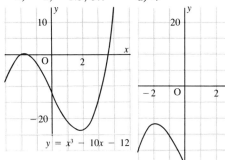

$y = x^3 - 10x - 12$

$y = x^3 - 10x - 24$

3. a) −3.5, −0.7, 4.2   **b)** 2.3

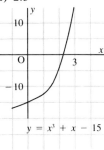

$y = x^3 - 15x - 10$

$y = x^3 + x - 15$

c) ± 1.2, ± 3.7   **d)** −2.3, 3.2

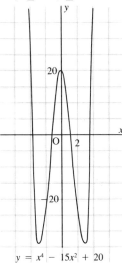

$y = x^4 - 15x^2 + 20$

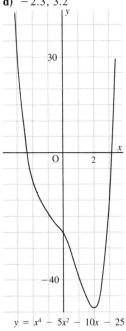

$y = x^4 - 5x^2 - 10x - 25$

4. a) 1.6   **b)** 3.5

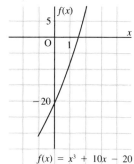

$f(x) = x^3 + 10x - 20$

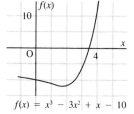

$f(x) = x^3 - 3x^2 + x - 10$

c) $-3.3, -0.6, 1.2, 2.7$ **d)** $-2.1, 3.2$

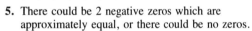

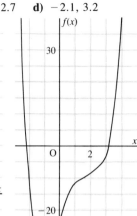

$f(x) = x^4 - 10x^2 + 5x + 7$

$f(x) = x^4 - 4x^3 + 16x - 25$

5. There could be 2 negative zeros which are approximately equal, or there could be no zeros.

6. Answers may vary.

7. Answers may vary.

a)

$f(x) = x^3$

b) See *Exercise 2b*.   **c)** See *Example 2b*.
d) See *Exercise 2d*.

8. Answers may vary.

a)   **b)**

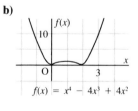

$f(x) = x^4$

$f(x) = x^4 - 4x^3 + 4x^2$

c)   **d)**

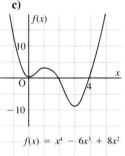

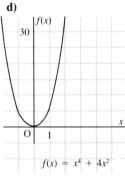

$f(x) = x^4 - 6x^3 + 8x^2$

$f(x) = x^4 + 4x^2$

9. About 4.5 s

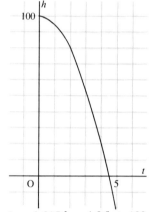

$h = 0.015t^3 - 4.9t^2 + 100$

10. a) i) $x^3 - 12x + 10 = 0$
  ii) $x^3 - 12x + 20 = 0$, $x^3 - 12x - 20 = 0$
  b) i) $-16 < k < 16$ **ii)** $k = \pm\, 16$
  iii) $k > 16$; $k < -16$

11. a)

n	1	2	3	4	5	6
$n^3 + n^2$	2	12	36	80	150	252

n	7	8	9	10
$n^3 + n^2$	392	576	810	1100

  b) 7   **c)** No

12. About 7.9 cm by 5.3 cm by 11.8 cm

Computer Power, page 47

1. a) $((5x + 2)x - 7)x + 8; 8, 42, 140, 332, 648$
   b) $((2x - 5)x + 3)x - 9; -9, -7, 9, 51, 131$
   c) $((6x + 1)x - 4)x + 12; 15, 56, 171, 396, 767$
   d) $(((2x + 3)x - 5)x + 6)x - 11; -5, 37, 205,$
   $637, 1519$
2. a) $24, 39, 56, 75, 96, 119, 144, 171, 200, 231$
   b) 7 **c) i)** 3 **ii)** 9 **iii)** 12
3. d) Linear function

Exercises 2-2, page 52

1. a) $x + 4$, R 2   **b)** $x - 1$, R 3
   c) $c - 2$, R 4   **d)** $n - 16$, R 86
2. a) $x^2 - 2x + 4$, R -3
   b) $m^2 - 3m - 7$, R -24
   c) $3s^2 - s - 2$, R -2
   d) $2x^2 - 5x - 12$
3. $x^3 - 2x^2 - 7x + 10$
4. $x^3 - x^2 - 11x + 12$
5. a) $2x + 3$, R -4 **b)** $3x + 8$, R 11
   c) $5u - 3$, R 10   **d)** $3x - 6$, R 21
   e) $4x + 3$, R 20   **f)** $3m - 2$, R -1
6. a) $c^2 + 4c + 3$, R -7
   b) $x^2 - 6x - 11$, R 15
   c) $1 + n - 2n^2$ **d)** $x^2 - 2x - 8$, R -4
   e) $5a^2 + 8a + 3$, R 6
   f) $m^2 + 3m - 10$, R -54
7. a) $x^2 - x - 2$, R 1   **b)** $-a^2 - 5a + 14$, R 2
   c) $-3m^2 + 13m + 10$, R -3
   d) $2s^2 - s - 6$
8. a) $(x - 3)(x - 4)$ **b)** $(3x + 1)(x - 1)$
   c) $-(x + 1)^2$ **d)** $(5x - 2)(x + 5)$
   e) $(2x + 3)(8x + 3)$ **f)** $(2x + 1)(-5x + 3)$
9. a) $x - 2$ **b)** $y - 3$, R $13y + 6$
   c) $2a^2 - a + 3$, R 8   **d)** $3t^2 + 2t + 1$
10. a) $x^2 + 5x + 6$ **b)** $m^2 - 2m - 3$
   c) $3x^2 - x - 10$, R -2 **d)** $a^2 - 4a - 12$, R 7
11. a) $(x - 3y)(x + 3y)$ **b)** $-(x + 4y)(x + 2y)$
   c) $-(8a + 3b)(a - 3b)$
   d) $-(3m + n)(m - 3n)$
12. a) $x^2 - 3$ **b)** $2a^2 + 3$ **c)** $3m^2 + 2$
   d) $2x^2 + 3$
13. $(4x + 3)(x + 5)$
14. $(2a + 3)(3a - 2)$
15. a) $x^2 - x + 1$ **b)** $-5 - 2a + 3a^2$
   c) $s^2 - 2s + 3$
16. a) $x^2 - x + 1$ **b)** $a^4 + a^3 + a^2 + a + 1$
   c) $s^2 - st + t^2$ **d)** $m^2 - 2mn + 2n^2$
17. $-21, -3$ **18.** -8 **19.** $x^2 + bx + c$

20. a) $x^2 + (b + c)x + bc$
   b) i) $x^2 + (a + c)x + ac$
   ii) $x^2 + (a + b)x + ab$

Investigate, page 53

1. a) 2   **b)** 2   **c)** $10, -70$
   d) When $f(x)$ is divided by $x - a$, the remainder is
   $f(a)$.

Exercises 2-3, page 56

1. a) $a^2 - 2a - 13 = (a + 3)(a - 5) + 2$
   b) $x^3 + x^2 + x + 11 = (x + 2)(x^2 - x + 3) + 5$
   c) $2p^3 + 5p^2 - 2p - 3$
   $= (p + 1)(2p^2 + 3p - 5) + 2$
   d) $2s^3 - 7s^2 + 16s - 22$
   $= (2s - 3)(s^2 - 2s + 5) - 7$
2. a) 3   **b)** 14   **c)** 43   **d)** 11   **e)** 18   **f)** 19
3. a) -4 **b)** 11   **c)** 0   **d)** 16   **e)** 21
   f) -43
4. a) 4   **b)** 44   **c)** 27   **d)** 7   **e)** 37   **f)** -1
5. a) 0   **b)** 8   **c)** -6 **d)** 1   **e)** 0   **f)** 2
6. a) 9   **b)** -9 **c)** 18   **d)** 43   **e)** 0
   f) -16
7. a) 4   **b)** 2   **c)** 3
8. $3, -1$ **9.** 1   **10. a)** 4   **b)** 3   **c)** 6
12. a) 11   **b)** -4 **c)** 5   **d)** $-\frac{3}{2}$
13. a) i), ii) No   **iii)** Yes   **b)** $7x - 5$
14. a) 1   **b)** $x + 10$ **c)** $x^2 - 2$
15. a) $f\left(-\dfrac{b}{a}\right)$ **b)** $\left(\dfrac{f(a) - f(b)}{a - b}\right)x + \dfrac{af(b) - bf(a)}{a - b}$

Exercises 2-4, page 61

4. 0   **5.** $x - 5$ **6.** a, b, d   **7.** a, c, d   **8.** b
9. a) $x^3 + 7x^2 + 7x - 15$
   b) $x^3 - 5x^2 - 17x + 21$
10. $(y + 1)(y - 2)(y + 3)$ **11.** a, c   **12.** c, d
13. a) Yes   **b)** Yes   **c)** No
14. a) $(a - 2)(a - 1)(a - 3)$
   b) $(a + 2)(a - 2)(a + 3)$
   c) $(x + 3)(x + 2)(x - 1)$
15. a) Yes   **b)** No   **c)** Yes   **d)** No   **e)** Yes
   f) Yes
16. a) $x - 1$ **b)** $x + 1$ **c)** $y + 1$ **d)** $x - 3$
   e) $y - 2$ **f)** $x + 1$
17. b) $x - 4$ **18. b)** $2x - 1$
19. a) $(x - 1)(x - 3)(x - 4)$
   b) $x^3 - 3x^2 + 3x - 1; x^3 - 3x + 2$

20. a) $(x - 1)(x + 2)(x + 4)$
b) $(x + 1)(x + 3)(x + 5)$
c) $(x + 1)(x - 4)(x + 5)$
d) $(x + 1)(x + 2)(x - 3)$
e) $(x - 1)^2(5x + 3)$ **f)** $(x - 2)(x^2 - 7x + 3)$
g) $(x + 1)(x + 2)(x + 5)$
h) $(x + 2)(x - 3)(2x + 1)$
21. a) $(x - 3)(x^2 - 5x + 2)$ **b)** $(x + 2)^2(x - 7)$
c) $(x + 1)(x - 4)(x + 9)$
d) $(x + 2)(x + 4)(x - 6)$
e) $(x + 1)(x - 2)(3x + 5)$
f) $(x - 2)(2x + 1)(5x - 3)$
g) $(x + 2)(x + 5)(x - 7)$
h) $(x - 3)(x + 4)(3x + 1)$
22. a) 11 **b)** -8 **c)** -4
23. Yes **24.** Yes **25.** Yes

26. a) $1, 5, -4$ **b)** $-2, 3, 7$ **c)** $1, -3, -\frac{1}{6}$
d) $-2, 5, -\frac{2}{5}$

Exercises 2-5, page 66

1. a) $0, 2, -5$ **b)** $0, -\frac{3}{2}, 4$ **c)** $0, -3, -7$
d) $0, -\frac{7}{3}, \frac{3}{2}$ **e)** $0, \pm 2$ **f)** $0, -2, -3$

2. a) 0 **b) i)** $-\frac{1}{2}, 3$ **ii)** $\pm\frac{3}{2}$ **iii)** $\frac{5}{2}, 3$
iv) $0, -\frac{2}{3}, -4$ **v)** $0, \pm\frac{5}{3}$ **vi)** $3, 4$

3. a) 2 **b)** $-5, \pm 3$ **c)** $-2, \frac{1}{2}, 3$ **d)** $\pm 2, \frac{2}{3}$

4. a) $-2, 3, -4$ **b)** 1 **c)** $1, 2, -\frac{3}{2}$
d) $-\frac{1}{2}, \pm\frac{3}{2}$

5. a) 2 **b)** $\pm 3, 2$ **c)** $-1, \dfrac{-4 \pm \sqrt{6}}{2}$ **d)** $\frac{2}{3}$

6. a) $-2, -3, -4$ **b)** $-4, -5, -6$
7. a) 3 **b)** -5

8. 10 cm by 6 cm by 1 cm or $\left(\dfrac{9 - \sqrt{21}}{2}\right)$ cm by
$(3 + \sqrt{21})$ cm by $(\sqrt{21} - 1)$ cm

9. $\pm 22, \pm 23$
10. a) $x^3 - 8x^2 + 17x - 10 = 0$
b) $x^3 - 3x^2 - 3x + 1 = 0$
c) $2x^4 - x^3 - 19x^2 + 9x + 9 = 0$
d) $4x^3 - 8x^2 - 23x - 11 = 0$

11. a) $13; 5, -\frac{1}{2}$ **b)** $-104; \pm\frac{2}{5}, -2$
c) $20; \dfrac{9 \pm \sqrt{57}}{6}$ **d)** $23; -\frac{1}{3}, 3 \pm \sqrt{2}$

12. a) $\pm 1, \pm 2$ **b)** $2, -1 \pm i$
13. a) $1, 5, 14, 30$ **b)** 24

Computer Power, page 70

1. $0.694\ 593, 3.064\ 178$
2. a) 1.1409 **b)** 1.5897 **c)** 2.2790
3. a) $-4.2916, -0.4283, 2.7180$
b) $-2.0205, 0.0636, 1.9364, 4.0204$
c) -2.4233
4. 88.7 m

The Mathematical Mind, page 71

1. a) $0.327\ 480\ 0$ **b)** $-0.673\ 593\ 1$
c) $-0.568\ 946\ 4$

Exercises 2-6, page 76

1. a) 3 **b)** 2 **c)** 3 **d)** 4 **e)** 3 **f)** 5
2. a) $(x-1)(x-2)(x-3) = 0$
b) $(x-2)^2(x-5) = 0$ **c)** $x(x+4)(x-1) = 0$
d) $(x-2)^3 = 0$
3. a) $(x-1)(x-2)(x-3)(x-4) = 0$
b) $(x-5)(x+2)(x-1)(x-2) = 0$
c) $(x-1)^2(x-2)^2(x-3)^2 = 0$
4. a) Degree 4 **b)** Degree 3 **c)** Degree 5
d) Degree 6 **e)** Degree 2 **f)** Degree 7
5.

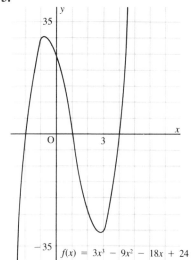

$f(x) = 3x^3 - 9x^2 - 18x + 24$

6. a)

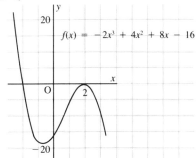

$f(x) = -2x^3 + 4x^2 + 8x - 16$

b)

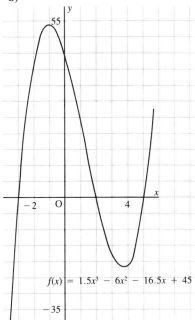

$f(x) = 1.5x^3 - 6x^2 - 16.5x + 45$

c)

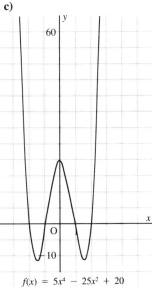

$f(x) = 5x^4 - 25x^2 + 20$

d)

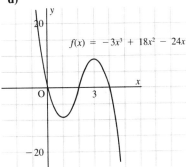

$f(x) = -3x^3 + 18x^2 - 24x$

7. a) 1

8. a) $\pm 1, \pm 5$ **b)** $\pm 1, \pm 2, \pm 4$
   c) $\pm 1, \pm 3, \pm 9$ **d)** $\pm 1, \pm 2, \pm 3, \pm 6$

9. a) $\pm 1, \pm 3$ **b)** $\pm 1, \pm 2, \pm 3, \pm 6$
   c) $\pm 1, \pm 2, \pm 5, \pm 10$ **d)** ± 1

12. a) $\pm 1, \pm \frac{1}{5}$ **b)** $\pm 1, \pm \frac{1}{2}$ **c)** $\pm 1, \pm 2, \pm \frac{1}{2}$

   d) $\pm 1, \pm \frac{1}{4}, \pm \frac{1}{2}$ **e)** $\pm 1, \pm 3, \pm \frac{1}{5}, \pm \frac{3}{5}$

   f) $\pm 1, \pm 2, \pm 4, \pm \frac{1}{2}, \pm \frac{1}{3}, \pm \frac{1}{6}, \pm \frac{2}{3}, \pm \frac{4}{3}$

13. a) ii, v   **b)** iii, iv, v   **c)** ii   **d)** i, ii, iii, iv, v
   e) iii, iv

14. a) $\frac{1}{2}, 2, -3$ **b)** $1, \dfrac{-1 \pm \sqrt{-3}}{2}$

   c) $-\frac{5}{2}, \dfrac{-3 \pm \sqrt{5}}{2}$ **d)** $1, -\frac{2}{3}, -\frac{3}{2}$

15. Answers may vary.

16. a) $y = x^3 - 9x^2 + 26x - 18$,
  $y = x^3 - 9x^2 + 27x - 19$,
  $y = x^3 - 9x^2 + 28x - 20$
  b) Answers may vary.
  c) $y = x^3 - 9x^2 + 22x - 14$,
  $y = x^3 - 9x^2 + 21x - 13$,
  $y = x^3 - 9x^2 + 20x - 12$
  d) Answers may vary.

Exercises 2-7, page 80

1. a) i) $\{x \mid -2 < x < 3\}$
   ii) $\{x \mid x < -2 \text{ or } x > 3\}$
   b) i) $\{x \mid x < -2\}$
   ii) $\{x \mid x > -2, x \neq 3\}$
2. a) $\{x \mid x > 2 \text{ or } x < -2\}$
   b) $\{x \mid -2 \leq x \leq -1\}$
   c) $\{x \mid x > 5 \text{ or } x < 0\}$
   d) $\{x \mid x \leq 0 \text{ or } 2 \leq x \leq 4\}$
   e) $\{a \mid a < 1 \text{ or } 2 < a < 3\}$
   f) $\{n \mid -5 \leq n \leq -1 \text{ or } n \geq 3\}$
3. a) $\{x \mid -2 < x < 2 \text{ or } x > 6\}$ **b)** $\{c \mid c < -4\}$
   c) $\{s \mid s \geq 0 \text{ or } -5 \leq s \leq -3\}$
   d) $\{x \mid -4 \leq x \leq 0 \text{ or } 2 \leq x \leq 4\}$
   e) $\{x \mid x \in R, x \neq -2, x \neq 5\}$ **f)** $\{u \mid u < 1\}$
4. a) $\{x \mid 0 < x < 5\}$ **b)** $\{m \mid m \leq -2 \text{ or } m \geq 4\}$
   c) $\{y \mid -6 \leq y \leq 3\}$ **d)** $x \mid x \neq 2\}$
   e) $\{x \mid x > 4\}$ **f)** $\{a \mid a \leq -5 \text{ or } 1 \leq a \leq 3\}$

5. a) $\{z \mid -2 < z < \frac{1}{2} \text{ or } z > 2\}$
   b) $\{x \mid x < -3 \text{ or } -3 < x < 3\}$
   c) $\{x \mid x < 0\}$ **d)** $n \in R$
   e) $\{x \mid x \leq -3 \text{ or } -1 \leq x \leq 1 \text{ or } x \geq 3\}$
   f) $\{r \mid 1 \leq r \leq 3\}$
6. $\{x \mid x < 1 \text{ or } x > 5\}$
7. $\{x \mid x > -1\}$
8. All real numbers between 0 and 1
10. Answers may vary; one example is $x^2 + 1 > 0$
11. Answers may vary; typical examples are:
   a) $(x - 3)^2 > 0$ **b)** $(x^2 - 9)^2 > 0$
12. a) $(x + 2)(x - 3) \leq 0$ **b)** $(x + 1)(x - 2) < 0$
   c) $(x + 2)(x - 1)(x - 4) < 0$
   d) $x(x + 2)(x - 2)(x - 4) \leq 0$
   e) $(x + 1)(x - 2)^2 \leq 0$
   f) $x^2(x + 3)(x - 3) < 0$

Problem Solving, page 83

1. a) Circular ring with outside radius $(x + y)$ cm
   and inside radius $(x - y)$ cm
   b) Circle with radius $(x + y)$ cm
2. b) Answers will vary. Typical answers are: $a = 2$,
   $b = 3, c = -2, d = -3; a = 0, b = 3, c = 0$,
   $d = 5$.
3. Not possible
4. $3\sqrt{3}$ cm
5. 72

Review Exercises, page 84

1. a) -2.9 **b)** $0, \pm 3$

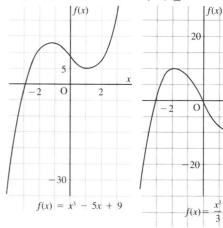

$f(x) = x^3 - 5x + 9$

$f(x) = \dfrac{x^3}{3} - 3x$

2. a) $(2a - 3)(a - 3)$ **b)** $(x + 2)(2x - 5)$
   c) $(3x - 2y)(2x - y)$
   d) $16x^2 - 16x - 1$, R 10
3. a) 5 **b)** -3 **c)** 5
4. 2 **5.** b, c, d
6. a) $(x - 2)(x + 2)(x + 3)$
   b) $(x + 1)(x + 1)(x - 2)$
   c) $(x - 1)(x + 2)(x + 4)$
   d) $(x + 1)(x - 3)(x + 3)$
7. -16
8. a) $-1, -3, -6, 2$ **b)** $-1, 2, 3$ **c)** $1, \pm 2$
   d) $1, \pm 2$
9. Answers may vary. $(x + 4)(x - 2)(x - 5) = 0$
11. a) $\pm 1, \pm 2, \pm 5, \pm 10, \pm \frac{10}{3}, \pm \frac{2}{3}, \pm \frac{5}{3}, \pm \frac{1}{3}$
   b) $\pm 1, \pm 3, \pm \frac{3}{2}, \pm \frac{3}{4}, \pm \frac{1}{2}, \pm \frac{1}{4}$
12. a) $\{x \mid -6 < x < -3 \text{ or } x > 4\}$
   b) $\{a \mid a \leq -2 \text{ or } 1 \leq a \leq 5\}$

Chapter 3

Exercises 3-1, page 88

1. a) The locus is a circle with centre $(0,0)$ and radius 2.
 b) The locus is a circle with centre $(0,2)$ and radius 2.
 c) The locus is a straight line with zero slope and y-intercept 3.
 d) The locus is a straight line with slope $\frac{1}{2}$ and y-intercept 3.
 e) The locus is a straight line with slope -1 and y-intercept 1.
 f) The locus is a pair of parallel lines with infinite slope and x-intercepts 2 and -2.

2. a) The locus is a straight line parallel to the x-axis, with y-intercept -5.
 b) The locus is a straight line parallel to the y-axis, with x-intercept -2.
 c) The locus is a circle, centre the origin and radius 7.
 d) The locus is a straight line with slope 1 and y-intercept 2.
 e) The locus is a circle, centre $(1,-4)$ and radius 4.
 f) The locus is a circle, centre $(1,0)$ and radius 1.

3. a) A circle, centre $B(0,3)$ and radius 6
 b) $x^2 + (y-3)^2 = 36$

4. a) $(x+1)^2 + (y-2)^2 = 25$
 b) A circle, centre $C(-1,2)$ and radius 5

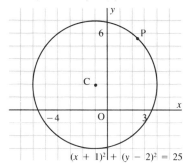

$(x + 1)^2 + (y - 2)^2 = 25$

 c) $5, -1$

5. a) A straight line with slope $\frac{2}{3}$, passing through $M(3,-1)$.

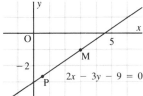

$2x - 3y - 9 = 0$

b) A parabola with vertex $(0,0)$ and axis of symmetry the y-axis. The parabola opens up.

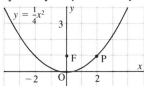

$y = \frac{1}{4}x^2$

 c) A parabola with vertex $(3,0)$ and axis of symmetry $x = 3$; it opens down, and is congruent to $y = -\frac{1}{4}x^2$.

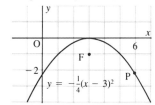

$y = -\frac{1}{4}(x - 3)^2$

6. a) $y = \frac{1}{4}(x - 2)^2 + 4$
 b) A parabola with vertex $(2,4)$ and axis of symmetry $x = 2$; it opens up and is congruent to $y = \frac{1}{4}x^2$.

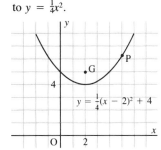

$y = \frac{1}{4}(x - 2)^2 + 4$

 c) 13

7. a) $5x - 2y - 13 = 0$; the perpendicular bisector of AB

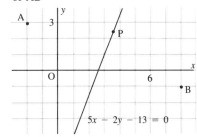

$5x - 2y - 13 = 0$

b) $x^2 + y^2 = 16$; a circle, centre (0,0) radius 4

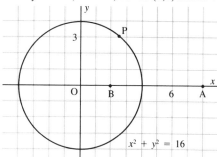

c) $x + y = 3$; a straight line through A and B

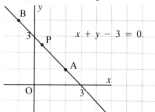

8. a) $y = \frac{1}{2}x^2 - 2$

b) A parabola, vertex $(0, -2)$, axis of symmetry the y-axis, which opens up and is congruent to $y = \frac{1}{2}x^2$

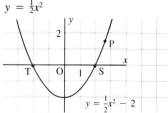

c) ± 6

9. a) $x^2 + y^2 = 25$

b) A circle, centre (0,0) and radius 5

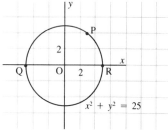

c) $\pm\sqrt{21}$

10. a) $x^2 + y^2 = 16$

b) A circle, centre (0,0) and radius 4

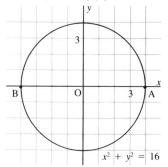

11. $x^2 + y^2 = 25$. See graph of *Exercise 9c)*.

12. a)

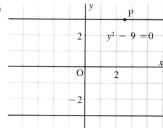

b)

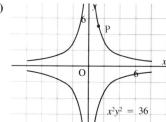

c)

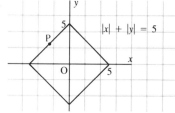

d)

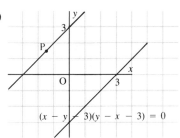

$(x - y - 3)(y - x - 3) = 0$

e)

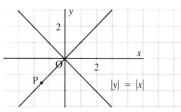

$|y| = |x|$

f)

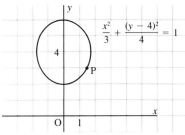

$$\frac{x^2}{3} + \frac{(y - 4)^2}{4} = 1$$

13.

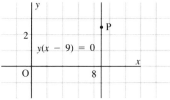

$y(x - 9) = 0$

14. a) $3x^2 + 4y^2 = 48$ **b)** $15x^2 - y^2 = 15$

15. $5x + 3y - 17 = 0$

Exercises 3-2, page 94

1. a, c, e, f

2. a) Circle

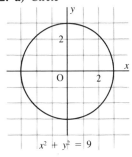

$x^2 + y^2 = 9$

b) Ellipse

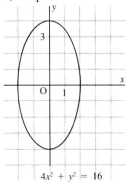

$4x^2 + y^2 = 16$

c) Hyperbola

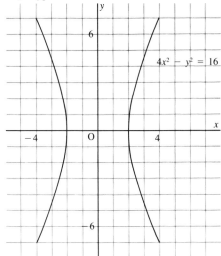

$4x^2 - y^2 = 16$

d) Parabola

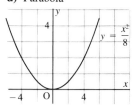

$y = \dfrac{x^2}{8}$

e) Ellipse

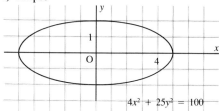

f) Hyperbola

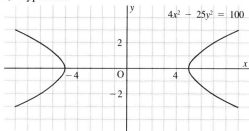

3. a) i)

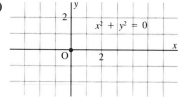

ii)

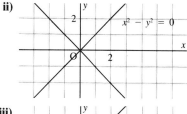

iii)

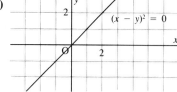

b) Answers may vary.

4. a) Hyperbola   **b)** Hyperbola, parabola or ellipse
c) Hyperbola

Exercises 3-3, page 98

See Teacher's Resource Book for graphs.

1. a) Yes   **b)** No   **c)** Yes   **d)** No

2. a) 8; (0,0)   **b)** $2\sqrt{3}$; (0,0)   **c)** 9; $(3,-4)$
d) $\sqrt{5}$; $(-2,1)$ **e)** $\sqrt{15}$; $(-4,0)$
f) $4\sqrt{3}$; (0,6)

3. a) $x^2 + y^2 = 9$ **b)** $x^2 + y^2 = 49$
c) $(x - 5)^2 + (y - 3)^2 = 16$
d) $(x + 2)^2 + (y - 6)^2 = 25$
e) $(x - 4)^2 + y^2 = 36$
f) $x^2 + (y + 3)^2 = 81$ **g)** $x^2 + y^2 = 5$
h) $(x - 3)^2 + (y + 5)^2 = 10$

4. a) $x^2 + y^2 - 6x + 4y - 12 = 0$
b) $x^2 + y^2 - 2x - 12y + 7 = 0$
c) $x^2 + y^2 + 8x - 4y + 9 = 0$
d) $x^2 + y^2 + 10x = 0$

5. a) $(x - 2)^2 + (y + 5)^2 = 16$
b) $(x + 4)^2 + (y - 3)^2 = 50$

7. a) $x^2 + y^2 = 36$ **b)** $\pm 2\sqrt{5}$

8. a) $3 \pm 2\sqrt{6}$ **b)** $2 \pm 2\sqrt{6}$

9. a) 3; $(5,-2)$ **b)** 5; $(3,1)$ **c)** Not a circle
d) $\sqrt{4.5}$; $\left(-\dfrac{1}{2}, -\dfrac{1}{2}\right)$ **e)** $\dfrac{\sqrt{65}}{4}$; $\left(1, -\dfrac{3}{4}\right)$
f) Not a circle

11. $G^2 + F^2 - C > 0$ **a) i)** $F = 0$ **ii)** $G = 0$
iii) $G = 0; F = 0$ **b)** $C = 0$
c) i) $C = G^2$ **ii)** $F^2 = C$ **iii)** $G^2 = F^2 = C$

12. To avoid fractions in the formulas for the coordinates of the centre, and the radius

13. a) $(x + 2)^2 + y^2 = 16$ **b)** Circle

14. a) $(x - 3)^2 + (y + 2)^2 = 25$
b) $(x - 1)^2 + (y - 2)^2 = 17$
c) $(x - 3)^2 + (y - 4)^2 = 5$

15. $x^2 + y^2 = 2x - 2y$

16. a) Not intersect   **b)** Not intersect
c) Intersect   **d)** Not intersect

17. $\sqrt{G_1^2 + F_1^2 - C_1} + \sqrt{G_2^2 + F_2^2 - C_2} \geqslant$
$\sqrt{(G_2 - G_1)^2 + (F_2 - F_1)^2} \geqslant$
$\left|\sqrt{G_1^2 + F_1^2 - C_1} - \sqrt{G_2^2 + F_2^2 - C_2}\right|$

18. $(x - 1)^2 + (y - 5)^2 = 25$

19. $\left(x - \dfrac{a}{2}\right)^2 + \left(y - \dfrac{b}{2}\right)^2 = \dfrac{a^2 + b^2}{4}$

20. $a_1 a_2 = b_1 b_2$

Exercises 3-4, page 103

See Teacher's Resource Book for graphs.

1. a) Yes **b)** No **c)** No **d)** Yes

2. a) $(1,0)$; $x = -1$ **b)** $(3,0)$; $x = -3$

  c) $\left(-\dfrac{3}{2},0\right)$; $x = \dfrac{3}{2}$ **d)** $(0,2)$; $y = -2$

  e) $\left(0,-\dfrac{1}{2}\right)$; $y = \dfrac{1}{2}$ **f)** $\left(0,\dfrac{3}{4}\right)$; $y = -\dfrac{3}{4}$

  g) $\left(-\dfrac{9}{4},0\right)$; $x = \dfrac{9}{4}$ **h)** $\left(0,-\dfrac{5}{4}\right)$; $y = \dfrac{5}{4}$

3. a) $(2,0)$; $x = -2$ **b)** $\left(-\dfrac{3}{4},0\right)$; $x = \dfrac{3}{4}$

  c) $(0,1)$; $y = -1$ **d)** $\left(0,-\dfrac{5}{2}\right)$; $y = \dfrac{5}{2}$

4. a) i) $y^2 = 16x$ **ii)** $y^2 = -24x$
  iii) $x^2 = 12y$ **b)** $x^2 = -32y$

5. a) $x^2 = \dfrac{1}{2}y$ **b)** $x^2 = \dfrac{8}{3}y$ **c)** $x^2 = \dfrac{8}{5}y$
  d) $x^2 = -8y$

6. a) $y^2 = \dfrac{16}{5}x$ **b)** $y^2 = \dfrac{25}{3}x$ **c)** $y^2 = \dfrac{36}{5}x$
  d) $y^2 = \dfrac{49}{3}x$

7. a) i) $x^2 = 8y$ **ii)** $x^2 = 5y$ **iii)** $x^2 = -3y$
  iv) $x^2 = -7y$
  b) If a parabola passes through (a,a), then
  $x^2 = ay$.

8. $y^2 = 20x$ **9.** $x^2 = 4py$

10. a) $A = x(25 - x)$

13. a) $(3p, \pm p\sqrt{12})$ **b)** $(p, \pm 2p)$

Exercises 3-5, page 107

See Teacher's Resource Book for graphs.

1. a) $(3,2)$; $y = 2$; right
  b) $(2,-1)$; $y = -1$; left
  c) $(-1,-5)$; $x = -1$; up
  d) $(4,1)$; $x = 4$; down **e)** $(0,3)$; $y = 3$; right
  f) $(0,2)$; $x = 0$; up

2. a) $y^2 + 6y - 2x + 11 = 0$
  b) $y^2 - 2y + x + 4 = 0$
  c) $x^2 + 10x + 4y + 17 = 0$
  d) $x^2 - 4x - 3y + 4 = 0$

3. a) $(x - 1)^2 = 3(y + 3)$
  b) $(x + 3)^2 = -5(y - 2)$
  c) $(y + 2)^2 = 4(x - 5)$
  d) $(y - 1)^2 = -3(x + 2)$

4. a) $(1,-2)$; $(2,-2)$; $y + 2 = 0$; $x = 0$

  b) $(-4,3)$; $\left(-\dfrac{9}{2},3\right)$; $y - 3 = 0$; $x = -\dfrac{7}{2}$

  c) $(3,-2)$; $\left(3,-\dfrac{3}{2}\right)$; $x - 3 = 0$; $y = -\dfrac{5}{2}$

  d) $(0,1)$; $\left(0,\dfrac{1}{4}\right)$; $x = 0$; $y = \dfrac{7}{4}$

  e) $(2,0)$; $(0,0)$; $y = 0$; $x = 4$
  f) $(0,-1)$; $(0,0)$; $x = 0$; $y = -2$

5. a) $(y - 2)^2 = 8(x - 1)$
  b) $(y - 3)^2 = -12(x + 1)$
  c) $(x - 2)^2 = 12(y + 3)$

6. a) $y^2 = 4(x - 2)$ **b)** Parabola

7. $(x + 1)^2 = -8(y - 4)$ **8.** $y^2 = 12x - 12$

10. a) $k = 0$; $h = -p$ **b)** $h = 0$; $k = -p$

Exercises 3-6, page 109

1. a) 11 **b)** 9 **c)** No real roots **d)** 4, 9
  e) 2 **f)** 3

2. a) 5,1 **b)** 4 **c)** 14 **d)** $\dfrac{13}{4}$ **e)** 18 **f)** 9,1

3. a) 1,0 **b)** 4 **c)** $\dfrac{25}{16}$ **d)** 5 **e)** 5 **f)** 2,6

4. 2.4 km **5.** 4.6 m **6.** 3.2 cm

7. a) 9 **b)** No real roots **c)** -3 **d)** 3

8. a) 1 **b)** 0,3 **c)** 13 **d)** 6

9. a) $75 - 50\sqrt{2}$ **b)** $26 - 2\sqrt{153}$
  c) $14 - 4\sqrt{11}$ **d)** 17

10. a)
$$\frac{\sqrt{(a + b + c)(-a + b + c)(a - b + c)(a + b - c)}}{2a}$$

11. a) 19.9 cm² **b)** 6.0 cm² **c)** 20.7 m²
  d) 10.8 m²

12. $x = \dfrac{s\sqrt{4R^2 - s^2}}{R}$

13. a) $10\sqrt{2}$ cm **b)** $(10\sqrt{2} - \sqrt{2})$ cm

14. a) $10\sqrt{3}$ cm **b)** 10 cm **15.** 5.78 m

16. a) i) $\dfrac{9 - \sqrt{21}}{2}$ **ii)** 2 **iii)** $\dfrac{9 - \sqrt{29}}{2}$
  iv) $\dfrac{9 - \sqrt{33}}{2}$ **b)** 2, 8, 16, 26, 38, ...

17. 2

Exercises 3-7, page 117

See Teacher's Resource Book for graphs.

1. a) Yes b) Yes c) No d) Yes

2. a) $(4,0),(-4,0); (\sqrt{7},0),(-\sqrt{7},0); 8; 6$
   b) $(6,0),(-6,0); (\sqrt{11},0),(-\sqrt{11},0); 12; 10$
   c) $(0,3),(0,-3); (0,\sqrt{5}),(0,-\sqrt{5}); 6; 4$
   d) $(0,7),(0,-7); (0,\sqrt{33}),(0,-\sqrt{33}); 14; 8$
   e) $(8,0),(-8,0); (4\sqrt{3},0),(-4\sqrt{3},0); 16; 8$
   f) $(0,5),(0,-5); (0,4),(0,-4); 10; 6$

3. a) $\dfrac{x^2}{25} + \dfrac{y^2}{9} = 1$ b) $\dfrac{x^2}{64} + \dfrac{y^2}{36} = 1$
   c) $\dfrac{x^2}{20} + \dfrac{y^2}{16} = 1$ d) $\dfrac{x^2}{49} + \dfrac{y^2}{9} = 1$
   e) $\dfrac{x^2}{25} + \dfrac{y^2}{9} = 1$ f) $\dfrac{x^2}{36} + \dfrac{y^2}{20} = 1$

4. a) i) $\dfrac{x^2}{9} + \dfrac{y^2}{4} = 1$ ii) $6; 4; (\pm 3,0); (\pm\sqrt{5},0)$
   b) i) $\dfrac{x^2}{16} + \dfrac{y^2}{4} = 1$ ii) $8; 4; (\pm 4,0); (\pm 2\sqrt{3},0)$
   c) i) $\dfrac{x^2}{9} + \dfrac{y^2}{16} = 1$ ii) $8; 6; (0,\pm 4); (0,\pm\sqrt{7})$
   d) i) $\dfrac{x^2}{16} + \dfrac{y^2}{25} = 1$ ii) $10; 8; (0,\pm 5); (0,\pm 3)$
   e) i) $\dfrac{x^2}{1} + \dfrac{y^2}{9} = 1$ ii) $6; 2; (0,\pm 3); (0,\pm 2\sqrt{2})$
   f) i) $\dfrac{x^2}{3} + \dfrac{y^2}{2} = 1$
   ii) $2\sqrt{3}; 2\sqrt{2}; (\pm\sqrt{3},0); (\pm 1,0)$

5. $\dfrac{x^2}{9} + \dfrac{y^2}{5} = 1$ 6. $\dfrac{x^2}{b^2} + \dfrac{y^2}{a^2} = 1$

7. a) $\dfrac{x^2}{100} + \dfrac{y^2}{25} = 1$ b) ± 8 c) $\pm\dfrac{5}{2}\sqrt{3}$

8. Yes 9. a) $\dfrac{x^2}{16} + \dfrac{y^2}{12} = 1$ b) Ellipse

14. a) $C < 0 < A < B$ or $B < A < 0 < C$
    b) $C < 0 < B < A$ or $A < B < 0 < C$

Exercises 3-8, page 126

See Teacher's Resource Book for graphs.

1. a) Yes b) No c) Yes d) No

2. a) $(2,0),(-2,0); (2\sqrt{5},0),(-2\sqrt{5},0); 4; 8$
   b) $(5,0),(-5,0); (\sqrt{34},0),(-\sqrt{34},0); 10; 6$
   c) $(9,0),(-9,0); (\sqrt{130},0),(-\sqrt{130},0); 18; 14$

3. a) $\dfrac{x^2}{36} - \dfrac{y^2}{9} = 1$ b) $\dfrac{x^2}{9} - \dfrac{y^2}{4} = 1$
   c) $\dfrac{x^2}{20} - \dfrac{y^2}{16} = 1$ d) $\dfrac{x^2}{25} - \dfrac{y^2}{49} = 1$
   e) $\dfrac{x^2}{4} - \dfrac{y^2}{5} = 1$ f) $\dfrac{x^2}{49} - \dfrac{y^2}{49} = 1$

4. a) i) $\dfrac{x^2}{4} - \dfrac{y^2}{9} = 1$
   ii) $4; 6; (\pm 2,0); (\pm\sqrt{13},0); y = \pm\dfrac{3}{2}x$
   b) i) $\dfrac{x^2}{36} - \dfrac{y^2}{4} = 1$
   ii) $12; 4; (\pm 6,0); (\pm 2\sqrt{10},0); y = \pm\dfrac{1}{3}x$
   c) i) $\dfrac{x^2}{9} - \dfrac{y^2}{25} = 1$
   ii) $6; 10; (\pm 3,0); (\pm\sqrt{34},0); y = \pm\dfrac{5}{3}x$
   d) i) $\dfrac{x^2}{4} - \dfrac{y^2}{16} = 1$
   ii) $4; 8; (\pm 2,0); (\pm 2\sqrt{5},0); y = \pm 2x$
   e) i) $\dfrac{x^2}{12} - \dfrac{y^2}{4} = 1$
   ii) $4\sqrt{3}; 4; (\pm 2\sqrt{3},0); (\pm 4,0); y = \pm\dfrac{1}{\sqrt{3}}x$
   f) i) $\dfrac{x^2}{5} - \dfrac{y^2}{4} = 20$
   ii) $2\sqrt{5}; 4; (\pm\sqrt{5},0); (\pm 3,0); y = \pm\dfrac{2}{\sqrt{5}}x$

5. $8x^2 - y^2 = 32$

6. a) $\dfrac{x^2}{6} - \dfrac{y^2}{2} = 1$ b) $\pm 3\sqrt{2}$ c) ± 1

7. a) $\dfrac{x^2}{9} - \dfrac{y^2}{9} = 1$ b) $(\pm 2\sqrt{3},0); y = x, y = -x$

8. a) $3x^2 - y^2 = 12$ b) Hyperbola

Exercises 3-9, page 130

See Teacher's Resource Book for graphs.

1. a) Yes b) Yes c) No d) Yes

2. a) $(0,3),(0,-3); (0,5),(0,-5); 6; 8$
   b) $(0,5),(0,-5); (0,\sqrt{29}),(0,-\sqrt{29}); 10; 4$
   c) $(0,6),(0,-6); (0,10),(0,-10); 12; 16$

3. a) $\dfrac{x^2}{16} - \dfrac{y^2}{9} = -1$ b) $\dfrac{x^2}{15} - \dfrac{y^2}{49} = -1$
   c) $\dfrac{x^2}{9} - \dfrac{y^2}{27} = -1$ d) $\dfrac{x^2}{7} - \dfrac{y^2}{25} = -1$
   e) $\dfrac{x^2}{4} - \dfrac{y^2}{16} = -1$

4. a) i) $\dfrac{x^2}{9} - \dfrac{y^2}{4} = -1$
   ii) $4; 6; (0,\pm 2); (0,\pm\sqrt{13}); y = \pm\dfrac{2}{3}x$
   b) i) $\dfrac{x^2}{16} - \dfrac{y^2}{4} = -1$
   ii) $4; 8; (0,\pm 2); (0,\pm 2\sqrt{5}); y = \pm\dfrac{1}{2}x$
   c) i) $\dfrac{x^2}{25} - \dfrac{y^2}{16} = -1$
   ii) $8; 10; (0,\pm 4); (0,\pm\sqrt{41}); y = \pm\dfrac{4}{5}x$
   d) i) $\dfrac{x^2}{25} - \dfrac{y^2}{100} = -1$
   ii) $20; 10; (0,\pm 10); (0,\pm 5\sqrt{5}); y = \pm 2x$

e) i) $\dfrac{x^2}{50} - \dfrac{y^2}{25} = -1$

ii) $10; 10\sqrt{2}; (0, \pm 5); (0, \pm 5\sqrt{3}); y = \pm\dfrac{1}{\sqrt{2}}x$

f) i) $\dfrac{x^2}{8} - \dfrac{y^2}{6} = -1$

ii) $2\sqrt{6}; 4\sqrt{2}; (0, \pm\sqrt{6}); (0, \pm\sqrt{14}); y = \pm\dfrac{\sqrt{3}}{2}x$

5. $\dfrac{x^2}{8} - \dfrac{y^2}{1} = -1$ **6.** $\dfrac{x^2}{b^2} - \dfrac{y^2}{a^2} = -1$

8. $A > 0, B < 0, C > 0$ or $A < 0, B > 0, C < 0$

9. a) Typical answer: $\dfrac{x^2}{4} - \dfrac{y^2}{9} = 1; \dfrac{x^2}{4} - \dfrac{y^2}{9} = -1$

b) Change the sign of the constant term.

Problem Solving, page 133

1. a) **Answers** may vary. Some typical answers are:
6^2 and 5^2; 3^3 and 4^3.
b) **Subtract 1, then divide by 2. Square this
number and the next one.**

2. $-0.5, 1, 1 \pm \sqrt{3}$

4. Answers may vary. One example is triangles with
sides of length 8, 12, 18 and 12, 18, 27 units.

6. See Teacher's Resource Book for graphs.

7. $\dfrac{2x^2}{7 + \sqrt{17}} + \dfrac{2y^2}{3 + \sqrt{17}} = 1$

8. $\dfrac{x^2}{72} + \dfrac{y^2}{8} = 1$ and $\dfrac{x^2}{28 + 4\sqrt{13}} + \dfrac{y^2}{12 + 4\sqrt{13}} = 1$

9. There are two possible ellipses:
$2(x - 3)(x - 2) + 3(y - 1)(y - 7) = 0$ and
$8(x - 3)(x + 1) + (y - 1)(y - 3) = 0$. There
is only one possible hyperbola:
$3(x - 2)(x + 1) - (y - 7)(y - 3) = 0$.

Exercises 3-10, page 136

1. a) $y = \dfrac{1}{2160}x^2$ **b)** 42 cm

2. $y = -\dfrac{1}{64}x^2$

3. Typical answers: **a)** $y = -\dfrac{15.3}{1225}x^2$ **b)** 14 m

4. a) $9x^2 + 25y^2 = 225$ **b)** About 5.50 m

5. a) $15\ 625x^2 + 22\ 500y^2 = 351\ 562\ 500$
b) About 123.9 m

6. 5.4 m

7. 44 m

8. a) 800 km   **b)** 2000 km

Exercises 3-11, page 140

1. a) $\dfrac{(x - 3)^2}{4} - (y - 2)^2 = 1$

b) $\dfrac{(x - 3)^2}{9} + \dfrac{(y + 2)^2}{4} = 1$

2. Coordinates of the centre, the vertices, and the foci
are listed.
a) Ellipse; $(2, -3)$; $(2,4), (2, -10)$;
$(2, \sqrt{33} - 3), (2, -\sqrt{33} - 3)$

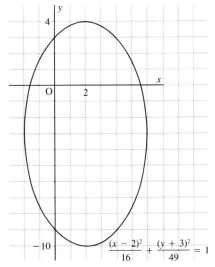

$\dfrac{(x - 2)^2}{16} + \dfrac{(y + 3)^2}{49} = 1$

b) Ellipse; $(-5,3)$; $(-1,3), (-9,3)$;
$(2\sqrt{3} - 5,3), (-2\sqrt{3} - 5,3)$

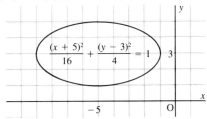

$\dfrac{(x + 5)^2}{16} + \dfrac{(y - 3)^2}{4} = 1$

c) Hyperbola; $(4, -6)$; $(7, -6), (1, -6)$;
$(\sqrt{13} + 4, -6), (-\sqrt{13} + 4, -6)$

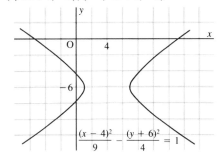

$\dfrac{(x - 4)^2}{9} - \dfrac{(y + 6)^2}{4} = 1$

d) Hyperbola; (2,0); (5,0), (−1,0);
$(\sqrt{34}+2,0), (−\sqrt{34}+2,0)$

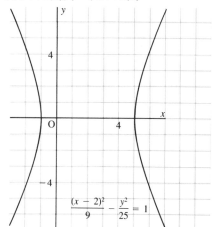

$$\frac{(x-2)^2}{9} - \frac{y^2}{25} = 1$$

e) Ellipse; (−3,−3); $(−3−3\sqrt{2},−3)$,
$(−3+3\sqrt{2},−3)$; (−6,−3), (0,3)

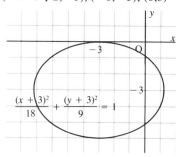

$$\frac{(x+3)^2}{18} + \frac{(y+3)^2}{9} = 1$$

f) Hyperbola; (5,1); (5,4), (5,−2);
$(5,3\sqrt{5}+1), (5,−3\sqrt{5}+1)$

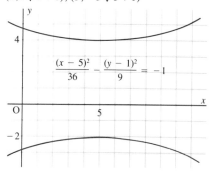

$$\frac{(x-5)^2}{36} - \frac{(y-1)^2}{9} = -1$$

3. Coordinates of the centre, the vertices, and the foci are listed.

a) Ellipse; (3,2); (6,2), (0,2);
$(\sqrt{5}+3, 2), (−\sqrt{5}+3, 2)$

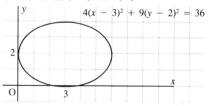

$4(x-3)^2 + 9(y-2)^2 = 36$

b) Hyperbola; (−1,3); (−3,3), (1,3);
$(−2\sqrt{5}−1,3), (2\sqrt{5}−1,3)$

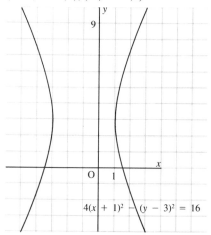

$4(x+1)^2 - (y-3)^2 = 16$

c) Hyperbola; (−5,−4); (−5,−1), (−5,−7);
$(−5,−3\sqrt{5}−4), (−5,3\sqrt{5}−4)$

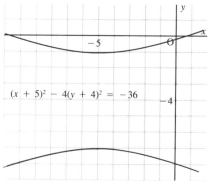

$(x+5)^2 - 4(y+4)^2 = −36$

d) Ellipse; (2,−2); $(2+2\sqrt{2},−2), (2−2\sqrt{2},−2)$;
$(2+\sqrt{2},−2), (2−\sqrt{2},−2)$
See Teacher's Resource Book for graph.

e) Hyperbola; (0,2); (3,2), (−3,2); (6,2), (−6,2)
See Teacher's Resource Book for graph.

f) Ellipse; (−5,0); (−11,0), (1,0);
($\sqrt{30}$ − 5,0), (−$\sqrt{30}$ − 5,0)

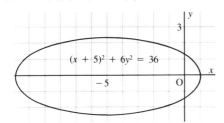

$(x + 5)^2 + 6y^2 = 36$

Exercises 3-12, page 143

1. a) $3x^2 + y^2 - 6x + 4y - 2 = 0$
b) $x^2 - 2y^2 + 10x + 4y + 13 = 0$
c) $3x^2 - 24x - y + 50 = 0$
d) $4x^2 + 9y^2 + 16x - 54y + 61 = 0$
e) $3x^2 - 6y^2 + 6x - 24y - 3 = 0$
f) $2y^2 + x - 12y + 22 = 0$

2. a) Ellipse **b)** Hyperbola **c)** Parabola
d) Circle

3. a)

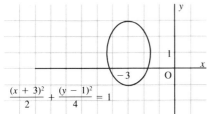

$$\frac{(x + 3)^2}{2} + \frac{(y - 1)^2}{4} = 1$$

b)

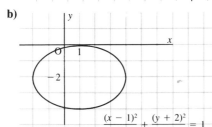

$$\frac{(x - 1)^2}{9} + \frac{(y + 2)^2}{4} = 1$$

c)

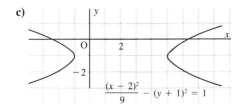

$$\frac{(x - 2)^2}{9} - (y + 1)^2 = 1$$

d)

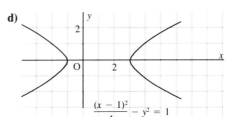

$$\frac{(x - 1)^2}{4} - y^2 = 1$$

e)

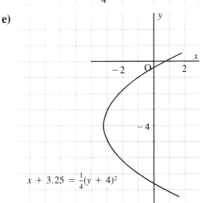

$x + 3.25 = \frac{1}{4}(y + 4)^2$

f)

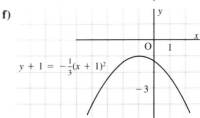

$y + 1 = -\frac{1}{3}(x + 1)^2$

4. a) $(x-4)^2 + (y+3)^2 = 16$; a circle, centre
(4,−3), radius 4

b) $\frac{(x-1)^2}{4} + (y+2)^2 = 1$; an ellipse, centre
(1,−2), length of major axis 4, length of minor
axis 2

c) $\frac{(x+3)^2}{4} + \frac{(y-2)^2}{3} = 1$; an ellipse, centre
(−3,2), length of major axis 4, length of minor
axis 2$\sqrt{3}$

d) $\frac{(x-6)^2}{4} - \frac{y^2}{6} = 1$; a hyperbola, centre (6,0),
length of transverse axis (which is horizontal) 4,
length of conjugate axis 2$\sqrt{6}$

e) $x+2 = \frac{1}{8}(y-4)^2$; a parabola, vertex (−2,4),
opening to the right, congruent to $x = \frac{1}{8}y^2$

f) $y + 5 = 6(x+2)^2$; a parabola, vertex
(−2,−5), opening up, congruent to $y = 6x^2$

5. a) $y + 3 = \frac{1}{6}(x - 3)^2$

b)

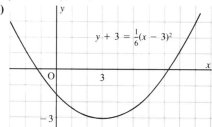

6. $y = -\frac{1}{8}(x - 3)^2 + 4$

7. $\frac{(x - 4)^2}{25} + \frac{(y - 3)^2}{9} = 1$

8. a) The lines $x = 1$ and $y = -4$
b) There is no graph.
c) The lines $2x - y + 2 = 0$ and $2x + y + 6 = 0$
d) Two coincident lines $x + y + 1 = 0$

Exercises 3-13, page 147

1. $3x^2 + 2y^2 - 6x + 8y - 1 = 0$
2. $5x^2 - 4xy + 8y^2 + 2x - 44y + 29 = 0$
3. a) Parabola **b)** Ellipse **c)** Hyperbola
d) Hyperbola **e)** Parabola **f)** Ellipse
4. Descriptions may vary.
a) See Teacher's Resource Book for graph.
b)

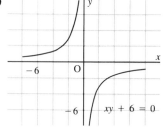

c) The graph $xy - 6 = 0$ translated 4 units right and 3 units down.

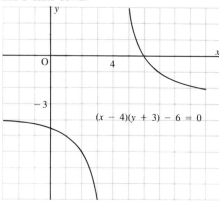

$(x - 4)(y + 3) - 6 = 0$

d) The graph $xy - 6 = 0$ translated 4 units left and 3 units up.

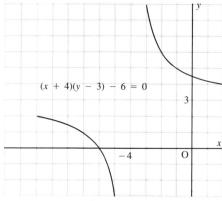

$(x + 4)(y - 3) - 6 = 0$

5. $x^2 + 2xy + y^2 - 22x + 10y - 7 = 0$
6. $x^2 - 2xy - y^2 + 10x - 10y = 0$

7. a) The equation is an ellipse if $AC - \frac{B^2}{4} > 0$

The equation is a hyperbola if $AC - \frac{B^2}{4} < 0$

The equation is a parabola if $AC - \frac{B^2}{4} = 0$

b) Answers may vary.
8. a) $3x^2 - 2xy + 3y^2 - 8 = 0$
b) $3x^2 - 2xy + 3y^2 - 4x - 4y - 4 = 0$
10. No; explanations may vary.

11. Assume that the first non-zero coefficient in the equation is positive. If it is not, then multiply both sides by -1.

a) $H = 0$, $A = B$, and $G^2 + F^2 - AC \geqslant 0$

b) i) $B > A > 0$, $H = F = 0$, and $G^2 - AC > 0$

ii) $A > B > 0$, $H = G = 0$, and $F^2 - BC > 0$

c) i) $A > 0$, $B < 0$, $H = F = 0$, and $G^2 - AC > 0$

ii) $A > 0$, $B < 0$, $H = G = 0$, and $F^2 - BC > 0$

d) i) $A = H = 0$ **ii)** $H = B = 0$

Review Exercises, page 149

1. a) Circle

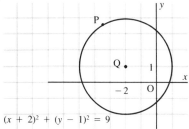

$(x + 2)^2 + (y - 1)^2 = 9$

b) Straight line

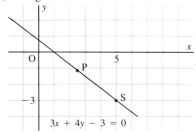

$3x + 4y - 3 = 0$

c) Parabola

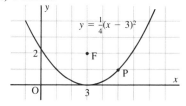

$y = \frac{1}{4}(x - 3)^2$

d) Straight line

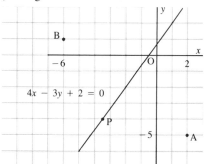

$4x - 3y + 2 = 0$

2. a) Ellipse

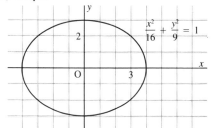

$\frac{x^2}{16} + \frac{y^2}{9} = 1$

b) Parabola

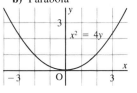

$x^2 = 4y$

c) Circle

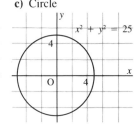

$x^2 + y^2 = 25$

d) Hyperbola

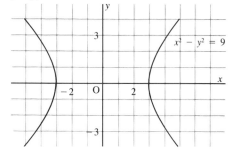

$x^2 - y^2 = 9$

e) Circle

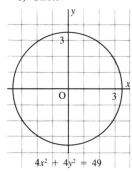

$4x^2 + 4y^2 = 49$

f) Hyperbola

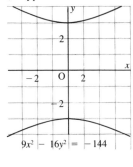

$9x^2 - 16y^2 = -144$

3. a) No; parabola   **b)** Yes; circle
c) No; hyperbola   **d)** No; ellipse
4. a) $(0,0)$; 2.5   **b)** $(2, -3)$; 5
5. a) $y = \dfrac{1}{8}x^2$ **b)** $y = -1.5x^2$

6. a) $\dfrac{x^2}{9} + \dfrac{y^2}{25} = 1$ **b)** $\dfrac{x^2}{9} + \dfrac{y^2}{36} = 1$

7. a) $\dfrac{x^2}{16} - \dfrac{y^2}{64} = 1$ **b)** $\dfrac{x^2}{16} - \dfrac{y^2}{49} = 1$

8. $y = -\dfrac{1}{64}x^2$ **9.** $\dfrac{x^2}{900} + \dfrac{y^2}{625} = 1$

10. $x^2 - y^2 = -380.25$
11. a) Circle   **b)** Ellipse   **c)** Parabola
d) Hyperbola

Cumulative Review, Chapters 1-3, page 150

1. a) R; R

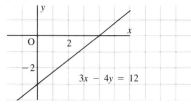

$3x - 4y = 12$

b) R; $\{y \mid y \geqslant 5, y \in R\}$

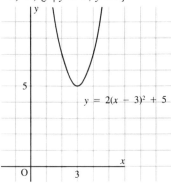

$y = 2(x - 3)^2 + 5$

c) $\{x \mid x \neq 0, x \in R\}$; $\{y \mid y \neq 2, y \in R\}$

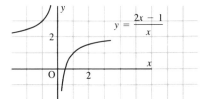

$y = \dfrac{2x - 1}{x}$

2. a) 13   **b)** -3 **c)** $12a - 2$ **d)** $3x^2 - 5$
e) $4x^2 + 2x - 3$ **f)** $3x^2 + 9x - 5$
3. a) R; R; yes

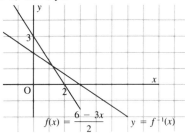

$f(x) = \dfrac{6 - 3x}{2}$ $y = f^{-1}(x)$

b) $\{x \mid x \neq 3, x \in R\}$; $\{y \mid y \neq 0, y \in R\}$; yes

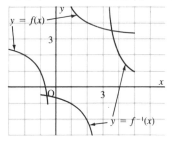

$y = f(x)$ $y = f^{-1}(x)$

4. a) 2 different real roots   **b)** No real roots
c) 2 equal real roots

5. a) $\dfrac{5 \pm \sqrt{57}}{2}$ **b)** $\dfrac{-3 \pm \sqrt{23}i}{4}$ **c)** $-1.8, 1$

6. a) $1.4, -3.4$ **b)** 0

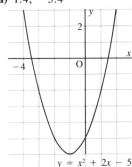
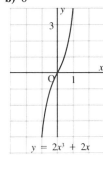

$y = x^2 + 2x - 5$

$y = 2x^3 + 2x$

7. a) $(x-5)(x+2)$ **b)** $(2x-1)(2x+1)$
c) $(x-1)(x+1)(x+2)$

8. a) Yes   **b)** No; -2

9. a) $(x-1)(x+3)(x+5)$
b) $(x-1)(x-2)(x+2)(x+3)$

10. a) $\pm 1, \pm 2, \pm 3, \pm 4, \pm 6, \pm 12$
b) $\pm 1, \pm 3, \pm \frac{1}{2}, \pm \frac{3}{2}$

11. a) $\{x \mid x < -3 \text{ or } -2 < x < 1\}$
b) $\{x \mid x \leqslant -2 \text{ or } -1 \leqslant x \leqslant 1 \text{ or } x \geqslant 3\}$

12. a) The perpendicular bisector of AB

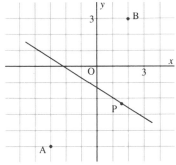

b) A circle, centre $Q(-2, -3)$, radius 4 units
   See Teacher's Resource Book for graph.

13. a) $\dfrac{x^2}{16} + y^2 = 1$ **b)** $\dfrac{x^2}{36} + \dfrac{y^2}{16} = 1$

14. $x^2 - y^2 = -28$

Chapter 4

Exercises 4-1, page 153

2. For example: pre-election opinion surveys; market research — new products; television ratings; monthly unemployment data; consumer price indices; Gallup, Harris, Angus Reid, Environics opinion polls; railway freight charges between rail companies; industrial quality control; traffic flow patterns in a city; environmental scientists; medical researchers

4. For example: political organizations; environmental organizations; network television; market research organizations; boards of school trustees; newspapers; Statistics Canada; sports organizations; consumer testing organizations; quality control departments

Exercises 4-2, page 154

2. c and d

3. a) Are you a male?
b) Did you spend more than $20 on a date in the last 2 weeks?
e) Did you smoke more than 5 cigarettes yesterday?
f) Did you miss at least 1 class last week?

4. Answers may vary.
a) . . . males in Algebra 12 classes.
b) . . . boys and girls who spent more than $20 on a date in the past 2 weeks.
e) . . . students in the school who smoked more than 5 cigarettes yesterday.
f) . . . students in the school who missed at least 1 class last week.

5. For example:
Are you over the legal drinking age?
Are you male?
Have you consumed alcohol at least once in the last 6 months?
Did you smoke at least 5 cigarettes last week?
Did you drink at least the equivalent of 8 bottles of beer on any day in the last 2 weeks?
Did you drink at least the equivalent of 2 bottles of beer on more than 4 separate days in the last 2 weeks?
Have you ever driven a car after drinking more than 3 bottles of beer?
Do your parents approve of your drinking habits?
Do either of your parents smoke at least 5 cigarettes per week?

6. a) A range of questions is possible depending on the particular emphasis of the survey; for example:
Do you have children in the public school system?
Do you have children in the private school system?
Do you think that the private schools provide a better education than the public schools?
If the fees were covered by your school tax payments, would you want your children to attend a private school of your choice?
Parents whose children attend a private school are required to pay taxes to support the public school systems. Would you support a proposal to allow such parents to use their schools taxes to support the private school instead?

Exercises 4-3, page 157

1. The distribution should be similar to that in the table on page 156, but it will not be an exact copy.

2., 3. Answers may vary.

4. You would not expect the percentage of yesses in your 100 samples to be exactly the same as the percentage of yesses in the population. You have taken a sample of size 2000 from the population and not a census. But because of the size of the sample, the difference between the population percentage and the samples percentage might be small.

Problem Solving, page 161

1. 14   **4.** 1, 51, 1176   **8. a)** 89   **9.** 44

Exercises 4-4, page 165

3. The sample chart should match that on page 189.

4. The differences between the chart for samples size 43 and the table at the end of the chapter may vary because of the randomise function in the computer program.

Exercises 4-5, page 171

1. a to e are likely proportions, f and g are unlikely proportions.

2. a) 10% to 40%   **b)** 20% to 55%
c) 40% to 75%   **d)** 50% to 85%
e) 70% to 95%

3. a) 0.25 to 0.65   **b)** 0.40 to 0.80   **c)** 0.65 to 0.95
d) 0.85 to 1.00

4. a) 15% to 50%   **b)** 35% to 70%   **c)** 40% to 70%
d) 55% to 85%

5. a) The boxes for 95% boxplots are longer than those for 90% boxplots.

b) The confidence intervals from charts of 95% boxplots are longer than the intervals from charts of 90% boxplots.

6. 0.20 to 0.60   **7.** 25% to 60%

8. b) 40% to 75%, yes   **c)** 45% to 80%, yes
d) 40% to 70%, yes   **e)** 35% to 65%, yes
f) 70% to 95%, no   **g)** 40% to 75%, yes
h) 35% to 70%, yes   **i)** 55% to 85%, yes
j) 40% to 75%

9. a) 60% to 90%, yes; 60% to 90%, yes; 50% to 85%, yes; 60% to 90%, yes; 70% to 95%, yes; 60% to 90%, yes; 60% to 90%, yes; 60% to 90%, yes; 55% to 85%, yes; 50% to 85%, yes
b) 20% to 55%, yes; 20% to 55%, yes; 15% to 45%, yes; 5% to 30%, no; 20% to 55%, yes; 20% to 55%, yes; 20% to 55%, yes; 15% to 45%, yes; 20% to 55%, yes; 15% to 50%, yes

Exercises 4-6, page 174

1. For a given population, the confidence interval for large sample sizes is shorter than the confidence interval for small sample sizes.

3. 22% to 60%; population between 67 and 182

4. 32% to 48%; population between 67 and 100

5. The confidence interval in *Exercise 4* is shorter because its sample size is larger than the sample size in *Exercise 3*.

6. 64% to 78%

7. a) 18% to 40%; 24% to 48%; 28% to 42%
b) 46% to 78%; 50% to 74%; 56% to 70%
c) 22% to 54%; 26% to 48%; 30% to 46%
d) 72% to 94%; 76% to 94%; 82% to 92%
e) 2% to 20%; 4% to 14%; 4% to 12%
f) 80% to 98%; 86% to 96%; 88% to 96%

8. a) I am 90% confident that between 60% and 74% of grade 11 and 12 boys spend more than $20 on a date.
b) I am 90% confident that between 36% and 52% of grade 11 and 12 girls spend more than $20 on a date.
c) I am 90% confident that between 4% and 10% of grade 11 and 12 boys smoke 10 or more cigarettes a day.
d) I am 90% confident that between 10% and 20% of grade 11 and 12 girls smoke more than 10 cigarettes a day.

9. a) No   **b)** . . . spend more than $20 on a date.

10. The confidence intervals do overlap so there does not seem to be a significant difference.

11. a) 4% to 20%; 6% to 14%; 6% to 18%
b) 150 to 750; 220 to 500; 170 to 500

12. 19 e's in the sentence; 14% to 26%

13. a)

Sample size	Confidence interval	Width
20	32% to 68%	36%
40	38% to 62%	24%
60	40% to 60%	20%
80	42% to 58%	16%
100	42% to 58%	16%

There is some inaccuracy because the tables only give data for even population percentages.

c) The relation is an inverse relation.

d) The graph of W against $\dfrac{1}{\sqrt{N}}$ is closest to being linear. **e)** $W = \dfrac{160}{\sqrt{N}}$

14. a) The student has a 20% chance of guessing the right phone number. The experiment is like obtaining a sample of size 20 from a 20% YES population. The likely number of correct guess is between 1 and 7.
b) The 90% confidence interval for a sample of 9 yesses out of 20 is 26% to 64%. We can be 90% confident that factors other than chance have affected this experiment.

Exercises 4-7, page 178

2. I am 95% confident that between 27% and 39% of the people in British Columbia approve of the performance of the leader of the Federal Progressive Conservative Party.

3. I am 95% confident that between 24% and 30% of Canadians believe that unemployment is the country's key problem.

4. I am 95% confident that between 47% and 67% of Canadians in Atlantic Canada believe that unemployment is the country's key problem.

5. I am 95% confident that between 40% and 46% of Canadians approve of the decision to grant the CBC a licence for an all-news television channel.

6. I am 95% confident that of the students in the three schools, between:
a) 26% and 34% spent more than $15 on a date
b) 41% and 49% had a part-time job
c) 7% and 15% worked more than 20 h a week
d) 12% and 20% watched TV more than 20 h a week
e) 46% and 54% spent more hours on school assignments than watching TV
f) 33% and 41% spent more than 10 h a week on assignments
g) 13% and 21% smoked
h) 48% and 56% had a driver's licence

7. a) A 95% confidence interval is no greater than 2.1% to 9.1%. A 95% confidence interval for the population size is no greater than 11 000 to 47 600.

8. 36% to 42%

9. a) 69% to 75%

10. We need to make some reasonable assumptions to answer this question. If we base these assumptions on the data in *Exercises 3* and *4*, it is reasonable to assume that 100 are from Atlantic Canada and 400 from Ontario. This gives a sampling error of 5% for Ontario and 10% for Atlantic Canada. The reported figure of 50% for Atlantic Canada is really a figure between 40% and 60%, and the figure of 36% is a figure between 31% and 41%. So it is conceivable that 41% of Ontario voters and 40% of Atlantic voters approved of Brian Mulroney's performance.

Exercises 4-8, page 183

2. a) Convenience sample
b) People who are at work or who are late risers.
c) No; if he only asked those who passed his store then the users of his store would be underrepresented. Also he would not ask anyone of school age, since they are normally at school at that time.
d) Since many people active in sports are either working or at school at that time, the survey would be biased against those active in sports.
e) He must include people who shop at all times in the week, not just at those times when he is not busy. If he wants to survey only those people active in sports then he should question, for example, every 20th person who enters his store during a given week. But this would exclude those who do not shop at his store. If he wants to include all shoppers who use the mall then he would assign someone to ask every nth person who passes a chosen spot (or spots) in the mall. Alternatively, he could position a person at each mall exit and ask every nth person leaving the mall.

3. a) Convenience sample
b) Students who had different course selections
c) The sample would be biased towards students who took the same kinds of courses as the student who conducted the survey. If the student had a concentration of business education courses, the survey would be biased towards the attitudes of business education students; similarly for other courses.
d) Use a simple random sample of all grade 12 students. Alternatively, if there is a course that is compulsory for grade 12 students, use a cluster sample using classes of that course.

4. a) Convenience sample
b) Convenience sample
c) Systematic sample
d) Convenience sample
e) Simple random sample

6. a) People who were unable to afford an automobile or a telephone
b) People who do not feel strongly enough about the issue to write a letter
c) Students who have no interest in math/science and avoid such courses
d) People who have no interest in any kind of sport as well as other groups who never attend baseball games
e) People who would rather watch sports on television than attend such games; also many other groups who are unable to attend B.C. Lions games
f) Students who were involved with sports activities after school

7. Typically, those who have enjoyed being parents might not be inclined to write to Ann Landers about this. Write-in polls are usually biased in favor of those who have strong opinions on the issue and who want their opinions known.

8. Answers may vary, for example:
a) Select a simple random sample of the students (using a numbered list of students and random digit tables), then send the survey to their parents.
b) Use a multi-stage technique to select elementary and secondary schools and then an appropriate number of students from the selected schools. The number of students selected from each level should be in proportion to the total number of students at that level.
c) If the area is such that almost every home has a telephone, then a phone survey is probably the most convenient. A more reliable method is a face-to-face interview.

d) Use a stratified random sample choosing some students from each secondary school in proportion to the number of students in the school.
e) Make a list of members of these professions from the Yellow Pages or Business Directory. Then use random digits to obtain a simple random sample.
f) A self-selected sample of listeners is the easiest method but it is not reliable. A phone survey using simple random sampling is better, but it may be necessary to ask many people before you find enough people who are listening to the radio show.
g) Position students near the exits of the mall. Ask every nth person. You will need to cover all exits and choose a randomly selected number of time intervals during which the interviews are conducted. Alternatively, select every nth person who crosses predetermined areas in the mall.

9. None of the samples would be representative of the entire population. Each sample is taken from a distinctive sub population.

Chapter 5

Section 5-1, page 194

Estimates may vary.

1. a) i) 17:00 h   **ii)** 20:00 h   **iii)** 17:00 h
b) Approximate dates: **i)** May 20, July 23
ii) April 12, Aug. 30   **iii)** Mar. 13, Sept. 29
iv) Feb. 20, Oct. 24

2. Answers may vary.

3. 10 to 11 years

4. Typical answers: **a)** 173 m, 58 m   **b)** 6 h

5. Answers may vary.   **6.** Answers may vary.

7. 5 s

8. Answers may vary.

9. Sunsets: 1 year; sunspots; 10.5 years; volume and pressure of blood: 0.8 s; volume of air: 5 s

10. 15 **11.** Sunspots

Exercises 5-2, page 200

1. a) $\dfrac{\pi}{6}$ **b)** $\dfrac{\pi}{4}$ **c)** $\dfrac{\pi}{3}$ **d)** $\dfrac{\pi}{2}$ **e)** $\dfrac{2\pi}{3}$ **f)** $\dfrac{3\pi}{4}$

g) $\dfrac{5\pi}{6}$ **h)** π **i)** $\dfrac{7\pi}{6}$ **j)** $\dfrac{5\pi}{4}$ **k)** $\dfrac{4\pi}{3}$

l) $\dfrac{3\pi}{2}$ **m)** $\dfrac{5\pi}{3}$ **n)** $\dfrac{7\pi}{4}$ **o)** $\dfrac{11\pi}{6}$ **p)** 2π

q) $\dfrac{13\pi}{6}$ **r)** $\dfrac{9\pi}{4}$

2. a) 90° **b)** 135° **c)** −120° **d)** 210°
e) 45° **f)** −270° **g)** 315° **h)** 360°
i) −300° **j)** 225° **k)** 30° **l)** −330°

3. a) 1.75 **b)** 3.93 **c)** 1.00 **d)** −2.18
e) $1.31x$ **f)** 0.33 **g)** −1.13 **h)** $0.43x$
i) 2.62 **j)** 0.52 **k)** 1.00 **l)** $-1.57x$

4. a) 114.6° **b)** −286.5° **c)** 183.3°
d) 103.1° **e)** −40.1° **f)** $80.2\theta°$ **g)** 383.9°
h) $-360x°$

5. a) 10 cm **b)** 15 cm **c)** 9 cm **d)** 30.5 cm
e) 21 cm **f)** 3 cm

6. a) 28.3 cm **b)** 15.7 cm **c)** 22.0 cm
d) 34.6 cm **e)** 50.3 cm **f)** 37.7 cm
g) 64.9 cm **h)** 41.9 cm

7. a) i) 15 m **ii)** 26 m **b) i)** 47 cm
ii) 353 cm **c) i)** 509 mm **ii)** 1131 mm

8. a) 2π **b)** π **c)** $\dfrac{\pi}{2}$

9. 15 m

10. 51 cm

11. $\dfrac{\pi x}{50}$

12. a) About 0.0172 **b)** 2 560 000 km

13. a) About 87 rad/s **b)** $\dfrac{500x}{9d}$ rad/s

14. a) i) $R\sqrt{2}$ **ii)** $\dfrac{\pi R}{2}$ **b)** $\dfrac{\pi}{2\sqrt{2}}$ **c)** $\dfrac{R^2(\pi - 2)}{4}$
d) $\dfrac{R\sqrt{2}}{2}$

Exercises 5-3, page 207

1. a) 0.939 69 **b)** −0.898 79 **c)** −4.331 48
d) −0.374 61 **e)** −0.809 02 **f)** −0.139 17
g) −0.424 47 **h)** −0.998 63

2. a) 0.295 52 **b)** 0.764 84 **c)** 5.797 88
d) 0.999 57 **e)** −0.998 29 **f)** −2.848 59
g) −0.345 89 **h)** −0.656 39

3. a) P is in the 4th quadrant.
b) −0.447 21; 0.894 43, −0.500 00

4. a) P is in the 2nd quadrant.
b) 0.832 05, −0.554 70, −1.500 00

5. a) 0.75, 5.53 **b)** 0.47, 3.61 **c)** 1.41, 4.88
d) 1.57, 4.71 **e)** 0.34, 2.80 **f)** 0.90, 5.38

6. a) P is in the 4th quadrant; $-\dfrac{6}{\sqrt{157}}, \dfrac{11}{\sqrt{157}}, -\dfrac{6}{11}$

b) P is in the 3rd quadrant; $-\dfrac{1}{\sqrt{26}}, -\dfrac{5}{\sqrt{26}}, \dfrac{1}{5}$

c) P is in the 2nd quadrant; $\dfrac{1}{\sqrt{5}}, -\dfrac{2}{\sqrt{5}}, -\dfrac{1}{2}$

d) P is in the 3rd quadrant; $-\dfrac{5}{\sqrt{41}}, -\dfrac{4}{\sqrt{41}}, \dfrac{5}{4}$

e) P is in the 4th quadrant; $-\dfrac{3}{\sqrt{34}}, \dfrac{5}{\sqrt{34}}, -\dfrac{3}{5}$

f) P is in the 1st quadrant; $\dfrac{8}{\sqrt{73}}, \dfrac{3}{\sqrt{73}}, \dfrac{8}{3}$

g) P is on the positive *y*-axis; 1, 0, undefined
h) P is on the negative *x*-axis; 0, −1, 0

7. a) 0.707 11
b) Answers may vary. 45°, 405°, 495°

8. a) −0.813 94
b) Answers may vary; to 5 decimal places,
8.741 59, 2.458 41, 11.883 19

9. a) 203°, 337° **b)** 139°, 221° **c)** 17°, 197°
d) 319°, 139° **e)** 119°, 241° **f)** 14°, 166°

10. a) 2.83, 5.98 **b)** 3.69, 5.73 **c)** 2.51, 3.77
d) 1.31, 4.98 **e)** 2.55, 5.69 **f)** 0.51, 2.63

11. a) i) 43°, 223° **ii)** 125°, 305° **iii)** 116°, 296°
b) i) 0.74, 3.88 **ii)** 2.18, 5.32
iii) 2.03, 5.17

12. b) P has coordinates (5,4), (10,8), (15,12), etc.
c) $\sin\theta = \dfrac{4}{\sqrt{41}}$, $\cos\theta = \dfrac{5}{\sqrt{41}}$

13. b) P has coordinates (−3,5), (−6,10),
(−9,15), etc.
c) $\sin\theta = \dfrac{5}{\sqrt{34}}$, $\cos\theta = -\dfrac{3}{\sqrt{34}}$

14. b) P has coordinates (−1,3), (−2,6), (−3,9), etc.
c) $\cos\theta = -\dfrac{1}{\sqrt{10}}$, $\tan\theta = -3$

15. Answers may vary.

Exercises 5-4, page 211

1. a) 3.420 **b)** 1.804 **c)** 2.281 **d)** 0.158
e) 1.836 **f)** 1.058 **g)** 5.145 **h)** 1.012
i) 0.754 **j)** 1.589 **k)** 1.086 **l)** 1.006

2. a) $\sin 25° = 0.423$, $\csc 25° = 2.366$;
$\cos 25° = 0.906$, $\sec 25° = 1.103$;
$\tan 25° = 0.466$, $\cot 25° = 2.145$
b) $\sin 50° = 0.766$; $\csc 50° = 1.305$;
$\cos 50° = 0.643$, $\sec 50° = 1.556$,
$\tan 50° = 1.192$, $\cot 50° = 0.839$
c) $\sin 75° = 0.966$, $\csc 75° = 1.035$;
$\cos 75° = 0.259$, $\sec 75° = 3.864$;
$\tan 75° = 3.732$, $\cot 75° = 0.268$
d) $\sin 30° = 0.500$, $\csc 30° = 2.000$;
$\cos 30° = 0.866$, $\sec 30° = 1.155$;
$\tan 30° = 0.577$, $\cot 30° = 1.732$
e) $\sin 45° = \cos 45° = 0.707$;
$\csc 45° = \sec 45° = 1.414$;
$\tan 45° = \cot 45° = 1.000$
f) $\sin 60° = 0.866$, $\csc 60° = 1.155$;
$\cos 60° = 0.500$, $\sec 60° = 2.000$;
$\tan 60° = 1.732$, $\cot 60° = 0.577$

3. a) 38° **b)** 56° **c)** 19° **d)** 61° **e)** 41°
f) 50° **g)** 15° **h)** 74° **i)** 23° **j)** 67°
k) 12° **l)** 52°

4. a), b) $\sin A = \cos B = \dfrac{a}{c}$; $\cos A = \sin B = \dfrac{b}{c}$;
$\tan A = \cot B = \dfrac{a}{b}$; $\csc A = \sec B = \dfrac{c}{a}$;
$\sec A = \csc B = \dfrac{c}{b}$; $\cot A = \tan B = \dfrac{b}{a}$

5. $\sin A = \cos B$, $\cos A = \sin B$, $\tan A = \cot B$,
$\csc A = \sec B$, $\sec A = \csc B$, $\cot A = \tan B$

6. a) $AB = 16.1$, $\angle A = 43.0°$; $\angle C = 47.0°$
b) $\angle N = 33°$, $PM = 26.1$, $PN = 40.3$
c) $\angle S = 57°$, $VS = 22.4$, $TS = 41.1$

7. a) $\sin \theta = \dfrac{q}{p}$, $\cos \theta = \dfrac{\sqrt{p^2 - q^2}}{p}$,
$\tan \theta = \dfrac{q}{\sqrt{p^2 - q^2}}$, $\sec \theta = \dfrac{p}{\sqrt{p^2 - q^2}}$,
$\cot \theta = \dfrac{\sqrt{p^2 - q^2}}{q}$
b) $\sin \phi = \dfrac{2\sqrt{x}}{x + 1}$, $\cos \phi = \dfrac{x - 1}{x + 1}$,
$\tan \phi = \dfrac{2\sqrt{x}}{x - 1}$, $\csc \phi = \dfrac{x + 1}{2\sqrt{x}}$,
$\cot \phi = \dfrac{x - 1}{2\sqrt{x}}$

c) $\sin \alpha = \dfrac{a + 1}{\sqrt{5a^2 + 2a + 1}}$,
$\cos \alpha = \dfrac{2a}{\sqrt{5a^2 + 2a + 1}}$, $\tan \alpha = \dfrac{a + 1}{2a}$,
$\csc \alpha = \dfrac{\sqrt{5a^2 + 2a + 1}}{a + 1}$,
$\sec \alpha = \dfrac{\sqrt{5a^2 + 2a + 1}}{2a}$

8. a) 31 cm **b)** 7.85 m **c)** 196.23 m
d) 9613 m

Exercises 5-5, page 215

1. a) 1 **b)** $\dfrac{2}{\sqrt{3}}$ **c)** $\dfrac{\sqrt{3}}{2}$ **d)** 0 **e)** 2 **f)** 1
g) $\sqrt{2}$ **h)** $\dfrac{1}{\sqrt{2}}$ **i)** $\sqrt{3}$ **j)** $\dfrac{\sqrt{3}}{2}$ **k)** 0
l) 1

2. a) $-\sqrt{2}$ **b)** $\dfrac{1}{2}$ **c)** 0 **d)** $\dfrac{1}{2}$ **e)** 1
f) Undefined **g)** $\dfrac{1}{\sqrt{2}}$ **h)** -2 **i)** $\dfrac{2}{\sqrt{3}}$
j) -1 **k)** $-\dfrac{1}{\sqrt{3}}$ **l)** $\dfrac{1}{\sqrt{3}}$

3. a) 3 **b)** 4 **c)** $\dfrac{1}{4}$ **d)** $\dfrac{4}{3}$ **e)** $-\dfrac{1}{2\sqrt{2}}$ **f)** $\dfrac{1}{3}$

4. a) $\dfrac{7\pi}{6}, \dfrac{11\pi}{6}$ **b)** $\dfrac{\pi}{4}, \dfrac{7\pi}{4}$ **c)** $\dfrac{2\pi}{3}, \dfrac{5\pi}{3}$ **d)** $\dfrac{\pi}{6}, \dfrac{5\pi}{6}$
e) $\dfrac{\pi}{4}, \dfrac{7\pi}{4}$ **f)** $\dfrac{3\pi}{4}, \dfrac{7\pi}{4}$ **g)** $\dfrac{\pi}{4}, \dfrac{3\pi}{4}$ **h)** $\dfrac{\pi}{6}, \dfrac{7\pi}{6}$
i) $\dfrac{2\pi}{3}, \dfrac{4\pi}{3}$ **j)** $\dfrac{3\pi}{2}$ **k)** $\dfrac{2\pi}{3}, \dfrac{4\pi}{3}$ **l)** $\dfrac{2\pi}{3}, \dfrac{5\pi}{3}$

5. a) $\dfrac{\pi}{4}, \dfrac{3\pi}{4}, \dfrac{5\pi}{4}, \dfrac{7\pi}{4}$ **b)** $\dfrac{\pi}{3}, \dfrac{2\pi}{3}, \dfrac{4\pi}{3}, \dfrac{5\pi}{3}$ **c)** $\dfrac{\pi}{4}, \dfrac{3\pi}{4}, \dfrac{5\pi}{4}, \dfrac{7\pi}{4}$
d) $\dfrac{\pi}{3}, \dfrac{2\pi}{3}, \dfrac{4\pi}{3}, \dfrac{5\pi}{3}$ **e)** $\dfrac{\pi}{3}, \dfrac{2\pi}{3}, \dfrac{4\pi}{3}, \dfrac{5\pi}{3}$ **f)** $\dfrac{2\pi}{3}, \dfrac{4\pi}{3}$
g) $\dfrac{7\pi}{6}, \dfrac{11\pi}{6}$ **h)** $\dfrac{\pi}{4}, \dfrac{3\pi}{4}, \dfrac{5\pi}{4}, \dfrac{7\pi}{4}$

6. a) $\csc \theta = -\dfrac{\sqrt{3}}{2}$, $\cos \theta = \pm\dfrac{1}{2}$, $\sec \theta = \pm 2$,
$\tan \theta = \pm\sqrt{3}$, $\cot \theta = \pm\dfrac{1}{\sqrt{3}}$
b) $\cot \theta = \dfrac{1}{\sqrt{3}}$, $\sin \theta = \pm\dfrac{\sqrt{3}}{2}$, $\csc \theta = \pm\dfrac{2}{\sqrt{3}}$,
$\cos \theta = \pm\dfrac{1}{2}$, $\sec \theta = \pm 2$
c) $\cos \theta = -\dfrac{\sqrt{3}}{2}$, $\sin \theta = \pm\dfrac{1}{2}$,
$\csc \theta = \pm 2$, $\tan \theta = \pm\dfrac{1}{\sqrt{3}}$, $\cot \theta = \pm\sqrt{3}$

7. a) $\sin(\pi + \theta) = -\dfrac{y}{r}$, $\csc(\pi + \theta) = -\dfrac{r}{y}$

$\cos(\pi + \theta) = -\dfrac{x}{r}$, $\sec(\pi + \theta) = -\dfrac{r}{x}$

$\tan(\pi + \theta) = \dfrac{y}{x}$, $\cot(\pi + \theta) = \dfrac{x}{y}$

b) $\sin(2\pi - \theta) = -\dfrac{y}{r}$, $\csc(2\pi - \theta) = -\dfrac{r}{y}$,

$\cos(2\pi - \theta) = \dfrac{x}{r}$, $\sec(2\pi - \theta) = \dfrac{r}{x}$,

$\tan(2\pi - \theta) = -\dfrac{y}{x}$, $\cot(2\pi - \theta) = -\dfrac{x}{y}$

Exercises 5-6, page 219

2. a) $\cos\theta = 1, 0.5, 0, -0.5, -1$
b) $\cos\theta = -0.5, 0, 0.5, 1$

5. a) $y = 1$ when $\theta = \dfrac{\pi}{2}$ and $-\dfrac{3\pi}{2}$

b) $y = -1$ when $\theta = \dfrac{3\pi}{2}$ and $-\dfrac{\pi}{2}$

c) $\{y \mid -1 \leqslant y \leqslant 1\}$ **d)** 0
e) $0, \pm\pi, \pm2\pi$

6. a) $y = 1$ when $\theta = 0$ and $\pm2\pi$
b) $y = -1$ when $\theta = \pm\pi$
c) $\{y \mid -1 \leqslant y \leqslant 1\}$ **d)** 1   **e)** $\pm\dfrac{\pi}{2}, \pm\dfrac{3\pi}{2}$

7. Answers may vary.
10. a)

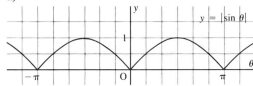

b)

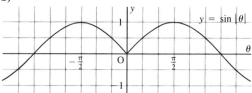

c)

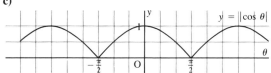

d)

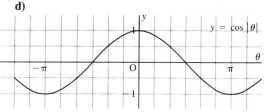

Exercises 5-7, page 224

3. a) No, explanations may vary; the graph goes to infinity at the asymptotes.
b) The domain is any angle in standard position. The range is any real number.
c) 0   **d)** $0, \pm\pi, \pm2\pi$, etc.
4. Answers may vary.
6. Odd
7. a)

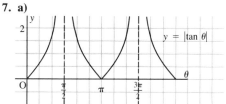

b)

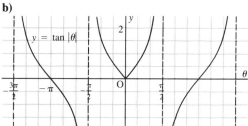

Exercises 5-8, page 230

2. a) $y = 1.5\sin\theta$; 1.5; -1.5; 1.5
b) $y = 2.5\sin\theta$; 2.5; -2.5; 2.5
c) $y = 0.5\cos\theta$; 0.5, -0.5, 0.5
3. a) $y = \sin\theta + 0.5$; 0.5; 1.5; -0.5; 0.5
b) $y = \cos\theta - 1$; -1; 0; -2; 0
4. a) 5; -5; $\{y \mid -5 \leqslant y \leqslant 5\}$

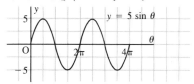

b) 3; −3; {*y* | −3 ⩽ *y* ⩽ 3}

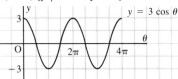

c) 7; 1; {*y* | 1 ⩽ *y* ⩽ 7}

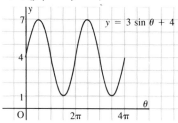

d) −1; −5; {*y* | −5 ⩽ *y* ⩽ −1}

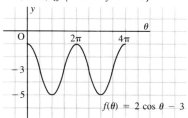

e) 2; −6; {*y* | −6 ⩽ *y* ⩽ 2}

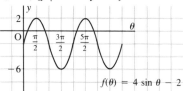

f) 3.5; 2.5; {*y* | 2.5 ⩽ *y* ⩽ 3.5}

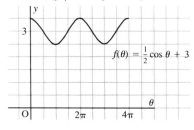

g) −0.5; −1.5; {*y* | −1.5 ⩽ *y* ⩽ −0.5}

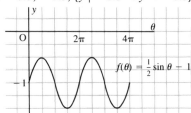

h) 4; 0; {*y* | 0 ⩽ *y* ⩽ 4}

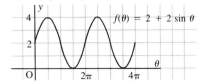

i) 6; 0; {*y* | 0 ⩽ *y* ⩽ 6}

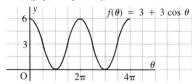

5. a) $a + q$; $\frac{\pi}{2}, \frac{5\pi}{2}, \ldots$ **b)** $q - a$; $\frac{3\pi}{2}, \frac{7\pi}{2}, \ldots$

6. a) $a + q$; $0, \pi, 2\pi, \ldots$
  b) $q - a$; $\pi, 3\pi, \ldots$

7. $y = \sin \theta + 1$; $y = \sin \theta - 1$

Exercises 5-9, page 235

2. Typical answers: $\frac{\pi}{3}$, $y = \sin \left(\theta - \frac{\pi}{3}\right)$;

  $-\frac{5\pi}{3}$, $y = \sin \left(\theta + \frac{5\pi}{3}\right)$

3. Typical answers: $\frac{5\pi}{6}$, $y = \cos \left(\theta - \frac{5\pi}{6}\right)$;

  $-\frac{7\pi}{6}$, $y = \cos \left(\theta + \frac{7\pi}{6}\right)$

4. a)

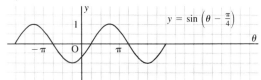

b)

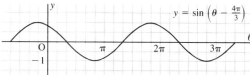

$y = \sin\left(\theta - \frac{4\pi}{3}\right)$

c)

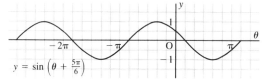

$y = \sin\left(\theta + \frac{5\pi}{6}\right)$

d)

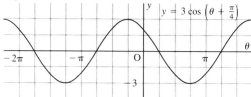

$y = 3\cos\left(\theta + \frac{\pi}{4}\right)$

e)

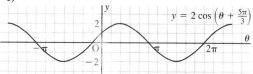

$y = 2\cos\left(\theta + \frac{5\pi}{3}\right)$

f)

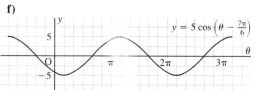

$y = 5\cos\left(\theta - \frac{7\pi}{6}\right)$

5. a)

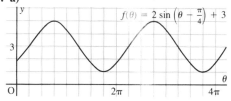

$f(\theta) = 2\sin\left(\theta - \frac{\pi}{4}\right) + 3$

b)

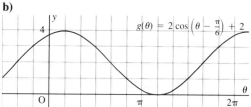

$g(\theta) = 2\cos\left(\theta - \frac{\pi}{6}\right) + 2$

c)

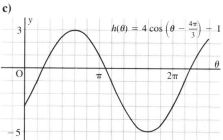

$h(\theta) = 4\cos\left(\theta - \frac{4\pi}{3}\right) - 1$

d)

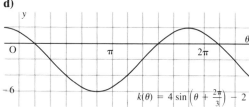

$k(\theta) = 4\sin\left(\theta + \frac{2\pi}{3}\right) - 2$

6. a)

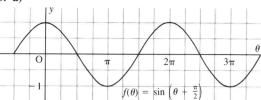

$f(\theta) = \sin\left(\theta + \frac{\pi}{2}\right)$

b)

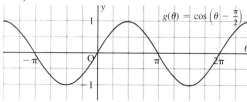

$g(\theta) = \cos\left(\theta - \frac{\pi}{2}\right)$

$f(\theta) = \sin\left(\theta + \frac{\pi}{2}\right)$ is the same graph as

$f(\theta) = \cos\theta$.

$g(\theta) = \cos\left(\theta - \frac{\pi}{2}\right)$ is the same graph as

$g(\theta) = \sin\theta$.

7. Answers may vary.   **a)** $\pm 2\pi,\ \pm 4\pi, \ldots$

   b) $-\frac{\pi}{2}, \frac{3\pi}{2}, \ldots$

8. Answers may vary.   **a)** $\frac{\pi}{2}, \frac{5\pi}{2}, \ldots$

   b) $\pm 2\pi,\ \pm 4\pi, \ldots$

9. **a)** $f(\theta) = a + q$ when $\theta = p + \frac{\pi}{2};\ p - \frac{3\pi}{2}, \ldots$

   b) $f(\theta) = -a + q$ when $\theta = p + \frac{3\pi}{2},$

     $p - \frac{\pi}{2}, \ldots$

10. **a)** $f(\theta) = a + q$ when $\theta = p;\ \pm 2\pi + p; \ldots$

   b) $f(\theta) = -a + q$ when $\theta = \pm \pi + p; \ldots$

11. Typical answer: $f(\theta) = \sin\left(\theta + \frac{\pi}{2}\right) + 2$

12. Typical answer: $f(\theta) = \cos(\theta + \pi) - 4$

Exercises 5-10, page 241

2. **a)** $y = \sin 3\theta$ **b)** $y = \sin 6\theta$

3. **a)** $2, \pi$ **b)** $3, 4\pi$

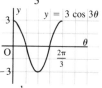

   c) $4, \pi$ **d)** $4, 4\pi$

   e) $5, \pi$ **f)** $3, \dfrac{2\pi}{3}$

4. **a)** $5; \frac{2\pi}{3}; \pi$ **b)** $2; \frac{\pi}{2}; -\frac{\pi}{2}$ **c)** $2.5; \frac{\pi}{3}; \frac{2\pi}{3}$

   d) $0.5; \frac{2\pi}{5}; -\frac{5\pi}{4}$

5. **a)** $1; \pi; \frac{\pi}{3}$

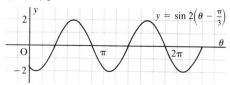

b) $2; \frac{2\pi}{3}; \frac{\pi}{2}$

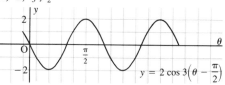

c) $4; 4\pi; -\pi$

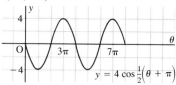

d) $0.5; 4\pi; \frac{5\pi}{4};$ only 1 cycle shown

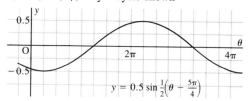

6. **a) i)**

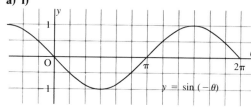

ii)

iii)

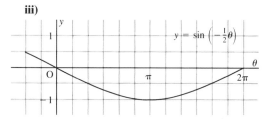

b) Answers may vary.

c) For $y = \sin k\theta$, see the graphs in part a).

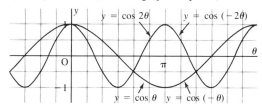

d) Answers may vary.

7. a) $\frac{2\pi}{3}$

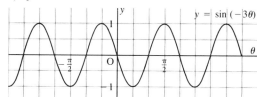

b) 4π

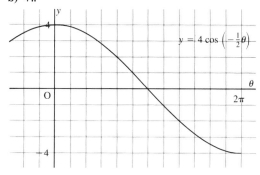

c) π

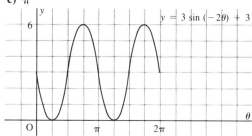

8. a) $y = \sin(-\theta)$ is a reflection of $y = \sin\theta$ in the y-axis.

b) $y = \cos(-\theta)$ is the same graph as $y = \cos\theta$.

The Mathematical Mind, page 243

1. a) 6 **b)** 120 **c)** 5040 **d)** 40 320
e) 362 880 **f)** 3 628 800

2. $\sin x = x - \dfrac{x^3}{6} + \dfrac{x^5}{120} - \dfrac{x^7}{5040}$
$+ \dfrac{x^9}{362\ 880} - \dfrac{x^{11}}{39\ 916\ 800};$
$\cos x = 1 - \dfrac{x^2}{2} + \dfrac{x^4}{24} - \dfrac{x^6}{720} + \dfrac{x^8}{40\ 320}$
$- \dfrac{x^{10}}{3\ 628\ 800}$

4. a) 3 **b)** 4 **c)** 5

Exercises 5-11, page 247

1. a) i) 2 **ii)** 2π
iii) Typical answer: $\frac{\pi}{4}$ for cosine function
iv) $y = 5$ when $\theta = \frac{\pi}{4}, \frac{9\pi}{4}, \ldots$
v) $y = 1$ when $\theta = \frac{5\pi}{4}, \ldots$ **vi)** 3
b) i) 3 **ii)** π
iii) Typical answer: $\frac{\pi}{2}$ for sine function
iv) $y = 6$ when $\theta = -\frac{\pi}{4}, \frac{3\pi}{4}, \frac{7\pi}{4}, \ldots$
v) $y = 0$ when $\theta = \frac{\pi}{4}, \frac{5\pi}{4}, \ldots$ **vi)** 3
c) i) 5 **ii)** 2π
iii) Typical answer: $\frac{\pi}{6}$ for cosine function
iv) $y = 20$ when $\theta = \frac{\pi}{6}, \frac{13\pi}{6}, \ldots$
v) $y = 10$ when $\theta = \frac{7\pi}{6}, \frac{19\pi}{6}, \ldots$ **vi)** 15

2. Typical answers: **a)** $y = 2\cos\left(\theta - \frac{\pi}{4}\right) + 3$

b) $y = 3 \sin 2\left(\theta - \frac{\pi}{2}\right) + 3$

c) $y = 5 \cos \left(\theta - \frac{\pi}{6}\right) + 15$

3. a) $\frac{\pi}{3}$; π **b)** 4; 2

c)

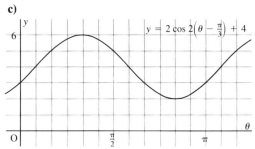

4. a) $\frac{\pi}{4}$, π **b)** 3; 3

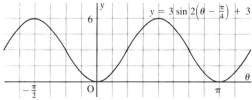

5. a) $\frac{\pi}{2}$; $\frac{2\pi}{3}$

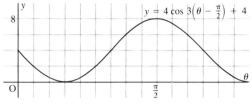

b) $-\pi$; $\frac{\pi}{2}$

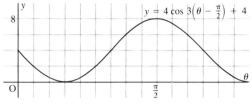

c) $-\frac{\pi}{6}$; π

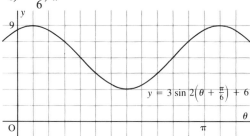

d) $\frac{\pi}{6}$, $\frac{2\pi}{3}$

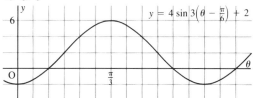

6. a)

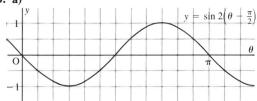

b)

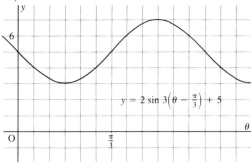

c)

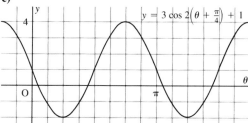

$y = 3 \cos 2\left(\theta + \frac{\pi}{4}\right) + 1$

d)

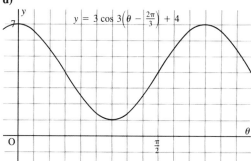

$y = 3 \cos 3\left(\theta - \frac{2\pi}{3}\right) + 4$

7. Answers may vary.

8. a) $\frac{\pi}{2}$; π

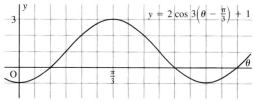

$y = \sin 2\left(\theta - \frac{\pi}{2}\right)$

b) $\frac{\pi}{3}$; $\frac{2\pi}{3}$

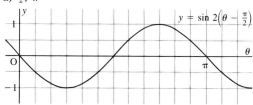

$y = 2 \cos 3\left(\theta - \frac{\pi}{3}\right) + 1$

c) $\frac{\pi}{3}$; $\frac{2\pi}{3}$; same shape as part b) but shifted 3 units up.

d) $-\frac{\pi}{4}$; $\frac{\pi}{2}$

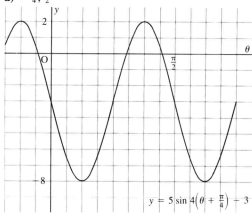

$y = 5 \sin 4\left(\theta + \frac{\pi}{4}\right) - 3$

9. a)

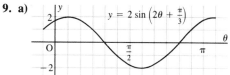

$y = 2 \sin\left(2\theta + \frac{\pi}{3}\right)$

b)

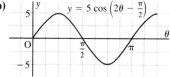

$y = 5 \cos\left(2\theta - \frac{\pi}{2}\right)$

c) Same shape as part b), but y-axis labelled with 3 in place of 5

d) Same shape as part a), but y-axis labelled with 5 in place of 2

10. a and c **11.** a and b

12. a) Typical answers: 0, $\pm\pi$, $\pm 2\pi$, $\pm 3\pi$
b) $n\pi$, where n is an integer

13. a) Typical answers:

$-\frac{11\pi}{4}$, $-\frac{7\pi}{4}$, $-\frac{3\pi}{4}$, $\frac{\pi}{4}$, $\frac{5\pi}{4}$, $\frac{9\pi}{4}$

b) $n\pi + \frac{\pi}{4}$, where n is an integer

14. Answers may vary.

15. a) 0; 1
 b)

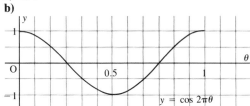

16. a) 0; 1

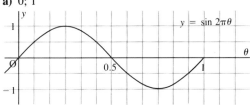

 b) 0; 4

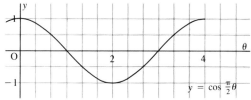

 c) 0; 4

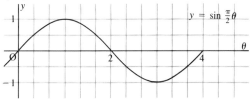

Exercises 5-12, page 254

1. a) 3; 5; 1; 4   **b)** 2; 4; 5; 6
2. a) 2; 12; typical answer: 2; 3
 b) 6; 4; typical answer: 0; 8
 c) 10; 40; typical answer: -5; 20
3. a) $y = 2 \sin \dfrac{2\pi(t - 2)}{12} + 3$

 b) $y = 6 \cos \dfrac{2\pi t}{4} + 8$

 c) $y = 10 \cos \dfrac{2\pi(t + 5)}{40} + 20$

4. a) $y = \sin \pi t$ **b)** $y = \cos \pi t$ **c)** $y = \cos \dfrac{\pi t}{2}$
 d) $y = \sin \dfrac{\pi t}{2}$
5. a) $y = 5 \cos 2\pi(t - 9) + 4$
 b) $y = 12 \cos 4\pi(t + 3) + 1.5$
 c) $y = 2.4 \cos \dfrac{2\pi(t - 19)}{27} + 15.1$

6. a)

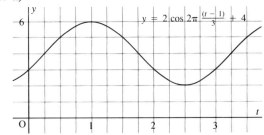

 b)

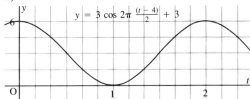

 c)

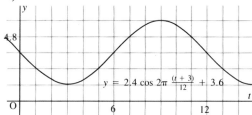

 d)

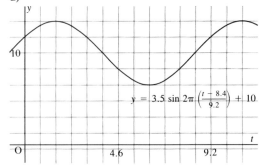

7. a) See page 250.

b)

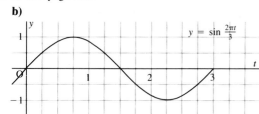

$y = \sin \frac{2\pi t}{3}$

c)

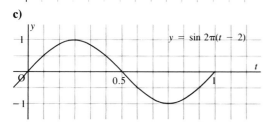

$y = \sin 2\pi(t - 2)$

d)

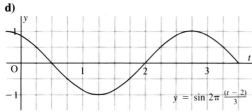

$y = \sin 2\pi \frac{(t - 2)}{3}$

e) See page 250.

f)

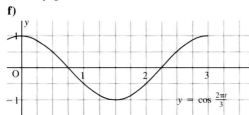

$y = \cos \frac{2\pi t}{3}$

g)

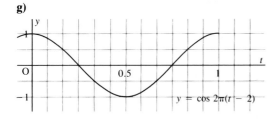

$y = \cos 2\pi(t - 2)$

h)

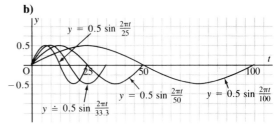

$y = \cos 2\pi \frac{(t - 2)}{3}$

8. a) $y = 5$ when $t = -5, -2, 1, 4$;
$y = 1$ when $t = -3.5, -0.5, 2.5$
b) $y = 0$ when $t = -0.75, 4.25$;
$y = -8$ when $t = -3.25, 1.75$
c) $y = 8$ when $t = -4.25, -1.25, 1.75, 4.75$;
$y = 4$ when $t = -2.75, 0.25, 3.25$
d) $y = 7$ when $t = -3, 3$; $y = -3$ when $t = 0$

9. a) $y = 6 \sin \dfrac{2\pi(t - 9)}{5} + 17$

b) $y = 4.3 \sin \dfrac{2\pi(t - 4.7)}{3.9} + 12.9$

10. Typical answer: $y = 2000 \sin \frac{\pi t}{5} + 3000$

11. a)

$y = 80 \sin \frac{2\pi t}{10}$

b) Typical answer: $y = 80 \sin \frac{\pi t}{5}$

12. a) i) 40 cm   **ii)** 0 cm   **iii)** 0.05 s   **b)** 72 000

13. a) $y = 0.5 \sin \frac{\pi t}{50}$; $y = 0.5 \sin \frac{\pi t}{25}$; $y = 0.5 \sin \frac{3\pi t}{50}$;
$y = 0.5 \sin \frac{2\pi t}{25}$

b)

$y = 0.5 \sin \frac{2\pi t}{25}$
$y = 0.5 \sin \frac{2\pi t}{50}$
$y = 0.5 \sin \frac{2\pi t}{100}$
$y \doteq 0.5 \sin \frac{2\pi t}{33.3}$

14. b and c

Exercises 5-13, page 261

1. a) About 4.0 m; 1.7 m
   b) 4.9 m at 7:06 A.M. and 7:30 P.M.

2. About 2.3 m

3. a) $y = 4 \cos \dfrac{2\pi(t - 8.00)}{12.4}$ **b)** About 2.1 m

4. a) $y = 4.6 \cos \dfrac{2\pi(t - 4.50)}{12.4} + 5$
   b) 1.2 m, 7.7 m

5. a) $y = 1.4 \cos \dfrac{2\pi(t - 4.50)}{12.4} + 5$
   b) 3.9 m, 5.8 m

6. a)

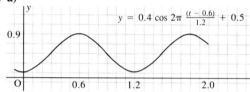

$$y = 0.4 \cos 2\pi \tfrac{(t - 0.6)}{1.2} + 0.5$$

b) Typical answer:
   $$y = 0.4 \cos \dfrac{2\pi(t - 0.6)}{1.2} + 0.5 \text{ or}$$
   $$y = 0.4 \sin \dfrac{2\pi(t - 0.3)}{1.2} + 0.5$$
   c) i) 0.50 m   **ii)** About 0.85 m   **iii)** 0.10 m

7. a)

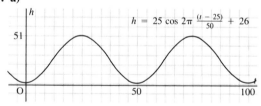

$$h = 25 \cos 2\pi \tfrac{(t - 25)}{50} + 26$$

b) Typical answer: $h = 25 \cos \dfrac{2\pi(t - 25)}{50} + 26$

   c) i) 18 m   **ii)** 46 m   **iii)** 18 m   **iv)** 18 m

8. a)

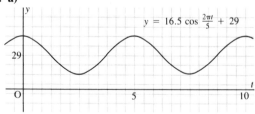

$$y = 16.5 \cos \tfrac{2\pi t}{5} + 29$$

b) Typical answer: $y = 16.5 \cos \tfrac{2\pi t}{5} + 29$
c) i) 45.5 cm   **ii)** 15.7 cm   **iii)** 15.7 cm

9. a) Typical answer:
   $$t = 2.5 \cos \dfrac{2\pi(n - 172)}{365} + 17.7$$
   b) i) 7:34 P.M.   **ii)** 8:10 P.M.   **iii)** 5:50 P.M.
   iv) 3:20 P.M.

10. a) Typical answer: $t = 2 \cos \dfrac{2\pi(n - 172)}{365} + 18.3$
   b) i) 5:19 P.M.   **ii)** 7:05 P.M.   **iii)** 7:58 P.M.
   iv) 4:53 P.M.

11. a) 5:28 A.M.   **b)** Answers may vary.

12. a) Typical answer:
   $$d = 2.5 \cos \dfrac{2\pi(n - 172)}{365} + 149.7$$
   b) i) 148.8 million km   **ii)** 151.3 million km
   iii) 150.5 million km

15. a) Answers may vary.   **b)** Feb. 16 and Oct. 23

16. a) 6:56 A.M.   **b)** 9:02 A.M.

Problem Solving, page 265

1. $y^2 = 2p(x + a^2)$

2. 4

3. $\dfrac{|Ax_1 + By_1 + C|}{\sqrt{A^2 + B^2}}$

4. 55°, 83°, 42°

7. b) Yes   **c) i)** $\tfrac{1}{2}\sqrt{2b^2 + 2c^2 - a^2}$

   ii) $\sqrt{bc\left(1 - \dfrac{a^2}{(b + c)^2}\right)}$

   iii) $\sqrt{c^2 - \left(\dfrac{a^2 - b^2 + c^2}{2a}\right)^2}$

8. 1:5

Review Exercises, page 266

1. a) 60°   **b)** −315°   **c)** 150°   **d)** 269.3°

2. a) $\tfrac{3\pi}{4}$ **b)** $\tfrac{3\pi}{2}$ **c)** $\tfrac{11\pi}{6}$ **d)** −0.82

3. About 35 cm

4. a) 0.914, 0.406, 2.250
   b) −0.882, 0.471, −1.875
   c) 0.868, −0.496, −1.75
   d) −0.640, −0.768, 0.833

5. **a)** **i)** 66.0°   **ii)** 1.153
  b) **i)** 298.1°   **ii)** 5.202
  c) **i)** 119.7°   **ii)** 2.090
  d) **i)** 219.8°   **ii)** 3.836

6. **a)** 47°, 133°   **b)** 113°, 293°   **c)** 101°, 281°

7. **a)** 1.30, 4.98   **b)** 0.82, 3.96   **c)** 5.80, 3.63

8. **a)** $\csc \theta = \dfrac{b}{a}$; $\cos \theta = \dfrac{\sqrt{b^2 - a^2}}{b}$;

$\sec \theta = \dfrac{b}{\sqrt{b^2 - a^2}}$; $\tan \theta = \dfrac{a}{\sqrt{b^2 - a^2}}$;

$\cot \theta = \dfrac{\sqrt{b^2 - a^2}}{a}$

b) $\sin \theta = \dfrac{p}{\sqrt{2p^2 + 2pq + q^2}}$;

$\csc \theta = \dfrac{\sqrt{2p^2 + 2pq + q^2}}{p}$;

$\cos \theta = \dfrac{p + q}{\sqrt{2p^2 + 2pq + q^2}}$;

$\sec \theta = \dfrac{\sqrt{2p^2 + 2pq + q^2}}{p + q}$; $\cot \theta = \dfrac{p + q}{p}$

c) $\sin \theta = \dfrac{\sqrt{3m^2 - 10m - 8}}{2m - 1}$;

$\csc \theta = \dfrac{2m - 1}{\sqrt{3m^2 - 10m - 8}}$; $\cos \theta = \dfrac{m + 3}{2m - 1}$;

$\tan \theta = \dfrac{\sqrt{3m^2 - 10m - 8}}{m + 3}$;

$\cot \theta = \dfrac{m + 3}{\sqrt{3m^2 - 10m - 8}}$

9. **a)** $\sin \frac{5\pi}{6} = \frac{1}{2}$; $\csc \frac{5\pi}{6} = 2$;

$\cos \frac{5\pi}{6} = -\frac{\sqrt{3}}{2}$; $\sec \frac{5\pi}{6} = -\frac{2}{\sqrt{3}}$;

$\tan \frac{5\pi}{6} = -\frac{1}{\sqrt{3}}$; $\cot \frac{5\pi}{6} = -\sqrt{3}$

b) $\sin \frac{\pi}{3} = \frac{\sqrt{3}}{2}$; $\csc \frac{\pi}{3} = \frac{2}{\sqrt{3}}$;

$\cos \frac{\pi}{3} = \frac{1}{2}$; $\sec \frac{\pi}{3} = 2$;

$\tan \frac{\pi}{3} = \sqrt{3}$; $\cot \frac{\pi}{3} = \frac{1}{\sqrt{3}}$

c) $\sin \frac{7\pi}{4} = -\frac{1}{\sqrt{2}}$; $\csc \frac{7\pi}{4} = -\sqrt{2}$;

$\cos \frac{7\pi}{4} = \frac{1}{\sqrt{2}}$; $\sec \frac{7\pi}{4} = \sqrt{2}$;

$\tan \frac{7\pi}{4} = -1$; $\cot \frac{7\pi}{4} = -1$

d) $\sin \frac{4\pi}{3} = -\frac{\sqrt{3}}{2}$; $\csc \frac{4\pi}{3} = -\frac{2}{\sqrt{3}}$;

$\cos \frac{4\pi}{3} = -\frac{1}{2}$; $\sec \frac{4\pi}{3} = -2$;

$\tan \frac{4\pi}{3} = \sqrt{3}$; $\cot \frac{4\pi}{3} = \frac{1}{\sqrt{3}}$

e) $\sin \frac{11\pi}{6} = -\frac{1}{2}$; $\csc \frac{11\pi}{6} = -2$;

$\cos \frac{11\pi}{6} = \frac{\sqrt{3}}{2}$; $\sec \frac{11\pi}{6} = \frac{2}{\sqrt{3}}$;

$\tan \frac{11\pi}{6} = -\frac{1}{\sqrt{3}}$; $\cot \frac{11\pi}{6} = -\sqrt{3}$

10. See page 218.

  a) $\sin \theta$: 1 at $-\frac{3\pi}{2}, \frac{\pi}{2}$; $\cos \theta$; 1 at 0, $\pm 2\pi$

  b) $\sin \theta$: -1 at $-\frac{\pi}{2}, \frac{3\pi}{2}$; $\cos \theta$: -1 at $\pm \pi$

  c) $\sin \theta$: y-intercept 0, θ-intercepts $\pm 2\pi$,
     $\pm \pi$, 0; $\cos \theta$: y-intercept 1,

     θ-intercepts $\pm \frac{3\pi}{2}, \pm \frac{\pi}{2}, 0$

11. **a)** 3; π; $\frac{\pi}{4}$; 4   **b)** 2; $\frac{2\pi}{5}$; $-\frac{\pi}{3}$; 1

12. **a)**

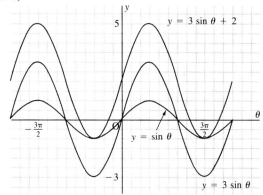

b)

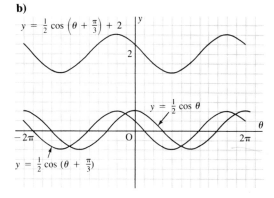

13. a)

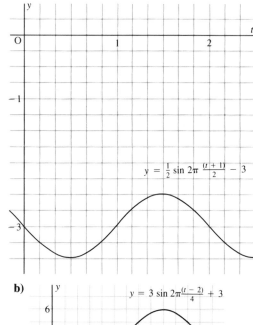

$$y = \tfrac{1}{2}\sin 2\pi\,\tfrac{(t+1)}{2} - 3$$

b)

$$y = 3\sin 2\pi\tfrac{(t-2)}{4} + 3$$

Chapter 6

Exercises 6-1, page 271

5. b) $\dfrac{\sin\theta + \tan\theta}{\csc\theta + \cot\theta} = \sin\theta\tan\theta$

6. b) $\dfrac{\cot\theta}{\csc\theta + 1} = \dfrac{\csc\theta - 1}{\cot\theta}$

7. b) $\dfrac{1}{1+\cos\theta} + \dfrac{1}{1-\cos\theta} = 2\csc^2\theta$

8. b) $\cot^2\theta(1 + \tan^2\theta) = \csc^2\theta$

15. a) $r\sqrt{2 - 2\cos\theta}$; $r\sqrt{2 + 2\cos\theta}$

16. $0, \pi, 2\pi$

Exercises 6-2, page 277

1. a) $-\tfrac{1}{2}$ **b)** $\tfrac{1}{\sqrt{2}}$ **c)** -1 **d)** -1 **e)** $-\tfrac{\sqrt{3}}{2}$

    f) $\tfrac{1}{\sqrt{2}}$ **g)** $\tfrac{\sqrt{3}}{2}$ **h)** $-\tfrac{1}{2}$

3. a) $-\sqrt{3}$ **b)** $\sqrt{2}$ **c)** -2 **d)** $-\tfrac{1}{\sqrt{3}}$

    e) $-\tfrac{\sqrt{3}}{2}$ **f)** $-\tfrac{1}{2}$ **g)** $-\tfrac{1}{2}$ **h)** 1

4. $\sin\theta = \sin(\pi - \theta)$;
    $\sin(\pi - \theta) = -\sin(\pi + \theta)$

6. $\sin\theta = \cos\left(\tfrac{\pi}{2} - \theta\right)$

7. b) $\sin(\pi + \theta) = -\sin(\pi - \theta)$;
    $\sin\left(\tfrac{3\pi}{2} + \theta\right) = \sin\left(\tfrac{3\pi}{2} - \theta\right)$;

    $\sin(2\pi + \theta) = -\sin(2\pi - \theta)$;
    $\cos(\pi + \theta) = \cos(\pi - \theta)$;

    $\cos\left(\tfrac{3\pi}{2} + \theta\right) = -\cos\left(\tfrac{3\pi}{2} - \theta\right)$;

    $\cos(2\pi + \theta) = \cos(2\pi - \theta)$

Exercises 6-3, page 283

2. a) 1 **b)** 0 **c)** $\tfrac{1}{2}$ **d)** $\tfrac{1}{2}$

3. a), b), c) $-\tfrac{1}{2}$

4. a), b), c) $\tfrac{1}{\sqrt{2}}$

5. b) $\cos\tfrac{\pi}{12} = \dfrac{\sqrt{3}+1}{2\sqrt{2}}$

6. a) $\dfrac{1-\sqrt{3}}{2\sqrt{2}}$ **b)** $\dfrac{\sqrt{3}-1}{2\sqrt{2}}$ **c)** $\dfrac{\sqrt{3}-1}{2\sqrt{2}}$

    d) $\dfrac{\sqrt{3}+1}{2\sqrt{2}}$

9. a) $-\cos\theta$ **b)** $\cos\theta$ **c)** $\sin x$ **d)** $\sin x$

10. a) $\dfrac{4\sqrt{3}+3}{10}$ **b)** $\dfrac{7}{5\sqrt{2}}$ **c)** $\dfrac{3+4\sqrt{3}}{10}$

11. a) $\dfrac{\sqrt{15}-2}{6}$ **b)** $\dfrac{-2-\sqrt{15}}{6}$ **c)** $\dfrac{\sqrt{5}-2}{3\sqrt{2}}$

12. a) $\dfrac{3-\sqrt{21}}{8}$ **b)** $\dfrac{3-\sqrt{21}}{8}$ **c)** $\dfrac{-\sqrt{7}-3}{4\sqrt{2}}$

13. b) i) $\cos\theta$ **ii)** $\sqrt{3}\cos\theta$
    c) $\sin(x+y) + \sin(x-y) = 2\sin x\cos y$

14. a) $-\tfrac{16}{65}$ **b)** $\tfrac{56}{65}$ **c)** $\tfrac{63}{65}$ **d)** $-\tfrac{33}{65}$

15. a) $\dfrac{4\sqrt{5}-6}{15}$ **b)** $\dfrac{4\sqrt{5}+6}{15}$ **c)** $\dfrac{-3\sqrt{5}-8}{15}$

    d) $\dfrac{-3\sqrt{5}+8}{15}$

16. Values do exist; some examples are:

    a) $\beta = 0$ **b)** $\alpha = \tfrac{\pi}{3}, \beta = -\tfrac{\pi}{3}$ **c)** $\beta = 0$

Exercises 6-4, page 287

3. a) $\sin 1.2$ **b)** $\sin 6$ **c)** $\sin 4$ **d)** $\cos 0.9$
   e) $\cos 10$ **f)** $\cos 6$

4. a) $\sin \frac{\pi}{3}$ **b)** $\cos \frac{\pi}{5}$ **c)** $\cos 1$

5. $\frac{\sqrt{3}}{2}$, $-\frac{1}{2}$

6. $1, 0$

7. Answers may vary.

8. a) $\frac{4\sqrt{2}}{9}$ **b)** $\frac{7}{9}$ **c)** $\frac{4\sqrt{2}}{7}$

9. a) $-\frac{\sqrt{3}}{2}$, $-\frac{1}{2}$, $\sqrt{3}$ **b)** $\frac{4\sqrt{5}}{9}$, $\frac{1}{9}$, $4\sqrt{5}$

   c) $\frac{24}{25}$, $\frac{7}{25}$, $\frac{24}{7}$

11. b) $\dfrac{1 + \cos 2\theta}{2}$

13. b) $\dfrac{(\sin \theta - \cos \theta)^2}{\sin 2\theta}$

14. a) $\tan \theta$ **b)** $\tan \theta$ **c)** $\cot \theta$

15. a) $-\frac{3}{4}$

16. a)

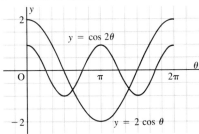

b) The graphs do not coincide.
c) $\theta = 0, \pm\pi, \pm 2\pi, \ldots$

17. a)

b) The graphs do not coincide.
c) Approximately 1.95, 4.34, . . .

Exercises 6-5, page 293

1. a) 0.52, 1.57, 2.62   **b)** 1.05, 5.24
   c) 0.46, 0.79, 3.61, 3.93
   d) 0.99, 2.43, 4.14, 5.57

2. a) 0, 1.05, 3.14, 5.24
   b) 0.45, 2.69, 4.02, 5.41
   c) 0.72, 5.56   **d)** 1.24, 2.03, 4.25, 5.04

3. a) $\frac{\pi}{3}$, $\frac{2\pi}{3}$ **b)** $\frac{\pi}{6}$, $\frac{5\pi}{6}$, $\frac{3\pi}{2}$ **c)** $\frac{3\pi}{4}$, $\frac{7\pi}{4}$ **d)** $0, \pi$

4. a) $\frac{7\pi}{12} + n\pi$, $\frac{11\pi}{12} + n\pi$ **b)** $\frac{7\pi}{24} + \frac{n\pi}{2}$, $\frac{11\pi}{24} + \frac{n\pi}{2}$
   c) No solution
   d) $\pi + n\pi$, $0.244\,978\,7 + n\pi$

5. 7:26 A.M., 7:50 P.M.

6. a)

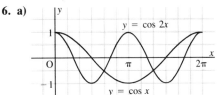

b) $\frac{\pi}{3}$, π, $\frac{5\pi}{3}$
c)

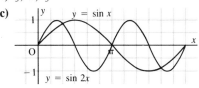

0, $\frac{2\pi}{3}$, π, $\frac{4\pi}{3}$

7. $46°$

8. Answers may vary. Typical answers are:
   a) $\sin x = 2$
   b) $\cos x = x^2 + 1$
   c) $\sin x = \frac{1}{2}x$

9. a) 0   **b)** 0.739 085   **c)** 0

Problem Solving, page 296

2. a) i) 2   **ii)** 4   **iii)** 7   **b)** No
   c) Answers may vary.

5. $3x - 4y - 9 = 0$ and $3x - 4y - 29 = 0$

6. $4x - 3y + 6 = 0$, $4x - 3y + 21 = 0$; or
   $4x + 3y - 6 = 0$, $4x + 3y - 21 = 0$

7. 22 square units

Review Exercises, page 297

3. a) $-\frac{\sqrt{3}}{2}$ **b)** $\sqrt{2}$ **c)** $\sqrt{3}$ **d)** $-\frac{\sqrt{3}}{2}$

4. a) $\frac{\sqrt{3}-1}{2\sqrt{2}}$ **b)** $\frac{\sqrt{3}-1}{2\sqrt{2}}$ **c)** $\frac{\sqrt{3}}{2}$ **d)** $\frac{\sqrt{3}}{2}$

5. a) $\frac{\sqrt{3}-1}{2\sqrt{2}}$ **b)** $\frac{-1-\sqrt{3}}{2\sqrt{2}}$ **c)** $\frac{1-\sqrt{3}}{2\sqrt{2}}$

  d) $\frac{1-\sqrt{3}}{2\sqrt{2}}$

6. a) $\frac{3\sqrt{7}-2}{10}$ **b)** $\frac{\sqrt{21}-2}{5\sqrt{2}}$

7. a) $\frac{3\sqrt{7}-12}{20}$ **b)** $\frac{3\sqrt{7}+12}{20}$ **c)** $\frac{-9-4\sqrt{7}}{20}$

  d) $\frac{-9+4\sqrt{7}}{20}$

8. a) $\cos\frac{\pi}{3}$ **b)** $\sin 1.6$ **c)** $\cos 0.7$

9. a) $-\frac{\sqrt{15}}{8}$ **b)** $\frac{7}{8}$ **c)** $-\frac{\sqrt{15}}{7}$

11. a) 0.25, 0.52, 2.62, 2.89   **b)** 2.30, 3.98
  c) 1.57, 3.67, 4.71, 5.76
  d) 1.15, 1.99, 4.29, 5.13

Cumulative Review, Chapters 5, 6, page 298

1. a) 135°   **b)** −210°   **c)** 154.70°   **d)** −660°

2. a) $\frac{7\pi}{6}$ **b)** $-\frac{5\pi}{4}$ **c)** 2.57 radians   **d)** $\frac{3\pi}{2}$

3. a) i) $\frac{1}{\sqrt{10}}, \frac{3}{\sqrt{10}}, \frac{1}{3}$ **ii)** $-\frac{2}{\sqrt{29}}, -\frac{5}{\sqrt{29}}, \frac{2}{5}$

  iii) $-\frac{2}{\sqrt{13}}, \frac{3}{\sqrt{13}}, -\frac{2}{3}$

  b) i) 18.4°   **ii)** 201.8°   **iii)** 326.3°

4. a) 0.87, 2.27   **b)** 2.16, 5.30   **c)** 0.52, 5.76

5. a) $\csc\theta = \frac{b-c}{a}$; $\cos\theta = \frac{\sqrt{(b-c)^2-a^2}}{b-c}$;

  $\sec\theta = \frac{b-c}{\sqrt{(b-c)^2-a^2}}$;

  $\tan\theta = \frac{a}{\sqrt{(b-c)^2-a^2}}$;

  $\cot\theta = \frac{\sqrt{(b-c)^2-a^2}}{a}$

b) $\tan\theta = \frac{q}{2p}$; $\sin\theta = \frac{q}{\sqrt{4p^2+q^2}}$;

  $\csc\theta = \frac{\sqrt{4p^2+q^2}}{q}$;

  $\cos\theta = \frac{2p}{\sqrt{4p^2+q^2}}$; $\sec\theta = \frac{\sqrt{4p^2+q^2}}{2p}$

6. a) $2, \frac{2\pi}{3}, \frac{\pi}{6}, 0$ **b)** $\frac{1}{2}, \pi, -\frac{\pi}{4}, -1$

8. a) $\frac{1+\sqrt{3}}{2\sqrt{2}}$ **b)** $\frac{1+\sqrt{3}}{2\sqrt{2}}$ **c)** $\frac{\sqrt{3}+1}{1-\sqrt{3}}$

9. a) $\frac{\sqrt{5}-2\sqrt{15}}{12}$ **b)** $\frac{5\sqrt{3}-2}{12}$ **c)** $\frac{1}{9}$

  d) $\frac{\sqrt{5}+2\sqrt{15}}{12}$

10. a) $\frac{\pi}{6}, \frac{5\pi}{6}$, 3.87, 5.55   **b)** 0.72, 1.23, 5.05, 5.56

Chapter 7

Exercises 7-1, page 302

1. a) About 9 years   **b)** About 14 years
3. About 45 years   **5.** About 6 bounces
7. About 27 m   **9.** $P = 80(2)^{\frac{n}{20}}$
10. $P = 300(2)^{\frac{d}{5}}$
11. $P = 100(0.95)^n$
12. $C = 100(0.5)^n$

Exercises 7-2, page 307

1. a) 1   **b)** $\frac{1}{5}$ **c)** $\frac{8}{125}$ **d)** $\frac{1}{8}$ **e)** $\frac{1}{16}$ **f)** 1
  g) 4   **h)** $\frac{16}{81}$ **i)** $\frac{1}{64}$ **j)** $\frac{9}{25}$ **k)** 81   **l)** $\frac{64}{27}$

2. a) 3   **b)** $\frac{1}{9}$ **c)** 2.5   **d)** 5   **e)** 5   **f)** $\frac{1}{2}$
  g) $\frac{1}{1000}$ **h)** 2   **i)** $\frac{7}{5}$ **j)** $\frac{1}{9}$ **k)** 0.5   **l)** 2

3. a) $\frac{1}{216}$ **b)** 9   **c)** 4   **d)** $\frac{1}{32}$ **e)** $\frac{1}{243}$ **f)** $\frac{27}{8}$
  g) $\frac{125}{27}$ **h)** $\frac{1}{1000}$ **i)** $\frac{4}{25}$ **j)** $\frac{125}{27}$ **k)** 32   **l)** $\frac{1}{27}$

4. a) 32   **b)** $\frac{1}{125}$ **c)** $\frac{1}{243}$ **d)** 8000   **e)** 8
  f) 8   **g)** 1   **h)** $\frac{32}{3125}$ **i)** 2   **j)** $\frac{16}{81}$ **k)** $\frac{8}{27}$
  l) 1

5. a) 3.278   **b)** 16.442   **c)** 5.481   **d)** 8.000
  e) 121.268   **f)** 3.386   **g)** 0.480   **h)** 0.170
  i) 68.470   **j)** 10.600   **k)** 0.150   **l)** 0.700

6. a) m^{-6} **b)** x^5 **c)** $-45a^7$ **d)** $-14s^{15}$
  e) $-9m^5$ **f)** $\frac{64n}{5}$

7. a) x^{-1} **b)** $s^{-\frac{1}{4}}$ **c)** $-3m^{-2}$ **d)** $-3a^{\frac{3}{5}}$
e) $n^{\frac{49}{60}}$ **f)** $-4x^{\frac{3}{4}}$

8. a) 5 **b)** 7 **c)** $\frac{17}{72}$ **d)** 0 **e)** 11 **f)** $\frac{1}{2}$
g) 256 **h)** $\frac{33}{16}$ **i)** 2.7

9. a) i) 8000 **ii)** 22 627 **iii)** 2828
b) i) 1000 **ii)** 1414 **iii)** 630

10. a) $P = 24.3(1.0185)^t$ **b)** 20.2 million

11. a) $N = 100(10)^{\frac{t}{7}}$ **b)** 3.7×10^8

12. a) $-7a^9b^{-8}$ **b)** $20m^{-7}n^3$ **c)** $9x^9y^{-12}$
d) $12a^3b^{-4}c^{-4}$ **e)** $10n^4$ **f)** $\frac{15x^{-4}z^5}{2}$

13. a) $-4b^{\frac{1}{3}}$ **b)** $\frac{5mn^{-1}}{2}$ **c)** $x^{\frac{4}{5}}y^{\frac{3}{5}}$ **d)** $a^{-\frac{9}{2}}b^{\frac{11}{4}}$
e) $m^{-\frac{5}{6}}n^{\frac{8}{9}}$ **f)** $a^{-1}b^2$

14. a) $-3m^{\frac{1}{3}}n^{-\frac{1}{2}}$ **b)** $-42a^{\frac{1}{6}}b^{\frac{1}{6}}$ **c)** $-2x^{-\frac{5}{4}}$
d) $2a^{-1}b^{\frac{3}{10}}c^{-\frac{7}{15}}$ **e)** $-\frac{2a^{\frac{1}{4}}c^{-3}}{21}$ **f)** $-\frac{40x^{-\frac{7}{4}}z^{\frac{7}{4}}}{9}$

15. a) 16 **b)** 32 **c)** $\frac{1}{1024}$ **d)** $\frac{1}{4096}$

16. a) $-\frac{16}{9}$ **b)** $\frac{59\,049}{4096}$ **c)** 1.5 **d)** 2187

17. a) $a^{\frac{9}{2}}$ **b)** $4a^{-4}$ **c)** $216a^{39}$

18. a) $6x^9$ **b)** $\frac{4x^{-12}}{27}$ **c)** $\frac{9x^3}{4}$

19. a) 1 **b)** s^{8n} **c)** a **d)** $m^{bc-ac-ab}$ **e)** x^{-2a+2}
f) $\frac{a^{x-4y}}{9}$ **g)** $x^{-\frac{a}{6}}$ **h)** $m^{-\frac{5n}{6}}n^{-\frac{3m}{4}}$ **i)** $a^{-\frac{10x}{3}}$

20. a) 31.544 **b)** 36.462 **c)** 25.955 **d)** 1.823
e) 0.013 **f)** 0.064 **g)** 3.416 **h)** 3.040

21. a) i) 4 **ii)** 0.25 **iii)** 0.25 **iv)** 4 **v)** 2
vi) 0.5 **vii)** 0.5 **viii)** 2

22. a) $5^{\frac{4}{3}}$ **b)** 2^{2x+1} **c)** 2^{2x+2}

Problem Solving, page 311

1. 7.75 cm²
2. a) Powers of 6 **b)** Powers of 12
3. $(20 + 10\sqrt{3})$ cm
4. $3x - 4y + 2 = 0$, $3x - 4y + 22 = 0$
5. There are two angles such that one is double the other.
6. a) $n!$ **c)** $\frac{(2n)!}{2^n(n!)}$
7. $\dfrac{b}{\sqrt{b^2\cos^2\theta + a^2\sin^2\theta}}$

Mathematics Around Us, page 312

1. a) 10 000 **b)** 10 000 000 **3. a)** 316
b) 10 000 **c)** 31 623 **4. a)** 8 **b)** 7943
5. a) Trumpet, clarinet
b) Bassoon, 3; flute, 5; trumpet, clarinet, 6
6. 316 **7. a)** 100 **b)** 2.5
8. a) $t = 8(0.5)^{\frac{d-90}{5}}$ **b) i)** 2 h **ii)** 2 min, 28 s

Exercises 7-3, page 317

1. a) iv **b)** iii **c)** i **d)** ii
2. Answers may vary.

3. a)

x	-2	-1	0	1	2
3^x	0.11	0.33	1	3	9
$\left(\frac{1}{3}\right)^x$	9	3	1	0.33	0.11

b)
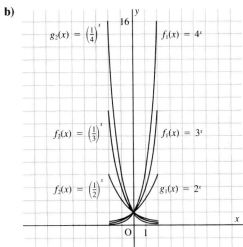

4.
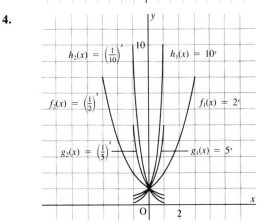

5. a) 6   **b)** 2   **c)** 8   **d)** 4   **e)** $\frac{1}{8}$ **f)** 6
g) 7   **h)** 27

8.

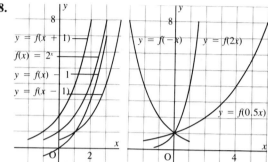

c)

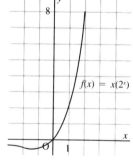

9. a) $a \in R$, $x = 0$ or $a = 1$, $x \in R$
    b) $a > 1$, $x > 0$ or $0 < a < 1$, $x < 0$
    c) $0 < a < 1$, $x > 0$ or $a > 1$, $x < 0$

10.

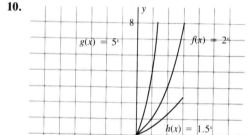

11. Answers may vary.

12. a)   **b)**

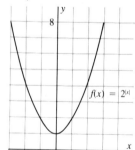 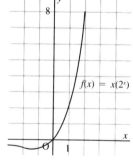

Exercises 7-4, page 323

1. a) 2   **b)** 3   **c)** 6   **d)** 1   **e)** -1 **f)** -3
    g) 0   **h)** $\frac{1}{3}$ **i)** 5   **j)** $\frac{1}{5}$ **k)** $\frac{2}{3}$ **l)** n

2. a) $10^{0.6990}$ **b)** $10^{1.2553}$ **c)** $10^{1.7952}$ **d)** $10^{3.6882}$
    e) $10^{-0.6021}$ **f)** $10^{-0.0969}$ **g)** $10^{-1.6990}$
    h) $10^{2.2218}$

3. a) 5   **b)** 9   **c)** 1

4. a) 12   **b)** -7 **c)** -12

5. a) $10\,000 = 10^4$ **b)** $10 = 10^1$
    c) $0.01 = 10^{-2}$

6. a) $\log 1000 = 3$ **b)** $\log 1 = 0$
    c) $\log 0.001 = -3$

7. 600

8. a) 100   **b)** 100 000   **c)** 0.001   **d)** 1   **e)** 10
    f) 10^{10}

9. a) 4   **b)** 5   **c)** -3 **d)** 100   **e)** 20
    f) 0.2

10. a) i) 0.301 03   **ii)** 1.301 03   **iii)** 2.301 03
     iv) 3.301 03   **v)** $-0.698\ 97$ **vi)** $-1.698\ 97$
     vii) $-2.698\ 97$ **viii)** $-3.698\ 97$
     b) Answers may vary.

Exercises 7-5, page 327

1. a) $\log 42$ **b)** $\log 4$ **c)** $\log 24$ **d)** $\log 7$
    e) $\log 84$ **f)** $\log 0.5$ **g)** $\log 10$ **h)** $\log 90$
    i) $\log 21$ **j)** $\log 28$

2. Answers may vary. Typical answers:
    a) $\log 2 + \log 5$ **b)** $\log 3 + \log 7$
    c) $\log 4 + \log 7$ **d)** $\log 3 + \log 12$
    e) $\log 3 + \log 3$ **f)** $\log 4 + \log 11$
    g) $\log 3 + \log 19$ **h)** $\log 11 + \log 11$

3. Answers may vary. Typical answers:
  a) $\log 10 - \log 2$ **b)** $\log 16 - \log 2$
  c) $\log 24 - \log 2$ **d)** $\log 26 - \log 2$
  e) $\log 20 - \log 2$ **f)** $\log 42 - \log 2$
  g) $\log 34 - \log 2$ **h)** $\log 80 - \log 2$

4. a) $2 \log 3$ **b)** $2 \log 5$ **c)** $3 \log 2$
  d) $3 \log 3$ **e)** $3 \log 10$ **f)** $5 \log 2$
  g) $3 \log 7$ **h)** $7 \log 2$

5. a) $\log 36$ **b)** $\log 64$ **c)** $\log 81$ **d)** $\log 49$
  e) $\log 243$ **f)** $\log 16$ **g)** $\log 216$
  h) $\log 100\,000$

6. a) $1.477\,12$ **b)** $3.477\,12$ **c)** $-0.522\,88$
  d) $-2.522\,88$ **e)** $0.954\,24$ **f)** $1.908\,48$
  g) $0.238\,56$ **h)** $0.095\,42$

7. a) $2.795\,88$ **b)** $0.232\,99$ **c)** $-0.698\,97$
  d) $-1.397\,94$

8. a) 0.8451 **b)** 2.8451 **c)** -1.1549
  d) -0.1549 **e)** 5.8451 **f)** -2.1549

9. a) $3 + \log a + \log b$ **b)** $2 \log a + \log b$
  c) $\log a + \frac{1}{2} \log b$ **d)** $\log a - 2 \log b$
  e) $\frac{1}{2} \log a - \log b$ **f)** $\frac{1}{3} \log a - 2 \log b$

10. a) $1 + 2 \log x$ **b)** $\frac{1}{2} \log x$ **c)** $\frac{1}{2} + \log x$
  d) $\frac{1}{2} + \frac{1}{2} \log x$ **e)** $1 + \frac{1}{2} \log x$

11. a) $\log \left(\dfrac{xy}{z} \right)$ **b)** $\log \left(\dfrac{m}{np} \right)$ **c)** $\log \left(\dfrac{ab}{cd} \right)$
  d) $\log \left(\dfrac{a^2 + ab}{a - b} \right)$

12. a) $\log (a^2 b^5)$ **b)** $\log (x^3 y^{\frac{1}{2}})$ **c)** $\log \left(\dfrac{m^2 n}{p^5} \right)$
  d) $\log \left(\dfrac{x^{\frac{1}{2}}}{y^2 z} \right)$ **e)** $\log \left(\dfrac{a^3 b^{\frac{1}{2}}}{c^{\frac{5}{4}}} \right)$ **f)** $\log \left(\dfrac{a^{10} c^{\frac{1}{2}}}{b^3 d} \right)$

13. a) $\log \left(\dfrac{x + 3}{x - 1} \right),\ x \neq 1$
  b) $\log \left(\dfrac{2x - 7}{x + 3} \right),\ x \neq -3$
  c) $\log \left(\dfrac{a + 2}{a - 2} \right),\ a \neq 2$
  d) $\log \left(\dfrac{8a + 15}{2a + 3} \right),\ a \neq -1.5$

14. a) $x + y$ **b)** $y - x$ **c)** $1 + x + y$
  d) $2x + y$ **e)** $x + 2y$ **f)** $2x + 2y$
  g) $2x + 2y - 1$ **h)** $-x - y$

15. a) $3^{1.7712437}$ **b)** $2^{2.3219281}$ **c)** $2^{4.8579809}$
  d) $8^{2.0889288}$ **e)** $0.5^{-1.5849625}$ **f)** $6^{-0.4456556}$

16. a) 3.459 **b)** 2.579 **c)** 0.898 **d)** 2.365
  e) -0.415 **f)** -0.398

17. a) $0.630\,929\,8$ **b)** $1.160\,964$ **c)** $-0.564\,575$
  d) $-0.464\,973\,5$ **e)** $-1.547\,952\,1$
  f) $0.769\,124$

18. a) $\log y = 1 + \log x$ **b)** $\log y = -\log x$
  c) $\log y = 2 \log x$ **d)** $\log y = \frac{1}{2} \log x$
  e) $\log y = 1 + \frac{1}{2} \log x$
  f) $\log y = \frac{1}{2} + \frac{1}{2} \log x$

19. a) $x > 2$ **b)** $x > 0$ **c)** $x > 5$
20. a) 3 **b)** 6 **c)** 101

21. a) $y = \dfrac{x + 2}{3x};\ \{x \mid x > 0, x \in \text{R}\}$
  b) $y = 100 + \dfrac{100}{x};\ \{x \mid x > 0, x \in \text{R}\}$
  c) $y = 10^x;\ \text{R}$

22. a) 3376 **b)** 6533 **c)** $39\,751$ **d)** $65\,050$
23. a) $3.056\,912 \times 10^{79}$ **b)** 80
24. a) 218 **b)** 2083 **c)** $20\,734$
  d) Answers may vary.

Mathematics Around Us, page 330

1. a) It's the logarithm of the distance in metres.
  b) The number increases by 3, the distance is 10^3
  times as great.
2. a) 3 **b)** 39
3. a) 5 **b)** km and cm
4. 2 cm **5.** 1 week **7.** 4.8
8. a) 6 **b)** 8 **c)** 12
9. 1.3×10^{26} m **10.** 2.0×10^{26} m **11.** 99.9%

Exercises 7-6, page 336

1. a) $x \doteq 3.3 \log \left(\dfrac{y}{5} \right)$ **b)** $x = \log \left(\dfrac{y}{1.3} \right)$
  c) $x \doteq 78 \log \left(\dfrac{y}{8.2} \right)$ **d)** $x \doteq -3.3 \log \left(\dfrac{y}{6.4} \right)$
  e) $x \doteq 2.3 \log \left(\dfrac{y}{3.5} \right)$
  f) $x \doteq -5.7 \log \left(\dfrac{y}{2.75} \right)$

2. a) $n \doteq 30 \log \left(\dfrac{A}{500} \right)$

b) i) 11.9 years; $500 will amount to $1250 in nearly 12 years

ii) -4.6 years; $350 invested about 4.6 years ago will amount to $500 now

c)

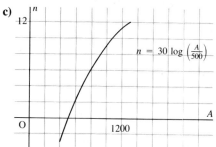

d) $\{A \mid A > 0, A \in R\}$; R

3. a) $n \doteq -6.5 \log \left(\dfrac{h}{2} \right)$

b) i) 3; after 3 bounces, the height is about 0.7 m

ii) 8; after 8 bounces, the height is about 0.12 m

c)

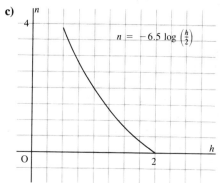

d) N

4. a) $P = 6800(1.018)^n$ **b)** $n \doteq 129 \log \left(\dfrac{P}{6800} \right)$

c) i) 17   **ii)** -12

d) They are inverses of each other.

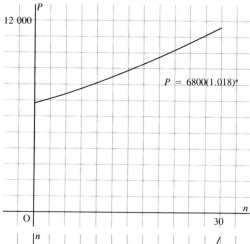

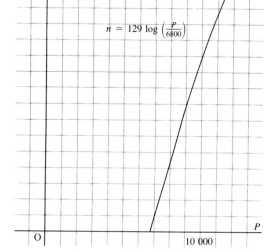

5. a) 3:20 P.M.   **b)** 5:04 P.M.   **c)** 8:57 A.M.

6.

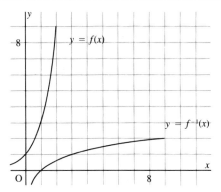

7. a) See page 338.

b)

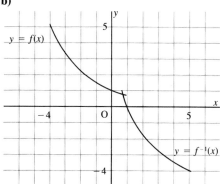

Exercises 7-7, page 340

1. a) $f^{-1}(x) = \log x$ **b)** $g^{-1}(x) = \log_3 x$
  c) $h^{-1}(x) = \log_7 x$ **d)** $f^{-1}(x) = \log_{0.4} x$
  e) $g^{-1}(x) = \log_{\frac{3}{2}} x$ **f)** $h^{-1}(x) = \log_{15} x$

2. a) $f^{-1}(x) = 10^x$ **b)** $g^{-1}(x) = 2^x$
  c) $h^{-1}(x) = 6^x$ **d)** $f^{-1}(x) = \left(\dfrac{1}{2}\right)^x$

  e) $g^{-1}x = \left(\dfrac{5}{4}\right)^x$ **f)** $h^{-1}(x) = 21^x$

3. a) $f^{-1}(x) = \log_5 x$

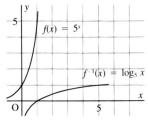

b) $g^{-1}(x) = \log_{\frac{3}{4}} x$

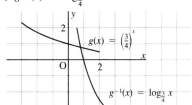

4. a), b) See Exercises 7-6, *Exercise 6.*
  c) $f^{-1}(x) = \log_3 x$
5. a), b)

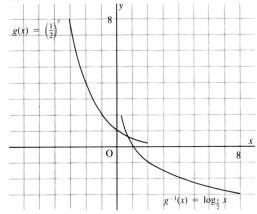

  c) $g^{-1}(x) = \log_{\frac{1}{2}} x$

6. a)   **b)**

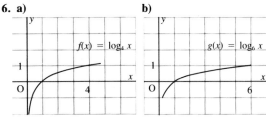

  c) See graph for *Exercise 5*.

d)

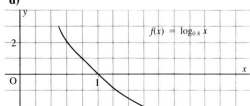

e)

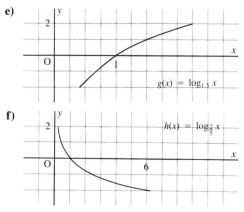

$g(x) = \log_{1.5} x$

f)

$h(x) = \log_{\frac{2}{5}} x$

9. (0.548, 0.548)

10. a) $0 < a < 1$ **b)** Answers may vary.

Exercises 7-8, page 343

1. a) $8 = 2^3$ **b)** $32 = 2^5$ **c)** $\frac{1}{4} = 2^{-2}$
   d) $625 = 5^4$ **e)** $9 = 3^2$ **f)** $3 = 9^{\frac{1}{2}}$

2. a) 4   **b)** 2   **c)** 3   **d)** 2   **e)** -1 **f)** 1
   g) 0   **h)** 4

3. a) 8; 6; 2; 1; -4, -8 **b)** 4; 3; 1; 0.5; -2, -4

4. a) $\frac{1}{2}$ **b)** 4   **c)** 2   **d)** 4   **e)** -3 **f)** -2
   g) 1.5   **h)** 6

5. a) 1.465   **b)** 0.712   **c)** 5.644   **d)** 1.544
   e) 2.377   **f)** 0.750

6. a) $\log_6 36 = 2$ **b)** $\log_4 \left(\frac{1}{16}\right) = -2$
   c) $\log_3 243 = 5$ **d)** $\log_7 343 = 3$
   e) $\log_8 2 = \frac{1}{3}$ **f)** $\log_2 1 = 0$
   g) $\log_5 0.04 = -2$ **h)** $\log_4 \left(\frac{1}{2}\right) = -\frac{1}{2}$
   i) $\log_{\frac{1}{2}} \left(\frac{1}{4}\right) = 2$ **j)** $\log_{\frac{2}{3}} \left(\frac{3}{2}\right) = -1$
   k) $\log_{\frac{1}{9}} \left(\frac{1}{81}\right) = 2$ **l)** $\log_x z = y$

7. a) $400 = 20^2$ **b)** $\frac{1}{49} = 7^{-2}$ **c)** $4 = 8^{\frac{2}{3}}$
   d) $36^2 = 6^4$ **e)** $8 = (0.5)^3$ **f)** $s = r^t$

8. a) 2   **b)** 0   **c)** 4   **d)** 9   **e)** 8   **f)** 81

9. a) 512   **b)** $\frac{1}{4}$ **c)** -1 **d)** 10   **e)** $\frac{1}{4}$ **f)** $\frac{1}{5}$

10. a) $3x + 2y$ **b)** $6x + 2y$

11. a) $2^x - x$ **b)** $\dfrac{2^x}{x}$

12. a) 0   **b)** 14

13. a) i) 3; $\frac{1}{3}$ **ii)** 2; $\frac{1}{2}$ **b)** $\log_a b = \dfrac{1}{\log_b a}$

Exercises 7-9, page 349

1. a) 2   **b)** 1   **c)** 3   **d)** 3   **e)** 3   **f)** 4

2. Answers may vary. Typical answers:
   a) $\log_3 10 + \log_3 2$ **b)** $\log_7 5 + \log_7 9$
   c) $\log_5 10 + \log_5 9$ **d)** $\log_{12} 2 + \log_{12} 3$
   e) $\log_8 5 + \log_8 15$ **f)** $\log_{20} 3 + \log_{20} 13$

3. Answers may vary. Typical answers:
   a) $\log_4 22 - \log_4 2$ **b)** $\log_3 24 - \log_3 2$
   c) $\log_9 10 - \log_9 2$ **d)** $\log_6 14 - \log_6 2$
   e) $\log_{11} 42 - \log_{11} 2$ **f)** $\log_2 26 - \log_2 2$

4. a) 2   **b)** 3   **c)** 2   **d)** 5

5. a) 7   **b)** 7   **c)** 6   **d)** 3   **e)** 2   **f)** 1

6. a) $3 \log_3 2$ **b)** $2 \log_5 6$ **c)** $3 \log_2 3$
   d) $5 \log_6 2$ **e)** $4 \log_{12} 3$ **f)** $3 \log_4 5$

7. a) $\log_2 125$ **b)** $\log_7 16$ **c)** $\log_3 262\,144$
   d) $\log_{12} 1024$ **e)** $\log_2 14\,348\,907$

8. a) 4   **b)** $\frac{5}{3}$ **c)** 1.5   **d)** 2.5   **e)** 1
   f) -1.5 **g)** 1.5   **h)** 1.75

9. a) 4.3219   **b)** 4.6438   **c)** 1.3219   **d)** 1.1610

10. a) 5   **b)** 3   **c)** 2   **d)** 1

11. a) 6.2877   **b)** 3.0959   **c)** $-0.547\,95$
   d) 2.1918

12. a) $y = x^2$; $\{x \mid x > 0, x \in R\}$
   b) $y = (x + 1)^2(x - 1)$; $\{x \mid x > 1, x \in R\}$
   c) $y = 3(x + 3)^2 + 3$; $\{x \mid x > -3, x \in R\}$

13. a) i) 11.550 747   **ii)** 8.228 819   **iii)** 4.906 891
   iv) 1.584 963   **v)** $-1.736\,966$
   vi) $-5.058\,894$ **vii)** $-8.380\,822$
   viii) $-11.702\,750$

14. a) $3x$ **b)** $1 + 3x$ **c)** $0.5x$ **d)** $1 + 1.5x$

15. a) $2 + x$ **b)** $2 + 2x$ **c)** $1 + 1.5x$
   d) $\frac{1}{3}x - 1$

16. a) 6   **b)** 4   **c)** 10   **d)** 12

17. a) 7   **b)** 11   **c)** 0   **d)** 4

18. a) 8   **b)** 9   **c)** 2   **d)** 6   **e)** 2   **f)** 5

19. a) 100   **b)** 18   **c)** 3   **d)** 4   **e)** 3   **f)** 2

20. a) 10.079   **b)** 114.036

21. b) $\dfrac{1}{\log_a x} + \dfrac{1}{\log_b x} = \dfrac{1}{\log_{ab} x}$

Exercises 7-10, page 354

1. $3814.48

2. About 12.9%

3. In 1990, about 3.52×10^{13}

4. Between 10 and 11 years

5. Between 6 and 7 years

6. **a)** $P = 100(0.65)^d$; $P = 100(0.95)^d$;
   $P = 100(0.975)^d$ **b)** 1.6 m; 13.5 m; 27.4 m
   c) 10.7 m; 89.8 m; 181.9 m

7. **a)** About 60%   **b)** About 90

8. 11 300   **9.** About 1.9%   **10.** 3960

11. 2620   **12.** 48 min

14. **a)** 93 years   **b)** 186 years

15. **a)**

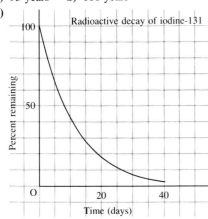

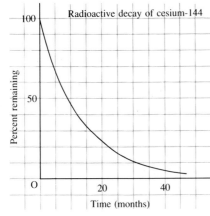

For iodine -131 **b) i)** $P = 100(0.5)^n$
ii) $P = 100(0.5)^{\frac{t}{8.1}}$ **c) i)** 55%   **ii)** 7.7%
iii) 2.7×10^{-12}%   **d) i)** 27 days   **ii)** 81 days
For cesium -144 **b) i)** $P = 100(0.5)^n$
ii) $P = 100(0.5)^{\frac{t}{282}}$ **c) i)** 98%   **ii)** 93%
iii) 41%   **d) i)** 937 days   **ii)** 2810 days

16. **a)** 99.7%   **b)** 97.2%   **c)** 74.9%   **d)** 5.6%

17. **a)** 8.8 g   **b)** 15 g   **c)** 4.1 g   **d)** 2.0 g

18. Between 9 and 10 years

19. **a)** $T = 80(0.5)^{\frac{t}{5}} + 20$ **b)** 15 min

20. **a)** $c = 100(0.5)^{\frac{t}{5}}$ **b) i)** 16.6 h   **ii)** 33.2 h

21. **a)** $L = 2.00(1.2)^n$ **b)** 18

22. **a)** $\frac{5}{6}$ **b)** $t = 0.120\left(\frac{5}{6}\right)^n$ **c)** 27   **d)** 240 m

23. **a)** 2018   **b) i)** 2065   **ii)** 2050
   iii) 2142 is the year when demand exceeds supply

Exercises 7-11, page 360

1. **a) i)** $P_4 = P_0(5)$ **ii)** $P_6 = P_0(5)^{1.5}$
   b) About 2.2

2. About 1.9   **3.** About 2.6   **4.** 5

5. **a)** About 4   **b)** About 3   **c)** About 13

6. **a)** 6 or 7 times as frequent   **b)** 36 to 49 times as
   frequent   **c)** 216 to 343 times as frequent

7. 20

8. **a)** 10   **b)** Answers may vary
   c) i) 50   **ii)** 501

9. 8

10. **a)** $\dfrac{P_2}{P_1} = (0.95)^{\frac{h_2 - h_1}{300}}$ **b)** About 15.7%

11. **a)** $\dfrac{N_2}{N_1} = 4^{\frac{t_2 - t_1}{3}}$ **b) i)** 10 times as many
   ii) 102 times as many   **iii)** 1024 times as many

Investigate, page 361

2.718 281 8

The Mathematical Mind, page 363

1. **a)** $e^{0.6931471} \doteq 2$ **b)** $e^{1.3862944} \doteq 4$
   c) $e^{3.4011974} \doteq 30$ **d)** $e^{4.6051702} \doteq 100$
   e) $e^{9.0768090} \doteq 8750$ **f)** $e^{-0.6931472} \doteq 0.5$
   g) $e^{-2.3025851} \doteq 0.1$ **h)** $e^{-7.7287358} \doteq 0.000\,44$

2. **a)** 1.609 437 9   **b)** 2.708 050 2
   c) 3.987 130 5   **d)** 5.583 496 3   **e)** 0
   f) $-1.386\,294\,4$ **g)** $-2.385\,966\,7$
   h) $-8.111\,728\,1$

3. **a)** 2.718 281 8   **b)** 4.953 032 4
   c) 20.085 537   **d)** 90.017 131   **e)** 1.390 968 1
   f) 0.367 879 4   **g)** 0.246 597 0
   h) 0.110 803 2

4. **a)** ln 15   **b)** ln 20   **c)** ln 36   **d)** ln 9
   e) ln 7   **f)** ln 5

5. **a) i)** 1   **ii)** 2   **iii)** -3 **iv)** 0.2
   b) $\ln e^n = n$

6. a) 4 **b)** 22 **c)** 145 **d)** 72 382
  e) 48 254 942
7. a) 4 **b)** 9 **c)** 42 **d)** 10 478
  e) 4 657 079
8. a) 3.912 023

Mathematics Around Us, page 366

1. a) 57 million; 0.7% **b)** 20 million; 3.0%
  c) 2.6 million; 3.8%
2. a) $P = 770e^{0.016t}$ **b) i)** 903.6 million
  ii) 2001 **iii)** 1958
3. a) 99.8% **b)** 4.53×10^9 years
4. a) 17 600 m; 25 500 m **b)** 5.9 kPa
  c) $h \doteq -6452 \ln \left(\dfrac{P}{130} \right)$

Review Exercises, page 367

1. a) $\frac{1}{4}$ **b)** 3 **c)** 8 **d)** 25 **e)** 3.375
  f) 3.375 **g)** 1 **h)** 0.000 32
2. a) i) 4000 **ii)** 45 255 **b) i)** 125 **ii)** 44
3. a) $5x^3y^{-2}$ **b)** $\dfrac{m^2n}{2}$ **c)** $\dfrac{25a^{-4}b^{-7}}{8}$
  d) $\dfrac{9y^{-\frac{4}{3}}}{25}$ **e)** $-\dfrac{3a^{-\frac{1}{4}}b^{-\frac{1}{3}}}{5}$ **f)** $\dfrac{3m^{-\frac{5}{2}}n^{-\frac{1}{6}}}{2}$
4. a) 1 **b)** $\dfrac{2m^{6x-4y}}{3}$ **c)** $a^x b^{\frac{x}{2}}$
5. $2351.18 **6.** About 20.7%
7. About 12.25 years
8. a) $1000 = 10^3$ **b)** $\sqrt{10} = 10^{\frac{1}{2}}$ **c)** $81 = 3^4$
9. a) $\log 10\,000 = 4$ **b)** $\log 0.001 = -3$
  c) $\log_5 625 = 4$
10. a) 100 **b)** 0.000 01 **c)** 8 **d)** 27 **e)** -2
  f) 32
11. a) $\log x + 2 \log y$ **b)** $\log x + \frac{1}{2} \log y$
  c) $1 + 3 \log x + 2 \log y$
  d) $\frac{1}{3} [\log x + 2 \log y]$
  e) $\log x - \frac{1}{2} \log y$
  f) $2 \log x - \frac{1}{3} \log y$
12. a) $\log \left(\dfrac{xy}{z} \right)$ **b)** $\log \left(\dfrac{x^2}{y} \right)$ **c)** $\log (x^3y^5)$
  d) $\log (x^{\frac{1}{2}}y^3)$ **e)** $\log (2x - 3)(y + 5)$
  f) $\log \dfrac{(x + y)^3}{x - y}$

13. a) $3^{1.8927893}$ **b)** $6^{1.7737056}$ **c)** $1.3^{9.4712085}$
  d) $2^{-0.358454}$
14. a) 1.3652 **b)** 0.7879 **c)** 1.9650 **d)** 2.2541
  e) 2.2876 **f)** 0.8072 **g)** -0.5204
  h) 3.5547
15. a) 4 **b)** 4 **c)** 5 **d)** -3 **e)** -3 **f)** 10
  g) -3 **h)** 3
16. a) 4 **b)** 4 **c)** 3 **d)** 3
17. a) See graph for Exercises 7-6, *Exercise 6*.
  b) See answers for Exercises 7-7, *Exercise 3a)*.
  c) See *Example 1*, page 339.
18. a) 76 days **b)** 116 days
19. a) 64.7% **b)** 536 days
20. a) $N = 1000(2)^{\frac{n}{2}}$ **b)** 1991
21. 19

Chapter 8

Exercises 8-1, page 371

1. Answers may vary.
2. a) K M O **b)** K P V **c)** F B G
3. a) Add 2: 10, 12, 14
  b) Multiply by 3: 81, 243, 729
  c) Add 5: 25, 30, 35
  d) Add the previous amount, plus 1: 16, 22, 29
  e) Divide by 2: 1, 0.5, 0.25
  f) Add 3: 14, 17, 20
4. a) 2, 4, 6, 8, 10 **b)** 11, 12, 13, 14, 15
  c) 3, 6, 9, 12, 15 **d)** 2, 4, 8, 16, 32
  e) 9, 8, 7, 6, 5 **f)** 1, 2, 3, 4, 5
5. a) Add 2: $2n - 1$ **b)** Add 5: $5n$
  c) Add 5: $5n - 1$ **d)** Multiply by 10: 10^n
6. a) 1, 4, 7, 10, 13 **b)** 1, 3, 7, 15, 31
  c) 18, 15, 12, 9, 6 **d)** 7, 9, 11, 13, 15
  e) $\frac{1}{4}, \frac{2}{7}, \frac{3}{10}, \frac{4}{13}, \frac{5}{16}$ **f)** $2, \frac{5}{2}, \frac{8}{3}, \frac{11}{4}, \frac{14}{5}$
7. a) 24, 34 **b)** 17, 53 **c)** 11, 76 **d)** 4, -32
8. a) v **b)** ii **c)** vi **d)** iii
9. a) $2n$ **b)** $2n + 3$ **c)** $2n - 5$ **d)** 2^n
  e) $2^n - 1$ **f)** $19 - 3n$ **g)** $\dfrac{n}{2n - 1}$
  h) $\dfrac{n}{n + 1}$
10. Answers may vary.
11. b and d are correct.
12. a) $f(x) = x^5, f(x) = x^6$
  b) $f(x) = ax^4 + bx^3 + cx^2 + dx + e$;
    $f(x) = ax^5 + bx^4 + cx^3 + dx^2 + ex + f$

13. a) 3, 4, 5

 b) $t_n = n - 1$, where n is the number of the polygon in the table; or $t_n = n - 3$, where n is the number of sides in the polygon

14. a) 120°, approximately 128.57°, 135°

 b) $t_n = 180° - \dfrac{360°}{n + 2}$, where n is the number of the polygon; or $t_n = 180° - \dfrac{360°}{n}$, where n is the number of sides

15. a) i) 3 **ii)** 7 **iii)** 15 **iv)** 31

 b) Answers may vary.

Investigate, page 373

i) The prime numbers greater than 1

ii) The difference between consecutive terms increases by 1.

iii) Beyond the second term, add the 2 previous terms to get the next term.

iv) Beyond the second term, add all the preceding terms to get the next term.

v) Beginning at 2, all numbers except those which are perfect squares

vi) Beyond the second term, multiply the 2 preceding terms and subtract 1.

Investigate, page 373

Another similar sequence is: 1, 31, 331, 3331, 33 331, 333 331, 3 333 331, 33 333 331, 333 333 331.
The first 8 terms are prime; the 9th term is not prime since 333 333 331 = 17 × 19 607 843.

Exercises 8-2, page 376

1. a) No **b)** Yes, 3 **c)** Yes, −1 **d)** No
 e) Yes, 0 **f)** Yes, 8

2. a) 3; 13, 16, 19 **b)** 4; 11, 15, 19
 c) −2; 8, 6, 4 **d)** −6; −26, −32, −38
 e) 5; 22, 27, 32 **f)** −3; −6, −9, −12

3. a) 2, 5, 8, 11, 14 **b)** 7, 11, 15, 19, 23
 c) −1, −4, −7, −10, −13
 d) 12, 8, 4, 0, −4 **e)** −8, −3, 2, 7, 12
 f) 25, 20, 15, 10, 5

4. a) 17 **b)** 51 **c)** $2n + 1$

5. a) −4 **b)** −46 **c)** $-3n + 14$

6. a) Answers may vary. 91 million years, 39 million years, 13 million years

 b) About 13 million years from now

7. a) i) No **ii)** Yes

 b) It is the 24th term of the sequence, with 1st term 1896 and common difference 4.

8. a) ii **b)** iv **c)** i **d)** v

9. a) 3, 10, 17, 24, 31 **b)** −3, 1, 5, 9, 13
 c) 5, 7, 9, 11, 13 **d)** 16, 11, 6, 1, −4
 e) −4, −1, 2, 5, 8
 f) −10, −14, −18, −22, −26

10. a) 71, 104 **b)** 51st term

11. a) 72, 202 **b)** 67th term

12. a) $4n - 3$; 65 **b)** $3n$; 63 **c)** $5n - 9$; 56
 d) $47 - 6n$; −61 **e)** $1 - 3n$; −29
 f) $17 - 8n$; −351

13. −3, 4 **14.** 7, 11, 15 **15.** 87, 81, 75

16. 3, 8, 13 **17.** 4, 11, 18

18. a) 24 **b)** 37 **c)** 20 **d)** 25

19. a) 2; 23; 30 **b)** 20; 14; −4 **c)** 17; 27; 32
 d) 10; 17; 31 **e)** 8; 0; −4 **f)** 6; −3; −12

20. $\frac{10}{3}$ **21.** $5x - 8y + 1 = 0$

22. 30 **23.** 10 or −2

24. a) $(2n - 1)(3n - 2)$ **b)** $6n^2$ **c)** $\dfrac{n}{2n + 1}$

 d) $\dfrac{(2n - 1)(2n + 1)}{2n(2n + 2)}$; none of the sequences is arithmetic.

25. a) 4th **b)** 3rd **c)** 1st **d)** 2nd

26. a) 3, 6, 11, 14, 19, 22, 27, 30, 35, 38
 b) i) 3rd **ii)** 4th **iii)** 3rd **iv)** 3rd

Investigate, page 378

There is an infinite number of 3 perfect squares in arithmetic sequence. Some examples are: 49, 169, 289; 4, 100, 196; 289, 625, 961; 1, 25, 49.

Computer Power, page 379

1. Answers may vary; for example, 5, 11, 17, 23, 29; 41, 47, 53, 59; 61, 67, 73, 79

2. Answers may vary.

3. 7, 157, 307, 457, 607, 757, 907

4. a) 5, 7; 11, 13; 17, 19 and 17, 19; 29, 31; 41, 43

 b) 41, 43; 461, 463; 881, 883; 1301, 1303; 1721, 1723; 2141, 2143

5. 276 615 587 107

6. $2 \times 3^2 \times 5 \times 7 \times 11^2 \times 13 \times 17 \times 19 \times 31$

Exercises 8-3, page 383

1. a) Yes, 2 **b)** No **c)** Yes, $-\frac{1}{2}$ **d)** Yes, 0.1
   e) No **f)** Yes, $-\frac{1}{3}$
2. a) 3; 81, 243, 729 **b)** -3; 405, -1215, 3645
   c) 2; 48, 96, 192 **d)** $\frac{1}{3}; \frac{2}{27}, \frac{2}{81}, \frac{2}{243}$
   e) $\frac{1}{4}; \frac{9}{64}, \frac{9}{256}, \frac{9}{1024}$ **f)** -4; 128, -512, 2048
3. a) 2, 6, 18, 54, 162 **b)** 5, 10, 20, 40, 80
   c) 3, -15, 75, -375, 1875
   d) 60, 30, 15, $\frac{15}{2}, \frac{15}{4}$
   e) -4, 8, -16, 32, -64
   f) 8, 24, 72, 216, 648
4. a) 96 **b)** 3072 **c)** $3(2)^{n-1}$
5. a) ii **b)** iv **c)** iii **d)** vi
6. a) No **b)** Yes **c)** No **d)** Yes
7. a) ±12 **b)** ±16 **c)** ±20 **d)** ±50
8. a) ±6, 12, ±24 **b)** ±8, 16, ±32
   c) ±10, 20, ±40 **d)** ±10, 50, ±250
9. a) 2, -6, 18, -54, 162
   b) 20, 10, 5, 2.5, 1.25 **c)** 3, 6, 12, 24, 48
   d) 7, 21, 63, 189, 567 **e)** $\frac{1}{8}, \frac{1}{2}$, 2, 8, 32
   f) -2, 10, -50, 250, -1250
10. a) 2^n; 1024 **b)** $5(2)^{n-1}$; 20 480
   c) $-3(-5)^{n-1}$; 234 375 **d)** $12\left(\frac{1}{2}\right)^{n-1}$; $\frac{3}{512}$
   e) $6\left(-\frac{1}{3}\right)^{n-1}$; $\frac{2}{2187}$ **f)** $3(6)^{n-1}$; 139 968
11. a) 196 608 **b)** 7th term
12. 2, ±6, 18, ±54, 162
13. 24 576, 12 288, 6144, 3072
14. a) ±8; ±32 **b)** 72, 432 **c)** ±6; ±24
   d) ±1; ±25 **e)** 8, 4 **f)** 15, 75
15. 1.25, 5 **16.** ±3; ±6, 18, ±54
17. a) 2, 18, 162, 1458
   b) 2, ±6, 18, ±54, 162, ±486, 1458
18. a) 6 **b)** 8 **c)** 11 **d)** 15
19. $\frac{1}{3}$ or 5 **20.** -1 or -6
21. About 22.8 million
22. 5, 125 **23.** $\frac{9}{5}, \frac{6}{5}, \frac{4}{5}, \frac{8}{15}$ or 9, -6, 4, $-\frac{8}{3}$
24. 1, 3, 9, 27, 81
25. $\frac{3}{7}, \frac{6}{7}, \frac{12}{7}, \frac{24}{7}, \frac{48}{7}$ or 1, -2, 4, -8, 16
27. 1, 3, 9 or 9, 3, 1 **28.** 1.41 **29. b)** t_{22}

Exercises 8-4, page 387

1. a) 5, 2, -1, -4 **b)** $\frac{1}{2}$, 1, 2, 4
   c) -2, 3, -2, 3 **d)** 1, 11, 111, 1111
   e) 1, 2, 3, 5
2. a) $t_1 = 1, t_n = t_{n-1} + 5, n > 1$
   b) $t_1 = 2, t_n = -3t_{n-1}, n > 1$
   c) $t_1 = 1, t_n = t_{n-1} + 2^{n-1}, n > 1$
   d) $t_1 = 1, t_n = t_{n-1} + 2n - 1, n > 1$
   e) $t_1 = 1, t_2 = 1, t_n = t_{n-1} + t_{n-2}, n > 2$
   f) $t_1 = 1, t_2 = 2, t_3 = 3,$
      $t_n = t_{n-1} + t_{n-2} + t_{n-3}, n > 3$
3. Examples may vary; for example, the sequence
   1, 4, 9, 16, ... can be defined by
   $t_1 = 1, t_n = t_{n-1} + 2n - 1, n > 1$ and by
   $t_1 = 1, t_n = (\sqrt{t_{n-1}} + 1)^2, n > 1$

Exercises 8-5, page 390

1. a) $2 + 6 + 10 + 14 + 18 + \ldots$
   b) $9 + 3 + 1 + \frac{1}{3} + \frac{1}{9} + \ldots$
2. a) Sequence **b)** Series **c)** Series **d)** Series
   e) Sequence **f)** Series
3. a) 4 **b)** 14 **c)** 16 **d)** -6
4. a) 4 **b)** 24 **c)** 40 **d)** -6
5. a) $3 + 3 + 3 + 3 + 3$
   b) $1 + 5 + 9 + 13 + 17$
   c) $-2 + 0 + 2 + 4 + 6$
   d) $3 + 5 + 5 + 5 + 5$
   e) $3 + 5 + 7 + 9 + 11$
   f) $13 - 6 - 10 - 14 - 18$
6. a) iii **b)** i **c)** v **d)** iv
7. a) $n(n-1)$; $2n$ **b)** $(n-1)(3n-8)$; $6n - 8$
   c) $2^{n-1} - 1$; 2^{n-1} **d)** $(n-1)(2n-5)$; $4n - 5$
   e) $2(3^{n-1} - 1)$; $4(3)^{n-1}$
   f) $(n-1)(n-5)$; $2n - 5$
8. $a + a + a + a + \ldots$
9. a) v **b)** iii **c)** vi **d)** i
10. a) $n^2 - 2n$ **b)** $2^n - 1$ **c)** $\dfrac{2^n - 1}{2^{n-1}}$ **d)** n^3
11. a) i) $n^2 + 2n$ **ii)** $n^2 + 4n$ **iii)** $n^2 + 6n$
   b) $n^2 + 8n$

Investigate, page 391

3. a) $n^2 + n$ **b)** $2^n - 1$ **c)** $\dfrac{n}{n+1}$ **d)** $\dfrac{n}{3n+1}$

Exercises 8-6, page 395

1. **a)** 210 **b)** 365 **c)** 290 **d)** 180 **e)** 600
   f) -60
2. **a)** 276 **b)** 375 **c)** 552 **d)** 1020
3. **a)** 104 **b)** 2750
4. **a)** 345 **b)** 15 **c)** -2670
5. **a)** ii **b)** vi **c)** v **d)** iii
6. Job A **7.** 68 **8.** $975
9. **a)** 893 **b)** 598 **c)** 3604 **d)** -400
10. $3 + 10 + 17$ **11.** $2 + 6 + 10$
12. $28 + 25 + 22$
13. 1.5; 405 **14.** $3 + 7 + 11$ **15.** 21
16. **a)** $n(n + 1)$ **b)** n^2
17. **a) i)** 79; $4n - 1$ **ii)** 820; $n(2n + 1)$
    b) i) 125 **ii)** 15
18. **a)** $n(n + 4)$ **b)** $n(3n - 11)$ **c)** $n(2n + 3)$
    d) $\frac{n}{2}(5n + 1)$ **e)** $\frac{n}{2}(21 - 3n)$ **f)** $\frac{n}{2}(15 + 7n)$
19. **b)** $21 + 23 + 25 + 27 + 29 = 5^3$
    c) $n^2 - n + 1$
20. **b)** $\frac{1}{2}(n^2 - n + 2)$ **c)** $\frac{1}{2}n(n^2 + 1)$
    d) $\frac{1}{2}n(n^2 + 1)$

Investigate, page 397

The list continues to give primes to $227 + 30 = 257$;
the next sum is $257 + 32 = 289 = 17^2$.
Another example: $11 + 2 = 13$; $13 + 4 = 17$;
$17 + 6 = 23$; etc., gives primes up to $57 + 16 = 73$;
the next sum is $73 + 18 = 91 = 13 \times 7$.

Investigate, page 397

210 letters

Exercises 8-7, page 400

1. **a)** 63 **b)** 1092 **c)** 682 **d)** 77.5
2. **a)** 1562 **b)** 484 **c)** 93 **d)** 46.5 **e)** 605
   f) 155
3. **a)** iv **b)** vi **c)** ii **d)** v
4. **a)** 0.093 75 **b)** 11.906 25
5. **a)** 1458 **b)** 2184
6. **a) i)** 8190 **ii)** 65 534 **b)** $2^{n+1} - 2$
7. 397 mg **8.** 63 **9.** $10 737 418.23
10. **a)** 2186 **b)** 3906 **c)** 95.625 **d)** $9841.\overline{3}$
    e) 27 305 **f)** 63.875
11. 9 **12.** $2 + 10 + 50$ or $72 - 60 + 50$

13. 2; 381 or -3; 1641
14. $3 + 15 + 75$ or $75 + 15 + 3$
15. **a)** $3^n - 1$ **b)** $5(2^n - 1)$ **c)** $4^n - 1$
    d) $4(2^n - 1)$
17. 2047

The Mathematical Mind, page 402

1. **a)** 65 536 : 17 **b)** 1 048 576 : 21
2. Answers may vary. **3.** 1.2×10^{24} : 81

Exercises 8-8, page 405

1. **a)** Yes, 16 **b)** Yes, 81 **c)** Not geometric
   d) Yes, $\frac{250}{9}$ **e)** No **f)** Yes, $-\frac{64}{7}$
2. **a)** 120 **b)** 10 **c)** $\frac{80}{7}$ **d)** $\frac{32}{3}$
3. **a)** $\frac{7}{3}$ **b)** $\frac{35}{11}$ **c)** $\frac{1520}{999}$ **d)** $\frac{1205}{198}$
4. **a)** 36 **b)** 51.2 **c)** Sum does not exist **d)** $\frac{48}{11}$
5. $\frac{2}{3}$ **6.** 6
7. **a)** 8 **b)** 0.031 25
8. 6 m **9.** About 11.3 m **10.** $(8 + 4\sqrt{2})$ m
11. **a)** $|x| < 1$ **b)** $|x| < 2$ **c)** $|x| < \sqrt{3}$
    d) $|x| > 1$

Exercises 8-9, page 412

1. **a)** $4 + 5 + 6 + 7 + 8$ **b)** $5 + 9 + 13 + 17$
   c) $2 + 4 + 6 + 8 + 10 + 12$
   d) $-5 - 2 + 1 + 4 + 7$
   e) $3 + 1 + \frac{1}{3} + \frac{1}{9} + \ldots$
   f) $-7 - 2 + 3 + 8$
2. **a)** $\sum_{i=1}^{7}(3i - 1)$ **b)** $\sum_{i=1}^{6}(2i + 1)$ **c)** $\sum_{i=1}^{\infty}\left(\frac{1}{5}\right)^{i-2}$
   d) $\sum_{i=1}^{4}(30 - 6i)$
3. **a)** iv **b)** ii **c)** iii **d)** vi
4. **a)** 192 **b)** 20 **c)** 210
5. **a)** 762 **b)** 252 **c)** 1092
6. **a)** $-1 + 0 + 3 + 8 + 15$
   b) $4 + 7 + 12 + 19 + 28 + 39 + 52$
   c) $0 + 11 + 28 + 51$
   d) $-3 - 2 + 3 + 12 + 25 + 42$
   e) $2 + 2 + 0 - 4 - 10$
   f) $4 + 12 + 22 + 34 + 48 + 64 + 82$

7. a) $\sum_{i=1}^{n}(3i - 1)$ **b)** $\sum_{i}(23 - 5i)$

c) $\sum_{i=1}^{16}(6i - 3)$ **d)** $\sum_{i=1}^{12}(4i - 2)$

e) $\sum_{i}2(3)^{i-1}$ **f)** $\sum_{i=1}^{9}3(2)^{n-1}$

8. a) $a + a^2 + a^3 + a^4$
b) $a + 2a^2 + 3a^3 + 4a^4$
c) $a + 4a + 27a + 256a$
d) $-a + 4a^2 - 27a^3 + 256a^4$

9. a) $\sum_{i=1}^{5}3i$ **b)** $\sum_{i=1}^{6}2^i$ **c)** $\sum_{i=1}^{5}\frac{1}{i}$ **d)** $\sum_{i=1}^{5}(-3)(-2)^{n-1}$

10. a) 338 **b)** 180 **c)** 363

11. a) 62 **b)** 2728 **c)** 1.9375

12. a) $\sum_{i=1}^{n}i$ **b)** $\sum_{i}i^2$ **c)** $\sum_{i=1}^{n}i^i$ **d)** $\sum_{i=1}^{n}3(2)^{i-1}$

13. a) -1 **b)** 0

14. a) $\sum_{i=1}^{n}[a + (i - 1)d]$ **b)** $\sum_{i=1}^{n}ar^{i-1}$

Computer Power, page 415

1. a) 9 cm, 12 cm, 16 cm, $21.\overline{3}$ cm, $28.\overline{4}$ cm
b) Approximately 3.897 11 cm², 6.495 19 cm², 7.072 54 cm², 7.200 84 cm², 7.229 35 cm²
c) $\dfrac{117\sqrt{3}}{28}$ cm²

2. a) Descriptions may vary.
b) $P_1 = 9$ cm, $P_n = \frac{4}{3}P_{n-1}$, $n > 1$
c) $A_1 = \dfrac{9\sqrt{3}}{4}$, $A_2 = \dfrac{15\sqrt{3}}{4}$, $A_n = A_{n-1} + \frac{2}{9}B_{n-1}$,
where $B_2 = \dfrac{6\sqrt{3}}{4}$, $n > 2$

4. 1.261 859 5

Exercises 8-10, page 422

1. a) $\dfrac{k + 1}{k + 2}$ **b)** $\dfrac{k + 1}{2k + 3}$ **c)** $\dfrac{k + 2}{k}$ **d)** $\dfrac{2k + 1}{3k + 2}$

e) $\frac{1}{2}(k + 1)(k + 2)$

f) $\frac{1}{3}(k + 1)(k + 2)(k + 3)$ **g)** $k(k + 2)$

h) $\frac{1}{2}(k + 1)(2k + 1)(2k + 3)$

6. a) $S_n = \dfrac{n}{2n + 1}$ **b)** $S_n = \dfrac{n}{3n + 1}$

c) $S_n = \dfrac{n}{4n + 1}$ **7.** $(n + 1)! - 1$

13. a) $n + 1$ **b)** $\dfrac{1}{n}$ **c)** $\dfrac{n + 1}{2n}$

Problem Solving, page 426

1. $na^2 + adn(n - 1) + \dfrac{d^2n(n - 1)(2n - 1)}{6}$

2. 129
438
567

3.
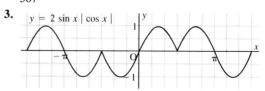

4. 24 cm²
6. Approximately 41.4° and 90°
7. b) Yes
8. $(\pm 1.410\ 533\ 616,\ \pm 1.765\ 143\ 358)$
9. 30°

Review Exercises, page 427

1. a) 4, 7, 10, 13 **b)** 0, 1, 4, 9 **c)** 3, 16, 39, 72
d) $-\frac{1}{2}, 0, \frac{1}{4}, \frac{2}{5}$

2. a) 23; 58 **b)** 29; 1021 **c)** $\frac{3}{8}; \frac{8}{23}$ **d)** 2; -54

3. a) 2, 9, 16, 23 **b)** 1, 3, 9, 27
c) 21, 17, 13, 9 **d)** $-2, -10, -50, -250$

4. a) Arithmetic; -4 **b)** Geometric; 2
c) Geometric; -0.5 **d)** Arithmetic; 8

5. a) $4n - 2$ **b)** $2(3)^{n-1}$ **c)** n^3 **d)** $\dfrac{n(n + 2)}{n + 1}$

6. a) $7n - 5$ **b)** $2(4)^{n-1}$ **c)** 5^{n-1} **d)** $24 - 5n$

7. a) 14, 20 **b)** 32, 128

8. a) -7 **b)** 0.128

9. a) 29 **b)** 81 **c)** $4n + 1$

10. 11.5; $26.5 - 1.5n$

11. a) 2916 **b)** 19 131 876 **c)** $4(3)^{n-1}$

12. 15 552; $2(6)^{n-1}$

13. a) 7 **b)** 29 **c)** 22 **d)** 9

14. 19 **15.** 153 **16.** 25, 22, 19

17. 2, 10, 50 **18.** 61 **19.** 3, 6, 12

20. a) 1, 7, 25, 79 **b)** $-0.5, 2, -8, 32$

21. a) Arithmetic **b)** Other **c)** Geometric
d) Geometric **e)** Arithmetic **f)** Other

22. a) 8   **b)** 23   **c)** −7

23. a) 2 + 2 + 2 + 2   **b)** 3 + 5 + 7 + 9
c) 4 + 3 + 3 + 3   **d)** 1 + 5 + 9 + 13

24. a) 40; $\frac{n}{2}(3n + 1)$ **b)** −10; $\frac{n}{2}(31 - 7n)$
c) 70; $n(2n + 4)$ **d)** 155; $5(2^n - 1)$
e) 23.25; $24(1 - (0.5)^n)$ **f)** 242; $3^n - 1$

25. a) 33   **b)** 432

26. a) 128   **b)** 2 097 151

27. 12   **28.** 8

29. a) 50 + 56 + 62   **b)** 4110

30. a) 2 + 6 + 18   **b)** 129 140 162

31. 1380   **32. a)** 80   **b)** −18

33. a) 102   **b)** −117   **c)** 0.968 75

Chapter 9

Exercises 9-1, page 434

See Teacher's Resource Book for graphs.

1. Answers may vary.
a) Over a number of years: total number of students in universities; total number of science courses available; number of students in each science course.
b) Over a number of years: population; number of AIDS victims; number of new AIDS victims; definition of "epidemic".
c) Over a number of years: the marks of Canadian and Japanese students on similar tests.
d) Over a number of years: the numbers of men and women in a company who are qualified for particular jobs; the numbers of men and women who have held these particular jobs; the numbers of men and women in management positions.
e) Over a number of years: population; the number of people who have mental disorders; the number of people who seek medical help; the number of new people who seek help.
f) Over a number of years: population; the number of people unemployed; the rate of unemployment; the factors that affect employment or produce unemployment.

2. a) 25   **b)** Japan, Thailand; England/Wales, Belgium (French)   **c)** No

3. Answers may vary.
a) i) 50%   **ii)** 28%   **b) i)** 58%   **ii)** 25%
c) Answers may vary. The number of students who look forward to taking more mathematics increased; the number who were undecided or disagreed decreased slightly.

4. Answers are approximate.
a) 7.0%, 7.5%, 7.8%   **b)** 22.3%
c) 7.6%, 11.0%   **d)** 20 to 30 years

5. c) 2

8. a)

Tens digit	Units digit
3	589
4	12334567788888999
5	00234468
6	0 1

d) 45 kg to 49 kg

10. c) Because each number is the percent of its age group.
d) "Percent of single Canadian males between 20 and 24" refers to the fraction of all single Canadian males who are between 20 and 24.
"Percent of Canadian males between 20 and 24 who are single" refers to the fraction of Canadian males between 20 and 24, who are single.

Exercises 9-2, page 440

See Teacher's Resource Book for graphs.

1. Answers may vary.
a) Median   **b)** Mode   **c)** Mean   **d)** Mode
e) Mean   **f)** Mean

2. a) R:5, 5, no mode; S: $2.\overline{6}$, 3, 4; T: 6, 2.5, 0
b) Mean and median are not; mode is.

3. a) 88.5%   **b)** 99%   **c)** No

4. Answers may vary; each hump represented the mode of each sex.

5. a) 98% of the scores occurred below Lesley's score.   **b)** 14 700

6. Answers may vary. 2, 3, 3, 6, 7, 7, 7

7. a)

Tens digit	Units digit
2	57778889
3	13344555666777788899999
4	00245668888899
5	01134669
6	048

b) 41.375 months; 39 months; 39 months, 48 months   **c)** 35 months, 48 months
d) 28 months, 56 months

8. a) 39 years   **b)** 39.2 years   **c)** 9, 17, 58, 71

9. b) 39.2 years   **c)** Results are the same.
d) Answers may vary. If the units digits were clustered at one end of the range

10. a) 5th percentile and 95th percentile
b) 2.5 h, 4 h, 4.8 h   **c)** 5%   **d)** 25%, 5%

11. 80.75

Exercises 9-3, page 447

1. Answers may vary. The extent to which data cluster around the mean.

2. 31 cm

3. Answers may vary.
   a) Range   b) Range
   c) Standard or mean deviation
   d) Standard or mean deviation
   e) Standard or mean deviation

4. Brand B

5. a) 5   b) $2.\overline{72}$ c) 3.16

6. a) V: 4; W: 4   b) V   c) 8
   d) V: $2.\overline{2}$; W: $0.\overline{8}$ e) V: 2.58; W: 1.89

7. i) a) 2.00 mm   b) 0.40 mm   c) 0.10 mm
   d) 0.12 mm
   ii) a) 1.97 mm   b) 0.60 mm   c) 0.17 mm
   d) 0.19 mm
   iii) a) 1.98 mm   b) 0.80 mm   c) 0.20 mm
   d) 0.24 mm
   No samples pass the standard.

8. a) 194 cm   b) 7.4 cm   c) 8.9 cm

9. a) 116   b) 116

10. a) 95 kg   b) 11.75 kg   c) 11.75 kg
    d) Answers may vary.   e) i) 94.2 kg
    ii) 11.10 kg, the second formula

11. a) Crispy Chips: 80 g, 26 g Special Spuds: 80 g, 27 g   b) Special Spuds

12. a) i   b) ii

Problem Solving, page 451

1. $f(x) = (\sqrt{2})^x$

2. $\dfrac{65\,535}{32\,768}$

3. a) i) 4   ii) 19   b) No

4. $\dfrac{\log 3}{\log 2}$

7. a) $\dfrac{1}{2}r^2\left(\dfrac{\theta\pi}{180} - \cos\theta\sin\theta\right)$

   b) $\dfrac{\theta\pi}{360}(x^2 + y^2) - \dfrac{1}{2}xy$

8. a) 45.5   b) 182

Exercises 9-4, page 455

See Teacher's Resource Book for scatterplots.

1. Explanations may vary.
   a) A scatterplot of the variables shows dots clustered along a line with positive slope.
   b) A scatterplot of the variables does not show a tendency to lie along a straight line.

2. a) Perfect positive correlation
   b) No correlation
   c) Perfect negative correlation
   d) Strong negative correlation

3. a) Strong positive correlation
   b) No correlation
   c) Strong negative correlation
   d) Weak positive correlation

4. a) 1; perfect positive correlation
   b) 0.89; strong positive correlation
   c) 0.60; positive correlation
   d) −1; perfect negative correlation
   e) −0.89; strong negative correlation
   f) 0; no correlation

5. Answers may vary.

6. a) 0   b) −0.95   c) 0.69

7. Answers may vary.

8. Answers may vary.   a) w, z b) $y, w; z, y$
   c) $z, w; y, w; z, y$ d) $y, x; w, x; x, z$

9. Yes

10. a) 0.998   b) −0.993   c) −0.994   11. z

12. a) 0.80
    b) 0.52 Answers may vary. There is a better correlation between marks on intelligence tests than there is between English and mathematics marks.

13. $20n$, where n is the number of measurements of x and y.

14. a) $\dfrac{1}{2}, \dfrac{1}{2}, 0$ 15. a) $\dfrac{1}{3}, \dfrac{1}{2}, \dfrac{1}{6}, 0$

Exercises 9-5, page 460

1. Answers may vary; the sum of the squares of the deviations.

2. Answers may vary.   a) 1   b) −1   c) 2

3. 11

4. a) 0.90   b) $y = 0.73x + 24.73$ c) 88

5. Answers may vary.   a) $y = 0.30x - 570$
   b) 27.3 million, 30.3 million   c) 300 000

Exercises 9-6, page 466

1. Answers may vary: faster, cheaper, and easier.

2. Answers may vary: the magazine probably has a political bias, and could not be relied upon.

3. Answers may vary: Melissa's friends will probably be biased towards her opinions, and the estimate would not be reasonable.

4. Answers may vary: if the salaries were selected from a range, the results would be reasonable.

5. Answers may vary: visit a parking lot and count the cars.

6. Answers may vary.

7. a) 34%   **b)** 68%   **c)** 48%   **d)** 2%

8. a) i) 98th   **ii)** 50th   **b)** About 0.13%
c) 36 400

9. a) About 37 months   **b)** About 6 months

10. a) 7.4 mm   **b)** 0.52 mm

11. a) 50%   **b)** 68%
c) About 6.88 mm and 7.92 mm

12. a) $\frac{4}{25}$ **b)** $\frac{49}{50}$ **c)** 30 to 70   **d) i)** 99.87th
ii) 50th   **iii)** 0.13th

13. 132

Exercises 9-7, page 474

1. The mean is 13 and the standard deviation is 4.

2. The mean is 0 and the standard deviation is 1.

3. a) 50%   **b)** 84%   **c)** 16%   **d)** 68%

4. a) N(0,3)   **b)** N(2,3)

5. Explanations may vary.

6. a) Yes, conversion from inches to centimetres does
not affect the distribution.   **b)** 164 cm, 6.6 cm

7. Symmetry

8. a) 0.8413   **b)** 0.0228   **c)** 0.1359   **d)** 0.50
e) 0.0668   **f)** 0.9332

9. a) 0.8413   **b)** 0.1587   **c)** 0.1587
d) 0.6826   **e)** 0.0228   **f)** 0.0228

10. a) 1.28   **b)** -0.67 **c)** 0.67   **d)** -1.28
e) -0.52 **f)** 0.84

11. a) 120.5   **b)** 89.3   **c)** 110.7   **d)** 91.7
e) 113.4   **f)** 79.5

12. Bell shape is preserved

13. 173 600   **14.** The second test   **15.** 74.2 h

Exercises 9-8, page 480

1. Explanations may vary.

2. a) 0   **b)** 0.67   **c)** 1.28   **d)** -0.25

3. Explanations may vary.

4. Explanations may vary.

5. P_{25} and P_{75}

6. a) 15   **b)** 21   **c)** 25   **d)** 29

7. a) Yes   **b)** Yes   **c)** No   **d)** No   **e)** Unlikely

8. 9.4 to 22.6   **9.** 151.6 cm to 174.4 cm

10. Prob $(11.0 \leqslant \mu \leqslant 46.2) = 0.95$

11. Prob $(3.4 \leqslant \mu \leqslant 42.6) = 0.95$

12. a) Prob $(X - 2.58\sigma \leqslant \mu \leqslant X + 2.58\sigma) = 0.99$
b) Prob $(148.1 \leqslant \mu \leqslant 177.9) = 0.99$

Review Exercises, page 482

1. a)

Tens digit	Ones digit
3	4
4	1 3
5	3 4
6	4 5 7 7 8 9
7	0 1 2 2 2 3 3 4 5 5 5 7 8
8	0 1 2 6 8
9	8

b) 34, 98   **c)** 72 and 75   **d)** $36.\overline{6}\%$, 20%
e) 72   **f)** 73, 78

2. a) $11.73   **b)** $12.00   **c)** 4

3. a) -0.50
b) There seems to be some negative correlation.

4. a) -0.90 **b)** Answers may vary.
$y = -0.24x + 28.8$; about 5 chin-ups

Chapter 10

Exercises 10-1, page 485

1. a) HT, HH, TH, TT
b) HHH, HHT, HTH, THH, TTT, TTH, THT, HTT

2. E, C, D; E, S, D; E, M, D; E, C, P; E, S, P;
E, M, P; H, C, D; H, S, D; H, M, D; H, C, P;
H, S, P; H, M, P

3. 1, 2, 3, 4; 1, 2, 4, 3; 1, 3, 2, 4; 1, 3, 4, 2;
1, 4, 2, 3; 1, 4, 3, 2; 2, 1, 3, 4; 2, 1, 4, 3;
2, 3, 1, 4; 2, 3, 4, 1; 2, 4, 1, 3; 2, 4, 3, 1;
3, 1, 2, 4; 3, 1, 4, 2; 3, 2, 4, 1; 3, 2, 1, 4;
3, 4, 1, 2; 3, 4, 2, 1; 4, 1, 3, 2; 4, 1, 2, 3;
4, 2, 1, 3; 4, 2, 3, 1; 4, 3, 1, 2; 4, 3, 2, 1

4. 12   **5.** 80   **6.** 45

7. a) 28   **b)** 32   **8. a)** 60   **b)** 120

9. 42   **10.** 336   **11.** 3840

12. 8 000 000   **13.** 657 720

14. a) 1 404 000   **b)** 1 757 600   **c)** 192

15. 20   **16.** 19   **17.** 205 320

18. a) 648   **b)** 4536   **c)** 27 216

19. a) 5.5×10^{26} **b)** About 6.7×10^{11} years
c) 5.5×10^{20} km

Exercises 10-2, page 489

1. a) 120   **b)** 5040   **c)** 3 628 800
d) 8.717 829 1 $\times 10^{10}$ **e)** 120   **f)** 3024
g) 1.005 903 4 $\times 10^{11}$ **h)** 3.218 124 3 $\times 10^{13}$

2. a) 6   **b)** 24   **c)** 120

3. a) 120   **b)** 720   **c)** 5040   **d)** 362 880

4. 5040   **5.** 120

6. a) 24   **b)** 720   **7.** $1.307\ 674\ 4 \times 10^{12}$
8. a) 120   **b)** 720   **c)** 121   **d)** 24

9. a) $(n + 2)(n + 1)$ **b)** $\dfrac{1}{n(n - 1)(n - 2)}$
c) $(n + 4)(n + 3)$ **d)** $2n(2n - 1)(2n - 2)$
10. a) 120   **b)** 151 200   **c)** $2.585\ 201\ 7 \times 10^{22}$
d) 4 151 347 200
11. 120   **12.** 3024
13. a) 210   **b)** 840   **c)** 2520
14. a) 120   **b)** 2520   **c)** 6720
15. 840   **16.** United States: 90 000;
Canada: 17 576 000
17. a) 120   **b)** 576   **c)** 144   **d)** 40 320
18. a) 6   **b)** 348   **c)** 10 266   **d)** 205 320
19. a) 9   **b)** 2   **c)** 3   **d)** 5   **e)** 8
20. 1710   **21. a)** 256   **b)** 340   **22. a)** 4   **b)** 12

Exercises 10-3, page 491

1. a) 5040   **b)** 720   **2. a)** 1440   **b)** 1440
3. a) 1440   **b)** 720   **4. a)** 4320   **b)** 14 400
5. a) 720   **b)** 144   **c)** 240   **d)** 480   **e)** 48
6. 2880   **7.** 2880   **8.** 967 680
9. a) 6   **b)** 120   **10. a)** 120   **b)** 1320   **c)** 1200
11. 103 680

Exercises 10-4, page 495

1. a) 30   **b)** 3360   **c)** 6 652 800   **d)** 37 800
e) 1260   **f)** 554 400   **g)** 1 441 440
h) 1 681 680
2. a) 2520   **b)** 45 360   **c)** 20 160
d) 1 814 400   **e)** 10 080   **f)** 604 800
g) 1 663 200   **h)** 39 916 800
3. 1260   **4.** 560   **5.** 1260
6. 24   **7.** 120   **8.** 362 880
9. $3.345\ 252\ 7 \times 10^{49}$
10. a) 1   **b)** 360   **11. a)** 120   **b)** 20   **12.** 2520
13. a) 360   **b)** 120   **c)** 24   **d)** 240   **e)** 96
14. 72   **15. a)** 10   **b)** 126
16. a) 144   **b)** 96   **c)** 96

Exercises 10-5, page 499

1. a) 10   **b)** 20   **c)** 56   **d)** 792   **e)** 5005
f) 8008   **g)** 350   **h)** 9900
2. 21   **3.** 35   **4.** 30 045 015
5. a) 125 970   **b)** 125 970
6. a) 4368   **b)** 1287   **c)** 376 992   **d)** 6
7. a) 3432   **b)** 1400   **c)** 168
8. 1620   **9.** 70   **10.** 163   **11.** 110

12. a) 845 000   **b)** 454 480   **c)** 1 299 480
13. 28   **14.** 70   **15.** 35
16. a) 190   **b)** 1140   **c)** 4845   **d)** 15 504
17. a) 9   **b)** 54   **c)** 170
18. a) 113 740   **b)** 133 672
19. $\dfrac{1}{11}$ **20.** 99   **21.** 56
23. 41   **24.** 8   **25.** 773
26. a) 23   **b)** 34   **c)** 863
27. a) 22   **b)** 46

Exercises 10-6, page 504

1. $\dfrac{1}{6}$ **2.** $\dfrac{1}{4}$ **3. a)** $\dfrac{1}{4}$ **b)** $\dfrac{1}{2}$ **4.** $\dfrac{1}{120}$ **5.** $\dfrac{1}{18}$
6. $\dfrac{1}{15}$ **7.** Explanations may vary.   **8.** $\dfrac{1}{17}$ **9.** $\dfrac{1}{4}$
10. $\dfrac{7}{22}$ **11.** $\dfrac{1}{7}$ **12. a)** $\dfrac{1}{3}$ **b)** $\dfrac{2}{15}$ **c)** $\dfrac{8}{15}$
13. a) $\dfrac{25}{102}$ **b)** $\dfrac{11}{221}$ **c)** $\dfrac{1}{17}$ **14.** 6
15. a) $\dfrac{1}{16}$ **b)** $\dfrac{1}{16}$ **c)** $\dfrac{1}{4}$ **16. a)** $\dfrac{1}{8}$ **b)** $\dfrac{7}{8}$
17. a) $\dfrac{77}{102}$ **b)** $\dfrac{8}{13}$ **18.** 0.9   **19.** $\dfrac{9}{14}$ **20.** 0.216
21. Yes   **22.** 0.0329   **23.** $_nC_r = \dfrac{_nP_r}{r!}$

Exercises 10-7, page 508

1. 15, 20, 15; 7, 21, 35, 35, 21, 7
2. $p^7 + 7p^6q + 21p^5q^2 + 35p^4q^3 + 35p^3q^4 + 21p^2q^5 + 7pq^6 + q^7$
3. a) 9   **b)** 8   **c)** 7   **d)** 8   **e)** 16
4. $2pq - q^2$
5. a) 9   **b)** 5   **c)** 11   **d)** 11   **e)** 0
6. 10 201
7. a) 6400, 560, 560, 49   **b)** 7569
c) They are the same; explanations may vary.
8. 1 030 301
9. $p^8 + 8p^7q + 28p^6q^2 + 56p^5q^3 + 70p^4q^4 + 56p^3q^5 + 28p^2q^6 + 8pq^7 + q^8$
10. $10p^4q + 20p^2q^3 + 2q^5$
11. a) $x^3 + 6x^2y + 12xy^2 + 8y^3$
b) $a^3 - 3a^2 + 3a - 1$
c) $a^4 + 8a^3b + 24a^2b^2 + 32ab^3 + 16b^4$
d) $16a^4 - 32a^3 + 24a^2 - 8a + 1$
12. $p^2 + 2pq + q^2$

13. $\frac{4}{3}\pi(3R^2r + 3Rr^2 + r^3)$

14. a) 2π **b)** $1 + 30R^{-1} + 300R^{-2} + 1000R^{-3} : 1$

15. a) i) \$5.23 **ii)** \$27.39

b) $1000\left(1 + \dfrac{I}{100}\right)^3$

c) $1000 + 30I + \dfrac{3I^2}{10} + \dfrac{I^3}{1000}$

Exercises 10-8, page 512

1. a) $a^3 + 3a^2b + 3ab^2 + b^3$
b) $x^4 - 4x^3y + 6x^2y^2 - 4xy^3 + y^4$
c) $x^5 + 5x^4y + 10x^3y^2 + 10x^2y^3 + 5xy^4 + y^5$
d) $x^7 - 7x^6 + 21x^5 - 35x^4 + 35x^3 - 21x^2 + 7x - 1$

2. a) 10 **b)** No **c)** If n is even.

3. Explanations may vary.

4. $x^{14} - 14x^{13}y + 91x^{12}y^2 - 364x^{11}y^3 + 1001x^{10}y^4 - 2002x^9y^5 + 3003x^8y^6 - 3432x^7y^7 + 3003x^6y^8 - 2002x^5y^9 + 1001x^4y^{10} - 364x^3y^{11} + 91x^2y^{12} - 14xy^{13} + y^{14}.$
For $(x + y)^{14}$, the terms are the same, but all positive.

5. $p^{10} + 10p^9q + 45p^8q^2$

6. $45p^2q^8 - 10pq^9 + q^{10}$

7. $a^7 + 7a^6b + 21a^5b^2 + 35a^4b^3 + 35a^3b^4 + 21a^2b^5 + 7ab^6 + b^7$
For $(2a + 2b)^7$, each term is multiplied by 2^7.

8. a) $2x^6 + 30x^4y^2 + 30x^2y^4 + 2y^6$
b) $12x^5y + 40x^3y^3 + 12xy^5$

9. a) $32a^5 + 80a^4b + 80a^3b^2 + 40a^2b^3 + 10ab^4 + b^5$
b) $x^{12} - 6x^{10} + 15x^8 - 20x^6 + 15x^4 - 6x^2 + 1$
c) $1 - \dfrac{7}{x} + \dfrac{21}{x^2} - \dfrac{35}{x^3} + \dfrac{35}{x^4} - \dfrac{21}{x^5} + \dfrac{7}{x^6} - \dfrac{1}{x^7}$

10. a) $p^{30} + 30p^{29}q + 435p^{28}q^2$
b) $a^{40} + 20a^{38} + 190a^{36}$
c) $1024x^{10} - 2560x^9y + 2880x^8y^2$

11. a) $-35\ 750x^{10}$ **b)** $-112\ 640a^9$

12. a) $448x^7$ **b)** 220 **c)** 20

13. a) i) 8 **ii)** 1024 **iii)** 2^k

14. a) $p^6 + 6p^5q + 15p^4q^2 + 20p^3q^3 + 15p^2q^4 + 6pq^5 + q^6$
c) $1 + n + \dfrac{n(n-1)}{2!} + \dfrac{n(n-1)(n-2)}{3!} + \dots + 1$

15. a) $\dfrac{1}{4}$ **b)** $\dfrac{729}{65\ 536}$ **c)** $\dfrac{729}{65\ 536}$ **d)** $\dfrac{5103}{16\ 384}$
e) $\dfrac{1701}{8192}$ **f)** $_8C_r\left(\dfrac{1}{4}\right)^r\left(\dfrac{3}{4}\right)^{8-r}$
g) The $(r + 1)$th term is $_8C_r p^{8-r}q^r$

Problem Solving, page 516

1. 12 714 km **4.** $x = \dfrac{s}{2 + \sqrt{2}}$

5. $x = \sqrt{\dfrac{1}{3}}s, y = \sqrt{\dfrac{2}{3}}s$ **6.** Yes, twin primes

7. $(3 + 3\sqrt{3}, 5 + 2\sqrt{3})$ and $(3 - 3\sqrt{3}, 5 - 2\sqrt{3})$

8. $x = (36 - 36\sqrt{3} + 12\pi)$ cm,
$y = (-36 + 18\sqrt{3} + 3\pi)$ cm,
$z = (36 - 9\sqrt{3} - 6\pi)$ cm

Review Exercises, page 517

1. 12 **2.** 24 **3.** 60

4. 144 **5.** 21 **6.** 20

7. 6 **8.** 120 **9.** 8 000 000

10. a) 5040 **b)** 1440 **c)** 120 **d)** 720 **e)** 1440

11. 12 **12.** 6 **13.** 210

Cumulative Review, Chapters 7-10, page 518

1. a) \$1265.32 **b)** \$8726.06 **c)** \$10 551.71

2. a) 27 **b)** 4 **c)** $\dfrac{1}{25}$ **d)** 1

3. a) $4ax^{-2}y^6$ **b)** $\dfrac{9m^{-13}n^{-2}}{2}$

4. a) 220.400 **b)** 0.013 **c)** 26.952 **d)** 1.833
e) 2.667 **f)** -4.000 **g)** 3.443 **h)** -0.8252

5. a) 0.01 **b)** 9 **c)** 128 **d)** 2.261 859 5
e) $-0.254\ 412$ **f)** 8.186 427 8

6. a) $\log 6$ **b)** $\log\left(\dfrac{2x^2 + 7x - 15}{x + 4}\right)$

7. a) $x - y$ **b)** $x - 2y$ **c)** $1 + x + y$
d) $3y - x$

8. a) 2.0828 **b)** 0.5207 **c)** 2.0414
d) -1.0414 **9. a)** 3 **b)** 3

10. a) Geometric, $r = 3$ **b)** Arithmetic, $d = 4$
c) Arithmetic, $d = -6$ **d)** Geometric, $r = \dfrac{2}{3}$

11. a) 3, 8, 13, 18 **b)** $-1, 2, 9, 20$
c) $3, \dfrac{4}{3}, 1, \dfrac{6}{7}$ **d)** 4, 5, 7, 11
e) $-4, -6, -8, -10$ **f)** $-16, 8, -4, 2$

12. a) $t_n = 8n - 13$ **b)** $t_n = 3(5)^{n-1}$
c) $t_n = -7n + 32$ **d)** $t_n = 48\left(\dfrac{3}{4}\right)^{n-1}$

13. a) i) 405 **ii)** 295 245 **iii)** $5(3)^{n-1}$
b) i) 12 **ii)** -54 **iii)** $-11n + 67$
c) i) 51 **ii)** 123 **iii)** $12n - 9$ **d) i)** 2.5
ii) 0.039 062 5 **iii)** $40\left(\dfrac{1}{2}\right)^{n-1}$

14. a) 15; 39   **b)** 9; 81

15. a) 9   **b)** 22   **c)** 38   **d)** 13

16. a) 2, 7, 17, 37   **b)** 12, 10, 9, 8.5

17. a) 60; $3n^2 - 8n$ **b)** 126; $2^{n+1} - 2$

c) $\dfrac{364}{9}$; $\dfrac{81\left(1 - \left(-\dfrac{1}{3}\right)^n\right)}{2}$ **d)** 87; $\dfrac{11}{2}n^2 - \dfrac{95}{2}n$

18. a) 48   **b)** 216

19. 32

20. a) 60   **b)** 8   **c)** 148

21. a)

Tens digit	Units digit
6	2 3 5 7 8
7	0 2 3 3 5 6 8 9 9
8	0 2 3 3 3 3 4 5 6 8
9	1 2 3 3 4 5 7 7 8
10	1 3

b) 82.6 kg, 83 kg, 83 kg

c) 41.0 kg, 9.1 kg, 11.1 kg

d) 73 kg, 93 kg

22. a) 0.98   **b)** $y = 0.99x - 2.32$ **c)** 76

23. 84   **24. a)** 720   **b)** 840   **c)** 34 650

25. a) 48   **b)** 40   **c)** 105

26. 2520   **27. a)** 4368   **b)** 65 780   **c)** 1287

28. 56   **29. a)** $\dfrac{2}{15}$ **b)** $\dfrac{2}{9}$

30. $x^7 + 7x^6y + 21x^5y^2 + 35x^4y^3 + 35x^3y^4 + 21x^2y^5 + 7xy^6 + y^7$

Index